토익 점수 마구 올려주는 토익

토마토 토익
PART 7 전략

토마토 토익
PART 7 전략

지은이	NE능률 영어교육연구소
선임 연구원	이보영
연구원	신이례 고은정 최연수 장유정 채민정
영문 교열	Danielle Josset
디자인	송현아 오솔길 DOTS
맥편집	김선희
영업	한기영 주성탁 박인규 장순용
마케팅	박혜선 김상민

First Published
Copyright ⓒ 2019 by NE Neungyule, Inc.
All rights reserved. No part of this publication may be reproduced, altered in a retrieval system, or transmitted in any form or by any means, electronic, mechanical, photocopying, recording, or otherwise, without the prior permission of the copyright owner.

✖ 본 교재의 독창적인 내용에 대한 일체의 무단 전재·모방은 법률로 금지되어 있습니다.
✚ 파본은 구매처에서 교환 가능합니다.

서문

토익 중급자들의 오래된 고민 중 하나가 바로 '아무리 공부해도 점수가 더 이상 오르지 않는' 점수 정체 현상이 아닐까 싶습니다. 수많은 어휘를 암기하고, 두꺼운 LC와 RC 기본서를 통독하고, 실전 문제를 반복해 풀어도 틀리는 문제는 여전히 틀리는 답답함을 많은 분들이 토로합니다. 사실 이런 현상은 기본 학습 없이 문제 은행식 학습법이 유행하면서 더욱 심해지고 있습니다.

예전처럼 '입문서 → 기본서 → 실전서'의 단계를 차근차근 밟아 갈 여력이 안 되는 수험자들의 고충을 백분 이해합니다. 그렇기에 점수 상승이라는 학습 효과도 중요하지만 단기간에 효율적으로 할 수 있는 학습 효율성을 고민했고 그 고민의 결과물로, 토마토 토익 브랜드에서 새롭게 파트별 전략서를 선보입니다. 모든 학습자가 900점 이상은 받을 필요가 없기에 자신이 원하는 구체적인 목표 점수를 받기 위한 최적의 점수대별 학습법을 제공합니다. 그중 800점대 이상의 점수 획득을 목표로 하는 전략서 시리즈는 하루 30분씩, 3주 만에, 800점대 완성을 목표로 하는 중급자들을 위한 파트별 전략서입니다. 특정 파트에서 점수가 오르지 않는 학습자들이 자신만의 취약한 파트를 선별해 필요한 학습만 할 수 있도록 하고, 파트별로 엄선된 핵심 전략과 다수의 실전 문제를 동시 수록한 신개념 학습서입니다.

토마토 토익 PART 7 전략은 800점대를 목표로 하는 PART 7 학습자에게 필수적인 35개의 독해 전략, 패러프레이징 훈련, 전략을 바로 적용해 볼 수 있는 훈련 문제와 실전 문제를 충분히 제공합니다. 하루 학습에 부담을 주지 않으면서도 알찬 구성으로 시간을 절약할 수 있는 것은 물론, 단 3주 만에 독해에 대한 실전 감각과 자신감을 기를 수 있습니다.

토익 고득점을 위해 아는 것은 확실히, 모르는 것은 정확히 익혀 내 것으로 만드는 스마트한 학습이 필요하며, 매일 꾸준한 학습이 뒷받침되어야 합니다. 토익 중급 학습자 여러분의 목표 달성을 위해 토마토 토익 파트별 전략서가 길잡이가 되어 드리겠습니다.

CONTENTS

서문	1
CONTENTS	2
책의 구성 및 특징	4
PART 7 최신 경향	6
학습 스케줄러	8
Warming up: 연결사와 패러프레이징	9

CHAPTER 1 문제 유형

UNIT 01	의도 파악 문제	12
UNIT 02	문장 위치 찾기 문제	18
UNIT 03	목적/주제 문제	24
UNIT 04	대상/출처 문제	30
UNIT 05	세부 정보 문제	36
UNIT 06	NOT/TRUE 문제	42
UNIT 07	추론 문제	48
UNIT 08	유의어 문제	54
UNIT 09	단서를 종합하는 문제	60
UNIT 10	연계 문제	66
CHAPTER TEST 1		74

CHAPTER 2　지문 유형

UNIT 11	문자메시지/SNS	86
UNIT 12	이메일/편지	94
UNIT 13	광고문	102
UNIT 14	기사문 (1)	110
UNIT 15	기사문 (2)	118
UNIT 16	회람/공지	126
UNIT 17	표/양식	134
UNIT 18	정보문	142
CHAPTER TEST 2		150

CHAPTER 3　실전 모의고사

UNIT 19	ACTUAL TEST 1	162
UNIT 20	ACTUAL TEST 2	182
UNIT 21	ACTUAL TEST 3	202

정답 및 해설
어휘 노트

책의 구성 및 특징

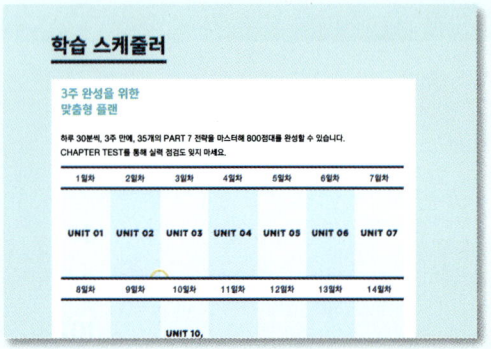

1 3주 만에 완성하는 학습 커리큘럼

토마토 토익 PART 7 전략은 하루 30분씩, 3주 만에, 800점대를 완성할 수 있는 학습 커리큘럼을 제시합니다. 부담 없는 분량과 콤팩트한 내용으로 단기간에 PART 7을 정복할 수 있습니다.

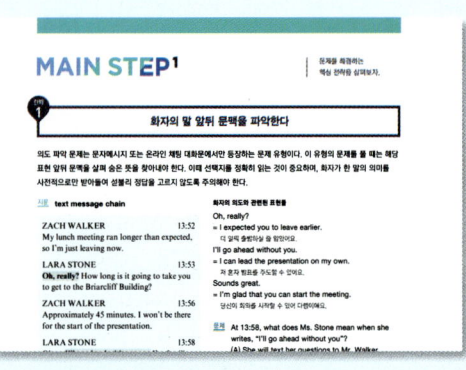

2 PART 7 독해 전략 제시

확실한 실력 향상을 보장하는, 엄선된 35개의 PART 7 독해 전략이 UNIT별로 고르게 제시됩니다. 요점만 쏙쏙 들어오는 구성으로 효과적인 학습이 가능합니다.

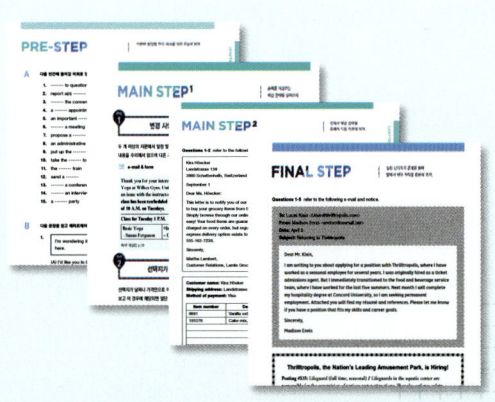

3 차근차근 실력 상승이 가능한 STEP별 구성

PART 7 주요 어휘 → 전략 학습 → 전략 적용 문제 풀이 → 실전 문제 풀이로 이어지는 STEP별 구성으로, PART 7 학습에 꼭 필요한 내용들을 단계별로 종합하였습니다.

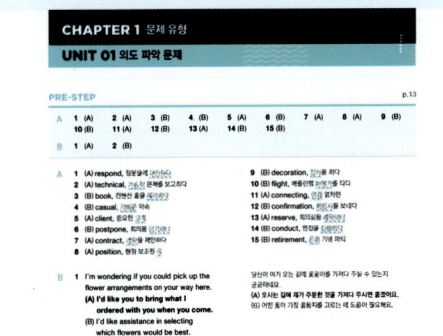

4 혼공족을 위한 상세하고 친절한 해석해설

정확한 본문과 문제 해석, 고득점에 꼭 필요한 패러프레이징 해설은 물론 오답 해설까지 수록하여, 혼자 공부하는 학습자도 교재를 완벽히 이해하고 활용할 수 있습니다.

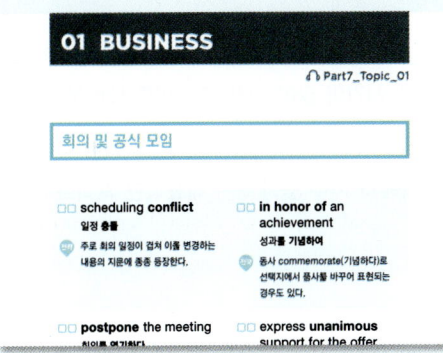

5 한 권으로 끝내는 PART 7 어휘

PART 7 주제별 어휘리스트, UNIT별 복습 어휘리스트를 언제 어디서나 한 손에 들고 다닐 수 있는 어휘 노트로 엮었습니다. 어휘 MP3 파일은 어휘 노트 내 QR코드를 이용하거나, 또는 토마토 토익 공식 홈페이지(www.tomatoclass.com)에서 무료로 다운로드 가능합니다.

PART 7 최신 경향

1 PART 7 구성

지문 종류	지문 개수	지문 당 문항 수	전체 문항 수
단일 지문	10개	2~4개	29개
이중 지문	2개	5개	10개
삼중 지문	3개	5개	15개

2 PART 7 최신 경향

PART 7에서는 e-mail(이메일) 지문이 압도적으로 높은 비율로 출제됩니다. 비슷한 양식의 letter(편지) 지문 역시 자주 출제되며, article(기사문), Web page(웹페이지), advertisement(광고문) 역시 매 시험마다 최소한 지문씩은 꼭 등장합니다.

단, 시험이 어려운 달의 경우 article(기사문)의 출제 비율이 높아지는 경향이 있는데, 기사문은 상대적으로 길이가 길며, 고난도 어휘를 많이 포함하고 있기 때문에 읽는 데 시간이 많이 걸립니다. 이를 대비하기 위해, 기사문의 특징, 빈출 소재 및 어휘를 알아두는 것이 좋습니다.

또 PART 7의 거의 모든 선택지는 패러프레이징되므로 토익에서 자주 출제되는 대표적인 패러프레이징 표현들을 숙지해 두면 문제 풀이 시간을 단축할 수 있습니다.

3 PART 7 시간 배분 및 풀이 전략

토익 전체 시험 시간인 120분 중에서 LC 45분을 빼면, 약 75분 정도가 RC에 할당됩니다. 그중에서 PART 5, 6를 푸는 데 걸리는 시간을 제외하면 PART 7에서 쓸 수 있는 시간은 약 55분 정도입니다.

PART 7이 54문항이므로 평균적으로 한 문제당 약 1분 정도를 기준으로 잡으면 됩니다. 하지만 앞쪽에 위치한 지문일수록 길이가 짧고 문제도 쉬운 경향이 있으므로, 이러한 문제는 1분 안쪽으로 풀고, 이중, 삼중 지문처럼 긴 지문이나 어려운 문제에는 시간을 더 투자하는 것이 좋습니다.

4 PART 7 신유형 지문

❶ 문자메시지, 온라인 채팅
주로 두 명의 화자 간에 주고받는 메시지 형태입니다. 일상/업무 관련 내용이 등장하며, 문제 제기 → 해결의 흐름으로 전개됩니다.

❷ 삼중 지문
내용상 서로 연관 있는 세 개의 지문이 출제됩니다. 이중 지문보다 지문 연계 양상이 복잡하므로 지문 간의 관계에 더 유의해서 읽어야 합니다.

5 PART 7 신유형 문제

❶ 의도 파악 문제

> At 4:46 P.M., what does Ms. Mitchell mean when she writes, "It's my first time"?
> (A) She can get a new customer discount.
> (B) She wants to sign up for a service.
> (C) She needs directions to a site.
> (D) She cannot recommend a business.

풀이 방법
의도 파악 문제는 문제 및 지문에서 주어진 표현의 앞뒤 문장을 읽고, 문맥을 통해 그 의미를 파악해야 합니다. 만약 앞뒤 문장을 읽어도 그 의도를 알 수 없다면 범위를 확장해서 살펴보아야 합니다.

❷ 문장 위치 찾기 문제

> In which of the positions marked [1], [2], [3] and [4] does the following sentence best belong?
> "He expressed concerns that methods that were effective a decade ago are no longer relevant."
> (A) [1]   (B) [2]   (C) [3]   (D) [4]

풀이 방법
문장 위치 찾기 문제는 주어진 문장의 의미를 정확히 파악한 후, 관련 내용이 언급되는 부분을 지문에서 찾아 대입해 보아야 합니다. 문장을 대입했을 때 흐름이 자연스럽다면 정답입니다.

학습 스케줄러

3주 완성을 위한 맞춤형 플랜

하루 30분씩, 3주 만에, 35개의 PART 7 전략을 마스터해 800점대를 완성할 수 있습니다.
CHAPTER TEST를 통해 실력 점검도 잊지 마세요.

1일차	2일차	3일차	4일차	5일차	6일차	7일차
UNIT 01	UNIT 02	UNIT 03	UNIT 04	UNIT 05	UNIT 06	UNIT 07

8일차	9일차	10일차	11일차	12일차	13일차	14일차
UNIT 08	UNIT 09	UNIT 10, CHAPTER TEST 1	UNIT 11	UNIT 12	UNIT 13	UNIT 14

15일차	16일차	17일차	18일차	19일차	20일차	21일차
UNIT 15	UNIT 16	UNIT 17	UNIT 18, CHAPTER TEST 2	UNIT 19	UNIT 20	UNIT 21

Warming up: 연결사와 패러프레이징

연결사와 패러프레이징은 PART 7 문제를 푸는 데 결정적 단서를 제공하기 때문에 그 개념과 종류를 꼭 알아 두어야 합니다.

1 연결사

연결사는 단락의 구조와 문장과 문장 사이의 논리적 흐름을 파악할 수 있게 해 줍니다.

❶ 역접·대조를 나타내는 연결사
but, however, yet, nevertheless, nonetheless, while, whereas, conversely, in contrast, on the contrary, on the other hand, on the opposite

❷ 원인을 나타내는 연결사
because, for this reason

❸ 결과를 나타내는 연결사
so, therefore, thus, hence, consequently, as a result, in conclusion

❹ 첨가를 나타내는 연결사
also, in addition, additionally, besides, furthermore, moreover, what's more

❺ 예시를 나타내는 연결사
for example, for instance, for one thing, as an illustration

2 패러프레이징

패러프레이징은 어떤 표현을 의미가 유사한 다른 표현으로 바꾸어 쓰는 것을 말합니다. 패러프레이징의 유형으로는 동의어 활용하기, 세부적인 항목을 상위어로 바꾸기, 문장 구조 바꾸기 등이 있습니다.

❶ 숫자의 단위가 나오면 동의어 떠올리기
시간이나 기간 등의 숫자 표현이 나왔을 때, 20 years → 2 decades처럼 단위를 환산하여 다른 의미인 것처럼 보이게 하는 것은 자주 등장하는 패러프레이징 유형입니다.

❷ 연락 수단이 나오면 일단 패러프레이징 예측하기
e-mail, call, reply, let me know 등 '연락을 바란다'는 표현은 'contact(연락하다)'를 포함한 구나 문장으로 패러프레이징됩니다.

❸ 부정적 접두사가 나오면 not 찾기
접두사 in-, im-, un- 등은 부정적인 의미를 내포하고 있습니다. 따라서 아래 접두사로 시작하는 단어가 지문에 나온다면 선택지에서 not- 형태로 패러프레이징될 확률이 높습니다.

invalid = not valid   **im**possible = not possible   **un**available = not available
disagree = not agree   **il**legal = not legal   **ir**regular = not regular

하루 30분씩 3주 만에
완성하는
PART 7

**CHAPTER 1
문제 유형**

CHAPTER

- [ ] **UNIT 01** 의도 파악 문제
- [ ] **UNIT 02** 문장 위치 찾기 문제
- [ ] **UNIT 03** 목적/주제 문제
- [ ] **UNIT 04** 대상/출처 문제
- [ ] **UNIT 05** 세부 정보 문제
- [ ] **UNIT 06** NOT/TRUE 문제
- [ ] **UNIT 07** 추론 문제
- [ ] **UNIT 08** 유의어 문제
- [ ] **UNIT 09** 단서를 종합하는 문제
- [ ] **UNIT 10** 연계 문제
- [ ] **CHAPTER TEST 1**

UNIT 01
의도 파악 문제

대화 흐름을 파악하면
의도가 보인다

PRE-STEP

지문에 등장할 주요 어휘를 미리 학습해 보자.

A 다음 빈칸에 들어갈 어휘로 알맞은 것을 고르시오.

1.	------- to questions	(A) respond	(B) book
2.	report a(n) ------- problem	(A) technical	(B) assistant
3.	------- the convention hall	(A) respond	(B) book
4.	a ------- appointment	(A) familiar	(B) casual
5.	an important -------	(A) client	(B) retirement
6.	------- a meeting	(A) fill	(B) postpone
7.	propose a -------	(A) contract	(B) flight
8.	an administrative assistant -------	(A) position	(B) decoration
9.	put up the -------	(A) position	(B) decoration
10.	take the ------- to Berlin	(A) retirement	(B) flight
11.	the ------- train	(A) connecting	(B) retirement
12.	send a -------	(A) connecting	(B) confirmation
13.	------- a conference room	(A) reserve	(B) postpone
14.	------- an interview	(A) respond	(B) conduct
15.	a ------- party	(A) confirmation	(B) retirement

B 다음 문장을 읽고 패러프레이징된 것으로 적절한 것을 고르시오.

1.
> I'm wondering if you could pick up the flower arrangements on your way here.

(A) I'd like you to bring what I ordered with you when you come.
(B) I'd like assistance in selecting which flowers would be best.

2.
> It needs to be filled as soon as possible, so I'd rather not delay it.

(A) The event must be postponed.
(B) The matter should be handled urgently.

MAIN STEP 1

문제를 해결하는
핵심 전략을 살펴보자.

 전략 1 화자의 말 앞뒤 문맥을 파악한다

의도 파악 문제는 문자메시지 또는 온라인 채팅 대화문에서만 등장하는 문제 유형이다. 이 유형의 문제를 풀 때는 해당 표현 앞뒤 문맥을 살펴 숨은 뜻을 찾아내야 한다. 이때 선택지를 정확히 읽는 것이 중요하며, 화자가 한 말의 의미를 사전적으로만 받아들여 섣불리 정답을 고르지 않도록 주의해야 한다.

지문 text message chain

ZACH WALKER　　　　　　　　13:52
My lunch meeting ran longer than expected, so I'm just leaving now.

LARA STONE　　　　　　　　　13:53
Oh, really? How long is it going to take you to get to the Briarcliff Building?

ZACH WALKER　　　　　　　　13:56
Approximately 45 minutes. I won't be there for the start of the presentation.

LARA STONE　　　　　　　　　13:58
Okay, **I'll go ahead without you.** I'm familiar with the information on the slides, and you can respond to questions when you arrive.

ZACH WALKER　　　　　　　　14:00
Sounds great. Thanks!

해석: 해설집 p.2

화자의 의도와 관련된 표현들

Oh, really?
= I expected you to leave earlier.
　더 일찍 출발하실 줄 알았어요.

I'll go ahead without you.
= I can lead the presentation on my own.
　저 혼자 발표를 주도할 수 있어요.

Sounds great.
= I'm glad that you can start the meeting.
　당신이 회의를 시작할 수 있어 다행이에요.

문제 At 13:58, what does Ms. Stone mean when she writes, "I'll go ahead without you"?
(A) She will text her questions to Mr. Walker.
(B) She agrees to lead a meeting on her own.

정답 (B)

 전략 2 의도 파악 문제에 등장하는 표현의 패턴을 알아 두자

의도 파악 문제에서 관용적 표현들이 항상 등장하는 것은 아니지만, 알아 두면 도움이 된다.

수락/긍정	Of course. / Certainly. / Sure (thing). / No problem. Why not? / Why wait? / Just go ahead. → 이 표현들이 나오면 바로 앞의 내용들을 살펴보자.
부정	I doubt it. / I'm afraid not. / I don't think so. / I can't believe it. → 이후에 화자가 본인의 의견이나 새로운 내용을 제안할 수 있으니, 이 표현들이 나오면 앞뒤 내용들을 살펴보자.
이해/수용	Got it. / I see. → 이 표현들이 나오면 그 바로 위 내용들을 살펴보자. 　단, 표현 앞뒤에 있는 어휘나 구문이 오답 함정으로 제시되기도 하니 주의해야 한다.

MAIN STEP 2

앞에서 배운 전략을 문제에 직접 적용해 보자.

Questions 1-2 refer to the following text message chain.

ANNE MITCHELL   4:36 P.M.
Thanks for booking the convention hall for Ms. Taylor's retirement party.

SUE CLAUSEN   4:37 P.M.
My pleasure. I think it will be a better place for the event than a restaurant.

ANNE MITCHELL   4:39 P.M.
I'm glad to hear that. Are you already setting up?

SUE CLAUSEN   4:40 P.M.
Yes, I'm here now, putting up the decorations. But I'm wondering if you could pick up the flower arrangements on your way here.

ANNE MITCHELL   4:43 P.M.
Sure. I'm leaving the office soon. They're at Gail's Flowers, right?

SUE CLAUSEN   4:44 P.M.
Actually, no. I used Diamond Florists instead. Have you been there before?

ANNE MITCHELL   4:46 P.M.
It's my first time.

SUE CLAUSEN   4:47 P.M.
It's really easy to find. I'll send you a map. And you can call me if you have any trouble.

---

1. Where most likely is Ms. Clausen now?

(A) At a restaurant
(B) At the writers' office
(C) At a meeting venue
(D) At a flower shop

2. At 4:46 P.M., what does Ms. Mitchell mean when she writes, "It's my first time"?

(A) She can get a new customer discount.
(B) She wants to sign up for a service.
(C) She needs directions to a site.
(D) She cannot recommend a business.

FINAL STEP

실전 난이도의 문제를 풀며 앞에서 배운 전략을 활용해 보자.

Questions 1-2 refer to the following text message chain.

ROXANNA BLACK 1:23 P.M.
Your hotel is reserved and I'm working on booking the flights for your trip to Berlin. Do you have any airline preferences?

ARTHUR COVEY 1:26 P.M.
I'm a member of the frequent flyer programs for Eagle Airways and World Air. One of those, if possible.

ROXANNA BLACK 1:31 P.M.
Okay. It looks like the lowest fare is $985.82, with World Air.

ARTHUR COVEY 1:33 P.M.
Perfect. And I'd like to arrive in Berlin as early as possible on that day.

ROXANNA BLACK 1:33 P.M.
This flight lands at 1:20 P.M.

ROXANNA BLACK 1:34 P.M.
But you'll stop in Brussels and then take the flight to Berlin. You'd only have 50 minutes. I'm worried there's not enough time for the connecting flight.

ARTHUR COVEY 1:36 P.M.
No, that's plenty.

ROXANNA BLACK 1:37 P.M.
All right. I'll send you a confirmation by e-mail.

---

1. Where does Ms. Black most likely work?

    (A) At an airline company
    (B) At a hotel
    (C) At a travel agency
    (D) At a theater

2. At 1:36 P.M., what does Mr. Covey mean when he writes, "No, that's plenty"?

    (A) He does not want too many connections.
    (B) He cannot pay a higher amount.
    (C) He has enough time to get a passport.
    (D) He is satisfied with the layover.

Questions 3-6 refer to the following online chat discussion.

Jun Tien 10:41 A.M.
Do you have a few minutes to talk? I noticed that both of you reserved the conference room for this afternoon. There was some kind of glitch in the system showing it was still available.

Sara Huber 10:42 A.M.
Did we reserve the exact same time? Maybe there isn't any overlap.

Jun Tien 10:44 A.M.
Unfortunately, both of you requested it at 3 P.M. So one of you will have to postpone or cancel your meeting for today.

Diego Costa 10:47 A.M.
I'm afraid I can't. I'm proposing a new supply contract to Leo Borrego. He's a very important client for us, and it's difficult to get a meeting with him. Ms. Huber, what do you need the room for?

Sara Huber 10:48 A.M.
I'm interviewing Stacey Pelham for the administrative assistant position. It needs to be filled as soon as possible, so I'd rather not delay it.

Jun Tien 10:50 A.M.
Ms. Huber, since your appointment is more casual, how about taking her to the coffee shop around the corner? It's usually quite empty at this time of day, so you could conduct the interview there.

Sara Huber 10:51 A.M.
I can make that work.

Diego Costa 10:52 A.M.
Thank you! And I guess someone needs to tell the IT department about the glitch so they can fix it. I'll take care of that.

Jun Tien 10:53 A.M.
All right. And, Ms. Huber, you should take the company credit card with you so you can buy the drinks. You can get it from me anytime before lunch.

Sara Huber 10:55 A.M.
Okay. I'll do that now.

---

3. What problem are the writers discussing?
(A) Some appointments have been canceled.
(B) A delivery will not arrive on time.
(C) Some presentation equipment is not working.
(D) A meeting space was double-booked.

4. At 10:51 A.M., what does Ms. Huber mean when she writes, "I can make that work"?
(A) She is willing to go off site.
(B) She will change an appointment time.
(C) She volunteers to contact Ms. Pelham.
(D) She can complete Mr. Costa's task.

5. What does Mr. Costa say he will do?
(A) Set up a conference room
(B) Report a technical problem
(C) Send Ms. Tien some information
(D) Make some repairs himself

6. Why will Ms. Huber visit Ms. Tien?
(A) To submit a schedule
(B) To sign a document
(C) To pick up a credit card
(D) To share a meal

UNIT 02
문장 위치 찾기 문제

지시어와 앞뒤 내용을
적극 활용하라

PRE-STEP

지문에 등장할 주요 어휘를 미리 학습해 보자.

A 다음 빈칸에 들어갈 어휘로 알맞은 것을 고르시오.

1. cause ------- damage   (A) high-quality   (B) permanent
2. a ------- period   (A) trial   (B) permanent
3. ------- population growth   (A) trial   (B) rapid
4. the new ------- year   (A) fiscal   (B) rapid
5. the ------- subway system   (A) fiscal   (B) existing
6. research creative -------   (A) concerns   (B) solutions
7. express ------- about safety (A) concerns   (B) passengers
8. accommodate more -------   (A) passengers   (B) solutions
9. ------- the market   (A) hit   (B) relieve
10. be ------- to be $3.2 million (A) hit   (B) estimated
11. make *one's* ------- on the industry (A) access (B) mark
12. ------- pressure   (A) relieve   (B) commemorate
13. increase employee ------- (A) mark   (B) productivity
14. create easy ------- to suburbs (A) access   (B) productivity
15. ------- 15 years in business (A) relieve   (B) commemorate

B 다음 문장을 읽고 패러프레이징된 것으로 적절한 것을 고르시오.

1.
> Being connected to Crafton and other major suburbs through the new lines will be convenient and cost-effective for a lot of commuters.

(A) Suburbs will be relocated in order to create a new transportation line.
(B) Travel to specific neighborhoods will become easy and inexpensive.

2.
> I was confident that its reputation for having high-quality and long-lasting goods was well-deserved.

(A) I knew that more expensive products are usually more durable.
(B) I knew that the company had worked hard to earn consumers' trust.

MAIN STEP¹

문제를 해결하는
핵심 전략을 살펴보자.

지시어를 활용해 주어진 문장이 들어갈 위치를 찾을 수 있다

문장 위치 찾기 문제는 기사문이나 보고서 등 서사 위주의 지문에서 주로 출제되며, 주어진 문장과 그 앞뒤의 지시어, 연결어, 시간의 전후 관계를 밝혀 주는 접속사나 부사를 단서로 활용해 풀 수 있다.

지문 article

Plans for New Community Center

City council chairperson Samantha Davies announced plans for the construction of **a community center** on Chesterton Avenue yesterday. — [1] — **In addition, it** will include a kitchen to accommodate luncheons and banquets. "The council felt that such facilities would really improve the quality of life in the city," Davies said.
— [2] — The city council approved the construction last month. The cost of the project is estimated to be $3.2 million. — [3] —

해석: 해설집 p.7

문제 "The new facility will feature a large event hall, three classrooms, and a conference room."

풀이 ① 주어진 문장 정확히 해석:
"새로운 시설은 대형 이벤트 홀과 세 개의 강의실, 그리고 회의실을 특징으로 할 것이다."
② 지문에서 'The new facility'를 가리키는 것 찾아보기:
New Community Center = a community center = The new facility = it
③ 적절한 위치에 문장을 넣고 최종 확인:
커뮤니티 센터 설립 발표 → 새로운 시설의 특징 → 시설의 추가적 특징 (In addition 이하)

정답 [1]

앞뒤 문맥을 활용해 주어진 문장이 들어갈 위치를 찾을 수 있다

지시어 등의 단서 없이, 주어진 문장과 그 앞뒤 문맥만을 보고 적절한 위치를 찾아야 하는 경우도 있다.

지문 article

Organics Market's Home Delivery Service

Health food retailer Organics Market has initiated a new service that provides customers with weekly deliveries of local, organic produce. — [1] — Spokesperson Jane Ryder claims that 주장 **the program will benefit both the community and the customers.**
— [2] — 근거 **For customers, they are assured that their produce is organic and fresh.** The region's director of health, Mark Swenson, supports this program, calling it an essential step in educating the public about the importance of choosing healthy, local foods.
— [3] —

해석: 해설집 p.8

문제 "The company can help farmers who would normally compete with industrial agriculture."

풀이 ① 주어진 문장 정확히 해석:
"회사는 주로 산업화된 농업과 경쟁하는 농부들에게 도움을 줄 수 있다."
② 지문에서 관련 내용 찾기
(주장) "이 프로그램은 지역사회와 고객 모두를 이롭게 할 것이다."
(근거) "고객은 농산물이 유기농이고 신선하다는 것을 확신할 수 있다."
→ 주어진 문장은 위 주장에 대한 근거의 하나로, 단서의 both the community and the customers 중 the community에 관한 내용임.
③ 적절한 위치에 문장을 넣고 최종 확인

정답 [2]

MAIN STEP 2

Questions 1-3 refer to the following article.

> Turtle Inc. to Institute Temporary Four-Day Workweek
> *By Mimi Favorman*
>
> Mr. Lance Fulchiron, the CEO of Turtle Inc., spoke formally to all of his employees yesterday, which was the first day of the company's new fiscal year. His carefully worded speech discussed the need to increase employee productivity through new techniques. — [1] — As a result, Mr. Fulchiron has researched creative solutions to address the problem of overworked personnel. He explained that he wanted to follow the example of states such as Utah and institute a four-day workweek as a pilot program. — [2] — Mr. Fulchiron went on to explain the theory behind the four-day workweek, which is that workers are propelled to work harder and accomplish more when they are given regular breaks. Businesses in turn save money on utility expenses when the office is closed for an extra day. According to Mr. Fulchiron, Turtle Inc. will spend the next four months testing this theory. — [3] — During this time, employees will no longer be required to work on Fridays (although their salaries will remain the same). At the end of the trial period, Turtle Inc. plans to re-evaluate the arrangement and determine whether or not to make it a permanent change. — [4] —

1. Why was the article written?
   (A) To introduce a new CEO
   (B) To announce an initiative
   (C) To promote a product
   (D) To respond to inquiries

2. What is NOT mentioned about the four-day workweek?
   (A) Employees will be off work Friday to Sunday.
   (B) Business expenses are projected to decrease.
   (C) Employee salaries will be adjusted as a result.
   (D) The change is being tested on a temporary basis.

3. In which of the positions marked [1], [2], [3] and [4] does the following sentence best belong?

   "He expressed concerns that methods that were effective a decade ago are no longer relevant."

   (A) [1]
   (B) [2]
   (C) [3]
   (D) [4]

FINAL STEP

실전 난이도의 문제를 풀며 앞에서 배운 전략을 활용해 보자.

Questions 1-3 refer to the following article.

Cordoba Games Celebrates 15th Anniversary

Video game developer Cordoba Games will celebrate its fifteen-year anniversary in April. The company initially focused on computer games in its early days, but it later branched out into developing its own gaming console. — [1] — It truly made its mark on the industry with the release of Dreamland Quest, which sold over three million copies in its first year. To commemorate its fifteen years in business, Cordoba Games is teaming up with Mesa Co. to create a line of limited-edition products featuring the characters from Dreamland Quest. — [2] — The line will include stationery sets, pencils, pencil cases, notebooks, and more.

With the products expecting to sell in the tens of millions, it is no surprise that a number of companies were interested in working with Cordoba Games. Executives at the company had a long list of options to choose from. — [3] — "I had previously worked for the marketing team at Mesa Co.," said Marketing Director Charles Rosario. "I know its products inside and out, and I was confident that its reputation for having high-quality and long-lasting goods was well-deserved. This is a special milestone for our company, and we didn't want to cut any corners."

The stationery is expected to hit the market on June 1 and will be sold internationally. — [4] — Whether you're a collector or just a fan of Dreamland Quest, you'll definitely want to get your hands on these unique products.

1. What does Cordoba Games plan to do?
   (A) Branch out into the international market
   (B) Release a sequel to a popular game
   (C) Provide discounts for its anniversary
   (D) Partner with another company

2. What is indicated about Mesa Co.?
   (A) It is seeking a new marketing director.
   (B) It is Cordoba Games' main competitor.
   (C) Its products are known for their durability.
   (D) It will celebrate a company milestone.

3. In which of the positions marked [1], [2], [3] and [4] does the following sentence best belong?

   "However, it was an employee's recommendation that helped them make the final decision."

   (A) [1]
   (B) [2]
   (C) [3]
   (D) [4]

Questions 4-7 refer to the following article.

MARCH 20—In a press conference held yesterday, Darby City transportation officials announced plans to add three new lines to the existing subway system to accommodate a larger number of passengers and to create easy access to suburbs such as Crafton. The city's rapid population growth over the past five years has resulted in pressure on public transportation, and the project is expected to relieve this pressure. — [1] — Construction is set to begin this summer, and the new lines will use automated trains that can be conducted without human operators. These trains are far more expensive than traditional ones, with an investment of $45 million needed for the trains alone. — [2] —

While many people are in favor of having more trains available, the city's decision to use unmanned trains is controversial. Passengers have expressed concerns about traveling in machine-operated trains, which they fear are more dangerous than those using trained operators. However, city officials say this is not the case, as these types of trains have been used by other cities for years and have proven themselves to be safe, fast, and efficient. — [3] —

Although the new trains do not require drivers, the city has no plans to lay off the existing workforce. — [4] — Skilled operators will still be needed for longer and more complex lines within the system, so personnel will be moved to these positions as necessary. "I'm pleased that the subway system is able to implement this new technology," said veteran operator Louis Belford. "Being connected to Crafton and other major suburbs through the new lines will be convenient and cost-effective for a lot of commuters."

4. According to the article, what will happen with Darby City's subway system?

   (A) Its network will be expanded.
   (B) Its fares will be doubled.
   (C) It will introduce larger cars.
   (D) Its platforms will be widened.

5. What are some passengers concerned about?

   (A) Unexpected delays
   (B) Crowded trains
   (C) Long wait times
   (D) Safety issues

6. What will happen to subway operators currently working for the city?

   (A) They will be transferred to other cities.
   (B) They will be given a retirement package.
   (C) They will be moved to other lines.
   (D) They will be retrained as technicians.

7. In which of the positions marked [1], [2], [3] and [4] does the following sentence best belong?

   "This initial expense will save money in the long run due to low labor costs."

   (A) [1]
   (B) [2]
   (C) [3]
   (D) [4]

UNIT 03
목적/주제 문제

단서의 위치는 제목과
첫 단락에 있다

PRE-STEP

지문에 등장할 주요 어휘를 미리 학습해 보자.

A 다음 빈칸에 들어갈 어휘로 알맞은 것을 고르시오.

1. a(n) ------- place to relax — (A) refreshing (B) overall
2. be selected to ------- in — (A) participate (B) remedy
3. be awarded a cash ------- — (A) prize (B) maintenance
4. ------- the situation — (A) participate (B) remedy
5. gain ------- experience — (A) valuable (B) uncomfortable
6. a ------- manager — (A) disruption (B) maintenance
7. in ------- for events — (A) preparation (B) disruption
8. ------- the final competition — (A) remedy (B) attend
9. ------- regarding parking spaces — (A) possessions (B) complaints
10. pack away one's ------- — (A) possessions (B) complaints
11. ------- the program — (A) join (B) gain
12. the overall landscape and park ------- — (A) requirements (B) facilities
13. hiring ------- — (A) possessions (B) requirements
14. a(n) ------- in the field — (A) expert (B) preparation
15. cause ------- or inconvenience — (A) disruption (B) requirement

B 다음 문장을 읽고 패러프레이징된 것으로 적절한 것을 고르시오.

1. I would like to apologize to employees on the upper floors for the uncomfortable working conditions in the last week or so.

   (A) I am sorry that some employees had to face a difficult working environment.
   (B) I am sorry for ignoring some of the employees' complaints.

2. One of the other contestants has a scheduling conflict and is now unable to attend the final competition.

   (A) The event is short one participant.
   (B) The venue is not available.

MAIN STEP¹

문제를 해결하는
핵심 전략을 살펴보자.

전략 1

90% 이상은 제목과 첫 단락에 목적이 드러난다

토익 지문은 글의 목적과 내용이 명확한 실용문으로, 대부분 그 목적과 주제가 첫 단락에 구체적으로 제시된다. 주제를 파악하면 다른 문제를 푸는 데 도움이 되므로 기본적으로 파악해 두어야 한다. 특히 이메일/편지, 회람, 광고문, 기사문의 경우 제목을 읽으면 큰 도움이 된다.

지문	memo	문제	What is the purpose of the memo? 회람이 보내진 목적은?

	MEMO
	
	 To: All employees
	 From: Maintenance department
	 ① **Subject: Parking lot expansion**
	
	 There have been a lot of complaints regarding the scarcity of parking spaces. Therefore, ② **we would like to inform you that our employee parking lot will be renovated next month.**
		풀이	① 제목에서 단서 찾기
			    "주차장 확장"
			 ② 첫 단락에서 단서 찾기
			    "직원용 주차장이 다음달에 개조된다"

		정답	To notify employees of a renovation project 직원들에게 개조 공사 계획에 대해 알리기 위해

해석: 해설집 p.13

전략 2

글쓴이의 의도가 드러나는 빈출 표현을 알아두자

이메일/편지에서 글쓴이의 의도는 지문 후반부에 제시될 수도 있다. 이하의 표현들과 연결사에 주목하도록 하자.

목적 알리기	This is a letter to ~ [I am writing to ~] 이는 ~하기 위한 편지입니다 This is to remind you that ~ 이는 ~를 상기시켜 드리기 위함입니다	We regret to inform you that ~ ~을 전하게 되어 유감입니다 I'd like to announce you that ~ ~를 알리고자 합니다
요청하기	We hope that you ~ 당신이 ~하기를 바랍니다 I would like to advise ~ ~를 조언하고 싶습니다	Please let us know whether ~ ~할 것인지 저희에게 알려주세요 Please note that ~ ~라는 점에 유의하세요
연결사	Therefore/So ~ 따라서 ~ (앞의 내용과 연결되는 내용이 온다.) I am sorry, but ~ 죄송하지만 ~	However ~ 그렇지만 ~ (앞의 내용과 반대되는 내용이 온다.)

MAIN STEP 2

앞에서 배운 전략을 문제에 직접 적용해 보자.

Question 1 refers to the following advertisement.

Maintenance Manager Needed

The construction of our new convention center is almost finished, and the center will reopen on April 30. Within the convention center grounds, there is a large park containing hundreds of trees, so it will be a refreshing place to relax with friends and family. Currently, we are looking for a maintenance manager to take care of the overall landscape and park facilities. If anyone is interested, please let us know by calling our supervisor, Mr. Scott at 100-134-5880. For specific information about duties, compensation, or hiring requirements, please visit www.southernhillconvention.net/recruit.

---

1. Why was the advertisement written?
   (A) To publicize a job vacancy
   (B) To promote a new facility
   (C) To introduce a new product
   (D) To announce an office move

보너스문제
① How can applicants get more details?

Question 2 refers to the following letter.

Laura Krause
922 Charack Road
Jasper, IN 47546

May 1

Dear Ms. Krause,

This is a letter to inform you that you have been selected to participate in Alma Industries' Summer Internship Program. Congratulations! During the internship, you will be working alongside experts in the field and will gain valuable experience. You will work with us from June 5 to August 31. You should confirm that you'll be joining in the program by calling my office at 555-8640 by May 10. I hope to hear good news from you soon.

Sincerely,

Walter Robbins
HR Director, Alma Industries

---

2. What is the purpose of the letter?
   (A) To inform Ms. Krause of a change
   (B) To schedule an interview with Ms. Krause
   (C) To offer Ms. Krause a position
   (D) To submit an application to Ms. Krause

보너스문제
② Why should Ms. Krause contact Mr. Robbins?

보너스문제 정답 ① By visiting a Web site ② To confirm a decision

FINAL STEP

실전 난이도의 문제를 풀며 앞에서 배운 전략을 활용해 보자.

Questions 1-2 refer to the following letter.

Ms. Charlotte Bass
100 Huntington Avenue
Boston, MA 02116

April 8

Dear Ms. Bass,

I am writing to congratulate you on making it to the final round of the Abra Bacon Prize in informative speaking. I understand that you finished fourth in your preliminary qualifying competition, of which only the top three speakers move forward. However, one of the other contestants has a scheduling conflict and is now unable to attend the final competition. Fortunately, this means that we are advancing you instead.

The final round of the contest will be held on Saturday, April 30, at 2 P.M. in the Donald Miller room of the Freeport Hotel in downtown Boston. You are expected to arrive by April 28 in preparation for a number of contestant events that will be held on April 28 and April 29. The person with the winning speech will be awarded a cash prize of $1,000.

Congratulations once again,

Nigel Ebner
Chairperson, Abra Bacon Prize

1. What is the purpose of Mr. Ebner's letter?
   (A) To update a contestant on her status
   (B) To provide directions to a competition
   (C) To solicit opinions on a tournament
   (D) To arrange the pick up of an award

2. When will the final speech take place?
   (A) On April 8
   (B) On April 28
   (C) On April 29
   (D) On April 30

Questions 3-5 refer to the following memo.

To: All staff
From: Alicia Wright
Date: July 17

I would like to apologize to employees on the upper floors for the uncomfortable working conditions in the last week or so. The air conditioning unit has been malfunctioning and, because the windows do not fully open on the 3rd, 4th, or 5th floors, it has been very stuffy and hot.

Please let me reassure you that management has taken steps to remedy the situation. A new air conditioner will be installed over the weekend. To protect belongings from dust and debris, employees on the upper floors are asked to pack away their possessions and equipment on Friday afternoon. I hope that this will not cause too much disruption or inconvenience. Thank you for your patience.

Kind regards,

Alicia Wright
Maintenance Manager

3. What is the purpose of the memo?
   (A) To request employee feedback on a matter
   (B) To announce a maintenance upgrade
   (C) To inform employees of safety guidelines
   (D) To report the results of a recent test

4. Why are upstairs workers experiencing difficulties?
   (A) Their windows are broken.
   (B) The temperature is uncomfortably warm.
   (C) The workspace is too crowded.
   (D) Their equipment is covered with dust.

5. What are upstairs workers requested to do on Friday?
   (A) Put their gear away
   (B) Stay out of the office
   (C) Dispose of old equipment
   (D) Work on a lower floor

UNIT 04
대상/출처 문제

지문의 내용을 알면
저절로 풀린다

PRE-STEP

지문에 등장할 주요 어휘를 미리 학습해 보자.

A 다음 빈칸에 들어갈 어휘로 알맞은 것을 고르시오.

1. ------- a time sheet   (A) submit   (B) refund
2. a ------- research assistant   (A) detailed   (B) short-term
3. ------- an arrival date   (A) indicate   (B) submit
4. ------- the documentation   (A) sign   (B) register
5. ------- a 40% discount   (A) sign   (B) receive
6. the place of -------   (A) form   (B) purchase
7. fill out a ------- accurately   (A) form   (B) purchase
8. a full -------   (A) refund   (B) purchase
9. a more ------- explanation   (A) detailed   (B) short-term
10. reliable -------   (A) refund   (B) transportation
11. ------- with the payroll department (A) upgrade (B) register
12. a ------- bank account number (A) valid   (B) detailed
13. ------- *one's* seat selection (A) submit   (B) upgrade
14. a few rules to -------   (A) follow   (B) submit
15. ------- the statement   (A) check   (B) upgrade

B 다음 문장을 읽고 패러프레이징된 것으로 적절한 것을 고르시오.

1.
> Forrester Farms initiated a voluntary recall of its frozen chicken breasts manufactured at the Oregon facility.

(A) Forrester Farms gives voluntary tours of its factory in Oregon.
(B) Forrester Farms is taking back products that may have problems.

2.
> A copy of the pay statement, including details about taxes and other withholdings, will be sent to you via e-mail.

(A) You will be sent financial information.
(B) You are expected to pay a tax bill.

MAIN STEP¹

| 문제를 해결하는 핵심 전략을 살펴보자.

대상 문제는 내용을 이해하면 자연스럽게 풀리므로 맨 마지막에 푼다

대상 문제는 주로 광고문, 상품 관련 정보문, 사용설명서에서 상품/서비스의 대상을 묻는 문제나, 공지문의 대상을 묻는 문제로 출제된다. 주제/목적 문제처럼 단서가 명확하지 않은 경우가 많으므로, 어휘를 종합해 유추해야 한다.

지문 information

If you want your **TXP132 hair dryer** to work properly, **there are a few rules you need to follow**:
— Do not cover or block any part when it is on
— Store it in a dry place

해석: 해설집 p.18

문제 For whom is the information intended?
정보의 의도된 대상은?

풀이 헤어드라이기 사용 시 주의 사항에 관한 내용으로, 헤어드라이기 구입자를 대상으로 하는 정보문이다.

정답 Owners of new hair dryers
새 헤어드라이기의 주인

글의 출처 문제는 광고, 정보문, 양식 등에서 주로 출제된다

해당 지문을 볼 수 있는 곳을 묻는 출처 문제가 광고문에 나오는 경우는 광고되는 상품/서비스가 무엇인지를, 정보문에 나오는 경우는 무엇에 관한 정보인지를 캐치하면 쉽게 풀 수 있다. 양식 지문에서는 양식의 구성 요소들을 살펴본다.

지문 form

Oaksville History Museum
Complimentary pass

Exhibition title: To the beginning of the human race
Issue date: July 10

해석: 해설집 p.19

문제 Where would this information most likely to be found?
이 정보가 있을 것 같은 곳은?

풀이 박물관, 무료 입장권, 전시 제목, 발급 날짜 등이 적혀 있으므로 티켓에서 볼 수 있는 내용이다.

정답 On a ticket
티켓

지문 information

Downtown Shuttle Service

For reliable transportation between the airport and downtown hotels, book your seat on our airport shuttle! Using our service, you can get from the airport to any hotel downtown within 30 minutes. **To book a ride on our shuttle, simply click the "Shuttle Reservations" button at the bottom of this page** and indicate your flight arrival date and time along with the flight number.

해석: 해설집 p.19

문제 Where does this information most likely appear?
이 정보가 있을 것 같은 곳은?

풀이 셔틀 버스 좌석 예약에 관한 정보문으로, 어느 매체에도 나올 수 있는 내용 같지만 끝부분에 "셔틀 버스 예약" 버튼을 클릭하라고 했으므로 출처는 웹사이트이다.

정답 On a Web site
웹사이트

MAIN STEP 2

앞에서 배운 전략을
문제에 직접 적용해 보자.

Question 1 refers to the following notice.

Forrester Farms initiated a voluntary recall of its frozen chicken breasts manufactured at the Portland, Oregon facility. If you have recently purchased frozen chicken, please check your freezer to see if your product has ALL of the following:
- Forrester Farms frozen chicken breasts label
- Product code T-44902
- Best before date of February 12

If this item is currently in your freezer, please return it to the place of purchase for a full refund. If you have any questions about the recall, please e-mail Richard Mayaski, who is in charge of customer service. His e-mail is richardmayaski@forresterfarms.com.

1. For whom was the notice written?
   (A) Meat purchasers
   (B) Factory workers
   (C) Grocery store cashiers
   (D) Chicken farmers

보너스문제
① Who most likely is Mr. Mayaski?

Question 2 refers to the following information.

Elliot's Bran Flakes: Great Taste in Every Bite!

Nutrition Facts
Serving Size: 3/4 cups

Amount per serving
Calories 101

| Fat 0.78g | Cholesterol 0mg | Sugars 4.82g | Calcium 16.2mg |
| Sodium 215.21mg | Dietary Fiber 5.31g | Protein 2.77g | Iron 6.6mg |

This product was manufactured in a facility that processes peanuts.

For further information, visit our Web site at www.elliotscereal.com.

2. Where would this information most likely appear?
   (A) On a nutritional Web site
   (B) In a recipe book
   (C) On a product's packaging
   (D) In an informational pamphlet

보너스문제
② What is true about Elliot's Bran Flakes?

보너스문제 정답 ① The head of customer service ② They have more dietary fiber than protein.

FINAL STEP

실전 난이도의 문제를 풀며 앞에서 배운 전략을 활용해 보자.

Questions 1-3 refer to the following form.

SECTION	ROW	SEAT
212	B	29

ALL GATE ACCESS   PRICE
LEVEL 4 CONCOURSE $21.50

VANCOUVER CANUCKS
VS
BOSTON BRUINS
ROGERS ARENA

THURSDAY, JUNE 15
Playing begins @ 7:00 P.M.
Doors open @ 6:00 P.M.

SEASON TICKET HOLDER: Milton Oxley

- Street parking during games is not provided.
- Games last three hours, including two intermissions.
- NO OUTSIDE FOOD OR DRINKS ARE PERMITTED.
- Do NOT lose this ticket. Only ticket holders will be admitted to hockey games.
- All season ticket holders receive a 40% discount on the purchase of arena merchandise.
- To upgrade your seat selection, visit www.majorleaguehockey.com at least two days before the game.

1. Where would this form most likely be found?

   (A) In a restaurant
   (B) In a parking lot
   (C) In a theater box office
   (D) In a hockey arena

2. What is indicated about Milton Oxley?

   (A) He can upgrade his seats at any time.
   (B) He can buy merchandise at a discounted price.
   (C) He can park underground below the stadium.
   (D) He can purchase alcohol on site.

3. What time will the game end?

   (A) 6:00 P.M.
   (B) 7:00 P.M.
   (C) 9:00 P.M.
   (D) 10:00 P.M.

Questions 4-7 refer to the following e-mail.

To: Elliot Franks <elliotfranks@twente.edu>, Javier Mendez <javiermendez@twente.edu>, Aluk Yousuf <alukyousuf@twente.edu>
From: James Cho <jamescho@twente.edu>
Date: March 14
Subject: Information for new recruits
Attachment: Payroll_registration.txt, Payroll_timesheets.txt

I understand that you have all been employed as short-term research assistants in the social science department as part of the Population Survey Project. In order to be paid for your work, you must first register with the payroll department. You will each need to fill out the forms accurately, providing the correct project code and a valid bank account number. Your project supervisor, Professor Herni Dwiliati, must sign these forms before you submit them to the payroll department. Once you are in the system, you should submit a time sheet at the end of each week. After doing so, please leave the time sheets at the reception desk of the Registry Building by 5:30 P.M. on Friday.

Provided that the details are all correct, your payment will be processed on Wednesday. You should receive the money in your nominated account by Thursday. A copy of the pay statement, including details about taxes and other withholdings, will be sent to you via e-mail. Please check the statement to ensure that everything is in order.

If you have further questions regarding this process, please contact me by e-mail.

James Cho
Payroll Administrator

4. For whom is the e-mail intended?
   (A) Temporary research employees
   (B) University administrators
   (C) Payroll department employees
   (D) Project supervisors

5. Where should employees leave their time sheets?
   (A) In the social science departmental office
   (B) In James Cho's office
   (C) In the payroll pigeon hole
   (D) In a reception area

6. Why have documents been attached to the e-mail?
   (A) To give a more detailed explanation of the project
   (B) To forward the paperwork the employees need to fill out
   (C) To explain the details of the employees' contracts
   (D) To provide examples about how the process works

7. What is NOT indicated about the payment system?
   (A) It operates on a weekly cycle.
   (B) It is administered by each individual department.
   (C) It provides detailed statements for employees.
   (D) It requires recording working hours.

UNIT 05
세부 정보 문제

키워드에 집중하라

PRE-STEP

지문에 등장할 주요 어휘를 미리 학습해 보자.

A 다음 빈칸에 들어갈 어휘로 알맞은 것을 고르시오.

1.	an industry -------	(A) apparel	(B) leader
2.	a(n) ------- investigator	(A) insurance	(B) reputation
3.	destroy most of the -------	(A) insurance	(B) inventory
4.	outdoor ------- and products	(A) apparel	(B) inventory
5.	a ------- seat upgrade	(A) loyal	(B) complimentary
6.	pass a ------- testing process	(A) tough	(B) complimentary
7.	a ------- customer	(A) loyal	(B) complimentary
8.	offer ------- tour deals	(A) tough	(B) exclusive
9.	------- with other professionals	(A) disclose	(B) network
10.	------- the situation	(A) disclose	(B) network
11.	estimate ------- costs	(A) repair	(B) reputation
12.	meals and -------	(A) repairs	(B) refreshments
13.	the ------- board	(A) exclusive	(B) executive
14.	------- to *one's* work	(A) dedication	(B) indication
15.	enhance a company's -------	(A) refreshment	(B) reputation

B 다음 문장을 읽고 패러프레이징된 것으로 적절한 것을 고르시오.

1.
> Unlike our other products, the lightweight design of our rain jacket makes it easy to fold up and store in a backpack without taking up much space.

(A) The jacket can withstand all types of weather.
(B) The jacket is compact for easy storage.

2.
> The executive board is meeting with the fire chief tomorrow to discuss the exact cause of the fire.

(A) The fire chief has caused a problem with officials.
(B) The reason for the fire will be examined by officials.

MAIN STEP¹

| 문제를 해결하는 핵심 전략을 살펴보자.

전략 1   문제에서 제시된 키워드 중심으로 빠르게 찾아 읽는다

세부 정보 문제의 경우, 문제가 출제되는 순서와 지문 내 단서의 위치는 대부분 일치한다. 따라서 문제의 키워드를 지문 내에서 순서대로 찾으며 하나씩 해결해 나가는 것이 좋다. 이때 지문의 내용이 문제의 선택지에서는 다른 표현으로 바뀌어 제시되므로, 같은 단어가 아닌 같은 의미를 알아채는 것이 관건이다.

지문   memo

The Better Tomorrow Association (BTA) is holding a workshop at the Hayward Plaza on Saturday, October 13. ①**The workshop will teach you practical methods for reducing your impact on the environment. From conserving resources to planting trees, you'll discover a number of ways in which you can make a difference.**

We would like many employees to attend this important event, so we are happy to announce that ②**we will be paying half of the registration fee for anyone who wishes to participate.** Simply send a copy of your registration receipt to the accounting department, and you will be reimbursed on your next paycheck.

해석: 해설집 p.24

문제①   What can participants learn about at the workshop?
참가자들이 워크숍에서 배울 수 있는 것은?

정답   Helping the environment
환경 살리기

문제②   What will the company do for its employees?
회사가 직원들을 위해 할 일은?

정답   Make a partial payment of the registration fee
등록비 일부 지불하기

전략 2   지문의 마지막 부분에 자주 나오는 세 가지 문제 유형이 있다

요청이나 수단, 방법, 연락처, 또는 추후의 일 관련 문제는 주로 지문의 마지막 부분에 나온다. 다음의 문제들이 나오면 지문 마지막 부분에서 단서를 찾아보자.

요청 문제 - 문제에 동사 ask, require가 등장	What is Ms. Churchill **asked** to present? 처칠 씨가 제출하도록 요청받은 것은? What document was **requested**? 요청받은 서류는?
수단, 방법, 연락처 문제 - 문제가 의문사 How로 시작	**How** can volunteers participate in the event? 자원봉사자들이 행사에 참석할 수 있는 방법은?
추후의 일 관련 문제 - 문제에 미래를 나타내는 시간 표현, 조동사 will이 등장	What **will** happen **next month**? 다음 달에 벌어질 일은?

MAIN STEP²

앞에서 배운 전략을 문제에 직접 적용해 보자.

Question 1 refers to the following advertisement.

For the last fifteen years, Nordic Athletic has been an industry leader in outdoor apparel and products. One of our most recent clothing items to pass our tough testing process is the Always-Dry rain jacket, which is made of waterproof material. The Always-Dry rain jacket is perfect for long hiking trips or camping weekends when you plan to be active, but need to be prepared for all weather conditions. Unlike our other products, the lightweight design of the Always-Dry rain jacket makes it easy to fold up and store in a backpack without taking up much space. We guarantee that if you buy this jacket you will not be disappointed.

1. What was the Always-Dry rain jacket designed for?
   (A) Outdoor activities
   (B) Winter sports
   (C) High-energy exercises
   (D) Short hiking trips

보너스문제
① How is the Always-Dry rain jacket different from other Nordic Athletic products?

Question 2 refers to the following e-mail.

To: Michael Naughton <naughton_mike@pmail.net>
From: Doral Airlines <noreply@doralairlines.com>
Date: November 1
Subject: Early bird rates

Dear Mr. Naughton,

Doral Airlines is offering exclusive tour deals to Europe. Take advantage of our early-bird offer by booking flights during the next several days. You will save thousands of dollars on the cost of tickets to any European destination! Our records indicate that you are a loyal customer who travels with us regularly. Because of your dedication to our airline, we will give you a complimentary seat upgrade during this promotion period. If you're interested in this offer, please respond to this e-mail as soon as possible.

Sincerely,
Doral Airlines Customer Service

2. How can Mr. Naughton get a free upgrade?
   (A) By sending an e-mail reply
   (B) By booking a ticket online
   (C) By calling the number provided
   (D) By presenting a loyalty card

보너스문제
② What is indicated about Mr. Naughton?

보너스문제 정답 ① It is very compact in size. ② He flies with Doral Airlines frequently.

FINAL STEP

실전 난이도의 문제를 풀며 앞에서 배운 전략을 활용해 보자.

Questions 1-3 refer to the following e-mail.

To: Anneke Rhodes <arhodes@yutaniindustries.com>
From: Barry Olson <barryolson@yutaniindustries.com>
Date: October 28
Subject: Urgent meeting tomorrow!

Hi Anneke,

I know you're on vacation, but we have a major issue, and consequently, I needed to let you know about it. Early yesterday morning, a fire erupted in the warehouse and destroyed most of our inventory. The executive board is meeting with the fire chief tomorrow to discuss the exact cause of the fire. The insurance investigator will also be present to outline what portion of the repair costs will be covered by our existing policy.

After that meeting tomorrow, our leadership team will also gather to determine how we intend to resolve several other problems. For instance, whereas there are three outstanding orders that need to be shipped, we now have no stock to fill them. I have contacted those three customers and disclosed the situation. But we must still develop a plan to cope with production delays. We are obviously going to have to rebuild and restock. As the warehouse superintendent, it's crucial that you be involved in this conversation. Are you available to call in and participate in the production meeting via phone at 11 A.M.?

Please let me know as soon as possible whether you can do this.

Barry Olson
Administrator

1. What is the purpose of the e-mail?
   (A) To inform a colleague about a crisis
   (B) To delegate various duties
   (C) To ask to have access to a telephone
   (D) To announce the results of a meeting

2. According to the e-mail, what is expected to happen on October 29?
   (A) An insurance payment will be processed.
   (B) A daily status meeting will be canceled.
   (C) A plan will be developed.
   (D) An inventory assessment will be conducted.

3. What is mentioned about the problem to be discussed?
   (A) Several customers called with complaints.
   (B) Three outstanding orders cannot be filled.
   (C) A shipment was delivered behind schedule.
   (D) Some orders were processed incorrectly.

Questions 4-6 refer to the following notice.

NOTICE

On behalf of the management team, I'm writing this notice to all employees who are planning to attend the National Journalism Conference in Seattle. The conference was originally scheduled for May 21 at the Bloomfield Convention Center. However, we've just been informed that it has been postponed due to a scheduling conflict at the venue. It will now be held on June 4, beginning at 8 A.M. All other plans, including the carpool arrangements, will remain the same.

As outlined in last month's newsletter, this conference is a great opportunity to network with other professionals in the industry as well as to enhance the company's reputation. There will be a number of lectures for participants to choose from, and meals and refreshments will be served throughout the day. In honor of the occasion, a live band will play in the evening, so we expect it to be an enjoyable event. Full details about the conference are posted on the bulletin board in the employee break room. Should you have questions, please refer to the materials there.

Thank you,

Richard Jordan, Office Manager

4. What is the purpose of the notice?
   (A) To announce a schedule change
   (B) To ask for assistance with an event
   (C) To organize carpool drivers
   (D) To thank employees for organizing an event

5. What is mentioned as a benefit of attending the conference?
   (A) Registrants can listen to every lecture.
   (B) Hotel accommodations are paid for.
   (C) Journalists might improve their writing ability.
   (D) Participants can make industry connections.

6. According to Mr. Jordan, how can employees get more information?
   (A) By reading a brochure
   (B) By checking a bulletin board
   (C) By visiting a Web site
   (D) By sending an e-mail

UNIT 06
NOT/TRUE 문제

대조 소거법을 이용하라

PRE-STEP

지문에 등장할 주요 어휘를 미리 학습해 보자.

A 다음 빈칸에 들어갈 어휘로 알맞은 것을 고르시오.

1. all ------- of expenses (A) attraction (B) documentation
2. ------- to the festival (A) admission (B) documentation
3. the product's main ------- (A) admission (B) attraction
4. ------- staff (A) supervise (B) unload
5. ------- cartons and store returns (A) feature (B) unload
6. ------- a handful of singers (A) feature (B) operate
7. a proven track ------- (A) delivery (B) record
8. prepare shipments for ------- (A) delivery (B) record
9. ------- warehouse equipment (A) feature (B) operate
10. one's ------- coworker (A) former (B) profitable
11. meet industry safety ------- (A) standards (B) reimbursements
12. an internationally ------- designer (A) recognized (B) former
13. a start of a ------- career (A) promising (B) handful
14. the processing of monthly ------- (A) standards (B) reimbursements
15. invest in a ------- business (A) handful (B) profitable

B 다음 문장을 읽고 패러프레이징된 것으로 적절한 것을 고르시오.

1.
> You should send me a copy of your driver's license so that we can add you to the company auto insurance policy.

(A) An ID is needed for some paperwork.
(B) A clean driving record is required.

2.
> By continuing to open stores in various countries, we are on our way to becoming the leading toy company in the world.

(A) We are developing more and more unique toys.
(B) We are growing our business internationally.

MAIN STEP¹

> 문제를 해결하는 핵심 전략을 살펴보자.

선택지를 하나씩 지문과 대조해 정답을 골라낸다

진위 여부를 묻는 NOT/TRUE 문제는 세부 정보가 나열된 부분에서 주로 출제된다. 정답은 대부분 패러프레이징되므로 선택지 (A)~(D)를 지문의 내용과 하나씩 대조해 가며 정답을 골라야 한다.

지문 advertisement

Enhance Your Office with the Kovar All-in-one Printer

Feature: Graves Electronics is the exclusive retailer for the Kovar-500 printer, which can ⁽ᶜ⁾scan, copy, fax, and print documents at the touch of a button. Its lightweight design and ⁽ᴮ⁾low-energy usage make it perfect for offices of any size. ⁽ᴬ⁾Customers who purchase the device this week will get an additional $50 off.

해석: 해설집 p.29

문제 What is **NOT** mentioned **as a feature of the printer**?
(A) Early purchase discounts (X)
(B) Energy efficiency (X)
(C) Document scanning (X)
(D) Wireless compatibility (O)

풀이 ① 키워드 확인: a feature of the printer
② 선택지 (A)~(D)를 순서대로 확인.
  → (D)의 무선 호환성에 관한 내용은 없음.

정답 (D)

대상에 대한 전반적 사항을 묻는 NOT/TRUE 문제는 마지막에 푼다

대상에 대해 전반적으로 묻는 NOT/TRUE 문제는 질문 자체가 광범위하기 때문에 단서가 여러 부분에 걸쳐 있다. 이러한 문제 유형은 지문 전체를 꼼꼼히 봐야 하기 때문에 시간이 많이 걸리므로 마지막에 푸는 것이 요령이다.

지문 advertisement

Having trouble keeping your home or office looking its best? Let Speed Cleaners make your space sparkle! We offer a variety of cleaning packages to fit your needs. Hourly rates start at just $20, and we're available Monday through Saturday from 7 A.M. to 8 P.M. And you won't have to worry about harsh cleaners or chemicals in your home. The cleaning products we use are chemical-free and won't cause harm to the environment. You'll be impressed by our respectful and courteous staff. Despite being the fastest in the business, they always get the job done right.

해석: 해설집 p.30

문제 What is **true about Speed Cleaners**?
(A) Its staff is highly experienced. (X)
(B) Its services are available every day. (X)
(C) It uses environmentally friendly products. (O)
(D) It has the lowest hourly rates in town. (X)

풀이 ① 키워드 확인: Speed Cleaners
② 선택지 (A)~(D)를 지문과 대조
  (A) 직원들의 경험이 풍부하다는 내용은 없음. (X)
  (B) 월~토요일까지 서비스 이용이 가능하므로 매일은 아님. (X)
  (C) 청소용품은 화학 성분이 없고 환경에 피해를 미치지 않음. (O)
  (D) 요금이 가장 낮다는 언급은 없음. (X)

정답 (C)

MAIN STEP 2

앞에서 배운 전략을 문제에 직접 적용해 보자.

Question 1 refers to the following memo.

> **MEMO**
>
> I have some news to share about our friend and former coworker. As you may remember, Allan Geere worked here at Cortex for three years before leaving to continue his education. Allan has gone on to complete graduate school and obtain his master's degree in vocal performance. He is now trying to establish himself as a musical theater actor, and he surely has the voice for it. Allan's unexpected concerts around the office were just a start to what will surely be a promising career!

1. What is NOT mentioned about Allan Geere?

(A) He is a former Cortex employee.
(B) He has received a graduate degree.
(C) He used to sing at work.
(D) He prefers acting in comedies.

보너스문제
① What is the purpose of the memo?

Question 2 refers to the following e-mail.

> **To:** Colleen Friske <friskecolleen@newmail.net>
> **From:** Riley Stendahl <rilst2@sfassociates.com>
> **Date:** April 30
> **Subject:** In response to your question
>
> Dear Ms. Friske,
>
> On behalf of Strehl-Friedman Associates, I wanted to answer your question about corporate travel. Yes, we will provide you with a company car for traveling to meet clients. Please ensure that all documentation of expenses related to the car or to your travel—gas, emergency repairs, tollbooth fees, overnight lodging, etc.—are carefully saved and dated to expedite the processing of monthly reimbursements for these expenditures. You should also send me a copy of your driver's license so that we can add you to the company auto insurance policy.
>
> Riley Stendahl, HR Manager
> Strehl-Friedman Associates

2. According to the e-mail, what is true about Strehl-Friedman Associates?

(A) It provides emergency repair services.
(B) It runs an auto insurance agency.
(C) It reimburses business travel expenses.
(D) It requires a passport copy.

보너스문제
② What can be inferred about Ms. Friske?

보너스문제 정답 ① To give an update on a colleague ② She asked Ms. Stendahl a question.

FINAL STEP

실전 난이도의 문제를 풀며 앞에서 배운 전략을 활용해 보자.

Questions 1-3 refer to the following article.

The 4th Annual Maceió Winter Jazz Festival is Approaching

December 3—Similarly to last year's event, more than 300 people are expected to attend the fourth annual Maceió Winter Jazz Festival from December 10 to 16 in Deodoro Park. Each day will have simultaneous performances. Years ago, this little jazz festival was no more than a one-day concert featuring a handful of singers and instrumentalists. Today, however, the festival has evolved into a week-long event that celebrates several dozen jazz musicians throughout Brazil. CDs, instruments, and other merchandise will be on sale for the entire festival.

Admission to the festival is $5 per day or $25 for the full week. Its hours of operation are from 9 A.M. to 9 P.M. on weekdays and 11 A.M. to 5 P.M. on weekends. The primary attraction for most attendees will be the performance of world-famous jazz singer Renée Byron. She will perform at 7 P.M. on the first evening of the festival.

1. What is the article mainly about?
   (A) A postponed instrumental performance
   (B) The opening of a music store
   (C) A popular once-a-year celebration
   (D) The results of a jazz competition

2. What is NOT mentioned as a feature of the event?
   (A) It was attended by more than 300 people last year.
   (B) Some performances will run concurrently.
   (C) Beverages will be sold near the stage.
   (D) Interested guests can purchase merchandise.

3. What is indicated about Ms. Byron?
   (A) She has been invited to close the festival.
   (B) She is the founder of the event.
   (C) She does not reside in Maceió, Brazil.
   (D) She will perform on December 10.

Questions 4-5 refer to the following job advertisement.

Toy World International

Toy World International, which was established by the internationally recognized toy designer Milo Lampen, is a Minnesotan toy manufacturer. Since its establishment seventy years ago, Toy World has expanded to sell merchandise in nearly 2,000 stores across the globe. By continuing to open stores in various countries, we are on our way to becoming the leading toy company in the world. With this plan, we are filling the following positions:

48989: Warehouse Operations Team Member (Minneapolis)
Warehouse operations team members unload all cartons and store returns. They also prepare shipments for delivery and load trailers. In order to meet industry safety standards, they must be certified to operate all warehouse equipment.

49464: Head, Facilities Department (Duluth)
This position is responsible for all aspects of facility maintenance such as assigning duties, supervising staff, monitoring equipment repairs, and ordering maintenance supplies.

59417: Store Manager (Rochester)
Store managers oversee the effective and profitable operations of each store. They manage customer satisfaction and staff development. Candidates must have a proven track record in management and generating significant revenue.

Interested applicants must send résumés to careers@toyworld.com with the position title and five-digit job number identified in the subject line.

4. What is indicated about Toy World International?
   (A) It sells products only in the United States.
   (B) It was founded by a famous designer.
   (C) It has a total of 2,000 employees on its staff.
   (D) It is hiring new staff for six available positions.

5. What is NOT included in the facilities department head's duties?
   (A) Assigning tasks to employees
   (B) Overseeing the operation of each store
   (C) Asking for necessary supplies
   (D) Supervising staff

UNIT 07
추론 문제

출제 유형을 알면
추론이 간단해진다

PRE-STEP

지문에 등장할 주요 어휘를 미리 학습해 보자.

A 다음 빈칸에 들어갈 어휘로 알맞은 것을 고르시오.

1.	------- an operation	(A) hesitate	(B) expand
2.	the ------- town	(A) brief	(B) entire
3.	be ------- to *do*	(A) encouraged	(B) handled
4.	a free ------- of wine	(A) variety	(B) bottle
5.	------- to contact	(A) hesitate	(B) expand
6.	be ------- to *do*	(A) excited	(B) presented
7.	have a ------- location	(A) brief	(B) secondary
8.	be just ------- the corner	(A) between	(B) around
9.	a ------- of wet weather	(A) likelihood	(B) bottle
10.	a fixed interest -------	(A) likelihood	(B) rate
11.	a(n) ------- description	(A) brief	(B) secondary
12.	a ------- for the loan	(A) guarantee	(B) variety
13.	a wide ------- of products	(A) guarantee	(B) variety
14.	a(n) ------- device	(A) brief	(B) efficient
15.	the data ------- in the table	(A) presented	(B) encouraged

B 다음 문장을 읽고 패러프레이징된 것으로 적절한 것을 고르시오.

1.
> I would like to discuss with you directly how we can ensure that future deliveries will arrive on time.

(A) I want to postpone a delivery that was scheduled for later.
(B) I want to make sure we don't receive our orders late again.

2.
> When you buy your tickets, there will be an opportunity to indicate your desire to participate in this special event.

(A) You can show your interest at the time of purchase.
(B) You can share your comments about what we offer.

MAIN STEP 1

문제를 해결하는
핵심 전략을 살펴보자.

 전략 1

추론 문제의 단서는 간접적으로 등장한다

What is inferred/implied/suggested about ~?의 형태로 등장하는 추론 문제는 세부 정보 문제와 헷갈리기 쉽다. 또한 단서가 간접적으로 등장하기 때문에 난이도가 다소 높다. 특히 양식과 같이 항목화된 내용에서 추론 문제가 자주 등장하므로 각 항목들이 의미하는 바를 주의 깊게 살펴야 한다.

지문 form

Current feedback form

Name: Takita Yumi
Purchase you made at Subtext Phones:
Hassler 4

Service Areas	Good	Satisfactory	Poor
Speed of service	×		
Friendliness of staff		×	
Staff knowledge of products			×

해석: 해설집 p.34

문제 What can be inferred about the service Ms. Takita received?
타키타 씨가 받은 서비스에 대해 추론할 수 있는 것은?

풀이 작성자인 타키타 씨가 Staff knowledge of products 항목의 Poor란에 체크함.
→ 해당 항목이 개선되어야 함을 의미

정답 Employees should have better product knowledge.
직원들이 제품 지식을 더 갖추어야 한다.

 전략 2

기간이나 시기를 추론하는 문제가 가장 많이 나온다

추론 문제로는 특정 기간 또는 시기를 추론해야 하는 문제가 가장 많이 출제된다.

기간, 시기와 관련해 자주 나오는 패러프레이징

기간 추론	지문	**For the second consecutive year**, China will be home to the conference. 연속 2년째, 중국은 그 회의의 주최국이 될 것이다.	정답	China has been holding a conference **for less than three years**. 중국은 3년 미만 동안 회의를 주최해 오고 있다.
과거 시기 추론	지문	The meeting **has just been canceled**. 회의가 방금 취소되었다.	정답	The meeting **was originally scheduled for today**. 회의가 원래 오늘로 예정되어 있었다.
미래 시기 추론	지문	The proposal was issued **at the end of the third quarter**, but it will be revised **early next quarter**. 그 제안은 3분기 말에 발표되었으나 다음 분기 초에 수정될 것이다.	정답	It will be changed **in the fourth quarter**. 4분기에 변경될 것이다.

MAIN STEP 2

앞에서 배운 전략을
문제에 직접 적용해 보자.

Question 1 refers to the following form.

Timbercrest Railway

Date of ticket acquisition: January 13
Frequent traveler number: 015 481 694

Passenger name: Randall Havisham
Paid by: Platinum Card XXXX XXXX XXXX 7534

Date	Train	Departure	Arrival	Seat
February 2, Mon	SWR 466	Toronto 6:05 A.M.	Ottawa 10:35 A.M.	10D
February 4, Wed	SWR 872	Ottawa 3:35 P.M.	Toronto 8:05 P.M.	12B

Printed tickets and personal identification must be presented upon boarding the train.

1. What is suggested about Mr. Havisham?
   (A) He paid for his ticket in cash.
   (B) He travels on the train regularly.
   (C) He will stay in Ottawa for three nights.
   (D) He will return to Toronto in the morning.

(보너스문제)
① When will Mr. Havisham depart for Toronto?

Question 2 refers to the following e-mail.

To: Derek Houston <dhouston@houstonsteel.com>
From: Heather Carlson <heather@sterling.com>
Subject: Re: Problem with Delivery Delays
Date: May 28

Dear Mr. Houston,

I'm contacting you today regarding your factory's recent shipments of steel pipes to our warehouse. I received each of the last three shipments between two and three days late. Our clients depend on Sterling Construction to finish the projects on time. Therefore, timely delivery of materials from our suppliers is essential to the success of our business. I am confident we can resolve this issue quickly and effectively. I am scheduled to visit your factory this coming month. I would like to discuss with you directly how we can ensure that future deliveries will arrive on time. I appreciate your attention to this matter.

Heather Carlson
Warehouse Manager, Sterling Construction

2. What can be inferred about the visit?
   (A) It will be about the new project.
   (B) It will take place in June.
   (C) It will involve many corporations.
   (D) It has been postponed.

(보너스문제)
② Why did Ms. Carlson contact Ms. Houston?

보너스문제 정답   ① On Wednesday afternoon   ② To complain about delivery delays

FINAL STEP

실전 난이도의 문제를 풀며 앞에서 배운 전략을 활용해 보자.

Questions 1-3 refer to the following flyer.

Averill Creek Wine Festival

The annual Averill Creek Wine Festival at Princeton Park is just around the corner! For one day only—June 28 from 7 A.M. to 9 P.M.—the entire town of Averill Creek will celebrate everything wine-related.

Vineyard and winery owners are encouraged to attend 'New Technologies in Wine Making' at 4 P.M., when a new machine will be demonstrated. Instead of crushing grapes, this efficient device is designed to split them open in a time-saving way.

During the famous 'Wine-Tasting' event held on the main stage, participants will be blindfolded and asked to taste and identify various types of wine. When you buy your tickets, there will be an opportunity to indicate your desire to participate in this special event.

Tickets cost $25 and include one free bottle of wine. As is typical for this time of year, there is a likelihood of wet weather. Just in case, we have a secondary indoor location prepared so that the festival can go on as planned.

---

1. For whom is this flyer most likely intended?
   (A) Princeton Park employees
   (B) Festival volunteers
   (C) Averill Creek residents
   (D) Event organizers

2. What can be inferred about the weather?
   (A) It is irrelevant because the event is always held indoors.
   (B) A poor weather plan has not yet been created.
   (C) It commonly rains at this time of year.
   (D) The festival will be rescheduled in the case of rain.

3. The word "way" in paragraph 2, line 3, is closest in meaning to
   (A) progress
   (B) method
   (C) direction
   (D) habit

Questions 4-6 refer to the following e-mail.

To: Jeffery Neal <jneal@email99.com>
From: Prime Bank <et@primebank1.net>
Date: January 29
Subject: RE: Your inquiry

Dear Mr. Neal,

Thank you for your inquiry about applying for a loan through Prime Bank. We have a wide variety of loans available for small businesses such as yours. After reading the brief description you gave of your need to finance a building upgrade, I think the Professional Construction Loan would be right for you. It can be used for any type of building project related to your business. We offer both a five-year term and a seven-year term, and you can borrow up to $15,000, which will have a fixed interest rate of 7.3% for the life of the loan.

Along with your loan application, you must submit documents such as your bank statements, tax records, or a business license. You will also have to provide a form of collateral—such as a vehicle or a house—as a guarantee for the loan. Furthermore, the loan agent will scrutinize your credit history to see how well you've handled credit in the past. If you have outstanding balances or delinquent loans, you may be denied.

Should you be approved for the loan, the funds will be deposited into the business checking account you currently hold with us. Please don't hesitate to contact me if you have any further questions.

Sincerely,

Eunice Trevino
Loan Agent, Prime Bank

4. Who is the e-mail aimed at?
   (A) A credit card holder
   (B) A student loan applicant
   (C) A new bank employee
   (D) A small business owner

5. What does Ms. Trevino indicate about the loan?
   (A) It will be issued in the form of a check.
   (B) Its interest rate will not change.
   (C) It requires proof of insurance.
   (D) It must be paid within seven months.

6. What is suggested about Mr. Neal?
   (A) He has an outstanding balance on his account.
   (B) His credit usage will be checked.
   (C) He is missing a document from his application.
   (D) His commercial buildings will be used as collateral.

UNIT 08
유의어 문제

단어 앞뒤의 문맥을 살펴라

PRE-STEP

지문에 등장할 주요 어휘를 미리 학습해 보자.

A 다음 빈칸에 들어갈 어휘로 알맞은 것을 고르시오.

#		(A)	(B)
1.	the ------- topic	(A) controversial	(B) trained
2.	an awards -------	(A) salary	(B) banquet
3.	show ------- in learning	(A) credit	(B) interest
4.	a(n) ------- balance	(A) salary	(B) outstanding
5.	raise a base -------	(A) salary	(B) banquet
6.	create more financial -------	(A) stability	(B) salary
7.	------- to support families	(A) struggle	(B) enroll
8.	------- student debt	(A) complete	(B) pay off
9.	------- in a marketing seminar	(A) undertake	(B) enroll
10.	------- various tasks	(A) complete	(B) pay off
11.	a(n) ------- on the software	(A) banquet	(B) opinion
12.	a(n) ------- time	(A) appropriate	(B) broader
13.	on an ------- basis	(A) appropriate	(B) experimental
14.	the ------- questionnaire	(A) attached	(B) skilled
15.	------- in a discussion	(A) engage	(B) undertake

B 다음 문장을 읽고 패러프레이징된 것으로 적절한 것을 고르시오.

1.
> This program will not only help to make you a trained promoter, but also enable you to have a broader view of the fast-changing market.

(A) There are advantages of being a formally trained professional.
(B) There are a couple of benefits of attending this event.

2.
> It currently bears the name of the corporation that invested the necessary finances to see the project through to completion.

(A) It is named after its main corporate sponsor.
(B) It changed its name throughout stages of the project.

MAIN STEP 1

문제를 해결하는 핵심 전략을 살펴보자.

 전략 1 대표적 의미는 문장만 보고도 답을 고를 수 있다

어휘의 대표적 의미를 고르는 유형은, 해당 어휘를 지문에서 찾아 문장을 해석해 보면 답을 바로 찾을 수 있다.

자주 출제되는 어휘

지문	annual **rates** have been discounted 연례 **요금**이 할인되었다	정답	prices 가격	지문	I can **assure** you that ~ ~을 당신에게 **약속할** 수 있습니다	정답	promise 약속하다
지문	sales **volume** is generally low 판매**량**이 대체적으로 적다	정답	numbers 수[량]	지문	show a high **degree** of increase 높은 **수준**의 상승세를 보이다	정답	level 수준, 정도
지문	**treat** your belongings with care 소지품을 주의해서 **다루세요**	정답	handle 다루다	지문	a feeling of **association** with the team 팀과의 **연관성**	정답	connection 관련

 전략 2 대표적 의미가 통하지 않으면 문맥을 자세히 살펴야 한다

어휘의 여러 의미 중 하나를 고르는 유형으로, 문맥을 통해 해당 어휘의 의미를 파악해야 하므로 난이도가 높다.

자주 출제되는 어휘

지문	During Tuesday's meeting, city council officials considered the opinions **raised** by others on this controversial topic. 화요일 회의에서, 시의회 의원들은 논란이 많은 사안에 대해 다른 이들에 의해 **제기된** 의견들을 검토했다.	정답	voice, express 나타내다	오답	increase 증가하다
지문	The person who receives the most votes in the election will formally **assume** the position of president. 선거에서 가장 많은 표를 받는 사람이 공식적으로 회장 직책을 **맡을** 것이다.	정답	undertake 맡다	오답	suppose, guess 추측하다
지문	Boyer Co.'s owner hosts an awards banquet every year in order to give employees **credit** for their hard work. 보이어 사의 소유주는 직원들의 노고를 **표창**하기 위해 매년 시상식 연회를 개최한다.	정답	recognition 인정, 표창	오답	balance 잔고
지문	As you showed interest in learning more about the class, I'd like to **extend** an invitation for you to attend our tour. 이 수업에 대해 더 배우는 것에 흥미를 보이셨기에, 관광에 참여하도록 초대장을 **보내고** 싶습니다.	정답	offer, give 제의하다	오답	expand 확장하다

MAIN STEP 2

앞에서 배운 전략을
문제에 직접 적용해 보자.

Question 1 refers to the following article.

> Industry Leader Focuses on Employee Satisfaction
>
> Insurance giant Ainsworth Industries has always had an outstanding reputation for customer service and dependable policies. Now, under the direction of newly appointed CEO Roger Nelson, the company is turning inward. It's seeking to improve working conditions for employees in an effort to retain skilled workers. Starting in the new year, the company will raise base salaries and bonuses across the board. The management team hopes this will help to create more financial stability for employees, many of whom are struggling to support their families or pay off student debts.

1. In the article, the word "raise" in paragraph 1, line 4, is closest in meaning to
   (A) earn
   (B) collect
   (C) bring
   (D) increase

   [보너스문제]
   ① What can be inferred about Mr. Nelson?

Question 2 refers to the following advertisement.

> Enroll in KreyTech's marketing seminar and you will see excellent outcomes! Our specially designed programs will give you an edge in the business world. You will learn how to manage profits and clients effectively. This will not only help to make you a trained promoter, but also enable you to have a broader view of the fast-changing market. It is scheduled to be held on December 12. Interested parties should register early to get in for free.

2. In the advertisement, the word "edge" in paragraph 1, line 2, is closest in meaning to
   (A) advantage
   (B) side
   (C) boundary
   (D) change

   [보너스문제]
   ② What benefit of advanced registration is mentioned?

보너스문제 정답 ① He wants to motivate employees. ② Complimentary admission

FINAL STEP

실전 난이도의 문제를 풀며 앞에서 배운 전략을 활용해 보자.

Questions 1-4 refer to the following e-mail.

From: Sergio Chicon <sergio.chicon@tamunatech.org>
To: All employees <allstaff@tamunatech.org>
Date: January 11
Subject: Software feedback
Attachment: Questionnaire_newsw.pdf

Hi everyone,

We recently installed a new office software program on an experimental basis. The program enables us to enter proposals and project details into a searchable database. It also contains time-tracking and budgeting components.

This program has been used in various capacities by nearly every department in our organization for approximately six months now. Thus, we feel it is an appropriate time to conduct a formal review of the software before we purchase it permanently. We want to hear directly from employees whether you think this software works for your position.

I need about 15–20 volunteers to meet on Saturday, January 25, and participate in a focus group. Ideally, we would like two individuals to act as representatives for each department. In the morning, you will engage in a discussion with coworkers sharing opinions on the software and its functionality. We want to know if any aspects are particularly useful, challenging, or difficult to understand. Conversely, during the afternoon session, you will complete various tasks using the software to determine whether or not additional training should be provided.

Please inform me if you wish to volunteer your time. Anyone who is interested in participating but is unavailable on January 25 can still help by completing and returning the attached questionnaire by January 20.

Regards,

Sergio Chicon
Vice-president, Tamunatech Inc.

1. Why did Mr. Chicon write the e-mail?
   (A) To organize a group of volunteers
   (B) To explain a new policy
   (C) To thank some participants
   (D) To reschedule an event

2. What can be inferred about Tamunatech?
   (A) It is a software development company.
   (B) It regularly conducts focus groups.
   (C) Its president is Mr. Chicon.
   (D) It solicits employee opinions.

3. In paragraph 3, line 2, the word "act" is closest in meaning to
   (A) perform
   (B) serve
   (C) pretend
   (D) deed

4. What are some recipients asked to do?
   (A) Recruit additional volunteers
   (B) Fill out a survey form
   (C) Place a call to a coworker
   (D) Rearrange their timetables

Questions 5-9 refer to the following article.

(Tulsa—May 25) Hyde Corporation is pleased to announce the opening of the newly rebuilt and rejuvenated city park. Located outside of the Parliament building, the area formerly known as Gotham Park has undergone a major transformation. On May 19, the park reopened as a modern and welcoming outdoor space now called Hyde Park. It currently bears the name of the corporation that invested the necessary finances to see the project through to completion. The Tulsa city council first proposed the idea before realizing halfway through that the construction costs would greatly exceed the original estimates. The two-year renovation would have been canceled if the Hyde Corporation hadn't stepped in to cover the outstanding costs.

Local resident Bill Hamilton, who has lived in Tulsa for forty-five years, declared that the new park is the best addition to the city that he's seen to date. "We've been desperate for a sophisticated common area for families to spend a Saturday afternoon," he said. "It's so refreshing to have extra green space in the middle of this city, which has been overrun by high-rises and concrete streets in other places."

The 130,668 square-foot park is now three times its former size. Many hope that it will become a dynamic and accessible new hub for pedestrians, commuters, and visitors. A multifaceted space, Hyde Park includes an enormous lawn to be used by the public for sporting events and dog walking. Surrounding the park are four tree groves that provide shade for people who wish to sit and read. In the middle of the park is a computer-programmed fountain to delight and entertain children. The park's seasonal areas contain a performance space for summer concerts as well as an ice-skating rink during the winter. Once it is opened, the skating rink will operate daily. Finally, Hyde Park includes an outdoor café, which has seating inside and outside on the terrace.

5. What is the article mainly about?
   (A) The naming of a new landmark
   (B) The closing of a commercial space
   (C) The alterations made to a public space
   (D) The plans for future infrastructure

6. What did the Hyde Corporation do in Tulsa?
   (A) It funded a community project.
   (B) It opened for business.
   (C) It invested in new property.
   (D) It changed its public relations team.

7. The word "bears" in paragraph 1, line 9, is closest in meaning to
   (A) exposes
   (B) uncovers
   (C) carries
   (D) endures

8. How long was Hyde Park under construction?
   (A) 6 months
   (B) 12 months
   (C) 18 months
   (D) 24 months

9. What is NOT suggested as a result of the renovation?
   (A) A name change has occurred.
   (B) Ice skating is possible in the winter.
   (C) An eating area was created.
   (D) Public transit is easily accessible.

UNIT 09
단서를 종합하는 문제

필요한 단서를 캐치하여
종합하라

PRE-STEP

지문에 등장할 주요 어휘를 미리 학습해 보자.

A 다음 빈칸에 들어갈 어휘로 알맞은 것을 고르시오.

1. be ------- for a position   (A) considered   (B) possessed
2. feedback will be -------   (A) solicited   (B) affiliated
3. be ------- with outlets   (A) solicited   (B) affiliated
4. ------- a new policy   (A) implement   (B) comply
5. enforce the -------   (A) expenses   (B) regulation
6. extend the ------- period   (A) prohibition   (B) demand
7. a higher ------- for the goods   (A) prohibition   (B) demand
8. have no ------- but to *do*   (A) choice   (B) charge
9. be in ------- of   (A) choice   (B) charge
10. ------- a deal   (A) confirm   (B) attend
11. ------- the trade   (A) secure   (B) implement
12. have ------- capital   (A) numerous   (B) sufficient
13. on ------- occasions   (A) numerous   (B) undergoing
14. the contract -------   (A) terms   (B) freeze
15. put the ------- on   (A) terms   (B) freeze

B 다음 문장을 읽고 패러프레이징된 것으로 적절한 것을 고르시오.

1.
> Investors are pleased that Eminence will be able to lower its cost of operations, as it will take over production facilities in countries where labor is more affordable.

(A) The savings on labor costs are appealing to investors.
(B) The goods are more popular in certain countries.

2.
> He has a bachelor's degree in business, so he possesses a deep understanding of how corporations operate.

(A) He is undergoing continuing education.
(B) He has sufficient knowledge for the position.

MAIN STEP

문제를 해결하는
핵심 전략을 살펴보자.

전략 1 — 문제의 키워드만으로 정답을 찾을 수 없다면 단서를 더 찾아라

문제의 키워드와 관련된 부분을 찾아 그 주변을 읽었는데도 정답을 찾을 수 없다면 다른 단서를 더 필요로 하는 고난도 문제이다. 주로 이메일, 편지, 기사문 등의 긴 지문에 등장하며, 시험당 한 문제씩은 꼭 출제된다.

지문 memo

In an effort to reduce expenses, our company has chosen to put a freeze on overtime work. ①**For the next month, we will run a pilot program during which no staff member will be permitted to work overtime hours.** From January 2 to 30, all electricity will be shut off at 6 P.M., and employees are expected to leave at that time. ②**Upon conclusion of the program, employee feedback will be solicited to determine whether we will extend this prohibition.**

해석: 해설집 p.44

문제 What will **employees** probably **do next month**?
(A) Reduce personal spending
(B) Stop using an in-house refrigerator
(C) Provide a detailed review of a program

풀이 단서①만 보았을 때 정답은 직원들이 pilot program에 참여하는 것이다. 하지만 이 내용이 선택지에 없다면 지문을 더 읽어 봐야 정답을 찾을 수 있다. 단서②를 읽고 이를 ①과 종합해 보면 직원들이 프로그램에 대한 평가를 내릴 것임을 알 수 있다.

정답 (C)

전략 2 — 문제의 패턴을 알아두면 문제 풀이 시간이 줄어든다

싱글 지문에서 단서를 종합하는 문제 유형에는 특히 자주 출제되는 두 가지 패턴이 있다. 이들을 익혀 두면, 지문을 읽을 때 해당 부분을 집중해서 읽음으로써 문제 풀이 시간을 줄일 수 있다.

인물에 대한 단서 종합	지문	①**In my managers' meeting this morning**, we decided to implement a new policy regarding employee evaluations. ②**Brianna Johnson, Sales Department**	문제 정답	What is true about Ms. Johnson? She is a department supervisor.
날짜에 대한 단서 종합	지문	①**July 25**, BROOMSBURG—A new regulation may reduce the number of cars illegally parked in loading zones in Broomsburg's downtown area. As part of the new measures, ②**the city's traffic police department will expand its workforce at the beginning of next month** to better enforce the regulation.	문제 정답	What will happen in Broomsburg in August? More city officials will be hired.

62

MAIN STEP 2

앞에서 배운 전략을
문제에 직접 적용해 보자.

Questions 1-3 refer to the following business article.

Eminence Manufacturing Confirms Deal
By Amina Barros

June 8—A spokesperson for athletics giant Eminence Manufacturing announced today that the company has acquired Lyndon Sports under a final agreement between the CEOs of both corporations. Investors are pleased that Eminence will be able to lower its cost of operations through this move, as it will take over production facilities in countries where labor is more affordable. In addition, because Lyndon Sports is affiliated with numerous retail outlets throughout Asia—a market in which Eminence has had consistently weak sales over the years—Eminence will now be well-positioned to become an industry leader worldwide.

The details of the transaction were organized by representatives from both companies. While Eminence was not the only company to make a bid for Lyndon, its competitors did not have sufficient capital to secure the winning offer. Operations will be entirely under the control of Eminence by the end of the month. Neal Harrington, the CEO of Lyndon Sports, estimates that Eminence's market share could increase by as much as 15 percent. He also mentioned that, with a higher demand for its goods, Eminence will have no choice but to expand its workforce, which is great news for the communities that house its facilities across the globe.

---

1. According to the article, what benefit is expected to come from the change?
   (A) Reducing operating expenses
   (B) Improving production speeds
   (C) Attracting new investors
   (D) Selling a wider variety of products

2. When will Eminence most likely take over control?
   (A) On June 10
   (B) On June 15
   (C) On June 30
   (D) On July 15

3. What can be inferred about Mr. Harrington?
   (A) He is sponsoring a sporting event.
   (B) He will hire more workers.
   (C) He is the CEO of Eminence.
   (D) He agreed to the merger.

FINAL STEP

실전 난이도의 문제를 풀며 앞에서 배운 전략을 활용해 보자.

Questions 1-3 refer to the following e-mail.

To: Michelle Ayala <michelleayala@waterviewind.com>
From: Carole Phillips <c_phillips@rosebudsolutions.com>
Date: December 9
Subject: RE: Brian Quinn

Dear Ms. Ayala,

I am the branch manager of Rosebud Solutions, and I am writing this e-mail as a letter of recommendation for Brian Quinn, who has applied for a sales position at Waterview Industries. I believe that Mr. Quinn is the ideal candidate for this job. He has a high degree of emotional intelligence along with a warm personality that people respond to positively.

Mr. Quinn started at Rosebud Solutions as a sales assistant, a job that he held with us for two years. He was then promoted to senior salesperson, where he served for another two years. In that role, he was in charge of multinational clients, and he negotiated one of the most lucrative contracts in our company's history. Everyone has been pleased with Mr. Quinn's work performance and reliability. He met or exceeded monthly sales targets consistently, and he always had a positive attitude. Moreover, he has a bachelor's degree in business, so he possesses a deep understanding of how corporations operate.

With his experience, education, and natural talent, Mr. Quinn is sure to be an invaluable asset to your team. I hope you will seriously consider him for this position. If you would like to speak further on this matter, please feel free to contact me at 555-2495, which is my direct office line.

Sincerely,

Carole Phillips

1. What is the purpose of the e-mail?
   (A) To apply for a position
   (B) To make a job offer
   (C) To recommend an employee
   (D) To accept an employment agreement

2. Who most likely is Ms. Ayala?
   (A) A branch manager
   (B) An HR worker
   (C) A sales director
   (D) A sales assistant

3. How long has Mr. Quinn worked at Rosebud Solutions for?
   (A) Two years
   (B) Four years
   (C) Five years
   (D) Six years

Questions 4-7 refer to the following advertisement.

Columbus University, Psychology Department
Distinguished Speaker Series

Date & time	Lecture title	Lecturer	Qualifications	Ticket price
January 15, 1 P.M. January 16, 1 P.M. January 20, 7 P.M.	*The Resilient Brain: Ageing, Memory, and Trauma*	Dr. Ira Corbett, PhD	Professor, Department of Psychology, University of Oxford	$20
January 22, 1 P.M.	*Your Child's Mind: Changes in Childhood Brain Development*	Dr. Natasha Bloomberg, PhD	Professor, Department of Psychology, University of Chicago	$25
January 24, 1 P.M. January 25, 1 P.M.	*Battling Dyslexia: The Trouble with Learning Words*	Mr. Pedro Fitzpatrick, MS	Psychologist/ Lead Instructor, Dyslexic Learning Center	Free admission
January 26, 7 P.M. January 29, 1 P.M.	*Without Shame: Helping Sufferers of Mental Illness*	Dr. Celina Robinson, PhD	Professor, Department of Psychology, Carnegie Mellon University	$35 *Child care will be provided for parents attending the lecture together. The cost is factored into the price of the ticket.

4. What is the purpose of the advertisement?
   (A) To describe a psychological experiment
   (B) To promote a series of upcoming talks
   (C) To introduce new university professors
   (D) To encourage the study of mental illness

5. Who is a practicing psychologist?
   (A) Ira Corbett
   (B) Natasha Bloomberg
   (C) Pedro Fitzpatrick
   (D) Celina Robinson

6. Which lecture can listeners attend without charge?
   (A) *The Resilient Brain*
   (B) *Your Child's Mind*
   (C) *Battling Dyslexia*
   (D) *Without Shame*

7. When will children most likely be brought to Columbus University?
   (A) On January 15
   (B) On January 22
   (C) On January 25
   (D) On January 29

UNIT 10
연계 문제

단서의 흐름을 따라가라

PRE-STEP

지문에 등장할 주요 어휘를 미리 학습해 보자.

A 다음 빈칸에 들어갈 어휘로 알맞은 것을 고르시오.

1. ------- customers of the change   (A) notify   (B) select
2. for a(n) ------- fee   (A) responsible (B) additional
3. ------- one's preference   (A) notify   (B) select
4. an express delivery -------   (A) comfort   (B) option
5. be ------- for a task   (A) responsible (B) additional
6. ------- safety procedures   (A) enforce   (B) rent
7. ------- a rehearsal space   (A) enforce   (B) rent
8. ------- health issues   (A) apply   (B) face
9. seek ------- employment   (A) permanent   (B) strategic
10. ------- for a position   (A) apply   (B) face
11. high-paying ------- jobs   (A) seasonal   (B) additional
12. ------- one's skills and goals   (A) comply   (B) fit
13. ------- with the standards   (A) comply   (B) face
14. the ideal -------   (A) admission   (B) candidate
15. ------- internal communication   (A) develop   (B) notify

B 다음 문장을 읽고 패러프레이징된 것으로 적절한 것을 고르시오.

1.
> I immediately transitioned to the food and beverage service team, where I have worked for the last five summers.

(A) I worked for the food and beverage service team for five years in a row.
(B) I am available to join the food and beverage service team this summer.

2.
> We allow new members to attend two sessions before deciding whether or not to join.

(A) New members can preview the sessions before making a decision.
(B) New members should attend at least two sessions a year.

MAIN STEP¹

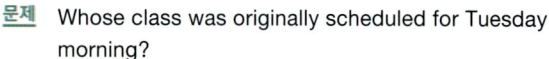

변경 사항에 대한 내용은 반드시 연계 문제로 문제화된다

두 개 이상의 지문에서 일정 및 계획 변경에 대한 내용이 등장하면 이는 반드시 연계 문제로 출제된다. 따라서 변경 내용을 주의해서 읽으며 다른 지문에서도 관련 내용을 찾아야 한다.

지문 e-mail & form

Thank you for your interest in ①**Intermediate Yoga** at Wilkes Gym. Unfortunately, due to an issue with the instructor's calendar, ①②**the class has been rescheduled for 1 P.M. instead of 10 A.M. on Tuesdays.**

Class for Tuesday 1 P.M.

Basic Yoga – Susan Ferguson	③**Intermediate Yoga** – **Carlene White**

해석: 해설집 p.50

문제 Whose class was originally scheduled for Tuesday morning?

풀이 ① 지문에서 변경 사항에 관한 내용 캐치
　→ 중급 요가 수업 일정 변경, 문제화 가능성 높음
② 변경 전과 변경 후 일정을 숙지
　→ 오전 10시에서 오후 1시로 변경
③ 두 번째 지문에서 변경된 중급 요가 수업의 강사 찾기

정답 Carlene White

선택지가 날짜, 가격만으로 이루어져 있으면 연계 문제이다

선택지가 날짜나 가격만으로 이루어져 있는 문제들은 연계 문제일 가능성이 매우 높다. 따라서 선택지를 미리 읽어 보고 이 경우에 해당되면 일단 연계 문제라고 생각하고, 각 지문에서 필요한 정보를 차례대로 찾아야 한다.

지문 notice & text message & form

National Entrepreneur Convention

We are holding the 3ʳᵈ National Entrepreneur convention ②**from April 26 to 29**. It starts at 10:00 A.M. and will run until 3 P.M. with just an hour lunch break at noon every day.

From: Mark Walter / To: Deborah Mason

Could you please send me a detailed schedule of my appointments at the end of this month? I'd like to attend a marketing convention but I need to check my schedule first.

③**Mark Walter's Plan**

April 26, 9 A.M. – Weekly executive meeting
April 28, 10 A.M. – Visiting manufacturers
April 29, 9 A.M. – Design Workshop

해석: 해설집 p.51

문제 When will Mr. Walter attend the convention?
(A) April 26
(B) April 27
(C) April 28
(D) April 29

풀이 ① 문제의 선택지가 날짜로만 이루어짐
　→ 연계 문제일 가능성이 높음을 염두에 둘 것
② 학회 일정 확인
　→ 4월 26-29일
③ 월터 씨의 일정 확인
　→ 27일에만 일정이 없음

정답 (B)

MAIN STEP 2

Questions 1-2 refer to the following letter and invoice.

Kira Höecker
Landstrasse 139
3860 Schattenhalb, Switzerland

September 1

Dear Ms. Höecker:

This letter is to notify you of our revolutionary online grocery shopping service. We enable you to buy your grocery items from the comfort of your own home with only the click of a button. Simply browse through our online aisles, select your items, and place your order. It's just that easy! Your food items are guaranteed to be delivered within seven days. A 15 percent tax is charged on every order, but regular delivery is free. However, for an additional fee, a next-day express delivery option exists for time-sensitive orders. If you have any questions, please call 555-163-7238.

Sincerely,

Martha Lambert,
Customer Relations, Lamla Grocers

Customer name: Kira Höeker   **Date of order:** September 19
Shipping address: Landstrasse 139, 3860 Schattenhalb, Switzerland
Method of payment: Visa   **Credit card number:** XXXX XXXX XXXX 4532

Item number	Description	Quantity	Cost
8691	Vanilla extract	2 bottles, 8 oz.	$13.96
195376	Cake mix, classic yellow	1 box	$2.10
		Subtotal	$16.06
		Tax amount (15%)	$2.41
		Delivery fee	$10.00
		Total cost	$28.47

1. According to the letter, what advantage does the Lamla Grocers provide?

    (A) Competitive pricing
    (B) Access to foreign foods
    (C) Convenient shopping
    (D) Organic produce

2. How much does next-day express delivery cost?

    (A) $10
    (B) $15
    (C) $25
    (D) $40

FINAL STEP

실전 난이도의 문제를 풀며 앞에서 배운 전략을 활용해 보자.

Questions 1-5 refer to the following e-mail and notice.

To: Lucas Klein <l.klein@thrilltropolis.com>
From: Madison Ennis <ennism@memail.net>
Date: April 3
Subject: Returning to Thrilltropolis

Dear Mr. Klein,

I am writing to you about applying for a position with Thrilltropolis, where I have worked as a seasonal employee for several years. I was originally hired as a ticket admissions agent. But I immediately transitioned to the food and beverage service team, where I have worked for the last five summers. Next month I will complete my hospitality degree at Concord University, so I am seeking permanent employment. Attached you will find my résumé and references. Please let me know if you have a position that fits my skills and career goals.

Sincerely,

Madison Ennis

Thrilltropolis, the Nation's Leading Amusement Park, is Hiring!

Posting #S35: Lifeguard (full time, seasonal) // Lifeguards in the aquatic center are responsible for the supervision of various water attractions. They also enforce safety procedures.

Posting #S48: Ride Attendant (full time, seasonal) // Ride attendants load and unload guests in a safe and hospitable manner. They comply with the ride operations standards of Thrilltropolis.

Posting #P67: Area Manager, Food and Beverage (full time, permanent) // The area manager will handle the daily functions of the park's food-service department. The ideal candidate should be a detail-oriented leader with a strong food and beverage background.

Posting #P76: Associate, Public Relations (full time, permanent) // The public relations associate will work to establish the Thrilltropolis brand throughout the world and strategically develop external and internal communications.

1. What is the purpose of the e-mail?
   (A) To verify application rules
   (B) To arrange an interview time
   (C) To inquire about a job opening
   (D) To schedule a tour of Thrilltropolis

2. How many summers did Ms. Ennis work at Thrilltropolis?
   (A) 2
   (B) 3
   (C) 5
   (D) 7

3. What is suggested about all of the jobs in the notice?
   (A) They each offer full-time hours.
   (B) They are permanent positions.
   (C) They are available at multiple locations.
   (D) They require previous experience.

4. What is true about Thrilltropolis?
   (A) It is a safari exhibit for tourists.
   (B) It contains a water park.
   (C) It is open to the public year-round.
   (D) It has the world's largest ride.

5. What job would probably best suit Ms. Ennis?
   (A) Posting #S35
   (B) Posting #S48
   (C) Posting #P67
   (D) Posting #P76

Questions 6-10 refer to the following advertisement, schedule, and e-mail.

The Laughs Never End with the Gilmore Improv Players!

The Gilmore Improv Players (GIP) was founded a decade ago and is dedicated to improvisation(improv), which is a type of theater in which the actors create unplanned scenes using suggestions from audience members. We get together weekly to play improv games, develop our acting skills, and—of course—have fun! We are currently looking for new members to join our group. No previous experience is necessary. If you're interested in joining, e-mail Megan Conaway at m.conaway@mcnallymail.net. We allow new members to attend two sessions before deciding whether or not to join. All members pay an annual fee of $50, which goes toward renting our rehearsal space.

We perform shows for the public regularly, and if you join GIP, your family members can get half-off tickets at these events. We are also hired for private shows, such as corporate parties. Join us today and don't miss out on the fun!

Gilmore Improv Players: Upcoming Events

Saturday, April 16, 7:30 P.M., Watson Hall   Public Performance
A Night of Improv — Enjoy hilarious scenes made up on-the-spot using ideas from you, the audience! (Tickets: $20)

Monday, April 18, 1:00 P.M., Grove Accounting Headquarters   Private Performance
Giggles Galore — A special performance for the Grove Accounting Employee Appreciation Luncheon

Saturday, April 23, 8:30 P.M., Perea Lounge   Public Performance
Battle for Laughs — Watch two teams battle it out with classic improv games. (Tickets: $16)

Tuesday, April 26, 3:00 P.M., Wiggins Children's Hospital   Private Performance
Tell Me More — A show with games designed specifically for children

Friday, April 29, 2:00 P.M., Dumont Community Center   Public Activity
Improv Workshop — Learn how to get started in improv and how to release your inner comedian in this three-hour workshop. (Tickets: $10)

E-MAIL MESSAGE

To: Megan Conaway <m.conaway@mcnallymail.net>
From: Jared Alvarez <jaredalvarez@inbox234.com>
Date: May 3
Subject: Gilmore Improv Players

Dear Ms. Conaway,

Thank you for your recent performance at the Wiggins Children's Hospital. I know that our young patients had a lot of fun watching the show, and staff members like me also had a great time. You brought so much joy to our patients, which is so important during a time when they are facing health issues. Some of our patients even made drawings and thank-you cards for your group that I would like to send to you. Please let me know where to do so.

Warmest regards,

Jared Alvarez

6. What is the purpose of the advertisement?
   (A) To recruit people to a group
   (B) To promote an upcoming show
   (C) To attract corporate sponsorship
   (D) To announce a competition

7. What is NOT indicated about GIP?
   (A) It only admits experienced actors.
   (B) It meets once a week.
   (C) It has been running for ten years.
   (D) It charges a membership fee.

8. How much would GIP members' relatives pay for *Battle for Laughs*?
   (A) $20
   (B) $16
   (C) $10
   (D) $8

9. When did Mr. Alvarez see a show?
   (A) April 16
   (B) April 18
   (C) April 26
   (D) April 29

10. What does Mr. Alvarez ask Ms. Conaway to do?
    (A) Perform at another event
    (B) Provide a mailing address
    (C) Report the group's availability
    (D) Give information about fees

CHAPTER TEST 1

제한시간 25분

Questions 1-2 refer to the following text message chain.

KATHERINE ZIEGLER 9:10 A.M.
I have a repair request for you. The printer in my office is acting up. The brand is Alto Co. and it's model #498-E.

GEORGE NOKES 9:16 A.M.
Can you describe the problem to me?

KATHERINE ZIEGLER 9:16 A.M.
The paper is loaded correctly, but the device isn't pulling the paper in from the tray.

GEORGE NOKES 9:17 A.M.
Maybe one of the components fell off.

KATHERINE ZIEGLER 9:19 A.M.
Are you busy this morning?

GEORGE NOKES 9:20 A.M.
Yes, quite a bit.

GEORGE NOKES 9:20 A.M.
I won't be able to look at it today. Is tomorrow all right?

KATHERINE ZIEGLER 9:22 A.M.
Okay. I have to take some other paperwork to one of my clients this afternoon anyway.

KATHERINE ZIEGLER 9:23 A.M.
But tomorrow I need to print some orientation materials, so please visit me first thing tomorrow, if possible.

---

1. At 9:20 A.M., what does Mr. Nokes mean when he writes, "quite a bit"?

    (A) He doesn't have time for a task.
    (B) He thinks a repair will be expensive.
    (C) His department keeps extra parts on hand.
    (D) His team has done similar work before.

2. What will Ms. Ziegler do after lunch today?

    (A) Conduct a staff orientation
    (B) Take something to Mr. Nokes
    (C) Print some materials
    (D) Visit a client in person

Questions 3-4 refer to the following notice.

NOTICE TO ALL EMPLOYEES

As previously announced at the conference, the cafeteria on the second floor will be closed for about four weeks beginning on March 7 in order for the building crew to renovate the facility. For your personal safety, please do not enter the area during this time. Should any of your colleagues be out of town to meet clients, please inform them of the contents of this notice so they may remain up-to-date.

We thank you in advance for your cooperative attitude in this matter. While we understand that this causes a major inconvenience at lunchtime, we believe the change will be well worth it. As part of the renovations, we will replace the walk-in refrigerator that is out of order and equip the kitchen with upgraded ovens. In addition, we will have room for four more dining tables, which will make lunch breaks less crowded for everyone. If you have any questions or concerns, please contact the maintenance department by dialing extension 48.

3. What is the purpose of this notice?
   (A) To get feedback on a proposed renovation
   (B) To give instructions regarding a project
   (C) To plan the distribution of safety gear
   (D) To remind employees of a conference

4. What is NOT included in the renovation?
   (A) Updated cooking appliances
   (B) Expanded eating space
   (C) Enhanced flooring
   (D) Improved refrigeration system

Questions 5-7 refer to the following e-mail.

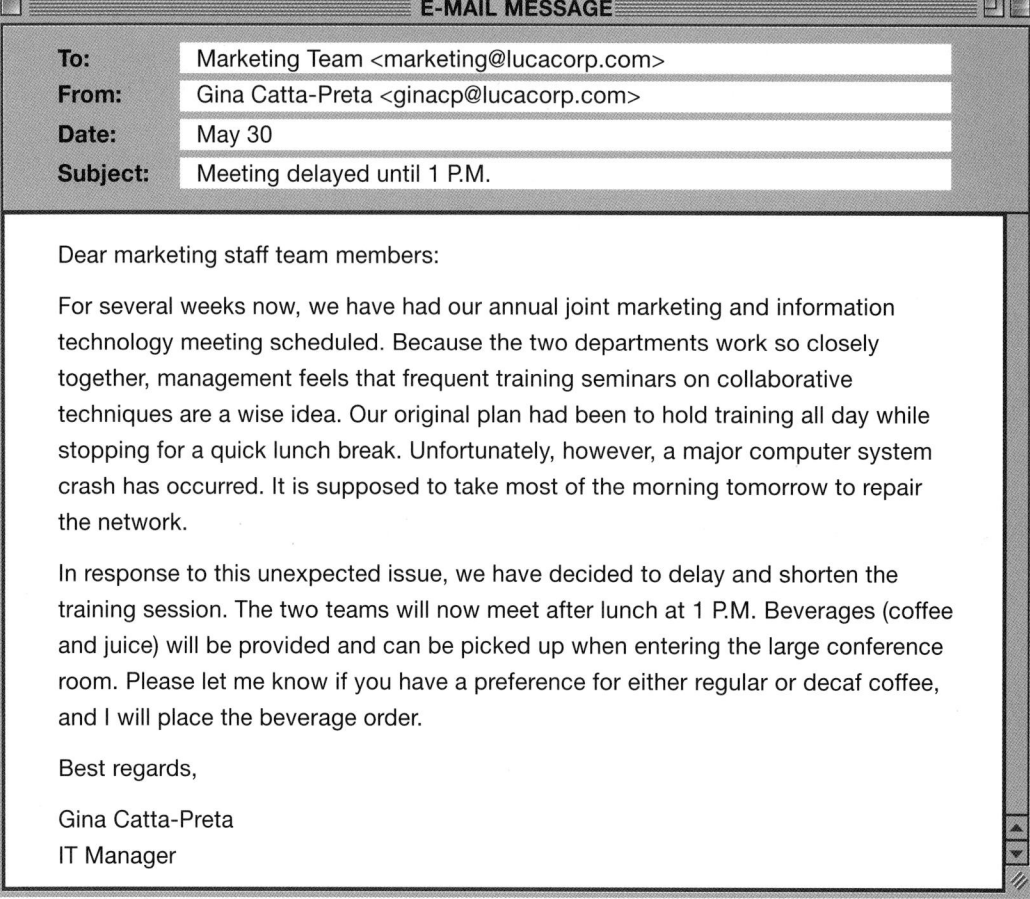

To: Marketing Team <marketing@lucacorp.com>
From: Gina Catta-Preta <ginacp@lucacorp.com>
Date: May 30
Subject: Meeting delayed until 1 P.M.

Dear marketing staff team members:

For several weeks now, we have had our annual joint marketing and information technology meeting scheduled. Because the two departments work so closely together, management feels that frequent training seminars on collaborative techniques are a wise idea. Our original plan had been to hold training all day while stopping for a quick lunch break. Unfortunately, however, a major computer system crash has occurred. It is supposed to take most of the morning tomorrow to repair the network.

In response to this unexpected issue, we have decided to delay and shorten the training session. The two teams will now meet after lunch at 1 P.M. Beverages (coffee and juice) will be provided and can be picked up when entering the large conference room. Please let me know if you have a preference for either regular or decaf coffee, and I will place the beverage order.

Best regards,

Gina Catta-Preta
IT Manager

5. Why did Ms. Catta-Preta send the e-mail?
   (A) To describe an unexpected delay
   (B) To reschedule a client meeting
   (C) To assign a team to a project
   (D) To order food items for lunch

6. What is mentioned about the meeting?
   (A) It was just scheduled this morning.
   (B) It will be changed to another day.
   (C) It will be delayed by a few hours.
   (D) It will include an afternoon meal.

7. What can be inferred about the drinks?
   (A) The company will handle the expense.
   (B) Staff members must bring their own cups.
   (C) There won't be enough for refills.
   (D) Only hot beverages are available.

Questions 8-10 refer to the following online chat discussion.

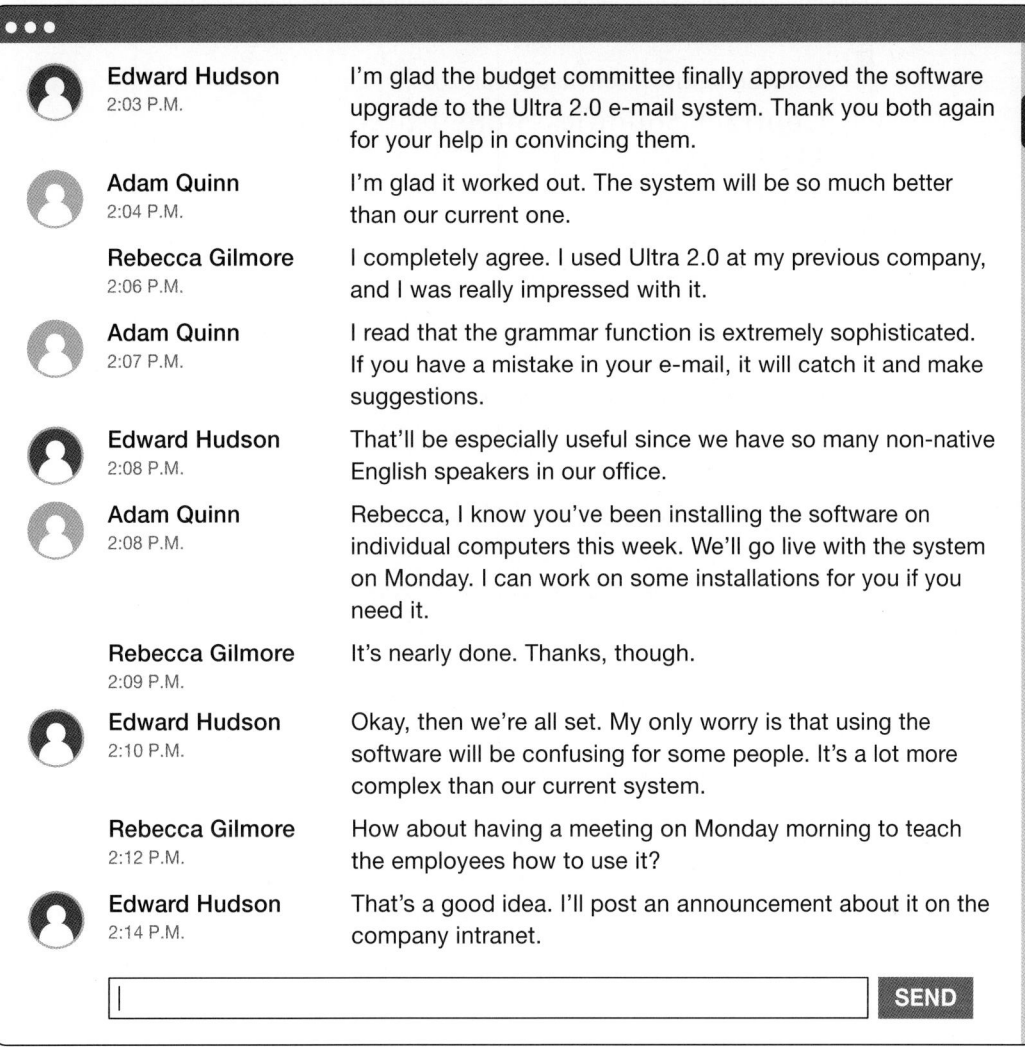

8. What benefit of the new software is mentioned?

   (A) Attracting customers
   (B) Cutting costs
   (C) Saving time
   (D) Reducing errors

9. At 2:09 P.M., what does Ms. Gilmore mean when she writes, "It's nearly done"?

   (A) She is conducting a test.
   (B) She wants to adjust a deadline.
   (C) She is rejecting an offer of help.
   (D) She has set up a meeting space.

10. What is the purpose of Monday's meeting?

    (A) To announce a change
    (B) To gather feedback
    (C) To train staff members
    (D) To introduce new employees

Questions 11-14 refer to the following article.

Stone Enterprises Newsletter–Vol. 209
Contract Solidifies Stone Enterprises' Market Position
By Keith Velarde

After seemingly endless market research and months of high-stakes negotiations, Stone Enterprises is pleased to announce that it has finalized an important contract with California manufacturer Baxley Solar. Becoming the exclusive distributor for Baxley's products has been the top priority of the company this year, as it is the key to positioning the company as an emerging global leader. — [1] —

Baxley Solar has made a name for itself through its dependable and sustainable energy systems, which make use of the latest technology in solar panels, monitoring systems, and long-life batteries. — [2] — Last year, when a spokesperson for the company indicated that it would be switching to a single distributor to simplify its internal processes, the race was on. — [3] — However, in the end, the Baxley Solar board of directors turned down the offers of other companies in favor of Stone Enterprises' ability to demonstrate sufficient capital. Earlier this month, business development manager Victor Wilburn drew up the agreement on behalf of Stone Enterprises, and Baxley's representatives gave consent to exclusive distribution rights for a five-year term. — [4] —

In honor of this monumental achievement, Stone Enterprises will hold a celebratory reception at the Woodward Hotel on July 8 at 8 P.M. It will feature speeches by company executives, including CEO Jamie Morris, and a stand-up comedy performance by Jed Reid. All employees are welcome to attend. We hope everyone will join the celebration.

11. What is the article mainly about?

(A) A corporate merger
(B) An industry trend
(C) A company accomplishment
(D) A negotiation workshop

12. What can be inferred about Baxley Solar?

(A) It will go out of business soon.
(B) It was seeking a distributor with financial stability.
(C) It is the largest company of its kind in the country.
(D) Its board members serve a five-year term.

13. According to the article, what did Mr. Wilburn do?

(A) Attended a global conference
(B) Planned a celebratory reception
(C) Created a contract
(D) Invented a long-life battery

14. In which of the positions marked [1], [2], [3] and [4] does the following sentence best belong?

"Several distributors negotiated with Baxley Solar representatives in an effort to secure this lucrative contract."

(A) [1]
(B) [2]
(C) [3]
(D) [4]

Questions 15-19 refer to the following form and memo.

Wentzville Factory Inspection Form 84B: General Safety Follow-up

Performance:
M=Meets expectations. No adjustments necessary.
R=Requires that revisions be made within a specified amount of time.
P=Poor. Required revisions were neglected during the initial grace period. Sanctions must be implemented.

Inspected by: Theo Challies
Inspection date: June 3

1. Accessible and proper number of fire exits	M
2. Adequate warning labels on machinery	M
3. Humidifiers free of hard water deposits	M
4. Appropriate storage of flammable materials	M
5. Safety clothing/equipment available and worn	P
6. Safety stations present: eye wash station, etc.	M
7. Walls, ceilings, and windows free of mold	M

Status: Sanction issued in the amount of a $225 fine*
Cause: Failure to revise #5. Safety equipment continues to be neglected by factory employees.

Theo Challies	Rozalyn Kozel
Theo Challies	*Rozalyn Kozel*
Safety inspector	Facilities manager

*Fines must be paid in full within 15 days after receiving the inspection report.

MEMO

To: All staff
From: Rozalyn Kozel
Date: June 7
Subject: Safety equipment

Dear factory staff members,

Recently, a safety inspection of our facilities was conducted, and I'm disappointed to report that we are being fined. The issue is with our safety gear. The safety inspector concluded that none of you are regularly wearing this equipment: your steel-toed boots, gloves, and—most importantly—safety goggles. Additionally, it is highly recommended that you also wear safety helmets. However, unlike the other items, helmets are optional.

All of this equipment must be worn at all times when inside the factory, as it prevents you from hurting yourselves. We have only two months from the time of our last inspection before our next visit. Wearing this equipment must become standard procedure for us by this time.

To understand the importance of following these procedures, I'm scheduling all employees to attend a safety equipment training session. It will educate each of you about what the purpose of this safety equipment is, why you must wear it, and how it should be properly stored.

Thank you in advance for your cooperation.

Rozalyn Kozel, Facilities Manager
Wentzville Factory

15. What is indicated about the Wentzville Factory inspection?
    (A) This was not the first safety inspection performed.
    (B) Numerous health code violations were found.
    (C) It was conducted by two inspectors.
    (D) A severe mold problem was discovered on the walls.

16. What was the result of the inspection?
    (A) All previous sanctions were removed.
    (B) A mandatory payment is expected.
    (C) All fire exits should be properly labeled.
    (D) An eye-washing station needs to be installed.

17. What is NOT mentioned as a necessary type of safety gear?
    (A) Boots
    (B) Gloves
    (C) Goggles
    (D) Helmets

18. When will the next inspection be conducted?
    (A) June 3
    (B) June 7
    (C) June 18
    (D) August 3

19. In the memo, what are the employees told to do?
    (A) Put warning labels on all machinery
    (B) Keep safety boots stored in the same place
    (C) Attend instructional training on safety
    (D) Replace the outdated humidifier

Questions 20-24 refer to the following advertisement, coupon, and online shopping cart.

Kitchen Sage
Create the kitchen of your dreams!

Kitchen Sage has been producing high-quality kitchen appliances for nearly fifty years. We are dedicated to helping make your daily tasks easier. From brewing your first cup of morning coffee to cleaning the last dinner plates in the dishwasher, we've got you covered.

At Kitchen Sage, we care about supporting the local economy. That's why we're committed to creating jobs here at home and never using overseas manufacturers. Our products are available at Kitchen Sage retail outlets, major department stores, and on our Web site. All products are guaranteed to last for ten years, or your money back.

Take advantage of these great deals until August 31!
- Buy any oven in our collection and get a free toaster.
- Get a free recipe book with any blender purchase.

Sign up for our monthly newsletter in May and get a coupon for 15% off your next order. Visit our Web site for a list of retail locations. Or order online, and we'll fill your order quickly. Make the most of every meal with Kitchen Sage!

15% Off Kitchen Sage Products
Coupon Code: D539R

Present this coupon at any Kitchen Sage retail outlet or input the code online to get 15% off your entire purchase. Coupon will not be accepted at department stores. Not valid when combined with any other offer. Cannot be used on clearance items. Expires July 31. No cash value.

---

http://www.kitchen-sage.com/shoppingcart

Review Your Order

Order date: August 5   **Delivery Date:** August 8
Shipping address: Anna Kennedy, 738 Murray Street SW, Phoenix, AZ 85021
Payment method: Skylar credit card XXXX-XXXX-XXXX-6870

Item	Price	Quantity
30″ stainless steel gas convection oven, 4 burners	$695.99	1
12-cup capacity coffee maker, red	$49.95	1
Shipping	$0.00	–
Installation (on day of delivery)	$79.95	–

Coupon Code: D539R
Error. Coupon not accepted. Please try another code or confirm order.

Total Due: $825.89

| CONFIRM |

---

20. What is indicated about Kitchen Sage products?

(A) They have energy-efficient designs.
(B) They come with a lifetime warranty.
(C) They are endorsed by professionals.
(D) They are produced domestically.

21. In the advertisement, the word "fill" in paragraph 4, line 2, is closest in meaning to

(A) supply
(B) crowd
(C) seal
(D) assure

22. What can be inferred about Ms. Kennedy?

(A) She is eligible for a free appliance.
(B) She is a regular customer.
(C) She will be sent a recipe book.
(D) She paid with a gift certificate.

23. Why was the coupon code rejected?

(A) It was applied to the wrong brand.
(B) Its expiration date had already passed.
(C) It cannot be used on multiple items.
(D) It can only be used in stores.

24. What will most likely happen on August 8?

(A) A sales period will end.
(B) Ms. Kennedy will pick up her goods.
(C) Kitchen Sage will send a catalog.
(D) A technician will install an appliance.

하루 30분씩 3주 만에
완성하는
PART 7

CHAPTER 2
지문 유형

CHAPTER

- [ ] **UNIT 11** 문자메시지/SNS
- [ ] **UNIT 12** 이메일/편지
- [ ] **UNIT 13** 광고문
- [ ] **UNIT 14** 기사문 (1)
- [ ] **UNIT 15** 기사문 (2)
- [ ] **UNIT 16** 회람/공지
- [ ] **UNIT 17** 표/양식
- [ ] **UNIT 18** 정보문
- [ ] **CHAPTER TEST 2**

UNIT 11
문자메시지/ SNS

상황 파악이 우선이다

PRE-STEP

지문에 등장할 주요 어휘를 미리 학습해 보자.

A 다음 빈칸에 들어갈 어휘로 알맞은 것을 고르시오.

1.	------- with customers	(A) interact	(B) count
2.	------- on close coworkers	(A) interact	(B) count
3.	stick to one's ------- limits	(A) activity	(B) budget
4.	attend a group -------	(A) activity	(B) issue
5.	at a ------- press conference	(A) recent	(B) severe
6.	offer ------- prices	(A) optimistic	(B) reasonable
7.	------- at a workshop	(A) present	(B) cover
8.	------- for someone	(A) spend	(B) cover
9.	------- a security code	(A) spend	(B) enter
10.	------- about the poor service	(A) complaints	(B) reimbursements
11.	be happy to ------- the comments	(A) spend	(B) share
12.	------- up brochures	(A) reimburse	(B) pick
13.	------- the intermission	(A) during	(B) between
14.	send someone more -------	(A) system	(B) information
15.	------- up a conference call	(A) set	(B) confirm

B 다음 짧은 지문을 읽고 패러프레이징 문장으로 적절한 것을 고르시오.

1.
> My team is experiencing so many issues because of the current system. We spend a lot of time sending reimbursement payments and confirming the receipts that people hand in.

(A) The system of reimbursing employees is inconvenient.
(B) The system of collecting payments is confusing.

2.
> MedMax is one of the nation's largest medical-related trade fairs. Major companies and medical experts alike look forward to this event every year to find out the latest trends in the industry.

(A) MedMax is recruiting more experts so it can grow in size.
(B) MedMax is an important event for those in the medical industry.

MAIN STEP[1]

> 문제를 해결하는
> 핵심 전략을 살펴보자.

 전략 1 문자메시지 지문에서는 정해진 스토리 라인이 출제된다

문자메시지(text message chain)는 두 인물 간에 주고 받는 대화문으로, 대부분 긴급한 업무 상황에서의 문제 공유 및 해결을 목적으로 한다. 내용이 비교적 간단하므로 빠르게 훑어가면 된다.

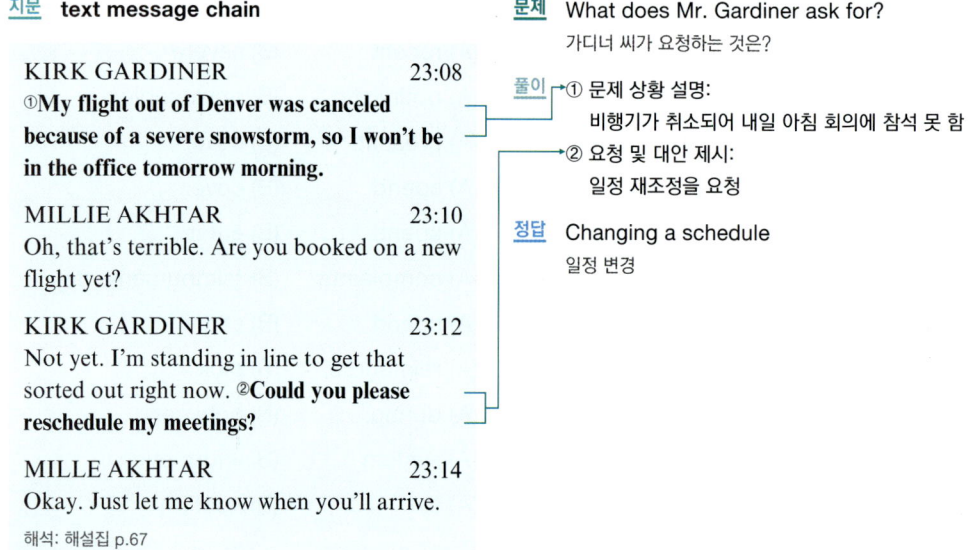

지문 **text message chain**

KIRK GARDINER 23:08
①**My flight out of Denver was canceled because of a severe snowstorm, so I won't be in the office tomorrow morning.**

MILLIE AKHTAR 23:10
Oh, that's terrible. Are you booked on a new flight yet?

KIRK GARDINER 23:12
Not yet. I'm standing in line to get that sorted out right now. ②**Could you please reschedule my meetings?**

MILLE AKHTAR 23:14
Okay. Just let me know when you'll arrive.

해석: 해설집 p.67

문제 What does Mr. Gardiner ask for?
가디너 씨가 요청하는 것은?

풀이
① 문제 상황 설명:
   비행기가 취소되어 내일 아침 회의에 참석 못 함
② 요청 및 대안 제시:
   일정 재조정을 요청

정답 Changing a schedule
일정 변경

 전략 2 온라인 채팅 대화문은 먼저 전체 흐름을 파악한 뒤, 필요한 정보를 찾는다

온라인 채팅 대화문(online chat discussion)에는 보통 3인 이상의 인물이 등장한다. 먼저 도입부에서 채팅의 주제와 인물 간 관계를 파악하고, 세부 정보 문제의 경우 지문에서 키워드를 찾아 해결하도록 한다.

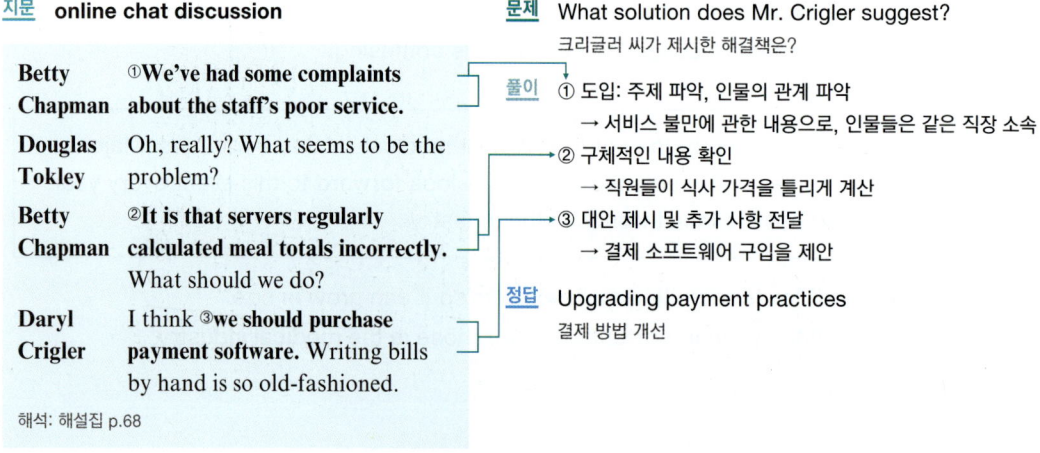

지문 **online chat discussion**

Betty Chapman	①**We've had some complaints about the staff's poor service.**
Douglas Tokley	Oh, really? What seems to be the problem?
Betty Chapman	②**It is that servers regularly calculated meal totals incorrectly.** What should we do?
Daryl Crigler	I think ③**we should purchase payment software.** Writing bills by hand is so old-fashioned.

해석: 해설집 p.68

문제 What solution does Mr. Crigler suggest?
크리글러 씨가 제시한 해결책은?

풀이
① 도입: 주제 파악, 인물의 관계 파악
   → 서비스 불만에 관한 내용으로, 인물들은 같은 직장 소속
② 구체적인 내용 확인
   → 직원들이 식사 가격을 틀리게 계산
③ 대안 제시 및 추가 사항 전달
   → 결제 소프트웨어 구입을 제안

정답 Upgrading payment practices
결제 방법 개선

MAIN STEP 2

앞에서 배운 전략을
문제에 직접 적용해 보자.

Questions 1-3 refer to the following online chat discussion.

Duncan, Kimberly 9:10 A.M.	I'm headed to the office supply store to pick up a few things. Do any of you need anything? I know you're all presenting at the workshop on fostering cooperation.
Kota, Jia 9:11 A.M.	I'm fine.
Hsu, Shan 9:12 A.M.	I could use a pack of new dry erase markers.
Geisler, Terry 9:12 A.M.	And I need a large foam board, size 40″ x 60″, if they have it.
Duncan, Kimberly 9:14 A.M.	Okay, I'll get both of those things.
Kota, Jia 9:16 A.M.	Terry, do you need any help? I know you had to cover for Mr. Rhodes at the last minute.
Geisler, Terry 9:17 A.M.	I'm nearly ready, but I just need someone to check my outline to see if my timing is okay. I'm worried I tried to fit in too many points.
Kota, Jia 9:18 A.M.	I can look it over. Just send it to me by e-mail.
Geisler, Terry 9:21 A.M.	Okay, thanks! It should be in your inbox now.
Hsu, Shan 9:23 A.M.	Does anyone have a copy of our catalog?
Kota, Jia 9:27 A.M.	I have a few in my office. Do you need them now?
Hsu, Shan 9:29 A.M.	Please just bring them to the workshop at 2:00. Thanks!

1. At 9:11 A.M., what does Ms. Kota mean when she writes, "I'm fine"?

   (A) She agrees with Ms. Duncan.
   (B) She doesn't need any supplies.
   (C) She feels optimistic about an event.
   (D) She is available to meet in person.

2. What can be inferred about Mr. Geisler?

   (A) He lost a copy of his outline.
   (B) He will go to the store with Ms. Duncan.
   (C) He is the newest member of the team.
   (D) He is filling in for another person.

3. Who will bring some catalogs to the event?

   (A) Ms. Duncan
   (B) Ms. Kota
   (C) Ms. Hsu
   (D) Mr. Geisler

FINAL STEP

> 실전 난이도의 문제를 풀며 앞에서 배운 전략을 활용해 보자.

Questions 1-2 refer to the following text message chain.

ALICE STANFIELD 1:56 P.M.
I'm setting up Conference Room A for the annual board meeting. I need some space for the refreshments, so I've got to move a few tables from other rooms. But they're too heavy. Could you give me a hand?

MINJUN BAEK 1:59 P.M.
Sure thing. Should I come up there now?

ALICE STANFIELD 2:01 P.M.
I have a few things to do before that, so could you come in about half an hour? I don't expect it to take more than fifteen minutes.

MINJUN BAEK 2:02 P.M.
Okay, I'll just meet you in the conference room. When does the meeting start?

ALICE STANFIELD 2:03 P.M.
It starts in about an hour, at 3 P.M., and will finish around 4 P.M. There's plenty of time. People usually don't arrive very early for it.

---

1. At 1:59 P.M., what does Mr. Baek mean when he writes, "Sure thing"?

   (A) He will help to move some furniture.
   (B) He will order some refreshments.
   (C) He will attend a board meeting.
   (D) He will set up a projector for Alice.

2. When will Mr. Baek meet Ms. Stanfield?

   (A) At 2:30 P.M.
   (B) At 3:00 P.M.
   (C) At 3:30 P.M.
   (D) At 4:00 P.M.

Questions 3-6 refer to the following online chat discussion.

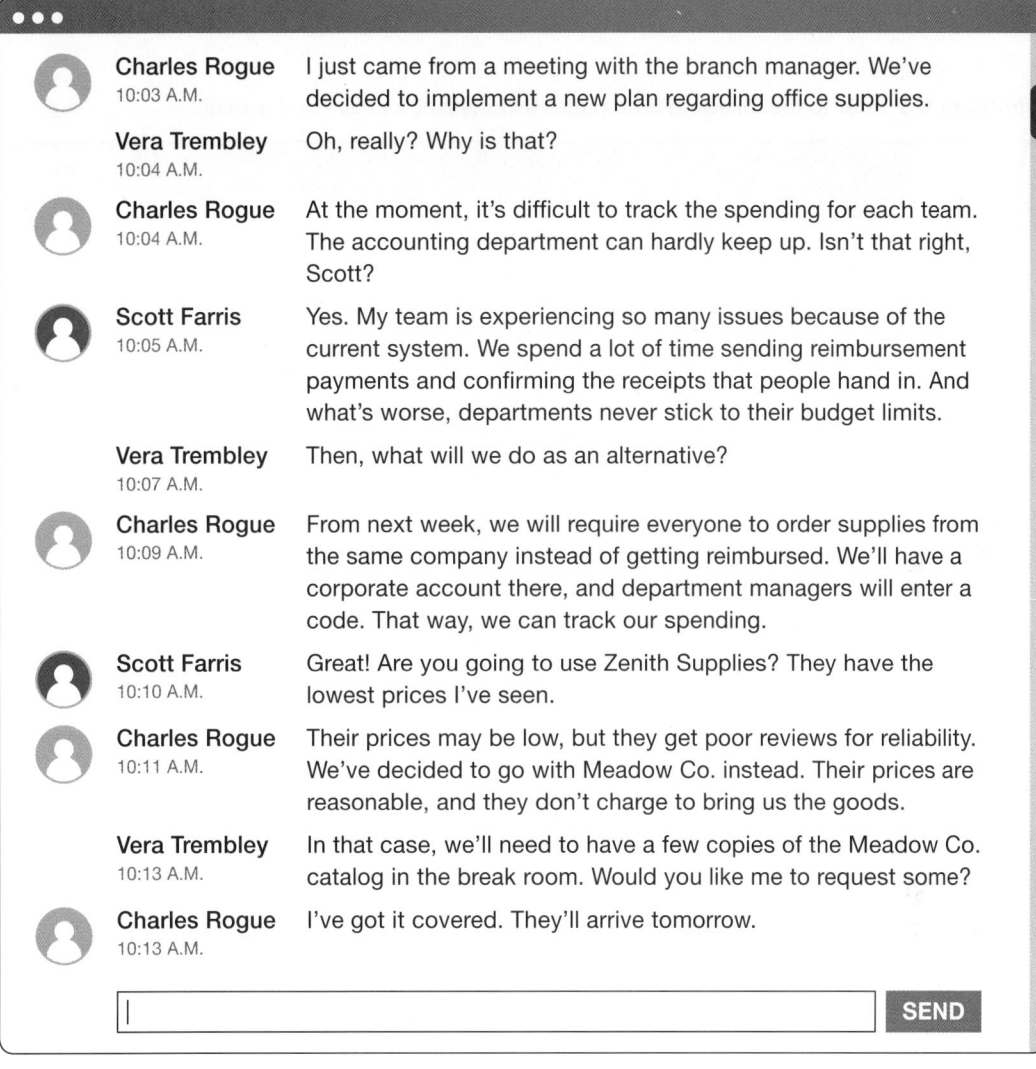

Charles Rogue 10:03 A.M.
I just came from a meeting with the branch manager. We've decided to implement a new plan regarding office supplies.

Vera Trembley 10:04 A.M.
Oh, really? Why is that?

Charles Rogue 10:04 A.M.
At the moment, it's difficult to track the spending for each team. The accounting department can hardly keep up. Isn't that right, Scott?

Scott Farris 10:05 A.M.
Yes. My team is experiencing so many issues because of the current system. We spend a lot of time sending reimbursement payments and confirming the receipts that people hand in. And what's worse, departments never stick to their budget limits.

Vera Trembley 10:07 A.M.
Then, what will we do as an alternative?

Charles Rogue 10:09 A.M.
From next week, we will require everyone to order supplies from the same company instead of getting reimbursed. We'll have a corporate account there, and department managers will enter a code. That way, we can track our spending.

Scott Farris 10:10 A.M.
Great! Are you going to use Zenith Supplies? They have the lowest prices I've seen.

Charles Rogue 10:11 A.M.
Their prices may be low, but they get poor reviews for reliability. We've decided to go with Meadow Co. instead. Their prices are reasonable, and they don't charge to bring us the goods.

Vera Trembley 10:13 A.M.
In that case, we'll need to have a few copies of the Meadow Co. catalog in the break room. Would you like me to request some?

Charles Rogue 10:13 A.M.
I've got it covered. They'll arrive tomorrow.

3. What is the online chat mainly about?
   (A) A weekly meeting
   (B) A new manager
   (C) A change in a procedure
   (D) A security plan

4. What problem does the company face?
   (A) Exceeding departmental budgets
   (B) Missing important deadlines
   (C) Losing experienced employees
   (D) Getting complaints from customers

5. What is suggested about Meadow Co.?
   (A) It offers free delivery.
   (B) It has the lowest prices.
   (C) It is near the writers' office.
   (D) It has recently opened.

6. At 10:13 A.M., what does Mr. Rogue mean when he writes, "I've got it covered"?
   (A) He will organize the break room.
   (B) He has arranged a brochure delivery.
   (C) He will cover Ms. Trembley's shift.
   (D) He has requested more workers.

FURTHER STEP

| 문자 메시지가 포함된 삼중 지문을 더 풀며 고득점을 노려보자.

Questions 1-5 refer to the following Web page, text message chain, and e-mail.

---

www.medmaxtradefair.com

MedMax Trade Fair

September 14-17 / Brownton Convention Center, Salt Lake City, Utah

MedMax is one of the nation's largest medical-related trade fairs. Major companies and medical experts alike look forward to this event every year to find out the latest trends in the industry. We have an exhibition space for nearly 1,000 booths, all of which were rented within the first week of announcing the dates, just like last year.

Our exhibitors will be displaying medical devices, specialty treatments, technical equipment, management systems, and more. One-, two-, and four-day passes are available to visitors and can be purchased through our Web site by clicking here. This year, for the first time ever, exhibitors will have the opportunity to give live presentations to show how their goods are used. We're also pleased to have Dr. Lisa McMillan, Dr. Vishall Kota, and Dr. Elias Quesada as the guest speakers for the first, second, and third evenings, respectively.

Don't miss the medical event of the year. Get your tickets to MedMax today!

LATASHA MORRIS	8:48 A.M.

Have you arrived at the convention center yet?

ARTURO ERWIN	8:55 A.M.

Yes, I just checked in. This is going to be a great opportunity for our journal. I hope I'll be able to interview representatives from the top medical companies.

LATASHA MORRIS	8:57 A.M.

I'm sure you will. When I went to the MedMax event in Los Angeles last year, I found that a lot of people were happy to share their comments.

LATASHA MORRIS	8:58 A.M.

While you're there, could you do something for me?

ARTURO ERWIN	9:03 A.M.

Sure. What is it?

LATASHA MORRIS	9:05 A.M.

Could you pick up as many brochures and catalogs at the booths as possible? A lot of companies provide special details to conference visitors that they don't share anywhere else.

ARTURO ERWIN	9:11 A.M.

All right. You can count on me.

To: Sherrie Wilson <s.wilson@therapexl.com>
From: Arturo Erwin <erwin_a@natmedicaljournal.org>
Date: September 24
Subject: MedMax

Dear Ms. Wilson,

It was a pleasure meeting you at the recent MedMax convention in Utah. As you may remember, I am a writer for the *National Medical Journal*. We publish medical research studies as well as articles about the latest on the commercial side of the industry. It was fascinating to see your colleague, Dr. Vishall Kota, discuss your company's new insulin pump during the speech. When I handled the prototype myself at your booth, I couldn't believe it because I was expecting it to be much heavier. I think it would be very comfortable for patients to wear. When you get the chance, could you please send me more information about this device? It was so popular that all of the brochures were gone by the time I got there.

Warmest regards,

Arturo Erwin

---

1. What is NOT indicated about last year's event?
   (A) It lacked demonstrations.
   (B) It was held in Los Angeles.
   (C) It lasted for four days.
   (D) Its booths were rented quickly.

2. On the Web page, the word "miss" in paragraph 3, line 1, is closest in meaning to
   (A) fail
   (B) lose
   (C) escape
   (D) skip

3. What does Ms. Morris ask Mr. Erwin for?
   (A) An interview schedule
   (B) Directions to the site
   (C) Some promotional materials
   (D) A free conference pass

4. When did Mr. Erwin see Ms. Wilson's coworker's speech?
   (A) September 14
   (B) September 15
   (C) September 16
   (D) September 17

5. What surprised Mr. Erwin about Therapexl's product?
   (A) Its numerous features
   (B) Its easy setup
   (C) Its low price
   (D) Its lightweight design

UNIT 12
이메일/편지

등장인물의 정보를
파악하면 절반이 풀린다

PRE-STEP

지문에 등장할 주요 어휘를 미리 학습해 보자.

A 다음 빈칸에 들어갈 어휘로 알맞은 것을 고르시오.

1. ------- for a job　　　　　　(A) approach　　(B) search
2. fill a job -------　　　　　　(A) vacancy　　(B) replacement
3. ------- an e-mail　　　　　　(A) draft　　(B) express
4. ------- displeasure　　　　　(A) draft　　(B) express
5. as a token of -------　　　　(A) goodwill　　(B) vacancy
6. a(n) ------- of the items　　(A) assistance　　(B) collection
7. in need of -------　　　　　　(A) assistance　　(B) collection
8. be ------- for the position　(A) corporate　　(B) eligible
9. ------- a letter to someone　(A) direct　　(B) deal
10. ------- with our client base　(A) direct　　(B) deal
11. walk ------- together　　　　(A) beyond　　(B) over
12. ------- for a membership　　(A) build　　(B) sign up
13. seek to ------- a partnership　(A) build　　(B) sign up
14. ------- a monthly newsletter　(A) receive　　(B) inquire
15. on ------- of McClain Consulting　(A) plan　　(B) behalf

B 다음 짧은 지문을 읽고 패러프레이징 문장으로 적절한 것을 고르시오.

1.
> I've hired a woman named Yasmin Sekar as our social responsibility specialist. With Thanksgiving approaching, her first task is to organize a company-wide donation drive for food, toiletries, and household items.

(A) A newly hired employee will arrange for the staff to donate goods.
(B) The social responsibility specialist is collecting money for basic necessities.

2.
> I thought you could come to my office about fifteen minutes before the meeting starts and we could just walk over together. Please let me know if you're interested in going.

(A) We can move the meeting to my office if that is more convenient.
(B) We can go to the meeting together if you plan on attending it.

MAIN STEP 1

문제를 해결하는
핵심 전략을 살펴보자.

발신자와 수신자 관련 문제가 자주 출제된다

이메일과 편지는 '목적 → 상황에 대한 구체적 설명 → 요청 사항'의 3단 구성으로 흐름이 고정되어 있어 내용 파악이 쉽다. 또한 발신자와 수신자가 따로 있어 이들의 정보를 활용해야 하는 문제가 자주 출제된다.

지문 e-mail

To: Clara Timber ^{수신인}
From: Michael Myers ^{발신인}
Subject: RE: Application

^{수신인}You also said that **you are working mornings** for a fashion magazine. ^{발신인}**I'm currently searching for a photographer for our design team.**

Warm regards,

Michael Myers, Director

해석: 해설집 p.76

1. 수신인 관련 문제

문제① What is true about **Ms. Timber**?
팀버 씨에 대해 사실인 것은?

정답 She is currently employed as a part-timer.
현재 시간제로 근무한다.

2. 발신인 관련 문제

문제② What is indicated about **Mr. Myers**?
마이어스 씨에 대해 시사된 바는?

정답 He is trying to fill a job vacancy.
공석을 채우려 하고 있다.

→ 발신인(From:)인 마이클 마이어스 씨는 본문에서 'I'로 바뀌어 표현되고 있으며, 수신인(To:)인 클라라 팀버 씨는 'You'로 표현되고 있다. 이메일은 To와 From부터 확인하자.

제3의 인물의 소속이 단골 오답 함정으로 등장한다

이메일에 수신자와 발신자 외에 제3의 인물이 등장할 경우, 그의 소속은 수신인 혹은 발신인의 소속과 다를 수 있다. 이를 이용한 오답 함정이 자주 등장하는 편이다.

지문 e-mail

To: Rachelle Hunter, Sales team ^{수신인}
From: Jason Diba ^{발신인}
Subject: New system

Hi Rachelle,

The new system was a recommendation we received from ^{제3의 인물}**Kenan Bayer, the outside consultant we hired** to improve the company's practices.

Jason Diba, Finance team ^{발신인}

해석: 해설집 p.76

문제 What is mentioned about Kenan Bayer?
키난 베이어 씨에 대해 언급된 것은?
(A) He works for Ms. Diba's company. (O)
   디바 씨의 회사를 위해 일한다.
(B) He is in the finance department. (X)
   재무팀 소속이다.

풀이 키난 베이어 씨는 디바 씨의 회사에서 고용한 외부 고문이다. 베이어 씨를 디바 씨의 Finance team(재무팀) 소속으로 오인하지 않도록 주의하자.

정답 (A)

MAIN STEP 2

Questions 1-2 refer to the following letter.

Stacey LeBlanc, Customer Service Manager
Fort Lauderdale, FL 33301
March 17

Dear Ms. LeBlanc,

I'm very disappointed with your company's service. I purchased a green-patterned dress online on March 4. When it arrived on March 9, it had several buttons missing. I e-mailed Kayla Doreo in the returns department asking to have a replacement shipped the next day, but she waited until today to reply. I plan to return the dress, but I also want to express my displeasure with the store's slow service.

Janet Gilbert

1. Why did Ms. Gilbert send the letter?
   (A) To request an exchange
   (B) To complain about a service
   (C) To place a new order
   (D) To inquire about a delivery

2. What can be inferred about Ms. Doreo?
   (A) She responds to e-mails immediately.
   (B) She is a customer service agent.
   (C) She processes returns and exchanges.
   (D) She repairs damaged clothing.

Questions 3-4 refer to the following e-mail.

To: Albert Kapp <a.kapp@trumail.com>
From: Centerville Bank <info@centerville.com>
Date: November 6
Subject: RE: Inquiry

Dear Mr. Kapp,

I'm writing in response to your inquiry about wiring money overseas. There is a daily transfer limit of $50,000. Attached is a document that explains how to send money abroad. The fee charged by our bank varies depending on the amount sent and the type of service chosen.

Linda Ayers
Centerville Bank, Foreign Accounts Manager

3. What is true about Mr. Kapp?
   (A) He sent an inquiry to Centerville Bank.
   (B) He called to confirm a wire transfer.
   (C) He was charged a late fee.
   (D) He reversed a transaction.

4. What was included with the e-mail?
   (A) An invoice for a transaction
   (B) Directions to a branch office
   (C) A promotion for a new service
   (D) Instructions for transferring funds

FINAL STEP

실전 난이도의 문제를 풀며 앞에서 배운 전략을 활용해 보자.

Questions 1-3 refer to the following e-mail.

To:	Vienna McCready <vmccr1@baumannenterprises.com>
From:	Elijah Machon <emach7@baumannenterprises.com>
Date:	November 4
Subject:	Corporate Social Responsibility Efforts

Dear Vienna,

As a token of goodwill to the community that provides us with so much business, the executive team of Baumann Enterprises has decided to institute a corporate social responsibility program. I've hired a woman named Yasmin Sekar as our social responsibility specialist. With Thanksgiving approaching, her first task is to organize a company-wide donation drive for food, toiletries, and household items. Staff participation is not mandatory, but will be strongly encouraged.

Attached is a letter that Yasmin has drafted to accompany the donations we will deliver to local food banks and shelters in need. I'd like for you to look it over and make sure there are no errors in spelling or grammar. Collection of the items will begin on November 10 and end on November 20. It would be ideal for you to finish editing this document by the time Ms. Sekar starts deliveries on November 22.

Finally, because you are the client relations manager, I'd like you to draft an e-mail to our full client list. Please inform them of this undertaking and encourage them to participate in their own collections. Do not tell them to drop off any items at our office. Instead, direct them to the charities in need of assistance. They should make their own donations separate from ours.

Kind regards,

Elijah Machon, Community Relations Manager

1. What is true about Yasmin Sekar?
    (A) She will organize the gathering of donations.
    (B) Her duties include proofreading the writing of others.
    (C) She supervises the work of Ms. McCready.
    (D) She will make deliveries starting November 10.

2. Who is Ms. McCready?
    (A) The community relations manager
    (B) A social responsibility specialist
    (C) The client relations manager
    (D) A donation center representative

3. What is included with the e-mail?
    (A) Directions to a charity
    (B) A draft of a letter
    (C) Ms. Sekar's contact information
    (D) A list of clients

Questions 4-5 refer to the following letter.

Brenda Silva
553 Archwood Avenue
Concord, NC 28025
March 8

Dear Ms. Silva,

Congratulations on passing the final interview! On behalf of McClain Consulting, I would like to offer you the position of junior associate. Our human resources team was pleased that you decided to apply for the job after visiting our booth at the job fair. We think you will be an ideal candidate for this position, and we were particularly impressed with the fact that you are bilingual in English and Spanish. This will be useful when dealing with our client base in South America.

In this role, you will be in charge of evaluating the needs of clients and working with your team leader to provide custom-made business solutions. After six months of employment, you will be eligible to switch to a full-time position if you have a satisfactory performance rating.

Enclosed you will find a copy of the employment contract. Please sign it and return it to our office in the envelope provided. Should you have questions regarding the terms of the contract, please contact me at 555-2045, extension 12.

I look forward to working with you.

Judy Arnold
Human Resources Representative, McClain Consulting

4. What is indicated about Ms. Silva?
   (A) She can speak two languages.
   (B) She applied for the job online.
   (C) She has a professional certification.
   (D) She was born in South America.

5. What is suggested about the position being offered?
   (A) It involves managing subordinates.
   (B) It is part-time employment.
   (C) It has competitive wages.
   (D) It required a written test.

FURTHER STEP

이메일이 포함된 삼중 지문을 더 풀며 고득점을 노려 보자.

Questions 1-5 refer to the following e-mail, Web page, and directory.

To: Leonard Akron <leonardakron@akronconsulting.com>
From: Genevieve Connelly <g_connelly@atro.net>
Date: February 19
Subject: Business Builders

Hi Leonard,

I'm glad we were finally able to get together for coffee to catch up. It was interesting hearing about your new consulting business, and I hope you continue to see growth. As you know, networking is a very important part of business, so I'm wondering if you would like to come to the Business Builders monthly meeting with me. You don't have to be a member to attend, and you can find more information at www.bizbuild.org.

The next meeting is on March 2 at 7 P.M. I thought you could come to my office about fifteen minutes before the meeting starts, and we could just walk over together. Please let me know if you're interested in going.

Talk to you soon,

Genevieve

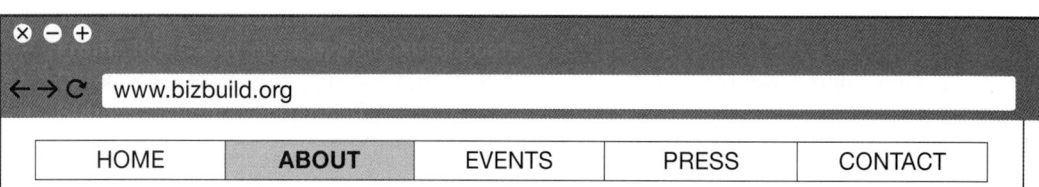

www.bizbuild.org

| HOME | ABOUT | EVENTS | PRESS | CONTACT |

Founded by Beth Crane in 2013, Business Builders is a network of business professionals in the Wilberville area who seek to share ideas and tips, provide advice, and build partnerships. We get together once a month. There is no cost to attend our meetings, and you can attend as many or as few as you'd like. We do recommend signing up for a free membership so you can receive our monthly newsletter and stay informed on group events. Meetings take place in Room 302 of the Evans Building (3939 Mahlon Street).

For inquiries, e-mail info@bizbuild.org.

Wilberville Business Directory

Search:
Jump to: A B C D E F G H I J **K** L M N O P Q R S T U V W X Y Z

----K----

Business	Address/Phone	Business Type	Notes
Karla's	3028 Cimarron Road 465-6594	Hair Salon	Owned by Karla Spencer Web site: hairbykarla.net
Kangaroo Café	431 Washburn Avenue 482-0022	Restaurant	Owned by Beth Crane Web site: mykcafe.com
Klein Inc.	4394 Parkway Street 482-2578	Landscaping	Owned by Simon Klein Web site: none
*Kuhn Appliances	508 18th Street N. 465-7641, 465-7642	Appliance Store	Owned by Kuhn Corporation Web site: kuhnappl.com

*Denotes recently added business.

---

1. What is the purpose of the e-mail?
   (A) To recommend a product to Mr. Akron
   (B) To invite Mr. Akron to an event
   (C) To confirm Mr. Akron's membership
   (D) To thank Mr. Akron for his assistance

2. What is NOT indicated about Business Builders on the Web page?
   (A) How many members it has
   (B) When it was started
   (C) How often it meets
   (D) What its purpose is

3. What can be inferred about Ms. Connelly?
   (A) She is a new Business Builders member.
   (B) She used to be Mr. Akron's coworker.
   (C) She has recently started a business.
   (D) She works near the Evans Building.

4. Who is the founder of Business Builders?
   (A) A salon owner
   (B) A restaurant owner
   (C) A landscaper
   (D) A retailer

5. What is true according to the business directory?
   (A) Karla's does not have a Web site.
   (B) Kangaroo Café has two phone numbers.
   (C) Klein Inc. is located on Washburn Avenue.
   (D) Kuhn Appliances has not been on the list long.

UNIT 13
광고문

제시된 조건과 관련된
오답 함정에 주의하자

PRE-STEP

지문에 등장할 주요 어휘를 미리 학습해 보자.

A 다음 빈칸에 들어갈 어휘로 알맞은 것을 고르시오.

		(A)	(B)
1.	------ *one's* online application	(A) fill up	(B) fill out
2.	------ *one's* team	(A) process	(B) join
3.	------ a marketing director	(A) look for	(B) fill out
4.	purchase in ------	(A) bulk	(B) field
5.	actual experience in the ------	(A) bulk	(B) field
6.	------ of certification	(A) environment	(B) proof
7.	ensure the ------ of *one's* services	(A) quality	(B) fair
8.	attend a job ------	(A) reference	(B) fair
9.	------ from three former clients	(A) references	(B) proofs
10.	a friendly work ------	(A) environment	(B) drawing
11.	restore ------ vehicles	(A) damaged	(B) desirable
12.	------ compensation package	(A) damaged	(B) desirable
13.	------ price	(A) affordable	(B) drawing
14.	------ monthly payments	(A) join	(B) process
15.	enter into a prize ------	(A) picking	(B) drawing

B 다음 짧은 지문을 읽고 패러프레이징 문장으로 적절한 것을 고르시오.

1.
> Although we do accept walk-in appointments, I suggest you schedule a session with us at least one week before your desired time slot so as to avoid disappointment.

(A) I recommend booking a longer session so you won't feel rushed.
(B) I recommend booking in advance so you can get the time you want.

2.
> We are now pleased to announce that we are adding another facility, across from the Atherton Mall. Celebrate the opening of this branch with us on Saturday, April 3. On that day, you can meet our staff, try free product samples, and enjoy some refreshments.

(A) The store's grand opening on April 3 will include complimentary items and a chance to meet employees.
(B) The new location is seeking staff who can begin work by April 3 and who are willing to work near the mall.

MAIN STEP¹

> 문제를 해결하는
> 핵심 전략을 살펴보자.

필수 요건 및 우대 요건과 관련된 오답 함정이 자주 출제된다

구인구직 광고문에서 꼭 등장하는 것이 바로 채용 요건이다. 채용 요건에는 구직자가 반드시 갖춰야만 하는 '필수 요건'과 갖추고 있으면 더 유리한 '우대 요건'이 있다. 이 두 요건은 오답 함정으로 자주 등장한다.

지문 | job advertisement

The ideal candidate must be certified as a civil engineer. Experience as a supervisor is an advantage but is not required for the position.

해석: 해설집 p.84

문제 | What is mentioned about the position?
(A) It is intended for certified professionals. (O)
(B) It requires management skills. (X)

풀이 | must be certified라고 했으므로 토목 기사 자격은 필수 요건이다. 감독으로서의 경험은 advantage라고 했으므로 우대 요건이다. 따라서 (B)는 오답이다.

정답 | (A)

필수 요건	You **must/should** have a bachelor's degree. 학사 학위가 있어야만 합니다. A degree is **required/necessary/mandatory**. 학위가 요구됩니다/필요합니다/필수입니다.
우대 요건	Field experience is **preferred/desirable/helpful**. 현장 경력이 **선호됩니다/바람직합니다/도움이 됩니다**. A master's degree is a(n) **advantage/plus**. 석사 학위는 우대 요건입니다.

구매 조건 관련 사항이 오답 함정으로 자주 출제된다

광고문에는 쿠폰 사용 조건, 일부 품목 세일 제외 혹은 특정 품목 세일, 세일 기간과 장소 등 구매 관련 조건들이 자주 등장한다. 이러한 조건들은 선택지에서 오답 함정으로 자주 쓰이므로 아래의 빈출 패턴을 알아보고 대비하자.

쿠폰 사용 조건	지문	Coupons **are not to be handed over**. 쿠폰은 양도되어서는 안 됩니다.	오답	Vouchers are transferable. 쿠폰은 양도 가능합니다.
일부 품목 세일 제외	지문	All the books will be 99 cents each **except for** art books. 미술서들을 **제외하고**, 모든 책은 권당 99센트일 것입니다.	오답	Art books will be sold for 99 cents. 미술서들은 99센트에 판매될 것입니다.
세일 기간 및 장소	지문	We are offering discounts on cookies **from May 1 to 25**. 5월 1일부터 25일까지 쿠키를 할인 판매합니다.	오답	They will be on sale throughout May. 그것들은 5월 내내 할인 판매될 것입니다.

MAIN STEP 2

Questions 1-2 refer to the following job advertisement.

Swanson Finance is looking for an accountant who is able to start working on April 1. We offer a friendly work environment along with a standard salary.

Duties include:
- Processing monthly payments for employees
- Tracking business expenses using spreadsheet software

Applicants must be certified by the state of Virginia. Proof of certification should be presented for verification at the time of the interview. Two years of experience in accounting is an advantage but is not required.

To apply for this position, visit our Web site at www.swansonfinance.com and fill out our online application.

1. What is mentioned as a requirement for the position?
(A) A flexible schedule
(B) State certification
(C) Two years' experience
(D) A business degree

2. What should candidates do to apply for the job?
(A) Send an e-mail
(B) Visit the office in person
(C) Complete an Internet form
(D) Attend a job fair

Questions 3-4 refer to the following advertisement.

Mission Auto Body and Paint offers award-winning Pro-Paint Services to restore damaged vehicles to their factory appearances.

The cost of this service will be charged to your insurance provider directly. And to celebrate 40 years in business, we're giving a complimentary Wax Coating Service to the first 40 customers who visit us this month.

To see our high-quality work for yourself, visit the gallery on our Web site at www.missionautobodyandpaint.com/gallery. If you are interested in our services, please send an e-mail to info@missionautobodyandpaint.com for a quote.

3. What should people do to get a free service?
(A) Be one of the first forty customers
(B) Call their insurance provider
(C) Visit the online photo gallery
(D) Pay for vehicle paint repairs

4. What is NOT true about Mission Auto Body and Paint?
(A) It has won an award for its services.
(B) It has been in operation for 4 decades.
(C) It provides samples of previous work.
(D) It offers estimates through its Web site.

FINAL STEP

실전 난이도의 문제를 풀며
앞에서 배운 전략을 활용해 보자.

Questions 1-2 refer to the following flyer.

Sugar & Spice Bakery
406 Rue Charlemagne

To get your office off to a great start each morning, you should consider using Sugar & Spice's delivery service! We bring freshly baked sourdough bread, pastries, cakes & brioche to your place of business. Our morning hours of delivery are between 7 A.M. and 10 A.M. on weekdays. On weekends, our delivery service is no longer available, although coffee and pastries can still be purchased in the store. We offer the following combinations, which all include a carafe of brewed coffee:

Item	Amount	Price
Hot sourdough	25 pieces	$85
Brioche & croissants	40 pieces	$110
Assorted French pastries	60 pieces	$160

*These options can be combined to accommodate any order size at an affordable price. Additionally, the following items can be purchased in bulk as needed: plastic forks, plastic knives, disposable plates and individual butter packages.

---

1. Who is the flyer most likely intended for?

(A) Baking instructors
(B) Local corporations
(C) Delivery drivers
(D) Coffee shops

2. What is true about Sugar & Spice Bakery?

(A) It offers delivery on weekends.
(B) It sells freshly baked pies.
(C) It provides utensils for free.
(D) It serves both coffee and pastries.

Questions 3-5 refer to the following job advertisement.

POSITION AVAILABLE: JUNIOR WEB DESIGNER

Job Description:
Woodbridge Web Design (WWD) is looking for a junior Web designer to join our team.

Responsibilities:
- Create prototypes and layouts for all new developments
- Design and develop graphics for Web applications
- Manage and maintain an internal image library

Requirements:
- Minimum one-year experience in Web site design
- Certification as a Web professional
- References from three former clients
- Strong time-management skills

Benefits:
WWD offers a desirable compensation package based on experience. One particular advantage of working for WWD is that all retirement contributions made by employees are doubled by the company each month.

To apply, please e-mail a cover letter, résumé, and link to a collection of previous work to the HR director, Walter Gatsby at gatsby_walter@woodbridgewebdesign.net, by October 8.

3. What is a duty of new employees?
   (A) Creating and updating an image database
   (B) Repairing damaged Web sites after they crash
   (C) Working unconventional hours including weekends
   (D) Sharing weekly design ideas in meetings

4. According to the advertisement, what is an advantage given to WWD employees?
   (A) A competitive starting salary
   (B) A generous retirement package
   (C) Extensive vacation days
   (D) Commission bonus payments

5. What is mentioned about the job application?
   (A) The submission deadline is October 10.
   (B) All documents must be received by mail.
   (C) It must be accompanied by at least two references.
   (D) The inclusion of a design sample is a requirement.

FURTHER STEP

| 광고문이 포함된 삼중 지문을 더 풀며 고득점을 노려 보자.

Questions 1-5 refer to the following advertisement, letter, and Web page.

Take a Break at Sierra Spa!

Sierra Spa, under the ownership of Nora Thomas, has served the Cambridge area for the past decade by providing luxury relaxation and beauty treatments. We are now pleased to announce that we are adding another facility, across from the Atherton Mall. Celebrate the opening of this branch with us on Saturday, April 3. On that day, you can meet our staff, try free product samples, and enjoy some refreshments. You can also be entered into a prize drawing for a Sierra Spa voucher if you register for our monthly e-mail.

For the best in professional massages, skincare treatments, manicures, and more, come to Sierra Spa!

1785 Lang Avenue and 305 16th Street / Open daily from 9 A.M. to 10 P.M.

Laurie Ekman
4509 Hillside Drive
Cambridge, MA 02141

April 5

Dear Ms. Ekman,

On behalf of Sierra Spa, I am pleased to inform you that you are the winner of the prize drawing from our April 3 event. Congratulations! Enclosed you will find a voucher for our services. It can be used for any of our spa packages except those that include a hot stone massage. The voucher does not expire, but we cannot replace it if it becomes lost, so please keep it in a safe place. You can use the voucher at either of our locations. Although we do accept walk-in appointments, I suggest you schedule a session with us at least one week before your desired time slot so as to avoid disappointment. We look forward to serving you!

Sincerely,

Sandra Robbins
Administrative Team, Sierra Spa

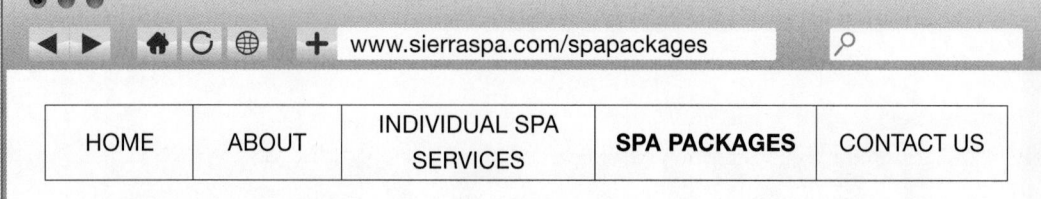

Spa Packages at Sierra Spa

Choose any spa package below for just $225. That gives you big savings over buying the services separately.

Revive and Refresh: 60-minute Thai massage + clarifying facial + aromatherapy body wrap
Nature Connect: brightening facial + seaweed body wrap + 60-minute hot stone massage
Cozy Comfort: antiaging body wrap + 60-minute deep tissue massage + sugar scrub facial
Big Night Out: 30-minute hair and scalp massage + oxygen infusion facial + moisturizing body wrap + manicure + pedicure

To ensure the quality of our services, all of our treatments are administered by massage therapists and beauty technicians with at least eight years of experience in the field.

1. Why is Sierra Spa holding a special event?
   (A) To promote a second location
   (B) To introduce a new owner
   (C) To celebrate a relocation
   (D) To launch a product line

2. What can be inferred about Ms. Ekman?
   (A) She is a regular customer.
   (B) She joined a mailing list.
   (C) She made a purchase.
   (D) She requested some samples.

3. What does Ms. Robbins advise Ms. Ekman to do?
   (A) Check an online schedule
   (B) Verify an expiration date
   (C) Use a certain location
   (D) Make a booking in advance

4. Which package is NOT available with the voucher?
   (A) Revive and Refresh
   (B) Nature Connect
   (C) Cozy Comfort
   (D) Big Night Out

5. What is true about Sierra Spa's services?
   (A) They come with a money-back guarantee.
   (B) They must be purchased as a package.
   (C) They are not available on weekends.
   (D) They are provided by experienced workers.

UNIT 14
기사문 (1)

단락별 중심 주제 파악이
먼저다

PRE-STEP

지문에 등장할 주요 어휘를 미리 학습해 보자.

A 다음 빈칸에 들어갈 어휘로 알맞은 것을 고르시오.

1.	------- the anniversary	(A) mark	(B) meet
2.	------- a need for a new space	(A) mark	(B) meet
3.	------- an organization	(A) sponsor	(B) submit
4.	more ------- to use	(A) convenient	(B) experienced
5.	a(n) ------- volunteer	(A) convenient	(B) experienced
6.	------- millions of dollars	(A) invest	(B) accomplish
7.	------- an aim	(A) invest	(B) accomplish
8.	------- the holiday season	(A) celebrate	(B) take part
9.	------- the local economy	(A) support	(B) celebrate
10.	------- in an event	(A) take part	(B) support
11.	an innovative -------	(A) conflict	(B) approach
12.	be in ------- as usual	(A) approach	(B) operation
13.	raise money for a(n) -------	(A) charity	(B) approach
14.	perform *one's* -------	(A) charities	(B) duties
15.	address some of the -------	(A) issues	(B) operations

B 다음 짧은 지문을 읽고 패러프레이징 문장으로 적절한 것을 고르시오.

1.
> A state-of-the-art community sports field opened in the center of town last month, and in a mere thirty days, its popularity among residents has grown dramatically.

(A) With assistance from residents, the facility can become more popular than ever.
(B) In a short time, many people living in the area have come to like the facility.

2.
> The council had hoped to make cycling more safe, convenient, and comfortable. To do so, it spent four months expanding the number of bicycle routes.

(A) More biking routes were added in an effort to improve conditions for cyclists.
(B) The project helped to improve the condition of outdated cycling trails.

MAIN STEP 1

문제를 해결하는 핵심 전략을 살펴보자.

전략 1 단락별 주제만 파악하면 빠른 읽기가 가능하다

기사문은 정보가 많아 난이도가 높지만, 중심 주제에 대해 '누가/언제/어디서/무엇을/왜/어떻게'의 육하원칙 정보가 명확히 제시된다는 특징이 있다. 각 단락은 아무리 길어도 중심 주제가 1개이며, 그 외의 내용은 중심 주제를 뒷받침하는 세부 설명들임을 알아두자.

지문 article

①Starius Plus, the Berlin-based ceramics manufacturer, announced its plans to improve market performance.

②Having posted losses of nearly 10 million euros over the last year, Starius Plus is proposing changes that should return it to profitability in nine months.

③The strategy centers on improving domestic operations. Executives believe that major savings could be made by organizational reshuffling and altering the supply chain.

④Investors anticipate that these measures will guarantee short-term profit growth.

해석: 해설집 p.90

1. 무엇을? → 기사의 전반적 주제
문제① What is the article mainly about?
기사의 주제는?
정답 A company's plans for improvement
회사의 개선 계획

2. 왜? → 언급된 사항이 시행되는 이유
문제② What can be inferred about Starius Plus?
스태리어스 플러스 사에 대해 추론할 수 있는 것은?
정답 Its recent sales have not been profitable.
최근 매출이 수익이 없었다.

3. 어떻게? → 시행 방법 및 구체적 계획
문제③ How does the company intend to improve domestic operations?
회사가 국내 사업을 개선하려고 하는 방법은?
정답 By handling administrative tasks efficiently
관리 업무를 효율적으로 함으로써

4. 무엇을? → 미래 전망
문제④ What do investors anticipate?
투자자들이 기대하는 것은?
정답 An increase in company profits 회사 수익 증대

전략 2 인터뷰/인용문에서 언급된 사항은 빈번하게 문제로 출제된다

관계자와의 인터뷰나 인용문에서 언급된 사항은 자주 문제로 출제되므로 주의 깊게 읽도록 한다.

지문 article

The CEO said, "We hope to meet more customers next year by opening 20 more stores abroad."

해석: 해설집 p.91

문제 What is the company planning to do?
회사가 계획하고 있는 것은?
정답 Open additional branches
추가 지점 개업

MAIN STEP 2

앞에서 배운 전략을
문제에 직접 적용해 보자.

Questions 1-2 refer to the following article.

San Francisco, A City that Cycles?

Yesterday, the San Francisco city council marked the completion of its green transportation program.

Recognizing that cycling is one of the cleanest and most energy-efficient forms of transportation, the council had hoped to make cycling more safe, convenient, and comfortable. To do so, it spent four months expanding the number of bicycle routes.

In order to encourage more people to take advantage of these new routes and start riding bicycles regularly, a second program will begin next month. For a small fee, shared bicycles will be available as short-term rentals from locations across the city.

1. What is the purpose of the article?

   (A) To announce a new policy
   (B) To change traffic signs
   (C) To promote bike sales
   (D) To point out walking paths

2. What will happen next month?

   (A) Toll fees will be collected.
   (B) More bike lanes will be added.
   (C) Public bicycles will be rentable.
   (D) Fuel prices will rise.

Questions 3-4 refer to the following article.

Changes on the Horizon for Volo Air

Italian-based air carrier Volo Air International is preparing for changes regarding its passenger class system and services. In a press release, spokesperson Bianca Lucci said the company plans to merge business and first class into one new class, which they will call "executive class." "To respond to the demand for economy class seats, every plane in the fleet will be expanding its economy class section by nearly 22 percent. The new executive class will offer all the comforts, services, and amenities that Volo Air's passengers have become accustomed to," said Lucci.

The work is scheduled to be completed by May 9, with the new pricing scheme for executive class going into effect on May 12. "Passengers can expect the cost of executive tickets to be around the same as what they currently pay for business class tickets," explained Lucci.

This is just the first step in the airline's plan to bring Volo Air up-to-date. The next project will be the addition of new uniforms for the staff and crew.

3. What is the article mainly about?

   (A) Current plans for an airline
   (B) The merger of two air carriers
   (C) A design competition for uniforms
   (D) An upcoming promotion for flight tickets

4. What is true about the executive class?

   (A) It will combine three classes.
   (B) Its cost will be about the same as business class.
   (C) It will offer new types of services.
   (D) Its seats will be created by a famous designer.

FINAL STEP

실전 난이도의 문제를 풀며 앞에서 배운 전략을 활용해 보자.

Questions 1-3 refer to the following article.

August 17—A state-of-the-art community sports field opened in the center of town last month, and in a mere thirty days, its popularity among residents has grown dramatically. The new facility can be used for a variety of outdoor sports like soccer and football, which meet a need for a new space to be allocated for local sporting events. — [1] — Athletes and their parents alike are thrilled to have such a place finally created. Tyler Duggan, a father of two, said that he's delighted to have a venue to which he can take his children for family outings in the evenings when other attractions are closed. He mentioned being particularly excited to take his young sons to watch the high school football games in the fall. The ticket prices for those competitions are only $5 for adults and $2 for children over the age of 5. — [2] —

Track-and-field coach Nolan Rossi is also thrilled because the facility makes athletic competitions easier on his colleagues and his students. As stated by Mr. Rossi, "The fields at my high school are too small to host the necessary track-and-field competitions in May." As a result, the teachers had to schedule each event on a different day. However, now that the new sports field is available, his school can hold the tournament there. This enables multiple events to be held simultaneously and creates one full day of competition for the students each spring. — [3] — Many participants agree that this is more convenient for everyone.

The final feature that the sports field boasts is the concession stand and snack bar underneath the stadium seating. Here, fans can purchase food and beverages while they enjoy watching games and practices. — [4] —

1. What is suggested about the stadium?
   (A) It is only open during daytime hours.
   (B) Its use is restricted to official games.
   (C) It was built with a food service center inside.
   (D) Its prices change according to the season.

2. What is true about Mr. Rossi?
   (A) He is a high school athletic coach.
   (B) He is a track-and-field competitor.
   (C) He is unhappy about the new project.
   (D) He has children under the age of five.

3. In which of the positions marked [1], [2], [3] and [4] does the following sentence best belong?

   "Therefore, it is an extremely affordable activity for families."

   (A) [1]
   (B) [2]
   (C) [3]
   (D) [4]

Questions 4-6 refer to the following article.

Wakefield Research Institute of Science and Technology Holds Annual Kids' Science Camp
By Chloé Yelding

Wakefield Research Institute of Science and Technology (WRIST) continues to sponsor its annual science camp for children aged 6 to 14. For one week every summer, WRIST invites 50 students, free of charge, to a campground two miles north of the city. Kids sleep on-site in cabins and spend their days engaged in interactive science experiments.

The origins of the WRIST camp began in 2000. Ethan Lazell—founding president of WRIST—decided that since his organization invested millions of dollars on research, it should also aim to pass the joy of science onto children. He envisioned craft programs that develop scientific literacy in kids who are not familiar with scientific concepts. His primary goal was to draw these participants to the world of science. He accomplished this aim, as his innovative approach to teaching motivated numerous children to later pursue careers in science, technology, engineering, and math. Although Mr. Lazell has since retired, WRIST continues to honor his vision and values to this day.

To maintain the functioning of the camp, WRIST relies heavily on educated volunteers. A range of science professionals serve as camp counselors and instructors. If you are interested in sharing your time and knowledge to help inspire children to become scientists, please send a completed volunteer form, a letter of reference, and a résumé to volunteers@wristsciencecamp.com.

4. What is the purpose of the article?
   (A) To encourage investment in a business
   (B) To announce a professional conference
   (C) To publicize an event for young people
   (D) To highlight an organizational achievement

5. What is true about Mr. Lazell?
   (A) His vision is still honored by WRIST today.
   (B) He opened the camp in 2010.
   (C) He hires the instructors.
   (D) He occasionally volunteers as a counselor.

6. What is suggested about volunteers?
   (A) They should have a background in engineering.
   (B) They must be recommended by a WRIST member.
   (C) They should send documents by e-mail.
   (D) They will receive on-site training.

FURTHER STEP

기사문이 포함된 삼중 지문을 더 풀며 고득점을 노려 보자.

Questions 1-5 refer to the following flyer, e-mail, and article.

Come Join the Fun at the Sherman City Winter Wonderland!
Saturday, December 12, 7 P.M.–10 P.M.

Sherman City is celebrating the holiday season with a Winter Wonderland event in the city center. We hope this will bring out-of-town shoppers to our town to support the local economy. In addition to the unique shops and cafés that will be in operation as usual, there will also be special activities for the whole family to enjoy:

- Victoria Cathedral: Free coffee and hot chocolate
- Hampton Station: Get your picture taken with a snowman
- Caradon Street: Booths where you can make holiday cards, ornaments, and more
- Crown Plaza: Live music by various performers
   (7 P.M. Sherman City Municipal Band, 8 P.M. Columbia Folk Singers, 9 P.M. Nellie Williams)

Admission is free to the public and no tickets are necessary. Please note that some of the downtown streets will be closed during the event, so driving routes and parking should be planned accordingly.

To: Undisclosed Recipients
From: Joel Casey <j.casey@inboxmail.com>
Date: December 6
Subject: Winter Wonderland

Dear Sherman Community Club Members,

I have been contacted by Laurie Domingo, the event planner for the Sherman City Winter Wonderland event this Saturday. I know many of you have already volunteered for this event, but Laurie is still looking for a few more volunteers for the arts and crafts booths. You would be partnered with an experienced volunteer, so you would not have to perform your duties alone. If you are interested, please contact Laurie as soon as possible at 555-2940. I hope you will seriously consider taking part in this event.

Sincerely,

Joel Casey
President, Sherman Community Club

Winter Wonderland Gets Cold Reaction

December 13—The Sherman City Winter Wonderland event held yesterday was considered a disappointment by many. Event planners had not anticipated the large crowds, which flooded the streets, making it difficult to move through the area and participate in activities and shopping. "The city center was like a wall of people," said Sherman City resident James Sims. "It took fifteen minutes just to move a few feet. I ended up just going home."

In addition, the live entertainment at Crown Plaza did not go on continuously as planned. The Columbia Folk Singers failed to show up for their performance. Although Nellie Williams was able to start half an hour early, that still left thirty minutes of silence.

"We've learned a lot from the difficulties with crowd control and planning," said Laurie Domingo, who was in charge of planning the event. "Next year we plan to have the activities more spread out to address some of these issues."

1. According to the flyer, what is one purpose of the event?
   (A) To attract visitors to the area
   (B) To raise money for a charity
   (C) To celebrate an achievement
   (D) To promote a shop opening

2. Where are more volunteers needed?
   (A) Victoria Cathedral
   (B) Hampton Station
   (C) Caradon Street
   (D) Crown Plaza

3. In the e-mail, the word "perform" in paragraph 1, line 5, is closest in meaning to
   (A) enforce
   (B) bring up
   (C) entertain
   (D) carry out

4. When did Nellie Williams begin her performance?
   (A) At 8:00 P.M.
   (B) At 8:30 P.M.
   (C) At 9:00 P.M.
   (D) At 9:30 P.M.

5. What does Ms. Domingo plan to do for the event next year?
   (A) Charge an admission fee
   (B) Use a larger area
   (C) Hold it earlier in the month
   (D) Recruit more volunteers

UNIT 15
기사문 (2)

주제별 지문의 흐름을
알아두자

PRE-STEP

지문에 등장할 주요 어휘를 미리 학습해 보자.

A 다음 빈칸에 들어갈 어휘로 알맞은 것을 고르시오.

1. ------- on strike (A) go (B) take
2. ------- seventy new employees (A) hire (B) book
3. negotiate an acquisition ------- (A) regulation (B) agreement
4. impose stricter ------- (A) wages (B) regulations
5. raise labor ------- (A) wages (B) agreements
6. ------- the store in person (A) stop by (B) unveil
7. reach new ------- (A) consumers (B) effects
8. take ------- on the first of next month (A) congestion (B) effect
9. traffic ------- (A) congestion (B) consideration
10. take the city's budget into ------- (A) consideration (B) effect
11. ------- a new logo (A) reach (B) unveil
12. ------- a wider market (A) launch (B) reach
13. ------- a Web site (A) launch (B) apply
14. ------- to all commercial enterprises (A) apply (B) comply
15. the ------- car manufacturer (A) sufficient (B) leading

B 다음 짧은 지문을 읽고 패러프레이징 문장으로 적절한 것을 고르시오.

1.
> Napier reports that downsizing its workforce is not likely. In fact, with the expected demand for its goods, Napier has plans to construct five more production plants, which are set to start operating late next year.

(A) To avoid cutting the number of employees, the company will focus on increasing its production levels next year.
(B) Instead of reducing the number of workers, the company will probably hire more, as it is opening more facilities.

2.
> Legislators passed a new environmental policy today that will make major changes to the current regulations. The new policy reflects an effort to lower the levels of contamination in soil and water in the region as well as to improve the overall air quality.

(A) Lawmakers enacted policies to monitor pollution levels.
(B) Lawmakers passed new regulations to get pollution under control.

MAIN STEP 1

> 문제를 해결하는
> 핵심 전략을 살펴보자.

 전략 1 기사의 주제별로 정해진 지문의 흐름이 있다

다음 토익 지문에 자주 등장하는 기사의 주제와 흐름을 파악해 두자.

1. 지역사회 - 공사 안내 / 정책 변경

Columbia Avenue to Undergo Construction

City officials have confirmed that construction will begin on May 2 to widen sections of Columbia Avenue, as the road can no longer accommodate the community's heavy traffic.

The construction will last for approximately four months, with lane closures between Hillview Boulevard and Stanton Street.

Although traffic congestion is expected for the duration of the project, motorists are pleased that driving conditions will be greatly improved upon its completion.

도입: 안내 사항 공지
- 공사/정책 변경의 대략적인 개요
- 시행 이유/배경

본론: 세부 내용
- 공사: 공사 구역/기간, 공사 중 불편에 대한 대책
- 정책 변경: 시행일, 세부 규정, 위반 시 불이익 등

결론: 기대 효과
- 긍정적인 효과 및 혜택

2. 비즈니스 - 신규 정책 / 기업체 합병

GT Electronics Makes Changes

John Miller, CEO of GT Electronics, unveiled a new logo for his corporation at an event held in Chicago on Monday.

The new logo features an orange circle, symbolizing the rising sun. Changing the logo on products and corporate materials is expected to cost nearly $24 million.

Miller and other company officials hope that the contemporary design of the logo will reflect the company's cutting-edge nature.

도입: 공지
- 신규 정책 또는 기업 합병의 대략적인 개요

본론: 세부 내용
- 신규 정책: 배경, 목적 설명
- 합병: 합병 이유, 합병 과정

결론: 기대 효과 / 미래 전망
- 기대 효과 및 향후 계획

3. 인물 - 인물/사업의 성공담

During her career as an industrial designer, Maryann Malone became increasingly interested in manufacturing efficiency. Six years ago, she decided to pursue this interest full-time.

She has recently published the results of her investigations in her first book. This work is expected to become the standard text for classrooms and manufacturing executives.

The book has sold over 50,000 copies so far, and the publisher is already planning a second edition.

해석: 해설집 p.99

도입: 인물/사업의 시초
- 인물: 성장 배경, 현재 위치에 온 계기
- 사업: 시작 배경, 초기 환경, 성공 계기

본론: 본격적인 성공
- 인물: 업적, 성공 에피소드, 명성을 얻게 된 과정
- 사업: 업체 성장, 수익 증대

결론: 현재 상태 / 미래 전망
- 현재 상태, 미래의 성장 계획

MAIN STEP 2

앞에서 배운 전략을 문제에 직접 적용해 보자.

Questions 1-2 refer to the following article.

The leading car manufacturer Napier has negotiated an acquisition agreement with RB Motors and announced it at a press conference yesterday.

For the past five decades, Napier has produced exquisite luxury vehicles, marketing its goods to high-end consumers. However, with the changing economic times, the company was searching for a way to reach a wider market. RB Motors was an attractive option for an acquisition deal, as its famous low-fuel hybrid vehicles are exactly the type of product that's missing from the current Napier line.

By making the acquisition, Napier can utilize RB Motors' technology and channel it through its existing distributors to reach millions of new consumers. Napier reports that downsizing its workforce is not likely. In fact, with the expected demand for its goods, Napier has plans to construct five more production plants, which are set to start operating late next year.

1. What is RB Motors known for?
   (A) Selling luxury vehicles
   (B) Entering foreign markets
   (C) Producing energy-efficient cars
   (D) Targeting wealthy consumers

2. According to the article, what will Napier do next year?
   (A) Recruit more distributors
   (B) Move its headquarters
   (C) Open more factories
   (D) Downsize existing structures

Questions 3-4 refer to the following article.

Demir Adnan and Saboro Mazhar, two Turkish-Americans, met in 2004 when they were both students at the Booth School of Business. After discovering their mutual love for food, the two resolved to popularize the Turkish doner kebab throughout Chicago.

The partners opened their first small take-out shop called Take-out Kebab in 2008. Two years later, they decided to try a food truck—and the success was almost immediate. "We opened the truck a month ago, and it became popular right away. We have people waiting in lines down the street and around the corner to be served," Demir Adnan stated in a 2010 interview.

Today, the business has grown to four stores and ten food trucks. The pair hopes to open four more stores and hire seventy new employees over the next five years.

3. What is the article mainly about?
   (A) The story of a shop's growth
   (B) The partnership of three people
   (C) The history of a business school
   (D) The food market in Chicago

4. What is indicated about Take-out Kebab's first food truck?
   (A) It opened in 2004.
   (B) It had lengthy wait times.
   (C) It employed seventy staff.
   (D) It served Indian food.

정답 및 해설 p.100   121

FINAL STEP

실전 난이도의 문제를 풀며
앞에서 배운 전략을 활용해 보자.

Questions 1-3 refer to the following article.

May 7—The subway employees' strike, which started on Monday, has brought subway operations to a standstill throughout the metropolitan area and has created chaos for commuters. — [1] — Union representatives called for its members to go on strike after an agreement between the union and government authorities could not be reached. Union workers complain about unfair working conditions in which hourly pay is barely above the minimum wage. — [2] — They also seek to increase pay for drivers, ticket takers, and security personnel. Meanwhile, government officials argue that the union refused to compromise and take the city's budget into consideration. — [3] —

This is not the first time a dispute of this sort has caused a citywide shutdown. Just last year, a similar case arose. — [4] — With strong emotions and compelling arguments on both sides, it is considered a controversial issue. However, in interviews with local residents, it seems that many people share a common opinion. They want the problem to be resolved so that these breaks in service will stop occurring. "If people can't get to their jobs, the entire local economy will crumble," said commuter Craig Laurel. "At this point, I just want to get to work." Ongoing meetings will be held until common ground can be found.

1. What is true about the strike?
   (A) It is being led by waste collection workers.
   (B) It has attracted more members to the union.
   (C) Its goal is to raise labor wages.
   (D) It started on May 7.

2. What is indicated about the event that occurred last year?
   (A) It lasted longer than a week.
   (B) It resulted in a service shutdown.
   (C) It was supported by local politicians.
   (D) It cost a lot of money to resolve.

3. In which of the positions marked [1], [2], [3] and [4] does the following sentence best belong?
   "Fortunately, parties were able to negotiate an agreement after just one day."
   (A) [1]
   (B) [2]
   (C) [3]
   (D) [4]

Questions 4-6 refer to the following article.

Drastic Changes Expected with Policy Implementation
By Axen Nieves

June 3—Legislators passed a new environmental policy today that will make major changes to the current regulations. The new policy reflects an effort to lower the levels of contamination in soil and water in the region as well as to improve the overall air quality. The policy will take effect on the first of next month and will apply to all commercial enterprises.

Last year, investigators found that many production plants in the area were not following the proper waste disposal procedures for hazardous materials. This allowed chemicals—often at toxic levels—to seep into the soil and water. After the findings of the investigations were released, citizens rallied to impose stricter regulations and politicians took notice.

The manufacturing industry is expected to take the hardest hit under the new regulations, as keeping pollutants under the allowable levels will be a difficult task. This especially applies to plants using older machinery and outdated production methods. Transportation companies, too, will struggle with regulations regarding exhaust emissions, and some have already made plans to file for an extension of the compliance deadline. Large corporations are calling the new policy unfair, saying it is "too much, too soon." Smaller companies have not protested as much, as they can make the necessary adjustments rapidly. A committee has been set up to assess how businesses are coping with the change and to advise lawmakers on future measures.

4. According to the article, why was the policy implemented?
   (A) To remove harmful substances
   (B) To deal with a shortage of resources
   (C) To reduce environmental pollution
   (D) To encourage more recycling

5. What is indicated about the policy?
   (A) It applies to business and residential sites.
   (B) It went into effect on June 1.
   (C) It was encouraged by residents.
   (D) It has the largest effect on transportation.

6. What is mentioned about smaller businesses?
   (A) They will not have to upgrade their facilities.
   (B) They will be able to make the change more quickly.
   (C) They have a longer compliance deadline.
   (D) They may not have the funds to follow regulations.

FURTHER STEP

기사문이 포함된 삼중 지문을 더 풀며 고득점을 노려 보자.

Questions 1-5 refer to the following article, e-mail, and report.

Local Spotlight: Quinn Printing
By Linda Pierce

Quinn Printing, founded a decade ago by Alan Quinn, has steadily grown its customer base by providing efficient service and high-quality printed materials. Mr. Quinn opened his first shop here in Meadow City, and he later expanded the business to three more sites. The company serves community groups, businesses, schools, and individuals who need professional printing services. Customers can bring in their own graphics or get help from one of the on-site designers. In addition, the business has recently launched a Web site, on which customers can place orders and have them delivered without ever having to stop by the store in person.

All locations can print brochures, flyers, business cards, and photos. In addition, Meadow City and Fairmont have equipment for printing large vinyl banners. While Carterville and Marshall do not provide this service on-site, they can process the order and have the banner sent by mail.

In a recent phone interview, owner Alan Quinn talked about his strategy for choosing the locations of his stores. "While we profit most from cities with many concerts and theater productions, we want to make sure we are in the right place to serve small business needs as well." Although opening a fifth branch is not planned at this time, Mr. Quinn says it's a strong possibility in the future.

E-MAIL MESSAGE

To: Linda Pierce <l.pierce@meadowcitytimes.com>
From: Alan Quinn <alan@quinnprinting.net>
Date: May 4
Subject: Quinn Printing article

Dear Ms. Pierce,

I read your recent article in the *Meadow City Times* about my business, Quinn Printing. I liked the quote you selected from our phone interview. Unfortunately, I'm afraid there's a piece of information in your article that is wrong. The article said that two of our branches don't have banner printing equipment. In fact, we are now using this equipment on-site at the Carterville location. Please change this information in the online version of your article as soon as possible.

Sincerely,

Alan Quinn

Quinn Printing Quarterly Profits Report

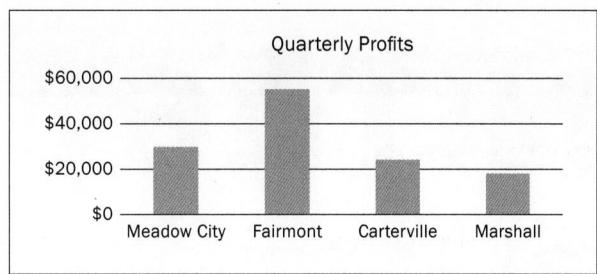

Figures compiled by Virginia Alexander. Staffing and building costs are factored for each branch individually. Advertising costs are spread equally among the four branches. Released April 2.

1. What is NOT true about Quinn Printing?
   (A) It offers graphic design services.
   (B) It has been online for a short time.
   (C) It is currently hiring more employees.
   (D) It has been in operation for ten years.

2. What is the purpose of the e-mail?
   (A) To correct an error
   (B) To schedule a phone interview
   (C) To thank Ms. Pierce
   (D) To make a job offer

3. Where is on-site banner printing unavailable?
   (A) Meadow City
   (B) Fairmont
   (C) Carterville
   (D) Marshall

4. What can be inferred about Fairmont?
   (A) It has only one printing company in town.
   (B) Its population is expected to grow.
   (C) It hosts a lot of performances.
   (D) It has Quinn Printing's oldest branch.

5. When will the next report most likely be released?
   (A) May
   (B) June
   (C) July
   (D) December

UNIT 16
회람/공지

구조가 명확해 빈출 문제가
정해져 있다

PRE-STEP

지문에 등장할 주요 어휘를 미리 학습해 보자.

A 다음 빈칸에 들어갈 어휘로 알맞은 것을 고르시오.

1. ------- the role of group leader (A) streamline (B) assume
2. ------- applications (A) assume (B) turn in
3. ------- the process (A) streamline (B) turn in
4. ------- injuries to workers (A) keep (B) prevent
5. ------- an asset in good condition (A) keep (B) prevent
6. ------- raw materials (A) store (B) collaborate
7. ------- with each other (A) store (B) collaborate
8. ------- an annual budget (A) allocate (B) appreciate
9. last ------- two weeks (A) reasonably (B) approximately
10. sales increase by ------- 15% (A) newly (B) nearly
11. be out of ------- for three days (A) efficiency (B) service
12. make ------- for the venue (A) arrangements (B) services
13. reduce equipment ------- (A) malfunction (B) arrangement
14. maximize ------- (A) efficiency (B) malfunction
15. ------- one's patience (A) allocate (B) appreciate

B 다음 짧은 지문을 읽고 패러프레이징 문장으로 적절한 것을 고르시오.

1.
> While the work itself was fine, the maintenance employee dripped paint on the floor of the room where he was painting and didn't clean it up. He also left some empty paint cans there.

(A) The painting job looked messy even though all of the paint was used.
(B) The worker did a good job on the project but left a mess behind.

2.
> From now on, you will no longer report maintenance issues to the rental office. Instead, you should fill out an online form at www.tcmaintenance.com.

(A) We are changing the method for making maintenance requests, which will now be done through an online system.
(B) We want to make maintenance work easier by allowing you to check the online system for updates.

MAIN STEP¹

> 문제를 해결하는 핵심 전략을 살펴보자.

회람/공지는 구조가 명확해 자주 출제되는 문제가 정해져 있다

회람과 공지는 그 구조가 비슷해 빈출 문제 유형도 비슷하다. 단 회람(memorandum)의 대상은 사내 직원들, 공지(notice)의 대상은 고객 또는 대중이라는 점을 기억해 두면 스토리 파악이 더 쉬워진다.

지문 notice

NOTICE

The Louisville Literary Society is ①holding its first ever short story contest.

To register, ②go to www.louisvillels.org/shortstory. There, you can print your own copy of the registration application.

③The deadline is March 18 and judges will assess the submissions on the following day.

해석: 해설집 p.107

1. 첫 단락: 주제/목적 및 대상 문제

문제① Why was the notice written? 공지가 쓰인 이유는?

정답 To announce a competition 대회를 알리기 위해

2. 중간 단락: 주제와 관련된 세부 내용 문제

문제② How can people get a registration form? 사람들이 등록 양식을 얻을 수 있는 방법은?

정답 By visiting a Web site 웹사이트에 방문으로써

3. 마지막 단락: 향후 일정, 요청 사항 등 추가 정보 문제

문제③ What will happen on March 19? 3월 19일에 일어나게 될 일은?

정답 A work evaluation 작품 심사

회람에서는 등장인물의 이름을 이용한 오답 함정이 등장할 수 있다

이메일 형식의 회람에는 수신자, 발신자, 날짜 및 제목(To, From, Date, Subject)이 등장한다. 이때 회람의 발신자와 문의 담당자가 서로 다른 경우가 많아, 이것이 오답 함정으로 이용된다.

지문 memo

To: Department Managers
From: Elle Lee, Director
Subject: Annual Seminar

The IT seminar will be held on Friday, November 8. Those who wish to participate should let me know by tomorrow. **Please direct any questions that you have to the program coordinator, Maria Rey.**

해석: 해설집 p.108

문제 To whom should questions be directed? 질문을 전달받아야 하는 사람은?
(A) Maria Rey, program coordinator (O)
    마리아 레이, 프로그램 담당자
(B) Elle Lee, director (X)
    엘 리, 관리자

풀이 회람을 보낸 사람은 리 씨이지만 회람과 관련한 질문을 전달받아야 하는 사람은 레이 씨이다.

정답 (A)

MAIN STEP 2

앞에서 배운 전략을 문제에 직접 적용해 보자.

Questions 1-2 refer to the following notice.

NOTICE TO RESIDENTS

Starting March 1, the two passenger elevators in our front lobby will be out of service for three days for repairs and upgrades.

We kindly ask that all residents use the stairs during this time. For anyone incapable of walking upstairs due to disability or injury, you may ride the north elevator in the rear of the building.

Normally, this elevator is used solely for the transportation of goods, but it will be accessible to certain people for those three days.

---

1. Who is this notice aimed at?
(A) Mechanics
(B) Delivery people
(C) Electricians
(D) Tenants

2. What is indicated about the north elevator?
(A) It failed to meet safety standards.
(B) It is near the building's stairs.
(C) It does not usually transport people.
(D) It requires a special code.

Questions 3-4 refer to the following memo.

To: Sales Department
From: Karl McFerren
Subject: Motivational speaker Adam Bock

Because many of you have requested more opportunities for professional development, we have hired motivational speaker Adam Bock to present a workshop on June 29.

He will teach you how to stand out and get your message heard. He was highly recommended by my former colleague, Ashley Varga, who said her team saw sales increase by nearly 15% after using his techniques. If you would like to sign up, you must do so no later than June 15 so that we can make arrangements for the venue.

Please submit any questions that you may have to my administrative assistant, Joann Moyers. This event is not mandatory, but we highly encourage everyone to take advantage of it.

---

3. What is indicated about Mr. Bock?
(A) He signed up for a workshop.
(B) He is an administrative assistant.
(C) His work was referred by Ms. Varga.
(D) He increased his team sales by 15%.

4. Who should be contacted regarding inquiries?
(A) Ashley Varga
(B) Karl McFerren
(C) Adam Bock
(D) Joann Moyers

FINAL STEP

실전 난이도의 문제를 풀며 앞에서 배운 전략을 활용해 보자.

Questions 1-3 refer to the following notice.

NOTICE

Renovations to our factory will begin on October 1 and will affect Sectors C and D. The purpose of the project is to deal with outdated equipment, which is contributing to a higher level of defective electronics coming out of our facility. Some of the machinery will be replaced completely, while the rest will be disassembled, cleaned thoroughly, and reassembled. This should reduce equipment malfunction in the future as well as help prevent injuries to workers. The refurbished interior will also have a designated space for storing raw materials in a climate-controlled area to keep them in good condition.

The renovation will last approximately two weeks, and we will provide updates as it progresses. We appreciate your patience and cooperation during this time.

1. Who most likely is the intended audience of the notice?

    (A) Employees at a production facility
    (B) Interior designers for a project
    (C) Visitors to an electronics factory
    (D) Members of a construction crew

2. What benefit of the renovation is mentioned?

    (A) Complying with government regulations
    (B) Preventing employees from getting hurt
    (C) Attracting new clients to a business
    (D) Saving money on raw materials

3. When is the project expected to be completed?

    (A) In the middle of October
    (B) At the end of October
    (C) In the middle of November
    (D) At the end of the year

Questions 4-6 refer to the following memo.

To: All employees
From: Richard Neely, Branch Manager
Date: March 8
Subject: To all employees

I'm writing to alert all employees to an opportunity to improve the viability of our company while reducing unnecessary expenditures. Currently, our spending on outsourcing is approximately 30% more than what was allocated in this year's budget. During last week's managerial meeting, the department heads expressed unanimous support for creating a task force to address the problem of overspending on external services. I urge your involvement in this important project.

The task force will be made up of 12 members and one leader. There will be at least one representative from each department. These people will collaborate with one another to find ways to deal with managing team members' time to maximize efficiency. This will be done by assigning work to their colleagues, observing productivity levels, and making adjustments according to individual employee strengths and weaknesses.

The task force will be modeled after those already used by some of the largest corporations in the industry, and Margaret Diaz has agreed to assume the role of group leader. If you are interested in finding out more about the responsibilities involved, please contact Margaret directly. To apply to take part in the task force, pick up an application from the reception desk. The deadline for turning in applications is the end of this month. Task force members will receive a quarterly bonus for their efforts. I hope all of you will consider participating in this essential undertaking. Thank you for your consideration.

4. What is the purpose of the memo?
   (A) To thank task force members for their work
   (B) To encourage employees to join a group
   (C) To ask coworkers to attend a managerial meeting
   (D) To congratulate a group on meeting a quota

5. What is NOT stated about the task force?
   (A) It will be made up of thirteen people.
   (B) It will be led by Margaret Diaz.
   (C) It will hold meetings once a week.
   (D) Its members will receive compensation.

6. What is suggested about applications?
   (A) They can be submitted until the end of April.
   (B) They can be picked up from Mr. Neely.
   (C) They will be accepted from all departments.
   (D) They must be signed by a supervisor.

FURTHER STEP

공지가 포함된 삼중 지문을 더 풀며 고득점을 노려 보자.

Questions 1-5 refer to the following notice, form, and survey.

NOTICE TO ALL TENANTS

Cochran Towers has hired a new maintenance company, TC Maintenance, to handle all building repairs. From now on, you will no longer report maintenance issues to the rental office. Instead, you should fill out an online form at www.tcmaintenance.com. The new system will streamline the process as well as allow you to make requests at your convenience, rather than only when the rental office is open. You should begin using the online system from March 1. If you call the rental office with a maintenance request, we will direct you to visit the site.

For tenants with pets, please be aware that for the safety of its employees, TC Maintenance does not allow pets (excluding birds kept in cages and fish) to be kept in the apartment during repair work unless the homeowner is present. If you will not be home during the repair work, you must remove your pet from the apartment. Should you fail to do so, TC Maintenance will not perform the work.

If you have any questions, please feel free to call the rental office at 555-3110.

Maintenance Request Form — TC Maintenance

Next Available Date for Repair Work: March 18 / 10 A.M. – 12:30 P.M.
In case of a maintenance emergency (gas leak, flooding, etc.), call (734) 555-6688 immediately.

Name: Andrea Weston   Phone Number: (734) 555-2950
Building: Cochran Towers   Unit #:   403

Description of Needed Repair(s):

> The faucet in the kitchen sink keeps dripping no matter how tightly I try to turn it off, the towel rack in the bathroom has become detached from the wall, and the bedroom ceiling needs to be repainted because the paint is flaking off.

Do you have any pets?   Yes   Pet Type(s):   Dog
Will you be home at the time and date indicated above?   No

TC Maintenance Feedback Survey

Your opinions matter! Please take a moment to tell us about your recent maintenance work.

Waiting time for receiving repairs: POOR   FAIR   AVERAGE   (GOOD)   EXCELLENT
Ease of using request form: POOR   FAIR   AVERAGE   GOOD   (EXCELLENT)
Professionalism of repair person: (POOR) FAIR   AVERAGE   GOOD   EXCELLENT
Quality of work: POOR   FAIR   AVERAGE   (GOOD)   EXCELLENT

Comments: While the work itself was fine, the maintenance employee dripped paint on the floor of the room where he was painting and didn't clean it up. He also left some empty paint cans there.

FOR OFFICE USE ONLY
Date: March 18
Employee: Daniel Derose

Building: Cochran Towers
Work Order #: 485606

---

1. What is the purpose of the notice?

   (A) To announce building renovations
   (B) To explain a change in procedure
   (C) To introduce a new employee
   (D) To request feedback on a task

2. In the notice, the word "direct" in paragraph 1, line 7, is closest in meaning to

   (A) train
   (B) instruct
   (C) oversee
   (D) focus

3. What can be inferred about Ms. Weston's pet?

   (A) It is usually kept in a cage during the day.
   (B) It caused some damage to her apartment.
   (C) It resulted in a higher rental deposit.
   (D) It was not in her apartment during the repair.

4. According to Ms. Weston, where did Mr. Derose leave a mess?

   (A) In the bedroom
   (B) In the kitchen
   (C) In the living room
   (D) In the bathroom

5. What was Ms. Weston most satisfied with?

   (A) The employee's qualifications
   (B) The completed repairs
   (C) The response time
   (D) The request process

UNIT 17
표/양식

인물 이름과 숫자 정보 등의 세부 정보가 관건이다

PRE-STEP

지문에 등장할 주요 어휘를 미리 학습해 보자.

A 다음 빈칸에 들어갈 어휘로 알맞은 것을 고르시오.

1.	------- to the security desk	(A) report	(B) display
2.	------- the receipt	(A) initiate	(B) retain
3.	------- necessary skills	(A) process	(B) possess
4.	------- in the main hall	(A) display	(B) retain
5.	registration ------- of $15	(A) fee	(B) order
6.	------- paid vacation	(A) accessible	(B) extra
7.	a(n) ------- shopper discount	(A) frequent	(B) accessible
8.	move to a new -------	(A) transfer	(B) location
9.	professional ------- training	(A) location	(B) development
10.	compensation for excellent -------	(A) transfer	(B) performance
11.	conduct an employee -------	(A) evaluation	(B) target
12.	bank -------	(A) transfer	(B) draft
13.	penalty for unexplained -------	(A) absences	(B) payments
14.	include tax -------	(A) targets	(B) payments
15.	meet output -------	(A) payments	(B) targets

B 다음 짧은 지문을 읽고 패러프레이징 문장으로 적절한 것을 고르시오.

1.
> On March 1 our head office will dispatch a team of employees to visit our site and conduct performance appraisals on all employees. This assessment is done annually.

(A) The headquarters will send employees to carry out the annual staff evaluations.
(B) The main office will assess employees to assign the annual work.

2.
> Residents of Delgado are invited to attend the city's inaugural art contest. The contest is open to all ages, and artists can enter pieces in the categories of Portrait, Nature, or Abstract.

(A) All local residents are encouraged to participate in the city's first-ever art competition.
(B) Artists of all ages are urged to make suggestions for the art contest.

MAIN STEP 1

> 문제를 해결하는
> 핵심 전략을 살펴보자.

전략 1 — 표와 양식의 성격을 파악하자

표와 양식의 특성은 정보가 압축적으로 표시된다는 것이다. 표와 양식 지문에서는 먼저 무엇에 관한 내용인지를 파악하고, 구성 요소 및 각 세부 항목을 파악한 뒤 문제를 푸는 것이 효과적이다.

지문 form

TEMPORARY PASS
Stiver Laboratories

This pass must be displayed at all times.

Daniel Loesch

Entry date: October 20
Entry time: 8:35 A.M.
Security clearance: Standard
Reason for visit: Media photography
Valid until: October 20, 12:05 P.M.

②*If you lose this pass,
report to the security desk immediately.
Other inquiries: 555-3950, extension 54

해석: 해설집 p.116

1. 문제 [목록 부분]
양식 목록의 세부 내용에 등장하는 인물에 대한 정보를 유추해야 하는 문제가 출제된다.

문제① What is indicated about Mr. Loesch?
래쉬 씨에 대해 시사된 바는?

정답 He arrived in the morning. 그는 아침에 도착했다.

2. 추가 사항 관련 문제 [마지막 부분]
보통 표나 양식 밑에는 부가 정보가 *Note 등의 내용으로 들어가 있는데 이 부분에서 문제가 출제된다.

문제② According to the form, what should Mr. Loesch do? 양식에 따르면, 래쉬 씨가 해야 하는 일은?

정답 Go to the security desk if the pass is lost
출입증 분실 시 보안 창구에 가기

전략 2 — 송장 지문에서는 인물 정보, 금액, 숫자 정보를 정확히 파악하자

지문 invoice

[1] 구매자와 수령인이 다를 수 있으니 유의해야 한다.

Ship to: Jennifer Parker	Bill to: Sarah Manning

[2] 금액과 관련된 다음 표현들을 알아두자.
Subtotal: $500 소계: 상품 구매 비용
Shipping: $10 배송료
Tax: $50 세금: 보통 subtotal의 10%

Total: $560 총계: 위의 금액을 모두 합산한 값
Deposit paid: $160 지불액: 미리 지불한 금액
②**Outstanding balance: $400** 미불액: 남은 지불 금액

해석: 해설집 p.116

문제① Who will receive the items? 상품을 받을 사람은?

풀이 ship to는 ~에게 보낸다는 뜻이므로 받는 사람, bill to는 ~에게 청구서를 보낸다는 뜻이므로 구매한 사람이다.

정답 Jennifer Parker 제니퍼 파커

문제② How much does Ms. Manning need to pay?
매닝 씨가 지불해야 하는 금액은?

풀이 총계 560달러 중 미리 지불한 금액이 160달러, 미불액이 400달러이므로 미불액 400달러만 지불하면 된다.

정답 $400 400달러

MAIN STEP²

앞에서 배운 전략을
문제에 직접 적용해 보자.

Questions 1-2 refer to the following invoice.

Stallion Supplies Wholesale Distributor	**Order Invoice**
Customer: Iris Harrop, Green Valley Ranch **Business ID:** 02-14131191	**Order date:** July 6 **Address:** 124 Gresham St., London, UK
Item(s) – Leather horse saddle, 16 in. – Animal blankets (5@ $76.79 each)	**Price** $639.99 $383.95
Total	$1,023.94
Payment: Visa XXXX XXXX XXXX 0153 (charged July 6) **Special instructions:** Imprint animal blankets with 'Green Valley.'	

1. What type of business does Ms. Harrop most likely work for?

    (A) A veterinarian's office
    (B) A pet store
    (C) A dog breeder
    (D) A facility for horses

2. What is suggested about the order?

    (A) Customization was requested.
    (B) An outstanding balance is due.
    (C) A 10% Internet discount was applied.
    (D) It was processed at the end of July.

Questions 3-4 refer to the following receipt.

SydneySports.com – Customer Receipt	
Bill to: Marie Ellis 865 Newbury Lane, Chicago, IL 60604	**Ship to:** Jan Eagan 394 Holloway Road, Seattle, WA 98116
Order date: April 7	**Estimated delivery:** April 10
Hylon tennis racket $135.99 Sydney Sports sweatshirt $19.99 Delivery charge $5.65	
Payment type: Credit card [ ] 　　　　　　　Bank transfer [✔] Please note that all listed prices include the applicable sales tax.	**Subtotal:** $161.63
	Frequent shopper discount: $16.50
	Total: $145.13

3. What is NOT true about the order?

    (A) It includes a clothing item.
    (B) It will be sent to Chicago.
    (C) It was placed on April 7.
    (D) It includes tax payments.

4. What can be inferred about Ms. Ellis?

    (A) She paid with a credit card.
    (B) She plans to move to a new location.
    (C) She paid extra for overnight shipping.
    (D) She has made a previous purchase.

FINAL STEP

실전 난이도의 문제를 풀며
앞에서 배운 전략을 활용해 보자.

Questions 1-2 refer to the following receipt.

833 Park Street
Phoenix, AZ 85034

Date: August 19
Reference #: 57934

Store ID: 082
Cashier: Jenny

Item	Description	Price
304943	#8 x 2 in. screws (box of 80)	$7.95
859606	1/8 in. x 48 in. x 96 in. prefinished wood paneling	$10.97
859606	1/8 in. x 48 in. x 96 in. prefinished wood paneling	$10.97
395821	16 oz. wood glue	$6.95
	Subtotal	$36.84
	Tax	$2.27
	Total	$39.11

Amount Tendered: $39.11
Credit Card: XXXX XXXX XXXX 7964

Delk's Deals: Retain this receipt and present it the next time you visit Delk's to get 10% off your purchase (excludes power tools).

1. What type of business most likely is Delk's?
   (A) A clothing store
   (B) A hardware store
   (C) A furniture store
   (D) A jewelry store

2. Why are customers encouraged to keep the receipt?
   (A) It can be used to get a discount.
   (B) It is required to honor the warranty.
   (C) It gives them entrance to a prize drawing.
   (D) It provides access to a survey.

Questions 3-5 refer to the following form.

On March 1 our head office will dispatch a team of employees to visit our site and conduct performance appraisals on all employees. This assessment is done annually. However, it is of particular importance this year because we have never been assessed under the new policies that were implemented in January. Please see the sample evaluation form below.

Name:
Department:

Category	Maximum Point Value
Overall contributions to the company – *Includes review of work tasks to date*	30
Teamwork – *Both with team members and other departments*	15
Attendance and punctuality – *Penalty for unexplained absences*	10
Professional development training – *Workshops, seminars, conferences, etc.*	10
Productivity – *Ability to meet output targets*	25
Job suitability – *Possessing necessary skills and knowledge*	10
Assessor 1: Assessor 2:	Total: _____ /100

The results of the appraisal will be announced on March 20. As an incentive, anyone who receives a score of 95 or more will receive special compensation for their extraordinary performance. You may choose either a cash bonus or extra paid vacation.

3. Why is the appraisal more important this time?

   (A) It was requested by a new owner.
   (B) It will determine who will be promoted.
   (C) It is the first assessment after a policy change.
   (D) It will be used to make layoff decisions.

4. For which skill will employees be given a maximum of fifteen points?

   (A) Cooperation
   (B) Creativity
   (C) Attitude
   (D) Leadership

5. What is mentioned about the incentive?

   (A) It will be evenly divided among team members.
   (B) It will be given to one person from each department.
   (C) It can be either financial compensation or extra vacation time.
   (D) It is for employees who receive perfect evaluation scores.

FURTHER STEP

양식이 포함된 삼중 지문을 더 풀며 고득점을 노려 보자.

Questions 1-5 refer to the following flyer, form, and voucher.

Delgado Amateur Art Contest

Residents of Delgado are invited to attend the city's inaugural art contest. The contest is open to all ages, and artists can enter pieces in the categories of Portrait, Nature, or Abstract. Thanks to sponsorship from a number of shops and restaurants in the area, we are pleased to offer the following prizes (four per category):

  1st Place: $300 voucher from Vox Electronics
  2nd Place: $150 voucher from Pennington Mall
  3rd Place: 2 one-year memberships to the Benson Art Museum
  4th Place: $50 voucher from Sam's Steakhouse

Entries will be accepted on June 14 at the Delgado Community Center from 9 A.M. to 4 P.M. Paintings will be displayed in the main hall while the auditorium's stage will accommodate the sculptures. The artwork can be viewed by the public until June 25, on which day the entries will be assessed by a judging panel made up of faculty from the Hillview University Art Department.

One entry per person. Registration fee of $15. For more information, or to register, visit www.delgadoart.org.

---

www.delgadoart.org/register

Name: Jeremy Ellington   **Phone number:** (495) 555-9094
E-mail address: j.ellington@dci9.com

Title of entry: *Waterfalls in Spring*
Type of entry: [✔] Painting   [   ] Sculpture
Age: [   ] Youth (under 18)   [✔] Adult
Category: [   ] Portrait   [✔] Nature   [   ] Abstract

Special instructions: Painting should be lit from the back instead of using the usual track lighting. I will provide the lamp for this.

Pennington Mall Voucher

Value: $150

Issued to: Jeremy Ellington   **Issue date:** June 27

This voucher can be used at any store in Pennington Mall. Change will be given in the form of another voucher if the amount is over $10. Change that is $10 or less will be given in cash.

Valid until December 31. See reverse side for restrictions.

1. What is NOT indicated about the competition?

   (A) Its winners will be notified by e-mail.
   (B) It is being held for the first time.
   (C) It is supported by local businesses.
   (D) It will be judged by university professors.

2. What is true about *Waterfalls in Spring*?

   (A) It is an abstract piece of art.
   (B) It was set up on June 25.
   (C) It was displayed in the main hall.
   (D) It was made by a professional artist.

3. What does Mr. Ellington request?

   (A) Changing the position of a light source
   (B) Keeping the artwork behind glass
   (C) Providing a brighter lamp
   (D) Hanging the artwork higher than usual

4. What place did Mr. Ellington receive in his category?

   (A) First place
   (B) Second place
   (C) Third place
   (D) Fourth place

5. What can be found on the back of the voucher?

   (A) A list of stores
   (B) Terms and conditions
   (C) An expiration date
   (D) Promotional offers

UNIT 18
정보문

문제 유형별로 단서가 되는
표현들을 익혀두자

PRE-STEP

지문에 등장할 주요 어휘를 미리 학습해 보자.

A 다음 빈칸에 들어갈 어휘로 알맞은 것을 고르시오.

		(A)	(B)
1.	now ------- for use	(A) steady	(B) ready
2.	receive a ------- sample	(A) free	(B) steady
3.	follow the -------	(A) steps	(B) periods
4.	the ------- of *one's* stay	(A) association	(B) duration
5.	reduce *one's* monthly -------	(A) spending	(B) term
6.	customer ------- rating	(A) duration	(B) satisfaction
7.	become a member of the -------	(A) association	(B) duration
8.	------- *one's* stay by one night	(A) expand	(B) extend
9.	driving ------- to the hotel	(A) attractions	(B) directions
10.	popular tourist -------	(A) attractions	(B) directions
11.	------- a start-up fee	(A) charge	(B) cater
12.	------- to *one's* every need	(A) charge	(B) cater
13.	newly ------- guest rooms	(A) renovated	(B) accommodated
14.	------- up to three people	(A) accommodate	(B) renovate
15.	early-bird registration -------	(A) spending	(B) period

B 다음 짧은 지문을 읽고 패러프레이징 문장으로 적절한 것을 고르시오.

1.
> We urge you to sign up for a membership before January 31 so that you can receive two complimentary tickets to the Annual Florida Boat Show.

(A) Take advantage of the discount on boat show tickets before January 31.
(B) Register for membership by January 31 in order to get free tickets.

2.
> We have several rooms for large gatherings, such as retirement parties, awards ceremonies, banquets, and conferences. We also have two on-site restaurants to suit even the most discerning tastes.

(A) Our staff can handle large groups, and there are several good restaurants in the area to choose from.
(B) We have facilities for a variety of events, including dining options that will appeal to everyone.

MAIN STEP¹

> 문제를 해결하는 핵심 전략을 살펴보자.

정보문에 자주 출제되는 지문이 있다

정보문은 제품/서비스/행사/시설 이용 안내문이 주를 이루며 그 외에 시간표, 브로셔, 목차 등도 출제된다. 하지만 이 중 사용설명서가 가장 높은 비율로 출제된다는 것을 기억해 두자.

지문 information

Thank you for purchasing a Westover coffee maker. ①**To keep your device in top condition, we recommend the following cleaning and preventive maintenance tips:**

– Use filtered water to decrease mineral buildup.
– Regularly wipe down the machine with a cloth.
– ②**Remove used coffee grounds after brewing.**

③**To order our exclusive Westover unbleached coffee filters,** visit www.westoverappl.com.

해석: 해설집 p.123

1. 첫 단락: 정보문의 출처를 묻는 문제

문제① Where would this information most likely be found? 이 정보문을 발견할 수 있을 것 같은 곳은?

정답 In a product manual 제품 사용설명서

2. 중간 단락: 세부 사항에 관한 문제

문제② What is NOT mentioned as a recommendation?
권고 사항으로 언급되지 않은 것은?

정답 Grinding beans before brewing
커피를 내리기 전에 커피콩 갈기

3. 마지막 단락: 추가 정보에 관한 문제

문제③ What is true about coffee filters?
커피 필터에 대해 사실인 것은?

정답 They must be purchased separately.
별도로 구매해야만 한다.

정보문에서는 유형별로 단서가 되는 표현이 있다

다음 표현들은 지문에서 어느 부분을 찾아 읽어야 할지 알려주는 단서들이다. 숙지해 두었다가 활용하도록 하자.

추천/권장 사항	We urge/advise/recommend you to ~ ~하는 것을 권고/권고/추천 드립니다	
제품의 사용 방법	You can use the product to ~ 이 제품은 ~하는 데 사용하실 수 있습니다	To install the product, ~ 제품 설치를 위해서는, ~
고객들이 받을 수 있는 것	~ is available at … …에서 ~가 이용 가능합니다 ~ can be picked up ~을 받으실 수 있습니다	~ will be given/distributed ~가 주어질/배부될 것입니다 You can receive ~ ~을 받으실 수 있습니다

MAIN STEP²

Questions 1-2 refer to the following product manual.

Thank you for purchasing the Topeka-3E microwave oven from Geo Appliances. We hope you enjoy using this product. When unpacking and setting up your microwave, please follow these steps:

1. Take off all materials used for shipping, such as paper and foam pieces.
2. Wipe the interior of the microwave with a damp cloth.
3. Place the device on a countertop or a steady shelf. It should be at least three inches away from a wall to allow for proper ventilation.

Your microwave is now ready for use.

To report any problems with your microwave, please call our Customer Care Hotline at 1-800-555-2940.

---

1. Where would this information most likely be printed?
   (A) On the side of a machine
   (B) In an employee manual
   (C) On a retail store's sign
   (D) In an instruction pamphlet

2. What is NOT mentioned as a step related to the Topeka-3E?
   (A) Inputting the time into the device
   (B) Removing packaging materials
   (C) Placing the device away from an outlet
   (D) Wiping the inside of the microwave

Questions 3-4 refer to the following information.

Join the Landis Sailing Association!

Enjoy these amazing benefits by becoming a member of the association.
* A free subscription to the *Sail the World* monthly magazine
* A 15% discount on all sailing clothes and equipment at Landis Heads retail store
* Free use of the Landis Sailing Club facilities throughout the year

Moreover, we urge you to sign up for a membership before January 31 so that you can receive two complimentary tickets to the Annual Florida Boat Show (valued at $150 each).

Call 1-800-555-0982 or visit us at www.landissailing.org.

---

3. What is the purpose of the information?
   (A) To advertise a local sailing apparel store
   (B) To announce a change in subscription fees
   (C) To promote a newly refurbished yacht club
   (D) To solicit new members for an association

4. What are the readers asked to do?
   (A) Volunteer for an event on a regular basis
   (B) Purchase their tickets in advance
   (C) Become a member before a certain date
   (D) Watch a show at the end of the month

FINAL STEP

실전 난이도의 문제를 풀며
앞에서 배운 전략을 활용해 보자.

Questions 1-2 refer to the following information.

Family Cell Phone Plans

Find the right plan for you and your family! Bundling the accounts of several family members can significantly reduce your monthly spending on smartphone services. Compare and save today!

	R&C	Metro 5	Conway Mobile	Atlas Communications
One-time start-up fee	None	$20 per line	$25 total	$15 per line
Monthly service cost (up to 4 lines)	$120/month	$100/month	$160/month	$100/month
Data usage limit	12GB	8GB	10GB	4GB
Talk minutes	Unlimited	3,000/month	Unlimited	Unlimited
Text messages	Unlimited	Unlimited	Unlimited	500/month
Percentage of dropped calls	4.2%	2.5%	1.8%	2.1%
Customer satisfaction rating	59%	72%	93%	76%

Note: Prices listed do not include taxes or device cost.

1. What is NOT true about R&C?

    (A) It does not charge a start-up fee.
    (B) It has the most expensive monthly plan.
    (C) It provides the highest data usage.
    (D) It offers unlimited text messages.

2. Which company most likely provides the best customer service?

    (A) R&C
    (B) Metro 5
    (C) Conway Mobile
    (D) Atlas Communications

Questions 3-5 refer to the following information.

4th Annual Human Resources Management Forum: Rates and Other Information

Pre-Forum Workshops on Monday, October 7
Registration includes a full-day workshop led by HR consulting gurus John Wang and Leah Fuentez, complimentary lunch and beverage breaks, and an e-document packet full of useful tips and links.

Forum from Tuesday to Thursday, October 8-10
Registration includes three days of conference sessions, complimentary lunch and beverage breaks, the conference dinner (October 9), and free admission to the exhibition area.

Rates

Early-Bird*	Standard
Member of IHRA Workshop only: $500 Conference only: $800 Workshop and conference: $1,100	**Member of IHRA** Workshop only: $650 Conference only: $950 Workshop and conference: $1,450
Non-member Workshop only: $650 Conference only: $950 Workshop and conference: $1,450	**Non-member** Workshop only: $750 Conference only: $1,050 Workshop and conference: $1,650

* The early-bird registration period begins July 13 and ends August 12.

3. What does forum registration NOT include?

(A) A special dinner
(B) An information package
(C) Entry to the exhibitions
(D) Free refreshments

4. How much would a member pay for a conference-only registration on July 31?

(A) $500
(B) $650
(C) $800
(D) $950

5. What will happen on August 13?

(A) A document will be distributed.
(B) The forum will conclude.
(C) Online registration will close.
(D) Discounted pricing will be unavailable.

FURTHER STEP

정보문에 포함된 삼중 지문을 더 풀며 고득점을 노려 보자.

Questions 1-5 refer to the following advertisement, information, and e-mail.

Make Memories at the Almeida Hotel

A memorable and pleasurable vacation starts with a remarkable hotel. At Almeida Hotel, we strive to ensure that you rest in comfort and luxury while our staff caters to your every need.

Known for having the most breathtaking vistas in the region, as many of our rooms overlook Vanna Beach's crystal-clear waters and white sand, our facility has modern amenities and a contemporary atmosphere. For $20 per person, our hotel will send a private car to pick you up from the airport and drive you into the city to our hotel. The charge also includes a return trip to the airport at the end of your stay.

Our spacious, newly renovated guest rooms are priced based on double occupancy, although most rooms can accommodate up to three people (or five for the largest suite).

Additionally, we have several rooms for large gatherings, such as retirement parties, awards ceremonies, banquets, and conferences. We also have two on-site restaurants to suit even the most discerning tastes. All guests may purchase a $15 voucher that entitles them to access our breakfast buffet each day of their stay. The buffet is served from 7 A.M. to noon every morning and features made-to-order options.

Almeida Hotel Spring Rates

Book a room for any date between March 1 and May 30 to take advantage of the off-peak rates listed below.

Room Type	Rate per Night*	Amenities Provided
Platinum Suite	$460	King-size bed, 50-inch HD flat-panel TV, high-speed Internet access, large balcony, fully equipped kitchen
Diamond Suite	$400	King-size bed, 50-inch HD flat-panel TV, high-speed Internet access, in-room safe, medium balcony
Gold Suite	$360	Queen-size bed, 37-inch HD flat-panel TV, high-speed Internet access, in-room safe
Silver Suite	$320	Queen-size bed, 37-inch HD flat-panel TV, high-speed Internet access

* If more than two people will be staying in the room, a surcharge of $85 will be added per person to have a portable cot in the room. Visit www.almeidahotel.com for a list of summer season rates, driving directions to the hotel, and details on popular tourist attractions.

To: Almeida Hotel <service@almeidahotel.net>
From: Bruno Pinto <brunop@usernet.mail>
Date: April 2
Subject: Upcoming stay

Dear Hotel Agent,

I recently reserved a room at your hotel for May 4 through May 20, and I need to make some minor changes to that booking. When I first called to make the reservation, I thought my return flight was on May 20, but I've just discovered that it is actually on May 21. I would like to extend my stay by one night. Does the rate of $400 still apply?

Also, my wife and I have decided to bring our ten-year-old son with us on this trip. We will need a cot in our room for the entire duration of our stay, and we also plan on using your airport transportation service. Please add the necessary charges to our bill.

Thank you for accommodating these changes.

I look forward to staying at your hotel,

Bruno Pinto

1. According to the advertisement, what is Almedia Hotel famous for?

   (A) Its attentive staff members
   (B) Its elegantly decorated suites
   (C) Its spectacular ocean views
   (D) Its on-site restaurants

2. What is suggested about the room rates?

   (A) They are lower for hotel club members.
   (B) They are higher for last-minute bookings.
   (C) They vary depending on the time of year.
   (D) They were increased to pay for renovations.

3. What is indicated about Mr. Pinto?

   (A) He made his original reservation by phone.
   (B) He found out about the hotel through a friend.
   (C) He must leave earlier than first planned.
   (D) He intends to recommend the hotel to others.

4. Which room did Mr. Pinto most likely reserve?

   (A) The Platinum Suite
   (B) The Diamond Suite
   (C) The Gold Suite
   (D) The Silver Suite

5. How much will Mr. Pinto pay for a transportation service?

   (A) $20
   (B) $40
   (C) $60
   (D) $85

CHAPTER TEST 2

Questions 1-2 refer to the following notice.

Biotech Laboratories

Welcome to the Biotech Laboratories family! We are very happy to have you join us. In accordance with company regulations, our laboratories are locked at all times of the day. Employees are issued a personalized five-digit passcode that they must type into the keypad before entering or exiting any laboratory. These codes take two weeks to process, however, so until yours has been granted, we request that you please use the temporary access code provided below. After your orientation has completed on November 4, you should be able to use your new code.

Temporary Access Information
Employee name: Stella Wilpstra
Password: 1234#
Valid through: November 4

1. What is the notice mainly about?
   (A) The protocol for accessing restricted areas
   (B) An orientation schedule for a new employee
   (C) Instructions to set up a computer password
   (D) Writing company regulations for approval

2. What can be inferred about the temporary passcode?
   (A) It is the same for every employee.
   (B) It will be updated at a later date.
   (C) It is selected by staff members.
   (D) It changes every two weeks.

Questions 3-4 refer to the following text message chain.

JILL BRAME — 11:25 A.M.
My phone shows a missed call from you. What's up?

LANDON COLE — 11:26 A.M.
Oh, I had my annual health checkup earlier this morning.

LANDON COLE — 11:27 A.M.
I needed to write down the company's insurance coverage number on the form, but I didn't know what it was.

JILL BRAME — 11:28 A.M.
But it's all sorted out now?

LANDON COLE — 11:29 A.M.
Yeah, I called Bert when you didn't answer. He was able to look up the information for me.

JILL BRAME — 11:30 A.M.
Oh, good. Sorry I wasn't available.

JILL BRAME — 11:31 A.M.
I've been in meetings all morning. I had my phone set to silent mode, so I didn't hear it ring.

LANDON COLE — 11:32 A.M.
I completely understand. I do the same thing. It's never good to have a phone call interrupt a meeting.

---

3. Why did Mr. Cole initially contact Ms. Brame?

   (A) To schedule a medical checkup
   (B) To request Bert's contact information
   (C) To inquire about insurance coverage
   (D) To ask for an account number

4. At 11:32 A.M., what does Mr. Cole mean when he writes, "I do the same thing"?

   (A) He schedules back-to-back meetings.
   (B) He regularly forgets his cell phone.
   (C) He prefers texting to answering calls.
   (D) He often turns off the ringer on his phone.

Questions 5-7 refer to the following advertisement.

Fitness World: Practically a Brand-new Gym!

After six long weeks of renovations, we have finally reopened! Fitness World remains in the same location where it started a decade ago, but it is now three times bigger. We kept the size of the sauna the same, but expanded the upstairs workout spaces used for yoga, kickboxing, and aerobics classes. We also added all new equipment on the main floor. These classes are offered several times a week for individuals who enjoy the motivation and support of working out in a group. Conversely, if you prefer to have individual assistance, our personal trainers are present five days a week. However, they're not available on weekends. Although personal trainers can be expensive, we have a trial policy that allows people to work out with a trainer once for free so they can see if it is worth the cost.

What our members like best about our gym is that we are open 24 hours a day for individuals who do not like to work out during regular hours. To see our membership rates, go to www.fitnessworld.org.

5. How long has Fitness World been in business?

   (A) Three years
   (B) Five years
   (C) Six years
   (D) Ten years

6. What is NOT true about personal trainers?

   (A) They are unavailable on weekdays.
   (B) Their rates are not cheap.
   (C) They provide one-on-one instruction.
   (D) They offer trial training sessions.

7. What is a popular feature of Fitness World?

   (A) Its rates are lower than other gyms.
   (B) It is conveniently located.
   (C) It lets people work out at any times.
   (D) Its instructors are former athletes.

Questions 8-10 refer to the following Web site.

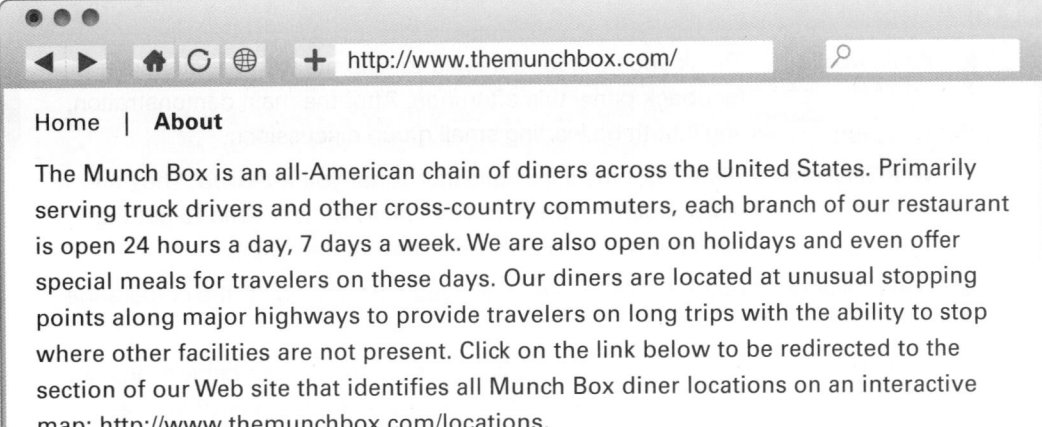

8. What is the Web site mainly about?

   (A) A chain of inexpensive hotels
   (B) A famous brand of gas stations
   (C) Well-known roadside landmarks
   (D) Food facilities across America

9. What can be inferred about the Munch Box?

   (A) It has tailored its business to travelers.
   (B) It does not operate on holidays.
   (C) It is located far from major highways.
   (D) It provides discounts to truck drivers.

10. What information is available at the link provided?

    (A) An image of the interstate
    (B) A map of diner locations
    (C) A number to use for reservations
    (D) A special discount on pricing

Questions 11-13 refer to the following online chat discussion.

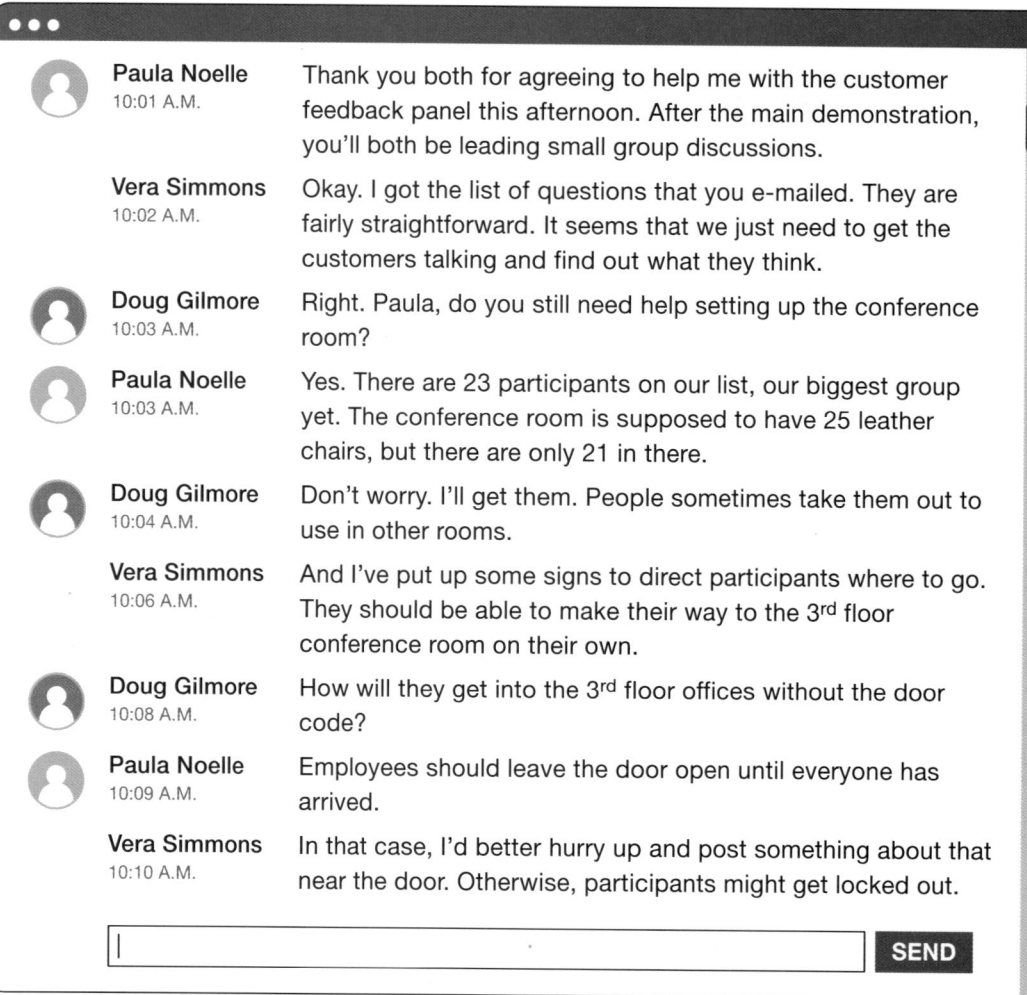

Paula Noelle 10:01 A.M.
Thank you both for agreeing to help me with the customer feedback panel this afternoon. After the main demonstration, you'll both be leading small group discussions.

Vera Simmons 10:02 A.M.
Okay. I got the list of questions that you e-mailed. They are fairly straightforward. It seems that we just need to get the customers talking and find out what they think.

Doug Gilmore 10:03 A.M.
Right. Paula, do you still need help setting up the conference room?

Paula Noelle 10:03 A.M.
Yes. There are 23 participants on our list, our biggest group yet. The conference room is supposed to have 25 leather chairs, but there are only 21 in there.

Doug Gilmore 10:04 A.M.
Don't worry. I'll get them. People sometimes take them out to use in other rooms.

Vera Simmons 10:06 A.M.
And I've put up some signs to direct participants where to go. They should be able to make their way to the 3rd floor conference room on their own.

Doug Gilmore 10:08 A.M.
How will they get into the 3rd floor offices without the door code?

Paula Noelle 10:09 A.M.
Employees should leave the door open until everyone has arrived.

Vera Simmons 10:10 A.M.
In that case, I'd better hurry up and post something about that near the door. Otherwise, participants might get locked out.

11. What is the purpose of the afternoon event?
   (A) To negotiate a business contract
   (B) To find out customer opinions
   (C) To train new employees
   (D) To discuss a policy change

12. At 10:04 A.M., what does Mr. Gilmore mean when he writes, "I'll get them"?
   (A) He is searching for some documents.
   (B) He can help to recruit more participants.
   (C) He plans to look for some chairs.
   (D) He will prepare a list of names.

13. What will Ms. Simmons most likely do next?
   (A) Check a door code
   (B) Put up a notice
   (C) Decorate a room
   (D) Repair a lock

Questions 14-17 refer to the following article.

Contam Corp. Sponsors Blue Glass Gallery
By Marissa Sagese

Contam Corp. recently announced its first-time sponsorship of the Blue Glass Gallery of Contemporary Art. The gallery's upcoming exhibit is a retrospective of works by the distinguished artist Eligio Calabrese. Opening night for the much-anticipated exhibit is scheduled for Saturday, April 20. — [1] —

Mr. Calabrese is a world-renowned sketch artist. Although he first entered the art world several decades ago as a watercolorist, it is his gray pencil drawings that eventually won him critical acclaim internationally. In particular, his abstract approach to objects alters the way people typically interpret drawings, and allows them to see everyday scenes in a completely new light. — [2] — As with all of our three-month exhibits, this collection has been designed to highlight the many themes used by Mr. Calabrese throughout his twenty-five year career. — [3] —

In gratitude for sponsoring the exhibition, the Blue Glass Gallery of Contemporary Art is extending free admission to Contam Corp. employees on opening night. All ushers will possess a copy of the staff directory, so employees need only identify themselves by name. — [4] — Anyone interested in viewing the exhibit can purchase tickets on the gallery's Web site at www.blueglassgallery.com or through the box office at 555-329-2814. You won't want to miss this must-see event.

14. What is mentioned about Mr. Calabrese?
    (A) He has changed his artistic style over time.
    (B) He will be in attendance on April 20.
    (C) He is known for drawing in bright colors.
    (D) He makes realistic-looking art.

15. What can be inferred about the Blue Glass Gallery?
    (A) It holds private viewings for special groups.
    (B) Its exhibits are typically 90 days long.
    (C) It earns a significant profit on shows.
    (D) It has a long-standing relationship with Contam Corp.

16. How can employees obtain complimentary admission?
    (A) By purchasing tickets in a large group
    (B) By printing a coupon from a Web site
    (C) By showing some ID to a gallery employee
    (D) By visiting the gallery on a specific night

17. In which of the positions marked [1], [2], [3] and [4] does the following sentence best belong?

    "Ticket pricing will return to the regular $21.00 amount for the remainder of the exhibit's run."

    (A) [1]
    (B) [2]
    (C) [3]
    (D) [4]

Questions 18-22 refer to the following invoice and e-mail.

CUSTOMER INVOICE

Date of Order: January 2
Invoice #: 959110
Customer Name/Address: Clifford Elston, 4650 Oakmound, Lombard, IL 60148

Origin of Order	Shipping Method	Estimated Delivery Date	Payment Type	Rewards Member
Web site	Standard	January 7	Credit Card	No

Quantity	Item #	Description	Unit Price	Line Total
1	A394	Revica Men's Thermal Ski Jacket – Large	$149.99	$149.99
1	S596	Revica Insulated Gloves – Large	$25.99	$25.99
2	P439	Woodland Co. Protective Ski Goggles	$15.99	$31.98

Subtotal	$207.96
Discounts/Coupons	-$0.00
Sales Tax	$12.49
Delivery	$8.95
Total	$229.40

Thank you for your purchase! We stand by all products sold at Harrison Co. If you are dissatisfied with your merchandise, please contact us at service@harrisonco.com.

To: Harrison Co. <service@harrisonco.com>
From: Clifford Elston <elstonc@wondermail.com>
Date: January 7
Subject: Invoice #959110

To Whom it May Concern:

I placed an order with your company on January 2 and received the merchandise this morning. Unfortunately, I purchased a large jacket, but I was sent a medium instead. I was planning on wearing the jacket on a ski trip this weekend. Because of this trip, I can receive a delivery at my house no later than January 9, after which time I will not be there. I hope you can use a courier that offers two-day or overnight delivery instead of using your usual shipping company because I need it exchanged as soon as possible.

In addition, I ordered two pairs of protective goggles. The flyer I received in the mail said that all goggles were buy-one-get-one-free this month without a coupon. However, I was charged for both, so the price of one of them should have been deducted on the invoice. Please e-mail me back with confirmation that you have received this message and explain how these issues will be resolved.

Sincerely,

Clifford Elston

18. What is NOT true about Mr. Elston's order?

(A) It was placed online.
(B) It included a delivery fee.
(C) It was sent by express shipping.
(D) It was paid for using a credit card.

19. What does Harrison Co. most likely sell?

(A) Medical device
(B) Heating equipment
(C) Camping gear
(D) Skiing supplies

20. Why did Mr. Elston send the e-mail?

(A) To complain about a damaged item
(B) To place an order for merchandise
(C) To report a problem with an order
(D) To ask about a payment deadline

21. How much will be deducted from Mr. Elston's payment?

(A) $8.95
(B) $12.49
(C) $15.99
(D) $25.99

22. What is suggested about Mr. Elston?

(A) He lost a required coupon.
(B) He purchased pants for a ski trip.
(C) He was overcharged for some gloves.
(D) He will go out of town on January 10.

Questions 23-27 refer to the following job posting, e-mail, and schedule.

Job Openings at Willow Co.

Willow Co., the leading supplier of corporate credit card services, is looking for motivated individuals to join its team. We have a solid reputation for excellence, and we offer some of the highest base salaries and commission rates in the industry. For applicants to be considered, we require excellent speaking and writing skills, the capacity to work well with others, and a positive attitude. Previous sales experience is preferred, but we are willing to train the right people. Please note that you must have your own vehicle for in-person visits.

To apply, please send a résumé and cover letter to Claire Harper at harper.c@willow-co.com by June 18. Interviews will be held from June 21 to 25. Successful candidates will report to their assigned branches for orientation sessions on July 6 (Lake City), July 7 (Winston), July 8 (Sherwood), and July 9 (Dawsonville).

To: Anthony Burris <a.burris@ridgepost.net>
From: Claire Harper <harper.c@willow-co.com>
Date: June 28
Subject: Contract

Dear Mr. Burris,

Welcome to the Willow Co. team! We are pleased you accepted the position. I will send you the sample employment contract sometime this week. Please look it over and let me know if you have any questions about it. You should bring a signed copy to the orientation session, which your branch is scheduled to hold on July 8. You should arrive at 8 A.M. and report to the head of human resources. You will train with various staff members throughout the day. I have attached a copy of the orientation schedule so you know in advance what will be covered. I look forward to working with you.

Warmest regards,

Claire Harper
Administrative Assistant, Willow Co.

Willow Co. New Employee Orientation

Time	Activity	Led by
8:00 A.M.	Arrival and Introductions	Administrative Assistant Claire Harper
8:30 A.M.	Welcome and Company Overview	Vice President Kevin Yoon
9:00 A.M.	Expectations and Company Policies	HR Director Margaret Daniels
10:30 A.M.	Break	
10:45 A.M.	Employee Benefits and Compensation	Finance Director Stephanie Lowe
11:15 A.M.	Security Procedures and ID Photos	Security Manager Dennis Mallory
noon	Lunch	

Please have a notebook or day planner with you to take notes during the orientation. After lunch, employees will receive training from their team leaders.

23. What benefit of the job is mentioned?
(A) A signing bonus
(B) A flexible work schedule
(C) Generous vacation time
(D) Competitive wages

24. What is NOT indicated as a requirement of the position?
(A) A personal form of transportation
(B) Experience in the field of marketing
(C) Strong communication skills
(D) The ability to cooperate

25. Where will Mr. Burris work?
(A) Lake City
(B) Winston
(C) Sherwood
(D) Dawsonville

26. Who should Mr. Burris find first when he arrives at the orientation?
(A) Claire Harper
(B) Kevin Yoon
(C) Margaret Daniels
(D) Dennis Mallory

27. What is suggested about the orientation program?
(A) Participants must bring something to write on.
(B) It will have a break time in between each session.
(C) It will be led by a single instructor.
(D) Team leaders will meet the new workers on the following day.

하루 30분씩 3주 만에
완성하는
PART 7

**CHAPTER 3
실전 모의고사**

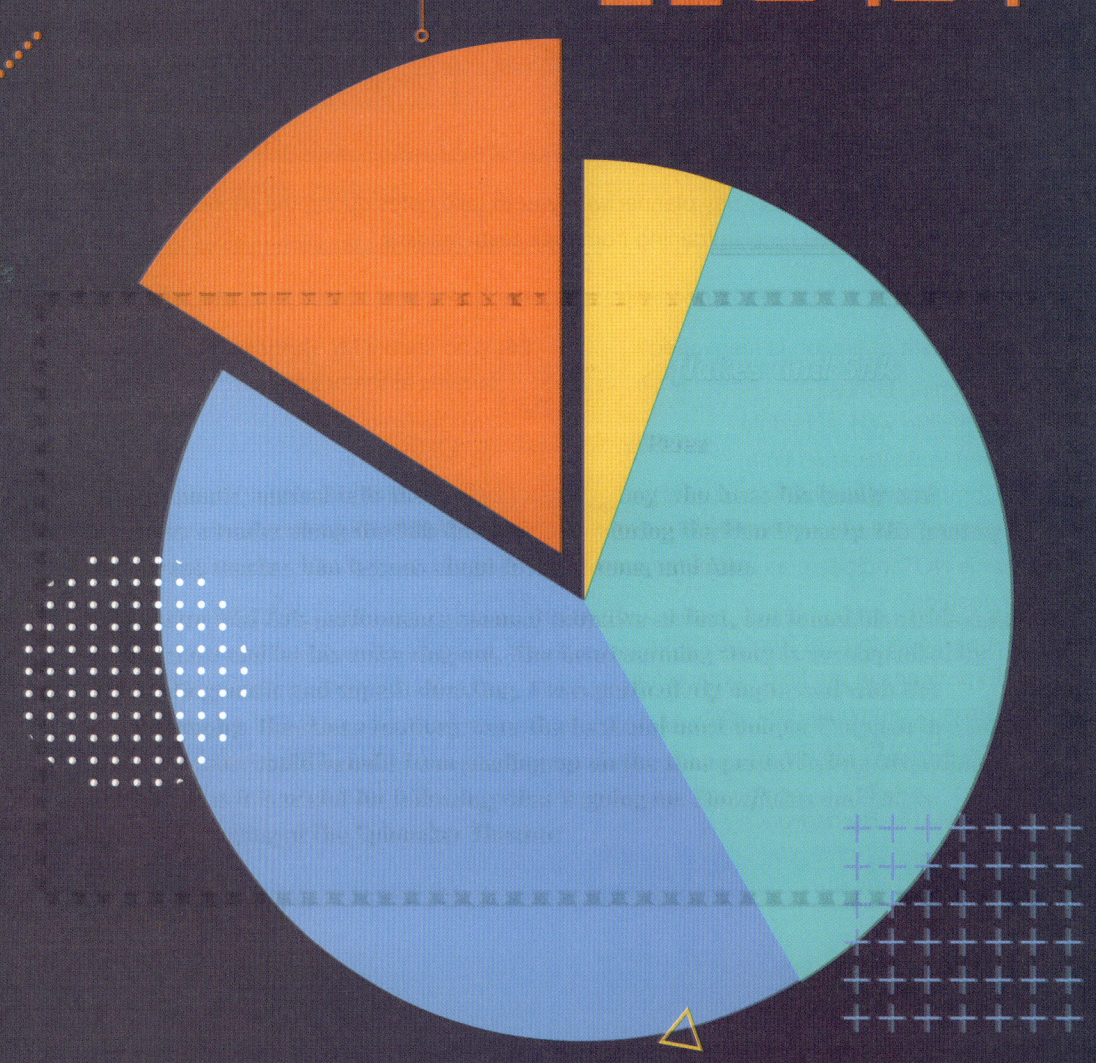

CHAPTER 3

- [ ] **UNIT 19** ACTUAL TEST 1
- [ ] **UNIT 20** ACTUAL TEST 2
- [ ] **UNIT 21** ACTUAL TEST 3

UNIT 19 ACTUAL TEST 1

⏱ 제한시간 50분

Directions: In this part, you will read a selection of texts, such as magazine and newspaper articles, e-mails, and instant messages. Each text or set of texts is followed by several questions. Select the best answer for each question and mark the letter (A), (B), (C), or (D) on your answer sheet.

Questions 147-148 refer to the following memo.

MEMO

Dear staff:

This memo is to share with you the updated schedule for the final quarter of our fiscal year. We request that you make note of the following special occasions and record these events in your agendas. If you are aware of any scheduling conflicts, please inform the management staff.

– Holiday in honor of the company's anniversary	May 7
– Computer system upgrade	June 19
– Pharmaceutical development convention	July 24-26
– Year-end financial audit	August 3

147. What is the purpose of the memo?
(A) To announce the departure of a CEO
(B) To instruct employees to change computers
(C) To inform staff of scheduled events
(D) To present a list of holidays

148. When will the drug convention commence?
(A) May 7
(B) June 19
(C) July 24
(D) July 26

Questions 149-151 refer to the following e-mail.

To: Felicity Caparulo <felicitycaparulo@capcorporation.com>
From: Mike Yard <mike.yard@trafalgarhall.com>
Date: February 20
Subject: Hall reservation confirmation
Attachment: Electronic receipt

Dear Ms. Caparulo,

First of all, I wish to congratulate you on your engagement! Second, I am writing to confirm receipt of your deposit for the wedding that you have booked with us at Trafalgar Hall. According to your file, you are taking advantage of our catering services in addition to our in-house party planner. To accommodate your 150 dinner guests, there will be eighteen round tables with eight people placed at each. Your head table will then seat the remaining six members of the wedding party. Be aware that our furniture arrangement is fixed and will not be changed.

I've attached an electronic copy of the receipt for the $1,000 deposit that you have already paid. The outstanding balance will be confirmed once you have determined your decoration preferences. The prices will then be calculated accordingly. Please visit our Web site www.trafalgarhall.com/decorations to view pictures of decoration choices we have available. Included on the same page are also photos of our floral centerpieces.

Warm regards,

Mike Yard, Reservation Director
Trafalgar Hall

149. What is the event being held for?
 (A) A wedding reception
 (B) A rehearsal dinner
 (C) A bridal lunch
 (D) An engagement ceremony

150. Which is NOT a service that Trafalgar Hall provides?
 (A) Food catering
 (B) Party planning
 (C) Furniture repositioning
 (D) Room decorating

151. What kind of information is available on the Web site?
 (A) Dinner and dessert menus
 (B) Images of decoration options
 (C) Blueprints of the banquet hall
 (D) Seating and table arrangements

Questions 152-153 refer to the following text message chain.

LEAH BORDERS — 08:12 A.M.
My alarm didn't go off this morning, so I just woke up! I'm so sorry to ask you this, but could you open the café for me?

LEAH BORDERS — 08:13 A.M.
With traffic, I'll never make it across town by 9:00 A.M. and you're the only other manager who has a key.

KEVIN JESTER — 08:16 A.M.
Okay, Leah. I can do that for you.

KEVIN JESTER — 08:17 A.M.
The only problem is that I can't stay for your entire shift. I have a dentist appointment at 10 A.M.

LEAH BORDERS — 08:18 A.M.
That's fine! I just need someone to open the doors and be there when the first customers arrive. I should be there by 9:30 A.M.

KEVIN JESTER — 08:20 A.M.
Okay. I'll work for you until then.

LEAH BORDERS — 08:20 A.M.
Thank you. I'm glad that you live so close to the café!

KEVIN JESTER — 08:21 A.M.
Yeah, it works out perfectly.

---

152. What is indicated about Ms. Borders?

(A) She got up late.
(B) She is stuck in traffic.
(C) She forgot a key.
(D) She lost a schedule.

153. At 08:18 A.M., what does Ms. Borders mean when she writes, "That's fine"?

(A) She will trade shifts with Mr. Jester.
(B) She can change a dental appointment.
(C) She only needs part of her shift covered.
(D) She is willing to pay Mr. Jester overtime.

Questions 154-156 refer to the following article.

Mexico Weekly
Business Reports

MEXICO CITY, July 8—Developer Jordan Callen has purchased additional land upon which he plans to begin expanding his dairy factory in Mexico City. — [1] — Callen's aim is to triple the current size of his factory's internal space in order to install sophisticated new equipment. — [2] — In addition to multiplying the number of Callen's assets, the new machinery will also enable him to create one of the first "zero water" manufacturing sites in the world. Callen Ltd. will be implementing these new processes at its Factory Viridiana in the water-deprived area of Mexico City. After the construction has been completed, the facility will be able to use water that has been recycled from its dairy operations. — [3] — Callen Ltd. plans to perfect this process and then replicate the approach in many of its other global factories. It is an important step toward creating sustainability in the industry. — [4] —

154. What is the article mainly about?
    (A) The profile of an international entrepreneur
    (B) The description of the inside of a factory
    (C) The details of an expansion project
    (D) The introduction of a company into Mexico

155. What is indicated about Callen Ltd.?
    (A) It owns factories around the world.
    (B) It is a water filtration company.
    (C) It has limited financial resources.
    (D) It copies the ideas of its competitors.

156. In which of the positions marked [1], [2], [3] and [4] does the following sentence best belong?

    "This then creates a location in which zero water is wasted."

    (A) [1]
    (B) [2]
    (C) [3]
    (D) [4]

Questions 157-158 refer to the following advertisement.

Adelphi Performances
Presents...
Moonlight Wishes
A ballet written and choreographed by Madame Cannato

The Bovim Ballet Company
Starring: Penelope Ramirez, Leo D'Avanzo, Tammy Matarese, and Leah Bonnema
February 19 at 8 P.M.
Cautley Hall
Auerspergstrasse 4, Salzburg 5020, Austria

General admission as well as VIP tickets can be purchased through the box office or online at www.cautlethall.com until 12 P.M. on the day of the performance. VIP passes allow patrons to receive autographs from the dancers after the show.

157. What type of performance is the information about?

(A) A symphony
(B) A choir
(C) A musical
(D) A dance

158. How can attendees receive an autograph?

(A) By visiting the box office
(B) By purchasing privileged tickets
(C) By meeting with individual performers
(D) By arriving early for the show

Questions 159-160 refer to the following schedule.

Destination	Departure Time	Arrival Time	Platform	Status
Calgary, AB	9:00 A.M.	11:55 A.M.	2	Boarding
Banff, AB	9:15 A.M.	1:20 P.M.	11	Delayed
Red Deer, AB	10:20 A.M.	12:05 P.M.	8	On schedule

Passenger instructions:
1) Travelers are encouraged to arrive at the bus terminal 45 minutes before their departure time. Tickets are sold without specific seats assigned, so passengers who arrive at the last minute may discover that the coach is already full.
2) Please line up at your designated platform with your ticket ready.

159. When will the bus to Red Deer arrive?

(A) 10:20 A.M.
(B) 11:55 A.M.
(C) 12:05 P.M.
(D) 1:20 P.M.

160. What is suggested about the bus to Banff?

(A) It will not leave on schedule.
(B) It has broken down.
(C) Its seats are already full.
(D) It will be the first to depart.

GO ON TO THE NEXT PAGE

Questions 161-163 refer to the following notice.

Attention West Wing Airlines Passengers

We require that all of our passengers familiarize themselves with the West Wing Airlines baggage policy. The total baggage allowance for all domestic flights is two checked bags and two carry-on bags per passenger. Any traveler who exceeds the acceptable number of bags is subject to a $50 fee to be charged at the discretion of the ticket agent. All small carry-on items, such as purses, must be stowed underneath the seat in front of you. Larger luggage items should be placed in the overhead compartments. Unidentified liquids in unmarked containers, firearms, and sharp objects are not allowed on the plane. For more information on the carry-on and checked baggage rules, please call us at 1-800-937-8946.

161. What is the purpose of the notice?
 (A) To identify a relevant policy
 (B) To outline evacuation procedures
 (C) To stipulate safety rules
 (D) To announce a pricing change

162. Why will passengers be charged a $50 fee?
 (A) They paid to bring an animal on the plane.
 (B) They failed to put their carry-ons underneath a seat.
 (C) They surpassed the stated baggage allowance.
 (D) They packed prohibited items in their checked luggage.

163. How can people get more information?
 (A) By watching an informative video
 (B) By reading a safety pamphlet
 (C) By asking a flight attendant
 (D) By contacting the airline directly

Questions 164-167 refer to the following letter.

Deidra Herndon
234 Cambine St.
Vancouver, BC V5A 4S3

Tiny Tots Hair Salon
849 Burrad Blvd.
Vancouver, BC V5A 0A1

1 November

Dear loyal customer:

Tiny Tots Hair Salon is moving to Burrad Blvd. Our new building is twice the size of our old one, which allows us to book more appointments and service more customers than we could in the past.

The new space will have a specifically designed area full of magazines and picture books available to keep children occupied and busy while they are waiting for their appointments. Reading materials will also be available for accompanying adults. — [1] —

To celebrate the opening of our new salon, we will be having a customer loyalty party on Saturday, November 20. — [2] — Starting the next day, we will extend our hours. Previously, our salon had been closed on Tuesdays, but now—in response to the high customer demand—it will be open every day of the week from 9 A.M. to 6 P.M. — [3] —

Additionally, we have created our own line of children's hair-care products. Enclosed is a pamphlet with pictures of the entire line of Tiny Tots merchandise that we will be selling at our new location. All of these items will be offered at 30% off the normal price until November 30. — [4] — Thus, even if you can't attend our party on the twentieth, be sure to drop by to check out these high-quality, chemical-free items.

We hope to see you at our new location sometime soon.

Tiny Tots Hair Salon

164. When will the business hours be extended?

(A) On November 1
(B) On November 21
(C) On November 25
(D) On November 30

165. What has been included with the letter?

(A) An advertising brochure
(B) A discount coupon
(C) An order form
(D) A business card

166. What is NOT stated as a change to the store?

(A) An increase in size
(B) The creation of a reading area
(C) The sale of new merchandise
(D) The addition of a second floor

167. In which of the positions marked [1], [2], [3] and [4] does the following sentence best belong?

"We're trying to make it easier for customers to get appointments that fit their busy schedules."

(A) [1] (B) [2] (C) [3] (D) [4]

Questions 168-171 refer to the online chat discussion.

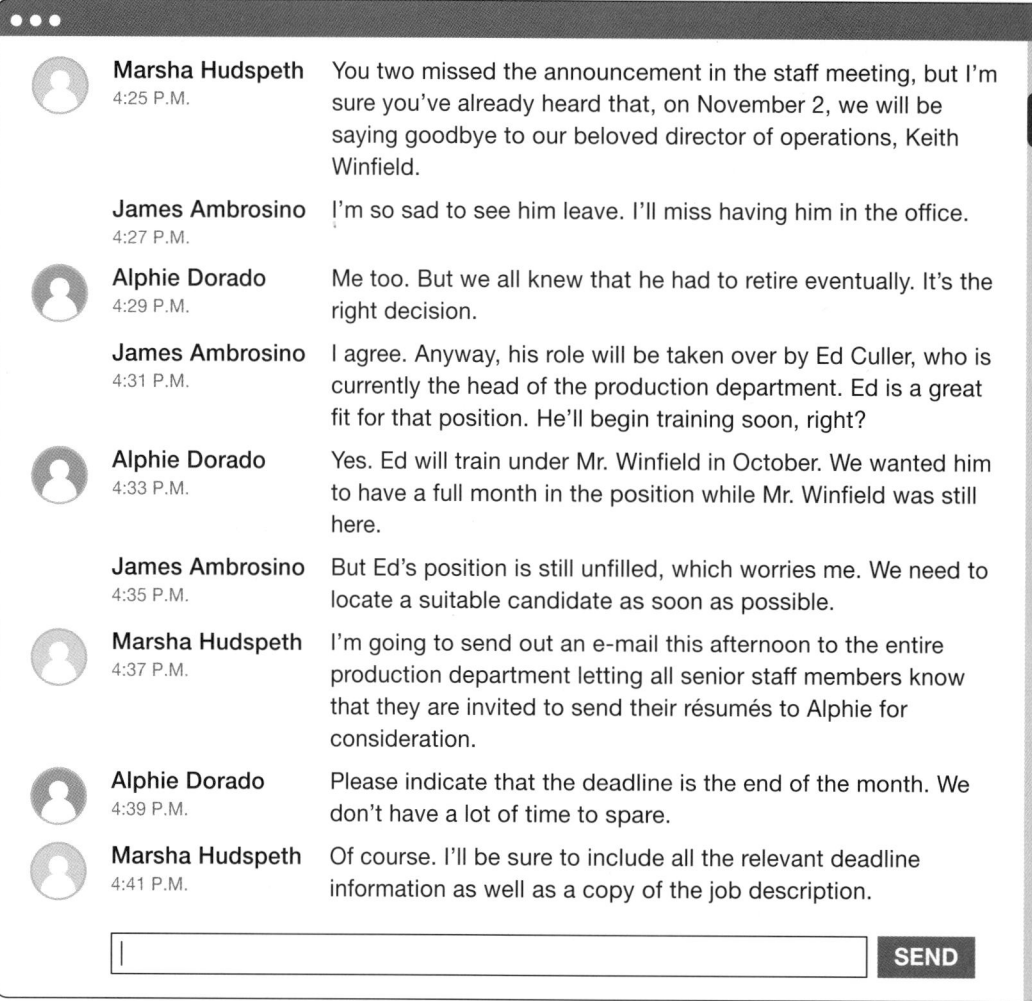

Marsha Hudspeth 4:25 P.M.	You two missed the announcement in the staff meeting, but I'm sure you've already heard that, on November 2, we will be saying goodbye to our beloved director of operations, Keith Winfield.
James Ambrosino 4:27 P.M.	I'm so sad to see him leave. I'll miss having him in the office.
Alphie Dorado 4:29 P.M.	Me too. But we all knew that he had to retire eventually. It's the right decision.
James Ambrosino 4:31 P.M.	I agree. Anyway, his role will be taken over by Ed Culler, who is currently the head of the production department. Ed is a great fit for that position. He'll begin training soon, right?
Alphie Dorado 4:33 P.M.	Yes. Ed will train under Mr. Winfield in October. We wanted him to have a full month in the position while Mr. Winfield was still here.
James Ambrosino 4:35 P.M.	But Ed's position is still unfilled, which worries me. We need to locate a suitable candidate as soon as possible.
Marsha Hudspeth 4:37 P.M.	I'm going to send out an e-mail this afternoon to the entire production department letting all senior staff members know that they are invited to send their résumés to Alphie for consideration.
Alphie Dorado 4:39 P.M.	Please indicate that the deadline is the end of the month. We don't have a lot of time to spare.
Marsha Hudspeth 4:41 P.M.	Of course. I'll be sure to include all the relevant deadline information as well as a copy of the job description.

168. Who will be leaving the company?
    (A) James Abrosino
    (B) Ed Culler
    (C) Marsha Hudspeth
    (D) Keith Winfield

169. At 4:29 P.M., what does Mr. Dorado mean when he writes, "It's the right decision"?
    (A) He agrees with Mr. Ambrosino's suggestion.
    (B) He understands the reason for a change.
    (C) He thinks the new director will do a good job.
    (D) He trusts the company's current leadership.

170. What does Ms. Hudspeth say she will do?
    (A) Write up a job description
    (B) E-mail a specific department
    (C) Determine a deadline for applications
    (D) Make arrangements for a training session

171. What will happen at the end of the month?
    (A) A retirement party will be held.
    (B) A training program will be conducted.
    (C) An application period will end.
    (D) A job opening will be posted.

Questions 172-175 refer to the following memo.

To: Graphic Design Team
From: Ella Parkinson
Date: March 2

Hello Everyone,

I am writing to inform you of an adjustment to the design workshop, which was originally scheduled for 9 A.M. on Friday, March 6, in conference room 3 of the Square Media headquarters building. Unfortunately, Jacqueline Wallace has to fly to Beijing to meet with a client, so she will not be able to attend the workshop. As a result, her 90-minute talk on using the Macrex Illustrator software program will be canceled because we were unable to find a replacement speaker. Since this was the first session of the talk, we have decided to start the workshop from the second session, which will be Joseph Bennett's talk. Please refer to the handout distributed earlier for the complete timetable and description of topics.

The workshop will cover a variety of topics including specific software programs, design trends, and common mistakes. All graphic design team employees at Square Media's three branches are expected to attend the workshop. If you are unable to do so for any reason, please e-mail me at ellap@squaremedia.net as soon as possible. This is so we can arrange for you to obtain the information in another way and also to have an accurate head count for the caterer. Any other questions may be directed to your immediate supervisor. They also have additional copies of the schedule should you need one. Please note that it is not necessary to bring your own laptop computer to the workshop.

This workshop was made possible by Square Media's Professional Development Fund. Should you have suggestions for future events that you believe would improve the skills of you and your colleagues, please send them to Amal Sykes at amals@squaremedia.net.

172. What is the purpose of the memo?

(A) To promote a new product
(B) To describe a company policy
(C) To report a schedule change
(D) To introduce a new manager

173. What can be inferred about Ms. Wallace?

(A) She will present a talk at a later time.
(B) She plans to transfer to the Beijing branch.
(C) She has requested to change her topic.
(D) She had a business trip at the last minute.

174. When was Ms. Wallace's talk originally scheduled to end?

(A) At 9:30 A.M.
(B) At 10:00 A.M.
(C) At 10:30 A.M.
(D) At 11:00 A.M.

175. Why should some recipients e-mail Ms. Parkinson?

(A) To reserve a laptop
(B) To report an absence
(C) To request a schedule
(D) To make a suggestion

Questions 176-180 refer to the following e-mail and receipt.

E-MAIL MESSAGE

To: Evangeline Hong <eviehong@netmail.com>
From: City of Saskatoon Parking Authority <noreply@cospa.com>
Subject: Obligatory parking pass
Date: March 2

Dear Ms. Hong:

Thank you for updating your address with the city database!

We hope you are settling into your new location comfortably. This e-mail is intended to inform you of a parking policy for people who own property in your current complex. All cars parked in the attached lots must have a parking permit displayed in their dashboard windows.

These parking passes are easily purchased through the City of Saskatoon. However, since your complex contains both residential as well as commercial units, there are two distinct types of parking passes. Business owners and their employees must apply for a $1,000/year purple parking pass. Purchasers of purple passes must keep their receipts if they wish to be reimbursed for this expense by their employers. Conversely, yellow passes are granted exclusively to residents. The cost of a yellow pass is $600/year. Each parking pass—regardless of category type—has the number of an assigned parking spot labeled on it. A $15 fine will be charged to the owner of any vehicle found parked in a spot that does not correspond to the number on the parking pass displayed.

Payments can be made by credit card, debit card, or check. Be aware that city employees are prohibited from accepting cash payments. When applying for a parking permit, you can select whether you would prefer to have your pass delivered to your home or be picked up at the City of Saskatoon Parking Authority center on Broadway Avenue. All passes are valid for one year from the date of purchase. An expiry date will be printed clearly on each pass.

Should you have any questions about the information details above, please call 555-567-1194. This is an automated message. Do not reply to this e-mail.

Regards,

City of Saskatoon Parking Authority

City of Saskatoon Parking Permit Receipt

Issue Date: March 4

Vehicle Information
Owner: Evangeline Hong
Address: 221 Idylwyld Dr. N, Saskatoon, SK
License plate number: 247 IVT

Permit Information
Pass Type: Yellow
Issue Type: New
Delivery Method: Mail

Payment Information
Amount Paid: $600
Payment Method: Credit card
Signature: *Evangeline Hong*

Card Number: XXXX XXXX XXXX 5465

Thank you for taking advantage of the City of Saskatoon's public parking service.

---

176. Why was the e-mail written?
(A) To welcome a new neighbor
(B) To update an address
(C) To describe a policy
(D) To request a payment

177. What is mentioned about the parking permits?
(A) Purchase is optional.
(B) Renewal occurs monthly.
(C) Commercial rates are cheaper.
(D) Payment is made to the City of Saskatoon.

178. How did Ms. Hong pay for her parking pass?
(A) By cash
(B) By bank transfer
(C) By check
(D) By credit card

179. What type of parking pass did Ms. Hong apply for?
(A) A residential pass
(B) A commercial pass
(C) A temporary pass
(D) A visitor's pass

180. What can be inferred about Ms. Hong?
(A) She had her pass delivered to her home.
(B) She was reimbursed for her payment.
(C) She is changing pass types.
(D) She is renewing her permit.

Questions 181-185 refer to the following Web site and notice.

Brooklyn Bridge Renovation Project

City of Brooklyn engineers have raised concerns about the structural soundness of the Brooklyn Bridge. In response, the bridge will be closed for construction for four months from May 1 to August 31. During this time, no public access will be granted to the bridge. Bridge use will be restricted solely to construction personnel and their equipment. Several detours will be established to help address any resulting traffic congestion in the surrounding area. Signposts for these alternate routes will be prominently displayed before entering the construction zone. Barring any unforeseen circumstances, we anticipate that this work will be completed before the first of September. Once it has begun, the City of Brooklyn will provide regular updates on the construction progress and any ensuing road closures throughout the repair period. To find these updates, simply click on the Brooklyn Bridge Renovation Project link here on the City of Brooklyn home page.

NOTICE: Brooklyn Bridge Renovation Project **UPDATE**

June 1

As part of our weekly updates on the Brooklyn Bridge Renovation Project, this notice is to confirm that construction has begun. Because of the severe weather conditions experienced by the City of Brooklyn throughout the month of May, any efforts to commence repair work on the Brooklyn Bridge were rendered impossible. However, yesterday's clear skies enabled work crews to finally complete their first full day of work. Because of the late start, we anticipate that work efforts will continue exactly a month longer than originally estimated. The Brooklyn Bridge will then be opened for use the very next day. All of the previous instructions and information remain in effect.

181. What does the Web site describe?
(A) A repair project
(B) A landscaping proposal
(C) A new bridge construction
(D) A traffic accident

182. What is NOT mentioned about the general public?
(A) It will be kept informed of scheduling progress.
(B) Its access to certain areas will be restricted.
(C) It will be provided with alternate travel routes.
(D) It will experience delays while driving.

183. What is indicated in the notice?
(A) The bridge is now safe for use.
(B) There has been a scheduling delay.
(C) The updates occur monthly.
(D) The cost is greater than anticipated.

184. According to the notice, what is the source of the problem?
(A) Poor weather conditions
(B) Mechanical failures
(C) Insufficient laborers
(D) Material shortages

185. When will the Brooklyn Bridge be reopened?
(A) On May 1
(B) On August 30
(C) On September 20
(D) On October 1

Questions 186-190 refer to the following flyer, review, and e-mail.

Spinnaker Theater Presents
Snowflakes and Silk

September 12-25 at 7:30 P.M. nightly

Starring: Wei Ku
Directed by: Sofia Gilman
Music and lyrics by: Yong Huang
Choreography by: Arnoldo Trentino

"Musical theater at its finest!" — Kent Wilson, *New York Artists Association*

Actors will be signing posters and CDs after the September 12 performance. Donations for the Willow Children's Hospital will be collected after the September 14 performance.

Purchase tickets at www.spinnakertheater.com. Discounts on refreshments for all Spinnaker Theater members.

Weekly Theater Review: *Snowflakes and Silk*
4.5/5 Stars
Reviewed by: Richard Perez

This dramatic musical tells the story of a young boy who loses his family and becomes a trader along the Silk Road in China during the Han Dynasty. His journey to success teaches him lessons about love, fortune, and fate.

Lead actor Wei Ku's performance seemed tentative at first, but found his stride later in the show and let his voice ring out. The heartwarming story is accompanied by enchanting music and superb directing. I was particularly impressed with the choreography. The dance routines were the best and most unique I've seen in a long time. Viewers would benefit from reading up on the time period before attending the show, as it is useful for following what is going on. *Snowflakes and Silk* is currently playing at the Spinnaker Theater.

To: Madison Aguilar <m.aguilar@ggcmail.com>
From: Kate Hayes <hayeskate@meridian1.com>
Date: September 14
Subject: *Snowflakes and Silk*

Dear Madison,

I'm wondering if you are still interested in going to see *Snowflakes and Silk* at the Spinnaker Theater. Most critics have really liked the show, so I think it's worth seeing. I know you had originally suggested going on September 18, but I just checked the Web site, and there are no tickets available for that night. In fact, the final performance is the only one that isn't sold out yet. So, I think we should go then and get our tickets as soon as possible. You're the perfect person to accompany me since you often go to shows like this. You can tell me how it compares to others you've seen!

Let me know if you're available,

Kate

---

186. What can visitors do at the opening performance?

(A) Make a donation
(B) Meet the show's director
(C) Get an autograph
(D) Buy a discounted ticket

187. Whose work did Mr. Perez like the most?

(A) Wei Ku's
(B) Sofia Gilman's
(C) Young Huang's
(D) Arnoldo Trentino's

188. In the review, the word "following" in paragraph 2, line 6, is closest in meaning to

(A) pursuing
(B) understanding
(C) monitoring
(D) supporting

189. When does Ms. Hayes propose going to the show?

(A) September 15
(B) September 18
(C) September 20
(D) September 25

190. What can be inferred about Ms. Aguilar?

(A) She attends musicals frequently.
(B) She prefers to go in a large group.
(C) She has already seen *Snowflakes and Silk*.
(D) She sent Ms. Hayes a review.

Questions 191-195 refer to the following article, program, and e-mail.

Collins, Inc.—November Newsletter

Spotlight on Achievement: Thomas Briggs

Sales Director Thomas Briggs is an integral part of the success of Collins, Inc., and we'd like to highlight his fine work in this month's column. Mr. Briggs first got to know Collins, Inc., during a summer internship with us ten years ago. Thanks to his hard work and his dedication to continually learning more about the market, he took on positions of increasing responsibility. He is now the head of the sales department, where his strong leadership and valuable insights have served the position well. In addition to growing the customer base, he has restructured the sales staff to promote cooperation and productivity.

Mr. Briggs will be presented with the prestigious Employee of the Year Award at the company's annual banquet. He is truly deserving of this honor, as he has spent his career working to meet the needs of Collins, Inc., and its investors. We can't thank him enough for his amazing work.

Collins, Inc., Annual Banquet
December 11, Sacramento Convention Hall

6:00 P.M.	Cocktail Reception, live music by the Archie Jazz Trio
7:00 P.M.	Welcome Speech by Vice President Carol Polk
7:30 P.M.	Best New Employee Award Presented to Brenda Bohn by Latanya Perry
7:45 P.M.	Best Team Award Presented to Human Resources by Emma Shaw
8:00 P.M.	Dinner Service and Year-in-Review Video
9:00 P.M.	Employee of the Year Award Presented to Thomas Briggs by President Troy Logan
9:15 P.M.	Future Projects Speech by President Troy Logan

To: Thomas Briggs <t.briggs@collinsinc.net>
From: Evelyn Wade <e.wade@collinsinc.net>
Date: December 12
Subject: Just a note

Hi Thomas,

I'm sorry I didn't have a chance to speak with you after the event last night. I had to catch a flight for a business trip, so I left right after your award presentation. I just want you to know how proud of you I am for this achievement. Great job! I can't think of anyone who deserves it more. It's a pleasure working with you on the management team, and I look forward to seeing more success from you in the years to come.

All the best,

Evelyn

191. What is NOT indicated about Mr. Briggs?
    (A) He reorganized the members of his department.
    (B) He is currently being considered for a promotion.
    (C) His first job with Collins, Inc., was as an intern.
    (D) He was presented an award by the Collins, Inc., president.

192. In the article, the word "meet" in paragraph 2, line 3, is closest in meaning to
    (A) connect
    (B) encounter
    (C) gather
    (D) fulfill

193. What is true about Collins, Inc.'s annual banquet?
    (A) It was held in the same venue as last year.
    (B) Dinner was served part-way through the evening.
    (C) Videos were shown of each award winner.
    (D) The evening concluded with a jazz performance.

194. What is the purpose of the e-mail?
    (A) To congratulate a colleague
    (B) To ask for a favor
    (C) To show appreciation
    (D) To give an invitation

195. What part of the program did Ms. Wade miss?
    (A) The Cocktail Reception
    (B) The Best New Employee Award
    (C) The Year-in-Review Video
    (D) The Future Projects Speech

Questions 196-200 refer to the following Web page, memo, and e-mail.

---

www.dixoncity.gov

| HOME | **ANNOUNCEMENTS** | EVENTS | CITY COUNCIL |

September is Homeless Assistance Month

The city council of Dixon City wants to raise awareness about homelessness and poverty in our region and to provide opportunities for the community to get involved. Below, you will find some suggested volunteer opportunities. More will be added at a later time.

Dixon City Outreach Association: Assist in cooking and serving a meal at one of our four locations throughout the city. Meals are served at the Webster Center (Mondays & Thursdays), Dawson Shelter (Tuesdays & Fridays), House of Hope (Wednesdays & Saturdays), and the 5th Street Soup Kitchen (Sundays). Contact Lena Becker at lena@dixoncityoa.org.

Helping Hands Warehouse: Volunteers are needed to sort the clothing gathered in our warehouse and organize it for both donations and for sale at our thrift store. Contact Walter Tirado at w_tirado@helpinghands1.org.

Dixon City Job Center: Assist those affected by homelessness and unemployment by tutoring them in reading, computer skills, interview skills, and more. Contact Angela Nichols at nichols.a@jobcenterdc.com.

To: Almazan, Inc., Staff
From: Andrew Bristow, Office Manager

September 5

In support of Homeless Assistance Month, our staff will work with the Dixon City Outreach Association to serve a meal to the homeless on Tuesday, September 14. Everyone is welcome to participate, and we need at least 20 people to volunteer. We will leave the office at 5 P.M. together, and we should be finished by 7:30 P.M. We will rent a charter bus to take us to the site so that everyone can ride together. You will be dropped off back at the office afterwards. Employees who take part in the activity do not have to come into the office the following day (September 15) until after lunch. This is our way of showing our appreciation for your support of this important project.

Please sign up with Jane in the HR office by September 10. You may also want to visit the Announcements page on the city's Web site to find other volunteer opportunities that you can do on your own.

Thank you.

To: Eric Canton <canton.e@almazaninc.com>
From: Angela Nichols <nichols.a@jcenterdc.com>
Date: September 21
Subject: Thank you
Attachment: timetable_sept-dec.pdf

Dear Mr. Canton,

Thank you for volunteering at our site this week. Your assistance truly makes a difference in the lives of others. While we've had a lot of volunteers so far this month thanks to the city's support of Homeless Assistance Month, we do need volunteers on an ongoing basis. If you'd like to visit us again, please feel free to contact me anytime. I've attached a timetable of our services, with the most short-staffed time slots marked in red. I hope you will consider working with us again soon.

Warmest regards,

Angela Nichols

196. Where most likely will Almazan, Inc.' employees volunteer?

(A) Webster Center
(B) Dawson Shelter
(C) House of Hope
(D) 5th Street Soup Kitchen

197. On the Web page, the word "gathered" in paragraph 3, line 1, is closest in meaning to

(A) constructed
(B) met
(C) collected
(D) assumed

198. What is true about Almazan, Inc.' employees?

(A) They will be given a half day off for participating.
(B) They will drive their own cars to the site.
(C) They are required to participate in the activity.
(D) They should contact Mr. Bristow to sign up.

199. What did Mr. Canton probably volunteer to do?

(A) Organized some clothes
(B) Worked at a thrift store
(C) Served some food
(D) Taught a skill

200. Why was the e-mail sent?

(A) To thank a financial contributor
(B) To encourage continued participation
(C) To offer a full-time position
(D) To explain the staffing process

UNIT 20 ACTUAL TEST 2

Directions: In this part, you will read a selection of texts, such as magazine and newspaper articles, e-mails, and instant messages. Each text or set of texts is followed by several questions. Select the best answer for each question and mark the letter (A), (B), (C), or (D) on your answer sheet.

Questions 147-148 refer to the following flyer.

Don't miss the biggest event ever at Oakland Home Center! We're relocating to a nearby building, so we're marking down most of the items in the store to get rid of our excess stock. The most popular brand names are on sale, with discounts you won't see anywhere else.

The sale starts this Saturday, September 6, and lasts through the weekend only, so stop by to browse our wide selection of items. Doors open at 8 A.M. Come early to get the merchandise you need before it sells out, and don't forget to keep your receipt to take advantage of the ten-year warranty on all products sold at Oakland Home Center. We hope you will take part in this great opportunity to add useful appliances to your home at a fraction of the cost. We thank you for your patronage, and we look forward to seeing you.

147. What is the advertisement about?

(A) A product launch
(B) A change in ownership
(C) A moving sale
(D) A grand opening

148. What is true about the event?

(A) It is held once a year.
(B) It ends on Sunday.
(C) It is a reward for card holders.
(D) It starts at 9 A.M.

Questions 149-151 refer to the following memo.

To: All Employees
From: Gloria Brown, HR Director
Date: October 20
Subject: Monthly Company Training

The monthly company training for November will take place on November 9 at 4 P.M. This month, we will have two programs rather than just one. As you know, Upton Enterprises has recently changed its benefits package for full-time employees. Many of you have contacted me with questions about how this affects your working hours, sales incentives, and severance pay. There is also some confusion about who is eligible for the on-site daycare facilities. The first program will allow me to give detailed information about these topics and offer clarification.

The second program will feature motivational speaker and business relations expert Jay Goulding. Some of you may remember Mr. Goulding from his time of employment here. He has gone on to become a highly respected consultant on interpersonal skills. His first book, *Workplace Connections*, will be published later this year, and it will be accompanied by an international speaking tour.

While the second session is scheduled to finish at 6 P.M., Mr. Goulding reports that the question-and-answer session following his talk has the tendency to go on for some time. If this happens, you will automatically be eligible for overtime pay. You will not need to fill out the usual paperwork, as this will be done for you by the accounting staff.

If you would like more information about the two programs, please view the detailed schedule posted on the company Web site.

149. According to Ms. Brown, what is the purpose of the first program?

(A) To explain the benefits package
(B) To introduce new employees
(C) To improve communication skills
(D) To negotiate sales incentives

150. What is mentioned about Mr. Goulding?

(A) He is currently on an international speaking tour.
(B) He used to work at Upton Enterprises.
(C) He is the writer of a best-selling book.
(D) He has a degree in communications.

151. What will happen if the session finishes after 6 P.M.?

(A) Employees will come in late the next day.
(B) Mr. Goulding will charge a fee.
(C) The company will order a meal.
(D) Staff members will be paid extra.

Questions 152-153 refer to the following text message chain.

LUCAS YANCEY   07:02 A.M.
Jackie, I'm afraid I'm feeling very ill today. I won't be coming into the office.

JACKIE KOVAR   07:03 A.M.
Oh, I'm sorry to hear that! I hope you feel better soon. Do you want me to let the department head know that you won't be here today?

LUCAS YANCEY   07:07 A.M.
Thanks, but I've already phoned Ms. Luther to let her know.

LUCAS YANCEY   07:10 A.M.
I do have one favor to ask, though. I'm supposed to submit the monthly status reports today. Do you remember helping me work on those?

JACKIE KOVAR   07:11 A.M.
Of course. Do you need me to submit them for you?

LUCAS YANCEY   07:12 A.M.
Yes, please. You'll have to print them all first, though. They're on the shared server.

JACKIE KOVAR   07:15 A.M.
All right. I'll take a look.

JACKIE KOVAR   07:21 A.M.
There's a folder under your name entitled *Monthly*.

LUCAS YANCEY   07:22 A.M.
That's the one. Thanks!

152. Why did Mr. Yancey contact Ms. Luther?
(A) To ask her to contact a coworker
(B) To report that he is too sick to come to work
(C) To rearrange a submission deadline
(D) To schedule a doctor's appointment

153. At 07:22 A.M., what does Mr. Yancey mean when he writes, "That's the one"?
(A) He is thanking Mr. Kovar for fixing an error.
(B) He is describing where to submit a report.
(C) He is telling Mr. Kovar to delete a folder.
(D) He is confirming where to find some files.

Questions 154-156 refer to the following e-mail.

To: All employees <allstaff@rankmedia.com>
From: Noah Mecurio <mecurionoah@rankmedia.com>
Date: September 26
Subject: Professional development opportunity

The Rank Media Professional Development Team is starting a new initiative for our employees. Because we require all staff members to regularly present marketing pitches and ideas to clients, communication is a critical skill for everyone employed here at Rank Media. — [1] — To further develop this skill in our employees, I highly encourage each of you to join the "Talking Points" program, which is designed for staff members interested in enhancing their speaking ability. Participants will meet weekly for six months and speak for five minutes on a randomly assigned topic pertinent to a corporate environment. — [2] — They will also increase their overall confidence while speaking in front of an audience.

Program meetings will be held on lunch breaks so that they don't interfere with work schedules. Additionally, because topics are assigned and delivered spontaneously, no 'homework' is necessary. — [3] — For those who are curious about the program, we will hold a demonstration meeting to illustrate what it is all about and why it is so popular with other companies. After the demonstration on November 15, you will have an opportunity to sign up. — [4] — If you determine that you are interested in participating at that time, please contact the "Talking Points" coordinator, Regina Grimes at grimes@rankmedia.com. We hope you will all consider being a part of this program.

Noah Mecurio
Professional Development Leader

154. What kind of business is Rank Media?

(A) An advertising agency
(B) A technology firm
(C) A communications firm
(D) A marketing company

155. Who is Regina Grimes?

(A) A potential client
(B) An external representative
(C) A program coordinator
(D) A personal assistant

156. In which of the positions marked [1], [2], [3] and [4] does the following sentence best belong?

"During this time, participants will undoubtedly notice a dramatic improvement in their presentation effectiveness."

(A) [1]
(B) [2]
(C) [3]
(D) [4]

Questions 157-158 refer to the following invitation.

LIMBURI HOTEL

Mr. and Mrs. Brillon
11 Xuan Dieu Road
Hanoi, Vietnam

February 17

We cordially extend an invitation for you to attend a farewell banquet being held in honor of Mr. Rudy Winslow. After 18 years of hard work and allegiance to serving the people here at the Limburi Hotel, Mr. Winslow is moving on to an exciting opportunity at another company. Please join us at the Haven Hill Country Club to celebrate his many years of service. Cocktail attire is mandatory. Please respond with your attendance and number of accompanying guests to the party organizer, Kathleen Jobrani, at kathleen.jobrani@limburi.com prior to March 22.

Regards,

Limburi Hotel Management

157. What type of event is Ms. Jobrani preparing?

(A) A retirement celebration
(B) A goodbye banquet
(C) An awards ceremony
(D) A cocktail reception

158. What is true about the event?

(A) Responses are due before February.
(B) The host venue is a hotel.
(C) The dress code is casual.
(D) Invitees can bring guests.

Questions 159-160 refer to the following notice.

Over the last 27 years, Malaprop Books has been a popular spot to buy used books and magazines in the East Park neighborhood. We are grateful for our many regular customers. However, we are sorry that we will soon be closing our doors temporarily to conduct some much-needed renovations. For three days, from April 22 to 24, we will be repairing some damaged pipes, repainting walls, rearranging furniture, and adding more shelving. Visit us again on April 25 when we reopen for business and show off our new interior. For one day only, we will be handing out free coffee to adults and chocolate milk to children with every book purchase.

159. What is suggested about Malaprop Books?

(A) It is a heavily visited neighborhood store.
(B) It has always been owned by the same person.
(C) It is open three days out of every week.
(D) It specializes in comic books and graphic novels.

160. According to the notice, when will the store reopen?

(A) On April 24
(B) On April 25
(C) On April 26
(D) On April 27

Questions 161-163 refer to the following letter.

The Pelican
107 Pearse Street
Dublin, Ireland

January 15

Dear Pelican Management,

I just wanted to send a note to extend a sincere thank you to the Pelican for hosting our banquet last week. I was impressed at how easily your team serviced our group in the ballroom while still ensuring that sufficient staff members were present to check in and care for your regular guests in the lobby downstairs. As you know, last month, we celebrated our twenty-fifth year in business. We consider this to be an important milestone. Thankfully, the Pelican made sure everything went according to the plan.

The most notable part of the evening was the decorations. Your decorators made the Starlight Ballroom look absolutely stunning. Specifically, I want to single out Declan Castor, who is a wonderful event coordinator. Having a very professional manner and polite tone, he addressed all of my questions fully over the phone. He made the whole planning process a delight for me. Overall, I'd have no hesitation in recommending the Pelican to others for similar events.

Again, thank you all so much!

Michael Calhoun
Venture Insurance

161. Why was the letter sent?
(A) To congratulate a staff member
(B) To arrange a set-up time
(C) To thank a business for its services
(D) To provide necessary instructions

162. What happened to Venture Insurance in December?
(A) A second location was opened.
(B) An anniversary was reached.
(C) A business deal was finalized.
(D) An important sales record was broken.

163. What is true about Mr. Castor?
(A) He answered questions politely.
(B) He decorated the ballroom.
(C) He recommended the Pelican hotel.
(D) He wrote a thank you note.

Questions 164-167 refer to the following job posting.

Everest Inc. offers a broad assortment of brand-name sporting equipment, apparel, and footwear in a specialty store environment. Our corporate office is headquartered in Binghamton, New York; our production plant is located in the nearby city of Ithaca; and our two most successful stores can be found in Madison, Wisconsin, and Frankfort, Kentucky. — [1] — However, we haven't finished expanding yet! We are hiring for the positions detailed below:

Administrator, Payroll (1 position): The payroll administrator helps the human resources manager with all functions related to maintaining personnel records and making salary payments. Specifically, s/he prepares and processes the biweekly payroll for nearly 15,000 employees.

Associate, Sales (1 position): The sales associate organizes and displays merchandise according to company standards. Associates must also keep all pricing, clearance discounts, and special promotions up-to-date.

Director, Public Relations (1 position): The public relations director develops and executes strategies intended to create a positive public image for Everest, Inc. — [2] — Managing crisis operations to protect Everest, Inc.'s reputation after negative incidents have occurred is an essential part of the role.

Operations Supervisor (1 position): The operations supervisor oversees and ensures the smooth and efficient performance of the operations department. — [3] — Because s/he is responsible for directing a large team, supervisory experience is required.

Plant Mechanic (2 positions): Working in the production plant, the mechanic performs skilled work related to building maintenance, such as welding, cutting, and electrical work. — [4] — S/he also conducts preventive maintenance procedures throughout the building and must be available on call as needed.

If you wish to apply for any of the above positions, please do so online by completing the fields at www.everest.com/careers. You will need to upload an updated résumé and a cover letter. Applications received by fax or e-mail will not be considered.

164. What is suggested about payroll administrators?
 (A) They operate financial computer software.
 (B) They schedule travel arrangements.
 (C) They pay salaries every two weeks.
 (D) They collect employee banking information.

165. Where will the plant mechanic work?
 (A) Binghamton
 (B) Frankfort
 (C) Ithaca
 (D) Madison

166. How should candidates apply?
 (A) By sending an e-mail
 (B) By calling a recruiter
 (C) By submitting a fax
 (D) By completing an online form

167. In which of the positions marked [1], [2], [3] and [4] does the following sentence best belong?

 "S/he forms relationships with the media, the government, and the community."
 (A) [1]
 (B) [2]
 (C) [3]
 (D) [4]

Questions 168-171 refer to the following online chat discussion.

Joel Forrest (3:39 P.M.): Good afternoon, everyone. Let's talk about the planned train drivers' strike on February 5 and how it is going to affect us at Oakridge Station.

Brenda Muse (3:43 P.M.): Obviously, some services will be canceled, and others will be delayed because of this. Has the management team determined what particular routes will be impacted?

Richard Dunnellon (3:45 P.M.): Yes. The cancellations will be: the Poppe Line to Toronto at 14:00, the Locklear Line to Ottawa at 09:30, and the Hickory Line to Brantford at 08:00. Furthermore, the 11:00 train to Brantford will be delayed by 15 minutes.

Joel Forrest (3:47 P.M.): The good news is that it affects fewer train lines than we initially feared, so that's encouraging.

Brenda Muse (3:49 P.M.): That's true, but one of the things we must keep in mind—and remind passengers about too—is that an event like this will also influence the services that are still running.

Joel Forrest (3:51 P.M.): Brenda's right. Many of the regular train departures will become jammed with passengers because people will be compensating for other routes that are not available.

Brenda Muse (3:53 P.M.): We should post a notice at the station reminding passengers to go to their platforms much earlier than the scheduled departure times in order to ensure that they get on their trains.

Richard Dunnellon (3:55 P.M.): That's a good plan. Obviously, we need to post the amended schedule as well. I can take care of both of those things.

---

168. What has caused the schedule changes at Oakridge Station?
(A) Some trains are out for regular maintenance.
(B) New travel routes are being introduced.
(C) Employees are refusing to go to work.
(D) Several new tracks are being constructed.

169. What time will the train to Brantford leave?
(A) 08:00
(B) 09:30
(C) 11:15
(D) 14:00

170. What problem does Mr. Forrest mention?
(A) Some of the workers are not experienced.
(B) There aren't enough funds to fix a problem.
(C) Some services will be overcrowded.
(D) Passengers are expected to complain.

171. At 3:55 P.M., what does Mr. Dunnellon mean when he writes, "That's a good plan"?
(A) He suggests posting a revised train schedule.
(B) He wants to advise passengers to arrive early.
(C) He is attempting to amend the timetable.
(D) He supports the idea of hiring new workers.

Questions 172-175 refer to the following cover letter.

August 26

Dear Staff,

On behalf of the management team at Cheshire Consulting, I would like to tell you about a decision that was recently made. Starting from September 1, we will implement a new regulation regarding Internet usage. Currently, employees are permitted to visit Web sites not related to work and to use personal e-mail accounts during working hours. Under the new policy, this will not be allowed. The decision was made in an effort to boost productivity, as we believe that employees are spending too much time on personal matters while at the office. I apologize for the short notice of this announcement. I planned to send this letter earlier but was delayed because a work crew is renovating my branch, which resulted in temporarily having no access to company records.

Details about the policy are outlined in Form 4861. We encourage all employees to read the information carefully so that they may be in compliance with the new rules. If you would like a copy of the new policy, you may request one by e-mailing Joshua Decker at j.decker@limaco.com. This form can also be downloaded from the company Web site, which you can access with your employee number and password. Please talk to your supervisor if you have problems logging in. Alternatively, we can mail you a printed copy to keep for your records, which can be done by making a formal request in writing to Mr. Decker.

We thank you in advance for complying with the new policy. We also value employee feedback about this and other matters. Therefore, Thomas Neely is forming a task force to monitor employee morale and elicit feedback from the staff. If you would like him to consider you for this group, please give him a call at extension 34.

Sincerely,

Elizabeth Simon

172. What is the purpose of the letter?

(A) To inform employees of a rule change
(B) To request some paperwork from employees
(C) To report a problem with an Internet connection
(D) To announce an upcoming management meeting

173. What caused Ms. Simon to send the letter late?

(A) A computer error
(B) A renovation project
(C) A lost file
(D) An employee absence

174. What is NOT indicated as a way to get access to Form 4861's information?

(A) Requesting a printed copy
(B) Sending an e-mail
(C) Signing into an online account
(D) Calling Mr. Decker's office

175. What is Mr. Neely responsible for doing?

(A) Appointing new managers
(B) Printing training materials
(C) Selecting committee members
(D) Creating meeting schedules

Questions 176-180 refer to the following advertisement and article.

Going Green with the Unozim Environmental Grant

Unozim is a company extremely concerned about the environment. Therefore, we are once again hosting an environment-preservation contest for businesses called the 'Unozim Grant.' The purpose of this contest is to provide businesses with an incentive to protect nature and reduce the environmental impact of their daily actions. All companies who register for the contest must develop a program in their communities that is related in some way to environmental preservation. The first-place winner will be awarded $100,000; second place, $50,000; and third place, $10,000. The prize money given should be used to fund the proposed initiative. The recipient of last year's grant was a law firm who assigned a team of lawyers to work with Congress to enact a new environmental policy. The legislation discourages water pollution through harsher penalties for corporations who get rid of chemical waste by dumping it into our water system. This year's applications must be received no later than June 18. The contest results will be e-mailed to all participating organizations by July 5.

Wegryn Enterprises Earns Congratulations!

By Whitney Caldwell

Congratulations should be extended to our very own local technology development company, Wegryn Enterprises, on becoming a recipient of the Unozim Grant. Wegryn Enterprises was awarded $10,000 to finance an electronic-waste management program. The company sells large volumes of technological devices and is therefore aware of the consumer trash that is produced when customers regularly upgrade their devices. Most of these items — used computers, cell phones, etc. — are simply thrown into the garbage, but this technological waste can be hazardous to the environment if it is not disposed of appropriately. To combat this issue, Wegryn Enterprises will place a dumpster outside its store for individuals to drop off outdated devices. Afterward, one of the hundreds of workers at Wegryn Enterprises will ensure that the items are discarded correctly. We should all be very proud of our local environmental heroes who entered this contest for the first time this year. What a pleasant surprise to see them win one of the top prizes.

176. What is the purpose of the advertisement?

(A) To encourage participation in a contest
(B) To publicize a company undertaking
(C) To announce the winner of an award
(D) To promote individual environmentalism

177. Which program was awarded the grant last year?

(A) An organized tree-planting effort
(B) A collection of used batteries
(C) An adopt-a-highway program
(D) A law against water pollution

178. What rank was Wegryn Enterprises awarded?

(A) First place
(B) Second place
(C) Third place
(D) Last place

179. What does Wegryn Enterprises plan to do?

(A) Reduce its reliance on chemicals
(B) Switch to energy-efficient electricity
(C) Encourage employees to carpool
(D) Gather consumers' discarded electronic items

180. What is NOT true about Wegryn Enterprises?

(A) It has several hundred employees.
(B) It has competed in this contest before.
(C) It is a firm that creates new technology.
(D) It sells technological devices in stores.

Questions 181-185 refer to the following notice and e-mail.

Attention Sailex Company

Are you a recent college graduate? Are you working your first permanent full-time job? If you answered yes to both of these questions, NOW is the time to start thinking seriously about your financial future. Learning the necessary skills to budget, save, and eliminate student debt should be your priority. Miskatonic College can do that for you! We offer a number of evening classes in financial planning and financial management. We will teach you how to make the most out of your new paycheck. Our goal is to position you well for a successful financial future.

Most of our classrooms are located in the Conniff Building on the south side of campus. However, there are some exceptions, so be sure to check the rooms indicated on the class schedule to verify where you must go.

Course title	Debt repayment planning	Learning how to save	The basics of budgeting	The need for investments
Dates	December 6, 8, 10	January 13, 15	January 20, 22, 24	January 20
Times	6 P.M.–9 P.M.	7 P.M.–10 P.M.	6 P.M.–9 P.M.	7 P.M.–10 P.M.
Pricing	$150	$100	$150	$50
Special notes		Held in Webb Hall		

(Due to classroom constraints, enrollment is limited to 30 people per class.)
Please submit a completed registration form to the recruitment coordinator James Cunningham at jcunningham@miskatoniccollege.com. Registration must be done a minimum of one month prior to the start date of your selected class. Once your enrollment has been confirmed, you must provide payment by either credit card or bank transfer within seven days of your first class.

To: James Cunningham <jcunningham@miskatoniccollege.com>
From: Elmira Monroe <emonroe@sailexcompany.net>
Date: November 17
Subject: Becoming a student
Attachment: Registration form

Dear Mr. Cunningham:

I noticed recently that a flyer for your school was displayed in my office break room. I am interested in joining your college. I've attached the registration form that I downloaded from your Web site. Although I like all of the courses listed, at the moment, I can only take the one offered in December. Could you please verify whether or not there is still an available seat in this class? Once I have received your confirmation I will proceed with my tuition payment. I'm very excited about taking a course from your institution.

Thank you,

Elmira Monroe

181. For whom is the notice most likely intended?
    (A) Entry-level employees
    (B) Current college students
    (C) University professors
    (D) Unemployed job seekers

182. What is indicated about the classes?
    (A) They are offered during daytime hours.
    (B) Their size is limited to twenty-five people.
    (C) They all cost the same price.
    (D) Their location occasionally changes.

183. According to the e-mail, where did Ms. Monroe get the attached form?
    (A) She picked it up from the college.
    (B) It was mailed to her after she requested it.
    (C) She printed it from the Web site.
    (D) It was posted in her office.

184. In the e-mail, the word "seat" in paragraph 1, line 5, is closest in meaning to
    (A) rear
    (B) time
    (C) base
    (D) place

185. In which course would Ms. Monroe like to enroll?
    (A) Debt repayment planning
    (B) Learning how to save
    (C) The basics of budgeting
    (D) The need for investments

GO ON TO THE NEXT PAGE

Questions 186-190 refer to the following e-mail, itinerary, and notice.

To	Carla Lambert <lambertc@fresnopost.net>
From	Kenny Warren <kenny@ace-travel.net>
Date	May 14
Subject	Your upcoming vacation

Dear Ms. Lambert,

Thank you for booking your vacation through Ace Travel! I have made all of the arrangements for your trip to White Sands Island. I was unable to book a suite for you and your husband for the entire trip, so you will be staying in a double room on your first night at Bay Resort. After that, you will be moved to a suite. As a result, the total price of the package will be slightly reduced.

All tickets for your activities on the island have been purchased, and these will be sent to you by mail this week. If anything gets canceled, just let me know when you get back, and I can help you to process a refund request. You do not need paper tickets for your flight. Simply show your passport at the time of check-in.

The deposit has already been paid, so there is a balance of $1,750. Please take care of this by May 30.

If I can be of service in any other way, please do not hesitate to contact me.

Sincerely,

Kenny Warren
Travel Agent, Ace Travel

Ace Travel Itinerary: White Sands Island
Customer: Lambert, Carla
Other Traveler(s): Lambert, Paul

DAY 1 [Saturday, June 3]
8:35 A.M.   Everton Air Flight EV304 departure from Walsh Airport
10:43 A.M. Arrival at White Sands Island, take shuttle to Bay Resort
8:00 P.M.   Banquet dinner, Bay Resort

DAY 2 [Sunday, June 4]
9:00 A.M.   Snorkeling Lesson at Vitali Beach
7:30 P.M.   Lyndon Folk Singers Concert, Upland Hall

DAY 3 [Monday, June 5]
2:00 P.M.   Guided hike through Comet Park
4:30 P.M.   Traditional basket-making lesson, Kerns Building
5:00 P.M.   Tour local art exhibit, Pearl Center

DAY 4 [Tuesday, June 6]
9:00 A.M.   Two-person spa package, Bay Resort
3:35 P.M.   Everton Air Flight EV650 departure from Mojica Airport

NOTICE TO ALL VISITORS

The Kerns Building will be closed from June 2 to June 10 due to unforeseen circumstances. All activities scheduled for these days have been canceled, and you should contact the ticket provider directly to seek a refund. The reason for this unexpected closure is the recent hurricane, which caused structural damage to a section of a building while passing through the area. This damage needs to be repaired for a safety inspection before the building can be reopened. We apologize for any inconvenience this may cause.

– The Management Team

186. When will Ms. Lambert stay in a double room?
    (A) June 3
    (B) June 4
    (C) June 5
    (D) June 6

187. What does Mr. Warren ask Ms. Lambert to do?
    (A) Confirm a mailing address
    (B) Send a copy of a passport
    (C) Make a final payment
    (D) Purchase travel insurance

188. What is NOT true about Ms. Lambert's trip?
    (A) Her return flight departs in the afternoon.
    (B) Her snorkeling lesson is scheduled for the weekend.
    (C) Her itinerary includes activities for every morning.
    (D) Her resort has a spa on the premises.

189. Which activity will Ms. Lambert be unable to participate in?
    (A) A nature hike
    (B) A craft lesson
    (C) A musical performance
    (D) An art tour

190. According to the notice, what are some visitors asked to do?
    (A) Listen to a weather forecast
    (B) Return after a reopening
    (C) Check the status of repairs
    (D) Request a reimbursement

GO ON TO THE NEXT PAGE

Questions 191-195 refer to the following advertisement, e-mail, and schedule.

Global Interpretation Enterprises–We speak your language!

At Global Interpretation Enterprises (GIE), we offer in-person professional interpreters for a variety of settings. We understand that in business situations, accuracy counts. That's why we only hire native speakers of the target language. All our interpreters are fully trained and have experience in a number of professional fields in addition to their language skills. Our services are perfect for negotiations, seminars, conferences, court hearings, and more.

Check out our competitive rates below:

Two-hour session	$290
Four-hour session	$560
Six-hour session	$780
Eight-hour session	$960
More than eight hours	Please contact us.

To book an interpreter for your next event, call (493) 555-7792 or e-mail us at booking@ginterpretation.com.

To: Global Interpretation Enterprises <booking@ginterpretation.com>
From: Shirley Lowry <lowrys@lumiomfg.com>
Date: October 3
Subject: RE: Lumio Manufacturing Conference

Dear Mr. Metz,

Thank you for your prompt reply. I am glad that your company will be able to supply an interpreter for our upcoming event. As I said in my original request, we would like a 4-hour session with a native English speaker who can translate French. Our own staff members will cover the Spanish and Mandarin sessions.

The interpreter's first talk will be at the Pomona Hotel on October 27 at 3 P.M. Someone at the registration booth will direct him or her where to go. Please also let the person know that he or she is welcome to come to the dinner after the final talk. This would, of course, be off the clock, but we would provide a complimentary ticket to get in.

Sincerely,

Shirley Lowry
Event Coordinator, Lumio Manufacturing

Lumio Manufacturing Conference
October 27, Pomona Hotel

Title	Speaker	Time	Location	Language*
Applying for Government Grants for Research Projects	Rachelle Uribe	3 P.M.	Pine Hall	Spanish
Trade Agreements and How They Affect You	Amabella Legault	3 P.M.	Oak Hall	French
Environmentally-Friendly Manufacturing	Timothy Bartlett	3 P.M.	Spruce Hall	English
The Key to Teamwork among Employees	Phillip Paradis	5 P.M.	Willow Hall	French
Making the Most of Modern Machinery	Lisa Stevens	5 P.M.	Spruce Hall	English
Waste Reduction in Materials Processing	Lei Chiang	5 P.M.	Pine Hall	Mandarin
Buffet Dinner – Ticket Required		7 P.M.	Main Ballroom	N/A

*All non-English talks will be translated into English.

191. How much will Lumio Manufacturing pay for a service?

(A) $290
(B) $560
(C) $780
(D) $960

192. In the advertisement, the word "counts" in paragraph 1, line 2, is closest in meaning to

(A) allows
(B) considers
(C) calculates
(D) matters

193. What does Ms. Lowry invite GIE's interpreter to do?

(A) Take part in a meal for free
(B) Pose in a group photograph
(C) Stay overnight at a hotel
(D) Meet a speaker in advance

194. Where should GIE's interpreter go on October 27 at 3 P.M.?

(A) Pine Hall
(B) Oak Hall
(C) Spruce Hall
(D) Willow Hall

195. What will Ms. Stevens give a talk about?

(A) Using technology
(B) Environmental issues
(C) Getting public funds
(D) Staff cooperation

GO ON TO THE NEXT PAGE

Questions 196-200 refer to the following job posting, e-mail, and memo.

Salesperson Needed

Grelton Pharmaceuticals, a leading supplier of prescription medications, is seeking self-motivated salespeople to join its team. The ideal candidate will want to develop a long-term career with us. The main responsibility of the position is maintaining our existing relationships with clinics and other medical facilities. A bachelor's degree in any field is required, and you must have worked in a sales environment for at least two years. You will often visit clients in person, so you must be able to go out of town regularly, often for a few days at a time.

We offer a competitive compensation package, which includes medical insurance, use of a company car, and a generous amount of paid vacation time. In addition, salespeople are eligible for a raise every three months, far sooner than most other companies.

To apply, send a résumé and cover letter to Adam Atwood at a.atwood@greltonpharma.com by March 28. If you are selected for an interview, you must also submit two letters of recommendation, a copy of your valid driver's license, and a copy of your university transcripts.

To: Suzanne Hirsch <suzanneh@securepost111.com>
From: Adam Atwood <a.atwood@greltonpharma.com>
Date: April 5
Subject: Interview with Grelton Pharmaceuticals

Dear Ms. Hirsch,

It was a pleasure speaking to you on the phone this morning, and I'm pleased that you are available for an interview. Our hiring committee was especially impressed with your cover letter. We believe that you can express yourself clearly in writing, and this is an important part of the job.

Your interview is scheduled for 10:30 A.M. on April 10 with sales director Paula Jakin and office manager Wendell Beckwith. I have attached a map to our office building. And you should come to the third floor. The office administrator, Jesse Tucker, will be in the reception area to direct you where to go.

Of the documents you need to submit prior to the interview, I still need the copy of your driver's license and your university transcripts. Feel free to send these to me anytime. I look forward to meeting you in person!

Sincerely,

Adam Atwood
HR Director, Grelton Pharmaceuticals

To: All Employees
From: Wendell Beckwith

April 6

The third-floor meeting room will be unavailable to employees from 9 A.M. to 4 P.M. on Tuesday, April 10, due to interviews for the open sales positions. Several rooms are available on other floors, but they must be reserved in advance. If you need to find a meeting space elsewhere in the building, please e-mail the office administrator, who will help you to make the necessary arrangements. For those of you working on the 3rd floor, please try to speak quietly and avoid using the copiers while interviews are being held. Thank you for your understanding.

196. What is NOT mentioned about the position?

(A) It requires previous experience.
(B) It includes a great deal of travel.
(C) It involves finding new clients.
(D) Its salary can increase quickly.

197. What has Ms. Hirsch already sent?

(A) A copy of a driver's license
(B) An outline of a sales strategy
(C) Some university transcripts
(D) Some letters of recommendation

198. What did the hiring committee find impressive about Ms. Hirsch?

(A) Her educational background
(B) Her written communication skills
(C) Her unique sales strategies
(D) Her former employer

199. Who should people contact about room availability?

(A) Adam Atwood
(B) Wendell Beckwith
(C) Paula Jakin
(D) Jesse Tucker

200. What are employees on the 3rd floor asked to do on April 10?

(A) Refrain from eating snacks
(B) Greet applicants eagerly
(C) Keep noise to a minimum
(D) Share their computers

UNIT 21   ACTUAL TEST 3   제한시간 50분

Directions: In this part, you will read a selection of texts, such as magazine and newspaper articles, e-mails, and instant messages. Each text or set of texts is followed by several questions. Select the best answer for each question and mark the letter (A), (B), (C), or (D) on your answer sheet.

Questions 147-148 refer to the following letter.

Tamara Lissow
66 Tunali Hilmi Caddesi
Ankara, Turkey 6680

May 21

Dear Ms. Lissow,

According to our records, you recently purchased a new, high-quality water filtration pump for your fish tank. After ordering it, we originally promised that the device would arrive within a week. Unfortunately, there was an error with the manufacturer who sends us products. I wanted to update you on your order and let you know that there will be a delay. I promise that your pump will be available for pickup sometime next week. To compensate you for the wait, please accept a complimentary bag of goldfish food. This is our gift to you.

Best wishes,

Caleb Mandelbaum
Manager, Pennington Pet Supply

147. Why did Mr. Mandelbaum send the letter?

(A) To ask a customer to visit the store
(B) To send a service reminder
(C) To provide details on an order
(D) To update some contact information

148. What will Ms. Lissow receive for free?

(A) Sample aquarium decorations
(B) A supply of food for her fish
(C) A water-purifying pump
(D) New glass-cleaning supplies

Questions 149-151 refer to the following advertisement.

Acclaimed novelist Jade Harvey has left the world of literature and successfully entered the realm of theater. Harvey's first-ever play, entitled *Portrait of a Lady*, is receiving compliments from audiences and critics alike. Inspired by the real-life story of artist Amelia Cotter, Harvey has written a play about a woman who becomes a famous painter after a car accident leaves her bedridden. Even the title, *Portrait of a Lady*, was taken from the name of one of Cotter's paintings. The show is two-hours long with a twenty-minute intermission.

The closing night performance will be on October 18 at 7 P.M. For this one night only, we have partnered with the nearby Savio Restaurant, known for its vegetarian dishes and exclusive use of local ingredients. After watching the play, simply present your theater ticket as a complimentary dinner voucher. The limit is one free meal per table.

With few show times remaining, seats at the box office are selling out fast. Get yours before they are all gone!

Rates:

Section	Child	Adult	Group Discount*
Dress Circle	$17.99	$39.99	$35.99
Balcony	$17.99	$49.99	$44.99
Orchestra	$17.99	$59.99	$50.39

*Groups of 20 or more will receive a 10% discount.

149. Who is Amelia Cotter?

(A) A fictional character
(B) A real-life painter
(C) A famous novelist
(D) A box office attendant

150. What will happen on October 18?

(A) The play *Portrait of a Lady* will open.
(B) The box office will be closed.
(C) Group discounts will not be available.
(D) The theater will partner with a restaurant.

151. What is indicated about ticket prices?

(A) Balcony seats are the least expensive.
(B) Groups are given a 15% discount.
(C) Children's ticket prices never change.
(D) Students are given special pricing.

Questions 152-153 refer to the following text message chain.

KIERA WADE   9:02 A.M.
Hi, Reese. Sorry for the short notice, but would it be all right if I didn't come into the office today? There's a water leak in my house, and I'm waiting for the plumber to arrive. I was hoping to work from home instead.

REESE BENTLEY   9:03 A.M.
That's fine as long as you're able to get your project done on time.

KIERA WADE   9:06 A.M.
Of course. My plan is to work on it all day.

KIERA WADE   9:08 A.M.
I've just logged into my work desktop through the remote server, but I can't access the folder with our subscriber information.

REESE BENTLEY   9:10 A.M.
Oh, that's because yesterday I asked Drake to clean up some of the files and update the spreadsheet. So the folder will be locked until he's finished with it.

KIERA WADE   9:12 A.M.
Well, I just need to get the address for one particular subscriber. Is it possible to have him change the settings to "view only" just long enough for me to get the information I need?

REESE BENTLEY   9:14 A.M.
Let me check with him, but I think that's possible.

KIERA WADE   9:15 A.M.
Thank you so much!

152. Why did Ms. Wade contact Mr. Bentley?

(A) To request a deadline extension
(B) To get clarification about an assignment
(C) To report an expected absence
(D) To reschedule a staff meeting

153. At 9:14 A.M., what does Mr. Bentley mean when he writes, "Let me check with him"?

(A) He will ask Drake to give Ms. Wade his address.
(B) He will tell Drake to make a folder publicly accessible.
(C) He will instruct Drake to change file settings temporarily.
(D) He will request permission from Drake to work at home.

Questions 154-155 refer to the following notice.

NOTICE

For the next eight weeks, this cafeteria will be closed for renovations. The construction is anticipated to last from September 1 to October 31. We understand that this is an inconvenience to employees who will not be able to use the facilities during this time. Therefore, we have negotiated relationships with several nearby restaurants. Until our cafeteria reopens, all employees will receive a 50% discount at all of the establishments listed on the attached document. At the time of order, just present your employee ID card to receive the discount.

154. Where would the notice most likely be found?

(A) In a storage room
(B) Outside a cafeteria
(C) In a parking area
(D) Inside an elevator

155. What are employees offered?

(A) Discounts at local eateries
(B) Complimentary meal delivery
(C) Reimbursement for food purchases
(D) Use of an alternate facility

Questions 156-158 refer to the following information.

Employee Profile: Tammy Wyatt

Tammy Wyatt currently serves as the director of marketing here at Indigo Apparel. She joined our company fifteen years ago as a summer intern while she was completing her master's degree. — [1] — Over the years, she has taken on positions of increasing responsibility, eventually working her way to the top of the department. She took over the director of marketing role four years ago. During this time, the company expanded internationally, creating unique marketing needs for each region. — [2] — Ms. Wyatt was able to handle these challenges with creativity and strong leadership, developing ad campaigns that suited the tastes of different audiences. This has helped us to increase our market share by as much as 30% in some areas.

Indigo Apparel has benefited greatly from Ms. Wyatt's hard work and expertise. — [3] — She developed an online system for customers that allowed them to enroll in weekly competitions at the touch of a button by sharing their ideas on social media. This helped to build brand awareness among our target demographic of young consumers. Her forward thinking also led to the company's creation of its own channel on the popular video-sharing Web site *Fashion View*. — [4] — Though it has now become common practice, this was innovative when she first came up with the idea, and popular videos with fashion tips and interviews with Indigo Apparel's designers have been viewed millions of times.

It is clear that Ms. Wyatt is an essential part of the Indigo Apparel team, and we look forward to seeing her latest ideas in marketing and public relations.

156. What is true about Indigo Apparel?
(A) It is currently recruiting new designers.
(B) Its director of marketing will retire soon.
(C) It is the largest clothing store in the industry.
(D) It operates in more than one country.

157. What did Ms. Wyatt make easier for customers to do?
(A) Place orders online
(B) Find a store branch
(C) Share their videos
(D) Sign up for contests

158. In which of the positions marked [1], [2], [3] and [4] does the following sentence best belong?

"We were one of the first companies in the industry to do so."

(A) [1]
(B) [2]
(C) [3]
(D) [4]

Questions 159-160 refer to the following Web site.

| HOME | **ABOUT US** | LECTURE SERIES | PRESS | CONTACT US |

Right Start Education (RSE) is a nonprofit educational organization founded by middle school teacher Lynn Flores. Throughout her career, Ms. Flores saw firsthand how students with learning difficulties fell further and further behind their peers. Many of these students came from low-income families who did not have the resources to provide the necessary additional support. RSE's mission is to offer one-on-one tutoring to students aged 5 to 14 at its head office downtown and at various learning centers throughout the area.

RSE relies on support from the public, as funding is not provided by the government. If you would like to donate to RSE, please click HERE and complete the donation form. Credit cards and bank transfers are accepted. If you are interested in becoming a volunteer for RSE, please contact Annette McGuire at amcguire@rightstartedu.org.

159. What is NOT true about RSE?

(A) It provides individual teaching.
(B) It is targeted at high school students.
(C) It was started by an instructor.
(D) Its headquarters is in the city center.

160. According to the Web site, how can people make a financial contribution?

(A) By sending a check
(B) By attending a banquet
(C) By e-mailing Ms. McGuire
(D) By filling out an online form

Questions 161-163 refer to the following job advertisement.

Opening: Technical Support Representative

TP Recruiting is filling a full-time position in the field of technology.

Working in an inbound call center environment, the technical support representative will be in charge of answering customer phone calls and providing resolution to technical and network problems. Technical support representatives are considered computer specialists and are expected to diagnose various problems through a series of questions and answers. Simultaneously, representatives must guide users step-by-step through solutions to various technological problems. These problems include—among other issues—recovering usernames and passwords, uninstalling/reinstalling basic software applications, and troubleshooting e-mail issues.

The ideal candidate will have a friendly attitude, a tendency toward the positive, and be able to clearly communicate technical solutions in a straightforward, professional manner. Candidates with previous call center experience are preferred and will be put at the top of the shortlist for consideration.

Interested individuals should apply for this position by e-mailing their credentials (cover letter, résumé, and one written recommendation) to the human resources director, Virgil Samuels, at vsamuels@tprecruiting.com by March 4. After carefully reviewing the qualifications and receiving verification of previous employment, candidates selected for an interview will be contacted.

161. How are the technical support representative's duties performed?

(A) Through in-person meetings
(B) Over the telephone
(C) Via e-mail correspondence
(D) By faxing documents

162. What is NOT mentioned as a desirable qualification of the position?

(A) Experience working in a call center
(B) A friendly demeanor
(C) The ability to communicate clearly
(D) A certificate in computer technology

163. What are candidates told to include in their applications?

(A) A document verifying their education
(B) A list of potential references
(C) A formal cover letter
(D) A completed application form

Questions 164-167 refer to the following article.

April 8—Washing, drying, and folding clothes is a chore that few people enjoy. That's where Ryan Co. comes in. The company was founded by two brothers, Douglas and Johnathan Ryan, who wanted to apply their entrepreneurial spirit to an everyday problem. — [1] — Their company has storage lockers for rent in apartment buildings and other sites all over town. Customers are assigned a locker on a monthly, quarterly, or annual basis. They put their dirty clothing in the secure locker and use a smartphone app to request the service. The clothes are then laundered by the company and returned to the locker. A text message informs the customer that their clothes are ready to be picked up.

"We came up with the idea one day when looking at the lockers after working out at the gym," says Douglas Ryan. "We were talking about how convenient it would be to have a drop-off point closer to home rather than making a special trip to the dry-cleaners." — [2] —

The two brothers originally tried a business model that offered dry-cleaning only, but they had trouble attracting customers because so many dry-cleaning businesses offer free delivery. The business ended in failure. However, this didn't stop the brothers from trying again. — [3] — It had a price point that was affordable for a larger number of people.

Ryan Co. has been in operation for just three months but has already become one of the hottest new businesses in town. In fact, the lockers are at full capacity, and there is a waiting list. — [4] — Since the current customers aren't expected to give up their lockers anytime soon, the Ryan brothers are looking for more sites to place lockers next month.

164. What kind of business is Ryan Co.?

(A) A clothing store chain
(B) A food delivery service
(C) A fashion studio
(D) A laundry cleaning service

165. Where did the founders get the idea for the business?

(A) From a business course
(B) From a television commercial
(C) From a friend's recommendation
(D) From a visit to a fitness facility

166. What will the company most likely do in May?

(A) Offer employee training
(B) Improve its smartphone app
(C) Increase its prices
(D) Add more locations

167. In which of the positions marked [1], [2], [3] and [4] does the following sentence best belong?

"The new business model, which became the basis for Ryan Co., focused on everyday clothing."

(A) [1]
(B) [2]
(C) [3]
(D) [4]

GO ON TO THE NEXT PAGE ➡ 209

Questions 168-171 refer to the following online chat discussion.

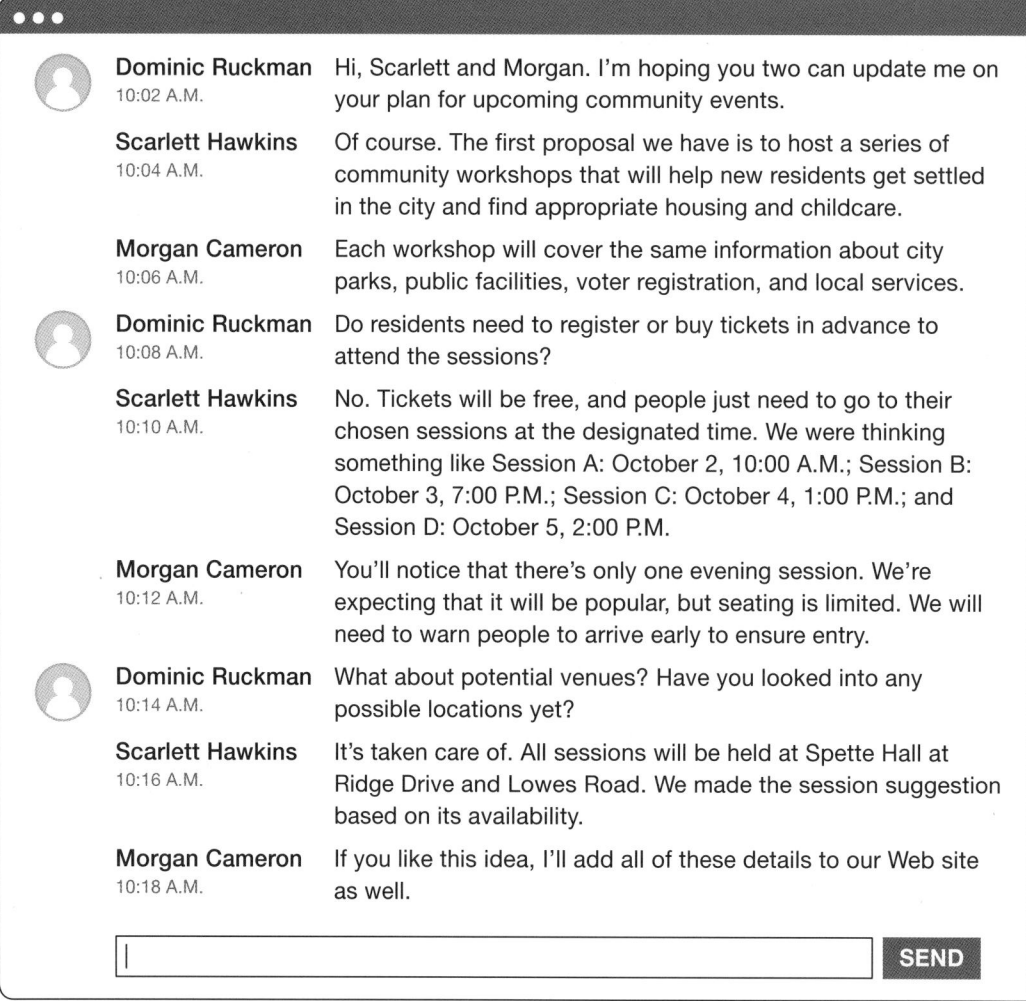

168. Who are the workshops intended for?

(A) People who have recently relocated
(B) Parents of young children
(C) Residents looking for work
(D) Visitors planning to tour the city

169. Which session is expected to fill up?

(A) Session A
(B) Session B
(C) Session C
(D) Session D

170. At 10:16 A.M., what does Ms. Hawkins mean when she writes, "It's taken care of"?

(A) She has confirmed speakers for each session.
(B) She has created an event advertisement.
(C) She has selected the location of the workshops.
(D) She has already set aside the tickets.

171. What does Ms. Cameron offer to do?

(A) Add photos to a Web site
(B) Tour possible venues
(C) Get some tickets printed
(D) Post information online

Questions 172-175 refer to the following letter.

Heather Ingram
1950 Jarvis Street
Buffalo, NY 14214

November 1

Dear Ms. Ingram,

I would like to bring to your attention an urgent matter regarding your account with Vine Satellite Television Services (VSTS). You have an outstanding balance of $59.50, which was due on October 15. This charge is for services you received at your residence at 1950 Jarvis Street. Our records show that you requested a service cancellation on September 14 and that the service was cut off on September 28, as two weeks' notice is required for all account changes. Therefore, the remaining charge is for the services rendered in September along with a $15 late fee.

I tried to contact you several times over the past few weeks. At first, I kept getting no answer at the phone number you provided when you signed up for the service last year. In the most recent call, I got a recorded message saying that the number was no longer in service. I do hope this letter reaches you, as it is important for you to settle this bill as quickly as possible.

Enclosed you will find an updated bill with the summary of the charges. This is the same as your previous bill but with the $15 late fee added. Please pay the amount in full to VSTS immediately. You can do so by visiting our Web site at www.vinests.com or by making a bank transfer. Detailed instructions are included on the back of the bill. If you do not make the payment by November 30, your account will be charged another late fee of $15. Therefore, I urge you to resolve the matter promptly.

Sincerely,

Leon Frost
Customer Service Agent, Vine Satellite Television Services

172. Why did Ms. Ingram receive the letter?

(A) She requested some company information.
(B) She failed to make a final payment.
(C) She may be interested in a new product.
(D) She made a complaint about a service.

173. According to the letter, what did Ms. Ingram do in September?

(A) Requested a repair
(B) Upgraded a package
(C) Canceled a service
(D) Moved to a new home

174. What did Mr. Frost have trouble doing?

(A) Contacting Ms. Ingram by phone
(B) Scheduling an installation appointment
(C) Finding Ms. Ingram's mailing address
(D) Accessing an online account

175. What will happen if Ms. Ingram does not take action by the end of November?

(A) She will be charged an additional fee.
(B) She will be contacted again by Mr. Frost.
(C) She will have her service cut off.
(D) She will miss out on a special promotion.

GO ON TO THE NEXT PAGE

Questions 176-180 refer to the following article and form.

Oxford (December 5)—The archives of prominent legal scholar and university professor Landon Fry are available in the Paragon Law Library, a research library located on Broad Street. The archives, which contain thousands of pages of documentation, are housed in the Brontë room. "Landon Fry was one of our nation's most brilliant legal minds," announced the archives facilitator, Ms. McDonald. His works analyzing the most significant aspects of constitutional law have been invaluable to law students and professors alike. The Paragon Law Library has recently compiled all his works into one large viewable assembly.

Within the Paragon Law library is a massive collection of case studies, legal briefs, rare legal books, and notable legal commentaries like that of Landon Fry.

This library is designed solely for on-site research purposes. It is mandatory for all new visitors to go to the reception desk to read and sign a form declaring that they understand the regulations of the library. Failure to follow the rules outlined in that declaration will result in confiscation of any banned items, immediate escort off the property, and possible fines or long-term suspensions.

Paragon Law Library Declaration Form

Name: Caroline Burr

As a library patron, I agree not to remove from the library archives—or to mark, deface, or injure in any way—any volume, document, or other object in their custody.

I promise to promote and protect an environment in the library that is conducive to legal research and study. I will do so by refraining from any activity or behavior that could disrupt and/or distract from the academic work of others. I will refrain from eating, smoking, or drinking in the library and will abstain from making noises through speech, music, or otherwise.

I, *Caroline Burr*, have read, understood, and agreed to the above terms and conditions. I further acknowledge and agree to the corresponding punishments for breaking these conditions.

Signature: *Caroline Burr*

176. What is the article mainly about?

(A) The organization of a law conference
(B) The research necessary for a trial
(C) The works of a brilliant man
(D) The disposal of archival material

177. What is NOT stated about Mr. Fry?

(A) He is a recognized legal scholar.
(B) He has written about constitutional law.
(C) He teaches courses at a university.
(D) He is retired from academia.

178. Who is Ms. McDonald?

(A) A library employee
(B) A research assistant
(C) A legal secretary
(D) A regular patron

179. What is true about the Paragon Law Library?

(A) Its employees have legal backgrounds.
(B) All of its documents must remain in the library.
(C) Its books are all available electronically.
(D) Its patrons are allowed to make photocopies.

180. What is NOT a punishment Ms. Burr risks by smoking in the library?

(A) Suspension from the library
(B) Prompt removal from the building
(C) Personal library card confiscation
(D) An assignment of fines

Questions 181-185 refer to the following article and Web site.

Dance is Back at the Majesty
By Loretta Benderly

Majesty Theater has announced its twelfth annual dance spectacle, entitled *The Festival of Movement*. In the springtime each year, the theater gathers dancers from around the world. Together, they showcase all that dance has to offer, encompassing all genres from tap to hip hop.

The highlight of this year's three-day festival will be a wordless play scheduled for May 9. This unique performance is entirely void of dialogue. Without any narrative, the story is told through the artistry of dance and music alone. The festival performances are traditionally held in Waltman Hall every year. However, the stage was closed earlier this year for some reconstructive work, and all shows were switched to one of the three smaller halls—McManus Hall, Gilderton Hall, and Alexandra Hall. This renovation project was expected to continue until June 15, but the work has progressed more rapidly than anticipated. As a result, all performances throughout the month of May will be moved back to Waltman Hall as originally planned.

As an exclusive privilege to Majesty Theater members, festival tickets can be purchased in advance and at 25% off the standard price. To take advantage of the discount, members must buy tickets before March 31. Starting of April 1, tickets to *The Festival of Movement* will be open to the general public.

---

www.majestytheater.com

| Home | Schedule | Ticket Info | **Contact** |

Name: Janet Vandersoek
Date: March 25
Subject: Ticket purchase

Message: I just completed my purchase of two tickets for the wordless dance performance. I followed the Web site's instructions, completed the order, and was able to print tickets without any difficulty. However, while looking at them I realized that I paid full price even though I should have received the 25% discount. I don't remember that being an option on the screen when I was processing the payment. Obviously, I have not missed the deadline, so I'm hoping someone can advise me on how to resolve the problem.

Thank you,

Janet Vandersoek

181. Why was the article written?

(A) To describe a renovation
(B) To advertise an annual event
(C) To promote a dance class
(D) To request funding from patrons

182. What is indicated about *The Festival of Movement*?

(A) Ballroom dancing is its focus.
(B) All dancers come from nearby cities.
(C) The performances will last for four days.
(D) A wide range of styles will be featured.

183. Where will the wordless performance be held?

(A) In Alexandra Hall
(B) In Gilderton Hall
(C) In McManus Hall
(D) In Waltman Hall

184. On what day will Ms. Vandersoek attend the theater?

(A) March 31
(B) April 1
(C) May 9
(D) June 15

185. What is suggested about Ms. Vandersoek?

(A) She overpaid for her tickets.
(B) She wants to cancel her purchase.
(C) She encountered problems printing tickets.
(D) She missed the member deadline.

Questions 186-190 refer to the following article, Web site and notice.

War of the Mountains Opens Friday
Dean Ziegler

The much-awaited second installment of the action-adventure *Mountaineer* has arrived! *War of the Mountains*, the second in a trilogy, opens in cinemas on Friday. Audiences have waited over a year for the release of this film. Although Padilla Studios spent a great deal of money on trailers and posters to promote the movie, very few details have been released about what will actually occur during the film's two hours and forty-five minutes. There has been much speculation that there will be one major death in this movie, but that claim remains unconfirmed by anyone involved with the film. When questioned, director Kristin Gaudet remained very tightlipped. "It's a rollercoaster ride of action and emotions. There is a lot that viewers won't see coming. That's all I'll reveal," she said.

Despite the lack of information about what will happen in the movie, fan anticipation is high, and the movie is expected to surpass the original in opening weekend ticket sales. Tickets for *War of the Mountains* are available online at www.movietickets.org or can be purchased at individual theaters. Prices vary according to the movie type, four of which are being offered for this film: 2D: $9.99, Imax: $12.99, 3D: $15.99, and 4D: $22.99.

---

www.movietickets.org

MOVIE SELECTION SCREEN

Name	Cell phone number	E-mail address
Daphne Dorsey	---	dapdorsey@netmail.org

■ I don't have a cell phone, so please send the reservation to my e-mail instead.

THEATER AND TICKET INFO

Bisenzio Cinema
War of the Mountains, 3D
April 2, 8:10 P.M., Cinema 9
Be sure to check your show time again before moving to the payment screen.

I prefer seats that are:

Column	☐ right side	■ center block	☐ left side
Row	☐ front	■ middle	☐ back

Proceed to payment

ATTENTION, MOVIEGOERS

Due to a technical issue, Cinemas 8 and 9 are unavailable for movie showings this evening.

Because we have another theater that can accommodate 3D movies, ticket holders for the 3D showings should go to Cinema 12 instead.

Unfortunately, Cinema 8 is our only 4D theater, so ticket holders for this film should visit the customer service desk. We apologize for the inconvenience and will not only refund these tickets in full, but will also give patrons free ticket passes to see this film at a later date.

186. What is indicated about *War of the Mountains*?

(A) It is a low-budget movie.
(B) It is the follow-up to a popular film.
(C) It is an animated picture for children.
(D) It has an all-star cast.

187. In the article, the word "deal" in paragraph 1, line 4, is closest in meaning to

(A) agreement
(B) bargain
(C) amount
(D) treatment

188. How much did Ms. Dorsey most likely pay for her ticket?

(A) $9.99
(B) $12.99
(C) $15.99
(D) $22.99

189. What is true about Ms. Dorsey?

(A) She is expected to arrive after 8:10 P.M.
(B) She made a reservation on the phone.
(C) She prefers an e-mail notification.
(D) She wants to sit near the back.

190. In what cinema will Ms. Dorsey see the movie?

(A) Cinema 5
(B) Cinema 8
(C) Cinema 9
(D) Cinema 12

Questions 191-195 refer to the following Web site, form and e-mail.

---

www.barnettcollege.edu

| **HOME** | MY COURSES | MY ACCOUNT | CONTACT US | LOG OUT |

We are excited to announce that your course instructor evaluations are now available under the "My Courses" section of your online account. While you will still receive an evaluation link via e-mail as usual, as a distance education student, you will also have the option to simply log into your online student account to complete and submit your course evaluation in a few simple steps. Our intention was to make the process of filling out evaluations for your classes easier and more convenient.

We wish to thank you in advance for your participation. Student feedback plays an essential role in helping Barnett College continue to improve its course offerings. We use the information to ensure that we're providing both courses and instructors that fit your educational needs and goals. Because your responses have a direct impact on the future of Barnett College, please take the time to give honest and accurate feedback.

TEACHING EVALUATION

Student Name: Cliffe Fonseca
Instructor Name: Dr. Susan Borre
Course Title: Medieval Poetry
Course Code: 3116E

	Strongly disagree	Disagree	Neutral	Agree	Strongly Agree
The syllabus was comprehensive, clear, and accurate.	☐	☐	☐	☐	■
The content of tests and assignments was consistent with content of lectures and readings.	☐	☐	☐	☐	■
The grading policies were clear and consistently followed.	☐	☐	☐	☐	■
The instructor showed concern for student learning and development.	☐	☐	■	☐	☐

Would you recommend this instructor to others? Why or why not?

Yes, I would recommend Dr. Borre. I've been in one of her classes on campus before (Restoration Literature). I thought both that class and my recently completed class were worthwhile and inspiring.

Please identify the aspects of the course you found most useful or valuable for learning.

The lectures were quite interesting and full of details that expanded upon the readings.

What suggestions would you make to the instructor for improving the course?

It's difficult to interact through distance studies courses, but overall, Dr. Borre did a great job. I think it might help if she encouraged more online discussions.

To: Susan Borre <borre@barnettcollege.edu>
From: Wanda Ringler <ringler@barnettcollege.edu>
Date: May 26
Subject: Returning next semester

Dear Dr. Borre,

As you are aware, at the end of each course, students are obligated to complete course evaluations that indicate their opinions of the course itself as well as of the instructor. We use these evaluations to help us recognize extraordinary members of our faculty. You have consistently received very positive teaching evaluations. We would, therefore, like to invite you to add another class, British Authors, to your teaching schedule for next semester. This would be in addition to the online course, Medieval Poetry. Since you've taught both of these classes before, I think the preparation time would be minimal.

We have tentatively scheduled the class for Tuesdays and Thursdays at 2 P.M. It would take place in room 207, which was originally scheduled for the Modern Shakespeare class taught by Professor Brian Rocco. We expect very low enrollment for that class, so we plan to move it to the spring semester next year.

If you are able to accept this additional responsibility, please let me know as soon as possible so that we may include the information in the course catalog.

Best wishes,

Wanda Ringler
HR Recruitment Manager,
Barnett College

---

191. Who is being asked to fill out evaluation forms?

(A) College students
(B) Course instructors
(C) Teaching assistants
(D) HR personnel

192. What can be inferred about Mr. Fonseca?

(A) He requested an e-mail-based evaluation.
(B) He recently transferred to Barnett College.
(C) He completed his course online.
(D) He plans to take a class from Dr. Borre again.

193. According to Mr. Fonseca, how could Dr. Borre improve her course in the future?

(A) By grading assignments more fairly
(B) By increasing the amount of discussion
(C) By making her lectures more entertaining
(D) By creating a more organized syllabus

194. What was the main purpose of the e-mail?

(A) To introduce a new policy
(B) To ask Dr. Borre to complete a survey
(C) To offer a teaching position
(D) To analyze evaluation results

195. What is NOT indicated as a course taught by Dr. Borre?

(A) British Authors
(B) Medieval Poetry
(C) Modern Shakespeare
(D) Restoration Literature

Questions 196-200 refer to the following e-mails and schedule.

To: Ryan Ashcroft <ashcroftr@newburncollege.net>
From: Anastasia Cusack <cusack@inspirekey.com>
Date: March 18
Subject: Scheduling Conflict

Dear Mr. Ashcroft,

I am writing to notify you that due to unforeseen circumstances, I will no longer be able to give the Wednesday afternoon talk at the 2nd Annual Newburn College Online Business Workshop Series. Unfortunately, I have been given a mandatory work assignment to meet with a client overseas, so I will be out of the country for the week during which you are holding the workshop. I would be happy to suggest some possible replacements for my talk, as I have several colleagues who might be interested in participating in your event.

I deeply regret that I cannot keep the commitment I made, especially since I so thoroughly enjoyed my participation in these workshops last year. I hope that you will still consider me as a speaker for next year.

My apologies again,

Anastasia Cusack
Inspirekey Marketing

To: Leila Wortham <leilawortham@inbound.plus>
From: Ryan Ashcroft <ashcroftr@newburncollege.net>
Date: March 22
Subject: Workshop Series
Attachment: Amended Schedule

Dear Ms. Wortham,

I want to inform you about some changes in the upcoming 2nd Annual Newburn College Online Business Workshop Series. I've attached the new schedule to this e-mail.

I'm disappointed to tell you that the Wednesday afternoon talk that you registered for, "Mobile Marketing," has been replaced with "Designs that Work." The original talk was canceled due to problems with the speaker's schedule. I apologize for any inconvenience this change may cause. Unfortunately, it was out of our control. You have been automatically enrolled in the replacement lecture. However, if you prefer not to attend it, please e-mail me back, and I will process a refund for you.

The rest of the talks on the schedule will remain the same, so there are no issues with the talk by Linda Rinaldi that you also signed up for on March 10. You may direct questions to my office at 555-2342.

Thank you for your understanding,

Ryan Ashcroft
Newburn College Workshops Organizer

Second Newburn College Online Business Workshop Series
AMENDED SCHEDULE

Time	Lecture	Speaker
Monday, 8 A.M.–12 P.M.	Customer Care	Customer Service Supervisor, Linda Rinaldi
Monday, 1 P.M.–5 P.M.	Planning Your Budget	Finance Manager, Iliza Waldron
Tuesday, 8 A.M.–12 P.M.	Maximizing Social Media	Advertising Director, Elsie Ocampo
Tuesday, 1 P.M.–5 P.M.	Measuring Results	Consultant, Larry Palmer
Wednesday, 8 A.M.–12 P.M.	Trends and Planning	Web Analyst, Cassandra Valle
Wednesday, 1 P.M.–5 P.M.	Designs that Work	Graphic Designer, Jean Breaux

196. What was the name of Ms. Cusack's lecture?

(A) Planning Your Budget
(B) Mobile Marketing
(C) Designs that Work
(D) Measuring Results

197. In the first e-mail, the word "keep" in paragraph 2, line 1, is closest in meaning to

(A) fulfill
(B) store
(C) retain
(D) prevent

198. What is the purpose of the second e-mail?

(A) To advertise a training program
(B) To invite a person to a workshop
(C) To confirm attendance at a lecture
(D) To give an update about an event

199. Which time slot was part of Ms. Wortham's March 10 registration?

(A) Monday morning
(B) Monday afternoon
(C) Tuesday morning
(D) Tuesday afternoon

200. Whose lecture would be best for those interested in online networking sites?

(A) Iliza Waldron's
(B) Elsie Ocampo's
(C) Larry Palmer's
(D) Cassandra Valle's

지은이

NE능률 영어교육연구소
NE능률 영어교육연구소는 혁신적이며 효율적인 영어교재를 개발하고
영어 학습의 질을 한 단계 높이고자 노력하는 NE능률의 연구 조직입니다.

토마토 토익 PART 7 전략

펴 낸 이	주민홍
펴 낸 곳	서울특별시 마포구 월드컵북로 396(상암동) 누리꿈스퀘어 비즈니스타워 10층 (주)NE능률 (우편번호 03925)
펴 낸 날	2019년 12월 2일 초판 제1쇄
전　　화	02 2014 7114
팩　　스	02 3142 0356
홈페이지	www.tomatoclass.com
등록번호	제 1-68호
정　　가	17,000원
I S B N	979-11-253-3122-3

NE능률

고객센터

교재 내용 문의 www.tomatoclass.com → 토마토교재 → 교재 Q&A
제품 구매, 교환, 불량, 반품 문의 (02-2014-7114)
☎ 전화 문의는 본사 업무 시간 중에만 가능합니다.

NE능률의 모든 교재가 한 곳에 - 엔이 북스
NE_Books

www.nebooks.co.kr ▼

NE능률의 유초등 교재부터 중고생 참고서,
토익·토플 수험서와 일반 영어까지!
PC는 물론 태블릿 PC, 스마트폰으로 언제 어디서나
NE능률의 교재와 다양한 학습 자료를 만나보세요.

- ✓ 필요한 부가 학습 자료 바로 찾기
- ✓ 주요 인기 교재들을 한눈에 확인
- ✓ 나에게 딱 맞는 교재를 찾아주는 스마트 검색
- ✓ 함께 보면 좋은 교재와 다음 단계 교재 추천
- ✓ 회원 가입, 교재 후기 작성 등 사이트 활동 시 NE Point 적립

건강한 배움의 즐거움

영어교과서 리딩튜터 능률보카 빠른독해 바른독해 수능만만 월등한 개념 수학 유형더블 토마토 토익 NE 클래스
NE_Build & Grow   NE_Times   NE_Kids(굿잡,상상수프)   NE_능률 주니어랩   아이챌린지

100% 토익 기출 어휘를 그대로 구운

토마토 토익
Vocachip

최신 토익
빈출 어휘
30일 완성!!

- 최신 빈출 어휘 3,000단어 수록 및 단어장 제공
- 파트 5&6 실전 내용 강화
- 3단계 반복학습 장치
  (망각방지 Test / Check up / Review Test)
- 미국식, 영국식 발음의 MP3 무료 다운로드
- 자가 테스트 및 Study 활용 가능한 문제 출제 마법사 및 온라인 어휘 테스트 제공

음성 MP3 / 문제 출제 마법사 / 온라인 어휘 테스트
토마토 토익 공식 홈페이지(www.tomatoclass.com)에서 이용 가능합니다.

정가 12,000원

NE
능률

토익 점수 마구 올려주는 토익

토마토 토익

TOMATO TOEIC ★ SINCE 2002

PART 7 전략

정답 및 해설

NE 능률

토마토 토익

PART 7 전략

정답 및 해설

CHAPTER 1 문제 유형
UNIT 01 의도 파악 문제

PRE-STEP p.13

A 1 (A) 2 (A) 3 (B) 4 (B) 5 (A) 6 (B) 7 (A) 8 (A) 9 (B)
   10 (B) 11 (A) 12 (B) 13 (A) 14 (B) 15 (B)

B 1 (A) 2 (B)

A
1 (A) respond, 질문들에 대답하다
2 (A) technical, 기술적 문제를 보고하다
3 (B) book, 컨벤션 홀을 예약하다
4 (B) casual, 가벼운 약속
5 (A) client, 중요한 고객
6 (B) postpone, 회의를 연기하다
7 (A) contract, 계약을 제안하다
8 (A) position, 행정 보조원 직
9 (B) decoration, 장식을 하다
10 (B) flight, 베를린행 비행기를 타다
11 (A) connecting, 연결 열차편
12 (B) confirmation, 확인서를 보내다
13 (A) reserve, 회의실을 예약하다
14 (B) conduct, 면접을 진행하다
15 (B) retirement, 은퇴 기념 파티

B
1 I'm wondering if you could pick up the flower arrangements on your way here.
(A) I'd like you to bring what I ordered with you when you come.
(B) I'd like assistance in selecting which flowers would be best.

당신이 여기 오는 길에 꽃꽂이를 가져다 주실 수 있는지 궁금하네요.
(A) 오시는 길에 제가 주문한 것을 가져다 주시면 좋겠어요.
(B) 어떤 꽃이 가장 좋을지를 고르는 데 도움이 필요해요.

2 It needs to be filled as soon as possible, so I'd rather not delay it.
(A) The event must be postponed.
(B) The matter should be handled urgently.

가능한 한 빨리 그 자리가 채워져야 해서, 그것을 연기하고 싶지 않아요.
(A) 행사가 연기되어야만 해요.
(B) 그 문제는 급히 처리되어야만 해요.

MAIN STEP 1 p.14

 회의 진행 관련 문자메시지

ZACH WALKER	13:52

My lunch meeting ran longer than expected, so I'm just leaving now.

LARA STONE 13:53
Oh, really? How long is it going to take you to get to the Briarcliff Building?

ZACH WALKER 13:56
Approximately 45 minutes. I won't be there for the start of the presentation.

LARA STONE 13:58
Okay, I'll go ahead without you. I'm familiar with the information on the slides, and you can respond to questions when you arrive.

ZACH WALKER 14:00
Sounds great. Thanks!

잭 워커 13:52
제 점심 회의가 예상보다 길어져서, 지금 막 출발할 거예요.

라라 스톤 13:53
아, 정말요? 당신이 브라이어클리프 빌딩에 도착하는 데 얼마나 걸릴까요?

잭 워커 13:56
약 45분 정도요. 발표 시작 시간에는 제가 그곳에 없을 거예요.

라라 스톤 13:58
그래요, 당신 없이 진행할게요. 제가 슬라이드의 내용을 잘 알고 있으니까, 당신은 도착해서 질문들에 대답하세요.

잭 워커 14:00
좋아요. 고마워요!

> **어휘** expect 예상하다 approximately 대략 presentation 발표, 프레젠테이션 go ahead 진행하다 be familiar with ~에 대해 잘 알다[익숙하다] respond to ~에 대답하다

13:58에, 스톤 씨가 "당신 없이 진행할게요"라고 하는 의도는?
(A) 워커 씨에게 질문을 문자로 보낼 것이다.
(B) 회의를 혼자 주도하는 데 동의한다.

해설 문제에서 주어진 표현 "I'll go ahead without you." 앞에서 워커 씨는 발표 시작 시간에 갈 수 없을 것이라 했다. 이에 대해 스톤 씨는 자신이 슬라이드의 내용을 잘 알고 있다고 했다. 따라서 "당신 없이 진행할게요"라는 스톤 씨의 말은 워커 씨 없이도 발표를 진행할 것이라는 뜻임을 알 수 있다. 정답은 (B).

MAIN STEP 2   p.15

1 (C)   **2** (C)

[1-2] 은퇴 기념 파티 준비에 관한 문자메시지

> **ANNE MITCHELL**   4:36 P.M.
> (1)Thanks for booking the convention hall for Ms. Taylor's retirement party.
>
> **SUE CLAUSEN**   4:37 P.M.
> My pleasure. I think it will be a better place for the event than a restaurant.
>
> **ANNE MITCHELL**   4:39 P.M.
> I'm glad to hear that. Are you already setting up?
>
> **SUE CLAUSEN**   4:40 P.M.
> (1)Yes, I'm here now, putting up the decorations. But I'm wondering if you could pick up the flower arrangements on your way here.
>
> **ANNE MITCHELL**   4:43 P.M.
> Sure. I'm leaving the office soon. They're at Gail's Flowers, right?
>
> **SUE CLAUSEN**   4:44 P.M
> Actually, no. I used Diamond Florists instead. (2)Have you been there before?
>
> **ANNE MITCHELL**   4:46 P.M.
> It's my first time.
>
> **SUE CLAUSEN**   4:47 P.M.
> (2)It's really easy to find. I'll send you a map. And you can call me if you have any trouble.
>
> **어휘** book 예약하다 retirement party 은퇴 기념 파티 set up ~을 준비하다 put up decorations 장식을 하다 flower arrangement 꽃꽂이

앤 미첼   오후 4:36
(1)테일러 씨의 은퇴 기념 파티를 위해 컨벤션 홀을 예약해 줘서 고마워요.

수 클로센   오후 4:37
천만에요. 레스토랑보다는 그곳이 이벤트에 더 나은 장소일 거라고 생각해요.

앤 미첼   오후 4:39
그 얘기를 들으니 기쁘네요. 벌써 준비하는 중인가요?

수 클로센   오후 4:40
(1)네, 여기서 장식을 하고 있어요. 그런데 당신이 여기 오는 길에 꽃꽂이를 가져다 주실 수 있는지 궁금하네요.

앤 미첼   오후 4:43
그럼요. 금방 사무실을 나갈 거예요. 그게 게일즈 플라워에 있죠, 그렇죠?

수 클로센   오후 4:44
실은 아니에요. 대신에 저는 다이아몬드 플로리스트를 이용했어요. (2)전에 거기 가 보신 적 있나요?

앤 미첼   오후 4:46
처음이에요.

수 클로센   4:47 P.M.
(2)그곳은 정말 찾기 쉬워요. 지도를 보내드릴게요. 문제가 있으면 저한테 전화하시면 돼요.

1 클로센 씨는 지금 어디에 있을 것 같은가?
(A) 레스토랑
(B) 화자들의 사무실
(C) 모임 장소
(D) 꽃집

해설 단서(1)에서 클로센 씨가 컨벤션 홀을 예약했다고 했고, 준비 중이냐는 미첼 씨의 질문에 여기서 장식을 하고 있다고 했으므로 클로센 씨는 지금 컨벤션 홀에 있음을 알 수 있다. 정답은 (C).

패러프레이징 지문의 convention hall이 정답에서 meeting venue로 패러프레이징되었다.

2 오후 4:46에, 미첼 씨가 "처음이에요"라고 하는 의도는?

  (A) 신규 고객 할인을 받을 수 있다.
  (B) 서비스에 가입하고 싶어 한다.
  (C) 위치에 대한 길 안내가 필요하다.
  (D) 업체를 추천해 줄 수 없다.

해설 문제에서 주어진 표현 "It's my first time" 앞의 단서(2)에서 클로센 씨는 미첼 씨에게 특정 장소에 전에 가 본 적이 있는지 물었다. 해당 표현 뒤의 단서(2)에서 클로센 씨가 그곳이 찾기 쉽다고 하면서 지도를 보낸다고 했으므로, "처음이에요"라는 미첼 씨의 말은 해당 장소까지의 길 안내가 필요하다는 뜻임을 알 수 있다. 정답은 (C).

FINAL STEP   p.16

1 (C)   2 (D)   3 (D)   4 (A)   5 (B)   6 (C)

[1-2] 비행기 티켓 예약에 관한 문자메시지

ROXANNA BLACK   1:23 P.M.
(1)Your hotel is reserved and I'm working on booking the flights for your trip to Berlin. Do you have any airline preferences?

ARTHUR COVEY   1:26 P.M.
I'm a member of the frequent flyer programs for Eagle Airways and World Air. One of those, if possible.

ROXANNA BLACK   1:31 P.M.
Okay. It looks like the lowest fare is $985.82, with World Air.

ARTHUR COVEY   1:33 P.M.
Perfect. And I'd like to arrive in Berlin as early as possible on that day.

ROXANNA BLACK   1:33 P.M.
This flight lands at 1:20 P.M.

ROXANNA BLACK   1:34 P.M.
But you'll stop in Brussels and then take the flight to Berlin. You'd only have 50 minutes. (2)I'm worried there's not enough time for the connecting flight.

ARTHUR COVEY   1:36 P.M.
No, that's plenty.

ROXANNA BLACK   1:37 P.M.
All right. I'll send you a confirmation by e-mail.

록사나 블랙   오후 1:23
(1)고객님의 호텔이 예약되어 고객님의 베를린 여행을 위한 항공편 예약을 처리하는 중입니다. 선호하시는 항공사가 있으신지요?

아서 코베이   오후 1:26
저는 이글 에어웨이즈와 월드 에어의 상용 고객 프로그램 회원입니다. 가능하다면 그중 한 곳으로요.

록사나 블랙   오후 1:31
알겠습니다. 가장 저렴한 요금은 월드 에어의 985.82달러입니다.

아서 코베이   오후 1:33
좋아요. 그리고 당일에 가능한 한 이르게 베를린에 도착하면 좋겠습니다.

록사나 블랙   오후 1:33
이 비행기는 오후 1시 20분에 착륙합니다.

록사나 블랙   오후 1:34
하지만 고객님께서는 브뤼셀에서 내리신 다음 베를린행 비행기를 타셔야 합니다. 50분밖에 없습니다. (2)연결 항공편으로 갈아타시는 데 시간이 충분하지 않을까 봐 염려가 되네요.

아서 코베이   오후 1:36
아니요, 충분합니다.

록사나 블랙   오후 1:37
알겠습니다. 이메일로 고객님께 확인서를 보내드리겠습니다.

어휘 reserve 예약하다 preference 선호하는 것 frequent flyer programs 상용 고객 프로그램 land 착륙하다 connecting flight 연결 항공편 confirmation 확인(서)

---

1 블랙 씨가 일할 것 같은 곳은?
  (A) 항공사
  (B) 호텔
  (C) 여행사
  (D) 극장

해설 단서(1)에서 블랙 씨는 아서 코베이 씨의 호텔을 예약하고 항공편 예약을 처리하는 중이라고 했으므로, 그녀가 여행사 직원임을 알 수 있다. 정답은 (C).
오답 피하기 hotel이나 flight이라는 단어만 보고 (A)나 (B)를 답으로 고르지 않도록 주의하자.

2 오후 1:36에, 코베이 씨가 "아니요, 충분합니다"라고 하는 의도는?
(A) 연결 항공편을 너무 많이 타고 싶지는 않다.
(B) 더 높은 요금을 치를 수 없다.
(C) 여권을 찾을 시간이 충분하다.
(D) 도중 하차에 만족한다.

해설 문제에서 주어진 표현 "No, that's plenty" 앞의 단서(2)에서 블랙 씨는 코베이 씨가 연결 항공편으로 갈아탈 시간이 충분치 않을 것을 우려하고 있다. 따라서 "아니요, 충분합니다"라는 코베이 씨의 말은 브뤼셀에 체류하는 도중 하차 시간(50분)에 만족한다는 뜻임을 알 수 있다. 정답은 (D).

[3-6] 회의실 예약에 관한 온라인 채팅 대화문

Jun Tien 10:41 A.M.
Do you have a few minutes to talk? (3)I noticed that both of you reserved the conference room for this afternoon. There was some kind of glitch in the system showing it was still available.

Sara Huber 10:42 A.M.
Did we reserve the exact same time? Maybe there isn't any overlap.

Jun Tien 10:44 A.M.
(3)Unfortunately, both of you requested it at 3 P.M. So one of you will have to postpone or cancel your meeting for today.

Diego Costa 10:47 A.M.
I'm afraid I can't. I'm proposing a new supply contract to Leo Borrego. He's a very important client for us, and it's difficult to get a meeting with him. Ms. Huber, what do you need the room for?

Sara Huber 10:48 A.M.
I'm interviewing Stacey Pelham for the administrative assistant position. It needs to be filled as soon as possible, so I'd rather not delay it.

Jun Tien 10:50 A.M.
Ms. Huber, since your appointment is more casual, (4)how about taking her to the coffee shop around the corner? It's usually quite empty at this time of day, so you could conduct the interview there.

Sara Huber 10:51 A.M.
I can make that work.

Diego Costa 10:52 A.M.
Thank you! (5)And I guess someone needs to tell the IT department about the glitch so they can fix it. I'll take care of that.

Jun Tien 10:53 A.M.
All right. And, Ms. Huber, (6)you should take the company credit card with you so you can buy the drinks. You can get it from me anytime before lunch.

Sara Huber 10:55 A.M.
Okay. (6)I'll do that now.

준 티엔 오전 10:41
잠깐 이야기하실 시간들 되세요? (3)두 분 다 오늘 오후에 회의실을 예약하신 것을 알았어요. 그곳이 아직 이용 가능하다고 안내하는 작은 오류가 시스템에 있었어요.

새라 후버 오전 10:42
우리가 똑같은 시간에 예약을 했다고요? 시간이 중복되지 않을 수도 있죠.

준 티엔 오전 10:44
(3)불행히도, 두 분 모두 3시에 그곳을 요청하셨어요. 그래서 두 분 중 한 분이 오늘 회의를 연기하거나 취소하셔야 해요.

디에고 코스타 오전 10:47
저는 안 될 것 같아요. 저는 리오 보레고 씨에게 새로운 공급 계약을 제안 중이에요. 그분은 우리에게 매우 중요한 고객이시고 그분과 회의를 잡는 것은 어렵거든요. 후버 씨, 회의실이 무엇 때문에 필요하세요?

새라 후버 오전 10:48
저는 행정 보조원 직에 스테이시 펠럼 씨 면접을 볼 거예요. 가능한 한 빨리 그 자리가 채워져야 해서, 그것을 연기하고 싶지 않아요.

준 티엔 오전 10:50
후버 씨, 당신의 약속이 좀 더 가벼운 것이니, (4)그분을 모퉁이 근처의 커피숍으로 모시고 가는 것은 어떠세요? 그곳은 이맘때쯤이면 거의 비어 있으니까, 그곳에서 면접을 진행하실 수 있을 거예요.

새라 후버 오전 10:51
그럴 수 있어요.

디에고 코스타 오전 10:52
고마워요! (5)그리고 누군가가 IT 부서에 오류에 대해 이야기해서 그걸 고치도록 해야 될 것 같아요. 제가 그것을 처리할게요.

준 티엔 오전 10:53
좋아요. 그리고 후버 씨, (6)회사 법인 카드를 가져가셔서 음료를 구입하도록 하세요. 점심 시간 전에 아무 때나 저한테 오셔서 가져가세요.

새라 후버 오전 10:55
네, (6)지금 할게요.

어휘 notice 알아채다, 인지하다 reserve 예약하다 glitch 작은 문제, 결함 available 이용 가능한 overlap 중복, 겹침 postpone 연기하다, 미루다 propose 제안하다 contract 계약 administrative assistant 행정 보조원 casual 가벼운, 격식을 차리지 않은 conduct 수행하다 fix 고치다

3 화자들이 논의 중인 문제는?
   (A) 몇몇 약속들이 취소되었다.
   (B) 배송이 제시간에 이루어지지 않을 것이다.
   (C) 일부 프레젠테이션 장비들이 작동하지 않는다.
   (D) 회의실이 이중 예약되었다.

   해설 단서(3)에서 두 사람이 같은 시간대에 회의실을 예약했다고 하고 있으므로 정답은 (D).

4 오전 10:51에, 후버 씨가 "그럴 수 있어요"라고 하는 의도는?
   (A) 기꺼이 장소를 피해 줄 것이다.
   (B) 약속 시간을 변경할 것이다.
   (C) 펠럼 씨에게 자청해서 연락을 취한다.
   (D) 코스타 씨의 업무를 완료할 수 있다.

   해설 문제에서 주어진 표현 "I can make that work" 앞의 단서(4)에서 티엔 씨는 후버 씨에게 면접 대상자인 펠럼 씨를 커피숍으로 데려가라고 제안하고 있고, 문맥상 이는 회의실 예약이 겹치는 문제를 해결하기 위한 것이다. 따라서 "그럴 수 있어요"라는 후버 씨의 말은 코스타 씨가 회의실을 쓸 수 있도록 자리를 피해 줄 것이라는 뜻임을 알 수 있다. 정답은 (A).

5 코스타 씨가 하겠다고 하는 일은?
   (A) 회의실 준비하기
   (B) 기술적 문제 보고하기
   (C) 티엔 씨에게 정보 전달하기
   (D) 직접 수리하기

   해설 코스타 씨가 한 말을 주의 깊게 살펴본다. 단서(5)에서 코스타 씨가 IT 부서에 오류에 대해 이야기하는 일을 하겠다고 자원하고 있으므로 정답은 (B).
   패러프레이징 지문의 tell the IT department about the glitch가 정답에서 report a technical problem으로 패러프레이징되었다.

6 후버 씨가 티엔 씨를 찾아가는 이유는?
   (A) 일정표를 제출하기 위해
   (B) 서류에 서명하기 위해
   (C) 신용카드를 받기 위해
   (D) 음식을 나누기 위해

   해설 단서(6)에서 티엔 씨가 후버 씨에게 회사 법인 카드를 가져가라고 했고, 후버 씨가 그러겠다고 했으므로 정답은 (C).
   패러프레이징 지문의 take the company credit card가 정답에서 pick up a credit card로 패러프레이징되었다.

UNIT 02 문장 위치 찾기 문제

PRE-STEP
p.19

A 1 (B)   2 (A)   3 (B)   4 (A)   5 (B)   6 (B)   7 (A)   8 (A)   9 (A)
   10 (B) 11 (B) 12 (A) 13 (B) 14 (A) 15 (B)

B 1 (B)   2 (B)

A 1 (B) permanent, 영구적인 손상을 초래하다
   2 (A) trial, 시범 기간
   3 (B) rapid, 급속한 인구 증가
   4 (A) fiscal, 새로운 회계 연도
   5 (B) existing, 기존의 지하철 시스템
   6 (B) solutions, 창조적인 해결 방안을 연구하다
   7 (A) concerns, 안전에 대한 우려를 표하다
   8 (A) passengers, 더 많은 수의 승객을 수용하다
   9 (A) hit, 시장에 출시하다[내다]
   10 (B) estimated, 320만 달러쯤으로 추정되다
   11 (B) mark, 업계에서 ~의 명성을 떨치다
   12 (A) relieve, 압박을 완화시키다
   13 (B) productivity, 직원들의 생산성을 향상시키다
   14 (A) access, 교외 지역으로의 용이한 접근을 제공하다
   15 (B) commemorate, 15주년 근무를 기념하다

B 1 Being connected to Crafton and other major suburbs through the new lines will be convenient and cost-effective for a lot of commuters.
      (A) Suburbs will be relocated in order to create a new transportation line.
      (B) Travel to specific neighborhoods will become easy and inexpensive.

새로운 노선을 통해 크래프턴과 다른 주요 교외 지역으로 연결되는 것은 많은 통근자들에게 편리하고 비용 효율이 높은 일이 될 것입니다.
(A) 교통 노선 신설을 위해 교외 지역이 재배치될 것입니다.
(B) 특정 지역으로의 이동이 쉽고 저렴해질 것입니다.

   2 I was confident that its reputation for having high-quality and long-lasting goods was well-deserved.
      (A) I knew that more expensive products are usually more durable.
      (B) I knew that the company had worked hard to earn consumers' trust.

저는 고품질에 오래가는 제품들을 보유한 그 회사의 명성이 그럴 만한 가치가 있다는 점을 확신했습니다.
(A) 저는 더 비싼 제품들이 대체로 더 오래간다는 것을 알고 있었습니다.
(B) 저는 그 회사가 고객들의 신뢰를 얻기 위해 열심히 노력했다는 것을 알고 있었습니다.

MAIN STEP 1
p.20

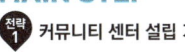 커뮤니티 센터 설립 기사

Plans for New Community Center

City council chairperson Samantha Davies announced plans for the construction of a community center on Chesterton Avenue yesterday. The new facility will feature a large event hall, three classrooms, and a conference room. In addition, it will include a kitchen to accommodate luncheons and banquets. "The council felt that such facilities would really improve the quality of life in the city,"

새로운 커뮤니티 센터 계획

시의회장 사만다 데이비스 씨는 어제 체스터튼 애비뉴에 새로운 커뮤니티 센터 건립 계획을 발표했다. 새로운 시설은 대형 이벤트 홀과 세 개의 강의실, 그리고 회의실을 특징으로 할 것이다. 또한, 그곳은 오찬과 연회를 열 수 있는 주방 또한 포함하게 될 것이다. "의회는 그러한 시설이 시의 삶의 질을 정말로 향상시킬 것이라고 여겼습니다."라고 데이비스 회장은 말했다.

Davies said.
The city council approved the construction last month. The cost of the project is estimated to be $3.2 million.

시의회는 지난달 건립을 승인했다. 프로젝트 비용은 320만 달러로 추산된다.

어휘 **feature** ~을 특징으로 하다 **accommodate** 공간을 제공하다 **banquet** 연회 **approve** 승인하다 **estimate** 추산하다

"새로운 시설은 대형 이벤트 홀과 세 개의 강의실, 그리고 회의실을 특징으로 할 것이다."

해설 주어진 문장은 새로운 시설의 특징에 관한 것인데, 그 앞의 문장에서 새로운 커뮤니티 센터에 관한 건립 계획이 발표되었다 했고, 뒤에서는 여기에 포함되는 주방에 관해 언급하고 있으므로 주어진 문장은 이 사이에 들어가야 알맞다. 커뮤니티 센터를 가리키는 표현과 in addition 등의 연결사를 주의 깊게 보도록 하자.

 식품업체의 신규 서비스 기사

Organics Market's Home Delivery Service

Health food retailer Organics Market has initiated a new service that provides customers with weekly deliveries of local, organic produce. Spokesperson Jane Ryder claims that the program will benefit both the community and the customers. The company can help farmers who would normally compete with industrial agriculture. For customers, they are assured that their produce is organic and fresh. The region's director of health, Mark Swenson, supports this program, calling it an essential step in educating the public about the importance of choosing healthy, local foods.

오가닉스 마켓의 가정 배달 서비스

건강식품 소매업체인 오가닉스 마켓이 고객들에게 현지 유기농 농산물을 주 단위로 배송하는 새로운 서비스를 시작했다. 대변인인 제인 라이더 씨는 이 프로그램이 지역사회와 고객 모두를 이롭게 할 것이라 주장한다. 회사는 주로 산업화된 농업과 경쟁하는 농부들에게 도움을 줄 수 있다. 고객들의 경우, 그들은 자신들의 농산물이 유기농이고 신선하다는 것을 확신할 수 있다. 그 지역의 건강 관리인 마크 스웬슨 씨는 이 프로그램을 지지하며, 대중에게 건강한 지역 식품을 선택하는 것의 중요성을 가르치는 데 있어 이것이 필수적인 조치라고 한다.

어휘 **retailer** 소매업체 **initiate** 시작하다 **produce** 농산물 **benefit** 이롭게 하다 **compete with** ~와 경쟁하다 **be assured that** ~에 확신이 있다

"회사는 주로 산업화된 농업과 경쟁하는 농부들에게 도움을 줄 수 있다."

해설 주어진 문장은 회사가 농부들을 도울 수 있다는 내용인데, 그 앞의 단서에서 식품업체의 프로그램이 지역사회와 고객들 모두를 이롭게 한다고 하였고, 뒤에서는 고객들에게 이로운 점에 대해 언급하고 있으므로 주어진 문장은 이 사이에 들어가야 알맞다. 해당 문장과 그 뒤의 문장은 앞의 주장(프로그램이 지역사회와 고객들을 이롭게 한다)에 대한 근거가 된다.

MAIN STEP 2   p.21

1 (B)   2 (C)   3 (A)

[1-3] 회사의 새 운영 정책에 대한 기사

(1) Turtle Inc. to Institute Temporary Four-Day Workweek
By Mimi Favorman

Mr. Lance Fulchiron, the CEO of Turtle Inc., spoke

(1) 터틀 사, 한시적 주 4일 근무제 도입
미미 페이버맨 작성

터틀 사 CEO 랑스 필시롱 씨는 어제 전 직원들에게 공식 발언을

formally to all of his employees yesterday, which was the first day of the company's new fiscal year. (3)His carefully worded speech discussed the need to increase employee productivity through new techniques. He expressed concerns that methods that were effective a decade ago are no longer relevant. As a result, Mr. Fulchiron has researched creative solutions to address the problem of overworked personnel. He explained that he wanted to follow the example of states such as Utah and institute a four-day workweek as a pilot program. Mr. Fulchiron went on to explain the theory behind the four-day workweek, which is that workers are propelled to work harder and accomplish more when they are given regular breaks. (2B)Businesses in turn save money on utility expenses when the office is closed for an extra day. According to Mr. Fulchiron, Turtle Inc. will spend the next four months testing this theory. (2A)During this time, employees will no longer be required to work on Fridays (2C)(although their salaries will remain the same). (2D)At the end of the trial period, Turtle Inc. plans to re-evaluate the arrangement and determine whether or not to make it a permanent change.

했는데, 어제는 회사의 새로운 회계 연도 첫날이었다. (3)신중하게 말을 고른 그의 연설은 새로운 기술을 통해 직원들의 생산성을 향상시킬 필요성에 대해 논했다. 그는 10년 전에 효율적이었던 방식들이 더 이상은 적절하지 않다고 우려를 표했다. 그 결과 퓔시롱 씨는 과중한 업무를 하고 있는 직원 문제를 해결할 창조적인 방안들을 연구하게 되었다. 그는 유타 주와 같은 주들의 선례를 따라 주 4일 근무를 시범적으로 운영하기를 원한다고 설명했다. 그는 이어서 주 4일 근무에 대한 이론적 배경을 설명하였는데, 이는 직원들은 정기적인 휴식이 부여될 때 추진력을 가지고 일을 더 열심히 하고 성취도도 더 올라간다는 것이다. (2B)결과적으로 기업들은 추가 요일에 사무실이 문을 닫게 되어 공공요금 비용을 줄이게 된다. 퓔시롱 씨에 따르면 터틀 사는 앞으로 4개월을 이 이론을 시험하는 데 보낼 생각이다. (2A)이 기간에 직원들은 더 이상 금요일에 일할 필요가 없다. (2C)(급여는 동일해도 말이다) (2D)시범 기간이 끝난 후 터틀 사는 이러한 조정에 대해 재평가하고 영구적으로 변경할 것인지 여부를 결정할 계획이다.

어휘 formally 공식적으로, 정식으로 fiscal year (기업 등 사업체의) 회계 연도 productivity 생산성 express concerns 우려를 표하다 decade 10년 relevant 적절한, 관련 있는 personnel 직원, 인사(과) pilot 시범의, 시험적인 propel to do ~하게 하다 in turn 결과적으로 utility expenses (보통 복수형) (수도, 가스, 전기세 등으로 지불하는) 공공요금 extra 추가의, 별도의 be required to do ~하는 것이 요구되다 permanent 영구적인, 지속적인

1 기사가 쓰인 이유는?
 (A) 새 CEO를 소개하기 위해
 (B) 계획을 발표하기 위해
 (C) 상품을 홍보하기 위해
 (D) 질문에 답하기 위해

해설 제목에서도 유추할 수 있듯이 이 기사는 터틀 사의 주 4일 근무제의 시범 운영에 대한 것이므로 정답은 (B).

2 주 4일 근무에 대해 언급되지 않은 것은?
 (A) 직원들은 금요일부터 일요일까지 쉴 것이다.
 (B) 기업의 지출이 감소할 것으로 예상된다.
 (C) 결과적으로 직원 봉급이 조정될 것이다.
 (D) 이러한 변화는 한시적으로 시험 운용 중이다.

해설 단서(2C)에서 주 4일 근무가 시행되는 기간 동안에도 직원들은 동일한 급여를 받게 될 것이라 하였으므로 (C)가 정답.

3 [1], [2], [3], [4]로 표시된 위치 중 다음 문장이 들어가기에 가장 알맞은 곳은?
 "그는 10년 전에 효율적이었던 방식들이 더 이상은 적절하지 않다고 우려를 표했다."
 (A) [1]
 (B) [2]
 (C) [3]
 (D) [4]

해설 주어진 문장은 과거의 방식들이 지금은 적절하지 않다는 퓔시롱 씨의 의견인데, 앞의 단서(3)에서 새로운 기술을 통한 생산성 향상의 필요성에 대해 언급하고, 뒤에서는 문제 해결을 위한 창조적 방안들을 연구하게 되었다고 했으므로 주어진 문장은 이 사이에 들어가야 알맞다. 연결사 As a result를 주의 깊게 보도록 하자. 정답은 (A).

FINAL STEP

p.22

1 (D) 2 (C) 3 (C) 4 (A) 5 (D) 6 (C) 7 (B)

[1-3] 게임 회사의 15주년 기념 제품 출시 기사

Cordoba Games Celebrates 15th Anniversary

Video game developer Cordoba Games will celebrate its fifteen-year anniversary in April. The company initially focused on computer games in its early days, but it later branched out into developing its own gaming console. It truly made its mark on the industry with the release of Dreamland Quest, which sold over three million copies in its first year. (1)To commemorate its fifteen years in business, Cordoba Games is teaming up with Mesa Co. to create a line of limited-edition products featuring the characters from Dreamland Quest. The line will include stationery sets, pencils, pencil cases, notebooks, and more.

With the products expecting to sell in the tens of millions, it is no surprise that a number of companies were interested in working with Cordoba Games. (3)Executives at the company had a long list of options to choose from. However, it was an employee's recommendation that helped them make the final decision. "I had previously worked for the marketing team at Mesa Co.," said Marketing Director Charles Rosario. "I know its products inside and out, and I was confident that (2)its reputation for having high-quality and long-lasting goods was well-deserved. This is a special milestone for our company, and we didn't want to cut any corners."

The stationery is expected to hit the market on June 1 and will be sold internationally. Whether you're a collector or just a fan of Dreamland Quest, you'll definitely want to get your hands on these unique products.

코르도바 게임즈 사가 15주년을 기념하다

비디오 게임 개발사인 코르도바 게임즈 사가 4월에 15주년을 기념할 것이다. 이 회사는 처음에 초창기에 컴퓨터 게임에 초점을 맞추었으나, 나중에는 자신만의 게임 콘솔을 개발하는 쪽으로 진출하였다. 이 회사는 드림랜드 퀘스트의 출시로 업계에 명성을 떨쳤으며, 그것은 출시 첫 해에 300만 부 이상이 판매되었다. (1)사업 15주년을 기념하기 위해, 코르도바 게임즈 사는 메사 사와 협력하여 드림랜드 퀘스트의 캐릭터들을 특징으로 하는 한정판 제품 라인을 만들어낼 것이다. 이 라인은 문구류 세트, 연필, 필통, 노트 등을 포함할 것이다.

이 제품은 수천만 개가 판매될 것으로 예상되는 만큼, 많은 회사들이 코르도바 게임즈 사와 함께 일하는 데 관심이 있었던 것은 놀랍지 않다. (3)당사의 임원들은 선택할 수 있는 긴 목록이 있었다. 그러나, 그들이 최종 결정을 내리게끔 도운 것은 한 직원의 추천이었다. "저는 이전에 메사 사의 마케팅 팀에서 일한 적이 있습니다." 마케팅 부장 찰스 로사리오가 말했다. "저는 그 회사의 제품들을 속속들이 알고 있고, (2)고품질에 오래가는 제품들을 보유한 그 회사의 명성이 그럴 만한 가치가 있다는 점을 확신했습니다. 이것은 우리 회사에 특별히 중요한 단계이며, 우리는 어떤 원칙도 무시하지 않았습니다."

문구류는 6월 1일에 시장에 출시될 예정이며 세계적으로 판매될 것이다. 당신이 드림랜드 퀘스트의 수집가이든 단순한 팬이든 간에, 이 특별한 제품을 틀림없이 손에 넣고 싶어할 것이다.

어휘 initially 처음에 focus on ~에 초점을 맞추다 branch out (새로운 분야로) 진출하다 make one's mark 명성을 떨치다 release 출시 commemorate 기념하다 stationery 문구류 recommendation 추천 previously 이전에 high-quality 고품질의, 고급의 long-lasting 오래가는 well-deserved 충분한 자격이 있는 milestone 중요한 단계, 이정표 cut corners (일을 쉽게 하려고) 원칙[절차]을 무시하다 hit the market 시장에 내다, 출시하다

1 코르도바 게임즈 사가 계획 중인 것은?
(A) 해외 시장으로의 진출
(B) 인기 있는 게임의 후속작 출시
(C) 기념일을 맞이한 할인 제공
(D) 타사와의 제휴

해설 단서(1)에서 코르도바 게임즈 사가 타사인 메사 사와 협력해 한정판 제품 라인을 만들 계획이라는 것을 확인할 수 있다. 따라서 정답은 (D).

패러프레이징 지문의 teaming up with Mesa Co.가 정답에서 Partner with another company로 패러프레이징되었다.

2 메사 사에 대해 시사된 바는?
(A) 새로운 마케팅 부장을 찾고 있다.
(B) 코르도바 게임즈 사의 주 경쟁사이다.
(C) 메사 사의 제품들은 내구성으로 알려져 있다.
(D) 회사의 중요한 단계를 축하할 것이다.

해설 지문에서 메사 사가 언급된 곳을 찾아본다. 단서(2)에서 찰스 로사리오 씨가 메사 사의 제품들이 고품질이고 오래간다고 했으므로, 정답은 (C).

패러프레이징 지문의 long-lasting이 정답에서 durability로 패러프레이징되었다.

3 [1], [2], [3], [4]로 표시된 위치 중 다음 문장이 들어가기에 가장 알맞은 곳은?
"그러나, 그들이 최종 결정을 내리게끔 도운 것은 한 직원의 추천이었다."
(A) [1]
(B) [2]
(C) [3]
(D) [4]

해설 주어진 문장은 직원의 추천으로 어떤 결정이 내려졌다는 내용으로, 연결어 However를 통해 그 앞에 결정을 내리는 데 어려움이 있었다는 내용이 와야 한다. 단서(3)에서 임원들에게 협력사 후보의 긴 목록이 있었다고 했고, 뒤에서 메사 사에서 일했던 직원의 경험이 제시되고 있으므로 주어진 문장은 이 사이에 들어가야 알맞다. 정답은 (C).

[4-7] 시 지하철 노선 추가 신설 기사

MARCH 20—In a press conference held yesterday, (4)Darby City transportation officials announced plans to add three new lines to the existing subway system to accommodate a larger number of passengers and to create easy access to suburbs such as Crafton. The city's rapid population growth over the past five years has resulted in pressure on public transportation, and the project is expected to relieve this pressure. (7)Construction is set to begin this summer, and the new lines will use automated trains that can be conducted without human operators. These trains are far more expensive than traditional ones, with an investment of $45 million needed for the trains alone. This initial expense will save money in the long run due to low labor costs.

While many people are in favor of having more trains available, the city's decision to use unmanned trains is controversial. (5)Passengers have expressed concerns about traveling in machine-operated trains, which they fear are more dangerous than those using trained operators. However, city officials say this is not the case, as these types of trains have been used by other cities for years and have proven themselves to be safe, fast, and efficient.

Although the new trains do not require drivers, the city has no plans to lay off the existing workforce. (6)Skilled operators will still be needed for longer and more complex lines within the system, so personnel will be moved to these positions as necessary. "I'm pleased that the subway system is able to implement this new technology," said veteran operator Louis Belford. "Being connected to Crafton and other major suburbs through the new lines will be convenient and cost-effective for a lot of commuters."

3월 20일—어제 열렸던 기자 회견에서, (4)다비 시 교통 당국 공무원들은 더 많은 수의 승객을 수용하고 크래프턴과 같은 교외 지역으로의 용이한 접근을 제공하기 위해 (4)기존 지하철 시스템에 세 개의 새로운 노선을 추가하는 계획을 발표했다. 지난 5년간의 시의 급속한 인구 증가는 대중교통에 대한 압박을 초래하였고, 이 계획은 이러한 압박을 완화시킬 것이라 기대된다. (7)공사는 올 여름에 시작하기로 정해졌고, 새로운 노선은 기관사 없이도 운행될 수 있는 자동화된 열차들을 이용할 것이다. 이 열차들은 전통적인 열차보다 훨씬 더 비싸며, 열차에만 단독으로 4천 5백만 달러의 투자가 필요할 것이다. 장기적으로 볼 때 이 초기 비용은 낮은 인건비 때문에 비용을 절감하는 셈이 될 것이다.

더 많은 열차가 이용 가능해지는 것에 대해 많은 이들이 호의적인 반면, 무인 열차를 이용한다는 시의 결정은 논란의 여지가 있다. (5)승객들은 기계가 운행하는 열차로 이동하는 것에 대해 우려를 표현했는데, 그들은 숙련된 기관사를 이용하는 열차보다 이것이 더 위험할 것이라고 불안해한다. 그러나, 시 공무원들은 그렇지 않다고 말하는데, 이러한 유형의 열차들은 수년간 다른 도시들에서도 이용되어 왔고 그 자체로 안전하고, 빠르고, 효율적이라는 것이 증명되었기 때문이다.

새로운 열차들이 운전사를 필요로 하지 않는다 하더라도, 시는 기존의 노동력을 해고할 계획이 전혀 없다. (6)숙련된 기관사들은 시스템 내에서 더 길고 더 복잡한 노선들을 위해 여전히 필요할 것이기 때문에, 직원들은 필요한 만큼 이러한 자리로 옮겨질 것이다. "지하철 시스템이 이러한 새 기술을 실행할 수 있어서 기쁩니다."라고 베테랑 기관사인 루이즈 벨포트는 말했다. "새로운 노선을 통해 크래프턴 및 기타 주요 교외 지역으로 연결되는 것은 많은 통근자들에게 편리하고 비용 효율이 높은 일이 될 것입니다."

어휘 **transportation** 교통수단, 교통기관 **official** 공무원, 관리 **existing** 기존의 **accommodate** 수용하다 **passenger** 승객 **access** 입장, 접근 **suburb** 교외 지역 **rapid** 급속한, 급격한 **population** 인구 **result in** ~을 낳다[초래하다] **relieve** 완화하다 **pressure** 중압, 압력 **automate** 자동화하다 **operator** (장비를) 조작하는 사람 **traditional** 전통적인 **investment** 투자 **unmanned** 무인의 **controversial** 논란이 많은 **fear** 두려워하다 **efficient** 효율적인 **workforce** 노동력 **implement** 시행하다 **cost-effective** 비용 효율이 높은 **commuter** 통근자

4 기사에 따르면, 다비 시의 지하철 시스템에 일어날 일은?
 (A) 노선망이 확장될 것이다.
 (B) 요금이 두 배가 될 것이다.
 (C) 더 넓은 열차를 도입할 것이다.
 (D) 승강장이 더 넓어질 것이다.

[해설] 단서(4)에서 시에서 기존 지하철 시스템에 노선 세 개를 추가 신설하는 계획을 발표했다고 했으므로, 정답은 (A).
[패러프레이징] 지문의 add three new lines to the existing subway system이 정답에서 network will be expanded로 패러프레이징되었다.

5 일부 승객들이 우려하는 바는?
 (A) 예기치 못한 지연
 (B) 붐비는 열차
 (C) 긴 대기 시간
 (D) 안전 문제

[해설] 승객들의 반응에 대해 언급한 두 번째 단락을 살펴본다. 단서(5)에서 승객들이 무인 열차가 위험할 것이라 불안해한다는 내용을 찾을 수 있다. 정답은 (D).

6 현재 시를 위해 일하는 지하철 기관사들에게 일어날 일은?
 (A) 다른 도시로 보내질 것이다.
 (B) 퇴직금을 받을 것이다.
 (C) 다른 노선으로 옮겨질 것이다.
 (D) 기술자로 재훈련을 받을 것이다.

[해설] 지하철 기관사들에 대해 언급된 마지막 단락을 살펴본다. 단서(6)에서 기관사들은 더 길고 복잡한 노선들에 필요해서 그 자리로 옮겨진다고 했으므로, 정답은 (C).

7 [1], [2], [3], [4]로 표시된 위치 중 다음 문장이 들어가기에 가장 알맞은 곳은?
 "장기적으로 볼 때 이 초기 비용은 낮은 인건비 때문에 비용을 절감하는 셈이 될 것이다."
 (A) [1]
 (B) [2]
 (C) [3]
 (D) [4]

[해설] 주어진 문장은 낮은 인건비가 비용을 절감하게 해 줄 것이라는 내용으로, 앞에는 낮은 인건비와 관련된 내용, 그리고 초기 비용이 높다는 내용이 와야 자연스럽다. 단서(7)에서 새로운 지하철 노선이 무인 열차를 도입할 것인데 이 열차들은 기존 열차들보다 훨씬 비싸지만 인건비가 적게 든다고 했으므로 주어진 문장은 이 뒤에 들어가야 한다. 정답은 (B).

UNIT 03 목적/주제 문제

PRE-STEP

p.25

A
1 (A) 2 (A) 3 (A) 4 (B) 5 (A) 6 (B) 7 (A) 8 (B) 9 (B)
10 (A) 11 (A) 12 (B) 13 (B) 14 (A) 15 (A)

B
1 (A) 2 (A)

A
1 (A) refreshing, 휴식하기에 쾌적한 장소
2 (A) participate, ~에 참가하도록 선발되다
3 (A) prize, 현금이 상으로 주어지다
4 (B) remedy, 상황을 개선하다
5 (A) valuable, 귀중한 경험을 얻다
6 (B) maintenance, 유지 보수 관리자
7 (A) preparation, 행사를 대비하여
8 (B) attend, 결승에 참가하다
9 (B) complaints, 주차 공간에 대한 불만
10 (A) possessions, ~의 소지품을 포장해서 치우다
11 (A) join, 프로그램에 합류하다
12 (B) facilities, 전반적인 조경과 공원 시설
13 (B) requirements, 고용 요건
14 (A) expert, 그 분야의 전문가
15 (A) disruption, 혼란이나 불편을 야기하다

B
1 I would like to apologize to employees on the upper floors for the uncomfortable working conditions in the last week or so.
   (A) I am sorry that some employees had to face a difficult working environment.
   (B) I am sorry for ignoring some of the employees' complaints.

위층 직원 분들께 지난주 즈음의 불편했던 근무 환경에 대해 사과 드리고 싶습니다.
(A) 몇몇 직원 분들이 어려운 업무 환경에 직면하셔야 했던 것이 유감입니다.
(B) 몇몇 직원 분들의 불만을 모른 척해서 죄송합니다.

2 One of the other contestants has a scheduling conflict and is now unable to attend the final competition.
   (A) The event is short one participant.
   (B) The venue is not available.

다른 참가자들 중 한 명이 일정상 충돌이 있어서 이번에 결승에 참가할 수 없게 되었습니다.
(A) 그 행사는 참가자가 한 명 부족합니다.
(B) 그 장소는 이용이 불가능합니다.

MAIN STEP 1

p.26

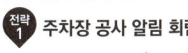 주차장 공사 알림 회람

MEMO

To: All employees
From: Maintenance department
Subject: Parking lot expansion

There have been a lot of complaints regarding the scarcity of parking spaces. Therefore, we would like to inform you that our employee parking lot will be renovated next month.

회람

수신: 전 직원
발신: 유지 보수팀
제목: 주차장 확장

주차 공간 부족에 대해 많은 불만들이 있었습니다. 그래서, 저희 직원 주차장이 다음 달에 개조될 것임을 알리고자 합니다.

회람이 보내진 목적은?
→ 직원들에게 개조 공사 계획에 대해 알리기 위해

해설 제목을 통해 회람이 주차장 확장에 관한 것이라는 것을 알 수 있으며, we would like to inform 이하에 이 내용이 더욱 자세히 나타나 있다. 따라서 회람을 보낸 목적은 직원들에게 개조 공사 계획에 대해 알리기 위함이다.

MAIN STEP 2   p.27

1 (A)   **2** (C)

[1] 유지 보수 관리자 구인 광고

(1)Maintenance Manager Needed

The construction of our new convention center is almost finished, and the center will reopen on April 30. Within the convention center grounds, there is a large park containing hundreds of trees, so it will be a refreshing place to relax with friends and family. (1)Currently, we are looking for a maintenance manager to take care of the overall landscape and park facilities. If anyone is interested, please let us know by calling our supervisor, Mr. Scott, at 100-134-5880. For specific information about duties, compensation, or hiring requirements, please visit www.southernhillconvention.net/recruit.

(1)유지 보수 관리자 구함

새 컨벤션 센터의 공사가 거의 끝났고 4월 30일에 다시 문을 열 것입니다. 컨벤션 센터 부지 내부에는 수백 그루의 나무가 있는 큰 공원이 있어서, 친구들 및 가족과 함께 휴식하기에 쾌적한 장소가 될 것입니다. (1)현재, 저희는 전반적인 조경과 공원 시설을 돌볼 유지 보수 관리자를 찾고 있습니다. 관심 있는 분이 있다면 저희 감독인 스캇 씨에게 100-134-5880으로 전화를 걸어 알려주십시오. 업무, 복지, 고용 요건에 대한 구체적인 정보를 위해서는 www.southernhillconvention.net/recruit에 방문해 주십시오.

어휘 construction 공사 refreshing 쾌적한 overall 전반적인 landscape 조경, 경치 facility (보통 복수형) 시설 supervisor 감독 duty 업무 compensation 복지, 보상 requirement 요건

1 광고가 쓰인 이유는?

(A) 공석인 일자리를 광고하기 위해
(B) 새로운 시설을 홍보하기 위해
(C) 신제품을 소개하기 위해
(D) 사무실 이전을 알리기 위해

해설 단서(1)에 따르면, 이 광고는 공사를 마친 새 컨벤션 센터의 공원에서 일할 유지 보수 관리자를 뽑기 위해 쓰였음을 알 수 있으므로 정답은 (A). 제목에 어느 정도 글의 목적이 드러난다.

보너스문제
① 지원자들이 더 상세한 정보를 얻을 수 있는 방법은?
→ 웹사이트를 방문함으로써

해설 지문 마지막 문장에 웹사이트 주소가 나와 있고 구체적인 정보를 위해서는 이 사이트에 방문하라고 하였다.

[2] 합격 안내 편지

Laura Krause
922 Charack Road
Jasper, IN 47546

May 1

Dear Ms. Krause,

(2)This is a letter to inform you that you have been selected to participate in Alma Industries' Summer Internship Program. Congratulations! During the internship, you will be working alongside experts in the field and will gain valuable experience. You will

로라 크라우스
차랙 가 922
인디애나 주, 재스퍼 47546

5월 1일

크라우스 씨께,

(2)이 편지는 귀하가 알마 산업의 하계 인턴십 프로그램에 참가하도록 선발되었음을 알려드리기 위한 것입니다. 축하 드립니다! 인턴십 기간 동안 귀하는 이 분야의 전문가들과 함께 일할 것이며 귀중한 경험을 얻게 될 것입니다. 귀하는 6월 5일부터 8월 31일까지 저희와 함께 일하게 될 것입니다. 5월

work with us from June 5 to August 31. You should confirm that you'll be joining in the program by calling my office at 555-8640 by May 10. I hope to hear good news from you soon.

Sincerely,

Walter Robbins
HR Director, Alma Industries

10일까지 제 사무실 555-8640으로 전화를 걸어서 프로그램에 합류하겠다는 것을 확정해 주셔야 합니다. 귀하로부터 곧 좋은 소식을 듣길 희망합니다.

알마 산업, 인사 부장
월터 로빈스 드림

어휘 inform 알리다   participate in ~에 참가하다   alongside ~와 함께   expert 전문가   field 분야   valuable 귀중한
confirm 확정하다

---

2 편지의 목적은?
(A) 크라우스 씨에게 변경 사항을 알려주기 위해
(B) 크라우스 씨와 면접 일정을 잡기 위해
(C) 크라우스 씨에게 일자리를 제안하기 위해
(D) 크라우스 씨에게 지원서를 제출하기 위해

보너스문제
② 크라우스 씨가 로빈스 씨에게 연락해야 하는 이유는?
→ 결정을 확정하기 위해

해설 편지의 서두 부분을 주의 깊게 보아야 한다. This is a letter to inform you that(이 편지는 귀하께 ~를 알려드리기 위한 것입니다.)이하를 통해 편지의 목적을 알 수 있는데, 크라우스 씨가 인턴십 프로그램에 선발되었음을 알리기 위해 편지를 쓴다고 하였으므로 정답은 (C).

해설 크라우스 씨는 편지의 수신인이고, 로빈스 씨는 편지의 발신인이다. 편지 마지막 부분에서, 로빈스 씨는 크라우스 씨에게 전화로 프로그램 합류 여부를 알려달라고 했다.

FINAL STEP

p.28

1 (A)   2 (D)   3 (B)   4 (B)   5 (A)

[1-2] 결승 진출 안내 편지

Ms. Charlotte Bass
100 Huntington Avenue
Boston, MA 02116

April 8

Dear Ms. Bass,

(1)I am writing to congratulate you on making it to the final round of the Abra Bacon Prize in informative speaking. I understand that you finished fourth in your preliminary qualifying competition, of which only the top three speakers move forward. However, one of the other contestants has a scheduling conflict and is now unable to attend the final competition. Fortunately, this means that we are advancing you instead.

(2)The final round of the contest will be held on Saturday, April 30, at 2 P.M. in the Donald Miller room of the Freeport Hotel in downtown Boston. You are expected to arrive by April 28 in preparation for a number of contestant events that will be held on April 28 and April 29. The person with the winning speech will be awarded a cash prize of $1,000.

샬럿 베이스 씨
헌팅턴 가 100
매사추세츠 주, 보스턴 02116

4월 8일

베이스 씨께,

(1)귀하께서 지식 연설로 에이브라 베이컨 상의 결승전 진출에 성공하신 것을 축하 드리기 위해 이 편지를 씁니다. 귀하께서는 상위 세 명만 다음 단계로 진출할 수 있는 예비 자격 심사에서 4위로 마무리를 하셨다고 알고 있습니다. 그러나, 다른 참가자들 중 한 명이 일정상 충돌이 있어서 현재 결승에 참가할 수 없게 되었습니다. 운 좋게도, 이는 우리가 귀하를 대신 진출시킨다는 뜻입니다.

(2)대회의 결승전은 보스턴 시내에 있는 프리포트 호텔의 도널드 밀러룸에서 4월 30일 토요일 오후 2시에 열립니다. 귀하께서는 4월 28일과 4월 29일에 열릴 다양한 참가자 행사를 대비하여 4월 28일까지 도착하셔야 합니다. 연설 우승자에게는 1천 달러의 현금이 상으로 주어집니다.

다시 한번 축하 드립니다,

에이브라 베이컨 수상협회, 회장
나이젤 에브너 드림

Congratulations once again,

Nigel Ebner
Chairperson, Abra Bacon Prize

어휘 **make it to** ~로 나아가는 데 성공하다　**final round** 결승전, 최종전　**informative** 설명하는, 정보를 제공하는　**preliminary** 예비의, 예선의　**qualify** 자격을 부여하다　**competition** 경연, 경합　**move forward** 진출하다, 앞으로 나아가다　**contestant** (대회, 시합 등의) 참가자, 경연자　**scheduling conflict** 일정상의 충돌

---

1 에브너 씨 편지의 목적은?
   (A) 참가자에게 그녀의 상황을 새로 알려주기 위해
   (B) 대회에 대한 지시 사항을 전달하기 위해
   (C) 토너먼트에 대한 의견을 요청하기 위해
   (D) 상품 수령 방식을 정하기 위해

해설 단서(1)의 I am writing to congratulate you on(~을 축하 드리기 위해 편지를 씁니다) 이하를 통해 베이스 씨가 새롭게 결승에 진출하게 되었음을 알리기 위해 에브너 씨가 이 편지를 썼음을 알 수 있다. 따라서 정답은 (A).

2 결승 연설이 열릴 예정인 때는?
   (A) 4월 8일
   (B) 4월 28일
   (C) 4월 29일
   (D) 4월 30일

해설 문제에서 결승 연설 날짜를 묻고 있으므로 결승전이 언급된 부분을 찾는다. 단서(2)에서 결승전 날짜가 4월 30일이라고 직접적으로 언급되어 있으므로 정답은 (D).

[3-5] 에어컨 설치 안내 회람

To: All staff
From: Alicia Wright
Date: July 17

I would like to apologize to employees on the upper floors for the uncomfortable working conditions in the last week or so. (4)The air conditioning unit has been malfunctioning and, because the windows do not fully open on the 3rd, 4th, or 5th floors, it has been very stuffy and hot.

(3)Please let me reassure you that management has taken steps to remedy the situation. A new air conditioner will be installed over the weekend. To protect belongings from dust and debris, (5) employees on the upper floors are asked to pack away their possessions and equipment on Friday afternoon. I hope that this will not cause too much disruption or inconvenience. Thank you for your patience.

Kind regards,

Alicia Wright
Maintenance Manager

받는 사람: 전 직원
보내는 사람: 알리시아 라이트
날짜: 7월 17일

위층 직원분들께 지난주 즈음의 불편했던 근무 환경에 대해 사과 드리고 싶습니다. (4)에어컨 설비가 고장 났고, 3층, 4층 그리고 5층의 창문이 완전히 열리지 않기 때문에, 매우 답답하고 더웠습니다.

(3)관리팀이 이 상황을 개선하기 위해 조치를 취했음을 재차 알려드리겠습니다. 새로운 에어컨이 이번 주말 동안에 설치될 것입니다. 먼지와 쓰레기로부터 소지품을 보호하기 위해, (5)위층 직원 분들은 금요일 오후에 여러분의 소지품과 장비들을 포장해서 치워 두시기를 바랍니다. 이것이 너무 많은 혼란이나 불편을 야기하지 않기를 바랍니다. 인내해 주셔서 감사합니다.

관리팀 팀장
알리시아 라이트 드림

어휘 **apologize** 사과하다　**uncomfortable** 불편한　**working conditions** 근무 환경　**malfunction** 고장 나다　**stuffy** 답답한　**reassure** 재차 알려주다, 안심시키다　**management** 관리(팀)　**take steps** 조치를 취하다　**remedy** 개선하다　**install** 설치하다　**protect** 보호하다　**belongings** 소지품　**debris** 쓰레기, 잔해　**disruption** 혼란　**inconvenience** 불편　**patience** 인내심

3 이 회람의 목적은?
(A) 문제에 대한 직원의 피드백을 요청하기 위해
(B) 유지 보수상의 개선 사항을 알리기 위해
(C) 직원들에게 안전 지침을 알리기 위해
(D) 최근 테스트의 결과를 보고하기 위해

[해설] 이메일 첫 부분에서 사과를 한 다음 단서(3)에서 문제에 대한 조치를 했다고 이야기하고 있다. 새로운 에어컨 설치를 할 것이라고 했으므로 정답은 (B). 첫 문단보다는 전체 내용을 보아야 풀 수 있는 문제이다.
[패러프레이징] 지문의 A new air conditioner will be installed가 정답에서 a maintenance upgrade로 패러프레이징되었다.

4 위층 직원들이 어려움을 겪는 이유는?
(A) 창문이 고장 났다.
(B) 온도가 불편할 정도로 높다.
(C) 업무 공간이 너무 빽빽하다.
(D) 장비가 먼지로 덮여 있다.

[해설] 단서(4)에서 에어컨이 고장 났고, 창문이 완전히 열리지 않아서 매우 답답하고 더웠다고 했으므로 정답은 (B).

5 위층 직원들이 금요일에 해 달라고 요청받은 일은?
(A) 장비 치우기
(B) 사무실에서 나가 있기
(C) 오래된 장비 버리기
(D) 아래층에서 일하기

[해설] 지문에서 Friday가 언급된 부분을 찾아보자. on Friday afternoon이 쓰인 단서(5)에서 요청을 나타내는 표현 are asked to 뒷부분에 소지품과 장비들을 치워 달라고 했다. 따라서 정답은 (A).
[패러프레이징] 지문의 equipment가 정답에서 gear로 패러프레이징되었다.

UNIT 04 대상/출처 문제

PRE-STEP p.31

A
1 (A) 2 (B) 3 (A) 4 (A) 5 (B) 6 (B) 7 (A) 8 (A) 9 (A)
10 (B) 11 (A) 12 (A) 13 (B) 14 (A) 15 (A)

B
1 (B) 2 (A)

A
1 (A) submit, 근무시간 기록표를 제출하다
2 (B) short-term, 단기 연구 보조원
3 (A) indicate, 도착 날짜를 표시하다
4 (A) sign, 서류에 서명하다
5 (B) receive, 40% 할인을 받다
6 (B) purchase, 구매처
7 (A) form, 양식을 정확히 작성하다
8 (A) refund, 전액 환불
9 (A) detailed, 더 자세한 정보
10 (B) transportation, 믿을 수 있는 교통수단
11 (B) register, 지급 부서에 등록하다
12 (A) valid, 유효한 은행 계좌번호
13 (B) upgrade, ~의 좌석을 업그레이드하다
14 (A) follow, 따라야 할 몇 가지 규칙
15 (A) check, 명세서를 확인하다

B
1 Forrester Farms initiated a voluntary recall of its frozen chicken breasts manufactured at the Oregon facility.
(A) Forrester Farms gives voluntary tours of its factory in Oregon.
(B) Forrester Farms is taking back products that may have problems.

포레스터 팜스 사는 오리건 주 시설에서 제조된 냉동 닭가슴살의 자발적 회수를 시작하였습니다.
(A) 포레스터 팜스 사는 오리건 주 공장의 자원 견학을 제공합니다.
(B) 포레스터 팜스 사는 문제가 있을지도 모르는 제품들을 거두어들이고 있습니다.

2 A copy of the pay statement, including details about taxes and other withholdings, will be sent to you via e-mail.
(A) You will be sent financial information.
(B) You are expected to pay a tax bill.

세금과 기타 원천 징수액에 대한 자세한 내용이 들어 있는 급여 명세서 한 부가 이메일로 귀하에게 보내질 것입니다.
(A) 여러분은 재무 정보를 받게 될 것입니다.
(B) 여러분은 세금 계산서를 지불해야 합니다.

MAIN STEP 1 p.32

 헤어드라이기 사용 정보

If you want your TXP132 hair dryer to work properly, there are a few rules you need to follow:

− Do not cover or block any part when it is on
− Store it in a dry place

TXP132 헤어드라이기를 제대로 작동시키고 싶으시다면, 따라야 할 몇 가지 규칙이 있습니다:

− 전원이 켜져 있을 때, 어떤 부품도 덮거나 가리지 마시오
− 건조한 장소에 보관하시오

정보의 의도된 대상은?
→ 새 헤어드라이기의 주인

해설 첫 문장에서 이 지문이 헤어드라이기 사용 시 주의 사항에 대한 내용임을 알아차릴 수 있다. 그 이하에 상세한 주의 사항이 나열되어 있으므로, 정보가 의도하는 대상은 헤어드라이기를 구입한 사람이다.

전략 2 · 박물관 티켓 양식

Oaksville History Museum
Complimentary pass

Exhibition title: To the beginning of the human race
Issue date: July 10

오크스빌 역사 박물관
무료 입장권

전시 제목: 인류의 시초로
발급 날짜: 7월 10일

이 정보가 있을 것 같은 곳은?
→ 티켓

해설 박물관 이름, 무료 입장권, 전시 제목, 발급 날짜 같은 정보는 티켓에 실려 있는 내용들이다.

전략 2 · 셔틀 버스 서비스 안내 정보문

Downtown Shuttle Service

For reliable transportation between the airport and downtown hotels, book your seat on our airport shuttle! Using our service, you can get from the airport to any hotel downtown within 30 minutes. To book a ride on our shuttle, simply click the "Shuttle Reservations" button at the bottom of this page and indicate your flight arrival date and time along with the flight number.

시내 셔틀 버스 서비스

공항과 시내 호텔 간의 믿을 수 있는 교통수단으로 저희 공항 셔틀 버스의 좌석을 예약하세요! 저희 서비스를 이용하시면 공항부터 시내의 어떤 호텔까지라도 30분 이내에 도착하실 수 있습니다. 저희 셔틀 버스 탑승 예약을 하시려면, 이 페이지 아래의 "셔틀 버스 예약" 버튼을 클릭하시고 항공기 번호와 함께 항공기 도착 날짜와 시간을 표시해 주시기만 하면 됩니다.

이 정보가 있을 것 같은 곳은?
→ 웹사이트

해설 지문은 셔틀 버스 좌석 예약에 관한 정보문으로, '이 페이지 아래의 "셔틀 버스 예약" 버튼을 클릭하라'는 문구를 통해 웹사이트에 실린 내용임을 알 수 있다.

MAIN STEP 2   p.33

1 (A)   2 (C)

[1] 식품 회수 공지

Forrester Farms initiated a voluntary recall of its frozen chicken breasts manufactured at the Portland, Oregon facility. (1)If you have recently purchased frozen chicken, please check your freezer to see if your product has ALL of the following:
- Forrester Farms frozen chicken breasts label
- Product code T-44902
- Best before date of February 12

If this item is currently in your freezer, (1)please return it to the place of purchase for a full refund. If you have any questions about the recall, please e-mail Richard Mayaski, who is in charge of customer service. His e-mail is richardmayaski@forresterfarms.com.

포레스터 팜스 사는 오리건 주 포틀랜드 시설에서 제조된 냉동 닭가슴살의 자발적 회수를 시작하였습니다. (1)최근에 냉동 닭을 구매하셨다면, 식품이 다음과 같은 특징을 모두 가지고 있는지를 보기 위해 냉동실 확인을 부탁 드립니다:
- 포레스터 팜스 냉동 닭가슴살 라벨
- 제품 코드 T-44902
- 유통기한 2월 12일

만약 이 식품이 현재 냉동실에 있다면 (1)전액 환불을 위하여 구매처에 가져다 주십시오. 제품 회수에 대해 궁금한 점이 있다면 고객 서비스를 맡고 있는 리차드 마야스키 씨에 이메일을 보내시기 바랍니다. 그의 이메일은 richardmayaski@forresterfarms.com입니다.

어휘 **initiate** 시작하다 **voluntary** 자발적인 **recall** 회수, 리콜 **manufacture** 제조하다 **facility** (보통 복수형) 시설 **freezer** 냉동실 **best before date** 유통 기한 **refund** 환불

1 공지가 쓰인 대상은?

(A) 고기 구매자
(B) 공장 근로자
(C) 식료품점 계산원
(D) 양계가

보너스문제
① 마야스키 씨는 누구일 것 같은가?
→ 고객 서비스 책임자

해설 공지문이 쓰인 대상을 찾는 문제이므로 본문의 전반적인 내용을 파악해야 한다. 본문 속 단서(1)을 통해 공지문이 냉동 닭가슴살 구매자를 대상으로 쓰였음을 알 수 있다. 따라서 정답은 (A).

해설 마야스키 씨의 이름, 곧 고유명사가 등장한 부분을 찾도록 한다. 마지막 문단을 보면 리차드 마야스키 씨가 고객 서비스를 맡고 있다는 것을 알 수 있다.

[2] 식품 영양 정보

(2)Elliot's Bran Flakes: Great Taste in Every Bite!

Nutrition Facts
Serving Size: 3/4 cups

Amount per serving			
Calories 101			
Fat 0.78g	Cholesterol 0mg	Sugars 4.82g	Calcium 16.2mg
Sodium 215.21mg	Dietary Fiber 5.31g	Protein 2.77g	Iron 6.6mg

This product was manufactured in a facility that processes peanuts.

For further information, visit our Web site at www.elliotscereal.com.

(2)엘리엇의 브랜 플레이크: 씹을 때마다 최고의 맛!

영양 성분
제공량: 3/4컵

1회 제공당 함량			
칼로리 101			
지방 0.78g	콜레스테롤 0mg	당분 4.82g	칼슘 16.2mg
나트륨 215.21mg	식이 섬유 5.31g	단백질 2.77g	철분 6.6mg

이 제품은 땅콩을 가공하는 시설에서 제조되었습니다.

더 자세한 정보를 얻으려면 저희 웹사이트 www.elliotscereal.com을 방문하세요.

어휘 **bite** 씹다; 한 입 **nutrition** 영양 **serving** 제공 **fat** 지방 **sodium** 나트륨 **dietary fiber** 식이 섬유 **protein** 단백질 **iron** 철분 **process** 가공하다

2 이 정보가 가장 있을 것 같은 곳은?

(A) 영양 웹사이트
(B) 요리책
(C) 제품 포장
(D) 정보 소책자

보너스문제
② 엘리엇의 브랜 플레이크에 대해 사실인 것은?
→ 식이섬유가 단백질보다 더 많다.

해설 제품의 홍보 문구나 영양 성분표 등으로 미루어 보아, 이 정보는 제품 포장의 영양 정보임을 알 수 있다. 따라서 정답은 (C).

해설 정보문에서는 제시된 정보들을 비교, 대조해야 풀 수 있는 문제들이 출제되기도 한다. 지문의 표에 의하면 식이섬유가 5.31g, 단백질이 2.77g이라고 했으므로 엘리엇의 브랜 플레이크는 단백질보다 식이섬유를 더 많이 함유하고 있음을 알 수 있다.

FINAL STEP

1 (D) 2 (B) 3 (D) 4 (A) 5 (D) 6 (B) 7 (B)

[1-3] 하키 경기 티켓

SECTION	ROW	SEAT
212	B	29

ALL GATE ACCESS　　PRICE
LEVEL 4 CONCOURSE　$21.50

VANCOUVER CANUCKS
VS
BOSTON BRUINS
ROGERS ARENA

THURSDAY, JUNE 15
(3)Playing begins @ 7:00 P.M.
Doors open @ 6:00 P.M.

(2)SEASON TICKET HOLDER: Milton Oxley

- Street parking during games is not provided.
- (3)Games last three hours, including two intermissions.
- NO OUTSIDE FOOD OR DRINKS ARE PERMITTED.
- (1)Do NOT lose this ticket. Only ticket holders will be admitted to hockey games.
- (2)All season ticket holders receive a 40% discount on the purchase of arena merchandise.
- To upgrade your seat selection, visit www.majorleaguehockey.com at least two days before the game.

구역	줄	좌석
212	B	29

모든 입구 입장　　가격
4층 중앙 홀　21.50달러

밴쿠버 캐넉스
VS
보스턴 브루인스
로저스 경기장

6월 15일 목요일
(3)경기 시작 저녁 7시
경기장 개장 저녁 6시

(2)시즌 티켓 소지자: 밀턴 옥슬리

- 경기 중 거리 주차는 제공되지 않습니다.
- (3)경기는 세 시간 동안 진행되며 두 번의 중간 휴식 시간이 포함되어 있습니다.
- 외부 음식이나 음료는 반입이 허용되지 않습니다.
- (1)이 티켓을 분실하지 마십시오. 티켓 소지자들만이 하키 경기에 입장할 수 있습니다.
- (2)모든 시즌 티켓 소지자들은 경기장 제품 구매에 40% 할인을 받습니다.
- 좌석을 업그레이드하시려면, 최소한 경기 이틀 전까지 www.majorleaguehockey.com을 방문해 주십시오.

어휘 section 구역　row 줄　access 입장, 접근　concourse 중앙 홀　arena 경기장　intermission 중간 휴식 시간　permit 허용하다, 허락하다　admit 입장시키다　at least 최소한

1 이 양식이 발견될 것 같은 장소는?
(A) 식당
(B) 주차장
(C) 영화관 매표소
(D) 하키 경기장

해설 양식의 전반적인 내용으로 보아, 특히 단서(1)로 보았을 때, 해당 양식이 하키 경기의 티켓이라는 것을 알 수 있으므로 정답은 (D).

2 밀턴 옥슬리 씨에 대해 시사된 바는?
(A) 언제라도 좌석을 업그레이드할 수 있다.
(B) 할인된 가격에 제품을 살 수 있다.
(C) 경기장 지하에 주차할 수 있다.
(D) 현장에서 주류를 구입할 수 있다.

해설 이름이 직접 언급된 곳을 중심으로 살펴본다. 첫 번째 단서(2)로 그가 시즌 티켓 소지자라는 것을 알 수 있고, 두 번째 단서(2)에서 시즌 티켓 소지자들은 할인가에 제품 구매를 할 수 있다고 했으므로 정답은 (B).

3 게임이 끝나는 시각은?
(A) 저녁 6시
(B) 저녁 7시
(C) 저녁 9시
(D) 저녁 10시

해설 지문 내 두 개의 단서(3)을 통해서 정답을 유추해 낼 수 있다. 경기가 시작하는 시간은 저녁 7시이며, 약 세 시간 동안 경기가 이어질 것이라고 했으므로 정답은 (D)이다.

[4-7] 급여 수령 안내 이메일

To: Elliot Franks <elliotfranks@twente.edu>, Javier Mendez <javiermendez@twente.edu>, Aluk Yousuf <alukyousuf@twente.edu>
From: James Cho <jamescho@twente.edu>
Date: March 14
Subject: Information for new recruits
(6)**Attachment:** Payroll_registration.txt, Payroll_timesheets.txt

(4)I understand that you have all been employed as short-term research assistants in the social science department as part of the Population Survey Project. (7B)In order to be paid for your work, you must first register with the payroll department. (6) You will each need to fill out the forms accurately, providing the correct project code and a valid bank account number. Your project supervisor, Professor Herni Dwiliati, must sign these forms before you submit them to the payroll department. Once you are in the system, (7A)(7D)you should submit a time sheet at the end of each week. (5)After doing so, please leave the time sheets at the reception desk of the Registry Building by 5:30 P.M. on Friday.

Provided that the details are all correct, (7A)your payment will be processed on Wednesday. You should receive the money in your nominated account by Thursday. (7C)A copy of the pay statement, including details about taxes and other withholdings, will be sent to you via e-mail. Please check the statement to ensure that everything is in order.

If you have further questions regarding this process, please contact me by e-mail.

James Cho
Payroll Administrator

수신: 엘리엇 프랭크 <elliotfranks@twente.edu>, 하비에르 멘데즈 <javiermendez@twente.edu>, 알룩 유수프 <alukyousuf@twente.edu>
발신: 제임스 조 <jamescho@twente.edu>
날짜: 3월 14일
제목: 신입 사원들에 대한 정보
(6)첨부: 급여_기록.txt, 급여_근무 시간 기록표.txt

(4)여러분이 인구 조사 프로젝트의 일환으로 사회과학부에 단기 연구 보조로 채용된 것으로 알고 있습니다. (7B)여러분의 업무에 대한 급여를 지급받으시려면, 먼저 급여 지급 부서에 등록을 해야 합니다. (6)각자 이 양식들을 정확하게 작성하고, 정확한 프로젝트 번호와 유효한 은행 계좌번호를 알려주세요. 여러분이 급여 지급 부서에 서류들을 제출하기 전에, 프로젝트 감독관인 헤르니 드와일리어티 교수가 그것들에 서명을 해야 합니다. 시스템에 등록이 되고 나면, (7A)(7D)매주 말에 근무 시간 기록표를 제출해야 합니다. (5)이렇게 한 후에, 근무 시간 기록표를 금요일 오후 5시 30분까지 등록소 건물의 안내 데스크로 가져다 주세요.

세부 정보가 모두 올바르다면, (7A)급여는 수요일에 처리될 것입니다. 목요일에는 정해진 계좌로 돈을 받으실 것입니다. (7C)세금과 기타 원천 징수액에 대한 자세한 내용이 들어 있는 급여 명세서는 이메일로 귀하에게 보내질 것입니다. 모든 것이 제대로 되어 있는지 확인하기 위해 명세서를 확인해 주세요.

이 절차에 관하여 더 질문이 있으시면, 저한테 이메일을 보내 주세요.

급여 지급 관리자
제임스 조 드림

어휘 short-term 단기의 assistant 보조 register with ~에 등록하다 payroll department 급여 지급 부서 fill out ~을 작성하다 form 양식 accurately 정확히 provide 제공하다 valid 유효한 account number 계좌번호 submit A to B A를 B에 제출하다 time sheet 근무 시간 기록표 provided that ~라면 detail (보통 복수형) 세부 사항 process 처리하다 receive 받다 nominate 지명[임명]하다 pay statement 급여 명세서 withholding 원천 징수액 ensure 확인하다 in order 제대로 된 regarding ~에 관하여

4 이 이메일이 의도한 대상은?
   (A) 임시 연구 직원들
   (B) 대학 관리자들
   (C) 급여 지급 부서 직원들
   (D) 프로젝트 감독관들

해설 이메일을 받는 대상은 지문에서 대명사 you로 표현된다. 단서(4)를 보면, you에 대한 정보가 as 이하에 언급되어 있다. 따라서 정답은 (A).
패러프레이징 지문의 short-term이 정답에서 temporary로, assistants가 employees로 각각 패러프레이징되었다.

5 직원들이 근무 시간 기록표를 두어야 하는 곳은?
(A) 사회과학부 사무실
(B) 제임스 조의 사무실
(C) 급여 지급 우편함
(D) 안내 데스크

해설 time sheets에 대한 구체적인 내용을 묻고 있으므로, 이 단어를 지문에서 찾아본다. 단서(5)에서 근무 시간 기록표를 등록소 건물의 안내 데스크에 가져다 놓으라고 했으므로 정답은 (D)이다.

6 이메일에 서류를 첨부한 이유는?
(A) 프로젝트에 대해 더 자세한 설명을 하기 위해
(B) 직원들이 작성해야 할 서류를 보내기 위해
(C) 직원 계약의 세부 사항을 설명하기 위해
(D) 절차가 진행되는 방법에 대한 예시를 보여주기 위해

해설 첨부된 서류에 대해 묻고 있으므로, 먼저 Attachment에 있는 첨부 파일들의 이름을 확인해 보자. 급여 기록과 근무 시간 기록표 파일인데, 단서(6)에서 이 양식들을 작성해 달라고 했으므로 정답은 (B)이다.

7 급여 시스템에 대해 언급되지 않은 것은?
(A) 주 단위로 처리된다.
(B) 각 개별 학과에 의해 관리된다.
(C) 직원들에게 자세한 명세서를 제공한다.
(D) 근무 시간 기록을 필요로 한다.

해설 NOT 문제는 지문과 선택지를 하나하나 대조해 가며 풀어야 한다. (A), (C), (D)는 모두 지문에서 언급된 내용이다. 단서(7B)를 보면 급여 처리는 급여 지급 부서에서 이루어진다는 것을 알 수 있으며, 각 학과에서 개별적으로 관리한다는 내용은 찾을 수 없다. 따라서 정답은 (B).

UNIT 05 세부 정보 문제

PRE-STEP
p.37

A 1 (B) 2 (A) 3 (B) 4 (A) 5 (B) 6 (A) 7 (A) 8 (B) 9 (B)
   10 (A) 11 (A) 12 (B) 13 (B) 14 (A) 15 (B)

B 1 (B) 2 (B)

A 1 (B) leader, 산업의 <u>선두 주자</u>
   2 (A) insurance, <u>보험</u> 조사원
   3 (B) inventory, <u>재고</u> 대부분을 소실시키다
   4 (A) apparel, 야외 활동 <u>의류</u>와 제품
   5 (B) complimentary, <u>무료</u> 좌석 업그레이드
   6 (A) tough, <u>혹독한</u> 시험 과정을 통과하다
   7 (A) loyal, <u>단골</u> 고객
   8 (B) exclusive, <u>고급</u> 여행 상품을 제공하다
   9 (B) network 다른 전문가들과 <u>인맥을 형성하다</u>
   10 (A) disclose, 상황을 <u>밝히다</u>
   11 (A) repair, <u>수리</u> 비용을 추정하다
   12 (B) refreshments, 식사와 <u>다과</u>
   13 (B) executive, <u>이사회</u>
   14 (A) dedication, ~의 일에 대한 <u>헌신</u>
   15 (B) reputation, 회사의 <u>명성</u>을 높이다

B 1 Unlike our other products, the lightweight design of our rain jacket makes it easy to fold up and store in a backpack without taking up much space.
   (A) The jacket can withstand all types of weather.
   (B) The jacket is compact for easy storage.

저희의 다른 제품들과 달리, 우리 비옷의 경량 디자인은 많은 공간을 차지하는 일 없이 접어서 배낭에 넣는 것을 매우 쉽게 만들어 줍니다.
(A) 이 재킷은 모든 종류의 날씨를 견딜 수 있습니다.
(B) 이 재킷은 소형 크기로 보관이 쉽습니다.

2 The executive board is meeting with the fire chief tomorrow to discuss the exact cause of the fire.
   (A) The fire chief has caused a problem with officials.
   (B) The reason for the fire will be examined by officials.

이사회는 내일 소방서장과 만나 화재의 정확한 원인에 대해 논의할 것입니다.
(A) 소방서장은 관리자들과 문제를 초래하였습니다.
(B) 화재 원인이 관리자들에 의해 조사될 것입니다.

MAIN STEP 1
p.38

 워크숍 개최 알림 회람

The Better Tomorrow Association (BTA) is holding a workshop at the Hayward Plaza on Saturday, October 13. ①The workshop will teach you practical methods for reducing your impact on the environment. From conserving resources to planting trees, you'll discover a number of ways in which you can make a difference.

미래 발전 협회(BTA)가 10월 13일 토요일에 헤이워드 플라자에서 워크숍을 개최합니다. ①워크숍에서는 여러분이 환경에 미치는 영향을 줄일 수 있는 실용적인 방법들을 가르쳐 드릴 것입니다. 자원 보존에서부터 나무 심기까지, 여러분은 변화를 가져올 수 있는 많은 방법들을 알게 될 것입니다.

We would like many employees to attend this important event, so we are happy to announce that ②we will be paying half of the registration fee for anyone who wishes to participate. Simply send a copy of your registration receipt to the accounting department, and you will be reimbursed on your next paycheck.

저희는 많은 직원들이 이 중요한 행사에 참여하기를 원하기 때문에 ②참석하고자 하는 분에게 등록비 절반을 지불한다는 것을 알려 드리게 되어 기쁩니다. 회계부로 등록비 영수증 사본을 보내시기만 하면, 다음 번 급여에 환급해 드리겠습니다.

어휘 **practical** 실용적인 **method** 방법 **impact** 영향 **conserve** 보존하다 **discover** 알다, 발견하다

① 참가자들이 워크숍에서 배울 수 있는 것은?
→ 환경 살리기

해설 첫 번째 문단에서 워크숍의 내용을 소개하고 있다. 참가자들은 환경에 미치는 영향을 줄일 수 있는 방법들을 배울 것이라 했으므로, 환경 살리기 방법에 대한 워크숍임을 알 수 있다.

② 회사가 직원들을 위해 할 일은?
→ 등록비 일부 지불하기

해설 회람은 회사의 직원들을 대상으로 하는 것이므로, we가 언급된 곳을 찾아본다. 두 번째 문단에서 참석 희망자에게 등록비의 절반을 지불해 준다고 했다.

MAIN STEP 2

p.39

1 (A)   **2** (A)

[1] 야외 활동 의류 광고

For the last fifteen years, Nordic Athletic has been an industry leader in outdoor apparel and products. One of our most recent clothing items to pass our tough testing process is the Always-Dry rain jacket, which is made of waterproof material. (1)The Always-Dry rain jacket is perfect for long hiking trips or camping weekends when you plan to be active, but need to be prepared for all weather conditions. Unlike our other products, the lightweight design of the Always-Dry rain jacket makes it easy to fold up and store in a backpack without taking up much space. We guarantee that if you buy this jacket you will not be disappointed.

지난 15년간, 노르딕 애틀레틱 사는 야외 활동 의류와 제품 산업에서 선두 주자였습니다. 혹독한 시험 과정을 거친 저희의 가장 최신 의류 품목들 중 하나는 바로 얼웨이즈-드라이 비옷인데, 이것은 방수 직물로 만들어졌습니다. (1)얼웨이즈-드라이 비옷은 활동적이고 싶지만 모든 종류의 기상 상황에 대비해야 하는 장기 산행이나 주말 캠핑에 최적화되어 있습니다. 저희의 다른 제품들과 달리, 얼웨이즈-드라이 비옷의 경량 디자인은 많은 공간을 차지하는 일 없이 접어서 배낭에 넣는 것을 매우 쉽게 만들어 줍니다. 이 비옷을 구입하시면 실망하지 않으실 것이라고 보장합니다.

어휘 **recent** 최신의, 최근의 **tough** 혹독한, 거친 **process** 과정 **be made of** ~으로 만들어지다 **waterproof** 방수의 **material** 직물, 천 **active** 활동적인 **be prepared for** ~에 대비하다 **lightweight** 경량의, 가벼운 **guarantee** 보장하다

1 얼웨이즈-드라이 비옷이 고안된 목적은?

 (A) 야외 활동
 (B) 겨울 스포츠
 (C) 고강도 운동
 (D) 짧은 산행

해설 단서(1)을 통해 알 수 있듯이, 얼웨이즈-드라이 비옷은 장기 산행이나 주말 캠핑과 같은 활동에 최적화되었다고 했으므로 정답은 (A).

패러프레이징 지문의 long hiking trips or camping weekends가 정답에서 Outdoor activities라는 상위어로 패러프레이징되었다.

해설 자사의 다른 제품들과 달리 이 비옷은 경량이라서 접어서 배낭에 넣기 쉽다고 했다.

보너스문제
① 얼웨이즈-드라이 비옷이 노르딕 애틀레틱 사의 다른 제품들과 다른 점은?
→ 크기가 초소형이다.

[2] 여행 상품 광고 이메일

To: Michael Naughton <naughton_mike@pmail.net>
From: Doral Airlines <noreply@doralairlines.com>
Date: November 1
Subject: Early bird rates

Dear Mr. Naughton,

Doral Airlines is offering exclusive tour deals to Europe. Take advantage of our early-bird offer by booking flights during the next several days. You will save thousands of dollars on the cost of tickets to any European destination! Our records indicate that you are a loyal customer who travels with us regularly. Because of your dedication to our airline, (2)we will give you a complimentary seat upgrade during this promotion period. If you're interested in this offer, please respond to this e-mail as soon as possible.

Sincerely,
Doral Airlines Customer Service

수신: 마이클 노튼 <naughton_mike@pmail.net>
발신: 도랄 항공사 <noreply@doralairlines.com>
날짜: 11월 1일
제목: 조기 예약 요금

노튼 씨께,

도랄 항공사가 유럽으로 가는 고급 여행 상품을 제공하고 있습니다. 다음 며칠간 비행기를 예약하셔서 저희 조기 예약 할인을 이용하세요. 유럽의 모든 목적지로 가는 티켓 비용에서 수천 달러를 절약하실 수 있습니다! 저희 기록은 고객님이 정기적으로 저희 항공사로 여행하시는 단골 고객임을 보여 주고 있습니다. 저희 항공사에 대한 고객님의 헌신 때문에, (2)저희는 이 판촉 기간 동안 고객님께 무료 좌석 업그레이드를 제공해 드릴 것입니다. 이 제안에 관심이 있으시다면, 가능한 한 빨리 이 이메일에 답장 주시기 바랍니다.

도랄 항공사 고객 서비스부 드림

어휘 early bird 조기 예약 offer 제공하다; 할인 exclusive 고급의; 독점적인 take advantage of ~을 이용하다 loyal customer 단골 고객 dedication 헌신 complimentary 무료의

---

2 노튼 씨가 무료 업그레이드를 받을 수 있는 방법은?
전략 2
(A) 이메일 답장을 보냄으로써
(B) 온라인으로 티켓을 예약함으로써
(C) 제공된 번호로 전화함으로써
(D) 단골 고객 카드를 제시함으로써

해설 문제가 How can ~? (~할 수 있는 방법은?)으로 시작하는 것으로 보아 수단, 방법을 묻는 문제이며, 이러한 문제의 단서는 지문의 후반부에 등장하는 경우가 많다. 단서(2)를 보면 무료 좌석 업그레이드에 대해 언급하며 이 제안에 관심이 있을 시 이메일에 답장을 하라고 했으므로 정답은 (A).

패러프레이징 지문의 respond to this e-mail이 정답에서 sending an e-mail reply로 패러프레이징되었다.

보너스문제
② 노튼 씨에 대해 시사된 바는?
→ 그는 도랄 항공사를 자주 이용한다.

해설 지문에서 노튼 씨가 도랄 항공사의 단골 고객이라고 하였으므로, 그가 도랄 항공사를 자주 이용한다는 것을 알 수 있다.

FINAL STEP
p.40

1 (A) 2 (C) 3 (B) 4 (A) 5 (D) 6 (B)

[1-3] 긴급 회의를 알리는 이메일

To: Anneke Rhodes <arhodes@yutaniindustries.com>
From: Barry Olson <barryolson@yutaniindustries.com>
(2)**Date:** October 28
Subject: Urgent meeting tomorrow!

Hi Anneke,

(1)I know you're on vacation, but we have a major

수신: 아넥 로즈 <arhodes@yutaniindustries.com>
발신: 베리 올슨 <barryolson@yutaniindustries.com>
(2)날짜: 10월 28일
제목: 내일 긴급 회의!

안녕하세요 아넥 씨,

(1)당신이 휴가 중인 걸 알지만, 우리에게 중요한 문제가 생겼고, 따라서 당신에게 이 사실을 알려야 할 필요가 있었습니다. 어제 이른 아침에, 창고에서 불이 났고 우리의 재고 대부분이

issue, and consequently, I needed to let you know about it. Early yesterday morning, a fire erupted in the warehouse and destroyed most of our inventory. The executive board is meeting with the fire chief tomorrow to discuss the exact cause of the fire. The insurance investigator will also be present to outline what portion of the repair costs will be covered by our existing policy.

(2)After that meeting tomorrow, our leadership team will also gather to determine how we intend to resolve several other problems. For instance, (3) whereas there are three outstanding orders that need to be shipped, we now have no stock to fill them. I have contacted those three customers and disclosed the situation. But we must still develop a plan to cope with production delays. We are obviously going to have to rebuild and restock. As the warehouse superintendent, it's crucial that you be involved in this conversation. Are you available to call in and participate in the production meeting via phone at 11 A.M.?

Please let me know as soon as possible whether you can do this.

Barry Olson
Administrator

소실되었습니다. 이사회는 내일 소방서장과 만나 정확한 화재의 원인에 대해 논의할 것입니다. 보험 조사원도 참석하여 어느 정도의 수리 비용이 기존 보험으로 보장될 것인지 대략적으로 설명할 것입니다.

(2)내일 그 회의 후에, 저희 지도부도 여러 가지 다른 문제들을 어떻게 해결할 것인지 정하기 위해 모입니다. 예를 들면, (3)배송되어야 하는 세 건의 미처리된 주문이 있지만, 우리는 현재 그것들을 처리할 재고가 하나도 없습니다. 저는 세 고객들에게 연락을 해서 상황을 밝혔습니다. 하지만 우리는 여전히 생산 지연에 대처할 계획을 세워야만 합니다. 우리는 확실히 시설을 다시 세우고 재고를 다시 채워야 할 것입니다. 창고 관리자로서, 당신이 이 대화에 참여하는 것은 중요합니다. 전화를 하셔서 오전 11시에 전화상으로 생산 회의에 참여하실 수 있습니까?

당신이 이것을 할 수 있는지 어떤지 가급적 빨리 알려주세요.

관리자
베리 올슨 드림

어휘 on vacation 휴가 중인   erupt 나다, 분출되다   warehouse 창고   executive board 이사회   insurance investigator 보험 조사원   present 참석한   cover 보장하다; 씌우다   determine 결정하다   outstanding 미처리된; 미불의   disclose 밝히다   cope with ~에 대처하다   superintendent 관리자   be involved in ~에 참여하다[관련되다]

1 이메일의 목적은?
   (A) 동료에게 위기에 대해 알리려고
   (B) 다양한 업무를 위임하려고
   (C) 전화기 사용을 요청하려고
   (D) 회의 결과를 알리려고

2 이메일에 따르면, 10월 29일에 일어날 것으로 예상되는 일은?
   (A) 보험료 납부가 처리될 것이다.
   (B) 일간 현황 회의가 취소될 것이다.
   (C) 계획이 세워질 것이다.
   (D) 재고 평가가 시행될 것이다.

3 논의될 문제에 대해 언급된 것은?
   (A) 여러 고객들이 불만 전화를 했다.
   (B) 세 건의 미처리된 주문이 이행되지 못하고 있다.
   (C) 수송품이 예정보다 늦게 배송되었다.
   (D) 일부 주문이 잘못 처리되었다.

해설 첫 단락의 연결사 consequently(결과적으로) 뒤에 이메일의 목적이 나와 있다. 휴가 중인 아넥 씨에게 이메일을 보낸 이유는 창고에 난 불로 재고가 소실된 것을 알리고 대책을 논의하는 회의에 참여할 것을 요청하기 위해서이다. 정답은 (A).

오답 피하기 이메일의 마지막 부분에서 아넥스 씨에게 전화 회의 참여 여부를 묻고 있긴 하지만 글쓴이인 올슨 씨가 본인의 전화기 사용을 요청하는 것은 아니기 때문에 (C)는 오답.

해설 두 개의 단서를 종합하여 풀어야 하는 문제이다. 이메일이 쓰인 날이 10월 28일이므로 10월 29일은 이메일을 쓴 다음날이다. 지문에서 내일(tomorrow)이 언급된 두 번째 단락을 보면 문제 해결을 위해 지도부가 모인다는 내용이 나와 있다. 따라서 정답은 (C).

해설 지문에서 문제점이 언급된 곳을 찾아야 한다. 단서(3)에서 미처리된 주문이 있지만 그것을 처리할 재고가 없다고 하였으므로 정답은 (B).

오답 피하기 생산이 지연되었다고는 했지만 늦은 배송에 대해 구체적으로 언급한 것은 아니므로 (C)는 오답.

[4-6] 외부 회의 공지

NOTICE

On behalf of the management team, I'm writing this notice to all employees who are planning to attend the National Journalism Conference in Seattle. (4)The conference was originally scheduled for May 21 at the Bloomfield Convention Center. However, we've just been informed that it has been postponed due to a scheduling conflict at the venue. It will now be held on June 4, beginning at 8 A.M. All other plans, including the carpool arrangements, will remain the same.

As outlined in last month's newsletter, (5)this conference is a great opportunity to network with other professionals in the industry as well as to enhance the company's reputation. There will be a number of lectures for participants to choose from, and meals and refreshments will be served throughout the day. In honor of the occasion, a live band will play in the evening, so we expect it to be an enjoyable event. (6)Full details about the conference are posted on the bulletin board in the employee break room. Should you have questions, please refer to the materials there.

Thank you,

Richard Jordan, Office Manager

알림

경영진을 대표하여, 시애틀에서 열리는 국제학술회의에 참석할 계획인 모든 직원들에게 이 공지를 씁니다. (4)회의는 원래 5월 21일에 블룸필드 컨벤션 센터에서 진행될 것으로 예정되어 있었습니다. 그러나, 우리는 장소가 겹쳐지는 문제 때문에 회의가 연기되었다고 통지 받았습니다. 회의는 이제 6월 4일에 열릴 것이며, 오전 8시에 시작할 것입니다. 카풀 예약을 포함한 다른 모든 계획은 그대로 유지될 것입니다.

지난달 사보에서 대략 설명해 드렸다시피, (5)이번 회의는 회사의 명성을 높일 수 있을 뿐만 아니라 업계 내의 다른 전문가들과 인맥을 형성할 수 있는 좋은 기회입니다. 참가자들이 선택할 수 있는 많은 강의들이 있을 것이며, 하루 종일 식사와 다과가 제공될 것입니다. 행사를 기념하여, 저녁에 라이브 밴드가 연주할 것이므로 굉장히 즐거운 행사가 될 것으로 기대하고 있습니다. (6)회의에 대한 모든 세부 사항은 직원 휴게실에 있는 게시판에 게시되어 있습니다. 문의 사항이 있으시면 그곳에 있는 자료를 참고해 주세요.

감사합니다,

사무장 리처드 조던 드림

어휘 on behalf of ~을 대표하여 management team 경영진 attend 참석하다 conference 회의 be scheduled for ~로 일정이 잡혀져 있다 postpone 연기하다 scheduling conflict 일정이 겹치는 것 venue 장소 carpool 카풀, 승용차 함께 타기 arrangement 준비, 합의 remain 계속 ~이다 outline 대략으로 설명하다; 개요 enhance 높이다 reputation 명성 refreshment (보통 복수형) 다과 bulletin board 게시판

---

4 공지의 목적은?
(A) 일정 변경을 알리기 위해
(B) 행사 보조를 요청하기 위해
(C) 카풀 운전자들을 구성하기 위해
(D) 행사를 준비한 직원들에게 감사를 표하기 위해

해설 공지의 목적을 묻고 있으므로 우선 지문의 첫 단락을 살펴본다. 단서(4)에 회의가 원래 5월 21일이었다가 장소가 겹쳐져서 연기된 사실이 언급되고 그 뒤에 변경된 일정이 설명되고 있으므로 정답은 (A).

5 회의 참석의 이점으로 언급된 것은?
(A) 등록자는 모든 강의를 들을 수 있다.
(B) 호텔 숙박료가 지불된다.
(C) 기자들은 글쓰기 실력을 향상시킬 수 있을 것이다.
(D) 참석자들은 업계 인맥을 맺을 수 있다.

해설 단서(5)에서 이번 회의가 회사의 명성을 높이고 업계 전문가들과 인맥을 형성할 수 있는 기회라고 했으므로 정답은 (D).
패러프레이징 지문의 network with other professionals in the industry가 정답에서 make industry connections로 패러프레이징되었다.

6 조던 씨에 의하면, 직원들이 더 많은 정보를 얻을 수 있는 방법은?
(A) 안내 책자를 읽음으로써
(B) 게시판을 확인함으로써
(C) 웹사이트를 방문함으로써
(D) 이메일을 보냄으로써

해설 단서(6)을 통해 알 수 있듯이, 회의에 관한 세부 사항은 직원 휴게실의 게시판에 게시되어 있으므로 정답은 (B).

UNIT 06 NOT/TRUE 문제

PRE-STEP   p.43

A 1 (B) 2 (A) 3 (B) 4 (A) 5 (B) 6 (A) 7 (B) 8 (A) 9 (B)
       10 (A) 11 (A) 12 (A) 13 (A) 14 (B) 15 (B)

B 1 (A) 2 (B)

A
1 (B) documentation, 모든 비용 서류
2 (A) admission, 축제의 입장료
3 (B) attraction, 제품의 특장점
4 (A) supervise, 직원을 감독하다
5 (B) unload, 상자와 매장 반품 상품을 내리다
6 (A) feature, 소수의 가수들을 출연시키다
7 (B) record, 검증된 실적
8 (A) delivery, 배달품의 수송을 준비하다
9 (B) operate, 창고 장비를 작동시키다
10 (A) former, ~의 전 직장 동료
11 (A) standards, 산업 안전 기준을 충족시키다
12 (A) recognized, 세계적으로 인정받은 디자이너
13 (A) promising, 유망한 경력의 시작
14 (B) reimbursements, 월별 상환 처리
15 (B) profitable, 수익성 있는 사업에 투자하다

B
1 You should send me a copy of your driver's license so that we can add you to the company auto insurance policy.
   (A) An ID is needed for some paperwork.
   (B) A clean driving record is required.

운전면허증의 사본도 저에게 주셔야 하는데 이는 회사 자동차 보험 정책에 귀하를 가입시키기 위함입니다.
(A) 몇몇 서류 작업을 위해 신분증이 필요합니다.
(B) 위법 사례가 없는 운전 기록이 필요합니다.

2 By continuing to open stores in various countries, we are on our way to becoming the leading toy company in the world.
   (A) We are developing more and more unique toys.
   (B) We are growing our business internationally.

다양한 국가에서 계속 매장을 개업함으로써, 우리는 세계 선두의 완구 기업으로 가는 중입니다.
(A) 우리는 점점 더 많은 독특한 장난감들을 개발하고 있습니다.
(B) 우리는 국제적으로 사업을 확장해 가고 있습니다.

MAIN STEP 1   p.44

 프린터 광고

Enhance Your Office with the Kovar All-in-one Printer

Feature: Graves Electronics is the exclusive retailer for the Kovar-500 printer, which can (C)scan, copy, fax, and print documents at the touch of a button. Its lightweight design and (B)low-energy usage make it perfect for offices of any size. (A)Customers who purchase the device this week will get an additional $50 off.

코바 올인원 프린터로 사무실의 가치를 높이세요.

특징: 그레이브스 전자는 버튼을 누르는 것만으로 서류를 (C)스캔, 복사, 팩스, 출력할 수 있는 코바-500 프린터의 독점 판매사입니다. 이것의 경량 디자인과 (B)낮은 에너지 사용률은 어떤 크기의 사무실에도 안성맞춤이 되게 해 줍니다. (A)이번 주에 이 기계를 구매하는 고객님께서는 추가로 50달러의 할인을 받으실 수 있습니다.

어휘 enhance 높이다, 강화하다   exclusive 독점적인   lightweight 경량의, 가벼운

프린터의 특징으로 언급되지 않은 것은?
(A) 조기 구매 할인
(B) 에너지 효율
(C) 문서 스캔
(D) 무선 호환성

해설 지문에 나열된 프린터의 특징들 중 무선 호환성에 관한 내용은 찾아볼 수 없다. 정답은 (D).

 청소 서비스 광고

Having trouble keeping your home or office looking its best? Let Speed Cleaners make your space sparkle! We offer a variety of cleaning packages to fit your needs. Hourly rates start at just $20, and we're available Monday through Saturday from 7 A.M. to 8 P.M. And you won't have to worry about harsh cleaners or chemicals in your home. The cleaning products we use are chemical-free and won't cause harm to the environment. You'll be impressed by our respectful and courteous staff. Despite being the fastest in the business, they always get the job done right.

가정이나 사무실이 최상의 상태로 보이도록 유지하는 데 어려움이 있으신가요? 스피드 클리너즈로 당신의 공간을 빛나게 하세요! 저희는 여러분의 요구에 부합하는 다양한 청소 패키지를 제공합니다. 시간당 요금은 단돈 20달러부터 시작하며, 월요일부터 토요일 오전 7시에서 오후 8시까지 이용 가능합니다. 그리고 집안에서 강한 세제나 화학 물질에 대해 걱정하실 필요가 없습니다. 저희가 사용하는 청소용품은 화학 성분이 없으며 환경에 피해를 주지 않습니다. 여러분은 저희의 공손하고 정중한 직원에게서 좋은 인상을 받으실 것입니다. 업계에서 가장 빠르면서도, 작업은 항상 제대로 합니다.

어휘 **hourly** 시간당의 **rate** 요금 **harsh** 너무 강한, 혹독한 **chemical** 화학 물질 **courteous** 정중한, 공손한

스피드 클리너즈에 대해 사실인 것은?
(A) 직원들의 경험이 매우 풍부하다.
(B) 서비스를 매일 이용할 수 있다.
(C) 환경 친화적인 제품을 사용한다.
(D) 지역에서 가장 저렴한 시간당 요금을 제공한다.

해설 지문에서 광고되고 있는 회사의 전반적 사항에 대해 묻고 있으므로, 지문 전체에 흩어진 단서들을 찾아 선택지와 대조해야 한다. 환경에 피해를 주지 않는 청소용품을 사용한다고 했으므로 정답은 (C).

오답 피하기 (A) 직원들의 경험이 풍부하다는 언급은 없고, (B) 서비스는 월~토요일까지만 이용 가능하다고 했으므로 매일은 아니고, (D) 요금이 지역에서 가장 낮다는 언급 또한 없으므로 모두 오답이다.

패러프레이징 지문의 The cleaning products we use are chemical-free and won't cause harm to the environment.가 정답에서 uses environmentally friendly products로 패러프레이징되었다.

MAIN STEP 2   p.45

1 (D)   **2** (C)

[1] 전 직장 동료의 소식에 관한 회람

MEMO

I have some news to share about our friend and former coworker. As you may remember, (1A)Allan Geere worked here at Cortex for three years before leaving to continue his education. Allan has gone on to complete graduate school and (1B)obtain his master's degree in vocal performance. He is now trying to establish himself as a musical theater actor, and he surely has the voice for it. (1C)Allan's unexpected concerts around the office were just a

회람

저는 우리의 친구이자 전 직장 동료에 대한 소식을 공유하고자 합니다. 기억하시는 바와 같이, (1A)앨런 기어 씨는 학업을 계속하기 위해 떠나기 전에 여기 코텍스 사에서 3년간 일했습니다. 앨런 씨는 이어서 대학원 과정을 마쳤고, (1B)성악 전공에서 석사 학위를 취득했습니다. 그는 현재 뮤지컬 연극 배우로서의 지위를 확고히 하기 위해 노력하고 있으며, 그는 분명히 그렇게 되기 위한 목소리를 갖고 있습니다. (1C)사무실에서의 앨런 씨의 깜짝 콘서트는 분명히 유망한 경력이 될 것의 시작에 불과한 것이었습니다!

start to what will surely be a promising career!

어휘 former 이전의 continue 계속하다 complete 끝마치다 graduate school 대학원 obtain 획득하다 master's degree 석사 학위 establish (~로서의 지위를) 확고히 하다 promising 유망한

---

1 앨런 기어 씨에 대해 언급되지 않은 것은?
(A) 코텍스 사의 전 직원이다.
(B) 석사 학위를 받았다.
(C) 직장에서 노래하곤 했다.
(D) 희극 연기를 선호한다.

보너스문제
① 이 회람의 목적은?
→ 동료의 최신 소식을 전하기 위해

해설 NOT 문제는 선택지를 하나하나 대조하며 풀어야 한다. 단서들을 통해 앨런 씨가 코텍스 사에서 일하다가 그만두고 석사 학위를 딴 후 뮤지컬 배우가 되려고 한다는 것을 알 수 있다. 하지만 그가 희극 연기를 선호한다는 내용은 찾아볼 수 없으므로 정답은 (D).

해설 회람 첫 줄에서 전 직장 동료의 소식을 공유하고자 한다고 했으므로, 글의 목적은 동료의 소식을 전하기 위한 것임을 알 수 있다.

---

[2] 출장비 환급 안내 이메일

To: Colleen Friske <friskecolleen@newmail.net>
From: Riley Stendahl <rilst2@sfassociates.com>
Date: April 30
Subject: In response to your question

Dear Ms. Friske,

On behalf of Strehl-Friedman Associates, I wanted to answer your question about corporate travel. Yes, we will provide you with a company car for traveling to meet clients. (2)Please ensure that all documentation of expenses related to the car or to your travel—gas, emergency repairs, tollbooth fees, overnight lodging, etc.—are carefully saved and dated to expedite the processing of monthly reimbursements for these expenditures. You should also send me a copy of your driver's license so that we can add you to the company auto insurance policy.

Riley Stendahl, HR Manager
Strehl-Friedman Associates

수신: 콜린 프리스키 <friskecolleen@newmail.net>
발신: 릴리 스텐달 <rilst2@sfassociates.com>
날짜: 4월 30일
제목: 문의 사항에 답하여

프리스키 씨께,

스트렐-프리드만 협회를 대표하여, 회사 출장에 대한 귀하의 문의에 답변해 드리겠습니다. 네, 저희는 고객을 만나러 가는 것에 대해 귀하께 회사 차량을 제공해 드릴 것입니다. (2)차량 또는 출장과 관련된 비용의 모든 서류 —연료, 긴급 수리, 톨게이트 요금, 숙박비 등— 를 잘 보관하고 날짜를 적어 이러한 경비의 월별 상환 처리가 신속하게 이루어지도록 해 주시기 바랍니다. 운전면허증의 사본도 저에게 주셔야 하는데 이는 회사 자동차 보험 정책에 귀하를 가입시키기 위함입니다.

스트렐-프리드만 협회
인사 담당자, 릴리 스텐달 드림

어휘 on behalf of ~을 대표하여 provide A with B A에게 B를 제공하다 documentation 서류 expenses (보통 복수형) 비용 emergency 긴급 lodging 숙소 expedite 신속히 처리하다 reimbursement 상환 insurance policy 보험 (증권)

---

2 이메일에 따르면, 스트렐-프리드만 협회에 대해 사실인 것은?
(A) 긴급 수리 서비스를 제공한다.
(B) 자동차 보험 대리점을 운영한다.
(C) 출장 비용을 상환해 준다.
(D) 여권 사본을 요구한다.

보너스문제
② 프리스키 씨에 대해 추론할 수 있는 것은?
→ 스텐달 씨에게 질문을 했다.

해설 단서(2)에 따르면, 출장 경비 관련 서류들을 통해 비용을 상환해 준다고 하였으므로 정답은 (C).
오답 피하기 선택지 (A)와 (D)에 본문에 등장한 emergency repair, copy와 같은 단어가 나왔다고 해서 이들을 정답으로 선택하지 않도록 한다.

해설 프리스키 씨가 이메일의 수신인이고, 스텐달 씨가 이메일의 발신인이라는 정보를 파악해 두어야 한다. 이메일 본문의 첫 문장에서 출장에 관한 문의에 답변해 드리겠다고 했으므로, 이전에 프리스키 씨가 스텐달 씨에게 질문을 했었음을 알 수 있다.

FINAL STEP

p.46

1 (C) **2** (C) **3** (D) **4** (B) **5** (B)

[1-3] 축제 소개 기사

(1)**The 4th Annual Maceió Winter Jazz Festival is Approaching**

December 3—(1)(2A)(3)Similarly to last year's event, more than 300 people are expected to attend the fourth annual Maceió Winter Jazz Festival from December 10 to 16 in Deodoro Park. (2B)Each day will have simultaneous performances. Years ago, this little jazz festival was no more than a one-day concert featuring a handful of singers and instrumentalists. Today, however, the festival has evolved into a week-long event that celebrates several dozen jazz musicians throughout Brazil. (2D) CDs, instruments, and other merchandise will be on sale for the entire festival.

Admission to the festival is $5 per day or $25 for the full week. Its hours of operation are from 9 A.M. to 9 P.M. on weekdays and 11 A.M. to 5 P.M. on weekends. The primary attraction for most attendees will be the performance of world-famous jazz singer Renée Byron. (3)She will perform at 7 P.M. on the first evening of the festival.

(1)제4회 연례 마세이오 겨울 재즈 축제가 다가오다

12월 3일 – (1)(2A)(3)작년의 행사와 마찬가지로, 12월 10일에서 16일까지 데오도로 공원에서 열릴 제4회 연례 마세이오 겨울 재즈 축제에 300명 이상의 사람들이 참석할 것으로 예상된다. (2B)매일 동시에 여러 공연들이 열릴 예정이다. 수년 전에, 이 작은 재즈 축제는 소수의 가수들과 연주자들이 출연하는 하루짜리 음악회에 지나지 않았다. 그러나, 오늘날 이 축제는 브라질 전역의 수십 명의 재즈 음악가들을 축하하는 일주일간의 행사로 발전했다. (2D)CD, 악기, 여타 다른 상품들이 축제 기간 내내 할인 판매될 것이다.

축제의 입장료는 하루 5달러, 일주일 전체는 25달러이다. 운영 시간은 평일에는 오전 9시부터 저녁 9시까지, 주말에는 오전 11시부터 오후 5시까지이다. 대부분의 참가자들의 주요 관심사는 세계적으로 유명한 재즈 가수 르네 바이런 씨의 공연일 것이다. (3)그녀는 축제 첫날 저녁 7시에 공연을 할 예정이다.

어휘 approach 다가오다, 접근하다 simultaneous 동시의, 같이 일어나는 no more than ~에 지나지 않는, ~ 이상이 아닌 a handful of 소수의, 적은 instrumentalist (악기) 연주자 evolve into ~으로 발전[진화]하다 be on sale 할인 판매 중인 entire 전체의 admission 입장료

1 기사의 주제는?
(A) 연기된 악기 연주회
(B) 음반 가게의 개업
(C) 유명한 연례 축제
(D) 재즈 경연의 결과

[해설] 제목과 서두의 단서(1)을 통해 알 수 있듯이 이 기사는 연례 마세이오 겨울 재즈 축제에 대한 것이므로 정답은 (C). 주제를 묻는 문제를 풀 때는 제목과 지문 첫 부분을 주의 깊게 보도록 하자.

2 행사의 특징으로 언급되지 않은 것은?
(A) 지난 해에 300명 이상의 사람들이 참여했다.
(B) 몇몇 공연은 동시에 열린다.
(C) 음료가 무대 근처에서 판매될 것이다.
(D) 관심 있는 손님들은 상품을 구매할 수 있다.

[해설] 행사의 특징이 나열되어 있는 기사의 첫 번째 문단을 통해 (A), (B), (D)가 언급된 부분을 찾아볼 수 있지만 음료 판매에 대한 내용은 없으므로 정답은 (C).

3 바이런 씨에 대해 시사된 바는?
(A) 축제를 마무리하기 위해 초대되었다.
(B) 행사의 창설자이다.
(C) 브라질의 마세이오에 거주하지 않는다.
(D) 12월 10일에 공연할 것이다.

[해설] 바이런 씨의 공연 날짜는 직접 언급되지 않았기 때문에 단서를 종합해 추론해야 한다. 마지막 문단의 단서(3)에서 그녀가 축제 첫날 공연할 예정임을 알 수 있고, 기사의 첫 문장의 단서(3)을 통해 12월 10일이 공연 첫날임을 알 수 있다. 정답은 (D).

[4-5] 완구 회사 구인 광고

Toy World International

(4)Toy World International, which was established by the internationally recognized toy designer Milo Lampen, is a Minnesotan toy manufacturer. Since its establishment seventy years ago, Toy World has expanded to sell merchandise in nearly 2,000 stores across the globe. By continuing to open stores in various countries, we are on our way to becoming the leading toy company in the world. With this plan, we are filling the following positions:

48989: Warehouse Operations Team Member (Minneapolis)
Warehouse operations team members unload all cartons and store returns. They also prepare shipments for delivery and load trailers. In order to meet industry safety standards, they must be certified to operate all warehouse equipment.

49464: Head, Facilities Department (Duluth)
This position is responsible for all aspects of facility maintenance such as (5A)assigning duties, (5D) supervising staff, monitoring equipment repairs, and (5C)ordering maintenance supplies.

59417: Store Manager (Rochester)
Store managers oversee the effective and profitable operations of each store. They manage customer satisfaction and staff development. Candidates must have a proven track record in management and generating significant revenue.

Interested applicants must send résumés to careers@toyworld.com with the position title and five-digit job number identified in the subject line.

어휘 recognized 인정된, 알려진 manufacturer 제조사 establishment 설립 expand 확장하다 merchandise 상품 warehouse 창고 operation 운영 unload (짐을) 내리다 carton 상자 shipment 수송품, 적하물 certify 자격증을 교부하다 equipment 장비 assign 할당하다 supervise 감독하다 oversee 감독하다 candidate 지원자, 후보자 significant 상당한; 중요한 revenue 수익

토이 월드 인터내셔널

(4)세계적으로 인정받은 완구 디자이너 밀로 램펜에 의해 설립된 토이 월드 인터내셔널은 미네소타에 있는 완구 제조사입니다. 70년 전에 설립된 이후로, 토이 월드는 확장을 거듭하여 전세계의 약 2,000여개의 매장에서 상품을 판매하고 있습니다. 다양한 국가에서 계속 매장을 개업함으로써, 우리는 세계 선두의 완구 기업으로 가는 중입니다. 이 계획을 가지고, 우리는 다음 일자리를 충원할 것입니다:

48989: 창고 운영 팀원 (미니애폴리스)
창고 운영 팀원은 모든 상자와 매장 반품 상품을 내립니다. 그들은 또한 배달품 수송도 준비하고 트레일러도 적재합니다. 산업 안전 기준을 충족시키기 위해서, 그들은 모든 창고 장비를 작동시킬 수 있는 자격을 갖추어야 합니다.

49464: 책임자, 설비 부서 (덜루스)
이 직책은 (5A)업무 분담, (5D)직원 감독, 설비 수리 감독, 그리고 (5C)유지 보수 물품 주문과 같은 시설 관리의 모든 부분을 책임져야 합니다.

59417: 매장 관리자 (로체스터)
매장 관리자는 각 매장의 효율적이고 수익성 있는 운영을 감독합니다. 그들은 고객 만족과 직원 계발을 관리합니다. 지원자는 관리와 상당한 수익을 창출했다는 검증된 실적을 갖고 있어야 합니다.

관심 있는 지원자는 careers@toyworld.com으로 직책명과 다섯 자리 직책 번호를 제목란에서 확인할 수 있게 하여 이력서를 보내면 됩니다.

---

4 토이 월드 인터내셔널 사에 대해 시사된 바는?
(A) 미국에서만 상품을 판매한다.
(B) 유명한 디자이너에 의해 설립되었다.
(C) 총 2,000명의 직원이 있다.
(D) 6개의 직무에서 신입 사원을 채용하고 있다.

해설 토이 월드 인터내셔널 사 구인 광고의 첫 문장의 which 이하를 보면 회사가 세계적인 디자이너에 의해 설립되었음을 알 수 있다. 따라서 정답은 (B).
오답 피하기 (C)의 2,000이라는 숫자는 전 세계에 있는 토이 월드 인터내셔널 사의 매장 개수이므로 오답.
패러프레이징 지문의 internationally recognized가 정답에서 famous로 패러프레이징되었다.

5 설비 부서 책임자의 업무로 포함되지 않은 것은?
(A) 직원들에게 업무 분담하기
(B) 각 상점의 운영 감독하기
(C) 필요한 보급품 요청하기
(D) 직원 감독하기

해설 설비 부서 책임자의 업무가 설명되어 있는 세 번째 문단을 보아야 한다. (A), (C), (D)에 해당하는 내용은 모두 찾아볼 수 있지만 각 매장의 운영을 감독하는 일은 매장 관리자의 업무이므로 정답은 (B).

UNIT 07 추론 문제

PRE-STEP   p.49

A 1 (B)   2 (B)   3 (A)   4 (B)   5 (A)   6 (A)   7 (B)   8 (B)   9 (A)
      10 (B) 11 (A) 12 (A) 13 (B) 14 (B) 15 (A)

B 1 (B)   2 (A)

A
1 (B) expand, 운영을 확대하다
2 (B) entire, 마을 전체
3 (A) encouraged, ~하도록 권장 받다
4 (B) bottle, 무료 와인 한 병
5 (A) hesitate, 연락하기를 망설이다
6 (A) excited, ~을 하게 되어 흥분되다
7 (B) secondary, 부차적인 장소를 마련해 두다
8 (B) around, 임박해 있다

9 (A) likelihood, 비가 올 가능성
10 (B) rate, 고정 이자율
11 (A) brief, 간략한 설명
12 (A) guarantee, 대출에 대한 보증
13 (B) variety, 아주 다양한 제품들
14 (B) efficient, 효율적인 기계
15 (A) presented, 표에 제시된 데이터

B
1 I would like to discuss with you directly how we can ensure that future deliveries will arrive on time.
   (A) I want to postpone a delivery that was scheduled for later.
   (B) I want to make sure we don't receive our orders late again.

2 When you buy your tickets, there will be an opportunity to indicate your desire to participate in this special event.
   (A) You can show your interest at the time of purchase.
   (B) You can share your comments about what we offer.

향후 배송품이 제시간에 도착하도록 할 수 있는 방법에 관해 당신과 직접 이야기하고 싶습니다.
(A) 다음에 예정된 배송을 더 늦추고 싶습니다.
(B) 저희의 배송품을 다시는 늦게 받는 일이 없도록 하게 하고 싶습니다.

표를 구입하실 때, 이 특별한 행사에 참여하겠다는 의사를 표현하실 기회가 있을 겁니다.
(A) 구매하실 때 관심을 보여 주시면 됩니다.
(B) 저희가 제공하는 것에 대한 의견을 공유하실 수 있습니다.

MAIN STEP 1   p.50

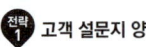 고객 설문지 양식

Current feedback form

Name: Takita Yumi
Purchase you made at Subtext Phones: Hassler 4

Service Areas	Good	Satisfactory	Poor
Speed of service	×		
Friendliness of staff		×	
Staff knowledge of products			×

최신 피드백 양식

이름: 타키타 유미
서브텍스트 폰에서 구매하신 것: 해슬러 4

서비스 분야	좋음	만족스러움	나쁨
서비스 속도	×		
직원의 친절도		×	
직원들의 제품 지식			×

타키타 씨가 받은 서비스에 대해 추론할 수 있는 것은?
→ 직원들이 제품 지식을 더 갖추어야 한다.

해설 양식 작성자인 타키타 씨가 Staff knowledge of products 항목의 Poor란에 체크했는데 이는 곧 제품에 대한 직원들의 지식이 부족하므로 이것이 개선되어야 한다고 생각한다는 뜻이다.

MAIN STEP 2

p.51

1 (B)　　2 (B)

[1] 기차표

Timbercrest Railway

Date of ticket acquisition: January 13
Passenger name: Randall Havisham
(1)**Frequent traveler number:** 015 481 694
Paid by: Platinum Card XXXX XXXX XXXX 7534

Date	Train	Departure	Arrival	Seat
February 2, Mon	SWR 466	Toronto 6:05 A.M.	Ottawa 10:35 A.M.	10D
February 4, Wed	SWR 872	Ottawa 3:35 P.M.	Toronto 8:05 P.M.	12B

Printed tickets and personal identification must be presented upon boarding the train.

팀버크레스트 철도

티켓 구매일: 1월 13일
승객 이름: 랜달 하비샴
(1)단골 승객 번호: 015 481 694
지불 방법: 플래티넘 카드 XXX XXXX XXXX 7534

날짜	기차	출발	도착	좌석
2월 2일 월요일	SWR 466	토론토 오전 6:05	오타와 오전 10:35	10D
2월 4일 수요일	SWR 872	오타와 오후 3:35	토론토 오후 8:05	12B

기차에 탑승하자마자 출력한 티켓과 개인 신분증을 제시하셔야 합니다.

어휘 acquisition 구매, 구입　passenger 승객　identification 신분증　upon *doing* ~하자마자　board 탑승하다

1 하비샴 씨에 대해 암시된 것은?
(A) 티켓 값을 현금으로 지불했다.
(B) 기차로 정기적으로 여행을 다닌다.
(C) 오타와에서 3박을 할 것이다.
(D) 아침에 토론토로 돌아올 것이다.

보너스문제
① 하비샴 씨가 토론토로 떠날 때는?
→ 수요일 오후

해설 티켓에 숨어 있는 단서를 찾아야 한다. 하비샴 씨는 티켓 구매자이며, 티켓의 Frequent traveler number(단골 승객 번호)라는 표현을 통해 하비샴 씨가 기차로 정기적으로 여행을 다닌다는 것을 추론할 수 있다. 따라서 정답은 (B).

해설 양식 사항을 보고 유추해 내야 하는 문제이다. 하비샴 씨는 수요일 오후 3시 35분에 오타와에서 토론토를 향해 떠나므로 정답은 '수요일 오후'이다.

[2] 배송 지연 문제 제기 및 방문 안내 이메일

To: Derek Houston <dhouston@houstonsteel.com>
From: Heather Carlson <heather@sterling.com>
Subject: Re: Problem with Delivery Delays
Date: (2)May 28

Dear Mr. Houston,

I'm contacting you today regarding your factory's recent shipments of steel pipes to our warehouse. I received each of the last three shipments between two and three days late. Our clients depend on Sterling Construction to finish the projects on

수신: 데렉 휴스턴 <dhouston@houstonsteel.com>
발신: 헤더 칼슨 <heather@sterling.com>
제목: 회신: 배달 지연의 문제
날짜: (2)5월 28일

휴스턴 씨께,

당신의 공장에서 최근에 저희 창고로 강철 파이프를 배송한 것과 관련하여 오늘 연락 드리게 됐습니다. 지난 세 번의 배송품을 각각 2~3일 늦게 받았습니다. 저희 고객들은 스털링 건설이 공사를 제시간에 끝낼 것으로 믿습니다. 따라서 공급업체로부터 자재를 적시에 배달받는 것은 저희 사업의 성공에 필수적입니다.

time. Therefore, timely delivery of materials from our suppliers is essential to the success of our business. I am confident we can resolve this issue quickly and effectively. (2)I am scheduled to visit your factory this coming month. I would like to discuss with you directly how we can ensure that future deliveries will arrive on time. I appreciate your attention to this matter.

Heather Carlson
Warehouse Manager, Sterling Construction

우리가 이 문제를 빨리 그리고 효과적으로 해결할 수 있을 거라고 확신합니다. (2)저는 다음 달에 당신의 공장을 방문하기로 예정되어 있습니다. 향후 배송품이 제시간에 도착하도록 할 수 있는 방법에 관해 당신과 직접 이야기하고 싶습니다. 이 문제에 주목해 주셔서 감사합니다.

스털링 건설, 창고 관리자
헤더 칼슨 드림

어휘 delivery delay 배송 지연 regarding ~와 관련하여 shipment 배송(품), 선적(품) depend on ~ to do ~이 …할 것으로 믿다 therefore 따라서, 그러므로 timely 적시의, 시기 적절한 supplier 공급업체 resolve an issue 문제를 해결하다 effectively 효과적으로 be scheduled to do ~할 예정이다 ensure that (반드시) ~하도록 하다 attention 주목, 관심

2 방문에 대해 추론할 수 있는 것은?
(A) 새로운 프로젝트에 대한 것일 것이다.
(B) 6월에 있을 것이다.
(C) 많은 기업들이 참여할 것이다.
(D) 연기되었다.

해설 이메일이 보내진 것은 5월 28일이다. 발신인인 헤더 칼슨 씨가, 다음 달에 공장을 방문할 예정이라고 했으므로 방문은 6월에 이루어질 것임을 추론할 수 있다. 따라서 정답은 (B).

보너스문제
② 칼슨 씨가 휴스턴 씨에게 연락한 이유는?
→ 배송 지연에 대해 불평하기 위해서

해설 칼슨 씨는 파이프 배송 건이 지연되는 것에 대해 불평하기 위해 이메일을 보낸 것이다.

FINAL STEP p.52

| 1 (C) | 2 (C) | 3 (B) | 4 (D) | 5 (B) | 6 (B) |

[1-3] 와인 축제 광고 전단지

Averill Creek Wine Festival

The annual Averill Creek Wine Festival at Princeton Park is just around the corner! (1)For one day only—June 28 from 7 A.M. to 9 P.M.—the entire town of Averill Creek will celebrate everything wine-related.

Vineyard and winery owners are encouraged to attend 'New Technologies in Wine Making' at 4 P.M., when a new machine will be demonstrated. Instead of crushing grapes, this efficient device is designed to split them open in a time-saving (3) way.

During the famous 'Wine-Tasting' event held on the main stage, participants will be blindfolded and asked to taste and identify various types of wine. When you buy your tickets, there will be an opportunity to indicate your desire to participate in this special event.

애버릴 크릭 와인 축제

프린스턴 공원에서의 연례 애버릴 크릭 와인 축제가 임박했습니다! (1)단 하루 동안, 6월 28일 오전 7시부터 저녁 9시까지, 애버릴 크릭 마을 전체가 와인과 관련된 모든 것을 축하할 것입니다.

포도밭과 와인 양조장 소유주들께서는 오후 4시에 있을 '와인 제조의 새로운 기술'에 참석하시기를 권해 드리는데, 이때 새로운 기계가 시연될 것입니다. 포도를 으깨는 것 대신, 이 효율적인 기계는 시간을 절약하는 (3)방식으로 포도를 쪼개어 벌리도록 설계되어 있습니다.

주 무대에서 열리는 그 유명한 '와인 시음' 행사 동안 참가자들은 눈가리개를 하고 다양한 종류의 와인을 맛본 뒤 맞히게 됩니다. 입장권을 구입하실 때 이 특별한 행사에 참여하겠다는 의사를 표현하실 기회가 있을 겁니다.

Tickets cost $25 and include one free bottle of wine. (2)As is typical for this time of year, there is a likelihood of wet weather. Just in case, we have a secondary indoor location prepared so that the festival can go on as planned.

입장권은 25달러이며 무료 와인 한 병의 가격이 포함되어 있습니다. (2)해마다 이때쯤 늘 그렇듯이 비가 올 가능성이 있습니다. 만약을 위해 우리는 축제가 예정대로 진행될 수 있도록 부차적인 실내 장소를 마련해 두었습니다.

어휘 around the corner 임박하여, 아주 가까운 vineyard 포도밭, 포도 농장 winery 와인 양조장 demonstrate (기계나 전자 제품 등의) 시연을 하다 crush 으깨다, 부수다 split 쪼개다, 가르다 time-saving 시간을 절약하는 blindfolded 눈가리개를 한 identify 식별하다 indicate a desire 의사를 표하다, 욕심(욕망)을 드러내다 likelihood of ~이 있을 가능성 wet weather 비 오는 날씨 just in case 만약을 위해 secondary 부차적인, 또 다른 indoor 실내의

1 이 전단지가 의도한 대상은?
 (A) 프린스턴 공원 직원
 (B) 축제 자원봉사자
 (C) 애버릴 크릭 거주자
 (D) 행사 기획자

해설 전단지 앞부분의 단서(1)을 통해 와인 축제가 애버릴 크릭 마을 내에서 열린다는 것을 알 수 있으므로, 이 전단지가 애버릴 크릭 마을의 거주자를 대상으로 쓰였음을 알 수 있다. 따라서 정답은 (C).

2 날씨에 대해 추론할 수 있는 것은?
 (A) 행사가 항상 실내에서 열리므로 무관하다.
 (B) 악천후 시의 계획은 아직 세워지지 않았다.
 (C) 해마다 이때쯤 보통 비가 내린다.
 (D) 비가 올 경우 축제 일정이 변경될 것이다.

해설 해마다 같은 시기에 비가 온다고 하였으므로 이를 통해 올해도 이 시기에 비가 내릴 것임을 유추할 수 있다. 정답은 (C).
패러프레이징 지문의 there is a likelihood of wet weather가 정답에서 It commonly rains로 패러프레이징되었다.

3 2단락, 세 번째 줄의 어휘 "way"와 의미상 가장 유사한 것은?
 (A) 친척
 (B) 방법
 (C) 방향
 (D) 습관

해설 유사 의미 어휘를 찾는 문제는 문맥 속에서 어휘의 적절한 뜻을 파악하는 것이 핵심이다. 새 기계는 포도를 쪼개는 '방식'을 사용한다고 해야 자연스러우므로 '방법'을 의미하는 (B)가 정답.

[4-6] 은행 고객 문의 응대 이메일

To: Jeffery Neal <jneal@email99.com>
From: Prime Bank <et@primebank1.net>
Date: January 29
Subject: RE: Your inquiry

Dear Mr. Neal,

(4)Thank you for your inquiry about applying for a loan through Prime Bank. We have a wide variety of loans available for small businesses such as yours. After reading the brief description you gave of your need to finance a building upgrade, I think the Professional Construction Loan would be right for you. It can be used for any type of building project related to your business. (5)We offer both a five-year term and a seven-year term, and you can borrow up to $15,000, which will have a fixed interest rate of 7.3% for the life of the loan.

Along with your loan application, you must submit documents such as your bank statements, tax records, or a business license. You will also have to provide a form of collateral—such as a vehicle or a house—as a guarantee for the loan. Furthermore, (6) the loan agent will scrutinize your credit history

수신: 제프리 닐 <jneal@email99.com>
발신: 프라임 은행 <et@primebank1.net>
날짜: 1월 29일
제목: 회신: 귀하의 문의 사항

닐 씨께,

(4)프라임 은행을 통해 대출 신청을 하는 것에 대해 문의를 해주셔서 감사 드립니다. 저희는 고객님의 기업과 같은 소기업들이 이용 가능한 다양한 종류의 대출 상품을 보유하고 있습니다. 건물 개조에 자금을 대야 할 필요성에 대해 고객님이 해주신 간략한 설명을 읽은 후, 저는 전문적인 건설 대출이 고객님께 적절할 것이라고 생각합니다. 이 대출은 고객님의 사업과 관련된 모든 종류의 건설 계획에 사용 가능합니다. (5)저희는 5년짜리와 7년짜리 둘 다를 제공하며, 고객님은 15,000달러까지 대출하실 수 있는데, 대출 기간 동안 7.3퍼센트의 고정 이자율을 가질 것입니다.

고객님의 대출 신청서와 함께 은행 명세서, 세무 기록이나 사업자 등록증과 같은 서류들을 제출하셔야 합니다. 또한 —자동차 또는 집과 같이—한 가지 형태의 담보를 대출에 대한 보증으로 제공하셔야 합니다. 뿐만 아니라, (6)대출 대리인이 고객님이 과거에 얼마나 신용을 잘 관리했는지 보기 위해서 신용 기록을 면밀히 조사할 것입니다. 미불 잔고나 연체된 융자금이 있으시다면 거부될 수도 있습니다.

to see how well you've handled credit in the past. If you have outstanding balances or delinquent loans, you may be denied.

Should you be approved for the loan, the funds will be deposited into the business checking account you currently hold with us. Please don't hesitate to contact me if you have any further questions.

Sincerely,

Eunice Trevino
Loan Agent, Prime Bank

대출 승인이 나면, 대출금이 현재 저희 은행에 갖고 계신 기업 당좌 예금 계좌로 예치될 것입니다. 문의 사항이 더 있으시면 주저 말고 제게 연락 주시기 바랍니다.

프라임 은행, 대출 상담사
유니스 트레비노 드림

어휘 inquiry 문의 apply for a loan 대출 신청을 하다 brief 간략한, 짧은 description 설명 finance 자금을 대다; 자금 interest rate 이자율 application 신청서 submit 제출하다 bank statement 은행 명세서 license 등록증; 면허증 collateral 담보물 guarantee 보증 scrutinize 면밀히 조사하다 handle 다루다 outstanding balance 미불 잔고 delinquent 연체된 deny 거부하다 approve 승인[허가]하다 deposit 예치하다 hesitate 주저하다

4 이메일이 대상으로 하는 사람은?
(A) 신용카드 소지자
(B) 학자금 대출 신청자
(C) 은행 신입 사원
(D) 소기업 소유주

해설 이메일 서두에 있는 단서(4)를 보면, 닐 씨가 소기업이 이용 가능한 대출에 대해 문의한 것에 대해 은행이 답장하는 것임을 알 수 있으므로 정답은 (D).

5 트레비노 씨가 대출에 대해 시사한 바는?
(A) 수표의 형태로 지급될 것이다.
(B) 이자율이 바뀌지 않을 것이다.
(C) 보험 확인증을 필요로 한다.
(D) 7개월 내에 상환해야 한다.

해설 단서(5)에 따르면, 대출 이율이 7.3%로 고정된다고 하였으므로 정답은 (B).
패러프레이징 지문의 a fixed interest rate가 정답에서 Its interest rate will not change로 패러프레이징되었다.

6 닐 씨에 대해 암시된 내용은?
(A) 계좌에 미불 잔고가 있다.
(B) 신용 사용 내역이 확인될 것이다.
(C) 신청서에 누락된 서류가 있다.
(D) 그의 상업용 건물들이 담보로 사용될 것이다.

해설 단서(6)에 따르면, 대출 신청자는 신용 기록을 조사받게 될 것이라 하였으므로 정답은 (B).
오답 피하기 신용 기록 조사에서 미불 잔고가 발견되면 대출 신청이 거부될 수도 있다는 것은 대출 조건 중 하나로 언급된 것이지 닐 씨가 그렇다는 내용은 아니므로 (A)는 오답.
패러프레이징 지문의 the loan agent will scrutinize ~ in the past가 정답에서 His credit usage will be checked로 패러프레이징되었다.

UNIT 08 유의어 문제

PRE-STEP
p.55

A 1 (A)   2 (B)   3 (B)   4 (B)   5 (A)   6 (A)   7 (A)   8 (B)   9 (B)
      10 (A) 11 (B) 12 (A) 13 (B) 14 (A) 15 (A)

B 1 (B)   2 (A)

A
1 (A) controversial, 논란이 많은 사안
2 (B) banquet, 시상식 연회
3 (B) interest, 배우는 것에 흥미를 보이다
4 (B) outstanding, 미지불된 잔액
5 (A) salary, 기본급을 올리다
6 (A) stability, 더 높은 재정 안정성을 도모하다
7 (A) struggle, 가족을 부양하려고 고군분투하다
8 (B) pay off, 학자금 대출을 갚다
9 (B) enroll, 마케팅 세미나에 등록하다
10 (A) complete, 다양한 과제를 완수하다
11 (B) opinion, 소프트웨어에 대한 의견
12 (A) appropriate, 적절한 시기
13 (B) experimental, 실험적 기반으로
14 (A) attached, 첨부된 설문지
15 (A) engage, 토론에 참여하다

B
1 This program will not only help to make you a trained promoter, but also enable you to have a broader view of the fast-changing market.
(A) There are advantages of being a formally trained professional.
(B) There are a couple of benefits of attending this event.

이 프로그램은 여러분을 훈련된 기획자로 만들어 줄 뿐 아니라 빠르게 변화하는 시장을 보는 더 넓은 시야를 가질 수 있게도 해줄 것입니다.
(A) 정식으로 훈련받은 전문가가 되는 것에는 장점이 있습니다.
(B) 이 행사에 참여하는 것에는 몇몇 이점이 있습니다.

2 It currently bears the name of the corporation that invested the necessary finances to see the project through to completion.
(A) It is named after its main corporate sponsor.
(B) It changed its name throughout stages of the project.

현재 그것은 프로젝트가 완료되는 것을 보기 위해 필요한 자금을 댔던 기업의 이름을 갖고 있다.
(A) 주요 후원업체의 이름을 따서 지어졌다.
(B) 프로젝트가 진행됨에 따라 이름을 바꾸었다.

MAIN STEP 2
p.57

1 (D)   2 (A)

[1] 기업 동향에 대한 기사

Industry Leader Focuses on Employee Satisfaction

Insurance giant Ainsworth Industries has always had an outstanding reputation for customer service and dependable policies. Now, under the direction of newly appointed CEO Roger Nelson, the

업계 선두가 직원 만족도에 집중하다

대기업 보험사인 아인즈워스 사는 고객 서비스와 신뢰할 수 있는 정책으로 항상 뛰어난 명성을 얻어 왔다. 이제, 새롭게 임명된 CEO 로저 넬슨 씨의 지휘하에, 회사는 내부를 되돌아보고

company is turning inward. It's seeking to improve working conditions for employees in an effort to retain skilled workers. Starting in the new year, the company will (1)raise base salaries and bonuses across the board. The management team hopes this will help to create more financial stability for employees, many of whom are struggling to support their families or pay off student debts.

있다. 회사는 숙련된 직원들을 보유하기 위한 노력으로 직원들의 근무 환경을 향상시킬 방안을 찾고 있다. 새해부터 시작하여, 회사는 전반적으로 기본급과 보너스를 (1)올릴 것이다. 가족을 부양하거나 학자금 대출을 갚으려고 고군분투하고 있는 직원들이 많으므로 경영팀은 이것이 그들의 더 높은 재정 안정성을 도모하는 데 도움이 되길 바라고 있다.

어휘 satisfaction 만족도 insurance 보험 outstanding 뛰어난 reputation 명성 dependable 신뢰할 수 있는 appoint 임명하다 working conditions 근무 환경 retain 보유하다 skilled 숙련된 across the board 전반적으로 stability 안정성 struggle to *do* ~하려고 고군분투하다 support 부양하다 pay off ~을 갚다

---

1 기사에서, 1단락 네 번째 줄의 어휘 "raise"와 의미상 가장 유사한 것은?
(A) 벌다
(B) 모으다
(C) 데려오다
(D) 증가시키다

해설 단서(1)에서 raise는 기본급과 보너스를 '올리다'라는 의미로 쓰였다. 따라서 그 의미가 비슷한 (D)가 정답. 어휘의 대표적 의미와 유사한 것을 고르는 문제이므로 어휘 주변 문장만 보고도 문제를 충분히 풀 수 있다.

보너스문제
① 넬슨 씨에 대해 추론할 수 있는 것은?
→ 그는 직원들을 고무시키고 싶어 한다.

해설 넬슨 씨는 숙련된 직원들을 보유하기 위해 근무 조건을 개선시킬 방법을 찾고 있다고 했으므로 직원들을 고무시키고 싶어 한다는 것을 유추할 수 있다.

[2] 마케팅 세미나 광고

Enroll in KreyTech's marketing seminar and you will see excellent outcomes! Our specially designed programs will give you an (2)edge in the business world. You will learn how to manage profits and clients effectively. This program will not only help to make you a trained promoter, but also enable you to have a broader view of the fast-changing market. It is scheduled to be held on December 12. Interested parties should register early to get in for free.

크레이테크 사의 마케팅 세미나에 등록하시면 훌륭한 결과를 보게 될 것입니다! 저희의 특별히 고안된 프로그램은 여러분에게 업계에서의 (2)유리함을 제공할 것입니다. 여러분은 수익과 고객을 효율적으로 관리하는 법을 배울 것입니다. 이 프로그램은 여러분을 훈련된 기획자로 만들어 줄 뿐 아니라 빠르게 변화하는 시장에 대해 더 넓은 시야를 가질 수 있게도 해줄 것입니다. 세미나는 12월 12일에 열리는 것으로 예정되어 있습니다. 관심이 있으신 단체는 무료로 참석할 수 있도록 조기 등록하시기 바랍니다.

어휘 enroll 등록하다 outcome 결과 designed 고안된 edge 유리함 manage 관리하다 profit 수익, 이익 broad 넓은 view 시야 party 단체 register 등록하다 for free 무료로

---

2 광고에서, 1단락 두 번째 줄의 어휘 "edge"와 의미상 가장 유사한 것은?
(A) 이점
(B) 옆
(C) 경계
(D) 변화

해설 edge는 '가장자리, 위기, 유리함' 등 그 의미가 여러 가지이므로 어휘 주변의 문맥을 유심히 읽어야 문제를 풀 수 있다. 세미나의 교육 프로그램이 제공해 줄 수 있는 것으로는 '유리함'이 적절하다. 따라서 정답은 (A).

보너스문제
② 조기 등록의 이점으로 언급된 것은?
→ 무료 입장

해설 무료로 참석할 수 있도록 조기 등록하라고 했으므로 조기 등록의 이점은 무료 입장이다.

FINAL STEP

p.58

| 1 (A) | 2 (D) | 3 (B) | 4 (B) | 5 (C) | 6 (A) | 7 (C) | 8 (D) | 9 (D) |

[1-4] 소프트웨어 평가 요청 이메일

From: Sergio Chicon <sergio.chicon@tamunatech.org>
To: All employees <allstaff@tamunatech.org>
Date: January 11
Subject: Software feedback
Attachment: Questionnaire_newsw.pdf

Hi everyone,

We recently installed a new office software program on an experimental basis. The program enables us to enter proposals and project details into a searchable database. It also contains time-tracking and budgeting components.

This program has been used in various capacities by nearly every department in our organization for approximately six months now. Thus, we feel it is an appropriate time to conduct a formal review of the software before we purchase it permanently. (2)We want to hear directly from employees whether you think this software works for your position.

(1)I need about 15–20 volunteers to meet on Saturday, January 25, and participate in a focus group. Ideally, we would like two individuals to (3)act as representatives for each department. In the morning, you will engage in a discussion with coworkers sharing opinions on the software and its functionality. We want to know if any aspects are particularly useful, challenging, or difficult to understand. Conversely, during the afternoon session, you will complete various tasks using the software to determine whether or not additional training should be provided.

Please inform me if you wish to volunteer your time. (4)Anyone who is interested in participating but is unavailable on January 25 can still help by completing and returning the attached questionnaire by January 20.

Regards,

Sergio Chicon
Vice-president, Tamunatech Inc.

발신: 세르지오 시콘 <sergio.chicon@tamunatech.org>
수신: 전 직원 <allstaff@tamunatech.org>
날짜: 1월 11일
제목: 소프트웨어 평가
첨부: Questionnaire_newsw.pdf

안녕하세요 여러분,

우리는 최근에 새로운 사무용 소프트웨어 프로그램을 시험적으로 설치했습니다. 이 프로그램은 우리가 제안서나 프로젝트 세부 내용들을 검색 가능한 데이터베이스에 입력할 수 있도록 해 줍니다. 이 프로그램은 또한 시간 추적과 예산 편성 기능을 포함하고 있습니다.

이 프로그램은 지금까지 약 6개월 동안 우리 회사의 거의 모든 부서에서 다양한 용도로 이용되어 왔습니다. 따라서, 지금이 우리가 그 소프트웨어를 영구적으로 구매하기 전에 공식적인 평가를 진행해야 할 적절한 시기라고 생각합니다. (2)우리는 이 소프트웨어가 여러분의 업무에 효용이 있다고 생각하는지 직원들로부터 직접 듣기를 원합니다.

(1)저는 1월 25일 토요일에 만나서 포커스 그룹에 참여할 15-20명 정도의 지원자들이 필요합니다. 바라건대, 각 부서의 대표 (3)역할을 해 주실 분이 두 명씩 있었으면 합니다. 오전에 여러분은 동료들과 토론에 참여하여 소프트웨어와 그 기능에 대한 의견을 나누게 될 것입니다. 우리는 특히 어느 부분이 유용하고, 어렵고, 이해하기가 힘든지 알고자 합니다. 반대로, 오후 시간에는 추가 교육이 제공되어야 하는지 아닌지 결정하기 위해 소프트웨어를 사용하여 다양한 과제를 완수하게 될 것입니다.

시간을 내 자원하고자 하시면 저에게 알려주십시오. (4)참여하는 것에 관심은 있지만 1월 25일에 시간이 안 되시는 분들은 1월 20일까지 첨부된 설문지를 작성하셔서 돌려주시는 것으로도 도와주실 수 있습니다.

타무나테크 사 부사장,
세르지오 시콘 드림

어휘 questionnaire 설문지　on an experimental basis 시험적으로, 실험적 기반으로　proposal 제안서, 기획서　searchable 검색이 가능한　tracking 추적, 탐색　component (구성) 요소　in various capacities 다양한 용도[역할]로　participate in ~에 참여하다　focus group 포커스 그룹 (시장 조사나 여론 조사를 위해 각 계층을 대표하도록 뽑은 소수의 사람들)　functionality 기능　challenging 어려운, 도전적인　conversely 반대로, 역으로　volunteer 자원하다

1 시콘 씨가 이메일을 쓴 목적은?
   (A) 지원자 그룹을 조직하기 위해
   (B) 새로운 정책을 설명하기 위해
   (C) 몇몇 참가자들에게 감사를 표하기 위해
   (D) 행사 일정을 다시 정하기 위해

해설 이메일의 목적이 초반부에 제시되어 있지 않아 유의해야 한다. 세 번째 단락의 단서(1)에서, 이메일을 쓴 사람의 요구 사항을 나타내는 표현 I need 이하에 이메일의 목적이 나타나 있다. 포커스 그룹에 참여할 지원자를 모집한다고 했으므로 정답은 (A).

2 타무나테크 사에 대해 추론할 수 있는 것은?
   (A) 소프트웨어 개발 회사이다.
   (B) 정기적으로 포커스 그룹을 운영한다.
   (C) 사장이 시콘 씨이다.
   (D) 직원들의 의견을 구한다.

해설 단서(2)에서 소프트웨어 프로그램에 대한 직원들의 의견을 구하고 싶다고 했으므로 정답은 (D).
오답 피하기 시콘 씨는 사장이 아니라 부사장(Vice-president)이므로 (C)는 오답이다.

3 3단락 두 번째 줄의 어휘 "act"와 의미상 가장 유사한 것은?
   (A) ~을 행하다
   (B) 역할을 하다
   (C) ~인 척하다
   (D) 양도하다

해설 act는 '행동하다, 수행하다, ~인 척하다' 등 여러 가지 뜻이 있으나 전치사 as와 함께 쓰였을 때는 '~의 역할을 하다'라는 의미로 사용된다. 정답은 (B).
오답 피하기 (A) perform은 특정한 업무나 과제를 수행한다는 의미이기 때문에 문맥상 적절하지 않다.

4 일부 수신자들이 하도록 요청받은 것은?
   (A) 지원자 추가로 모집하기
   (B) 설문지 작성하기
   (C) 동료에게 전화하기
   (D) 일정표 재조정하기

해설 마지막 단락의 단서(4)를 보면, 25일 당일에 참여할 수 없는 사람은 설문지를 작성하여 보냄으로써 도움을 줄 수 있다고 했으므로 정답은 (B)이다.
패러프레이징 지문의 completing and returning the attached questionnaire가 정답에서 Fill out a survey form으로 패러프레이징되었다.

[5-9] 공원 개장에 대한 기사

(Tulsa—May 25) (5)Hyde Corporation is pleased to announce the opening of the newly rebuilt and rejuvenated city park. Located outside of the Parliament building, the area formerly known as Gotham Park has undergone a major transformation. On May 19, the park reopened as a modern and welcoming outdoor space now called Hyde Park. (6)(9A)It currently (7)bears the name of the corporation that invested the necessary finances to see the project through to completion. The Tulsa city council first proposed the idea before realizing halfway through that the construction costs would greatly exceed the original estimates. (8)The two-year renovation would have been canceled if the Hyde Corporation hadn't stepped in to cover the outstanding costs.

Local resident Bill Hamilton, who has lived in Tulsa for forty-five years, declared that the new park is the best addition to the city that he's seen to date. "We've been desperate for a sophisticated common area for families to spend a Saturday afternoon," he said. "It's so refreshing to have extra green space in the middle of this city, which has been overrun by high-rises and concrete streets in other places."

The 130,668 square-foot park is now three times its former size. Many hope that it will become a dynamic and accessible new hub for pedestrians, commuters, and visitors. A multifaceted space,

(털사 — 5월 25일) (5)하이드 사는 새로이 지어져 활기를 되찾은 시립 공원의 개장을 알리게 되어 기쁘하고 있다. 의회 건물 외부에 위치한 이곳은, 이전에는 고담 공원으로 알려져 있었는데, 큰 변화를 겪었다. 이 공원은 5월 19일에 이제 하이드 공원이라고 불리는 현대적이고 아늑한 외부 공간으로 재개장했다. (6)(9A)현재 이 공간은 프로젝트가 완료되는 것을 보기 위해 필요한 자금을 댔던 회사의 이름을 (7)갖고 있다. 털사 시위원회는 공사비가 당초의 예상치를 훨씬 초과할 것이라는 것을 중간에 깨닫기 전에 이 아이디어를 처음 제안했다. (8)하이드 사가 미지불된 비용을 충당하기 위해 개입하지 않았다면 2년간의 보수 공사는 취소되었을 것이다.

지역 주민인 빌 해밀턴 씨는 털사에서 45년간 살았는데, 이 새로운 공원이 이제껏 자신이 본 시의 시설 중 최고라고 단언했다. 그는 "우리는 토요일 오후에 가족들이 시간을 보낼 수준 높은 공공 장소가 절실히 필요했습니다."라고 했고 "다른 공간에 고층 빌딩과 콘크리트 도로로 꽉 찬 도심 한가운데에 별도의 녹지 공간을 갖는다는 것은 정말 재충전이 되는 일입니다."라고 말했다.

130,668 평방 피트의 이 공원은 현재 이전 크기의 세 배이다. 많은 이들이 이곳이 보행자들, 통근자들, 그리고 방문객들에게 활기차고 쉽게 갈 수 있는 새로운 중심지가 되기를 바란다. 다면적 공간인 하이드 공원은 대중들이 스포츠 행사나 반려견 산책용으로 쓸 수 있는 넓은 잔디밭을 보유하고 있다. 공원을 둘러싼 네 개의 나무 숲은 앉아서 독서하기를 원하는 사람들에게 그늘을 제공해 준다. 공원 한가운데에는 아이들이 즐겁고 신나게 할 컴퓨터로 조종되는 분수가 있다. (9B)공원의 계절 영역은 통절기 아이스 스케이팅은 물론 하계 음악회를 위한 공연장도 보유하고 있다. 일단 개장을 하게 되면 스케이트장은 매일 운영될 것이다. 마지막으로, (9C)하이드 공원에는 야외

Hyde Park includes an enormous lawn to be used by the public for sporting events and dog walking. Surrounding the park are four tree groves that provide shade for people who wish to sit and read. In the middle of the park is a computer-programmed fountain to delight and entertain children. (9B)The park's seasonal areas contain a performance space for summer concerts as well as an ice-skating rink during the winter. Once it is opened, the skating rink will operate daily. Finally, (9C)Hyde Park includes an outdoor café, which has seating inside and outside on the terrace.

카페가 있는데, 이곳은 테라스 내외부에 좌석을 갖추고 있다.

어휘 rejuvenated 활기를 되찾은, 다시 젊어진　**formerly** 이전에, 예전에　**undergo** 겪다, 경험하다　**transformation** 변화, 전환　**bear** 가지다, 품다　**finance** 자금, 재정　**estimate** 예상치, 견적　**step in** 개입하다, 돕기 위해 나서다　**cover** (금전적으로) 충당하다, (돈을) 대다　**outstanding** 미지불된　**to date** 이제껏, 지금까지　**sophisticated** 수준 높은, 세련된　**be overrun by** ~이 꽉 들어차다, ~으로 넘쳐나다　**accessible** 접근 가능한　**pedestrian** 보행자　**commuter** 통근자　**multifaceted** 다면적인, 다면성의　**surround** 둘러싸다　**operate** 운영하다; 조작하다

5 기사의 주제는?
 (A) 새로운 대형건물의 작명
 (B) 상업적 공간의 폐쇄
 (C) 공공 장소에 이루어진 변화
 (D) 향후 사회 기반 시설 계획

[해설] 기사의 주제는 주로 도입부에서 찾을 수 있다. 단서(5)에서 알 수 있듯이 기사는 시립 공원의 개장과 변화에 관한 내용이므로 정답은 (C).
[패러프레이징] 지문의 the opening of the newly rebuilt and rejuvenated city park가 The alterations made to a public space로 패러프레이징되었다.

6 하이드 사가 털사에서 한 일은?
 (A) 지역사회 프로젝트에 자금을 지원했다.
 (B) 사업을 시작했다.
 (C) 새로운 부동산에 투자했다.
 (D) 홍보팀을 변경했다.

[해설] 단서(6)을 보면, 하이드 공원의 이름이 자금을 댔던 회사의 이름을 따서 지어진 것이라고 했으므로 이를 통해 하이드 사가 털사 시의 보수 공사 프로젝트에 자금을 지원했다는 사실을 알 수 있다. 정답은 (A).
[오답 피하기] 하이드 사가 공원 개장에 필요한 자금을 댔지만 회사의 부동산은 아니므로 (C)는 오답.

7 1단락, 아홉 번째 줄의 어휘 "bears"와 의미상 가장 유사한 것은?
 (A) 노출하다
 (B) 드러내다
 (C) 가지다
 (D) 인내하다

[해설] 지문의 bears는 동사로 '견디다'라는 의미도 있지만 특정한 이름을 '갖다'라는 의미 역시 있다. 지문에서는 하이드 사의 이름을 '갖다'라는 의미로 쓰여 이와 의미가 가장 가까운 것은 (C)이다.

8 하이드 공원의 공사 기간은?
 (A) 6개월
 (B) 12개월
 (C) 18개월
 (D) 24개월

[해설] 단서(8)에서 '2년간의 보수 공사(The two-year renovation)'라고 했으므로 공사가 2년간 진행되었다는 것을 알 수 있다. 따라서 정답은 (D)이다.

9 개조 공사의 결과로 암시된 것이 아닌 것은?
 (A) 이름 변경이 있었다.
 (B) 겨울에는 아이스 스케이팅을 할 수 있다.
 (C) 식사를 할 수 있는 곳이 생겼다.
 (D) 대중 교통으로 쉽게 접근 가능하다.

[해설] 단서(9A), (9B), (9C)를 통해 선택지 (A), (B), (C)를 모두 확인해 볼 수 있지만 대중교통에 대한 이야기는 언급되지 않았으므로 정답은 (D).

UNIT 09 단서를 종합하는 문제

PRE-STEP
p.61

A
| 1 (A) | 2 (A) | 3 (B) | 4 (A) | 5 (B) | 6 (A) | 7 (B) | 8 (A) | 9 (B) |
| 10 (A) | 11 (A) | 12 (B) | 13 (A) | 14 (A) | 15 (B) | | | |

B 1 (A)　　2 (B)

A
1 (A) considered, 일자리 <u>고려 대상이 되다</u>
2 (A) solicited, 의견이 <u>구해질</u> 예정이다
3 (B) affiliated, 매장들과 <u>제휴하고</u> 있다
4 (A) implement, 새로운 제도를 <u>도입하다</u>
5 (B) regulation, <u>규제</u>를 강화하다
6 (A) prohibition, <u>금지</u> 기간을 연장하다
7 (B) demand, 증가된 제품 <u>수요</u>
8 (A) choice, 다른 <u>선택</u>의 여지가 없다
9 (B) charge, ~을 <u>담당</u>하다
10 (A) confirm, 거래를 <u>확정하다</u>
11 (A) secure, 거래를 <u>확보하다</u>
12 (B) sufficient, <u>충분한</u> 자본을 보유하다
13 (A) numerous, <u>많은</u> 경우에
14 (A) terms, 계약 <u>조건</u>
15 (B) freeze, ~을 <u>금지</u>하다

B
1 Investors are pleased that Eminence will be able to lower its cost of operations, as it will take over production facilities in countries where labor is more affordable.
   (A) The savings on labor costs are appealing to investors.
   (B) The goods are more popular in certain countries.

투자자들은 인건비가 더 저렴한 국가들의 생산 시설을 인수할 예정이기 때문에 운영 비용을 낮출 수 있을 것이라며 기뻐하고 있다.
(A) 인건비 절감이 주주들에게 매력적으로 느껴진다.
(B) 상품은 특정 국가들 사이에서 더 인기 있다.

2 He has a bachelor's degree in business, so he possesses a deep understanding of how corporations operate.
   (A) He is undergoing continuing education.
   (B) He has sufficient knowledge for the position.

그는 경영학 학위를 갖고 있어서 어떻게 기업이 운영되는지에 대해 깊이 이해하고 있습니다.
(A) 그는 계속해서 교육을 받고 있습니다.
(B) 그는 그 직책에 대한 충분한 지식을 가지고 있습니다.

MAIN STEP 1
p.62

전략 1 새로운 프로그램 도입에 대한 회람

In an effort to reduce expenses, our company has chosen to put a freeze on overtime work. For the next month, we will run a pilot program during which no staff member will be permitted to work overtime hours. From January 2 to 30, all electricity will be shut off at 6 P.M., and employees are expected to leave at that time. Upon conclusion of the program, employee feedback will be solicited to determine whether we will extend this prohibition.

비용을 줄이기 위한 노력의 일환으로, 우리 회사는 초과 근무를 전면 중단하는 쪽을 택했습니다. 다음 달 동안, 우리는 어떠한 직원에게도 초과 근무가 허가되지 않는 프로그램을 시범적으로 운영할 것입니다. 1월 2일부터 30일까지, 저녁 6시에 모든 전기가 끊길 것이며, 직원들은 이 시간에 퇴근해야 합니다. 이 프로그램이 종료되면, 이 금지를 연장할지에 대해 결정하기 위해 직원들의 의견이 요청될 예정입니다.

44

어휘 reduce 줄이다, 축소하다 expense 비용, 돈 put a freeze on ~을 전면 중단하다[동결하다] solicit 요청하다

직원들이 다음 달에 할 것 같은 일은?
(A) 개인 지출 줄이기
(B) 사내 냉장고 사용 멈추기
(C) 프로그램에 대한 상세한 평가 제공하기

해설 다음 달부터 초과 근무를 중지하는 프로그램이 실시되는데, 프로그램이 종료된 후 직원들에게 프로그램에 대해 의견을 구할 것이라고 했으므로 두 개의 단서를 종합해 보면 정답은 (C).
패러프레이징 지문의 employee feedback이 정답에서 detailed review로 패러프레이징되었다.

 인물에 대한 단서 종합

In my managers' meeting this morning, we decided to implement a new policy regarding employee evaluations.

Brianna Johnson,
Sales Department

오늘 아침 우리 부서장 회의에서, 우리는 직원 평가와 관련하여 새로운 정책을 도입하기로 결정했습니다.

영업부
브리아나 존슨 드림

존슨 씨에 대해 사실인 것은?
→ 그녀는 부서장이다.

해설 회람의 발신인인 존슨 씨가 in my manager's meeting (우리 부서장 회의)이라고 했으므로 그녀가 영업부의 부서장임을 알 수 있다.

 날짜에 대한 단서 종합

July 25, BROOMSBURG—A new regulation may reduce the number of cars illegally parked in loading zones in Broomsburg's downtown area.

As part of the new measures, the city's traffic police department will expand its workforce at the beginning of next month to better enforce the regulation.

7월 25일, 브룸스버그 — 새로운 규제는 브룸스버그 시내 지역의 적재 구간에 불법적으로 주차된 차량의 수를 줄일 것이다.

새로운 조치의 일환으로, 시의 교통 경찰 부서는 규제를 더욱 강화하기 위해 다음 달 초에 더 많은 직원을 고용할 예정이다.

어휘 regulation 규제, 규정 illegally 불법적으로 measure 조치, 정책 enforce 강화하다

8월에 브룸스버그에서 일어날 일은?
→ 시 공무원들이 더 채용될 것이다.

해설 기사가 쓰인 시기는 7월인데, 기사 본문에서 다음 달에 더 많은 교통 경찰 부서 직원을 고용할 예정이라고 했으므로 시 공무원들이 더 채용될 것임을 알 수 있다.

MAIN STEP 2

p.63

1 (A) **2** (C) **3** (D)

[1-3] 기업 합병 기사

Eminence Manufacturing Confirms Deal
By Amina Barros

(2)June 8—(3)A spokesperson for athletics giant Eminence Manufacturing announced today that the company has acquired Lyndon Sports

에미넌스 제조사가 거래를 확정하다
아미나 바로스 작성

(2)6월 8일 — (3)스포츠 용품 대기업인 에미넌스 제조사의 대변인은 오늘 당사가 두 기업의 CEO들 간의 최종 합의하에 린던 스포츠 사를 인수하였다고 알렸다. (1)투자자들은

under a final agreement between the CEOs of both corporations. (1)Investors are pleased that Eminence will be able to lower its cost of operations through this move, as it will take over production facilities in countries where labor is more affordable. In addition, because Lyndon Sports is affiliated with numerous retail outlets throughout Asia—a market in which Eminence has had consistently weak sales over the years—Eminence will now be well-positioned to become an industry leader worldwide.

The details of the transaction were organized by representatives from both companies. While Eminence was not the only company to make a bid for Lyndon, its competitors did not have sufficient capital to secure the winning offer. (2)Operations will be entirely under the control of Eminence by the end of the month. (3)Neal Harrington, the CEO of Lyndon Sports, estimates that Eminence's market share could increase by as much as 15 percent. He also mentioned that, with a higher demand for its goods, Eminence will have no choice but to expand its workforce, which is great news for the communities that house its facilities across the globe.

이번 조치를 통하여 인건비가 더 저렴한 국가들의 생산 시설을 인수할 예정이기 때문에 운영 비용을 낮출 수 있을 거라며 기뻐하고 있다. 게다가, 린든 스포츠 사는 에미넌스 사가 수년간 끊임없이 판매 약세를 보였던 시장인 아시아 전역에 걸쳐 수많은 소매점들과 제휴하고 있기 때문에 에미넌스 사는 이제 전 세계적으로 잘 자리잡은 업계 선두 주자가 될 것이다.

거래 세부 사항은 두 회사의 대표에 의해 정리되었다. 에미넌스 사가 린든 사를 입찰하려고 했던 유일한 회사는 아니었지만, 경쟁사들은 마음을 끄는 제안을 확보할 만큼의 충분한 자본을 갖고 있지 않았다. (2)운영은 이달 말에는 전적으로 에미넌스 사에 넘어갈 것이다. (3)린든 스포츠 사의 대표인 닐 해링턴 씨는 에미넌스 사의 시장 점유율이 15%만큼이나 증가할 수 있을 것이라고 추정하고 있다. 그는 또한, 증가된 제품 수요 때문에, 에미넌스 사는 인력을 확장할 수밖에 없는데, 이는 전 세계적으로 생산 시설을 수용하고 있는 지역사회에 좋은 소식이라고 말했다.

어휘 confirm 확정하다 spokesperson 대변인 announce 알리다, 발표하다 acquire 인수하다 cost of operation 운영 비용 labor 노동력 affordable (가격이) 저렴한, 알맞은 be affiliated with ~와 제휴하고 있다 numerous 수많은 throughout ~ 전역에[도처에] sufficient 충분한 capital 자본 secure 확보하다 under the control of ~의 관리하에 estimate 추정하다 market share 시장 점유율 have no choice but to do ~할 수밖에 없다 expand 확장하다 workforce 인력

1 기사에 따르면, 변화에서 비롯될 것으로 예상되는 혜택은?
(A) 운영 비용 감소
(B) 생산 속도 향상
(C) 새 투자자 유치
(D) 더 다양한 상품 판매

2 에미넌스 사가 관리를 맡게 될 것 같은 때는?

(A) 6월 10일
(B) 6월 15일
(C) 6월 30일
(D) 7월 15일

3 해링턴 씨에 대해 추론할 수 있는 것은?
(A) 스포츠 행사를 후원하고 있다.
(B) 더 많은 직원을 채용할 것이다.
(C) 에미넌스 사의 CEO이다.
(D) 합병에 동의했다.

해설 단서(1)에 따르면 투자자들이 이번 변화를 통해 운영 비용을 낮출 수 있을 것이라 기대한다고 하였기 때문에 정답은 (A).
패러프레이징 지문의 lower its cost of operations가 정답에서 Reducing operating expenses로 패러프레이징되었다.

해설 날짜에 관한 두 개의 단서를 찾아 종합해야 풀 수 있는 문제이다. 두 번째 단락 단서(2)의 에미넌스 사가 이달 말까지 완전히 운영권을 넘겨받을 것이라는 것에서 첫 번째 힌트를 얻고, 기사 첫머리 단서(2)에서 기사가 쓰인 날짜가 6월 8일임을 통해 두 번째 힌트를 얻을 수 있다. 두 개의 단서를 종합하면 정답은 (C).

해설 인물에 대한 단서를 종합해야 풀 수 있는 문제이다. 두 번째 단서(3)에서 해링턴 씨가 린든 스포츠 사의 CEO라는 것을 알 수 있는데, 첫 번째 단서(3)에서 합병이 두 기업의 CEO들 간의 합의하에 이루어졌다고 했으므로 정답은 (D).
오답 피하기 더 많은 직원을 채용할 계획인 회사는 에미넌스 사이므로 (B)는 오답. 해링턴 씨는 린든 스포츠 사의 대표이므로 (C)도 오답.

FINAL STEP

p.64

1 (C)   **2** (C)   **3** (B)   **4** (B)   **5** (C)   **6** (C)   **7** (D)

[1-3] 직원 추천 이메일

To: Michelle Ayala <michelleayala@waterviewwind.com>
From: Carole Phillips <c_phillips@rosebudsolutions.com>
Date: December 9
Subject: RE: Brian Quinn

Dear Ms. Ayala,

(1)(2)I am the branch manager of Rosebud Solutions, and I am writing this e-mail as a letter of recommendation for Brian Quinn, who has applied for a sales position at Waterview Industries. I believe that Mr. Quinn is the ideal candidate for this job. He has a high degree of emotional intelligence along with a warm personality that people respond to positively.

(3)Mr. Quinn started at Rosebud Solutions as a sales assistant, a job that he held with us for two years. He was then promoted to senior salesperson, where he served for another two years. In that role, he was in charge of multinational clients, and he negotiated one of the most lucrative contracts in our company's history. Everyone has been pleased with Mr. Quinn's work performance and reliability. He met or exceeded monthly sales targets consistently, and he always had a positive attitude. Moreover, he has a bachelor's degree in business, so he possesses a deep understanding of how corporations operate.

(2)With his experience, education, and natural talent, Mr. Quinn is sure to be an invaluable asset to your team. I hope you will seriously consider him for this position. If you would like to speak further on this matter, please feel free to contact me at 555-2495, which is my direct office line.

Sincerely,

Carole Phillips

수신: 미쉘 아얄라 <michelleayala@waterviewwind.com>
발신: 카롤 필립스 <c_phillips@rosebudsolutions.com>
날짜: 12월 9일
제목: 회신: 브라이언 퀸

아얄라 씨께

(1)(2)저는 로즈버드 솔루션 사의 지점장이며, 워터뷰 산업의 판매직에 지원한 브라이언 퀸 씨를 위한 추천장으로 이메일을 보냅니다. 저는 퀸 씨가 이 일자리에 이상적인 지원자라고 믿습니다. 그는 사람들이 긍정적으로 반응하는 따뜻한 성격에 덧붙여 높은 감성 지능을 갖고 있습니다.

(3)퀸 씨는 로즈버드 솔루션 사에서 판매 보조로 일을 시작하였고, 2년간 저희와 함께하였습니다. 그는 그 후에 정사원으로 승진하여 2년간 더 일하였습니다. 그 직무에서, 그는 다국적 고객들을 담당하였고 회사 창사 이래 가장 수익성이 좋은 계약들 중 하나를 협상하였습니다. 모두들 퀸 씨의 근무 실적과 믿음직스러움에 기뻐하였습니다. 그는 지속적으로 월별 판매 목표량을 충족시키거나 초과하였고, 항상 긍정적인 태도를 갖고 있었습니다. 더욱이, 그는 경영학 학위를 갖고 있어서 어떻게 기업이 운영되는지에 대해 깊이 이해하고 있습니다.

(2)그의 경험과 교육, 천부적인 재능으로 퀸 씨는 반드시 귀하의 팀에 귀중한 자산이 될 것입니다. 저는 당신이 이 일자리에 그를 진지하게 고려해 보시길 바랍니다. 이 건에 대해 더 이야기하길 원하신다면, 제 사무실 직통 전화인 555-2945로 언제든 연락 주시길 바랍니다.

카롤 필립스 드림

어휘 apply for ~에 지원하다   ideal 이상적인   candidate 지원자   assistant 보조   promote 승진시키다   be in charge of ~을 담당하다   multinational 다국적인   negotiate 협상하다   lucrative 수익성이 좋은   reliability 믿음직함   exceed 초과하다   consistently 지속적으로   positive 긍정적인   attitude 태도   bachelor's degree 학사 학위   possess 소유하다   operate 운영되다   natural talent 천부적인 재능   invaluable 귀중한   asset 자산

1 이메일의 목적은?
   (A) 직책에 지원하기 위해서
   (B) 일자리 제안을 하기 위해서
   (C) 직원을 추천하기 위해서
   (D) 고용 계약을 받아들이기 위해서

해설 이메일의 목적은 주로 첫 단락에서 찾을 수 있다. 단서(1)에서 필립스 씨는 퀸 씨를 위한 추천장으로 이메일을 보낸다고 했으므로 정답은 (C). 목적을 나타내는 표현인 I am writing this e-mail 이하를 주의 깊게 보자.

2 아얄라 씨는 누구일 것 같은가?
   (A) 지점장
   (B) 인사팀 직원
   (C) 판매부 부장
   (D) 판매부 보조

해설 첫 번째 단서(2)에 따르면 이메일은 판매직에 지원한 브라이언 퀸 씨를 위한 추천장이다. 두 번째 단서(2)에 따르면 퀸 씨가 귀하의 팀(your team), 즉 추천장을 받는 사람의 팀에 귀중한 자산이 될 것이라고 했으므로 아얄라 씨는 판매부의 임직원임을 알 수 있다. 정답은 (C).

3 퀸 씨가 로즈버드 솔루션 사에서 일한 기간은?
   (A) 2년
   (B) 4년
   (C) 5년
   (D) 6년

해설 단서(3)을 보면 퀸 씨는 판매 보조로 2년, 정사원으로 2년간 일했으므로 총 4년 동안 일했다. 정답은 (B).
오답 피하기 단서(3)의 앞부분만 보고 (A)를 정답으로 선택하지 않도록 조심해야 한다.

[4-7] 심리학과 강연에 대한 광고

Columbus University, Psychology Department
(4)Distinguished Speaker Series

Date & time	Lecture title	Lecturer	Qualifications	Ticket price
January 15, 1 P.M. January 16, 1 P.M. January 20, 7 P.M.	The Resilient Brain: Ageing, Memory, and Trauma	Dr. Ira Corbett, PhD	Professor, Department of Psychology, University of Oxford	$20
January 22, 1 P.M.	Your Child's Mind: Changes in Childhood Brain Development	Dr. Natasha Bloomberg, PhD	Professor, Department of Psychology, University of Chicago	$25
January 24, 1 P.M. January 25, 1 P.M.	Battling Dyslexia: The Trouble with Learning Words	(5) Mr. Pedro Fitzpatrick, MS	(5) Psychologist/ Lead Instructor, Dyslexic Learning Center	(6)Free admission
(7) January 26, 7 P.M. January 29, 1 P.M.	Without Shame: Helping Sufferers of Mental Illness	Dr. Celina Robinson, PhD	Professor, Department of Psychology, Carnegie Mellon University	$35 *(7)Child care will be provided for parents attending the lecture

콜럼버스 대학교, 심리학과
(4)명 강사 시리즈

날짜 & 시간	강연 제목	강연자	약력	강연료
1월 15일 오후 1시 1월 16일 오후 1시 1월 20일 저녁 7시	〈탄력적인 두뇌: 노화, 기억, 그리고 정신적 외상〉	아이라 콜벳 박사, 박사 학위 소지자	옥스퍼드 대학교 심리학과 교수	20달러
1월 22일 오후 1시	〈자녀의 정신 세계: 유년기 두뇌 발달 과정에서의 변화들〉	나타샤 블룸버그 박사, 박사 학위 소지자	시카고 대학교 심리학과 교수	25달러
1월 24일 오후 1시 1월 25일, 오후 1시	〈난독증 이겨내기: 단어 학습의 어려움〉	(5) 페드로 피츠패트릭 씨, 이공계 석사	(5) 심리학자/ 난독증 학습 센터 수석 강사	(6) 무료 입장
(7) 1월 26일 저녁 7시 1월 29일 오후 1시	〈수치심 없애기: 정신 질환자들 돕기〉	셀리나 로빈슨 박사, 박사 학위 소지자	카네기멜론 대학교 심리학과 교수	35달러 *(7)아이들과 함께 강연에 참석하는 부모들을 위해 탁아 서비스가 제공됩니다. 가격은 티켓 가격에 포함되어 있습니다.

| | | | | together. The cost is factored into the price of the ticket. |

어휘 **psychology** 심리학 **distinguished** 성공적인, 눈에 띄는 **qualification** (보통 복수형) (특정 분야에 대한) 약력, 기술, 지식 **resilient** 탄력성 있는, 회복력 있는 **ageing** 노화 **trauma** (정신적) 외상 **battle** ~과 싸우다, ~을 이기려고 애쓰다 **dyslexia** 난독증 **psychologist** 심리학자 **lead** 선두, 우위 **admission** 입장, 허가 **shame** 수치, 부끄러움 **sufferer** 환자, 고통 받는 사람

4 광고의 목적은?
(A) 심리학 실험을 설명하기 위해
(B) 곧 있을 강연 시리즈를 홍보하기 위해
(C) 새로 부임한 대학 교수들을 소개하기 위해
(D) 정신 질환 연구를 독려하기 위해

해설 주제, 목적을 묻는 문제는 지문의 첫 부분을 집중해서 보아야 하는데 위 광고의 제목에서도 알 수 있다시피, 이 광고는 강의 주제, 강연자, 가격, 특별 서비스 등을 자세히 설명해 주고 있으므로 곧 있을 강연 시리즈를 홍보하기 위해서 쓰였다는 것을 쉽게 유추할 수 있다. 정답은 (B).

5 현업에 재직 중인 심리학자는 누구인가?
(A) 아이라 콜벳
(B) 나타샤 블룸버그
(C) 페드로 피츠패트릭
(D) 셀리나 로빈슨

해설 약력란의 단서(5)를 보면 다른 강연자들은 대학 교수인 반면에 페드로 피츠패트릭 씨는 난독증 센터에서 근무하고 있는 심리학자임을 알 수 있으므로 정답은 (C).

6 청중이 무료로 참여할 수 있는 강연은?
(A) 〈탄력적인 두뇌〉
(B) 〈자녀의 정신 세계〉
(C) 〈난독증 이겨내기〉
(D) 〈수치심 없애기〉

해설 광고에서 '강연료' 정보가 있는 열을 집중해서 보아야 한다. Battling Dyslexia 강연의 참가비가 무료이므로 정답은 (C).
패러프레이징 지문의 Free admission이 문제에서 without charge로 바꾸어 표현되었다.

7 콜럼버스 대학교에 어린이들이 올 가능성이 가장 큰 날은?
(A) 1월 15일
(B) 1월 22일
(C) 1월 25일
(D) 1월 29일

해설 단서(7)을 보면, 1월 26일과 29일의 강연에 탁아 서비스가 제공된다고 했으므로 이때 어린이들이 올 가능성이 높다는 것을 추론할 수 있다. 따라서 정답은 (D).

UNIT 10 연계 문제

PRE-STEP
p.67

A 1 (A) 2 (B) 3 (B) 4 (B) 5 (A) 6 (A) 7 (B) 8 (B) 9 (A)
   10 (A) 11 (A) 12 (B) 13 (A) 14 (B) 15 (A)

B 1 (A) 2 (A)

A 1 (A) notify, 고객에게 변경 사항을 알려주다
   2 (B) additional, 추가 비용으로
   3 (B) select, ~가 선호하는 것을 선택하다
   4 (B) option, 익일 특급 배송 선택권
   5 (A) responsible, 일에 대해 책임이 있다
   6 (A) enforce, 안전 절차를 실시하다
   7 (B) rent, 리허설 장소를 대여하다
   8 (B) face, 건강 문제에 직면하다
   9 (A) permanent, 정규직 일자리를 구하다
   10 (A) apply, 일자리에 지원하다
   11 (A) seasonal, 고수익의 계절직 일자리
   12 (B) fit, ~의 기술과 목표에 맞다
   13 (A) comply, 기준을 따르다
   14 (B) candidate, 이상적인 후보자
   15 (A) develop, 내부 의사소통 방식을 개발하다

B 1 I immediately transitioned to the food and beverage service team, where I have worked for the last five summers.
       (A) I worked for the food and beverage service team for five years in a row.
       (B) I am available to join the food and beverage team this summer.

       저는 즉시 식음료 서비스팀으로 옮겼고, 그곳에서 지난 5년 동안 여름마다 일해 왔습니다.
       (A) 저는 5년 연속으로 식음료 서비스팀에서 근무했습니다.
       (B) 저는 이번 여름에 식음료 서비스팀에 합류 가능합니다.

   2 We allow new members to attend two sessions before deciding whether or not to join.
       (A) New members can preview the sessions before making a decision.
       (B) New members should attend at least two sessions a year.

       우리는 신입 회원들이 가입 여부를 결정하기 전에 두 번의 세션에 참석하도록 허용하고 있습니다.
       (A) 신입 회원들은 결정을 내리기 전에 세션을 미리 볼 수 있습니다.
       (B) 신입 회원들은 1년에 최소한 두 차례의 세션에 참가해야 합니다.

MAIN STEP 1
p.68

 강의 일정 변경 이메일 & 변경된 시간표 양식

Thank you for your interest in Intermediate Yoga at Wilkes Gym. Unfortunately, due to an issue with the instructor's calendar, the class has been rescheduled for 1 P.M. instead of 10 A.M. on Tuesdays.

월크스 체육관의 중급 요가 수업에 대한 여러분의 관심에 감사드립니다. 안타깝게도, 강사의 일정상의 문제 때문에 수업 일정이 화요일 오전 10시가 아닌 오후 1시로 변경되었습니다.

Class for Tuesday 1 P.M.

Basic Yoga	Intermediate Yoga
– Susan Ferguson	– Carlene White

화요일 오후 1시 수업

초급 요가	중급 요가
– 수잔 퍼거슨	– 칼렌 화이트

원래 화요일 오전으로 예정되어 있었던 수업의 강사는?
→ 칼렌 화이트

해설 변경 사항 관련 내용은 변경 전후의 내용을 종합해 풀어야 하므로 자주 출제되는 연계 문제 유형이다. 변경 사항이 지문에 등장하면 연계 문제가 아닌지 의심해 본다. 이메일에서 중급 요가 수업이 오전에서 오후로 변경되었다고 했고, 시간표를 통해 이 수업의 강사가 칼렌 화이트 씨라는 것을 알 수 있다.

전략 2 학회 공지 & 일정 문의 문자메시지 & 일정표

National Entrepreneur Convention

We are holding the 3rd National Entrepreneur convention from April 26 to 29. It start at 10:00 A.M. and will run until 3 P.M. with just an hour lunch break at noon every day.

From: Mark Walter
To: Deborah Mason

Could you please send me a detailed schedule of my appointments at the end of this month? I'd like to attend the marketing convention but I need to check my schedule first.

Mark Walter's Plan

| April 26, 9 A.M – Weekly executive meeting |
| April 28, 10 A.M. – Visiting manufacturers |
| April 29, 9 A.M. – Design Workshop |

국내 기업가 학회

우리는 4월 26일부터 29일까지 제3회 국내 기업가 학회를 개최합니다. 학회는 매일 오전 10시에 시작해서 오후 3시까지 정오에 한 시간의 점심 휴식 시간만을 가진 채 쭉 진행될 예정입니다.

발신: 마크 월터
수신: 데보라 메이슨

이달 말 제 세부 약속 일정을 보내 주실 수 있나요? 마케팅 학회에 참석하고 싶은데, 먼저 제 일정을 확인해야 해서요.

마크 월터 씨의 계획

| 4월 26일, 오전 9시 – 주간 임원 회의 |
| 4월 28일, 오전 10시 – 생산 공장 방문 |
| 4월 29일, 오전 9시 – 디자인 워크숍 |

월터 씨가 학회에 참석하게 될 날짜는?
(A) 4월 26일
(B) 4월 27일
(C) 4월 28일
(D) 4월 29일

해설 공지에 따르면, 학회는 4월 26일부터 29일까지 열리는데, 일정표에서 월터 씨는 27일을 제외한 모든 날짜에 일정이 있으므로, 27일에 학회에 참석할 가능성이 가장 높다.

MAIN STEP 2   p.69

1 (C)   2 (A)

[1-2] 식료품 주문 안내 편지 & 주문 송장

Kira Höecker
Landstrasse 139
3860 Schattenhalb, Switzerland

September 1

Dear Ms. Höecker:

This letter is to notify you of our revolutionary online grocery shopping service. (1)We enable you to buy your grocery items from the comfort of your own home with only the click of a button. Simply browse through our online aisles, select your items, and

키라 회커
란트스트라세 139
스위스, 샤텐할브 3860

9월 1일

회커 씨께:

귀하께 우리의 혁신적인 온라인 식료품 쇼핑 서비스에 대해 알려드리기 위해 이 편지를 보냅니다. (1)저희는 버튼을 클릭하는 것만으로 귀하가 자택에서 편안하게 식료품을 살 수 있게 해 드립니다. 그저 저희 가게의 온라인상의 진열대를 둘러보시고 물건을 고르신 후 주문하시기만 하면 됩니다. 정말

place your order. It's just that easy! Your food items are guaranteed to be delivered within seven days. A 15 percent tax is charged on every order, but (2-1) regular delivery is free. However, for an additional fee, a next-day express delivery option exists for time-sensitive orders. If you have any questions, please call 555-163-7238.

Sincerely,

Martha Lambert,
Customer Relations, Lamla Grocers

쉽습니다! 귀하의 식료품은 7일 이내 배송이 보장됩니다. 15%의 세금이 주문마다 부과되지만 (2-1)일반 배송은 무료입니다. 하지만, 추가 비용을 내시면 긴급한 주문을 위한 익일 특급 배송 옵션이 있습니다. 질문이 있으시다면, 555-163-7238로 전화 주세요.

람라 식료품점, 고객관리팀
마르타 램버트 드림

Customer name: Kira Höeker
Date of order: September 19
Shipping address: Landstrasse 139, 3860 Schattenhalb, Switzerland
Method of payment: Visa
Credit card number: XXXX XXXX XXXX 4532

고객명: 키라 회커
주문 날짜: 9월 19일
배송지 주소: 스위스, 샤텐할브 3860, 란트스트라세 139
지불 방법: 비자
신용카드 번호: XXXX XXXX XXXX 4532

Item number	Description	Quantity	Cost
8691	Vanilla extract	2 bottles, 8 oz.	$13.96
195376	Cake mix, classic yellow	1 box	$2.10
		subtotal	$16.06
		Tax amount (15%)	$2.41
		(2-2)Delivery fee	$10.00
		Total cost	$28.47

상품 번호	세부사항	수량	가격
8691	바닐라 추출액	2병, 8온즈	13.96달러
195376	전형적인 노란색 케이크 가루	1상자	2.10달러
	소계		16.06달러
	세금 (15%)		2.41달러
	(2-2)배송비		10달러
	합계		28.47달러

어휘 notify A of B A에게 B를 알리다[공지하다] revolutionary 혁신적인, 혁명적인 browse through (가게 안의 물건을) 둘러보다 aisle (진열대 사이의) 통로 place an order 주문하다 charge (금액, 수수료 등을) 부과하다 regular 일반, 보통의 time-sensitive 긴급한, 분초를 다투는 extract 추출액, 엑기스 subtotal 소계

---

1 편지에 따르면, 람라 식료품점이 제공하는 혜택은?
 (A) 경쟁력 있는 가격
 (B) 수입 식품 구매 접근성
 (C) 편리한 쇼핑
 (D) 유기농 농산물

해설 단서(1)에서 람라 식료품점의 혁신적인 온라인 쇼핑 서비스가 고객들이 자택에서 편안하게 쇼핑하도록 해 준다고 했으므로 정답은 (C).

2 익일 특급 배송의 비용은?

 (A) 10달러
 (B) 15달러
 (C) 25달러
 (D) 40달러

해설 편지의 단서(2-1)을 보면, 일반 배송은 무료이지만 익일 특급 배송에 추가 비용이 붙는다고 하였다. 송장의 단서(2-2)를 보면 배송비 10달러가 추가되었는데, 이는 익일 특급 배송 비용이므로 정답은 (A)이다.

FINAL STEP

| 1 (C) | 2 (C) | 3 (A) | 4 (B) | 5 (C) | 6 (A) | 7 (A) | 8 (D) | 9 (C) | 10 (B) |

[1-5] 구직 이메일 & 구인 공지문

To: Lucas Klein <l.klein@thrilltropolis.com>
From: Madison Ennis <ennism@memail.net>
Date: April 3
Subject: Returning to Thrilltropolis

Dear Mr. Klein,

(1)I am writing to you about applying for a position with Thrilltropolis, where I have worked as a seasonal employee for several years. (5-1)I was originally hired as a ticket admissions agent. But I immediately transitioned to the food and beverage service team, (2)where I have worked for the last five summers. Next month I will complete my hospitality degree at Concord University, so I am seeking permanent employment. Attached you will find my résumé and references. (1)Please let me know if you have a position that fits my skills and career goals.

Sincerely,

Madison Ennis

Thrilltropolis, the Nation's Leading Amusement Park, is Hiring!

Posting #S35: Lifeguard ((3)full time, seasonal) // (4)Lifeguards in the aquatic center are responsible for the supervision of various water attractions. They also enforce safety procedures.

Posting #S48: Ride Attendant ((3)full time, seasonal) // Ride attendants load and unload guests in a safe and hospitable manner. They comply with the ride operations standards of Thrilltropolis.

(5-2)**Posting #P67:** Area Manager, Food and Beverage ((3)full time, permanent) // The area manager will handle the daily functions of the park's food-service department. The ideal candidate should be a detail-oriented leader with a strong food and beverage background.

Posting #P76: Associate, Public Relations ((3)full time, permanent) // The public relations associate will work to establish the Thrilltropolis brand throughout the world and strategically develop external and internal communications.

수신: 루카스 클라인 <l.klein@thrilltropolis.com>
발신: 매디슨 이니스 <ennism@memail.net>
날짜: 4월 3일
제목: 쓰릴트로폴리스로의 복귀

클라인 씨께,

(1)저는 쓰릴트로폴리스에 있는 일자리에 지원하는 것과 관련하여 귀하께 이메일을 드리는데, 그곳에서 저는 몇 년간 계절직 직원으로 일해 왔습니다. (5-1)저는 원래 입장권을 받는 직원으로 고용됐었습니다. 하지만 즉시 식음료 서비스팀으로 옮겼고, (2)그곳에서 지난 5년 동안 여름마다 일해 왔습니다. 다음 달이면 저는 콩코드 대학에서 호텔학 학위를 받게 되므로 정규직 일자리를 구하고 있습니다. 제 이력서와 추천서를 첨부하였습니다. (1)제 기술과 경력 목표에 맞는 직책이 있다면 제게 알려주시기 바랍니다.

매디슨 이니스 드림

국내의 선도적인 놀이공원 쓰릴트로폴리스에서 채용을 진행합니다!

게시물 S35번: 안전요원 ((3)상근, 계절 고용직) // (4)물놀이장의 안전요원은 다양한 물놀이 기구들의 감독을 책임집니다. 또한 안전 절차를 실시합니다.

게시물 S48번: 탑승 보조원 ((3)상근, 계절 고용직) // 탑승 보조원은 안전하고도 친절한 태도로 승객들을 탑승시키고 하차시킵니다. 쓰릴트로폴리스의 탑승 운영 규정을 따릅니다.

(5-2)게시물 P67번: 식음료 구역 관리자 ((3)상근, 정규직) // 구역 관리자는 공원 음식 서비스 부서의 일상적인 운영을 처리합니다. 가장 이상적인 후보는 식음료에 대해 매우 잘 알고 있는 꼼꼼한 관리자이어야 합니다.

게시물 P76번: 홍보팀 직원 ((3)상근, 정규직) // 홍보팀 직원은 전 세계에 쓰릴트로폴리스의 브랜드를 확립하고 대내외적인 의사소통 방식을 전략적으로 개발하기 위해 일하게 될 것입니다.

어휘 seasonal 계절의, 기간 한정적인   transition to ~로 위치를 옮기다, ~로 이동하다   hospitality (호텔 서비스 등의) 접객업; 환대   permanent employment 정규직   reference 추천서, 추천인   full time 상근직의, 정규 근무 시간에 일하는   aquatic 수중의, 수생의   enforce (강제적으로) 실시하다, 집행하다   safety procedures 안전 절차   comply with (법이나 규정 등을) 따르다, 준수하다   establish 확립하다   strategically 전략적으로, 계획적으로

1 이메일의 목적은?
   (A) 지원 규정을 확인하기 위해
   (B) 면접 시간을 정하기 위해
   (C) 공석에 대해 문의하기 위해
   (D) 쓰릴트로폴리스 견학 일정을 잡기 위해

   해설 이메일 본문 도입부의 단서(1)에 나온 표현 I am writing to you about(~와 관련하여 이메일을 씁니다)에서 목적이 명시된다. 일자리 지원과 관련해서 이메일을 쓴다고 했으므로 정답은 (C).
   패러프레이징 지문의 position이 단서에서 job opening으로 패러프레이징되었다.

2 이니스 씨가 쓰릴트로폴리스에서 일한 여름의 횟수는?
   (A) 2회
   (B) 3회
   (C) 5회
   (D) 7회

   해설 문제의 키워드인 summers(여름)가 직접 언급된 단서(2)를 보면, 그녀가 지난 5년 동안 여름마다 일해 왔다고 했으므로 정답은 (C).

3 공지에 있는 직무 전반에 대해 암시된 내용은?
   (A) 각각 상근 업무 시간을 제공한다.
   (B) 정규직이다.
   (C) 여러 지점에서 구인 중이다.
   (D) 이전 경력을 요구한다.

   해설 공지문의 모든 직무가 상근(full time)이라고 언급되어 있으므로 정답은 (A).
   오답 피하기 앞의 두 직무는 계절 고용직(seasonal)이므로 (B)는 오답이다.

4 쓰릴트로폴리스에 대해 사실인 것은?
   (A) 관광객들을 위한 사파리 전시장이다.
   (B) 물놀이장을 보유하고 있다.
   (C) 연중 내내 대중에게 공개된다.
   (D) 세계에서 제일 큰 놀이기구가 있다.

   해설 단서(4)에 나와 있는 aquatic center(물놀이장)와 water attractions(물놀이 기구) 등의 표현으로 보아 놀이공원에 물놀이장이 있다는 것을 추론할 수 있다. 따라서 정답은 (B).

5 이니스 씨에게 가장 적합할 것 같은 직종은?
   (A) S35번 게시물
   (B) S48번 게시물
   (C) P67번 게시물
   (D) P76번 게시물

   해설 이니스 씨에게 맞는 구체적인 직종을 묻는 문제이므로 두 지문을 모두 보아야 한다. 이니스 씨가 쓴 이메일의 단서(5-1)을 통해 그가 식음료 제공팀에서 일한 경력이 있다는 것을 알 수 있다. 공지문에서 식품과 관련된 직무를 찾으면 정답은 (C)이다.

[6-10] 극단 회원 모집 광고 & 행사 일정 & 감사 이메일

The Laughs Never End with the Gilmore Improv Players!

(7C)The Gilmore Improv Players (GIP) was founded a decade ago and is dedicated to improvisation (improv), which is a type of theater in which the actors create unplanned scenes using suggestions from audience members. (7B)We get together weekly to play improv games, develop our acting skills, and—of course—have fun! (6)We are currently looking for new members to join our group. (7A)No previous experience is necessary. If you're interested in joining, e-mail Megan Conaway at m.conaway@mcnallymail.net. We allow new members to attend two sessions before deciding whether or not to join. (7D)All members pay an annual fee of $50, which goes toward renting our rehearsal space.

We perform shows for the public regularly, (8-1)and if you join GIP, your family members can get half-off tickets at these events. We are also hired for private shows, such as corporate parties. Join us today and don't miss out on the fun!

길모어 즉흥극 연기자들과 함께라면 웃음이 끊이지 않습니다!

(7C)길모어 즉흥극 연기자(GIP)는 10년 전에 창설되었으며, 즉흥극에 전념하고 있는데, 즉흥극이란 관객들의 제안을 이용하여 계획되지 않은 장면들을 배우들이 연출해 내는 연극의 한 형태입니다. 우리는 (7B)일주일에 한 번 모여 즉흥극 게임을 하고, 연기 실력을 발전시키며, 당연히 재미도 누립니다! (6)우리는 현재 모임에 가입할 신입 회원들을 찾고 있습니다. (7A)이전 경력은 필요하지 않습니다. 만약 가입에 관심이 있으시다면, 메간 코너웨이 씨에게 m.conaway@mcnallymail.net로 이메일을 보내시면 됩니다. 우리는 새로운 회원들이 가입 여부를 결정하기 전에 두 번의 세션에 참석하도록 허용하고 있습니다. (7D)모든 회원들은 50달러의 연회비를 납부하며, 이는 우리의 리허설 장소를 대여하는 데 쓰입니다.

우리는 대중들을 위해 정기적으로 공연하며, (8-1)만약 GIP에 가입하시면, 여러분의 가족은 이 행사의 티켓을 반값에 구입할 수 있습니다. 우리는 또한 기업 연회와 같은 사설 공연을 위해서도 고용됩니다. 오늘 가입하셔서 재미를 놓치지 마세요!

Gilmore Improv Players: Upcoming Events

Saturday, April 16, 7:30 P.M., Public Performance
Watson Hall
A Night of Improv—Enjoy hilarious scenes made up on-the-spot using ideas from you, the audience! (Tickets: $20)

Monday, April 18, 1:00 P.M., Private Performance
Grove Accounting Headquarters
Giggles Galore—A special performance for the Grove Accounting Employee Appreciation Luncheon

Saturday, April 23, 8:30 P.M., Public Performance
Perea Lounge
(8-2)*Battle for Laughs*—Watch two teams battle it out with classic improv games. (Tickets: $16)

(9-2)Tuesday, April 26, 3:00 P.M., Private Performance
Wiggins Children's Hospital
Tell Me More—A show with games designed specifically for children

Friday, April 29, 2:00 P.M., Public Activity
Dumont Community Center
Improv Workshop—Learn how to get started in improv and how to release your inner comedian in this three-hour workshop. (Tickets: $10)

To: Megan Conaway <m.conaway@mcnallymail.net>
From: Jared Alvarez <jaredalvarez@inbox234.com>
Date: May 3
Subject: Gilmore Improv Players

Dear Ms. Conaway,

(9-1)Thank you for your recent performance at the Wiggins Children's Hospital. I know that our young patients had a lot of fun watching the show, and staff members like me also had a great time. You brought so much joy to our patients, which is so important during a time when they are facing health issues. (10)Some of our patients even made drawings and thank-you cards for your group that I would like to send to you. Please let me know where to do so.

Warmest regards,

Jared Alvarez

어휘 found 창설하다 decade 10년 be dedicated to ~에 전념하다 improv(= improvisation) 즉흥극 suggestion 제안 necessary 필수적인 attend 참석하다 annual fee 연회비 rent 대여하다 public 대중 hire 고용하다 private 개인적인, 사적인 miss out on ~을 놓치다 hilarious 아주 재미있는 audience 관객 galore 많은, 풍성한 appreciation 감사; 감상 luncheon 오찬 specifically 특별히

6 광고의 목적은?
(A) **사람들을 모임에 모으기 위해**
(B) 다가오는 공연을 홍보하기 위해
(C) 회사 후원을 모으기 위해
(D) 대회를 알리기 위해

해설 단서(6)에서 현재 즉흥극 모임에 가입할 사람을 찾고 있다고 했으며, 그 뒤에 모임의 운영 방식에 대해 설명하고 있으므로 정답은 (A)이다. 글의 목적이 지문 중간에 온 유형으로, 이처럼 앞부분에 명확한 목적이 보이지 않으면 지문 전체를 살펴봐야 한다.

7 GIP에 대해 시사되지 않은 바는?
(A) **경험이 풍부한 배우들만 허용한다.**
(B) 일주일에 한 번 만난다.
(C) 10년째 운영 중이다.
(D) 회비를 청구한다.

해설 단서(7A)를 보면 경험이 없어도 가입이 가능하다고 하였으므로 정답은 (A). 나머지 선택지는 모두 지문에 언급되어 있다.

8 GIP 회원의 친척이 〈웃음 대결〉에 내야 하는 금액은?
(A) 20달러
(B) 16달러
(C) 10달러
(D) **8달러**

해설 광고의 단서(8-1)을 보면 GIP 회원의 가족들은 티켓을 반값에 구입할 수 있다고 했고, 공연 일정의 단서(8-2)를 보면 〈웃음 대결〉의 원래 티켓 가격이 16달러이므로 정답은 반값인 (D).

9 알바레즈 씨가 공연을 본 때는?
(A) 4월 16일
(B) 4월 18일
(C) **4월 26일**
(D) 4월 29일

해설 단서(9-1)을 통해 알바레즈 씨가 본 공연은 위긴스 아동 병원에서 이루어졌음을 알 수 있다. 단서(9-2)를 보면 병원에서 이루어진 공연은 4월 26일의 공연임을 알 수 있다. 따라서 정답은 (C).

10 알바레즈 씨가 콘웨이 씨에게 하도록 요청하는 일은?
(A) 다른 행사에서 공연하기
(B) **우편 주소 제공하기**
(C) 극단의 이용 가능 시간을 알려주기
(D) 요금에 대한 정보 제공하기

해설 알바레즈 씨가 근무하는 병원의 환자들이 만든 그림과 감사 카드를 어디로 보내야 하는지 알려 달라고 했으므로 우편 주소를 요청하고 있음을 알 수 있다. 정답은 (B). 요청을 나타내는 표현 Please let me ~를 주의 깊게 보아야 한다.

CHAPTER TEST 1

p.74

1 (A)	2 (D)	3 (B)	4 (C)	5 (A)	6 (C)	7 (A)	8 (D)	9 (C)
10 (C)	11 (C)	12 (B)	13 (C)	14 (C)	15 (A)	16 (B)	17 (D)	18 (D)
19 (C)	20 (D)	21 (A)	22 (A)	23 (B)	24 (D)			

[1-2] 프린터기 수리 요청 문자메시지

KATHERINE ZIEGLER 9:10 A.M.
I have a repair request for you. The printer in my office is acting up. The brand is Alto Co. and it's model #498-E.

GEORGE NOKES 9:16 A.M.
Can you describe the problem to me?

KATHERINE ZIEGLER 9:16 A.M.
The paper is loaded correctly, but the device isn't pulling the paper in from the tray.

GEORGE NOKES 9:17 A.M.
Maybe one of the components fell off.

KATHERINE ZIEGLER 9:19 A.M.
(1)Are you busy this morning?

GEORGE NOKES 9:20 A.M.
Yes, quite a bit.

GEORGE NOKES 9:20 A.M.
(1)I won't be able to look at it today. Is tomorrow all right?

KATHERINE ZIEGLER 9:22 A.M.
Okay. (2)I have to take some other paperwork to one of my clients this afternoon anyway.

KATHERINE ZIEGLER 9:23 A.M.
But tomorrow I need to print some orientation materials, so please visit me first thing tomorrow, if possible.

캐서린 지글러 오전 9:10
수리를 요청할 게 있어요. 제 사무실의 프린터기가 제대로 작동하지 않아요. 브랜드는 알토 사이고, 모델 번호는 498-E번이에요.

조지 녹스 오전 9:16
문제점을 제게 설명해 주시겠어요?

캐서린 지글러 오전 9:16
용지는 제대로 끼워지는데, 기기가 트레이에서 용지를 끌어들이지 못하고 있어요.

조지 녹스 오전 9:17
아마 부품 중 하나가 떨어져 나갔나 보네요.

캐서린 지글러 오전 9:19
(1)오늘 오전에 바쁘세요?

조지 녹스 오전 9:20
네, 상당히요.

조지 녹스 오전 9:20
(1)오늘은 그걸 봐 드릴 수 없어요. 내일 괜찮으세요?

캐서린 지글러 오전 9:22
괜찮아요. (2)어차피 오늘 오후에는 고객 중 한 분에게 다른 서류를 갖다 줘야 하니까요.

캐서린 지글러 오전 9:23
하지만 내일은 오리엔테이션 자료를 출력해야 하니, 가능하면 내일은 제일 먼저 저한테 와 주세요.

어휘 act up 제대로 작동하지 않다 load 끼우다, 장착하다 correctly 제대로, 바르게 component 부품 fall off 떨어져 나가다 quite a bit 상당히, 꽤 paperwork 서류 (작업) material 자료 first thing 제일 먼저

1 오전 9:20에, 녹스 씨가 "상당히요"라고 하는 의도는?
(A) 일을 할 시간이 없다.
(B) 수리비가 많이 들 것이라고 생각한다.
(C) 그의 부서는 수중에 여분의 부품이 있다.
(D) 그의 팀은 전에 유사한 작업을 한 적이 있다.

해설 문제에서 주어진 표현 "quite a bit" 앞의 단서(1)에서 지글러 씨는 녹스 씨에게 오전에 바쁜지를 물었고, 뒤의 단서에서 녹스 씨가 오늘은 고장난 프린터기를 봐 줄 수 없다고 했다. 따라서 "상당히요"라는 녹스 씨의 말은 지글러 씨를 위해 일을 할 시간이 없다는 뜻임을 알 수 있다. 정답은 (A).

2 지글러 씨가 오늘 점심시간 후에 할 일은?
(A) 직원 오리엔테이션 실시하기
(B) 녹스 씨에게 뭔가를 갖다주기
(C) 자료 출력하기
(D) 고객을 직접 방문하기

해설 지글러 씨는 오늘 오후에 고객에게 서류를 갖다 줘야 한다고 했으므로, 고객을 직접 방문한다는 (D)가 정답이다.
오답 피하기 자료 출력하기는 지글러 씨가 내일 해야 하는 일이므로 (C)는 오답.
패러프레이징 지문의 this afternoon이 문제에서 after lunch today로 패러프레이징되었다.

[3-4] 건물 수리 공지

NOTICE TO ALL EMPLOYEES

(3)As previously announced at the conference, the cafeteria on the second floor will be closed for about four weeks beginning on March 7 in order for the building crew to renovate the facility. For your personal safety, please do not enter the area during this time. Should any of your colleagues be out of town to meet clients, please inform them of the contents of this notice so they may remain up-to-date.

We thank you in advance for your cooperative attitude in this matter. While we understand that this causes a major inconvenience at lunchtime, we believe the change will be well worth it. As part of the renovations, (4D)we will replace the walk-in refrigerator that is out of order and (4A)equip the kitchen with upgraded ovens. (4B)In addition, we will have room for four more dining tables, which will make lunch breaks less crowded for everyone. If you have any questions or concerns, please contact the maintenance department by dialing extension 48.

전 직원들에게 알림

(3)이전에 회의에서 알려드렸다시피, 건물 관리팀이 시설을 보수할 수 있도록 2층의 구내식당이 3월 7일부터 약 4주간 폐쇄될 것입니다. 개인의 안전을 위하여, 이 기간 동안에는 이 구역에 들어가지 마십시오. 고객을 만나러 출장 중인 동료가 있다면, 최신 정보를 알 수 있도록 이 공지 내용을 알려주십시오.

이 문제에 대한 여러분의 협조적인 태도에 미리 감사 드립니다. 이번 보수 공사가 점심시간에 큰 불편을 일으킨다는 것을 알고 있지만 변화는 그만큼의 가치가 있을 것이라 믿습니다. 개조의 일환으로 (4D)고장 난 대형 냉장고를 교체하고 (4A)더 좋은 오븐을 주방에 설치할 것입니다. (4B)또한, 네 개의 식탁을 더 놓을 공간이 생길 것인데, 이는 모두의 점심시간을 덜 혼잡하게 만들어 줄 것입니다. 문의사항이나 염려되는 점이 있으시다면 내선번호 48번을 누르셔서 관리부에 연락 주세요.

어휘 previously 이전에 crew (함께 일을 하는) 팀, 조 renovate 보수하다 be out of town 출장 중이다 client 고객 inform A of B A에게 B를 알리다 content (보통 복수형) 내용 in advance 미리 cooperative 협조적인 attitude 태도 replace 교체하다 equip A with B A에 B를 설치하다 crowded 혼잡한 maintenance department 관리부 extension 내선

3 공지의 목적은?
(A) 제안된 보수 공사에 대한 피드백을 얻기 위해
(B) 프로젝트에 대해 설명하기 위해
(C) 안전 장비 배부를 계획하기 위해
(D) 직원들에게 회의를 상기시키기 위해

해설 목적을 묻는 문제이므로 지문의 도입부를 주의 깊게 읽어야 한다. 단서(3)에 따르면 보수 공사가 4주 동안 이루어질 것이라 했다. 이어서 두 번째 단락에서는 보수 공사의 구체적인 내용에 대하여 설명하고 있으므로 정답은 (B)다.

4 보수에 포함되지 않는 것은?
(A) 더 좋아지는 조리 기구
(B) 확장되는 식사 공간
(C) 강화되는 바닥재
(D) 개선되는 냉장 장치

해설 보수 공사의 세부 항목이 서술되어 있는 두 번째 문단을 참고해서 풀어야 한다. 지문을 보면 냉장고가 교체되고, 더 좋은 오븐이 설치되고, 식탁 네 개가 추가로 설치된다는 설명이 있으므로 선택지 (A), (B), (D)를 소거할 수 있다. 반면 flooring(바닥재)에 대한 언급은 없으므로 정답은 (C)다.

[5-7] 교육 일정 변경 안내 이메일

To: Marketing Team <marketing@lucacorp.com>
From: Gina Catta-Preta <ginacp@lucacorp.com>
Date: May 30
Subject: Meeting delayed until 1 P.M.

Dear marketing staff team members:

For several weeks now, we have had our annual joint marketing and information technology meeting scheduled. Because the two departments work so closely together, management feels that frequent training seminars on collaborative techniques are a wise idea. Our original plan had been to hold training all day while stopping for a quick lunch break. (5)Unfortunately, however, a major computer system crash has occurred. It is supposed to take most of the morning tomorrow to repair the network.

(5)(6)In response to this unexpected issue, we have decided to delay and shorten the training session. The two teams will now meet after lunch at 1 P.M. (7)Beverages (coffee and juice) will be provided and can be picked up when entering the large conference room. Please let me know if you have a preference for either regular or decaf coffee, and I will place the beverage order.

Best regards,

Gina Catta-Preta
IT Manager

수신: 마케팅 부서 <marketing@lucacorp.com>
발신: 지나 카타-프레타 <ginacp@lucacorp.com>
날짜: 5월 30일
제목: 오후 1시로 회의 연기

마케팅 부서 직원 여러분들께:

지금 몇 주째 우리는 마케팅과 정보 기술 연례 합동 모임 일정이 잡혀 있었습니다. 두 부서가 함께 매우 긴밀하게 일하고 있기 때문에 경영진은 협력 기술에 관한 교육 세미나를 자주 갖는 것이 좋은 아이디어라고 생각하고 있습니다. 원래 우리의 계획은 점심시간에만 잠시 쉬는 것을 제외하고는 하루 종일 교육을 진행하는 것이었습니다. (5)그런데 불행히도, 주요 컴퓨터 시스템 고장이 발생했습니다. 네트워크를 복구하는 데 내일 오전 내내 걸릴 것으로 보입니다.

(5)(6)이 예상치 못한 사안에 대응하여, 우리는 교육 과정을 연기하고 단축시키기로 결정했습니다. 두 팀은 이제 점심 식사 후 오후 1시에 만나게 될 것입니다. (7)음료(커피와 주스)가 제공될 것이고 대회의장으로 들어가실 때 받으실 수 있습니다. 일반 커피와 디카페인 커피에 대한 선호 여부를 저에게 알려주시면 제가 음료 주문을 해 드리겠습니다.

IT 책임자
지나 카타-프레타 드림

어휘 management 경영진; 관리 frequent 자주 있는, 빈번한 collaborative 협력하는, 공동의 crash 고장, 사고 occur 발생하다, 일어나다 be supposed to do ~하기로 되어 있다 in response to ~에 대한 대응으로, ~에 반응하여 preference 선호하는 것

---

5 카타-프레타 씨가 이메일을 보낸 이유는?
(A) 예상치 못한 지연에 대해 설명하기 위해
(B) 고객 회의 일정을 재조정하기 위해
(C) 팀에 프로젝트를 배정하기 위해
(D) 점심으로 음식을 주문하기 위해

[해설] 카타-프레타 씨는 주요 컴퓨터 시스템이 고장 나서 회의를 연기해야 한다고 하였으므로 정답은 (A). 지문 중간에 목적이 나오므로 신중하게 읽어야 한다.
[오답 피하기] 고객 회의가 아니므로 (B)는 오답.

6 모임에 대해 언급된 것은?
(A) 오늘 오전에 막 일정이 정해졌다.
(B) 다른 날로 변경될 것이다.
(C) 몇 시간 연기될 것이다.
(D) 오후 식사가 포함될 것이다.

[해설] 단서(6)에 따르면, 갑자기 생긴 문제로 인해 교육 과정을 연기 및 단축하기로 결정했다고 했으므로 정답은 (C).

7 음료에 대해 추론할 수 있는 것은?
(A) 회사가 비용을 지불할 것이다.
(B) 직원들은 자신의 컵을 가져와야 한다.
(C) 리필할 만큼 양이 충분하지 않을 것이다.
(D) 뜨거운 음료만 이용 가능하다.

[해설] 지문에서 음료가 언급된 부분을 찾아야 한다. 회의장에 입장할 때 음료가 제공될 것이라 하였으므로 회사에서 비용을 지불하는 것임을 유추할 수 있다. 정답은 (A).
[패러프레이징] 지문의 Beverages(coffee and juice)가 문제에서 drinks로 패러프레이징되었다.

[8-10] 이메일 시스템 변경에 대한 온라인 채팅 대화문

Edward Hudson   2:03 P.M.
I'm glad the budget committee finally approved the software upgrade to the Ultra 2.0 e-mail system. Thank you both again for your help in convincing them.

Adam Quinn   2:04 P.M.
I'm glad it worked out. The system will be so much better than our current one.

Rebecca Gilmore   2:06 P.M.
I completely agree. I used Ultra 2.0 at my previous company, and I was really impressed with it.

Adam Quinn   2:07 P.M.
I read that the grammar function is extremely sophisticated. (8)If you have a mistake in your e-mail, it will catch it and make suggestions.

Edward Hudson   2:08 P.M.
That'll be especially useful since we have so many non-native English speakers in our office.

Adam Quinn   2:08 P.M.
Rebecca, I know you've been installing the software on individual computers this week. We'll go live with the system on Monday. (9)I can work on some installations for you if you need it.

Rebecca Gilmore   2:09 P.M.
It's nearly done. (9)Thanks, though.

Edward Hudson   2:10 P.M.
Okay, then we're all set. My only worry is that using the software will be confusing for some people. It's a lot more complex than our current system.

Rebecca Gilmore   2:12 P.M.
(10)How about having a meeting on Monday morning to teach the employees how to use it?

Edward Hudson   2:14 P.M.
That's a good idea. I'll post an announcement about it on the company intranet.

어휘 budget committee 예산위원회 approve 승인하다 convince 설득하다, 납득시키다 work out (일이) 잘되다 current 현재의 previous 이전의 extremely 굉장히, 매우 be impressed with ~에 감명받다 sophisticated 수준 높은, 정교한 make a suggestion 제안하다 non-native 모국어 사용자가 아닌 nearly 거의 confusing 혼란스러운

8 새로운 소프트웨어 프로그램의 이점으로 언급된 것은?
(A) 고객 유치
(B) 비용 절감
(C) 시간 절약
(D) 오류 감소

해설 새로운 프로그램은 문법 기능이 뛰어나서 이메일에 오류가 있으면 찾아내서 올바른 표현을 제안해 준다고 했으므로, 오류를 줄여 주는 장점이 있음을 알 수 있다. 정답은 (D).
패러프레이징 지문의 a mistake가 정답에서 errors로 패러프레이징되었다.

9 오후 2:09에, 길모어 씨가 "거의 끝났어요"라고 하는 의도는?
(A) 테스트를 시행 중이다.
(B) 마감일을 조정하기를 원한다.
(C) 도움 제안을 거절하고 있다.
(D) 회의 장소를 마련했다.

해설 문제에서 주어진 표현 "It's nearly done" 앞의 단서(9)에서 퀸 씨가 길모어 씨에게 시스템 설치 작업을 도와주겠다고 제안했고, 뒤의 단서(9)에서 길모어 씨는 그래도 고맙다고 하였다. 따라서 "거의 끝났어요"는 설치 작업을 도와주겠다는 퀸 씨의 제안을 사양하는 말임을 알 수 있다. 정답은 (C).

10 월요일 회의의 목적은?
(A) 변경 사항을 알리기 위해
(B) 의견을 모으기 위해
(C) 직원들을 교육하기 위해
(D) 신입 직원들을 소개하기 위해

해설 월요일 회의를 소집하는 이유는 직원들에게 새로운 프로그램 사용법을 가르치기 위함이므로 정답은 (C).
패러프레이징 지문의 teach the employees가 정답에서 train staff members로 패러프레이징되었다.

[11-14] 계약 성사를 알리는 기업 소식지의 기사

Stone Enterprises Newsletter–Vol. 209
Contract Solidifies Stone Enterprises' Market Position
By Keith Velarde

(11)After seemingly endless market research and months of high-stakes negotiations, Stone Enterprises is pleased to announce that it has finalized an important contract with California manufacturer Baxley Solar. Becoming the exclusive distributor for Baxley's products has been the top priority of the company this year, as it is the key to positioning the company as an emerging global leader.

Baxley Solar has made a name for itself through its dependable and sustainable energy systems, which make use of the latest technology in solar panels, monitoring systems, and long-life batteries. (14)Last year, when a spokesperson for the company indicated that it would be switching to a single distributor to simplify its internal processes, the race was on. Several distributors negotiated with Baxley Solar representatives in an effort to secure this lucrative contract. (12)(14)However, in the end, the Baxley Solar board of directors turned down the offers of other companies in favor of Stone Enterprises' ability to demonstrate sufficient capital. (13)Earlier this month, business development manager Victor Wilburn drew up the agreement on behalf of Stone Enterprises, and Baxley's representatives gave consent to exclusive distribution rights for a five-year term.

In honor of this monumental achievement, Stone Enterprises will hold a celebratory reception at the Woodward Hotel on July 8 at 8 P.M. It will feature speeches by company executives, including CEO Jamie Morris, and a stand-up comedy performance by Jed Reid. All employees are welcome to attend. We hope everyone will join the celebration.

스톤 사 소식지–209호
계약이 스톤 기업의 시장 입지를 굳히다
키스 벨라르데 작성

(11)끝이 없어 보이던 시장 조사와 수개월간의 고위험의 협상을 거쳐서 스톤 사는 캘리포니아 제조사인 백슬리 솔라 사와 중요한 계약을 마무리 짓게 된 것을 알리게 되어 기쁩니다. 백슬리 사의 독점 유통업자가 되는 것은 우리 회사가 세계적인 신흥 선두 주자로 자리잡는 데 있어 핵심이었기 때문에 올해 우리 회사의 최우선 과제였습니다.

백슬리 솔라 사는 신뢰할 수 있는 지속 가능 에너지 시스템을 통하여 유명해졌는데, 그것은 태양 전지판과 점검 시스템, 그리고 수명이 긴 배터리의 최첨단 기술을 이용한 것입니다. (14)작년에 그 회사의 대변인이 내부 절차를 단순화하기 위해 독점 유통사로 바꾸겠다는 것을 시사했을 때, 경쟁은 시작되었습니다. 여러 유통업체가 이 수익성 있는 계약을 따내려고 백슬리 솔라 사의 대표들과 협상하였습니다. (12)(14)하지만, 결국 백슬리 솔라 사의 이사회는 충분한 자본력을 보여주는 스톤 사를 선호하여 다른 회사들의 제안을 거절하였습니다. (13)이달 초에, 사업 개발부 책임자 빅터 윌번 씨가 스톤 사를 대표하여 계약서를 작성하였고 백슬리 사의 대표들이 5년간의 독점 유통권에 동의하였습니다.

이 기념비적인 업적을 기리기 위해 스톤 사는 7월 8일 저녁 8시에 우드워드 호텔에서 축하 연회를 열 예정입니다. CEO인 제이미 모리스 씨를 포함한 회사 간부들이 연설을 할 것이고 제드 레이드 씨의 스탠드업 코미디 공연이 있을 것입니다. 모든 직원들의 참석을 환영합니다. 모두가 축하 연회에 참석해 주시길 바랍니다.

어휘 contract 계약 high-stake 고위험의 negotiation 협상 manufacturer 제조사 exclusive 독점적인 distributor 유통업자 priority 우선순위 make a name for *oneself* 유명해지다 dependable 신뢰할 수 있는 sustainable 지속 가능한 spokesperson 대변인 indicate 시사하다 simplify 단순화하다 negotiate 협상하다 representative 대표 in an effort to *do* ~해보려는 노력으로 secure 확보하다 lucrative 수익성이 좋은 board of directors 이사회 turn down ~을 거절하다 demonstrate 보여주다; 설명하다 capital 자금 draw up the agreement 계약서를 작성하다 on behalf of ~를 대표하여 monumental 기념비적인 celebratory 축하하는

---

11 기사의 주제는?
 (A) 회사 합병
 (B) 업계 동향
 (C) 회사 업적
 (D) 협상 워크숍

해설 지문의 첫 부분을 통해 회사가 중요한 계약을 성사시킨 것을 알리기 위해 이 기사가 쓰였음을 알 수 있으므로 정답은 (C).
패러프레이징 지문의 it has finalized an important contract 이하가 정답에서 상위어인 A company accomplishment로 패러프레이징되었다.

12 백슬리 솔라 사에 대해 추론할 수 있는 것은?
 (A) 곧 폐업할 것이다.
 (B) 재정 안전성을 갖춘 유통업자를 찾고 있었다.
 (C) 국내 동종 업계의 최대 회사이다.
 (D) 이사회 임원은 5년의 임기를 수행한다.

해설 단서(12)에 따르면, 백슬리 솔라 사가 다른 기업들의 제안을 거절하고 스톤 사를 선택한 이유는 충분한 자본 때문이었음을 알 수 있으므로, 백슬리 솔라 사가 재정 안전성을 갖춘 회사를 찾고 있었다는 것을 유추할 수 있다. 정답은 (B).
패러프레이징 지문의 sufficient capital이 정답에서 financial stability로 패러프레이징되었다.

13 기사에 따르면, 월번 씨가 한 일은?
 (A) 국제 회의에 참가했다
 (B) 축하 연회를 계획했다
 (C) 계약서를 작성했다
 (D) 수명이 긴 배터리를 발명했다

해설 지문에서 월번 씨가 언급된 부분을 빠르게 찾아야 한다. 단서(13)에 의하면 월번 씨는 이달 초에 계약서를 작성했고 백슬리 사의 대표가 이에 동의했으므로 정답은 (C).
패러프레이징 지문의 drew up the agreement가 정답에서 Created a contract로 패러프레이징되었다.

14 [1], [2], [3], [4]로 표시된 위치 중 다음 문장이 들어가기에 가장 알맞은 곳은?
 "여러 유통업체가 이 수익성 있는 계약을 따내려고 백슬리 솔라 사의 대표들과 협상하였습니다."
 (A) [1]
 (B) [2]
 (C) [3]
 (D) [4]

해설 주어진 문장은 여러 회사에서 백슬리 솔라 사와 계약을 따내려고 했다는 내용으로, 그 앞에는 계약의 배경이, 뒤에는 계약의 결과가 와야 자연스럽다. 앞의 단서(14)에서 백슬리 솔라 사의 독점 유통 계획이 제시되고 있고, 뒤의 단서(14)에서 백슬리 솔라 사가 스톤 사를 선호했다고 언급하고 있으므로 주어진 문장은 이 사이에 와야 알맞다. 정답은 (C).

[15-19] 공장 점검 양식 & 점검 결과 알림 회람

Wentzville Factory Inspection Form 84B:
(15)General Safety Follow-up

Performance:
M=Meets expectations. No adjustments necessary.
R=Requires that revisions be made within a specified amount of time.
P=Poor. (15)Required revisions were neglected during the initial grace period. Sanctions must be implemented.

Inspected by: Theo Challies
(18-1)Inspection date: June 3

1. Accessible and proper number of fire exits	M
2. Adequate warning labels on machinery	M
3. Humidifiers free of hard water deposits	M
4. Appropriate storage of flammable materials	M
5. Safety clothing/equipment available and worn	P

웬츠빌 공장 점검 양식 84B:
(15)일반 안전 후속 조치

수행 성적:
M=기대치를 충족시킴. 개선 필요 없음.
R=명시된 기간 내에 개선을 요함.
P= 열악함. (15)최초 유예 기간에 요청한 변경 사항이 등한시됨. 제재가 가해져야 함.

점검 수행자: 테오 찰리스
(18-1)점검일: 6월 3일

1. 접근이 가능한, 적정 수의 화재 비상구	M
2. 기계류에 적절한 경고 라벨 표시	M
3. 경수 침전물이 없는 가습기	M
4. 가연성 물질의 적절한 보관	M
5. 안전 의류/장비 이용 가능 여부 및 착용 여부	P
6. 안전 설비 구비: 구급용 세안기 등	M
7. 곰팡이가 없는 벽과 천장, 창문	M

6. Safety stations present: eye wash station, etc.	M
7. Walls, ceilings, and windows free of mold	M

Status: (16)Sanction issued in the amount of a $225 fine*
Cause: (15)Failure to revise #5. Safety equipment continues to be neglected by factory employees.

Theo Challies	Rozalyn Kozel
Theo Challies	*Rozalyn Kozel*
Safety inspector	Facilities manager

*Fines must be paid in full within 15 days after receiving the inspection report.

MEMO

To: All staff
From: Rozalyn Kozel
Date: June 7
Subject: Safety equipment

Dear factory staff members,

Recently, a safety inspection of our facilities was conducted, and I'm disappointed to report that we are being fined. The issue is with our safety gear. The safety inspector concluded that none of you are regularly wearing this equipment: (17A)your steel-toed boots, (17B)gloves, (17C)and— most importantly—safety goggles. Additionally, it is highly recommended that you also wear safety helmets. (17D)However, unlike the other items, helmets are optional. All of this equipment must be worn at all times when inside the factory, as it prevents you from hurting yourselves. (18-2) We have only two months from the time of our last inspection before our next visit. Wearing this equipment must become standard procedure for us by this time.

To understand the importance of following these procedures, (19)I'm scheduling all employees to attend a safety equipment training session. It will educate each of you about what the purpose of this safety equipment is, why you must wear it, and how it should be properly stored.

Thank you in advance for your cooperation.

Rozalyn Kozel, Facilities Manager
Wentzville Factory

어휘 inspection 점검, 시찰   follow-up 후속 조치   adjustment 개선, 수정   revision 변경, 개정   specify 명시하다   neglect 등한시하다, 무시하다   grace period 유예 기간   sanction 제재, 처벌   implement 시행하다   accessible 접근 가능한   adequate 적절한, 충분한   humidifier 가습기   storage 보관, 저장   flammable 가연성의   eye wash station 구급용 세안기   mold 곰팡이   status 상태; 지위   fine 벌금(을 물다)   facility (보통 복수형) 시설   conduct 실시하다; 지휘하다   gear 장비   conclude 판단[결론]을 내리다   optional 선택적인   procedure 절차   schedule 일정을 세우다   in advance 미리   cooperation 협조, 협력

15 웬츠빌 공장 점검에 대해 시사된 바는?
 (A) **이번이 처음으로 이루어진 안전 조사는 아니었다.**
 (B) 여러 가지 보건법 위반 사항이 발견되었다.
 (C) 두 명의 조사관에 의해 실시되었다.
 (D) 벽에서 심한 곰팡이 문제가 발견되었다.

해설 점검 양식 속 세 군데의 단서(15)를 보자. 양식 제목에 쓰인 표현 follow-up(후속 조치)으로 어느 정도 정답이 유추 가능하며, 성적 기준의 P가 최초 유예 기간에 대해 언급하고 있고, 점검 결과에서 5번 사항을 개선하는 데에 실패했으므로 벌금을 내야 한다고 설명하고 있다. 이를 통해서 공장 점검이 이번이 처음 이루어진 게 아니라는 것을 추측할 수 있다. 따라서 정답은 (A).

16 점검 결과는?
 (A) 이전의 모든 제재들이 거두어졌다.
 (B) **의무적인 지불이 예상된다.**
 (C) 모든 화재 비상구들에 적절한 표시가 되어야 한다.
 (D) 구급용 세안기가 설치되어야 한다.

해설 점검 양식에서 항목별 점수와 점검 상태를 집중해서 보아야 한다. 단서(16)에서 점검 항목을 제대로 따르지 않은 것에 대해 225달러의 벌금이 가해질 것이라 하였으므로 정답은 (B).
패러프레이징 지문의 we are being fined가 정답에서 A mandatory payment is expected.로 패러프레이징되었다.

17 필수 안전 장비 유형으로 언급되지 않은 것은?
 (A) 부츠
 (B) 장갑
 (C) 고글
 (D) **헬멧**

해설 안전 장비가 언급된 이메일을 보아야 한다. 이메일의 발신자 코젤 씨는 안전 장비 착용을 강조하면서 부츠, 장갑, 안전 고글, 안전 헬멧을 착용할 것을 권장하였다. 하지만 헬멧은 필수가 아닌 선택 사항이라고 하였으므로 정답은 (D).

18 다음 점검이 시행되는 때는?
 (A) 6월 3일
 (B) 6월 7일
 (C) 6월 18일
 (D) **8월 3일**

해설 두 개 이상의 지문에서 문제의 선택지가 모두 날짜로 되어 있으면 연계 문제이다. 점검 양식에 따르면, 단서(18-1)에서 보듯이 제재가 가해진 점검 일자가 6월 3일이었는데, 이메일 속 단서(18-2)에서 지난번 점검 시기부터 다음 점검까지 두 달이 남아 있다고 하였으므로 다음 점검이 8월 3일임을 알 수 있다. 따라서 정답은 (D).

19 회람에서, 직원들이 하도록 당부받은 것은?
 (A) 모든 기계에 경고 라벨 붙이기
 (B) 안전 부츠를 동일한 장소에 보관하기
 (C) **안전 교육 훈련에 참가하기**
 (D) 구식 가습기 교체하기

해설 단서(19)에서 안전 장비 착용의 중요성을 강조하기 위해 전 직원이 안전 교육에 참가할 것이라고 하였으므로 정답은 (C).
패러프레이징 지문의 safety equipment training session이 정답에서는 instructional training on safety로 패러프레이징되었다.

[20-24] 가전제품 광고 & 할인 쿠폰 & 장바구니

Kitchen Sage
Create the kitchen of your dreams!

Kitchen Sage has been producing high-quality kitchen appliances for nearly fifty years. We are dedicated to helping make your daily tasks easier. From brewing your first cup of morning coffee to cleaning the last dinner plates in the dishwasher, we've got you covered.

At Kitchen Sage, we care about supporting the local economy. (20)That's why we're committed to creating jobs here at home and never using overseas manufacturers. Our products are available at Kitchen Sage retail outlets, major department stores, and on our Web site. All products are guaranteed to last for ten years, or your money back.

(22-2)Take advantage of these great deals until August 31!

키친 세이지
꿈의 주방을 만드세요!

키친 세이지는 거의 50년간 고품질의 주방 가전제품을 생산해 오고 있습니다. 저희는 여러분이 매일 하는 일들을 더 간편하게 만드는 데 도움을 드리는 데에 헌신하고 있습니다. 모닝 커피 첫 잔을 끓이는 일부터 마지막 저녁 식사 접시들을 식기 세척기에서 씻는 일까지, 저희가 알아서 해 드리겠습니다.

저희 키친 세이지는 지역 경제 후원에도 관심을 갖고 있습니다. (20)그래서 저희는 여기 국내에서 일자리를 창출하는 데 전념하고 해외 제조업체를 절대 이용하지도 않습니다. 저희 제품은 키친 세이지 소매점과 주요 백화점, 그리고 저희 웹사이트에서 구입하실 수 있습니다. 모든 제품은 10년 이상 지속됨을 보장하며, 그렇지 않을 경우 환불해 드립니다.

(22-2)8월 31일까지 이번 대박 행사를 이용하십시오!
 – 저희 제품 중 어떤 오븐이든 구입하시고 무료로 토스터를 받으세요.
 – 믹서기를 구입하시고 무료 요리 책자를 받으세요.

– Buy any oven in our collection and get a free toaster.
– Get a free recipe book with any blender purchase.

Sign up for our monthly newsletter in May and get a coupon for 15% off your next order. Visit our Web site for a list of retail locations. Or order online, and we'll (21)fill your order quickly. Make the most of every meal with Kitchen Sage!

15% Off Kitchen Sage Products
Coupon Code: D539R

Present this coupon at any Kitchen Sage retail outlet or input the code online to get 15% off your entire purchase. Coupon will not be accepted at department stores. Not valid when combined with any other offer. Cannot be used on clearance items. (23-1)Expires July 31. No cash value.

---

http://www.kitchen-sage.com/shoppingcart

Review Your Order

(22-1)(23-2)**Order date:** August 5
(24)**Delivery Date:** August 8
Shipping address: Anna Kennedy, 738 Murray Street SW, Phoenix, AZ 85021
Payment method: Skylar credit card XXXX-XXXX-XXXX-6870

Item	Price	Quantity
(22-1)30″ stainless steel gas convection oven, 4 burners	$695.99	1
12-cup capacity coffee maker, red	$49.95	1
Shipping	$0.00	–
(24)Installation (on day of delivery)	$79.95	–

Coupon Code: D539R
Error. Coupon not accepted. Please try another code or confirm order.

Total Due: $825.89

[CONFIRM]

5월에 저희 월간 소식지를 신청하시고 다음 주문 시 15%가 할인되는 쿠폰을 받으십시오. 소매점 목록을 보시려면 저희 웹사이트를 방문하십시오. 또는 온라인으로 주문하시면, 신속하게 고객님의 주문을 (21)처리해 드리겠습니다. 키친 세이지와 함께 여러분의 모든 식사를 최대한 즐기시기 바랍니다!

키친 세이지 제품 15% 할인
쿠폰 번호: D539R

키친 세이지 소매점 어느 곳에서든 이 쿠폰을 제시하거나 인터넷에 쿠폰 번호를 입력하여 전체 구매품에 대해 15% 할인을 받으세요. 백화점에서는 쿠폰을 받지 않습니다. 다른 할인과 함께 쓰이면 유효하지 않습니다. 재고 정리 제품에는 사용할 수 없습니다. (23-1)유효기간은 7월 31일까지입니다. 현금으로 돌려드리지 않습니다.

---

http://www.kitchen-sage.com/shoppingcart

주문 확인

(22-1)(23-2)**주문일:** 8월 5일
(24)**배송일:** 8월 8일
배송 주소: 85021, 애리조나 주 피닉스, 머레이 가 남서쪽 738번지, 애나 케네디
지불 방법: 스카일라 신용카드 XXXX-XXXX-XXXX-6870

제품	가격	수량
(22-1)점화구 4개짜리 30인치 스테인리스 스틸 컨벡션 가스 오븐	695.99달러	1
12컵 용량 커피 메이커, 빨강	49.95달러	1
배송료	0.00달러	–
(24)설치비(배송 당일)	79.95달러	–

쿠폰 번호: D539R
오류. 쿠폰 입력되지 않음. 다른 쿠폰 번호를 입력하거나 주문을 확정하시기 바랍니다.

총액: 825.89달러

[확인]

어휘   be dedicated[committed] to *doing* ~하는 데 헌신[전념]하다   care about ~에 관심을 갖다   overseas 해외의, 해외에   manufacturer 제조업체   retail outlet 소매점   take advantage of ~을 이용하다   fill *one's* order ~의 주문을 처리하다   make the most of ~을 최대한 활용하다[즐기다]   present 제시하다   input 입력하다   valid 유효한   combined with ~와 결합된   clearance (sale) 재고 정리 세일   expire 만료하다   shipping 배송   capacity 용량   installation 설치   total due 총액

20 키친 세이지 제품에 대해 시사된 바는?
 (A) 디자인이 에너지 효율적이다.
 (B) 평생 보증이 따른다.
 (C) 전문가들이 보증한다.
 (D) 국내에서 생산된다.

21 광고에서, 4단락, 두 번째 줄의 "fill"과 의미상 가장 유사한 것은?
 (A) 공급하다
 (B) 가득 메우다
 (C) 밀봉하다
 (D) 보장하다

22 케네디 씨에 대해 추론할 수 있는 것은?
 (A) 무료 가전제품을 받을 자격이 있다.
 (B) 단골 고객이다.
 (C) 요리책을 받게 될 것이다.
 (D) 상품권으로 지불했다.

23 쿠폰 번호가 거부된 이유는?
 (A) 엉뚱한 브랜드에 적용했다.
 (B) 유효기간이 이미 지났다.
 (C) 여러 제품에 사용할 수 없다.
 (D) 매장에서만 사용할 수 있다.

24 8월 8일에 일어날 가능성이 큰 일은?
 (A) 세일 기간이 끝난다.
 (B) 케네디 씨가 제품을 찾으러 갈 것이다.
 (C) 키친 세이지에서 책자를 보낼 것이다.
 (D) 기술자가 가전제품을 설치할 것이다.

해설 광고에서 키친 세이지는 국내에서 일자리를 창출하고, 해외 제조업체를 이용하지 않는다고 했으므로 제품을 국내에서 생산한다는 것을 알 수 있다. 정답은 (D).
패러프레이징 지문의 at home이 정답에서 domestically로 패러프레이징되었다.

해설 지문에서 fill your order는 '주문을 처리하다, 주문대로 이행하다'라는 뜻이다. 선택지 중에서는 '주문한 제품을 공급하다'라는 뜻으로 fill 대신 supply가 가장 어울리는 어휘이다. 정답은 (A).

해설 두 지문 연계 문제이다. 케네디 씨의 장바구니에 있는 단서(22-1)을 보면 8월 5일에 가스 오븐을 구입했는데, 광고에서 8월 31일까지 오븐을 구입하면 무료로 토스터를 준다고 했다. 따라서 케네디 씨는 무료로 가전제품을 받을 자격이 있으므로 정답은 (A).

해설 두 지문 연계 문제이다. 단서(23-1)에서 쿠폰 유효 기간이 7월 31일까지라고 했는데, 단서(23-2)를 보면 케네디 씨의 주문일자는 8월 5일이다. 따라서 유효 기간이 경과해서 쿠폰 이용이 거부된 것임을 알 수 있다. 정답은 (B).

해설 장바구니 양식에서 필요한 단서를 찾아 종합해야 하는 문제이다. 8월 8일은 케네디 씨가 주문한 가전 제품이 배송되는 날인데, 비용 내역에 배송 당일 설치비가 청구된 것으로 보아, 8월 8일에 가전제품이 설치될 것이라 볼 수 있다. 정답은 (D).

CHAPTER 2 지문 유형
UNIT 11 문자메시지/SNS

PRE-STEP
p.87

A 1 (A) 2 (B) 3 (B) 4 (A) 5 (A) 6 (B) 7 (A) 8 (B) 9 (B)
   10 (A) 11 (B) 12 (B) 13 (A) 14 (B) 15 (A)

B 1 (A) 2 (B)

A 1 (A) interact, 고객과 소통하다
   2 (B) count, 가까운 동료들에게 의지하다
   3 (B) budget, ~의 예산 한도액을 지키다
   4 (A) activity, 그룹 활동에 참가하다
   5 (A) recent, 최근의 기자 회견에서
   6 (B) reasonable, 합리적인 가격을 제시하다
   7 (A) present, 워크숍에서 발표하다
   8 (B) cover, 누군가를 대신해 주다
   9 (B) enter, 보안 코드를 입력하다
   10 (A) complaints, 형편없는 서비스에 대한 불만
   11 (B) share, 기꺼이 의견을 교환하다
   12 (B) pick, 안내 책자를 가져오다
   13 (A) during, 중간 휴식 시간 동안
   14 (B) information, 누군가에게 정보를 더 보내주다
   15 (A) set, 전화 회담을 준비하다

B 1 My team is experiencing so many issues because of the current system. We spend a lot of time sending reimbursement payments and confirming the receipts that people hand in.
   (A) The system of reimbursing employees is inconvenient.
   (B) The system of collecting payments is confusing.

   저희 팀은 현재 시스템으로 인해 많은 문제를 겪고 있어요. 우리는 환급액을 보내주는 것과 사람들이 제출하는 영수증들을 확인하는 것에 많은 시간을 소비하고 있어요.
   (A) 직원 환급 시스템이 불편합니다.
   (B) 수금 시스템이 혼란스럽습니다.

   2 MedMax is one of the nation's largest medical-related trade fairs. Major companies and medical experts alike look forward to this event every year to find out the latest trends in the industry.
   (A) MedMax is recruiting more experts so it can grow in size.
   (B) MedMax is an important event for those in the medical industry.

   메드맥스는 국내 최대의 의학 관련 무역박람회 중 하나입니다. 주요 기업들과 의학 전문가들 모두 업계의 최신 동향을 알아내기 위하여 매년 이 행사를 기대하고 있습니다.
   (A) 메드맥스는 규모를 늘리고자 더 많은 전문가를 모집하고 있습니다.
   (B) 메드맥스는 의료 업계에 있는 사람들에게 중요한 행사입니다.

MAIN STEP 1
p.88

 일정 조정 요청 문자메시지

KIRK GARDINER   23:08
My flight out of Denver was canceled because of a severe snowstorm, so I won't be in the office tomorrow morning.

커크 가디너   23:08
덴버에서 출발하는 제 비행편이 심한 눈보라로 취소되어서, 내일 아침에 사무실에 가지 못할 것 같아요.

MILLIE AKHTAR 23:10 Oh, that's terrible. Are you booked on a new flight yet?		밀리 아크타 23:10 아, 그거 안됐네요. 새로운 비행편을 예약했나요?	
KIRK GARDINER 23:12 Not yet. I'm standing in line to get that sorted out right now. Could you please reschedule my meetings?		커크 가디너 23:12 아직요. 그것을 해결하려고 지금 줄 서 있어요. 회의 일정을 다시 잡아 주시겠어요?	
MILLE AKHTAR 23:14 Okay. Just let me know when you'll arrive.		밀리 아크타 23:14 알겠어요. 언제 오실지만 알려주세요.	

가디너 씨가 요청하는 것은?
→ 일정 변경

해설 비행기가 취소되어 제시간에 사무실에 도착하지 못하게 된 가디너 씨가 회의 일정을 다시 잡아 달라고 요청하고 있다.

 서비스 개선 관련 온라인 채팅 대화문

Betty Chapman
We've had some complaints about the staff's poor service.

Douglas Tokley
Oh, really? What seems to be the problem?

Betty Chapman
It is that servers regularly calculated meal totals incorrectly. What should we do?

Daryl Crigler
I think we should purchase payment software. Writing bills by hand is so old-fashioned.

베티 챕맨
우리 직원들의 형편없는 서비스에 대해 일부 불만이 있어 왔습니다.

더글라스 토클리
아, 정말요? 문제가 무엇인 것 같나요?

베티 챕맨
종업원들이 식사 가격을 자주 틀리게 계산한다는 거죠. 어떻게 하면 좋을까요?

대럴 크리글러
제 생각에 우리는 결제 소프트웨어를 구입해야 돼요. 손으로 계산서를 적는 것은 너무 구식이에요.

크리글러 씨가 제시한 해결책은?
→ 결제 방법 개선

해설 크리글러 씨가 말한 부분을 집중해서 보아야 하는 문제이다. 문제 해결책을 묻는 챕맨 씨의 말에 크리글러 씨는 새로운 결제 소프트웨어를 구입해야 한다고 했으므로 정답은 '결제 방법 개선'이다.

MAIN STEP 2

p.89

1 (B)   **2** (D)   **3** (B)

[1-3] 워크숍 준비에 관한 온라인 채팅 대화문

Duncan, Kimberly 9:10 A.M.
(1)I'm headed to the office supply store to pick up a few things. Do any of you need anything? I know you're all presenting at the workshop on fostering cooperation.

Kota, Jia 9:11 A.M.
I'm fine.

Hsu, Shan 9:12 A.M.
I could use a pack of new dry erase markers.

던컨, 킴벌리 오전 9:10
(1)저는 물건 몇 개를 사러 사무용품점에 가고 있어요. 여러분들 중 필요한 것 있으신 분 있나요? 협동심 발전시키기에 관한 워크숍에서 여러분 모두 발표하신다고 알고 있는데요.

코타, 지아 오전 9:11
저는 괜찮아요.

슈, 산 오전 9:12
마커펜 한 팩이 필요할 것 같은데요.

Geisler, Terry   9:12 A.M.
And I need a large foam board, size 40˝ x 60˝, if they have it.

Duncan, Kimberly   9:14 A.M.
Okay, I'll get both of those things.

Kota, Jia   9:16 A.M.
(2)Terry, do you need any help? I know you had to cover for Mr. Rhodes at the last minute.

Geisler, Terry   9:17 A.M.
I'm nearly ready, but I just need someone to check my outline to see if my timing is okay. I'm worried I tried to fit in too many points.

Kota, Jia   9:18 A.M.
I can look it over. Just send it to me by e-mail.

Geisler, Terry   9:21 A.M.
Okay, thanks! It should be in your inbox now.

Hsu, Shan   9:23 A.M.
(3)Does anyone have a copy of our catalog?

Kota, Jia   9:27 A.M.
(3)I have a few in my office. Do you need them now?

Hsu, Shan   9:29 A.M.
(3)Please just bring them to the workshop at 2:00. Thanks!

가이슬러, 테리   오전 9:12
그리고 저는, 만약 있다면, 40×60인치짜리 대형 보드판이 필요해요.

던컨, 킴벌리   오전 9:14
알겠어요. 두 개 다 사 갈게요.

코타, 지아   오전 9:16
(2)테리, 도움 필요한 것 없어요? 당신이 막판에 로즈 씨를 대신해야 했다고 알고 있어요.

가이슬러, 테리   오전 9:17
저는 거의 다 준비됐는데요, 시간이 괜찮은지 제 개요를 확인해 줄 사람이 필요해요. 너무 많은 요점을 담으려고 한 것 같아 걱정스럽네요.

코타, 지아   오전 9:18
제가 봐 드릴 수 있어요. 제 이메일로 보내 주시기만 하면 돼요.

가이슬러, 테리   오전 9:21
네, 고마워요! 지금쯤 수신함에 있을 거예요.

슈, 샨   오전 9:23
(3)혹시 누구 우리 책자 사본 하나 가지고 있는 분 있나요?

코타, 지아   오전 9:27
(3)제 사무실에 몇 개 있어요. 지금 필요한가요?

슈, 샨   오전 9:29
(3)그냥 2시 워크숍에 그것들을 가져와 주세요. 감사해요!

어휘 **head** 향하게 하다; 향하다   **office supply store** 사무용품점   **present** 발표하다   **foster** 발전시키다   **cooperation** 협동심   **cover for** ~를 대신하다   **at the last minute** 막판에, 임박해서   **look over** ~을 살펴보다

---

1 오전 9:11에, 코타 씨가 "저는 괜찮아요"라고 하는 의도는?

(A) 던컨 씨의 말에 동의한다.
(B) 아무 물품도 필요하지 않다.
(C) 행사에 대해 긍정적으로 느낀다.
(D) 직접 만날 시간이 된다.

해설 필요한 물건이 없냐고 묻는 던컨 씨의 말에 코타 씨가 "저는 괜찮아요"라고 말했으므로 이는 곧 아무것도 필요하지 않다는 뜻임을 알 수 있다. 따라서 정답은 (B).

2 가이슬러 씨에 대해 추론할 수 있는 것은?
(A) 그의 개요 서류를 잃어버렸다.
(B) 던컨 씨와 함께 상점에 갈 것이다.
(C) 팀에서 가장 신입이다.
(D) 다른 사람을 대신하고 있다.

해설 지문에서 가이슬러 씨 또는 그와 대화를 나눈 사람의 말을 유심히 보아야 한다. 단서(2)를 보면, 가이슬러 씨가 로즈 씨를 대신해 발표하게 되었다는 사실을 알 수 있다. 정답은 (D).
패러프레이징 지문의 cover가 정답에서 filling in으로 패러프레이징되었다.

3 행사에 책자를 가져올 사람은?
(A) 던컨 씨
(B) 코타 씨
(C) 슈 씨
(D) 가이슬러 씨

해설 단서(3)을 보면, 슈 씨가 코타 씨에게 워크숍이 시작할 때 책자를 가지고 와 달라고 부탁하고 있으므로 정답은 (B)이다.

FINAL STEP

p.90

| 1 (A) | 2 (A) | 3 (C) | 4 (A) | 5 (A) | 6 (B) |

[1-2] 회의실 준비에 관한 문자메시지

ALICE STANFIELD   1:56 P.M.
I'm setting up Conference Room A for the annual board meeting. I need some space for the refreshments, (1)so I've got to move a few tables from other rooms. But they're too heavy. Could you give me a hand?

MINJUN BAEK   1:59 P.M.
Sure thing. Should I come up there now?

ALICE STANFIELD   (2)2:01 P.M.
(2)I have a few things to do before that, so could you come in about half an hour? I don't expect it to take more than fifteen minutes.

MINJUN BAEK   2:02 P.M.
Okay, I'll just meet you in the conference room. When does the meeting start?

ALICE STANFIELD   2:03 P.M.
It starts in about an hour, at 3 P.M., and will finish around 4 P.M. There's plenty of time. People usually don't arrive very early for it.

앨리스 스탠필드   오후 1:56
연례 이사회를 위해 A 회의실에 자리를 마련하는 중이에요. 다과를 위한 공간이 약간 필요해서, (1)다른 회의실에서 테이블 몇 개를 옮겨와야 해요. 그렇지만 그것들이 너무 무겁네요. 도와주실 수 있나요?

민준 백   오후 1:59
물론이죠. 지금 그리로 올라가면 될까요?

앨리스 스탠필드   (2)오후 2:01
(2)그전에 몇 가지 해야 할 일이 있으니, 30분 정도 후에 와 주실 수 있어요? 15분 이상 걸리지는 않을 거라고 예상해요.

민준 백   오후 2:02
알겠어요, 회의실에서 만나요. 회의가 언제 시작하죠?

앨리스 스탠필드   오후 2:03
한 시간 정도 후인 오후 3시에 시작하고 오후 4시 정도에 끝날 거예요. 시간은 많이 있어요. 사람들은 보통 그렇게 일찍 도착하지 않거든요.

어휘 set up ~을 마련하다[설치하다]   board meeting 이사회   space 공간   refreshment (보통 복수형) 다과   give a hand 도와주다

1 오후 1:59에, 백 씨가 "물론이죠"라고 하는 의도는?
 (A) 가구 옮기는 것을 도와주겠다.
 (B) 약간의 다과를 주문하겠다.
 (C) 이사회에 참석하겠다.
 (D) 앨리스 씨를 위해 프로젝터를 설치하겠다.

해설 테이블을 옮겨야 하는데 너무 무거우니 좀 도와줄 수 있겠냐는 말에 백 씨가 "물론이죠"라고 대답하고 있다. 따라서 정답은 (A).

2 백 씨가 스탠필드 씨를 만날 때는?
 (A) 오후 2시 30분
 (B) 오후 3시
 (C) 오후 3시 30분
 (D) 오후 4시

해설 백 씨와 스탠필드 씨가 문자를 주고받는 시간은 약 2시이다. 스탠필드 씨가 백 씨에게 30분 정도 후에 와 달라고 부탁하고 있으므로 정답은 (A).

[3-6] 사무용품 주문 시스템 관련 온라인 채팅 대화문

Charles Rogue   10:03 A.M.
I just came from a meeting with the branch manager. (3)We've decided to implement a new plan regarding office supplies.

Vera Trembley   10:04 A.M.
Oh, really? Why is that?

찰스 로그   오전 10:03
방금 지점장과의 회의에 다녀왔어요. (3)우리는 사무용품과 관련하여 새로운 계획을 도입하기로 했어요.

베라 트렘블리   오전 10:04
아, 그래요? 그게 뭐죠?

Charles Rogue	10:04 A.M.

At the moment, it's difficult to track the spending for each team. The accounting department can hardly keep up. Isn't that right, Scott?

Scott Farris	10:05 A.M.

Yes. My team is experiencing so many issues because of the current system. We spend a lot of time sending reimbursement payments and confirming the receipts that people hand in. And what's worse, (4)departments never stick to their budget limits.

Vera Trembley	10:07 A.M.

Then, what will we do as an alternative?

Charles Rogue	10:09 A.M.

From next week, (3)we will require everyone to order supplies from the same company instead of getting reimbursed. We'll have a corporate account there, and department managers will enter a code. That way, we can track our spending.

Scott Farris	10:10 A.M.

Great! Are you going to use Zenith Supplies? They have the lowest prices I've seen.

Charles Rogue	10:11 A.M.

Their prices may be low, but they get poor reviews for reliability. We've decided to go with (5)Meadow Co. instead. Their prices are reasonable, and (5) they don't charge to bring us the goods.

Vera Trembley	10:13 A.M.

In that case, (6)we'll need to have a few copies of the Meadow Co. catalog in the break room. Would you like me to request some?

Charles Rogue	10:13 A.M.

I've got it covered. (6)They'll arrive tomorrow.

찰스 로그 오전 10:04
현재, 각 팀의 지출을 추적하기가 어려워요. 회계 부서가 거의 따라잡을 수가 없습니다. 그렇지 않나요, 스캇?

스캇 패리스 오전 10:05
맞아요. 저희 팀은 현재 시스템으로 인해 많은 문제를 겪고 있어요. 환급액을 보내주는 것과 사람들이 제출하는 영수증들을 확인하는 것에 많은 시간을 소비하고 있어요. 그리고 더 안 좋은 것은, (4)부서들이 절대 예산 한도액을 지키지 않는다는 거예요.

베라 트렘블리 오전 10:07
그렇다면 대안으로 우리가 무엇을 하게 되죠?

찰스 로그 오전 10:09
다음 주부터, (3)환급 받는 것 대신에 같은 회사에서 물품을 주문하도록 모든 이에게 요청할 거예요. 우리는 그 회사에 기업 계정을 만들 것이고, 부서장들은 암호를 입력할 겁니다. 그렇게 하면, 우리가 지출을 추적할 수 있어요.

스캇 패리스 오전 10:10
좋네요! 제니스 용품을 이용할 예정인가요? 그들은 제가 본 것 중 가격이 가장 저렴해요.

찰스 로그 오전 10:11
가격은 낮을지 몰라도, 그들은 신뢰도 면에서 나쁜 평가를 받고 있어요. 우리는 대신 (5)미도우 사와 거래하기로 결정했어요. 가격이 합리적이고, (5)물품을 가져다 주는 데 요금을 청구하지 않아요.

베라 트렘블리 오전 10:13
그렇다면, (6)휴게실에 미도우 사의 책자 사본 몇 부가 있어야겠네요. 제가 몇 부 요청할까요?

찰스 로그 오전 10:13
제가 처리했어요. (6)내일 도착할 겁니다.

어휘 branch manager 지점장 implement 도입하다 reimbursement 환급 confirm 확인하다 hand in ~을 제출하다 stick to ~을 지키다[고수하다] budget 예산 alternative 대안 corporate account 기업 계정 track 추적하다 reliability 신뢰성 reasonable 합리적인 charge 청구하다 request 요청하다 cover 처리하다

3 온라인 채팅 대화문의 주제는?
  (A) 주간 회의
  (B) 새로운 관리자
  (C) 절차 변경
  (D) 보안 계획

4 회사가 직면한 문제는?
  (A) 부서 예산을 초과하는 것
  (B) 중요한 기한을 놓치는 것
  (C) 숙련된 직원을 잃는 것
  (D) 고객들의 불만을 받는 것

[해설] 단서(3)을 종합해 보면, 사무용품과 관련하여 새로운 계획을 도입할 예정이라고 한 뒤, 이에 따른 구체적인 실행 방안에 관한 이야기를 하고 있으므로 정답은 (C).
[패러프레이징] 지문의 implement a new plan이 정답에서 A change in a procedure로 패러프레이징되었다.

[해설] 현재의 시스템으로 인해 환급 과정이 번거로우며, 또한 부서들이 예산 한도액을 지키지 않는다고 했으므로 정답은 (A).
[패러프레이징] 지문의 departments never stick to their budget limits가 정답에서 Exceeding departmental budgets로 패러프레이징되었다.

5 미도우 사에 대해 암시된 바는?
(A) 무료 배달을 제공한다.
(B) 가장 가격이 낮다.
(C) 화자들의 사무실에서 가깝다.
(D) 최근에 문을 열었다.

해설 미도우 사는 물품을 배달해 주는 데 요금을 받지 않는다고 했으므로 정답은 (A).
오답 피하기 가장 가격이 낮은 회사는 미도우 사가 아니라 제니스 용품이므로 (B)는 오답.
패러프레이징 지문의 they don't charge to bring us the goods가 정답에서 It offers free delivery로 패러프레이징되었다.

6 오전 10:13에, 로그 씨가 "제가 처리했어요"라고 하는 의도는?
(A) 휴게실을 정리할 것이다.
(B) 책자 배달을 신청해 놓았다.
(C) 트렘블리 씨의 근무 시간을 대신할 것이다.
(D) 더 많은 직원들을 요청했다.

해설 미도우 사의 책자를 구비해 놓는 게 어떻겠냐는 트렘블리 씨의 말에, 로그 씨가 "제가 처리했어요"라고 말하는 것으로 보아 이는 곧 책자 배달을 미리 신청했다는 뜻임을 유추해 볼 수 있다. 따라서 정답은 (B).

FURTHER STEP

p.92

1 (C) **2** (D) **3** (C) **4** (B) **5** (D)

[1-5] 박람회 관련 웹 페이지 & 자료 요청 문자메시지 & 정보 요청 이메일

www.medmaxtradefair.com

Medmax Trade Fair
(4-2)September 14-17 /
Brownton Convention Center, Salt Lake City, Utah

MedMax is one of the nation's largest medical-related trade fairs. Major companies and medical experts alike look forward to this event every year to find out the latest trends in the industry. We have an exhibition space for nearly 1,000 booths, **(1D) all of which were rented within the first week of announcing the dates, just like last year.**

Our exhibitors will be displaying medical devices, specialty treatments, technical equipment, management systems, and more. One-, two-, and four-day passes are available to visitors and can be purchased through our Web site by clicking here. **(1A)This year, for the first time ever, exhibitors will have the opportunity to give live presentations to show how their goods are used. (4-2)We're also pleased to have Dr. Lisa McMillan, Dr. Vishall Kota, and Dr. Elias Quesada as the guest speakers for the first, second, and third evenings, respectively.**

Don't **(2)miss** the medical event of the year. Get your tickets to MedMax today!

LATASHA MORRIS 8:48 A.M.
Have you arrived at the convention center yet?

ARTURO ERWIN 8:55 A.M.
Yes, I just checked in. This is going to be a great opportunity for our journal. I hope I'll be able to interview representatives from the top medical companies.

www.medmaxtradefair.com

메드맥스 산업 박람회
(4-2)9월 14-17일 /
유타 주, 솔트레이크 시티 시, 브라운턴 컨벤션 센터

메드맥스는 국내 최대의 의학 관련 산업박람회 중 하나입니다. 주요 기업들과 의학 전문가들 모두 업계의 최신 동향을 알아내기 위하여 매년 이 행사를 기대하고 있습니다. 거의 1,000개의 부스가 들어갈 만한 전시장을 마련하고 있는데, (1D)이 부스들 전부가 작년과 마찬가지로 날짜를 발표한 첫 주 안에 대여되었습니다.

저희 박람회 참가자들은 의료 기기, 전문 치료법, 기술 장비, 관리 시스템 등등을 전시할 예정입니다. 방문객들은 1일, 2일, 4일 입장권을 이용할 수 있으며 여기를 클릭하셔서 저희 웹사이트를 통해 구입할 수 있습니다. (1A)올해는 사상 처음으로, 박람회 참가자들이 제품 사용 방식을 보여주기 위해 현장에서 프레젠테이션을 하는 기회를 갖게 됩니다. (4-2)또한 리사 맥밀란 박사님과 바이샬 코타 박사님, 엘리아스 퀘사다 박사님을 각각 첫날, 둘째 날, 셋째 날 저녁의 초청 연사로 모시게 되어 기쁘게 생각합니다.

올해의 의료 행사를 (2)놓치지 마세요. 오늘 메드맥스 티켓을 구입하세요!

라타샤 모리스 오전 8:48
컨벤션 센터에 도착했어요?

아투로 어윈 오전 8:55
네, 방금 등록했어요. 이건 우리 잡지에 아주 좋은 기회가 될 거예요. 일류 의료 기업들의 대표와 인터뷰를 할 수 있으면 좋겠어요.

LATASHA MORRIS   8:57 A.M.

I'm sure you will. (1B)When I went to the MedMax event in Los Angeles last year, I found that a lot of people were happy to share their comments.

LATASHA MORRIS   8:58 A.M.

While you're there, could you do something for me?

ARTURO ERWIN   9:03 A.M.

Sure. What is it?

LATASHA MORRIS   9:05 A.M.

(3)Could you pick up as many brochures and catalogs at the booths as possible? A lot of companies provide special details to conference visitors that they don't share anywhere else.

ARTURO ERWIN   9:11 A.M.

All right. You can count on me.

To: Sherrie Wilson <s.wilson@therapexl.com>
From: (5)Arturo Erwin <erwin_a@natmedicaljournal.org>
Date: September 24
Subject: MedMax

Dear Ms. Wilson,

It was a pleasure meeting you at the recent MedMax convention in Utah. As you may remember, I am a writer for the *National Medical Journal*. We publish medical research studies as well as articles about the latest on the commercial side of the industry. (4-1)It was fascinating to see your colleague, Dr. Vishall Kota, discuss your company's new insulin pump during the speech. (5)When I handled the prototype myself at your booth, I couldn't believe it because I was expecting it to be much heavier. I think it would be very comfortable for patients to wear. When you get the chance, could you please send me more information about this device? It was so popular that all of the brochures were gone by the time I got there.

Warmest regards,

Arturo Erwin

어휘 trade fair 산업[무역] 박람회 expert 전문가 exhibitor 전시 출품자[참가자] specialty 전문 treatment 치료, 요법 guest speaker 초청 연사 respectively 각각 check in 수속하다, 등록하다 representative 대표, 대리인 brochure 안내 책자 count on ~을 믿다 latest 최신의 commercial 상업적인 fascinating 대단히 흥미로운 insulin pump 인슐린 펌프[주입 장치] prototype 원형, (상품화에 앞서 제작하는) 시제품

1 작년 행사에 대해 시사되지 않은 바는?
(A) 시연이 없었다.
(B) 로스앤젤레스에서 열렸다.
(C) 4일 동안 계속되었다.
(D) 부스가 신속하게 대여되었다.

해설 선택지의 내용이 한 개 이상의 지문에 걸쳐 언급되고 있으므로, 선택지에 해당하는 내용을 지문에서 재빨리 찾아내어 대조하는 것이 문제 풀이의 관건이다. (C)는 작년이 아닌 올해 행사에 대한 것이며, 작년 행사가 며칠 동안 개최되었는지는 언급되지 않으므로 정답은 (C).

오답 피하기 (A)와 (D)는 첫 번째 지문에서, (B)는 두 번째 지문에서 언급되었으므로 모두 오답.

2 웹페이지에서, 3단락, 첫 번째 줄의 어휘 "miss"와 의미상 가장 유사한 것은?
(A) 실패하다
(B) 잃다
(C) 달아나다
(D) 거르다

해설 본문의 miss는 '놓치다'라는 뜻으로 쓰이고 있다. 선택지 중에서는 '거르다, 빼먹다'라는 뜻의 skip이 이와 가장 유사한 의미이다. 따라서 정답은 (D).

3 모리스 씨가 어윈 씨에게 요청한 것은?
(A) 인터뷰 일정
(B) 장소까지의 약도
(C) 일부 홍보 자료
(D) 무료 학회 입장권

해설 모리스 씨와 어윈 씨가 주고받는 문자메시지 지문을 보아야 한다. 모리스 씨는 안내 책자와 카탈로그를 가져다 달라고 부탁하고 있다. 이것들을 홍보 자료라고 표현한 (C)가 정답. 요청을 나타내는 Could you 이하를 주의 깊게 보아야 한다.

4 어윈 씨가 윌슨 씨 동료의 강의를 본 때는?
(A) 9월 14일
(B) 9월 15일
(C) 9월 16일
(D) 9월 17일

해설 두 지문 연계 문제로, 우선 문제에서 언급된 어윈 씨가 이메일 발신자이고 윌슨 씨가 이메일 수신자라는 점을 파악해야 한다. 이메일에서 어윈 씨는 윌슨 씨의 동료인 바이샬 코타 박사의 강연에 대해 이야기하는데, 웹 페이지에서 바이샬 코타 박사가 강연을 한 날은 박람회 둘째 날인 15일임을 알 수 있다. 정답은 (B).

5 어윈 씨는 테라펙슬 사 제품의 어떤 점에 놀랐는가?
(A) 수많은 사양
(B) 간편한 설치
(C) 저렴한 가격
(D) 경량 디자인

해설 이메일 지문에서 윌슨 박사의 메일 주소를 보고 테라펙슬이 윌슨 박사의 회사임을 알아채야 한다. 어윈 씨는 테라펙슬 사의 인슐린 펌프 시제품이 훨씬 무거울 거라고 예상했기에 놀랐다고 했다. 즉 예상보다 훨씬 가벼운 무게에 놀란 것이므로 정답은 (D).

UNIT 12 이메일/편지

PRE-STEP
p.95

A 1 (B) 2 (A) 3 (A) 4 (B) 5 (A) 6 (B) 7 (A) 8 (B) 9 (A)
    10 (B) 11 (A) 12 (B) 13 (A) 14 (A) 15 (B)

B 1 (A) 2 (B)

A
1 (B) search, 일자리를 <u>찾다</u>
2 (A) vacancy, 일자리 <u>공석</u>을 채우다
3 (A) draft, 이메일 <u>초안을 작성하다</u>
4 (B) express, 불쾌함을 <u>표현하다</u>
5 (A) goodwill, <u>호의</u>의 표시로
6 (B) collection, 물품 한 <u>더미</u>
7 (A) assistance, <u>도움</u>이 필요한
8 (B) eligible, 직책에 대해 <u>자격이 되다</u>
9 (A) direct, 누군가에게 편지를 <u>보내다</u>
10 (B) deal, 고객층을 <u>상대하다</u>
11 (B) over, 함께 <u>건너</u>가다
12 (B) sign up, 회원 <u>가입하다</u>
13 (A) build, 협력 관계 <u>구축</u>을 추구하다
14 (A) receive, 월간 소식지를 <u>받다</u>
15 (B) behalf, 맥클레인 컨설팅을 <u>대표</u>하여

B
1 I've hired a woman named Yasmin Sekar as our social responsibility specialist. With Thanksgiving approaching, her first task is to organize a company-wide donation drive for food, toiletries, and household items.
   (A) A newly hired employee will arrange for the staff to donate goods.
   (B) The social responsibility specialist is collecting money for basic necessities.

저는 우리 책임 전문가로 야스민 세카라는 이름의 여성을 채용했습니다. 추수감사절이 다가오는 가운데, 그녀의 첫 번째 업무는 식품과 세면도구, 가정용품의 전사적 기부 운동을 조직하는 것입니다.
(A) 새로 채용된 직원은 직원들이 물품을 기증하게 하는 일을 조직할 것입니다.
(B) 사회적 책임 전문가는 기본적 필수품들을 위한 자금을 모으고 있습니다.

2 I thought you could come to my office about fifteen minutes before the meeting starts and we could just walk over together. Please let me know if you're interested in going.
   (A) We can move the meeting to my office if that is more convenient.
   (B) We can go to the meeting together if you plan on attending it.

모임이 시작하기 약 15분 전에 제 사무실로 오셔서 함께 건너가시면 될 것 같습니다. 가실 의향이 있으신지 알려주시기 바랍니다.
(A) 그쪽이 더 편리하시다면 제 사무실로 회의를 옮길 수 있습니다.
(B) 만약 회의에 가실 예정이라면 저와 함께 가셔도 됩니다.

MAIN STEP 1   p.96

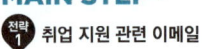 취업 지원 관련 이메일

①**To:** Clara Timber
②**From:** Michael Myers
Subject: RE: Application

You also said that ①you are working mornings for a fashion magazine. ②I'm currently searching for a photographer for our design team.

Warm regards,

Michael Myers, Director

①**수신:** 클라라 팀버
②**발신:** 마이클 마이어스
제목: 회신: 지원

①당신은 또한 패션 잡지사에서 오전 근무를 한다고도 말했습니다. ②저는 현재 내부 디자인 팀을 위한 사진 작가를 찾고 있습니다.

책임자,
마이클 마이어스 드림

① 팀버 씨에 대해 사실인 것은?
→ 현재 시간제로 근무한다.

해설 팀버 씨는 편지의 수신인이므로 You와 관련된 내용에 집중하여 문제를 푼다. you are working mornings를 통해 그녀가 현재 시간제로 근무하고 있음을 알 수 있다.

② 마이어스 씨에 대해 시사된 바는?
→ 공석을 채우려 하고 있다.

해설 마이어스 씨는 편지의 발신인이므로 I와 관련된 내용을 찾아 읽도록 한다. I'm currently searching for 이하를 보면 그가 현재 사진 작가를 찾고 있음을 알 수 있다.

전략 2 회사 결정을 알리는 이메일

To: Rachelle Hunter, Sales team
From: Jason Diba
Subject: New system

Hi Rachelle,

The new system was a recommendation we received from Kenan Bayer, the outside consultant we hired to improve the company's practices.

Jason Diba, Finance team

수신: 레이첼 헌터, 영업팀
발신: 제이슨 디바
제목: 새로운 시스템

안녕하세요, 레이첼.

새로운 시스템은 회사의 관행을 개선하기 위해 우리가 고용한 외부 고문인 키난 베이어 씨로부터 받은 추천 사항이었습니다.

제이슨 디바, 재무팀

키난 베이어 씨에 대해 언급된 것은?
(A) 디바 씨의 회사를 위해 일한다.
(B) 재무팀 소속이다.

해설 수신인인 영업팀의 레이첼 헌터 씨와 발신인인 재무팀의 디바 씨 외에 제3의 인물인 키난 베이어 씨가 더 등장한다. 이때 키난 베이어 씨의 소속을 수신인이나 발신인의 소속과 헷갈려서는 안 된다. 디바 씨의 회사에서 고용한 외부 고문이라고 했으므로 그는 디바 씨의 회사를 위해 일하는 것이다.

MAIN STEP 2   p.97

1 (B)   2 (C)   3 (A)   4 (D)

[1-2] 서비스에 대한 고객의 항의 편지

Stacey LeBlanc, Customer Service Manager
Fort Lauderdale, FL 33301

스테이시 르블랑, 고객 서비스 관리자
플로리다 주 포트 로더데일, 33301

March 17

Dear Ms. LeBlanc,

(1)I'm very disappointed with your company's service. I purchased a green-patterned dress online on March 4. When it arrived on March 9, it had several buttons missing. (2)I e-mailed Kayla Doreo in the returns department asking to have a replacement shipped the next day, but she waited until today to reply. I plan to return the dress, (1)but I also want to express my displeasure with the store's slow service.

Janet Gilbert

3월 17일

르블랑 씨께,

(1)귀사의 서비스에 저는 몹시 실망했습니다. 저는 3월 4일에 온라인으로 초록색 무늬 원피스 하나를 구입했습니다. 3월 9일에 옷이 도착했을 때, 단추 몇 개가 떨어져 있었습니다. 저는 다음날 교환품 발송을 요청하고자 (2)반품 부서의 카일라 도레오 씨에게 이메일을 보냈지만, 그녀는 오늘에서야 답장을 했습니다. 저는 그 원피스를 반품할 계획이지만, (1)매장의 느린 서비스에 대한 저의 불쾌감도 표현하고 싶습니다.

재닛 길버트 드림

어휘 be disappointed with ~에 실망하다   missing 없어진   returns department 반품 부서   replacement 교환[대체]품
displeasure 불쾌감, 불만

1 길버트 씨가 편지를 보낸 이유는?
(A) 교환을 요청하기 위해
(B) 서비스에 대해 불만을 표시하기 위해
(C) 새로운 주문을 하기 위해
(D) 배송에 관해 문의하기 위해

해설 문제에서 편지의 발신인에 관해 묻고 있음을 파악한 후 대명사 I로 시작하는 문장을 찾아보면 된다. 느린 서비스에 대한 불쾌감을 표출하기 위해 편지를 쓴 것이므로 정답은 (B).

2 도레오 씨에 대해 추론할 수 있는 것은?
(A) 이메일에 즉시 답장을 한다.
(B) 고객 서비스 직원이다.
(C) 반품과 교환을 처리한다.
(D) 손상된 옷을 수선한다.

해설 도레오 씨는 수신자도 발신자도 아니며 편지에 등장하는 제3의 인물이다. 단서(2)에 도레오 씨가 언급된 부분을 통해 정답 (C)를 추론할 수 있다.
오답 피하기 고객 서비스 직원은 편지의 수신자인 르블랑 씨이므로 (B)는 오답이다.

[3-4] 해외 송금에 관한 이메일

To: Albert Kapp <a.kapp@trumail.com>
From: Centerville Bank <info@centerville.com>
Date: November 6
(3)**Subject:** RE: Inquiry

Dear Mr. Kapp,

(3)I'm writing in response to your inquiry about wiring money overseas. There is a daily transfer limit of $50,000. (4)Attached is a document that explains how to send money abroad. The fee charged by our bank varies depending on the amount sent and the type of service chosen.

Linda Ayers
Centerville Bank, Foreign Accounts Manager

수신: 앨버트 캡 <a.kapp@trumail.com>
발신: 센터빌 은행 <info@centerville.com>
날짜: 11월 6일
(3)제목: 회신: 문의

캡 씨께,

(3)해외 송금에 대한 귀하의 문의에 답변 드립니다. 하루 5만 달러의 이체 한도가 있습니다. (4)첨부되어 있는 것은 해외로 송금하는 방법을 설명하는 문서입니다. 저희 은행이 부과하는 수수료는 송금 액수나 선택하신 서비스 유형에 따라 다릅니다.

센터빌 은행, 해외 계좌 관리자
린다 에이어스 드림

어휘 in response to ~에 답하여, ~에 응하여   wire (전자 시스템을 이용하여) 송금하다; (전선을) 연결하다   vary 다르다, 다양하다

3 캡 씨에 대해 사실인 것은?
   (A) 센터빌 은행에 문의를 보냈다.
   (B) 송금을 확인하려고 전화를 걸었다.
   (C) 연체료가 청구되었다.
   (D) 거래를 취소했다.

해설 단서(3)에서 알 수 있듯이 이 이메일은 해외 송금에 대한 고객의 문의에 답변하기 위한 것이므로 캡 씨가 사전에 문의를 보냈다는 것을 알 수 있다. 정답은 (A).

4 이메일에 포함된 것은?
   (A) 거래 송장
   (B) 지점으로 가는 길 안내
   (C) 새로운 서비스 홍보
   (D) 자금 이체에 대한 설명

해설 단서(4)에서 첨부를 나타내는 표현인 attached(첨부된) 뒤를 보면 해외 송금 방법을 설명하는 문서를 첨부했다고 하였으므로 정답은 (D).

FINAL STEP
p.98

1 (A)   2 (C)   3 (B)   4 (A)   5 (B)

[1-3] 기부 운동에 관한 이메일

To: Vienna McCready <vmccr1@baumannenterprises.com>
From: Elijah Machon <emach7@baumannenterprises.com>
Date: November 4
Subject: Corporate Social Responsibility Efforts

Dear Vienna,

As a token of goodwill to the community that provides us with so much business, the executive team of Baumann Enterprises has decided to institute a corporate social responsibility program. (1)I've hired a woman named Yasmin Sekar as our social responsibility specialist. With Thanksgiving approaching, her first task is to organize a company-wide donation drive for food, toiletries, and household items. Staff participation is not mandatory, but will be strongly encouraged.

(3)Attached is a letter that Yasmin has drafted to accompany the donations we will deliver to local food banks and shelters in need. I'd like for you to look it over and make sure there are no errors in spelling or grammar. Collection of the items will begin on November 10 and end on November 20. It would be ideal for you to finish editing this document by the time Ms. Sekar starts deliveries on November 22.

Finally, (2)because you are the client relations manager, I'd like you to draft an e-mail to our full client list. Please inform them of this undertaking and encourage them to participate in their own collections. Do not tell them to drop off any items at our office. Instead, direct them to the charities in need of assistance. They should make their own donations separate from ours.

수신: 비엔나 맥크레디 <vmccr1@baumannenterprises.com>
발신: 엘리야 메이천 <emach7@baumannenterprises.com>
날짜: 11월 4일
제목: 기업의 사회적 책임 노력

비엔나 씨께,

우리에게 아주 많은 사업을 제공하는 지역사회에 대한 호의의 표시로, 바우만 사의 경영진은 기업의 사회적 책임 프로그램을 도입하기로 결정했습니다. (1)저는 우리의 사회적 책임 전문가로 야스민 세카라는 이름의 여성을 채용했습니다. 추수감사절이 다가오는 가운데, 그녀의 첫 번째 업무는 식품과 세면도구, 가정용품의 전사적 기부 운동을 조직하는 것입니다. 직원 참여는 의무는 아니지만 강력히 권장됩니다.

(3)첨부된 것은 야스민 씨가 초안을 작성한 편지로, 어려움에 처한 지역 푸드 뱅크와 보호소에 우리가 전달하게 될 기증품에 동봉하기 위한 것입니다. 저는 귀하가 편지를 한번 살펴보고 철자나 문법적 오류가 없는지 확인해 주시기를 바랍니다. 물품 수집은 11월 10일에 시작해 11월 20일에 끝날 것입니다. 세카 씨가 기증품 전달을 시작하는 11월 22일까지 귀하께서 이 문서의 수정을 완료해 주시면 좋겠습니다.

마지막으로, (2)귀하께서는 고객 관리 운영자이므로, 우리 고객들 전원에게 보낼 이메일 원고 초안을 작성해 주셨으면 합니다. 고객분들께 이 일에 대해 알려 드리고, 고객들이 각자의 기증품 수집에 참여하도록 독려하여 주십시오. 고객들에게 우리 사무실에 물건을 두고 가라고 하지 마십시오. 대신, 고객들께 도움이 필요한 자선 단체들을 안내해 드리십시오. 고객들은 우리와 별도로 고객들 스스로 기증해야 합니다.

지역사회 관리 운영자
엘리야 메이천 드림

Kind regards,

Elijah Machon, Community Relations Manager

어휘 corporate social responsibility 기업의 사회적 책임　as a token of ~의 표시로　goodwill 호의　enterprise 기업, 회사　institute 도입하다　donation 기부, 기증(품)　toiletry 세면도구　participation 참여, 참가　mandatory 의무적인　draft 초안[원고]을 작성하다　shelter 보호소, 쉼터　in need 어려움에 처한, 궁핍한　edit 수정[편집]하다　client relations manager 고객 관리 운영자　undertaking 일, 프로젝트　direct 안내하다　separate from ~와는 별도인

1 야스민 세카 씨에 대해 사실인 것은?
　(A) 기증품 수집을 조직할 것이다.
　(B) 그녀의 업무는 다른 사람들의 글 교정을 포함한다.
　(C) 맥크레디 씨의 일을 감독한다.
　(D) 11월 10일부터 전달을 시작할 것이다.

해설 문제가 이메일의 수신인, 발신인이 아닌 제3의 인물에 관한 것이므로, 지문에서 야스민 세카 씨가 언급된 부분을 찾아야 한다. 단서(1)에 따르면, 그녀는 전사적인 기부 운동을 조직할 것이므로 정답은 (A).

2 맥크레디 씨는 누구인가?
　(A) 지역사회 관리 운영자
　(B) 사회 책임 전문가
　(C) 고객 관리 운영자
　(D) 기부 센터 대표

해설 맥크레디 씨가 이 이메일의 수신인이므로 지문에서 you와 관련된 내용을 보아야 한다. 단서(2)에 보면 '귀하께서는 고객 관리 운영자이므로'라고 직접적으로 그녀의 직책을 언급하고 있으므로 정답은 (C).

3 이메일에 포함되어 있는 것은?
　(A) 자선 단체로 가는 약도
　(B) 편지의 초안
　(C) 세카 씨의 연락처
　(D) 고객 명단

해설 이메일이나 편지에 첨부된 것을 나타낼 때 자주 쓰이는 표현인 attached(첨부된)가 쓰인 부분을 주의해서 읽어야 한다. 단서(3)을 보면 야스민 세카 씨가 작성한 편지의 초안을 첨부했다고 했으므로 정답은 (B).

[4-5] 최종 합격 통보 편지

Brenda Silva
553 Archwood Avenue
Concord, NC 28025
March 8

Dear Ms. Silva,

Congratulations on passing the final interview! On behalf of McClain Consulting, I would like to offer you the position of junior associate. Our human resources team was pleased that you decided to apply for the job after visiting our booth at the job fair. (4)We think you will be an ideal candidate for this position, and we were particularly impressed with the fact that you are bilingual in English and Spanish. This will be useful when dealing with our client base in South America.

In this role, you will be in charge of evaluating the needs of clients and working with your team leader to provide custom-made business solutions. (5)After six months of employment, you will be eligible to switch to a full-time position if you have a satisfactory performance rating.

브렌다 실바
아치우드 가 553
노스캐롤라이나 주 콩코드, 28025
3월 8일

실바 씨께,

최종 면접을 통과하신 것을 축하드립니다! 맥클레인 컨설팅 사를 대표하여, 귀하께 일반사원 직을 제안하고 싶습니다. 저희 인사팀은 귀하가 채용 박람회에서 저희 부스를 방문한 후에 이 일에 지원할 것을 결심하였다는 사실에 기뻤습니다. (4)저희는 귀하가 이 직위에 가장 적합한 지원자라고 생각하며 특히 귀하가 영어와 스페인어 두 언어를 사용한다는 사실이 인상 깊었습니다. 이는 귀하가 남미의 고객층을 상대할 때 유용할 것입니다.

이 직위에서, 귀하는 고객 맞춤의 비즈니스 솔루션을 제공하기 위해 고객의 요구를 감정하고 팀장과 협업하는 일을 담당할 것입니다. (5)6개월의 근무 후에, 귀하가 만족스러운 인사 고과 등급을 받는다면, 정규직으로 전환될 자격이 생길 것입니다.

Enclosed you will find a copy of the employment contract. Please sign it and return it to our office in the envelope provided. Should you have questions regarding the terms of the contract, please contact me at 555-2045, extension 12.

I look forward to working with you.

Judy Arnold
Human Resources Representative, McClain Consulting

채용 계약서 사본이 동봉된 것을 보실 수 있을 겁니다. 서명한 후 제공된 봉투에 넣어 저희 사무실로 반송해 주십시오. 계약 조건에 대해 질문이 있으시면, 555-2045 내선번호 12로 저에게 연락 주세요.

함께 일하길 고대하고 있겠습니다.

맥클레인 컨설팅 사, 인사팀 대표
쥬디 아놀드 드림

어휘 position 직위 junior associate 일반 사원 apply for ~에 지원하다 job fair 채용 박람회 ideal candidate 가장 적합한 지원자 bilingual 두 언어를 사용하는 client 고객 custom-made 고객 맞춤의 employment 채용 be eligible to do ~할 자격이 있다 full-time position 상근직 satisfactory 만족스러운 enclosed 동봉된 term (계약) 조건; 용어 look forward to doing ~하기를 고대하다

4 실바 씨에 대해 시사된 바는?
(A) 두 언어를 할 수 있다.
(B) 온라인으로 일자리에 지원했다.
(C) 전문 자격증을 갖고 있다.
(D) 남미에서 태어났다.

해설 단서(4)에 따르면, 맥클레인 컨설팅 사의 인사팀은 실바 씨가 영어와 스페인어 둘 다 한다는 사실이 인상 깊었다고 했으므로 정답은 (A).
오답 피하기 실바 씨는 채용 박람회에서 맥클레인 컨설팅 사의 부스를 방문하여 지원했다고 했으므로 (B)는 오답.
패러프레이징 지문의 bilingual이 정답에서 speak two languages로 패러프레이징되었다.

5 제공된 직위에 대해 암시된 것은?
(A) 부하 직원 관리를 포함한다.
(B) 임시직 고용이다.
(C) 임금이 경쟁력이 있다.
(D) 필기 시험 응시가 요구되었다.

해설 실바 씨는 6개월간 근무한 후에 만족스러운 인사 고과 등급을 받는다면 정규직으로 전환될 것이라 하였으므로 현재 제공된 직위는 임시직임을 추론할 수 있다. 따라서 정답은 (B).

FURTHER STEP

p.100

1 (B)   2 (A)   3 (D)   4 (B)   5 (D)

[1-5] 모임에 초대하는 이메일 & 관련 웹페이지 & 주소록

To: Leonard Akron <leonardakron@akronconsulting.com>
From: Genevieve Connelly <g_connelly@atro.net>
Date: February 19
Subject: Business Builders

Hi Leonard,

I'm glad we were finally able to get together for coffee to catch up. It was interesting hearing about your new consulting business, and I hope you continue to see growth. As you know, networking is a very important part of business, (1)so I'm wondering if you would like to come to the Business Builders monthly meeting with me. You don't have to be a member to attend, and you can find more information at www.bizbuild.org.

The next meeting is on March 2 at 7 P.M. (3-1)I

수신: 레너드 아크론 <leonardakron@akronconsulting.com>
발신: 제너비브 코넬리 <g_connelly@atro.net>
날짜: 2월 19일
제목: 비즈니스 빌더즈

안녕하세요, 레너드.

우리가 마침내 만나서 커피를 마시며 못다 한 얘기를 나눌 수 있어서 기뻤습니다. 아크론 씨의 새로운 컨설팅 업체에 대해 흥미롭게 들었으며, 계속 발전하기를 바랍니다. 아시다시피, 인적 네트워크 형성은 사업에서 매우 중요한 부분이라서, (1)아크론 씨가 매월 저와 같이 비즈니스 빌더즈 회의에 오시는 게 좋지 않을까 생각합니다. 참석을 위해 회원 가입을 하실 필요는 없으며, www.bizbuild.org에서 더 많은 정보를 얻으실 수 있습니다.

다음 모임은 3월 2일 저녁 7시에 있습니다. (3-1)모임이

thought you could come to my office about fifteen minutes before the meeting starts, and we could just walk over together. Please let me know if you're interested in going.

Talk to you soon,

Genevieve

---

www.bizbuild.org

| HOME | **ABOUT** | EVENTS | PRESS | CONTACT |

(2B)(4-1)Founded by Beth Crane in 2013, Business Builders is a network of business professionals in the Wilberville area who (2D)seek to share ideas and tips, provide advice, and build partnerships. (2C)We get together once a month. There is no cost to attend our meetings, and you can attend as many or as few as you'd like. We do recommend signing up for a free membership so you can receive our monthly newsletter and stay informed on group events. (3-2)Meetings take place in Room 302 of the Evans Building (3939 Mahlon Street).

For inquiries, e-mail info@bizbuild.org.

Wilberville Business Directory

Search:
Jump to: A B C D E F G H I J **K** L M N O P Q R S T U V W X Y Z

---K---

Business	Address/Phone	Business Type	Notes
Karla's	3028 Cimarron Road 465-6594	Hair Salon	Owned by Karla Spencer Web site: hairbykarla.net
Kangaroo Café	431 Washburn Avenue 482-0022	**(4-2) Restaurant**	**Owned by Beth Crane** Web site: mykcafe.com
Klein Inc.	4394 Parkway Street 482-2578	Landscaping	Owned by Simon Klein Web site: none
(5)*Kuhn Appliances	508 18th Street N. 465-7641, 465-7642	Appliance Store	Owned by Kuhn Corporation Web site: kuhnappl.com

(5)*Denotes recently added business.

시작하기 약 15분 전에 제 사무실로 오셔서 함께 건너가시면 될 것 같습니다. 가실 의향이 있으신지 알려주시기 바랍니다.

조만간 뵙겠습니다,

제너비브 드림

---

www.bizbuild.org

| 홈 | 소개 | 행사 | 기사 | 연락처 |

(2B)(4-1)2013년에 베스 크레인 씨가 설립한 비즈니스 빌더즈는 윌버빌 지역의 사업 전문가들로 이루어진 네트워크로 (2D)아이디어와 정보를 공유하고 조언을 제공하며 협력 관계 구축을 추구합니다. (2C)우리는 한 달에 한 번 모임을 갖습니다. 모임 참석에는 비용이 없으며, 원하는 만큼 많이 혹은 적게 모임에 참석할 수 있습니다. 우리의 월간 소식지를 받아보시고 단체 행사에 대한 정보를 계속 제공받으시도록 무료 회원에 가입하실 것을 권해 드립니다. (3-2)모임은 에반스 빌딩 302호(말론 가 3939번지)에서 열립니다.

문의하시려면, info@bizbuild.org로 이메일을 주십시오.

윌버빌 사업체 주소록

검색:
건너뛰기: A B C D E F G H I J **K** L M N O P Q R S T U V W X Y Z

---K---

사업체	주소/전화	사업체 종류	메모
칼라즈	시머론 로 3028 465-6594	미용실	소유주: 칼라 스펜서 웹사이트: hairbykarla.net
캥거루 카페	워시번 가 431 482-0022	**(4-2)식당**	소유주: 베스 크레인 웹사이트: mykcafe.com
클라인 사	파크웨이 가 4394 482-2578	조경업체	소유주: 사이먼 클라인 웹사이트: 없음
(5)*쿤 가전제품	18번 가 북쪽 508 465-7641, 465-7642	가전제품 매장	소유주: 쿤 코퍼레이션 웹사이트: kuhnappl.com

(5)*최근에 추가된 업체를 의미함.

어휘 get together 만나다, 모이다 catch up 못다 한 얘기를 나누다 networking 인적 네트워크 형성 found 설립하다 seek to do ~하는 것을 추구하다 partnership 협력 관계, 동업 newsletter 소식지 inquiry 문의 directory 주소록, 전화번호부 landscaping 조경 appliance 가전제품 denote 의미하다, 나타내다

1 이메일의 목적은?
   (A) 아크론 씨에게 제품을 추천하기 위해
   (B) 아크론 씨를 행사에 초대하기 위해
   (C) 아크론 씨의 회원 자격을 확인하기 위해
   (D) 아크론 씨의 도움에 대해 감사하기 위해

[해설] 권유를 나타내는 표현인 I'm wondering if you would like 이하에 이메일의 목적이 나타나 있다. 코넬리 씨는 아크론 씨에게 비즈니스 빌더즈라는 정기 모임에 참석할 것을 권하고 있으므로 정답은 (B).

2 웹페이지에서 비즈니스 빌더즈에 대해 시사되지 않은 바는?
   (A) 회원이 몇 명인지
   (B) 언제 시작되었는지
   (C) 얼마나 자주 모이는지
   (D) 목적이 무엇인지

[해설] 웹페이지에서 비즈니스 빌더즈는 2013년에 설립되었고, 한 달에 한 번 모임을 가지며, 아이디어 및 정보 공유, 조언 제공, 협력 관계 구축을 목적으로 한다는 내용이 나오지만, 회원 수에 대한 언급은 없다. 따라서 정답은 (A).

3 코넬리 씨에 대해 추론할 수 있는 것은?
   (A) 비즈니스 빌더즈의 신입 회원이다.
   (B) 예전에 아크론 씨의 동료였다.
   (C) 최근에 사업을 시작했다.
   (D) 에반스 빌딩 근처에서 근무한다.

[해설] 두 지문 연계 문제로, 우선 코넬리 씨가 발신인인 이메일을 보아야 한다. 이메일에서 코넬리 씨가 모임이 시작하기 15분 전에 자기 사무실에서 만나서 같이 걸어가자고 제안하는 것으로 보아, 비즈니스 빌더즈의 모임 장소가 코넬리 씨의 사무실에서 가깝다는 것을 짐작할 수 있다. 두 번째 지문에서 비즈니스 빌더즈의 모임 장소가 에반스 빌딩이라고 했으므로 정답은 (D).

4 비즈니스 빌더즈의 설립자는?
   (A) 미용실 소유주
   (B) 식당 소유주
   (C) 조경사
   (D) 소매업자

[해설] 두 지문 연계 문제이다. 웹페이지에 비즈니스 빌더즈의 설립자는 베스 크레인이라고 나와 있으므로, 주소록에서 이 이름을 찾으면 된다. 베스 크레인은 캥거루 카페라는 식당의 소유주이므로 정답은 (B).

5 사업체 주소록에 따르면 사실인 것은?
   (A) 칼라즈는 웹사이트가 없다.
   (B) 캥거루 카페에는 전화번호가 두 개 있다.
   (C) 클라인 사는 워시번 가에 위치해 있다.
   (D) 쿤 가전제품은 주소록에 올라온 지 얼마 되지 않았다.

[해설] 주소록에 쿤 가전제품이 최근에 주소록에 추가된 업체라고 명시되어 있으므로 정답은 (D).
[오답 피하기] 웹사이트가 없는 업체는 클라인 사이고, 전화번호가 두 개인 업체는 쿤 가전제품, 워시번 가에 위치한 업체는 캥거루 카페이므로 (A)~(C)는 모두 오답이다.

UNIT 13 광고문

PRE-STEP
p.103

A 1 (B) 2 (B) 3 (A) 4 (A) 5 (B) 6 (B) 7 (A) 8 (B) 9 (A)
    10 (A) 11 (A) 12 (B) 13 (A) 14 (B) 15 (B)

B 1 (B) 2 (A)

A
1 (B) fill out, ~의 온라인 지원서를 <u>작성하다</u>
2 (B) join, ~의 팀에 <u>합류하다</u>
3 (A) look for, 마케팅 책임자를 <u>구하다</u>
4 (A) bulk, <u>대량</u>으로 구매하다
5 (B) field, 그 <u>분야</u>에서의 실제 경험
6 (B) proof, 자격 <u>증명</u>
7 (A) quality, ~의 서비스의 <u>질</u>을 보장하다
8 (B) fair, 취업 <u>박람회</u>에 참석하다
9 (A) references, 이전 고객들 세 명의 <u>추천서</u>
10 (A) environment, 친화적인 업무 <u>환경</u>
11 (A) damaged, <u>파손된</u> 차량을 복구하다
12 (B) desirable, <u>바람직한</u> 보수
13 (A) affordable, <u>저렴한</u> 가격
14 (B) process, 월 급여를 <u>처리하다</u>
15 (B) drawing, 경품 <u>추첨</u>에 응모하다

B
1 Although we do accept walk-in appointments, I suggest you schedule a session with us at least one week before your desired time slot so as to avoid disappointment.
   (A) I recommend booking a longer session so you won't feel rushed.
   (B) I recommend booking in advance so you can get the time you want.

예약 없이 방문하셔도 되지만, 실망스러운 일을 피하기 위해서 원하시는 시간대보다 최소 일주일 전에 저희와 시간을 정하실 것을 권해 드립니다.
(A) 급박한 느낌을 받지 않도록 더 긴 세션을 예약하시는 것을 추천해 드립니다.
(B) 원하시는 시간을 누리실 수 있도록 미리 예약하시는 것을 추천해 드립니다.

2 We are now pleased to announce that we are adding another facility, across from the Atherton Mall. Celebrate the opening of this branch with us on Saturday, April 3. On that day, you can meet our staff, try free product samples, and enjoy some refreshments.
   (A) The store's grand opening on April 3 will include complimentary items and a chance to meet employees.
   (B) The new location is seeking staff who can begin work by April 3 and who are willing to work near the mall.

이제 애서턴 몰 맞은편에 또 하나의 시설을 추가하게 됨을 알려드리게 되어 기쁘게 생각합니다. 4월 3일 토요일에 이 지점의 개장을 저희와 함께 축하해 주십시오. 그날, 저희 직원들을 만나 무료 견본 제품을 테스트해 보시고 다과를 즐기실 수 있습니다.
(A) 4월 3일에 있을 매장의 개점 행사는 무료 물품들과 직원들과 만날 수 있는 기회를 포함합니다.
(B) 새 지점은 4월 3일부터 근무를 시작할 수 있고 몰 근처에서 일할 의향이 있는 직원을 찾고 있습니다.

MAIN STEP 1 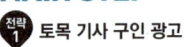 p.104

전략 1 토목 기사 구인 광고

> The ideal candidate must be certified as a civil engineer. Experience as a supervisor is an advantage but is not required for the position.

> 이상적인 후보자는 반드시 토목 기사로서 공인을 받아야 합니다. 관리자로서의 경력이 우대 사항이긴 하지만 그 직책을 위해 필수는 아닙니다.

어휘 ideal 이상적인 candidate 후보자 certify 자격증[면허증]을 교부하다 supervisor 관리자 advantage 유리한 점, 장점 position (일)자리, 직위

직무에 관해 언급된 사항은?
(A) 공인된 전문직 종사자를 대상으로 한다.
(B) 관리 기술을 필요로 한다.

해설 must be certified라고 했으므로 토목 기사 자격은 필수 요건이다. 감독으로서의 경험은 advantage라고 했으므로 우대 요건이다. 따라서 management skills(관리 기술)가 필수라는 선택지는 오답이다.

MAIN STEP 2 p.105

1 (B)　**2** (C)　**3** (A)　**4** (D)

[1-2] 회계사 채용 공고

> Swanson Finance is looking for an accountant who is able to start working on April 1. We offer a friendly work environment along with a standard salary.
>
> **Duties include:**
> - Processing monthly payments for employees
> - Tracking business expenses using spreadsheet software
>
> (1)Applicants must be certified by the state of Virginia. Proof of certification should be presented for verification at the time of the interview. Two years of experience in accounting is an advantage but is not required.
>
> (2)To apply for this position, visit our Web site at www.swansonfinance.com and fill out our online application.

> 스완슨 금융에서 4월 1일부터 근무를 시작하실 수 있는 회계사를 구하고 있습니다. 저희는 평균 수준의 급여와 함께 친화적인 업무 환경을 제공합니다.
>
> 업무 내용:
> - 직원 월 급여 처리
> - 스프레드시트 소프트웨어를 이용한 사업 비용 추적
>
> (1)지원자들은 버지니아 주에서 교부한 자격증이 있어야 합니다. 검증을 위해 면접 시 이를 증명하는 문서가 제시되어야 합니다. 회계 분야에서 2년간의 경력이 있으시면 유리하지만 필수는 아닙니다.
>
> (2)이 자리에 지원하시려면, 저희 웹사이트 www.swansonfinance.com을 방문하셔서 온라인 지원서를 작성해 주십시오.

어휘 accountant 회계사 track 추적하다 expenses 비용, 경비 certification 증명(서) present 제시[제출]하다 verification 증명, 입증, 검증

1 이 일자리의 자격 요건으로 언급된 것은?
전략 1 (A) 유연한 일정
(B) 주 발급 자격증
(C) 2년간의 경력
(D) 경영학 학위

해설 자격 요건을 묻는 문제이므로 지문에서 지원자들이 갖춰야 하는 항목이 언급된 부분을 찾아야 한다. 지원자들은 버지니아 주에서 교부된 자격증이 있어야 하므로 정답은 (B).
오답 피하기 (C)의 경우 경력은 우대 요건일 뿐이므로 오답이다. must와 advantage를 구분하도록 하자.

2 지원자들이 이 일자리에 지원하기 위해 해야 하는 일은?
   (A) 이메일 보내기
   (B) 직접 사무실 방문하기
   (C) 인터넷 양식 작성하기
   (D) 취업 박람회 참가하기

해설 구인구직 광고문에서 지원 방법과 관련된 내용은 지문의 마지막 부분에서 언급되는 경우가 많다. 단서(2)에서 지원하려면 웹사이트를 방문해서 온라인 지원서를 작성하라고 했으므로 정답은 (C).

[3-4] 자동차 정비소의 서비스에 관한 광고

Mission Auto Body and Paint offers (4A)award-winning Pro-Paint Services to restore damaged vehicles to their factory appearances.

The cost of this service will be charged to your insurance provider directly. And (4B)to celebrate 40 years in business, (3)we're giving a complimentary Wax Coating Service to the first 40 customers who visit us this month.

(4C)To see our high-quality work for yourself, visit the gallery on our Web site at www.missionautobodyandpaint.com/gallery. If you are interested in our services, (4D)please send an e-mail to info@missionautobodyandpaint.com for a quote.

미션 오토 바디 앤 페인트는 손상된 차량을 공장 출고 시의 모습으로 복구해 주는, (4A)수상 경력이 있는 프로 페인트 서비스를 제공합니다.

서비스 비용은 귀하의 보험 회사로 직접 청구될 것입니다. 또한 (4B)창업 40주년을 기념하기 위해, (3)저희는 이번 달에 방문해 주시는 최초 40분의 고객 여러분께 무료 왁스 코팅 서비스를 제공해 드립니다.

(4C)저희의 고품격 작업물을 직접 보시려면, 저희 웹사이트의 사진첩 www.missionautobodyandpaint.com/gallery를 방문해 주십시오. 저희 서비스에 관심이 있으시다면, (4D)견적을 위해 info@missionautobodyandpaint.com 으로 이메일을 보내 주십시오.

어휘 award-winning 수상 경력이 있는 restore 복구하다 appearance 모습, 외관 charge 청구하다; 요금 insurance provider 보험 회사 directly 직접적으로, 바로 celebrate 기념하다, 축하하다 complimentary 무료의 high-quality 고품질의, 고급의 quote 견적

3 무료 서비스를 받기 위해 고객들이 해야 할 일은?
   (A) 최초 40명 중 한 명의 고객이 되기
   (B) 보험 회사에 전화하기
   (C) 온라인 사진첩 방문하기
   (D) 차량 페인트 수리 비용 지불하기

해설 단서(3)을 보면, 최초 40명의 고객들에게 무료 왁스 코팅 서비스를 제공한다고 했으므로 정답은 (A).
오답 피하기 온라인 사진첩에서 볼 수 있는 것은 작업물 사진이므로 (C)는 오답.

4 미션 오토 바디 앤 페인트에 대해 사실이 아닌 것은?
   (A) 서비스로 상을 받은 적이 있다.
   (B) 40년째 영업을 해 오고 있다.
   (C) 이전 작업물의 샘플을 제공한다.
   (D) 웹사이트로 견적을 제공한다.

해설 (A), (B), (C)에 해당하는 내용은 모두 지문에서 확인할 수 있지만, 단서(4D)를 보면 견적을 받기 위해서는 이메일 문의를 해야 한다고 했으므로 정답은 (D). 웹사이트에서 할 수 있는 일은 작업물을 보는 것이다.

FINAL STEP

p.106

1 (B)   **2** (D)   **3** (A)   **4** (B)   **5** (D)

[1-2] 베이커리의 배달 서비스 광고 전단

Sugar & Spice Bakery
406 Rue Charlemagne

(1)To get your office off to a great start each morning, you should consider using Sugar & Spice's delivery service! We bring freshly baked sourdough bread, pastries, cakes & brioche to your

슈거 & 스파이스 베이커리
뤼 샤를마뉴 406

(1)여러분의 사무실이 매일 아침 멋진 시작을 할 수 있도록, 슈거 & 스파이스의 배달 서비스 이용을 고려해 보세요! 여러분의 사무실까지 갓 구운 사워도우 빵과 패스트리, 케이크와 브리오슈를 가져다 드립니다. 아침 배달 시간은 평일 오전

place of business. Our morning hours of delivery are between 7 A.M. and 10 A.M. on weekdays. On weekends, our delivery service is no longer available, (2)although coffee and pastries can still be purchased in the store. We offer the following combinations, which all include a carafe of brewed coffee:

Item	Amount	Price
Hot sourdough	25 pieces	$85
Brioche & croissants	40 pieces	$110
Assorted French pastries	60 pieces	$160

*These options can be combined to accommodate any order size at an affordable price. Additionally, the following items can be purchased in bulk as needed: plastic forks, plastic knives, disposable plates and individual butter packages.

7시부터 오전 10시까지입니다. 주말에는 배달 서비스 제공이 불가능하지만, (2)커피와 패스트리는 매장에서 여전히 구입 가능합니다. 저희는 다음과 같은 세트를 제공하며, 여기에는 전부 커피 한 병이 포함되어 있습니다:

품목	수량	가격
따뜻한 사워도우	25개	85달러
브리오슈 & 크루아상	40개	110달러
갖가지 프랑스식 패스트리류	60개	160달러

*이 선택사항들은 저렴한 가격에 어떤 양의 주문으로도 결합이 가능합니다. 추가로, 다음의 품목들도 필요에 따라 대량 구입이 가능합니다: 플라스틱 포크, 플라스틱 나이프, 일회용 접시, 낱개 포장 버터.

어휘 get A off to B A를 B가 되게 하다 sourdough 사워도우, 시큼한 맛이 나는 빵 available 이용 가능한 carafe (식탁용의) 유리병 assorted 갖가지의 combine 결합하다 accommodate (요구 등에) 부응하다 affordable (가격 등이) 알맞은 following 다음[아래]에 언급되는 in bulk 대량으로 disposable 일회용의

---

1 이 전단이 의도할 것 같은 대상은?
(A) 제빵 강사
(B) 지역 기업
(C) 배달 기사
(D) 커피숍

해설 단서(1)에서 슈거 & 스파이스가 고객들의 사무실까지 빵을 배달해 준다고 한 것으로 미루어 보아 근처 직장인들이 타깃임을 유추할 수 있다. 따라서 정답은 (B).

2 슈거 & 스파이스 베이커리에 대해 사실인 것은?
(A) 주말에 배달 서비스를 제공한다.
(B) 갓 구운 파이를 판매한다.
(C) 주방용품을 무료로 제공한다.
(D) 커피와 패스트리 둘 다 제공한다.

해설 단서(2)를 통해서 슈거 & 스파이스 베이커리가 커피와 패스트리 둘 다 판매한다는 것을 알 수 있으므로 정답은 (D).
오답 피하기 (A)는 주말에는 매장 구매만 가능하다고 했고, (B)는 파이가 광고에서 언급되지 않아서, (C)는 주방용품이 대량으로 구매 가능하다고 했기 때문에 각각 오답이다.

[3-5] 웹 디자이너 구인 광고

POSITION AVAILABLE: JUNIOR WEB DESIGNER

Job Description:
Woodbridge Web Design (WWD) is looking for a junior Web designer to join our team.

Responsibilities:
- Create prototypes and layouts for all new developments
- Design and develop graphics for Web applications
- (3)Manage and maintain an internal image library

Requirements:
- Minimum one-year experience in Web site design
- Certification as a Web professional
- References from three former clients
- Strong time-management skills

Benefits:
WWD offers a desirable compensation package

지원 가능 직무: 사원급 웹 디자이너

일자리 개요:
우드브릿지 웹 디자인 (WWD)은 팀에 합류하실 사원급 웹 디자이너를 찾고 있습니다.

업무:
- 모든 새로운 개발물들의 원형 및 레이아웃 개발
- 웹 어플리케이션을 위한 그래픽 디자인 및 개발
- (3)내부 이미지 장서 관리 및 유지

자격 요건:
- 최소 1년간의 웹사이트 디자인 경력
- 웹 전문 자격증
- 이전 고객들 세 명의 추천서
- 뛰어난 시간 관리 능력

혜택:
WWD는 경력에 기반하여 바람직한 보수를 제공합니다.

based on experience. (4)One particular advantage of working for WWD is that all retirement contributions made by employees are doubled by the company each month.

To apply, please e-mail a cover letter, résumé, (5) and link to a collection of previous work to the HR director, Walter Gatsby at gatsby_walter@woodbridgewebdesign.net, by October 8.

(4)WWD에서 일하는 것의 한 가지 특별한 이점은 직원들의 모든 퇴직금이 회사에 의해 매달 두 배로 산정된다는 것입니다.

지원하시려면, 자기소개서, 이력서, (5)그리고 지난 업무 결과물들의 모음으로 연결되는 링크를 인사 부장인 월터 개츠비 씨에게 gatsby_walter@woodbridgewebdesign.net으로 10월 8일까지 보내 주세요.

어휘 junior 사원급의, 청소년의 responsibility 업무, 책임 prototype 원형, 샘플 maintain 유지하다 internal 내부의 minimum 최소의 reference 추천서, 추천인 former 이전의 desirable 바람직한 compensation 보상(금) based on ~에 기반하여 particular 특별한, 특정한 retirement 퇴직, 은퇴 cover letter 자기소개서 previous 이전의

3 신규 직원의 업무는?
 (A) 이미지 데이터베이스 생성 및 업데이트
 (B) 고장으로 손상된 웹사이트 복구
 (C) 주말을 포함한 자유 시간제 근무
 (D) 회의에서 매주 디자인 아이디어 공유

4 광고에 따르면, WWD 직원들에게 주어지는 혜택은?
 (A) 경쟁력 있는 초봉
 (B) 후한 퇴직금
 (C) 더 긴 휴가 일수
 (D) 상여금 지급

5 일자리 지원에 대해 언급된 것은?
 (A) 제출 기한은 10월 10일까지이다.
 (B) 모든 서류는 우편으로 수신되어야 한다.
 (C) 최소 2개의 추천서가 동봉되어야 한다.
 (D) 디자인 샘플 포함이 필수 사항이다.

해설 신규 직원의 업무가 나열된 곳을 보면, 내부 이미지 장서 관리 및 유지 업무를 맡게 된다고 했으므로 정답은 (A)이다.
패러프레이징 지문의 Manage and maintain an internal image library가 지문에서는 Creating and updating an image database로 패러프레이징되었다.

해설 WWD 직원들에게 주어지는 혜택 중 하나가 두 배로 산정되는 퇴직금이므로 정답은 (B)이다.
패러프레이징 지문의 retirement contributions made by employees are doubled가 정답에서는 generous retirement package로 패러프레이징되었다.

해설 마지막 단락의 단서(5)에서 지원 시 지난 업무 결과물들을 링크 형식으로 제출하여야 한다고 했으므로 정답은 (D).
오답 피하기 제출 기한은 10월 8일까지이고, 서류는 이메일로 제출해야 하며, 추천서 3장이 필수 요건으로 언급되었기 때문에 (A), (B), (C)는 모두 오답.

FURTHER STEP

p.108

1 (A) **2** (B) **3** (D) **4** (B) **5** (D)

[1-5] 스파 광고 & 경품 당첨 안내 편지 & 서비스 소개 웹페이지

Take a Break at Sierra Spa!

Sierra Spa, under the ownership of Nora Thomas, has served the Cambridge area for the past decade by providing luxury relaxation and beauty treatments. (1)We are now pleased to announce that we are adding another facility, across from the Atherton Mall. Celebrate the opening of this branch with us on Saturday, April 3. On that day, you can meet our staff, try free product samples, and enjoy some refreshments. (2-2)You can also be entered into a prize drawing for a Sierra Spa voucher if you register for our monthly e-mail.

시에라 스파에서 휴식을 취하세요!

노라 토마스 씨의 소유하에 있는 시에라 스파는 지난 10년간 캠브리지 지역에 고급스러운 휴식과 미용 관리를 제공하는 서비스를 제공해 왔습니다. (1)이제 애서턴 몰 맞은편에 또 하나의 시설을 추가하게 됨을 알려드리게 되어 기쁘게 생각합니다. 4월 3일 토요일에 이 지점의 개장을 저희와 함께 축하해 주십시오. 그날, 저희 직원들을 만나 무료 견본 제품을 테스트해 보시고 다과를 즐기실 수 있습니다. (2-2)저희의 월간 이메일 수신을 신청하시면 시에라 스파의 쿠폰을 드리는 경품 추첨에도 응모하실 수 있습니다.

For the best in professional massages, skincare treatments, manicures, and more, come to Sierra Spa!

1785 Lang Avenue and 305 16th Street / Open daily from 9 A.M. to 10 P.M.

Laurie Ekman
4509 Hillside Drive
Cambridge, MA 02141

April 5

Dear Ms. Ekman,

On behalf of Sierra Spa, (2-1)I am pleased to inform you that you are the winner of the prize drawing from our April 3 event. Congratulations! Enclosed you will find a voucher for our services. (4-1)It can be used for any of our spa packages except those that include a hot stone massage. The voucher does not expire, but we cannot replace it if it becomes lost, so please keep it in a safe place. You can use the voucher at either of our locations. Although we do accept walk-in appointments, (3)I suggest you schedule a session with us at least one week before your desired time slot so as to avoid disappointment. We look forward to serving you!

Sincerely,

Sandra Robbins
Administrative Team, Sierra Spa

---

www.sierraspa.com/spapackages

HOME	ABOUT	INDIVIDUAL SPA SERVICES	SPA PACKAGES	CONTACT US

Spa Packages at Sierra Spa

Choose any spa package below for just $225. That gives you big savings over buying the services separately.

Revive and Refresh: 60-minute Thai massage + clarifying facial + aromatherapy body wrap

(4-2)Nature Connect: brightening facial + seaweed body wrap + 60-minute hot stone massage

Cozy Comfort: antiaging body wrap + 60-minute deep tissue massage + sugar scrub facial

Big Night Out: 30-minute hair and scalp massage + oxygen infusion facial + moisturizing body wrap + manicure + pedicure

To ensure the quality of our services, (5)all of our treatments are administered by massage therapists and beauty technicians with at least eight years of experience in the field.

전문 마사지, 피부 관리, 손톱 손질 등에서 최고를 찾으신다면, 시에라 스파로 오세요!

랭 가 1785번지와 16번 가 305번지 / 매일 오전 9시부터 저녁 10시까지 개점

로리 에크만
힐사이드 로 4509
매사추세츠 주 캠브리지, 02141

4월 5일

에크만 씨께,

시에라 스파를 대표하여, (2-1)귀하께서 저희의 4월 3일 행사에서 경품 추첨에 당첨되셨음을 알려드리게 되어 기쁩니다. 축하드립니다! 저희 서비스를 받을 수 있는 쿠폰을 동봉합니다. (4-1)핫 스톤 마사지가 포함된 패키지만 제외하고 저희 스파 패키지 어느 것에도 사용하실 수 있습니다. 쿠폰은 만기일이 없지만, 분실 시 재발급해 드리지 않으니, 안전한 곳에 보관하시기 바랍니다. 쿠폰은 저희 지점 두 곳 중 어디에서나 사용하실 수 있습니다. 예약 없이 방문하셔도 되지만, 실망스러운 일을 피하기 위해서 (3)원하시는 시간대보다 최소 일주일 전에 저희와 시간을 정하실 것을 권해 드립니다. 귀하를 모시기를 고대하고 있겠습니다!

시에라 스파, 관리팀
산드라 로빈스 드림

---

www.sierraspa.com/spapackages

홈	소개	개인 스파 서비스	스파 패키지	연락처

시에라 스파의 스파 패키지

단돈 225달러로 아래 스파 패키지 중 아무것이나 선택하세요. 개별적으로 서비스를 구입하시는 것보다 훨씬 절약됩니다.

리바이브 앤 리프레쉬: 60분간의 태국식 마사지 + 맑게 해주는 얼굴 마사지 + 아로마테라피 바디 랩

(4-2)네이쳐 커넥트: 얼굴 미백 마사지 + 해초 바디 랩 + 60분간의 핫 스톤 마사지

코지 컴포트: 안티에이징 바디 랩 + 60분간의 심부 조직 마사지 + 설탕 스크럽 얼굴 마사지

빅 나잇 아웃: 30분간의 헤어 및 두피 마사지 + 산소 주입 얼굴 마사지 + 보습 바디 랩 + 손톱 손질 + 발 관리

서비스의 질을 보장하기 위해서, (5)저희 관리는 전부 이 분야에 최소 8년의 경력을 지닌 마사지 전문가와 미용 전문가에 의해 이루어집니다.

어휘 **ownership** 소유(권) **relaxation** 휴식 **treatment** 관리, 치료 **refreshment** (보통 복수형) 다과 **prize drawing** 경품 추첨 **register for** ~에 등록하다 **on behalf of** ~을 대표[대신]하여 **voucher** 상품권, 쿠폰 **expire** 만료되다 **walk-in** 예약 없이 방문하는 **schedule** 일정을 잡다 **time slot** 시간대 **avoid** 피하다 **saving** 절약 **separately** 따로따로, 별도로 **revive** 활기를 되찾다 **clarifying** 맑게 해주는 **deep tissue** 심부 조직 **scalp** 두피 **infusion** 주입 **moisturizing** 보습(의) **ensure** 보장하다 **administer** 관리하다

1 시에라 스파가 특별 행사를 하는 이유는?
(A) 2호점을 홍보하기 위해
(B) 새로운 주인을 소개하기 위해
(C) 이전을 축하하기 위해
(D) 제품을 출시하기 위해

[해설] 광고문에서 시에라 스파의 새로운 지점 개장을 알리며, 이를 축하하는 개장식에 초대하고 있으므로 정답은 (A). adding another facility, opening of this branch는 모두 지점 개장을 의미하는 표현이다.

2 에크만 씨에 대해 추론할 수 있는 것은?
(A) 단골 고객이다.
(B) 우편물 수신자 명단에 가입했다.
(C) 구매를 했다.
(D) 샘플을 요청했다.

[해설] 두 지문 연계 문제이다. 편지의 수신인인 에크만 씨는 경품 추첨 당첨자인데, 광고문에서 경품 추첨에 응모하려면 이메일 수신을 신청해야 한다고 했다. 따라서 에크만 씨가 이메일 수신을 신청했음을 알 수 있으므로 정답은 (B). mailing list는 업체나 기관 등에서 광고물 등을 보내기 위해 갖고 있는 우편물 수신자 명단을 뜻한다.

3 로빈스 씨가 에크만 씨에게 하도록 권고한 것은?
(A) 온라인상의 일정 확인하기
(B) 만료일 확인하기
(C) 특정 지점 이용하기
(D) 미리 예약하기

[해설] 권고하는 일이 무엇인지를 묻는 문제이므로, 이메일 후반부의 I suggest you라는 표현이 힌트가 된다. 편지에서 로빈스 씨는 에크만 씨에게 원하는 시간대보다 최소 일주일 전에 미리 예약할 것을 제안했으므로 정답은 (D).

4 쿠폰으로 이용할 수 없는 패키지는?
(A) 리바이브 앤 리프레쉬
(B) 네이처 커넥트
(C) 코지 컴포트
(D) 빅 나잇 아웃

[해설] 두 지문 연계 문제이다. 편지에서 쿠폰은 핫 스톤 마사지가 포함된 패키지만 제외하고 모든 패키지에 사용할 수 있다고 했는데, 웹 페이지에서 핫 스톤 마사지가 포함되어 있는 패키지는 네이쳐 커넥트라는 것을 확인할 수 있다. 따라서 정답은 (B).

5 시에라 스파의 서비스에 대해 사실인 것은?
(A) 환불 보장 규정이 있다.
(B) 반드시 패키지로 구입해야 한다.
(C) 주말에는 이용할 수 없다.
(D) 경험 많은 직원들이 제공한다.

[해설] 시에라 스파의 모든 관리는 최소 8년의 경력을 지닌 전문가들에 의해 이루어진다고 했으므로 정답은 (D).
[오답 피하기] 패키지로 구입하면 절약할 수 있다는 것이지, 반드시 패키지로 구입해야 한다는 것은 아니므로 (B)는 오답이다.

UNIT 14 기사문 (1)

PRE-STEP
p.111

A 1 (A) 2 (B) 3 (A) 4 (A) 5 (B) 6 (A) 7 (B) 8 (A) 9 (A)
10 (A) 11 (B) 12 (B) 13 (A) 14 (B) 15 (A)

B 1 (B) 2 (A)

A 1 (A) mark, 기념일을 축하하다
2 (B) meet, 새 공간에 대한 필요를 충족시키다
3 (A) sponsor, 단체를 후원하다
4 (A) convenient, 사용하기 더 편리한
5 (B) experienced, 경험 많은 자원봉사자
6 (A) invest, 수백만 달러를 투자하다
7 (B) accomplish, 목적을 달성하다
8 (A) celebrate, 휴가 시즌을 기념하다
9 (A) support, 지역 경제를 후원하다
10 (A) take part, 행사에 참여하다
11 (B) approach, 혁신적인 방법
12 (B) operation, 평소대로 영업을 하다
13 (A) charity, 자선단체를 위해 모금하다
14 (B) duties, ~의 임무를 수행하다
15 (A) issues, 몇몇 문제들을 다루다

B 1 A state-of-the-art community sports field opened in the center of town last month, and in a mere thirty days, its popularity among residents has grown dramatically.
(A) With assistance from residents, the facility can become more popular than ever.
(B) In a short time, many people living in the area have come to like the facility.

최신식 지역사회 운동장이 지난달 시내 중심가에 개장하였고, 단 30일 만에 주민들 사이에서 그 인기가 굉장해졌다.
(A) 주민들의 도움으로, 시설은 그 어느 때보다도 인기가 많아질 수 있다.
(B) 짧은 시간 내에, 지역에 거주하는 많은 사람들이 시설을 좋아하게 되었다.

2 The council had hoped to make cycling more safe, convenient, and comfortable. To do so, it spent four months expanding the number of bicycle routes.
(A) More biking routes were added in an effort to improve conditions for cyclists.
(B) The project helped to improve the condition of outdated cycling trails.

시의회는 자전거 타기를 보다 안전하고 편리하고 편안한 것으로 만들기를 바라 왔다. 그렇게 하기 위해, 의회는 자전거 도로의 수를 확장시키는 데에 4개월을 들였다.
(A) 자전거 타는 사람들의 환경을 개선하기 위한 노력으로 더 많은 자전거 도로가 추가되었다.
(B) 이 프로젝트는 낙후된 자전거 도로의 상태를 개선하는 데 도움이 되었다.

MAIN STEP 1
p.112

 회사의 성과 향상 방안에 대한 기사

①Starius Plus, the Berlin-based ceramics manufacturer, announced its plans to improve market performance.

①베를린에 본사를 둔 도자기 제조사인 스태리어스 플러스 사는 시장 성과를 향상시킬 계획을 발표했다.

②Having posted losses of nearly 10 million euros over the last year, Starius Plus is proposing changes that should return it to profitability in nine months.

③The strategy centers on improving domestic operations. Executives believe that major savings could be made by organizational reshuffling and altering the supply chain.

④Investors anticipate that these measures will guarantee short-term profit growth.

②작년 거의 천만 유로의 손실을 공표한 스태리어스 플러스 사는 9개월 안에 수익률을 회복하는 변화를 꾀하고 있다.

③계획은 국내 사업 개선에 초점을 맞춘다. 경영진은 조직 개편과 공급망 변경으로 크게 절약을 할 수 있을 것이라고 생각한다.

④투자자들은 이 조치가 단기 수익 성장을 보장할 것이라고 예상하고 있다.

어휘 manufacturer 제조사 market performance 시장 성과 post 공표[발표]하다 nearly 거의 profitability 수익률, 수익성 strategy 계획, 전략 center on ~에 초점을 맞추다 executive 경영진 organizational 조직(상)의 reshuffle (조직을) 개편하다 alter 바꾸다, 고치다 measure 조치, 정책 guarantee 보장하다

① 기사의 주제는?
→ 회사의 개선 계획

해설 첫 문단에 스태리어스 플러스 사가 시장 성과를 향상시키려고 한다는 내용이 나오고, 그 이유와 방법, 전망에 대한 내용이 이어지므로 '회사의 개선 계획'이 주제이다.

② 스태리어스 플러스 사에 대해 추론할 수 있는 것은?
→ 최근 매출이 수익이 없었다.

해설 회사가 작년에 천만 유로에 달하는 손실을 입었다고 했는데, 이는 즉 수익이 없었다는 말이다.

③ 회사가 국내 사업을 개선하려고 하는 방법은?
→ 관리 업무를 효율적으로 함으로써

해설 조직 개편으로 절약을 하려는 계획이 언급된 부분을 통해 회사가 관리 업무를 효율적으로 할 것임을 알 수 있다.

④ 투자자들이 기대하는 것은?
→ 회사 수익 증대

해설 전망이 나타나 있는 마지막 문단에서 투자자들이 기대하는 바를 찾을 수 있다.

전략 2 회사 CEO의 인터뷰 내용

The CEO said, "We hope to meet more customers next year by opening 20 more stores abroad."

CEO는 "내년에는 해외에 20개의 매장을 추가로 개점하여 더 많은 고객을 만나기를 바랍니다."라고 말했다.

어휘 abroad 해외에

회사가 계획하고 있는 것은?
→ 추가 지점 개업

해설 해외에 매장 20개를 개점한다고 했으므로 지점을 추가로 개업한다는 것을 알 수 있다.

MAIN STEP 2   p.113

1 (A)   **2** (C)   **3** (A)   **4** (B)

[1-2] 시의회의 자전거 이용 독려 계획에 관한 기사

(1)**San Francisco, A City that Cycles?**

Yesterday, (1)the San Francisco city council marked the completion of its green transportation program.

(1)샌프란시스코, 자전거를 타는 도시?

어제 (1)샌프란시스코 시의회는 녹색 교통수단 프로그램의 완성을 축하했다.

Recognizing that cycling is one of the cleanest and most energy-efficient forms of transportation, the council had hoped to make cycling more safe, convenient, and comfortable. To do so, it spent four months expanding the number of bicycle routes.

In order to encourage more people to take advantage of these new routes and start riding bicycles regularly, (2)a second program will begin next month. For a small fee, shared bicycles will be available as short-term rentals from locations across the city.

시의회는 자전거 타기가 가장 깨끗하고 가장 에너지 효율적인 교통수단 형태 중 하나라는 것을 알고 있기 때문에, 자전거 타기를 보다 더 안전하고 편리하고 편안한 것으로 만들기를 바라 왔다. 그렇게 하기 위해, 의회는 자전거 도로의 수를 확장시키는 데에 4개월을 들였다.

더 많은 사람들이 이 새로운 도로를 이용해 정기적으로 자전거 타기를 시작하도록 독려하기 위해, (2)두 번째 프로그램이 다음 달에 시작될 것이다. 값싼 요금으로, 도시 전역에서 공용 자전거가 단기 대여로 이용 가능해질 것이다.

어휘 council 의회 mark (중요 사건을) 축하하다 transportation 교통 수단 recognize 인식하다, 인정하다 energy-efficient 에너지 효율적인 expand 확장하다 route 도로, 길 take advantage of ~을 이용하다, 기회로 활용하다 available 이용 가능한 short-term 단기간의

1 이 기사의 목적은?

(A) 새로운 정책을 알리기 위해
(B) 교통 표지판 변경을 위해
(C) 자전거 할인 판매를 홍보하기 위해
(D) 산책로를 알려 주기 위해

해설 기사의 목적은 제목과 첫 문단에 주로 나타난다. 단서(1)을 통해 시의 새로운 계획 시행을 알리는 기사임을 알 수 있다. 따라서 정답은 (A).

2 다음 달에 일어날 일은?

(A) 통행료가 징수될 것이다.
(B) 자전거 도로가 더 추가될 것이다.
(C) 공공 자전거가 대여 가능해질 것이다.
(D) 연료비가 인상될 것이다.

해설 단서(2)에서 다음 달부터 공용 자전거 대여가 가능해진다고 했으므로 정답은 (C). 보통 앞으로의 일에 관한 문제는 기사의 후반부에서 단서를 찾아볼 수 있으므로 지문의 후반부를 중점적으로 읽도록 하자.

[3-4] 항공사의 서비스 변경에 관한 기사

Changes on the Horizon for Volo Air

Italian-based air carrier (3)Volo Air International is preparing for changes regarding its passenger class system and services. In a press release, spokesperson Bianca Lucci said the company plans to merge business and first class into one new class, which they will call "executive class." "To respond to the demand for economy class seats, every plane in the fleet will be expanding its economy class section by nearly 22 percent. The new executive class will offer all the comforts, services, and amenities that Volo Air's passengers have become accustomed to," said Lucci.

The work is scheduled to be completed by May 9, with the new pricing scheme for executive class going into effect on May 12. (4)"Passengers can expect the cost of executive tickets to be around the same as what they currently pay for business class tickets," explained Lucci.

This is just the first step in the airline's plan to bring Volo Air up-to-date. The next project will be the addition of new uniforms for the staff and crew.

볼로 항공에 임박한 변화

이탈리아에 본사를 둔 항공사 (3)볼로 에어 인터내셔널은 승객 등급 체계와 서비스에 관한 변화를 준비하고 있다. 보도 자료에서 대변인 비앙카 루씨 씨는 회사가 비즈니스 석과 일등석을 하나의 새로운 등급으로 합칠 계획이라고 말했고, 그것을 "이그제큐티브 석"으로 부를 예정이다. 루씨 씨는 "이코노미 석에 대한 수요에 응답하기 위해, 항공사의 모든 비행기는 일반석 칸을 거의 22%까지 확대할 것입니다. 새로운 이그제큐티브 석은 볼로 항공 승객들이 익숙한 모든 편의 시설, 서비스, 오락 시설을 제공할 것입니다."라고 말했다.

작업은 5월 9일까지 완료될 예정이며, 이그제큐티브 석에 대한 새 가격 체계는 5월 12일에 발효될 것이다. 루씨 씨는 (4)"승객들은 이그제큐티브 석 티켓의 가격을 현재 비즈니스 석 티켓에 지불하는 가격과 거의 같을 것으로 예상하면 됩니다."라고 설명했다.

이것은 볼로 항공을 최신화하려는 항공사 계획의 첫 단계일 뿐이다. 다음 프로젝트는 직원과 승무원을 위한 새 유니폼 추가가 될 것이다.

어휘 **on the horizon** 임박한, 곧 일어날 듯한 **air carrier** 항공사 **regarding** ~에 관해 **press release** 보도 자료 **spokesperson** 대변인 **merge** 합치다, 병합하다 **fleet** 한 회사 소유의 모든 비행기[선박, 차량] **expand** 확장하다 **amenities** 오락 시설 **become accustomed to** ~에 익숙해지다 **pricing scheme** 가격 체계 **go into effect** 발효하다, 효력이 발생되다 **around the same as** ~와 거의 같은 **bring ~ up-to-date** ~을 최신화하다

3 기사의 주제는?
 (A) 항공사의 현재 계획
 (B) 두 항공사의 합병
 (C) 유니폼 디자인 대회
 (D) 다가오는 비행기 티켓 할인

해설 기사의 첫 문장에서 볼로 항공이 승객 등급 체계와 서비스에 관한 변화를 준비하고 있다고 했으므로 정답은 (A).

4 이그제큐티브 석에 대해 사실인 것은?
 (A) 세 개 등급을 합칠 것이다.
 (B) 비용이 비즈니스 석과 거의 같을 것이다.
 (C) 새로운 종류의 서비스를 제공할 것이다.
 (D) 좌석이 유명 디자이너에 의해 제작될 것이다.

해설 지문에서 executive class가 언급된 부분을 찾는다. 두 번째 단락에서 이그제큐티브 석의 가격은 현재 비즈니스 석 가격과 거의 동일할 것이라는 언급이 있으므로 정답은 (B).

FINAL STEP

p.114

1 (C) 2 (A) 3 (B) 4 (C) 5 (A) 6 (C)

[1-3] 새로운 지역사회 운동장에 관한 기사

August 17—A state-of-the-art community sports field opened in the center of town last month, and in a mere thirty days, its popularity among residents has grown dramatically. The new facility can be used for a variety of outdoor sports like soccer and football, which meet a need for a new space to be allocated for local sporting events. Athletes and their parents alike are thrilled to have such a place finally created. Tyler Duggan, a father of two, said that he's delighted to have a venue to which he can take his children for family outings in the evenings when other attractions are closed. (3)He mentioned being particularly excited to take his young sons to watch the high school football games in the fall. The ticket prices for those competitions are only $5 for adults and $2 for children over the age of 5. Therefore, it is an extremely affordable activity for families.

(2)Track-and-field coach Nolan Rossi is also thrilled because the facility makes athletic competitions easier on his colleagues and his students. As stated by Mr. Rossi, "(2)The fields at my high school are too small to host the necessary track-and-field competitions in May." As a result, the teachers had to schedule each event on a different day. However, now that the new sports field is available, his school can hold the tournament there. This enables multiple events to be held simultaneously and creates one full day of competition for the students each spring. Many participants agree that

8월 17일—최신식 지역사회 운동장이 지난달 시내 중심가에 개장하였고, 단 30일 만에 주민들 사이에서 그 인기가 굉장해졌다. 새로운 시설은 축구나 미식축구 같은 다양한 야외 운동에 이용될 수 있는데, 이 시설은 지역 스포츠 행사를 위해 배정되어야 하는 새 공간에 대한 필요를 충족시킨다. 운동선수와 선수의 부모들은 모두 그런 장소가 마침내 마련되어 신이 나 있다. 두 자녀의 아버지인 타일러 듀건 씨는 다른 명소들이 문을 닫은 저녁 시간 가족 나들이에 아이들을 데려갈 장소가 생겨 기쁘다고 말했다. (3)그는 특히 가을에 고등학교 미식축구 경기 관람에 어린 아들을 데려가게 되어 흥분된다고 했다. 그 경기의 입장권 가격은 성인은 단돈 5달러, 5세 이상의 어린이는 2달러이다. 따라서, 그것은 가족들을 위한 매우 알맞은 금액의 활동이다.

(2)육상 경기 코치인 놀란 로시 씨도, 그 시설이 그의 동료와 학생들에게 체육 대회를 더욱 쉬운 것으로 만들어주어 매우 기뻐하고 있다. "(2)저희 고등학교 운동장은 5월에 필수 육상 경기를 개최하기에는 규모가 너무 작습니다."라고 로시 씨는 말했다. 그 결과, 교사들은 각각의 행사를 다른 날로 정해야 했다. 하지만 이제 새로운 운동장이 이용 가능해졌으므로, 그의 학교는 그곳에서 토너먼트를 개최할 수 있다. 이로 인해 여러 행사들이 동시에 열리는 것이 가능해졌고, 매해 봄 꼬박 하루간의 학생 경기가 열릴 것이다. 많은 참가자들이 이것이 모두에게 더 편리하다는 것에 동의한다.

this is more convenient for everyone.

(1)The final feature that the sports field boasts is the concession stand and snack bar underneath the stadium seating. Here, fans can purchase food and beverages while they enjoy watching games and practices.

(1)운동장이 자랑하는 마지막 특징은 경기장 좌석 아래의 구내 매점과 스낵 바이다. 이곳에서, 팬들은 경기나 연습을 관람하는 동안 식음료를 구매할 수 있다.

어휘 state-of-the-art 최신식의, 최첨단의　resident 주민　allocate 배정하다　be thrilled to *do* ~하게 되어 신나다　venue 장소　outing 나들이, 소풍　attraction 명소, 명물　affordable (가격이) 적당한, 감당할 수 있는　track-and-field 육상 경기　simultaneously 동시에　participant 참가자　boast 자랑하다, 뽐내다　concession stand 구내 매점

---

1 경기장에 대해 암시된 것은?
 (A) 낮 시간에만 개장한다.
 (B) 이용은 공식 경기에만 국한되어 있다.
 (C) 내부에 음식 서비스 센터가 함께 지어졌다.
 (D) 가격이 계절에 따라 바뀐다.

해설 단서(1)에서 경기장 좌석 아래쪽에 매점과 스낵 바가 있다고 하였으므로 정답은 (C).
패러프레이징 지문의 concession stand and snack bar가 정답에서 food service center로 패러프레이징되었다.

2 로시 씨에 대해 사실인 것은?
 (A) 고등학교 운동부 코치이다.
 (B) 육상 경기 참가자이다.
 (C) 새로운 프로젝트에 대해 불만스러워한다.
 (D) 5세 미만의 자녀들이 있다.

해설 지문에서 로시 씨가 언급된 두 번째 문단의 초입과 그의 인터뷰 부분을 보아야 한다. 단서(2)를 종합해 보면 로시 씨가 고등학교 육상 경기 코치임을 알 수 있으므로 정답은 (A).

3 [1], [2], [3], [4]로 표시된 위치 중 다음 문장이 들어가기에 가장 알맞은 곳은?
 "따라서, 그것은 가족들을 위한 매우 알맞은 금액의 활동이다."
 (A) [1]
 (B) [2]
 (C) [3]
 (D) [4]

해설 주어진 문장의 연결사 Therefore와 대명사 it이 가리키는 것을 주의 깊게 보아야 한다. 주어진 문장은 어떤 것이 가족을 위해 알맞은 활동이라는 의미인데, affordable이 주로 '(가격이) 알맞은, 저렴한'이라는 뜻을 고려할 때 해당 문장 앞에는 가격에 관한 내용이 와야 한다. 단서(3)에서 미식축구 경기 입장권 가격 정보를 볼 수 있으므로 정답은 (B). 주어진 문장의 it은 to take his young sons to watch the high school football games를 의미한다.

[4-6] 어린이 과학 캠프를 알리는 기사

(4)**Wakefield Research Institute of Science and Technology Holds Annual Kids' Science Camp**
By Chloé Yelding

(4)Wakefield Research Institute of Science and Technology (WRIST) continues to sponsor its annual science camp for children aged 6 to 14. For one week every summer, WRIST invites 50 students, free of charge, to a campground two miles north of the city. Kids sleep on-site in cabins and spend their days engaged in interactive science experiments.

The origins of the WRIST camp began in 2000. Ethan Lazell—founding president of WRIST—decided that since his organization invested millions of dollars on research, it should also aim to pass the joy of science onto children. He envisioned craft programs that develop scientific literacy in kids who are not familiar with scientific concepts. His primary

(4)웨이크필드 과학 기술 연구소가 연례 어린이 과학 캠프를 개최하다
클로에 옐딩 작성

(4)웨이크필드 과학 기술 연구소 (WRIST)는 6-14세 어린이들을 위한 연례 과학 캠프를 지속적으로 후원한다. 매해 여름 1주일간, WRIST는 50명의 학생들을 도심에서 북쪽으로 2마일 떨어진 야영지에 무료로 초대한다. 어린이들은 현장의 오두막집에서 잠자면서, 쌍방향 과학 실험에 참여하며 여러 날을 보낸다.

WRIST 캠프의 유래는 2000년에 시작되었다. WRIST의 창립 회장인 에단 라젤 씨는 그의 조직이 연구에 수백만 달러를 투자했으니, 과학의 즐거움을 어린이들에게 전수하는 것 또한 목표로 삼아야 한다고 결심했다. 그는 과학 개념에 친숙하지 않은 어린이들의 과학적 소양을 계발해 주는 기술 프로그램을 마음속에 그렸다. 그의 주된 목표는 이 참가자들을 과학의 세계로 이끄는 것이었다. 그는 이 목적을 달성했는데, 그의 혁신적인 교육 방법은 수많은 어린이들로 하여금 나중에 과학, 기술, 공학, 그리고 수학 분야에서 직업을 찾도록 동기 부여를 해 주었기 때문이다. (5)비록 라젤 씨는 그 후 은퇴했으나,

goal was to draw these participants to the world of science. He accomplished this aim, as his innovative approach to teaching motivated numerous children to later pursue careers in science, technology, engineering, and math. (5)Although Mr. Lazell has since retired, WRIST continues to honor his vision and values to this day.

To maintain the functioning of the camp, WRIST relies heavily on educated volunteers. A range of science professionals serve as camp counselors and instructors. (6)If you are interested in sharing your time and knowledge to help inspire children to become scientists, please send a completed volunteer form, a letter of reference, and a résumé to volunteers@wristsciencecamp.com.

WRIST는 오늘날까지도 계속해서 그의 비전과 가치관을 기념하고 있다.

캠프의 운영을 지속하기 위해, WRIST는 학식 있는 자원 봉사자들에게 상당히 의존하고 있다. 여러 과학 전문가들이 캠프 상담사나 강사로 활동한다. (6)어린이들이 과학자가 되도록 고무시키는 일에 시간과 지식을 공유하는 데 관심이 있다면, 완성된 자원 봉사 양식과 추천서, 이력서를 volunteers@wristsciencecamp.com으로 보내면 된다.

어휘 **on-site** 현장의, 현지의 **engage in** ~에 참여[관여]하다 **interactive** 쌍방향의, 상호적인 **founding president** 창립 회장 **organization** 조직 **pass A onto B** A를 B에게 전수하다 **envision** 마음에 그리다 **literacy** 소양, 능력, 지식 **primary** 주된, 제일의 **accomplish** 달성하다, 완수하다 **motivate** 동기를 부여하다 **pursue** 추구하다 **value** (보통 복수형) 가치관 **maintain** 지속[유지]하다 **heavily** 상당히, 심하게 **educated** 학식[교양] 있는, 많이 배운 **a range of** 여럿의, 다양한 **inspire** 고무시키다, 영감을 주다 **a letter of reference** 추천서

4 기사의 목적은?
(A) 사업에의 투자를 촉구하기 위해
(B) 전문 학회를 알리기 위해
(C) 어린이들을 위한 행사를 홍보하기 위해
(D) 조직의 업적을 강조하기 위해

해설 보통 기사문의 목적은 제목과 도입부에서 드러나는 경우가 많다. 도입부에서 어린이 과학 캠프를 소개 및 설명하고 있으므로 정답은 (C).

5 라젤 씨에 대해 사실인 것은?
(A) 그의 비전은 오늘날 여전히 WRIST에 의해 기념된다.
(B) 그는 2010년에 캠프를 열었다.
(C) 그는 강사들을 고용한다.
(D) 그는 가끔 상담가로서 봉사 활동을 한다.

해설 단서(5)에서 그가 은퇴한 지금까지도 WRIST가 그의 비전과 가치관을 기념한다고 했으므로 정답은 (A)이다.
오답 피하기 라젤 씨가 캠프를 시작한 것은 2010년이 아닌 2000년이므로 (B)는 오답. 또한 강사들은 캠프에서 자원 봉사를 하는 것이지 돈을 받고 고용되는 것이 아니므로 (C)도 오답.

6 자원 봉사자들에 대해 암시된 것은?
(A) 공학 분야에 이력이 있어야 한다.
(B) WRIST 회원의 추천을 받아야 한다.
(C) 이메일로 서류를 보내야 한다.
(D) 현장 훈련을 받을 것이다.

해설 자원 봉사자에 대해 언급하는 기사의 마지막 문단을 집중해서 보아야 한다. 관심 있는 사람들은 서류를 이메일로 보내야 한다고 했으므로 정답은 (C).
패러프레이징 지문의 a completed volunteer form, a letter of reference, and a résumé가 정답에서 상위어인 documents로 패러프레이징되었다.

FURTHER STEP
p.116

1 (A)　　2 (C)　　3 (D)　　4 (B)　　5 (B)

[1-5] 지역 행사 광고 전단 & 자원 봉사자 모집 이메일 & 행사에 대한 후속 기사

Come Join the Fun at the Sherman City Winter Wonderland!
Saturday, December 12, 7 P.M.–10 P.M.

Sherman City is celebrating the holiday season with a Winter Wonderland event in the city center. (1)We

셔먼 시 윈터 원더랜드에 오셔서 함께 즐기세요!
12월 12일 토요일 저녁 7시-10시

셔먼 시에서는 도심부에서 윈터 원더랜드 행사를 열어 연말 휴가 시즌을 기념하고자 합니다. (1)이 행사로 다른 도시의 쇼핑객들이 우리 시를 찾아 지역 경제를 후원하게 되기를 바라고

95

hope this will bring out-of-town shoppers to our town to support the local economy. In addition to the unique shops and cafés that will be in operation as usual, there will also be special activities for the whole family to enjoy:

- Victoria Cathedral: Free coffee and hot chocolate
- Hampton Station: Get your picture taken with a snowman
- (2-2)Caradon Street: Booths where you can make holiday cards, ornaments, and more
- Crown Plaza: Live music by various performers (7 P.M. Sherman City Municipal Band, 8 P.M. Columbia Folk Singers, (4-1)9 P.M. Nellie Williams)

Admission is free to the public and no tickets are necessary. Please note that some of the downtown streets will be closed during the event, so driving routes and parking should be planned accordingly.

To: Undisclosed Recipients
From: Joel Casey <j.casey@inboxmail.com>
Date: December 6
Subject: Winter Wonderland

Dear Sherman Community Club Members,

I have been contacted by Laurie Domingo, the event planner for the Sherman City Winter Wonderland event this Saturday. I know many of you have already volunteered for this event, but (2-1)Laurie is still looking for a few more volunteers for the arts and crafts booths. You would be partnered with an experienced volunteer, so you would not have to (3)perform your duties alone. If you are interested, please contact Laurie as soon as possible at 555-2940. I hope you will seriously consider taking part in this event.

Sincerely,

Joel Casey
President, Sherman Community Club

Winter Wonderland Gets Cold Reaction

December 13—The Sherman City Winter Wonderland event held yesterday was considered a disappointment by many. Event planners had not anticipated the large crowds, which flooded the streets, making it difficult to move through the area and participate in activities and shopping. "The city center was like a wall of people," said Sherman City resident James Sims. "It took fifteen minutes just to move a few feet. I ended up just going home."

In addition, the live entertainment at Crown Plaza did not go on continuously as planned. The Columbia Folk Singers failed to show up for their performance. (4-2)Although Nellie Williams was able to start half an hour early, that still left thirty minutes of silence.

"We've learned a lot from the difficulties with crowd control and planning," said Laurie Domingo, who was in charge of planning the event. "(5)Next year we plan to have the activities more spread out to address some of these issues."

(4-2)넬리 윌리엄즈가 30분 일찍 시작할 수 있었지만, 그럼에도 불구하고 30분간은 정적이 흘렀다.

"저희는 군중 통제와 기획의 어려움으로부터 많은 것을 배웠습니다."라고 행사 기획 책임자였던 로리 도밍고 씨는 말했다. "(5)내년에는 이런 몇몇 문제들에 대처하기 위해 행사들이 더 넓은 공간을 쓰게 할 계획입니다."

어휘 out-of-town 다른 곳에서 온 be in operation 영업하다 as usual 평소대로 ornament 장식품, 장신구 municipal 시의 admission 입장(료) accordingly 그에 맞춰 undisclosed 밝혀지지 않은 recipient 수신인, 수령인 arts and crafts 공예 partner 파트너가 되다 experienced 경험이 있는, 능숙한 take part in ~에 참여하다 anticipate 예상하다 flood 넘쳐나다, 밀려들다 end up doing 결국 ~하다 show up 나타나다 be in charge of ~을 책임지다 spread out 넓은 공간을 쓰다 address an issue 문제를 해결하다

---

1 전단에 따르면, 행사의 한 가지 목적은?
  (A) 지역에 관광객을 유치하기 위해
  (B) 자선단체를 위해 모금하기 위해
  (C) 업적을 기념하기 위해
  (D) 상점 개업을 홍보하기 위해

해설 전단에서 윈터 원더랜드 행사를 통해 다른 도시의 쇼핑객들이 찾아와 지역 경제에 보탬이 되기를 바란다고 했는데, 이를 행사의 목적으로 볼 수 있으므로 정답은 (A).
패러프레이징 지문의 bring out-of-town shoppers to our town이 정답에서 attract visitors to the area로 패러프레이징되었다.

2 더 많은 자원 봉사자가 필요한 곳은?
  (A) 빅토리아 성당
  (B) 햄튼역
  (C) 케라돈 거리
  (D) 크라운 광장

해설 두 지문 연계 문제이다. 단서(2-1)에서 공예 부스에 자원 봉사자가 더 필요하다고 했는데, 단서(2-2)에서 장식품 부스가 있는 곳이 케라돈 거리임을 알 수 있다. 따라서 정답은 (C).
패러프레이징 전단의 Booths where you can make holiday cards, ornaments가 이메일에서는 arts and crafts booths로 표현되었다는 것을 알아야 한다.

3 이메일에서, 1단락, 다섯 번째 줄의 어휘 "perform"과 의미상 가장 유사한 것은?
  (A) 집행하다
  (B) 꺼내다
  (C) 즐겁게 해주다
  (D) 수행하다

해설 지문에서 perform은 your duties를 목적어로 하여 '일[임무]를 수행하다'라는 뜻으로 쓰였다. 선택지 중에서는 carry out과 바꿔쓸 수 있으므로 정답은 (D).
오답 피하기 (A)의 enforce는 법률 등을 집행한다는 의미로 문맥과 맞지 않아 오답.

4 넬리 윌리엄즈가 공연을 시작한 때는?
  (A) 저녁 8시
  (B) 저녁 8시 30분
  (C) 저녁 9시
  (D) 저녁 9시 30분

해설 두 지문 연계 문제이다. 전단에 따르면 넬리 윌리엄즈의 예정된 공연 시간은 저녁 9시부터였지만, 기사에서 공연이 30분 일찍 시작되었다고 했으므로 정답은 (B).

5 도밍고 씨가 내년 행사를 위해 계획한 일은?
  (A) 입장료 부과하기
  (B) 더 넓은 장소 이용하기
  (C) 월초에 더 일찍 개최하기
  (D) 더 많은 자원 봉사자 모집하기

해설 기사의 마지막 문장에서 도밍고 씨가 혼잡 문제를 해결하기 위해 내년에는 행사들이 더 넓은 장소를 쓰게 할 계획이라고 했으므로 정답은 (B).
패러프레이징 지문의 have the activities more spread out이 정답에서는 Use a larger area로 패러프레이징되었다.

UNIT 15 기사문 (2)

PRE-STEP p.119

A
1 (A)	2 (A)	3 (B)	4 (B)	5 (A)	6 (A)	7 (A)	8 (B)	9 (A)
10 (A)	11 (B)	12 (B)	13 (A)	14 (A)	15 (B)			

B 1 (B) 2 (B)

A
1 (A) go, 파업에 <u>돌입하다</u>
2 (A) hire, 70명의 새 직원을 <u>고용하다</u>
3 (B) agreement, 인수 <u>계약</u>을 타결하다
4 (B) regulations, 더 엄격한 <u>규제</u>를 가하다
5 (A) wages, 노동 <u>임금</u>을 인상하다
6 (A) stop by, 매장에 직접 <u>들르다</u>
7 (A) consumers, 신규 <u>소비자들</u>에게 다가서다
8 (B) effect, 다음 달 1일부터 <u>효력</u>을 발휘하다
9 (A) congestion, 교통 <u>체증</u>
10 (A) consideration, 시의 예산을 <u>고려하다</u>
11 (B) unveil, 새 로고를 <u>발표하다</u>
12 (B) reach, 더 큰 시장에 <u>도달하다</u>
13 (A) launch, 웹사이트를 <u>개설하다</u>
14 (A) apply, 모든 영리 기업에 <u>적용하다</u>
15 (B) leading, <u>선두적인</u> 자동차 제조업체

B
1 Napier reports that downsizing its workforce is not likely. In fact, with the expected demand for its goods, Napier has plans to construct five more production plants, which are set to start operating late next year.
(A) To avoid cutting the number of employees, the company will focus on increasing its production levels next year.
(B) Instead of reducing the number of workers, the company will probably hire more, as it is opening more facilities.

네이피어 사는 인력 감축은 없을 가능성이 크다고 발표했다. 사실, 제품의 예상 수요로 인해, 네이피어 사는 내년 말에 가동을 시작할 생산 공장을 5개 더 건설할 계획이다.
(A) 노동자 수 삭감을 피하기 위해, 회사는 내년의 생산 수준을 높이는 데 주력할 것이다.
(B) 근로자 수를 줄이는 대신, 회사는 시설을 더 많이 만들 것이므로 아마도 더 많은 직원을 고용할 것이다.

2 Legislators passed a new environmental policy today that will make major changes to the current regulations. The new policy reflects an effort to lower the levels of contamination in soil and water in the region as well as to improve the overall air quality.
(A) Lawmakers enacted policies to monitor pollution levels.
(B) Lawmakers passed new regulations to get pollution under control.

오늘 국회의원들은 현 규제에 주요한 변화를 가져올 새 환경 정책을 통과시켰다. 새 정책은 전반적인 공기의 질을 향상시킬 뿐만 아니라 지역의 토양과 물의 오염 정도를 낮춰 줄 노력을 반영한 것이다.
(A) 국회위원들은 오염 수준을 감시하기 위한 정책들을 제정했다.
(B) 국회위원들은 오염을 통제하기 위한 새 규제를 통과시켰다.

MAIN STEP 1

p.120

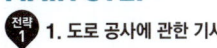 1. 도로 공사에 관한 기사

Columbia Avenue to Undergo Construction

City officials have confirmed that construction will begin on May 2 to widen sections of Columbia Avenue, as the road can no longer accommodate the community's heavy traffic.

The construction will last for approximately four months, with lane closures between Hillview Boulevard and Stanton Street.

Although traffic congestion is expected for the duration of the project, motorists are pleased that driving conditions will be greatly improved upon its completion.

콜롬비아 가, 공사에 들어가다

시 공무원들은 콜롬비아 가의 구획을 확장하는 공사가 5월 2일에 시작될 것이라는 것을 확인해 주었는데, 이는 도로가 지역 사회의 교통 체증을 더 이상 수용할 수 없기 때문이다.

공사는 약 4개월간 지속될 것이며, 힐뷰 대로와 스탠튼 가의 도로가 폐쇄될 것이다.

프로젝트가 지속되는 동안 교통 정체가 예상되지만, 운전자들은 완공과 동시에 운전 환경이 크게 개선될 것에 기뻐하고 있다.

어휘 undergo 겪다, 받다　confirm 확인해 주다　widen 확장하다　accommodate 수용하다　approximately 대략　traffic congestion 교통 정체　duration (지속되는) 기간　motorist (승용차) 운전자

 2. 기업의 새 로고 발표에 대한 기사

GT Electronics Makes Changes

John Miller, CEO of GT Electronics, unveiled a new logo for his corporation at an event held in Chicago on Monday.

The new logo features an orange circle, symbolizing the rising sun. Changing the logo on products and corporate materials is expected to cost nearly $24 million.

Miller and other company officials hope that the contemporary design of the logo will reflect the company's cutting-edge nature.

GT 전자 사, 변화를 꾀하다

GT 전자 사의 최고경영자인 존 밀러 씨는 월요일에 시카고에서 열린 행사에서 회사의 새 로고를 발표했다.

새 로고는 떠오르는 태양을 상징하는 주황색 원이 특징이다. 제품과 기업 자료 로고 변경에 거의 2천 4백만 달러가 들 것으로 예상된다.

밀러 씨와 다른 회사 임원들은 로고의 현대적인 디자인이 회사의 최첨단적인 면을 나타내주길 바라고 있다.

어휘 unveil 발표하다　feature ~의 특징을 이루다　symbolize 상징하다　corporate 기업의　material 자료　nearly 거의　official 임원　contemporary 현대의　reflect 나타내다, 반영하다　cutting-edge 최첨단의

 3. 산업 디자이너의 성공에 대한 기사

During her career as an industrial designer, Maryann Malone became increasingly interested in manufacturing efficiency. Six years ago, she decided to pursue this interest full-time.

She has recently published the results of her investigations in her first book. This work is expected to become the standard text for classrooms and manufacturing executives.

산업 디자이너로서의 경력 동안, 마리안 멀론 씨는 생산 효율성에 점점 더 관심을 가지게 되었다. 6년 전에, 그녀는 이 관심사를 전업으로 밀고 나가기로 결정했다.

그녀는 그녀의 연구 결과를 첫 번째 책으로 출간했다. 이 작품은 학교와 제조업 간부들을 위한 권위 있는 책이 될 것으로 기대된다.

The book has sold over 50,000 copies so far, and the publisher is already planning a second edition.

책은 현재까지 5만 부가 넘게 판매되었으며, 출판사는 벌써 재판을 계획하고 있다.

어휘 increasingly 점점 더 efficiency 효율성 pursue 밀고 나가다, 해 나가다 investigation 조사

MAIN STEP 2   p.121

1 (C)   2 (C)   3 (A)   4 (B)

[1-2] 두 기업의 합병 기사

The leading car manufacturer Napier has negotiated an acquisition agreement with RB Motors and announced it at a press conference yesterday.

For the past five decades, Napier has produced exquisite luxury vehicles, marketing its goods to high-end consumers. However, with the changing economic times, the company was searching for a way to reach a wider market. (1)RB Motors was an attractive option for an acquisition deal, as its famous low-fuel hybrid vehicles are exactly the type of product that's missing from the current Napier line.

By making the acquisition, Napier can utilize RB Motors' technology and channel it through its existing distributors to reach millions of new consumers. Napier reports that downsizing its workforce is not likely. In fact, with the expected demand for its goods, (2)Napier has plans to construct five more production plants, which are set to start operating late next year.

선두적인 자동차 제조업체인 네이피어 사는 RB 모터스 사와 인수 계약을 타결했고 이것을 어제 기자 회견에서 발표했다.

지난 50년 동안, 네이피어 사는 상류층 소비자들을 겨냥해 제품을 출시하며 정교한 고급 차량들을 생산해 왔다. 하지만, 변화하는 경제 상황으로 회사는 더 큰 시장에 도달하기 위한 방법을 모색해 왔다. (1)RB 모터스 사는 인수 계약으로 매력적인 선택권이었는데, RB 모터스 사의 그 유명한 저연료 하이브리드 차량이 바로 현재 네이피어 사의 작업 라인에서 빠져 있는 종류의 상품이기 때문이다.

인수를 함으로써, 네이피어 사는 RB 모터스 사의 기술을 활용하고 이를 기존 유통업자들을 통해 수백만 명의 신규 소비자들에게 다다르게 할 수 있다. 네이피어 사는 인력 감축은 없을 가능성이 크다고 발표했다. 사실, 제품의 예상 수요로 인해, (2)네이피어 사는 내년 말에 가동을 시작할 생산 공장을 5개 더 건설할 계획이다.

어휘 leading 선두적인 negotiate 타결하다, 성사시키다 acquisition 인수 exquisite 정교한, 매우 아름다운 market (상품을) 내놓다 high-end 고급의 utilize 활용하다 channel ~을 통해 보내다 downsize 축소하다 be set to do ~할 준비가 되어 있다

1 RB 모터스 사는 무엇으로 알려져 있는가?
 (A) 고급 차량 판매
 (B) 해외 시장 진입
 (C) 에너지 효율적인 자동차 생산
 (D) 부유한 소비자 겨냥

해설 단서(1)에서 RB 모터스 사의 저연료 하이브리드 차량이 유명하다고 했으므로 정답은 (C).
오답 피하기 (A)와 (D)는 네이피어 사에 대한 내용이기 때문에 오답.
패러프레이징 지문의 famous가 문제에서 known for로, low-fuel hybrid vehicles가 정답에서 energy-efficient cars로 각각 패러프레이징되었다.

2 기사에 따르면, 네이피어 사가 내년에 할 일은?
 (A) 유통업체 추가 모집하기
 (B) 본사 이전하기
 (C) 공장 추가 개설하기
 (D) 기존 조직 감축하기

해설 마지막 문장에 공장을 더 열 것이라는 언급이 있으므로 정답은 (C).
패러프레이징 지문의 production plants가 정답에서는 factories로 패러프레이징되었다.

[3-4] 사업 성공담에 관한 기사

Demir Adnan and Saboro Mazhar, two Turkish-Americans, met in 2004 when they were both students at the Booth School of Business. After discovering their mutual love for food, the two resolved to popularize the Turkish doner kebab throughout Chicago.

The partners opened their first small take-out shop called Take-out Kebab in 2008. Two years later, they decided to try a food truck—and the success was almost immediate. (4)"We opened the truck a month ago, and it became popular right away. We have people waiting in lines down the street and around the corner to be served," Demir Adnan stated in a 2010 interview.

(3)Today, the business has grown to four stores and ten food trucks. The pair hopes to open four more stores and hire seventy new employees over the next five years.

두 터키계 미국인인 데미르 아드난 씨와 사보로 마즈하르 씨는 2004년에 부스 경영 학교에 함께 재학 중일 때 만났다. 음식을 향한 두 사람의 공통적인 애정을 발견한 뒤, 두 사람은 시카고 전역에 터키식 도너 케밥을 대중화시키로 결심했다.

두 동업자는 테이크-아웃 케밥이라고 불리는 그들 최초의 작은 테이크아웃 케밥 가게를 2008년에 개업했다. 2년 뒤, 그들은 푸드 트럭에 도전하기로 결심했고 — 성공은 거의 즉각적이었다. (4)"우리는 한 달 전에 트럭을 개업했고, 바로 유명해졌어요. 사람들이 음식을 사려고 길을 따라 모퉁이까지 줄을 서 있습니다." 2010년의 인터뷰에서 데미르 아드난 씨가 말했다.

(3)오늘날, 사업은 4개의 매장과 10개의 푸드 트럭으로 성장했다. 두 동업자는 앞으로 5년 동안 4개의 매장을 더 개업하고 70명의 새 직원을 고용하게 되기를 희망한다.

어휘 discover 발견하다 mutual 공통적인, 상호의 resolve to do ~하기로 결심하다 (= decide to do) popularize 대중화하다 immediate 즉시의, 즉각적인 around the corner 모퉁이를 돌아

3 기사의 주제는?
(A) 가게의 성장 이야기
(B) 세 사람의 동업
(C) 경영 학교의 역사
(D) 시카고의 식료품점

해설 첫 단락에서 두 동업자가 처음 조우하게 된 계기를 밝히고 있으며, 결론적으로 가게가 성공을 거두었다는 것을 알 수 있다. 두 사람이 함께한 케밥 사업의 성장 이야기를 다루고 있으므로 정답은 (A). 첫 단락만 봐서는 바로 정답을 찾기 어려우므로 전체적인 흐름을 파악해야 한다는 점에 주의하자.

4 테이크-아웃 케밥의 첫 푸드 트럭에 대해 시사된 바는?
(A) 2004년에 개업했다.
(B) 대기 시간이 길었다.
(C) 70명의 직원을 고용했다.
(D) 인도 음식을 제공했다.

해설 테이크-아웃 케밥이 언급된 두 번째 단락에서 손님들의 대기 시간이 길었다는 내용을 확인할 수 있다. 정답은 (B). 단서(4)와 같이 기사문의 인용문이나 인터뷰에서 언급된 사항은 문제화될 확률이 높으니 주의 깊게 읽자.

FINAL STEP

p.122

1 (C)　**2** (B)　**3** (D)　**4** (C)　**5** (C)　**6** (B)

[1-3] 지하철 파업 기사

May 7—The subway employees' strike, which started on Monday, has brought subway operations to a standstill throughout the metropolitan area and has created chaos for commuters. Union representatives called for its members to go on strike after an agreement between the union and government authorities could not be reached. (1) Union workers complain about unfair working

5월 7일—월요일에 시작된 지하철 직원들의 파업은 대도시 지역 전체의 지하철 운영을 멈추게 하였고 통근자들에게 혼란을 일으켰다. 조합의 대표는 조합과 정부 당국 간에 합의에 도달하지 못한 후에 조합원들에게 파업에 돌입할 것을 요청했다. (1)조합원들은 시급이 간신히 최저 임금을 넘는 불공평한 근무 환경에 대해 불만을 표한다. 그들은 또한 기관사, 티켓 검수원, 보안 요원의 임금을 인상할 것을 추구하고 있다. 한편, 정부 공무원은 조합이 타협하고 시의 예산을 고려하는 것을

101

conditions in which hourly pay is barely above the minimum wage. They also seek to increase pay for drivers, ticket takers, and security personnel. Meanwhile, government officials argue that the union refused to compromise and take the city's budget into consideration.

(2)(3)This is not the first time a dispute of this sort has caused a citywide shutdown. Just last year, a similar case arose. Fortunately, parties were able to negotiate an agreement after just one day. With strong emotions and compelling arguments on both sides, it is considered a controversial issue. However, in interviews with local residents, it seems that many people share a common opinion. They want the problem to be resolved so that these breaks in service will stop occurring. "If people can't get to their jobs, the entire local economy will crumble," said commuter Craig Laurel. "At this point, I just want to get to work." Ongoing meetings will be held until common ground can be found.

거부했다고 주장한다.

(2)(3)이러한 종류의 분쟁이 도시 전체의 폐쇄를 야기한 것은 이번이 처음이 아니다. 바로 작년에, 비슷한 경우가 발생했었다. 다행히도, 양측은 불과 하루 만에 계약을 체결할 수 있었다. 양측의 격한 감정과 강력한 논쟁 때문에, 이는 논란이 많은 이슈로 여겨진다. 그러나, 지역 주민들과의 인터뷰에서 많은 사람들이 공통된 견해를 갖고 있는 것 같다. 그들은 이러한 서비스 중단이 그만 일어나도록 문제가 해결되길 바랐다. "만약 사람들이 출근을 못 하게 되면 지역 경제 전체가 무너질 것입니다."라고 통근자 크레이그 로렐 씨는 말했다. "이 시점에서, 저는 단지 일을 하러 가고 싶습니다." 협의점을 찾을 때까지 회의는 계속 열릴 예정이다.

어휘 strike 파업 standstill 멈춤 metropolitan 대도시의 commuter 통근자 union 조합 representative 대표 government authorities 정부 당국 minimum wage 최저 임금 seek to do ~하는 것을 추구하다 refuse to do ~하는 것을 거부하다 compromise 타협하다 take ~ into consideration ~를 고려하다 budget 예산 dispute 분쟁, 논쟁 shutdown 폐쇄 arise 발생하다 party 단체, 정당 compelling 강력한 controversial 논란이 많은 resolve 해결하다 occur 발생하다 crumble 무너지다 common ground 협의점

---

1 파업에 대해 사실인 것은?
(A) 쓰레기 집하 직원들에 의해 진행되고 있다.
(B) 조합으로 더 많은 조합원들을 유치했다.
(C) 노동 임금 인상을 목적으로 한다.
(D) 5월 7일에 시작됐다.

2 작년에 일어난 일에 대해 시사된 바는?
(A) 일주일 이상 지속되었다.
(B) 서비스 중단을 초래했다.
(C) 지역 정치인들의 지지를 받았다.
(D) 해결하는 데 많은 돈이 들었다.

3 [1], [2], [3], [4]로 표시된 위치 중 다음 문장이 들어가기에 가장 알맞은 곳은?
"다행히도, 양측은 불과 하루 만에 계약을 체결할 수 있었다."
(A) [1]
(B) [2]
(C) [3]
(D) [4]

해설 단서(1)에서 조합원들이 낮은 시급에 대해 불평하고 처우 개선을 추구하고 있다고 했으므로 정답은 (C).
오답 피하기 기사가 쓰인 날짜가 5월 7일인데 파업은 월요일에 시작됐다고(which started on Monday) 과거 시제로 이야기하고 있으므로 (D)는 오답이다.

해설 작년의 일에 대해 언급한 두 번째 문단을 보고 문제를 풀어야 한다. 작년에도 도시 전체의 폐쇄가 일어난 적이 있었다고 했으므로 정답은 (B).
패러프레이징 본문의 caused a citywide shutdown이 정답에서 resulted in a service shutdown으로 패러프레이징되었다.

해설 주어진 문장은 양측이 협상에 다다랐다는 내용으로, 해당 문장의 연결어 Fortunately를 통해 그 앞에는 이와 상반되는 내용이 온다는 것을 유추할 수 있다. 단서(3)에서 분쟁에 대해 언급하고, 작년에도 비슷한 경우가 발생했었다고 하므로, 주어진 문장은 [4]에 와야 알맞다. 따라서 정답은 (D).

[4-6] 새 환경 정책 시행 기사

Drastic Changes Expected with Policy Implementation
By Axen Nieves

June 3—Legislators passed a new environmental policy today that will make major changes to the current regulations. (4)The new policy reflects an effort to lower the levels of contamination in soil and water in the region as well as to improve the overall air quality. The policy will take effect on the first of next month and will apply to all commercial enterprises.

Last year, investigators found that many production plants in the area were not following the proper waste disposal procedures for hazardous materials. This allowed chemicals—often at toxic levels—to seep into the soil and water. (5)After the findings of the investigations were released, citizens rallied to impose stricter regulations and politicians took notice.

The manufacturing industry is expected to take the hardest hit under the new regulations, as keeping pollutants under the allowable levels will be a difficult task. This especially applies to plants using older machinery and outdated production methods. Transportation companies, too, will struggle with regulations regarding exhaust emissions, and some have already made plans to file for an extension of the compliance deadline. Large corporations are calling the new policy unfair, saying it is "too much, too soon." (6)Smaller companies have not protested as much, as they can make the necessary adjustments rapidly. A committee has been set up to assess how businesses are coping with the change and to advise lawmakers on future measures.

정책 시행으로 기대되는 급격한 변화
악센 니에브스 작성

6월 3일—오늘 국회의원들은 현 규제에 주요한 변화를 가져올 새 환경 정책을 통과시켰다. (4)새 정책은 전반적인 공기의 질을 향상시킬 뿐만 아니라 지역의 토양과 물의 오염 정도를 낮춰줄 노력을 반영한 것이다. 이 정책은 다음 달 1일부터 효력을 발휘할 것이며, 모든 영리 기업에 적용될 것이다.

작년에, 연구원들은 지역에 있는 많은 생산 공장이 위험 물질에 대한 적절한 폐기물 처리 절차를 따르지 않는다는 것을 발견했다. 이는 화학 물질—종종 유독한 수준의—이 토양과 물에 스며들게 했다. (5)조사 결과가 발표된 후에, 시민들은 더 엄격한 규제를 부과해야 한다며 결집했고 정치가들은 이를 주목했다.

제조업은 새로운 규제하에서 가장 큰 타격을 입을 것으로 예상되는데, 이는 허용치 미만으로 오염 물질을 유지하는 것은 어려운 일이기 때문이다. 이는 특히 오래된 기계와 구식의 생산 방식을 사용하는 공장들에 해당된다. 운수 회사 또한 배기 가스에 대한 규제로 고군분투할 것이며, 몇몇 회사는 이미 준수 기한을 연장해 달라고 신청할 계획을 세웠다. 대기업들은 새로운 정책이 "너무 많고, 너무 빠르다"고 말하면서 그것이 불공평하다고 말하고 있다. (6)소기업들은 필요한 조정을 빨리 할 수 있기 때문에 그만큼 항의하지는 않았다. 기업들이 변화에 어떻게 대처하는지 평가하고 입법자들에게 향후 조치에 대해 자문하기 위하여 위원회가 수립되었다.

어휘 drastic 급격한 implementation 시행, 집행 regulation 규제 reflect 반영하다; 숙고하다 contamination 오염 overall 전반적인 take effect 효력을 발휘하다 disposal 처리 procedure 절차 hazardous 위험한 allow ~ to do ~가 …하는 것을 허락하다 seep into ~로 스며들다 investigation 조사 release 발표하다 rally 결집하다 impose 부과하다 strict 엄격한 take the hardest hit 가장 큰 타격을 입다 pollutant 오염 물질 allowable 허용되는 outdated 구식인 struggle with ~로 고군분투하다 exhaust emission 배기 가스 file for ~을 신청하다 extension 연장 compliance 준수 assess 평가하다 cope with ~에 대처하다

4 기사에 따르면, 정책이 시행된 이유는?
 (A) 유해 물질을 제거하기 위해서
 (B) 자원 부족에 대처하기 위해서
 (C) 환경 오염을 줄이기 위해서
 (D) 더 많은 재활용을 장려하기 위해서

해설 새 정책의 도입 배경을 묻는 질문이므로 기사 초반에서 단서를 찾아야 한다. 단서(4)에 따르면, 정책은 공기의 질을 향상시키고 토양, 수질의 오염 정도를 낮추기 위해 시행되는 것이므로 정답은 (C).

패러프레이징 지문의 lower the levels of contamination in soil and water가 정답에서 reduce environmental pollution으로 패러프레이징되었다.

5 정책에 대해 시사된 바는?
(A) 상업 및 주거 단지에 적용된다.
(B) 6월 1일에 발효되었다.
(C) 주민들에 의해 장려되었다.
(D) 운송업에 가장 큰 영향을 미친다.

해설 단서(5)에 따르면, 지역의 폐기물 처리 절차 조사 결과를 보고 시민들이 더 엄격한 규제를 부과해야 한다고 주장하며 집회를 열었으며 정치가들이 이에 주목하여 새 정책을 만든 것이므로 정답은 (C).
오답 피하기 새로운 정책의 시행으로 인해 가장 큰 타격을 입는 것은 제조업이므로 (D)는 오답.

6 소기업들에 대해 언급된 것은?
(A) 시설을 개선하지 않아도 될 것이다.
(B) 더 빨리 변화할 수 있을 것이다.
(C) 준수 기한이 더 길다.
(D) 규제를 따르기 위한 자금이 없을 수도 있다.

해설 단서(6)에 따르면 소기업들은 대기업보다 필요한 조정을 더 빨리 할 수 있다고 했으므로 정답은 (B).
패러프레이징 지문의 can make the necessary adjustments rapidly가 정답에서 be able to make the change more quickly로 패러프레이징되었다.

FURTHER STEP
p.124

1 (C)   2 (A)   3 (D)   4 (C)   5 (C)

[1-5] 인쇄소 소개 기사 & 기사의 오류 정정 요청 이메일 & 수익 보고서

Local Spotlight: Quinn Printing
By Linda Pierce

(1D)Quinn Printing, founded a decade ago by Alan Quinn, has steadily grown its customer base by providing efficient service and high-quality printed materials. Mr. Quinn opened his first shop here in Meadow City, and he later expanded the business to three more sites. The company serves community groups, businesses, schools, and individuals who need professional printing services. (1A)Customers can bring in their own graphics or get help from one of the on-site designers. In addition, (1B)the business has recently launched a Web site, on which customers can place orders and have them delivered without ever having to stop by the store in person.

All locations can print brochures, flyers, business cards, and photos. In addition, (3-1)Meadow City and Fairmont have equipment for printing large vinyl banners. While Carterville and Marshall do not provide this service on-site, they can process the order and have the banner sent by mail.

In a recent phone interview, owner Alan Quinn talked about his strategy for choosing the locations of his stores. "(4-1)While we profit most from cities with many concerts and theater productions, we want to make sure we are in the right place to serve small business needs as well." Although opening a fifth branch is not planned at this time, Mr. Quinn says it's a strong possibility in the future.

지역 집중 조명: 퀸 프린팅 사
린다 피어스 작성

(1D)10년 전 앨런 퀸 씨가 설립한 퀸 프린팅 사는 효율적인 서비스와 양질의 인쇄물을 제공함으로써 꾸준히 고객층을 늘려 오고 있다. 퀸 씨는 이곳 메도우 시에 첫 매장을 열었으며, 이후에 추가로 세 곳에 사업을 확장했다. 이 회사는 전문 인쇄 서비스를 필요로 하는 지역 단체와 사업체, 학교, 개인들에게 서비스를 제공한다. (1A)고객들은 자신들의 그래픽을 직접 가져오거나, 사내 디자이너들로부터 도움을 얻을 수 있다. 게다가, (1B)이 업체는 최근에는 웹사이트를 개설했는데, 이 웹사이트에서 고객들은 직접 매장에 들를 필요 없이 주문을 하고 배송을 시킬 수 있다.

모든 지점에서 안내 책자 및 광고 전단지, 명함, 사진 인쇄가 가능하다. 또한, (3-1)메도우 시와 페어몬트는 대형 비닐 현수막을 인쇄할 수 있는 장비를 갖추고 있다. 카터빌과 마샬에서는 매장에서 이 서비스를 제공하지는 않지만, 주문을 받아 현수막을 우편으로 보내 주는 것이 가능하다.

최근의 전화 인터뷰에서, 소유주 앨런 퀸 씨는 그의 매장 위치 선정 전략에 대해서 말했다. "(4-1)우리가 콘서트 및 연극 공연이 많은 도시들에서 가장 많은 이윤을 얻고 있기는 하지만, 소기업의 수요 또한 맞출 수 있는 적절한 장소에도 꼭 있었으면 합니다." 현재 5호점 개장은 아직 계획된 바 없지만, 퀸 씨는 개장 가능성이 앞으로 매우 크다고 밝히고 있다.

To: Linda Pierce <l.pierce@meadowcitytimes.com>
From: Alan Quinn <alan@quinnprinting.net>
Date: May 4
Subject: Quinn Printing article

Dear Ms. Pierce,

I read your recent article in the *Meadow City Times* about my business, Quinn Printing. I liked the quote you selected from our phone interview. Unfortunately, I'm afraid there's a piece of information in your article that is wrong. The article said that two of our branches don't have banner printing equipment. (3-2)In fact, we are now using this equipment on-site at the Carterville location. (2) Please change this information in the online version of your article as soon as possible.

Sincerely,

Alan Quinn

Quinn Printing (5)Quarterly Profits Report

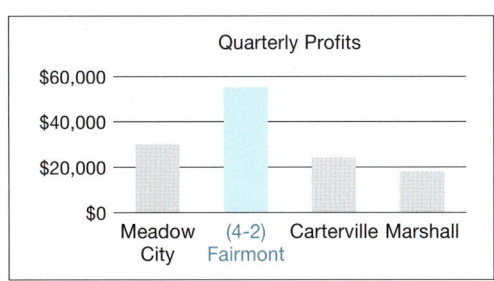

Figures compiled by Virginia Alexander. Staffing and building costs are factored for each branch individually. Advertising costs are spread equally among the four branches. (5)Released April 2.

3 매장 내에서 현수막 인쇄기를 이용할 수 없는 곳은?
(A) 메도우 시
(B) 페어몬트
(C) 카터빌
(D) 마샬

4 페어몬트에 대해 추론할 수 있는 것은?
(A) 시내에 인쇄소가 하나밖에 없다.
(B) 인구가 증가할 것으로 예상된다.
(C) 공연을 많이 개최한다.
(D) 퀸 프린팅 사의 가장 오래된 지점이 있다.

5 다음 보고서가 발표될 확률이 가장 높은 때는?
(A) 5월
(B) 6월
(C) 7월
(D) 12월

[해설] 기사와 이메일 두 지문의 내용을 모두 참조해야 하는 연계 문제이다. 기사에서는 메도우 시와 페어몬트에 이 장비가 있다고 했고, 이메일에서 퀸 씨는 카터빌에도 현재는 이 장비가 갖춰져 있다고 했다. 따라서 정답은 (D)이다.

[해설] 기사와 수익 보고서의 내용을 종합해서 풀어야 한다. 기사에서 콘서트 및 극장 공연이 많은 도시에 있는 지점의 수익이 가장 높다고 했는데, 수익 보고서를 보면 가장 많은 수익을 얻는 곳은 페어몬트 지점이다. 따라서 페어몬트에서 공연이 많이 열린다고 짐작할 수 있으므로 정답은 (C).

[해설] Quarterly Profits Report(분기 수익 보고서)라는 제목이 말해 주듯이 이 수익 보고서는 분기별로, 즉 3달마다 작성되는 것이다. 이 보고서가 4월에 공개되었다고 했으므로, 다음 보고서 공개는 3달 후인 7월이다. 정답은 (C).

UNIT 16 회람/공지

PRE-STEP
p.127

A 1 (B) 2 (B) 3 (A) 4 (B) 5 (A) 6 (A) 7 (B) 8 (A) 9 (B)
   10 (B) 11 (B) 12 (A) 13 (A) 14 (A) 15 (B)

B 1 (B) 2 (A)

A
1 (B) assume, 그룹 대표 역할을 맡다
2 (B) turn in, 신청서를 제출하다
3 (A) streamline, 절차를 간소화하다
4 (B) prevent, 작업자들의 부상을 방지하다
5 (A) keep, 자신을 양호한 상태로 유지하다
6 (A) store, 원자재를 보관하다
7 (B) collaborate, 서로 협업하다
8 (A) allocate, 연간 예산을 할당하다
9 (B) approximately, 대략 2주 동안 지속되다
10 (B) nearly, 15%에 가까운 매출 신장
11 (B) service, 3일간 이용 불가능하다
12 (A) arrangements, 장소를 마련하다
13 (A) malfunction, 기기 오작동을 줄이다
14 (A) efficiency, 효율성을 극대화하다
15 (B) appreciate, ~의 인내에 감사하다

B
1 While the work itself was fine, the maintenance employee dripped paint on the floor of the room where he was painting and didn't clean it up. He also left some empty paint cans there.
(A) The painting job looked messy even though all of the paint was used.
(B) **The worker did a good job on the project but left a mess behind.**

작업 자체는 괜찮았지만, 관리 직원이 페인트칠하던 방바닥에 페인트를 흘리고 닦지 않았습니다. 또한 그곳에 페인트통들도 두고 갔습니다.
(A) 페인트 전부가 사용되었음에도 불구하고 페인트 작업이 지저분해 보였습니다.
(B) 작업자는 프로젝트는 잘해주셨지만 현장을 지저분하게 해놓고 가셨습니다.

2 From now on, you will no longer report maintenance issues to the rental office. Instead, you should fill out an online form at www.tcmaintenance.com.
(A) **We are changing the method for making maintenance requests, which will now be done through an online system.**
(B) We want to make maintenance work easier by allowing you to check the online system for updates.

지금부터는 더 이상 보수 문제를 임대 사무실에 신고하지 마십시오. 대신에, www.tcmaintenance.com에서 온라인 양식을 작성하셔야 합니다.
(A) 저희는 보수 요청을 하는 방법을 바꾸고 있는데, 이것은 이제 온라인 시스템을 통해 이루어질 것입니다.
(B) 저희는 여러분이 온라인 시스템에서 업데이트된 사항을 확인할 수 있도록 함으로써 보수 작업을 더 용이하게 하고자 합니다.

MAIN STEP 1
p.128

 단편 소설 대회 개최를 알리는 공지

NOTICE	공지
The Louisville Literary Society is ①holding its first ever short story contest.	루이빌 문학회는 ①문학회 최초로 단편 소설 대회를 개최합니다.

107

To register, ②go to www.louisvillels.org/shortstory. There, you can print your own copy of the registration application.

③The deadline is March 18 and judges will assess the submissions on the following day.

어휘 registration 등록 application 신청(서) assess 평가하다 submission 제출(물) following (시간상으로) 다음의

등록하기 위해서는, ②www.louisvillels.org/shortstory에 접속해 주세요. 거기서 등록 신청서 사본을 인쇄하실 수 있습니다.

③마감일은 3월 18일이며 심사위원들은 다음 날 제출물을 평가할 것입니다.

① 공지가 쓰인 이유는?
→ 대회를 알리기 위해

② 사람들이 등록 양식을 얻을 수 있는 방법은?
→ 웹사이트에 방문함으로써

③ 3월 19일에 일어나게 될 일은?
→ 작품 심사

해설 첫 단락에 단편 소설 대회 개최를 알리는 문구가 나오므로 이 공지의 목적은 대회를 알리는 것이다.

해설 두 번째 단락에 웹사이트에서 등록 신청서 사본 인쇄가 가능하다고 명시되어 있다.

해설 참가 신청 마감일은 3월 18일이며, 그 다음날 작품들이 평가된다고 했으므로 3월 19일에는 작품 심사가 있을 것이다.

전략 2 세미나 개최를 알리는 회람

To: Department Managers
From: Elle Lee, Director
Subject: Annual Seminar

The IT seminar will be held on Friday, November 8. Those who wish to participate should let me know by tomorrow. Please direct any questions that you have to the program coordinator, Maria Rey.

어휘 annual 연례의 participate 참가하다 direct ~ to ~을 …로 보내다

수신: 부서장들
발신: 엘 리, 관리자
제목: 연례 세미나

IT 세미나가 11월 8일 금요일에 열릴 예정입니다. 참가를 희망하는 분들은 내일까지 제게 알려주세요. 질문이 있으신 분은 프로그램 담당자인 마리아 레이 씨에게 직접 전달해 주세요.

질문을 전달받아야 하는 사람은?
(A) 마리아 레이, 프로그램 담당자
(B) 엘 리, 관리자

해설 회람을 보낸 사람은 리 씨이지만 회람과 관련된 질문을 전달받아야 하는 사람은 레이 씨이다.

MAIN STEP 2   p.129

1 (D)   2 (C)   3 (C)   4 (D)

[1-2] 엘리베이터 이용 제한에 관한 공지

(1)NOTICE TO RESIDENTS

Starting March 1, the two passenger elevators in our front lobby will be out of service for three days for repairs and upgrades.

We kindly ask that all residents use the stairs during this time. For anyone incapable of walking upstairs due to disability or injury, you may ride the north elevator in the rear of the building.

(1)주민 여러분께 드리는 공지

3월 1일부터, 정문 로비의 승객용 엘리베이터 두 대가 수리 및 기능 향상을 위해 3일간 이용 불가능할 것입니다.

이 기간 동안 모든 주민 여러분께서는 계단을 이용해 주시기를 부탁 드립니다. 장애나 부상 때문에 계단을 오르지 못하는 분들은, 건물 뒤에 있는 북쪽 엘리베이터를 타시면 됩니다.

(2)Normally, this elevator is used solely for the transportation of goods, but it will be accessible to certain people for those three days.

(2)보통, 이 엘리베이터는 물품 운반을 위해서만 사용되지만, 이 3일간은 특정 분들이 이용하실 수 있을 것입니다.

어휘 passenger 승객 out of service 이용[서비스] 불가능 상태인 disability 장애 injury 부상, 상처 rear 뒤 solely 오로지, 단지 transportation 운반, 수송 accessible 이용[접근] 가능한

---

1 이 공지의 대상은?
(A) 정비사들
(B) 배송 기사들
(C) 전기 기사들
(D) 세입자들

해설 공지의 제목과 내용을 통해서 이 공지가 주민들을 대상으로 하는 안내문임을 알 수 있다. 따라서 정답은 (D).
패러프레이징 지문의 RESIDENTS가 정답에서는 Tenants로 패러프레이징되었다.

2 북쪽 엘리베이터에 대해 시사된 바는?
(A) 안전 기준을 충족시키지 못했다.
(B) 건물 계단 근처에 있다.
(C) 보통은 사람들을 실어 나르지 않는다.
(D) 특정 암호를 필요로 한다.

해설 지문에서 북쪽 엘리베이터가 언급된 부분을 찾아야 한다. 마지막 단락에서 북쪽 엘리베이터는 원래 물품 운반을 위해서만 사용된다고 했으므로 정답은 (C).
패러프레이징 지문의 is used solely for the transportation of goods가 정답에서는 does not usually transport people로 패러프레이징되었다.

[3-4] 워크숍에 관한 회람

To: Sales Department
From: Karl McFerren
Subject: Motivational speaker Adam Bock

Because many of you have requested more opportunities for professional development, we have hired motivational speaker Adam Bock to present a workshop on June 29.

He will teach you how to stand out and get your message heard. (3)He was highly recommended by my former colleague, Ashley Varga, who said her team saw sales increase by nearly 15% after using his techniques. If you would like to sign up, you must do so no later than June 15 so that we can make arrangements for the venue.

(4)Please submit any questions that you may have to my administrative assistant, Joann Moyers. This event is not mandatory, but we highly encourage everyone to take advantage of it.

수신: 영업부
발신: 칼 맥퍼렌
제목: 동기 부여 강사 애덤 보크

많은 분들께서 더 많은 전문성 개발 기회를 요청하셔서, 저희는 동기 부여 강사인 애덤 보크 씨를 기용해 6월 29일에 워크숍을 제공하기로 했습니다.

그분은 여러분들에게 눈에 띄는 방법과 여러분들의 메시지가 잘 전달되게 하는 방법을 알려 주실 것입니다. (3)그분은 제 전 직장 동료인 애쉴리 바르가 씨로부터 적극 추천을 받았으며, 애쉴리 씨는 그녀의 팀이 그분의 기법을 활용한 후 15%에 가까운 매출 신장을 목격했다고 했습니다. 등록을 원하신다면 늦어도 6월 15일까지는 등록하셔서 저희가 장소를 준비할 수 있게 해 주시기 바랍니다.

(4)질문이 있으시면 제 행정 보조인 조앤 모이어스 씨에게 제출해 주십시오. 이 행사는 의무는 아니지만, 저희는 모든 분들께서 이를 이용하시기를 강력히 권장합니다.

어휘 motivational 동기를 부여하는 stand out 눈에 띄다, 두드러지다 no later than 늦어도 ~까지는 make arrangements for ~을 준비하다 venue 장소 mandatory 의무적인 encourage 권장하다 take advantage of ~을 이용하다

---

3 보크 씨에 대해 시사된 바는?
(A) 워크숍에 등록했다.
(B) 행정 보조이다.
(C) 바르가 씨가 그의 업무를 추천했다.
(D) 그의 팀 매출을 15% 증가시켰다.

해설 특정 대상에 대한 질문이므로 지문에서 보크 씨에 대해 언급된 중간 부분을 유심히 봐야 한다. 단서(3)에 따르면 애쉴리 바르가 씨가 보크 씨를 추천하였으므로 정답은 (C).
오답 피하기 직업이 행정 보조인 사람은 모이어스 씨이므로 (B)는 오답이다. 15% 오른 것은 보크 씨의 팀 매출이 아니라 바르가 씨의 소속인 영업부의 매출이므로 (D) 역시 오답.

4 문의 사항에 대해 연락해야 하는 사람은?

(A) 애쉴리 바르가
(B) 칼 맥퍼렌
(C) 애덤 보크
(D) 조앤 모이어스

해설 회람의 마지막 부분에서 워크숍에 대한 질문은 조앤 모이어스 씨에게 보내달라고 하였으므로 정답은 (D). 회람에는 수신자/발신자 정보가 상단에 있는데, 이 지문처럼 여러 인물이 등장하는 경우 혼동하기 쉬우므로 유의해야 한다.

FINAL STEP
p.130

1 (A) 2 (B) 3 (A) 4 (B) 5 (C) 6 (C)

[1-3] 공장 보수 공사를 알리는 공지

NOTICE

(3)Renovations to our factory will begin on October 1 and will affect Sectors C and D. (1)The purpose of the project is to deal with outdated equipment, which is contributing to a higher level of defective electronics coming out of our facility. Some of the machinery will be replaced completely, while the rest will be disassembled, cleaned thoroughly, and reassembled. (2)This should reduce equipment malfunction in the future as well as help prevent injuries to workers. The refurbished interior will also have a designated space for storing raw materials in a climate-controlled area to keep them in good condition.

(3)The renovation will last approximately two weeks, and we will provide updates as it progresses. We appreciate your patience and cooperation during this time.

공지

(3)우리 공장의 보수 공사가 10월 1일에 시작되어 C와 D 구역에 영향을 미칠 것입니다. (1)이 프로젝트의 목적은 구식 장비를 처리하는 것으로, 이 장비는 우리 시설에서 높은 수치의 불량 전자 제품이 나오는 한 원인이 되고 있습니다. 몇몇 기계는 완전히 교체될 것이며, 나머지는 해체되어 완전히 청소가 된 후 다시 조립될 것입니다. (2)이는 작업자들의 부상을 방지하는 데 도움이 될 뿐 아니라 나중에 있을 기기 오작동도 줄여 줍니다. 또한 재단장된 내부에는 원자재를 좋은 상태로 보관하기 위해 냉난방이 되는 구역에 이것들을 보관할 수 있는 지정 공간이 생길 것입니다.

(3)보수는 대략 2주 동안 지속될 것이고 진행됨에 따라 최신 정보를 제공하겠습니다. 이 기간 동안 여러분의 인내와 협조에 감사드립니다.

어휘 renovation 보수 affect 영향을 미치다 deal with ~을 처리하다; 다루다 outdated 구식인(= old-fashioned) contribute to ~의 한 원인이 되다, ~에 기여하다 defective 결함이 있는 electronics 전자 제품 disassemble 해체하다 thoroughly 완전히 reassemble 재조립하다 malfunction 오작동 injury 부상 refurbish 재단장하다 designate 지정하다 store 보관하다 raw material 원자재 climate-controlled 냉난방이 되는 approximately 대략

1 공지가 의도된 대상으로 가장 알맞은 사람은?
  (A) 생산 시설의 직원
  (B) 프로젝트의 인테리어 디자이너
  (C) 전자 제품 공장에 온 방문객
  (D) 공사 작업반의 인부

해설 공지문의 전반적인 내용이 공장 시설의 보수 공사를 알리는 것임을 파악해야 한다. 단서(1)에 따르면 보수 공사의 목적은 구식 장비를 처리하는 것이라 하였고 이어서 그 이유가 제시되므로, 공지가 생산 시설 직원을 대상으로 쓰였음을 알 수 있다. 정답은 (A).

2 보수 공사의 이점으로 언급된 것은?
  (A) 정부 규제를 따르는 것
  (B) 직원들이 다치지 않도록 하는 것
  (C) 사업체에 새 고객들을 유치하는 것
  (D) 원자재 비용을 절약하는 것

해설 단서(2)에서 보수 공사를 통해 작업자의 부상을 방지한다고 하였으므로 정답은 (B).
패러프레이징 지문의 prevent injuries to workers가 정답에서는 Preventing employees from getting hurt로 패러프레이징되었다.

3 프로젝트가 완료될 것으로 예상되는 때는?
(A) 10월 중순
(B) 10월 말
(C) 11월 중순
(D) 연말

해설 흩어진 단서를 종합해서 풀어야 하는 문제이다. 공장의 보수 공사가 시작되는 때는 10월 1일이며 약 2주간 지속된다고 했으므로 10월 중순쯤에 프로젝트가 완료된다는 것을 알 수 있다. 따라서 정답은 (A).

[4-6] 프로젝트 팀 운영을 알리는 회람

To: All employees
From: Richard Neely, Branch Manager
Date: March 8
Subject: To all employees

I'm writing to alert all employees to an opportunity to improve the viability of our company while reducing unnecessary expenditures. Currently, our spending on outsourcing is approximately 30% more than what was allocated in this year's budget. During last week's managerial meeting, (4)the department heads expressed unanimous support for creating a task force to address the problem of overspending on external services. I urge your involvement in this important project.

(5A)The task force will be made up of 12 members and one leader. (6)There will be at least one representative from each department. These people will collaborate with one another to find ways to deal with managing team members' time to maximize efficiency. This will be done by assigning work to their colleagues, observing productivity levels, and making adjustments according to individual employee strengths and weaknesses.

(5B)The task force will be modeled after those already used by some of the largest corporations in the industry, and Margaret Diaz has agreed to assume the role of group leader. If you are interested in finding out more about the responsibilities involved, please contact Margaret directly. To apply to take part in the task force, pick up an application from the reception desk. The deadline for turning in applications is the end of this month. (5D)Task force members will receive a quarterly bonus for their efforts. I hope all of you will consider participating in this essential undertaking. Thank you for your consideration.

수신: 전 직원
발신: 지점장, 리차드 닐리
날짜: 3월 8일
제목: 전 직원들께

불필요한 지출을 줄이면서 우리 회사의 생존력을 향상시킬 기회를 전 직원 여러분께 알리기 위해 이 글을 씁니다. 현재 우리가 외부 위탁에 쓰는 지출은 올해 예산에 할당된 것의 약 30% 이상입니다. 지난주 경영 회의 때, (4)부서장들은 외주 서비스에 대한 낭비 문제를 해결하기 위해 프로젝트 팀을 만드는 것에 만장일치의 지지를 표했습니다. 이 중요한 프로젝트에 여러분의 참여를 강력히 권고합니다.

(5A)프로젝트 팀은 12명의 팀원과 한 명의 대표로 이루어질 것입니다. (6)각 부서에서 최소한 한 명의 대표가 있어야 합니다. 이 사람들은 효율성을 극대화하기 위해 팀원들의 시간을 관리할 방법을 찾기 위하여 서로 협업하게 될 것입니다. 이는 그들의 동료들에게 일을 할당하고, 생산성 수준을 관찰하고, 직원 개개인의 강점과 약점에 따라 조정을 함으로써 이루어질 것입니다.

(5B)프로젝트 팀은 업계 내 대기업에서 이미 활용된 사례들을 본떠 만들어질 것이며, 마가렛 디아즈 씨가 팀의 대표 역할을 맡기로 동의했습니다. 관련된 책무에 대해 더 아는 것에 관심이 있다면 마가렛 씨에게 직접 연락하십시오. 프로젝트 팀 참여에 지원하시려면 안내 데스크에서 신청서를 가져가십시오. 신청서 제출 기한은 이번 달 말입니다. (5D)프로젝트 팀 팀원들은 그들의 수고에 대해 분기별 상여금을 받게 될 것입니다. 여러분 모두가 이 중요한 일에 참여하는 것을 고려해 보길 바랍니다. 고려해 주셔서 감사합니다.

어휘 **alert** 알리다; 기민한 **viability** 생존력 **expenditure** 지출(= spending) **allocate** 할당하다(= assign) **budget** 예산 **unanimous** 만장일치의 **task force** (특정 문제를 해결하기 위한) 프로젝트 팀 **address** (문제, 상황 등을) 다루다 **overspending** 낭비 **urge** 강력히 권고하다 **involvement** 참여 **collaborate with** ~와 협업하다 **efficiency** 효율성 **adjustment** 조정 **model after** ~을 본떠서 만들다 **assume** 맡다 **turn in** ~을 제출하다(= submit) **quarterly** 분기별의 **effort** 수고, 노력 **undertaking** 일

4 회람의 목적은?
   (A) 프로젝트 팀 팀원들의 업무에 대해 감사하기 위해
   (B) 직원들이 팀에 참여하도록 격려하기 위해
   (C) 동료들이 경영회의에 참여하도록 요청하기 위해
   (D) 할당량을 채운 팀을 축하기 위해

   해설 회람은 회사의 불필요한 지출을 줄이기 위해 프로젝트 팀을 만들기로 했다는 것을 전 직원에게 알리고 참여를 독려하는 내용이므로 정답은 (B).

5 프로젝트 팀에 대해 언급되지 않은 것은?
   (A) 13명의 인원으로 구성될 것이다.
   (B) 마가렛 디아즈 씨가 지휘할 것이다.
   (C) 일주일에 한 번 회의를 열 것이다.
   (D) 팀원들은 보상을 받을 것이다.

   해설 12명의 팀원과 1명의 대표로 팀이 이루어진다 하였으므로 총 인원은 13명이다. 또한, 마가렛 디아즈 씨가 대표직을 맡는다고 했으며, 팀원들은 분기별로 상여금을 받게 될 것이라 했으므로 (A), (B), (D) 모두 지문에서 언급된 내용이다. 하지만 회의 주기에 대한 내용은 나오지 않았기 때문에 정답은 (C).

6 지원서에 대해 암시된 것은?
   (A) 4월 말까지 제출하면 된다.
   (B) 닐리 씨에게 받아가면 된다.
   (C) 모든 부서로부터 접수될 것이다.
   (D) 상사에게 서명 받아야 한다.

   해설 단서(6)에 따르면, 각 부서에서 최소 한 명의 대표가 있어야 한다고 했으므로 정답은 (C).
   오답 피하기 공지문이 쓰인 때가 3월 8일이고, 제출 기한이 이달 말까지라고 하였으므로 (A)는 오답. 지원서는 닐리 씨가 아니라 안내데스크에서 배포한다고 했으므로 (B) 역시 오답이다.

FURTHER STEP

p.132

1 (B) 2 (B) 3 (D) 4 (A) 5 (D)

[1-5] 수리 요청 방법 변경 공지 & 보수 요청 양식 & 보수 작업에 대한 설문 조사

NOTICE TO ALL TENANTS

Cochran Towers has hired a new maintenance company, TC Maintenance, to handle all building repairs. (1)From now on, you will no longer report maintenance issues to the rental office. Instead, you should fill out an online form at www.tcmaintenance.com. The new system will streamline the process as well as allow you to make requests at your convenience, rather than only when the rental office is open. You should begin using the online system from March 1. If you call the rental office with a maintenance request, we will (2)direct you to visit the site.

(3-1)For tenants with pets, please be aware that for the safety of its employees, TC Maintenance does not allow pets (excluding birds kept in cages and fish) to be kept in the apartment during repair work unless the homeowner is present. If you will not be home during the repair work, you must remove your pet from the apartment. Should you fail to do so, TC Maintenance will not perform the work.

If you have any questions, please feel free to call the rental office at 555-3110.

모든 세입자에게 알립니다

코크란 타워즈에서는 모든 건물 수리를 처리할 새로운 관리회사로 TC 메인터넌스를 고용했습니다. (1)지금부터는 더 이상 보수 문제를 임대 사무실에 신고하지 마십시오. 대신에, www.tcmaintenance.com에서 온라인 양식을 작성하셔야 합니다. 새로운 시스템은 임대 사무실이 열려 있을 때만이 아니라, 여러분이 편할 때 요청하실 수 있도록 해 드리고 또한 절차도 간소하게 해줄 겁니다. 3월 1일부터 온라인 시스템 사용이 시작됩니다. 임대 사무실에 관리 요청 건으로 전화하시면, 사이트를 방문하도록 (2)안내해 드릴 것입니다.

(3-1)애완동물을 키우는 세입자들께는, TC 메인터넌스에서는 직원들의 안전을 위해서 집주인이 계시지 않을 경우 수리 작업 동안 아파트 내에 애완동물을 두는 것(새장에 있는 새와 물고기는 제외)을 허용하지 않는다는 것을 알려 드립니다. 수리 작업 동안 집에 계시지 않을 경우, 애완동물은 아파트에서 내보내셔야 합니다. 그렇게 하지 않을 경우, TC 메인터넌스는 작업을 수행하지 않습니다.

문의 사항이 있으시면, 언제든지 555-3110로 전화를 걸어 임대 사무실로 연락 주십시오.

Maintenance Request Form – TC Maintenance

Next Available Date for Repair Work: March 18 / 10 A.M. – 12:30 P.M.
In case of a maintenance emergency (gas leak, flooding, etc.), call (734) 555-6688 immediately.

Name: Andrea Weston   Phone Number: (734) 555-2950
Building: Cochran Towers   Unit #: 403
Description of Needed Repair(s):

> The faucet in the kitchen sink keeps dripping no matter how tightly I try to turn it off, the towel rack in the bathroom has become detached from the wall, and (4-2)the bedroom ceiling needs to be repainted because the paint is flaking off.

(3-2)Do you have any pets? Yes   Pet Type(s): Dog
Will you be home at the time and date indicated above? No

TC Maintenance Feedback Survey

Your opinions matter! Please take a moment to tell us about your recent maintenance work.

Waiting time for receiving repairs:
POOR   FAIR   AVERAGE   (GOOD)   EXCELLENT
(5)Ease of using request form:
POOR   FAIR   AVERAGE   GOOD   (EXCELLENT)
Professionalism of repair person:
(POOR)   FAIR   AVERAGE   GOOD   EXCELLENT
Quality of work:
POOR   FAIR   AVERAGE   (GOOD)   EXCELLENT

Comments: While the work itself was fine, (4-1)the maintenance employee dripped paint on the floor of the room where he was painting and didn't clean it up. He also left some empty paint cans there.

FOR OFFICE USE ONLY
Date: March 18   Building: Cochran Towers
(4-1)Employee: Daniel Derose   Work Order #: 485606

보수 요청서 – TC 메인터넌스

다음 가능한 수리 작업 날짜: 3월 18일 / 오전 10시부터 오후 12시 30분까지
긴급 보수(가스 누출, 하수 넘침 등)가 발생할 경우, 즉시 (734) 555-6688로 전화하십시오.

이름: 안드레아 웨스턴   전화번호: (734) 555-2950
건물: 코크란 타워즈   호수: 403

필요한 수리 작업 내용:

> 아무리 꽉 잠그려 해도 주방 싱크대 수도꼭지에서 계속 물이 떨어지고, 욕실 수건걸이가 벽에서 떨어졌으며, (4-2)침실 천장의 페인트칠이 벗겨져 다시 페인트칠 해야 합니다.

(3-2)애완동물이 있습니까? 네   애완동물 종류: 개
위에 명시된 날짜와 시간에 댁에 계십니까? 아니오

TC 메인터넌스 피드백 설문 조사

여러분의 의견은 중요합니다! 잠시 시간을 내어 여러분이 받으신 최근의 보수 작업에 대해 말씀해 주십시오.

수리 대기 시간:
나쁨   나쁘지 않음   보통   (좋음)   매우 좋음
(5)요청서 이용의 간편성:
나쁨   나쁘지 않음   보통   좋음   (매우 좋음)
수리 기사의 전문성:
(나쁨)   나쁘지 않음   보통   좋음   매우 좋음
작업 품질:
나쁨   나쁘지 않음   보통   (좋음)   매우 좋음

의견: 작업 자체는 괜찮았지만, (4-1)관리 직원이 페인트칠하던 방바닥에 페인트를 흘리고 닦지 않았습니다. 또한 그곳에 페인트통도 두고 갔습니다.

사무실 전용
날짜: 3월 18일   건물: 코크란 타워즈
(4-1)직원: 대니얼 데로스   작업 요청 번호: 485606

어휘 tenant 세입자 maintenance 유지 보수, 관리 fill out a form 양식을 작성하다 streamline 간소화하다 at one's convenience ~가 편리한 때에 direct 안내하다, 지시하다 aware 알고 있는 excluding ~을 제외하고 in case of ~이 발생한 경우 leak 누출 flooding 범람 description 서술 faucet 수도꼭지 drip 방울방울 흐르다 detached 분리된, 떨어진 flake off 벗겨지다, 떨어지다 matter 중요하다 ease 용이함, 편의성

---

1 공지의 목적은?
(A) 건물 보수 작업을 알리기 위해
(B) 절차상의 변경 사항을 설명하기 위해
(C) 신입 직원을 소개하기 위해
(D) 업무에 대한 피드백을 요청하기 위해

해설 공지의 목적을 묻는 문제이므로, 도입부를 중점적으로 살펴야 한다. From now on, will no longer, Instead 등의 표현에서 앞으로 변경 사항이 있음을 알리고 있다는 것을 알 수 있다. 건물 보수 문제를 신고하는 절차상의 변경 사항에 대한 것이므로 정답은 (B).

2 공지에서, 1단락, 일곱 번째 줄의 어휘 "direct"와 의미상 가장 유사한 것은?
(A) 훈련시키다
(B) 지시하다
(C) 감독하다
(D) 초점을 맞추다

3 웨스턴 씨의 애완동물에 대해 추론할 수 있는 것은?
(A) 낮 동안에는 대개 우리 안에 넣어 둔다.
(B) 그녀의 아파트에 손상을 입혔다.
(C) 더 많은 임대 보증금을 내게 했다.
(D) 수리 작업 동안 그녀의 아파트에 없었다.

4 웨스턴 씨에 따르면, 데로스 씨가 어질러 놓고 간 곳은?
(A) 침실
(B) 주방
(C) 거실
(D) 욕실

5 웨스턴 씨가 가장 만족한 부분은?
(A) 직원의 자격
(B) 완료된 수리 작업
(C) 응답 시간
(D) 요청 절차

해설 지문에서 direct는 '(~하도록) 지시하다'라는 뜻이므로 정답은 (B).
오답 피하기 direct에 '감독하다'라는 뜻도 있으므로 문맥을 제대로 보지 않고 (C)를 정답으로 고르지 않도록 주의한다.

해설 두 지문 연계 문제이다. 공지의 단서(3-1)에서 수리 작업 동안 집주인이 집에 없을 경우, 새나 물고기를 제외한 애완동물은 집에서 내보내야 한다는 규정을 알리고 있다. 양식의 단서(3-2)에서 웨스턴 씨는 수리 작업 동안 집에 없을 것이라고 했으므로, 규정상 그녀의 애완견도 집에 없었을 것임을 짐작할 수 있다. 정답은 (D).

해설 두 지문 연계 문제이다. 설문 조사의 단서(4-1)을 종합해 보면 데로스 씨는 웨스턴 씨 집의 보수 작업을 한 직원인데, 웨스턴 씨는 관리 직원이 방바닥에 페인트를 흘리고 치우지 않았다고 불만을 제기하고 있다. 양식의 단서(4-2)에서 페인트칠이 필요한 곳은 침실이라고 했으므로 정답은 (A).

해설 피드백 설문 조사에서 웨스턴 씨가 EXCELLENT(매우 좋음)로 평가를 한 항목은 '요청서 이용의 간편성'이므로 (D)가 정답이다.
패러프레이징 지문의 Ease of using request form이 정답에서 request process로 패러프레이징되었다. 선택지 (A), (B), (C)는 각각 지문의 Professionalism of repair person, Quality of work, Waiting time for receiving repairs를 다르게 표현한 것이다.

UNIT 17 표/양식

PRE-STEP
p.135

A 1 (A) 2 (B) 3 (B) 4 (A) 5 (A) 6 (B) 7 (A) 8 (B) 9 (B)
      10 (B) 11 (A) 12 (A) 13 (A) 14 (B) 15 (B)

B 1 (A) 2 (A)

A
1 (A) report, 보안 창구에 알리다
2 (B) retain, 영수증 보관하다
3 (B) possess, 필수 기술을 보유하다
4 (A) display, 본관에 전시하다
5 (A) fee, 15달러의 등록비
6 (B) extra, 추가적인 유급 휴가
7 (A) frequent, 단골 고객 할인
8 (B) location, 새로운 곳으로 이사하다
9 (B) development, 전문성 개발 교육
10 (B) performance, 훌륭한 성과에 대한 보상
11 (A) evaluation, 직원 평가를 진행하다
12 (A) transfer, 은행 이체
13 (A) absences, 사유 없는 결근에 대한 불이익
14 (B) payments, 세금 납부를 포함하다
15 (B) targets, 생산량 목표를 달성하다

B
1 On March 1 our head office will dispatch a team of employees to visit our site and conduct performance appraisals on all employees. This assessment is done annually.
   (A) The headquarters will send employees to carry out the annual staff evaluations.
   (B) The main office will assess employees to assign the annual work.

3월 1일, 본사는 우리 현장을 방문하여 모든 직원을 대상으로 업무 평가를 실행하기 위해 한 팀의 직원들을 파견할 것입니다. 이 평가는 매년 실시됩니다.
(A) 본사는 직원들을 보내 연례 직원 평가를 시행할 것입니다.
(B) 본사는 연례 업무를 할당하기 위해 직원들을 평가할 것입니다.

2 Residents of Delgado are invited to attend the city's inaugural art contest. The contest is open to all ages, and artists can enter pieces in the categories of Portrait, Nature, or Abstract.
   (A) All local residents are encouraged to participate in the city's first-ever art competition.
   (B) Artists of all ages are urged to make suggestions for the art contest.

델가도 주민들께서는 우리 시의 첫 번째 미술 대회에 참가해 주시기 바랍니다. 대회는 모든 연령에 열려 있으며, 초상화, 풍경화, 추상화 부문에 출품할 수 있습니다.
(A) 모든 지역 주민들은 시의 사상 첫 미술 대회에 참가하시길 권장합니다.
(B) 모든 연령대의 화가들에게 미술 대회에 대한 제안을 해 주시길 권고 드립니다.

115

MAIN STEP 1

p.136

전략 1 실험실 임시 출입증 양식

TEMPORARY PASS
Stiver Laboratories

This pass must be displayed at all times.

Daniel Loesch

Entry date: October 20
①Entry time: 8:35 A.M.
Security clearance: Standard
Reason for visit: Media photography
Valid until: October 20, 12:05 P.M.

②*If you lose this pass,
report to the security desk immediately.
Other inquiries: 555-3950, extension 54

임시 출입증
스티버 실험실

이 출입증은 항상 보여져야 함.

다니엘 래쉬

출입 날짜: 10월 20일
①출입 시간: 오전 8시 35분
보안 허가: 표준
방문 사유: 언론 사진 촬영
유효 기간: 10월 20일 오후 12시 5분

②*이 출입증을 분실하셨을 시에는,
즉시 보안 창구에 알려주세요.
기타 문의 사항: 555-3950, 내선번호 54

어휘 temporary 임시의, 일시적인 pass 출입[통행]증 display 내보이다 clearance 허가, 승인 valid 유효한 report to ~에 알리다 extension 내선번호

① 래쉬 씨에 대해 시사된 바는?
→ 그는 아침에 도착했다.

해설 출입 시간이 오전 8시 35분이라고 기재된 것으로 보아 래쉬 씨가 아침에 도착했다는 것을 알 수 있다.

② 양식에 따르면, 래쉬 씨가 해야 하는 일은?
→ 출입증 분실 시 보안 창구에 가기

해설 출입증 분실 시 보안 창구에 알리라고 나와 있으므로 정답은 Go to the security desk if the pass is lost이다.
패러프레이징 지문의 report to와 pass가 정답에서 각각 Go to와 form으로 패러프레이징되었다.

전략 2 [1] 구매 송장

①Ship to:	Bill to:
Jennifer Parker	Sarah Manning

①수령인:	구매인:
제니퍼 파커	새라 매닝

① 상품을 받을 사람은?
→ 제니퍼 파커

해설 ship to는 ~에게 보낸다는 뜻이므로 받는 사람(수령인), bill to는 ~에게 청구서를 보낸다는 뜻이므로 구매한 사람이다. 받는 사람의 이름을 보면 정답은 Jennifer Parker라는 것을 알 수 있다.

전략 2 [2] 구매 송장

Subtotal: $500
Shipping: $10
Tax: $50

Total: $560
Deposit paid: $160
②Outstanding balance: $400

소계: 500달러
배송료: 10달러
세금: 50달러

총계: 560달러
지불액: 160달러
②미불액: 400달러

② 매닝 씨가 지불해야 하는 금액은?
→ 400달러

해설 총계 560달러 중 미리 지불한 160달러를 제외한 미불액 400달러가 정답이다.

MAIN STEP 2   p.137

1 (D)   **2** (A)   **3** (B)   **4** (D)

[1-2] 마구 주문 송장

Stallion Supplies Wholesale Distributor	Order Invoice	스탤리언 서플라이즈 도매업자	주문 송장
(1)**Customer:** Iris Harrop, Green Valley Ranch **Business ID:** 02-14131191	**Order date:** July 6 **Address:** 124 Gresham St., London, UK	(1)**고객명:** 아이리스 해로프, 그린 밸리 목장 **사업자 번호:** 02-14131191	**주문일:** 7월 6일 **주소:** 그리샴 가 124, 영국, 런던
Item(s) – (1)Leather horse saddle, 16 in. – Animal blankets (5@ $76.79 each)	**Price** $639.99 $383.95	**물품** – (1)가죽 말 안장, 16인치 – 동물 덮개 (5장, 각 76.79달러)	**가격** 639.99달러 383.95달러
Total	$1,023.94	총계	1,023.94달러
Payment: Visa XXXX XXXX XXXX 0153 (charged July 6) **Special instructions:** (2)Imprint animal blankets with 'Green Valley.'		결제: 비자카드 XXXX XXXX XXXX 0153 (7월 6일 청구) 특별 주문 사항: (2)동물 덮개에 '그린 밸리'라고 인쇄해 주세요.	

어휘 wholesale 도매의   distributor 도매업자   saddle 안장   imprint 인쇄하다, 찍다, 새기다

1 해로프 씨가 종사할 것 같은 업종은?
(A) 동물 병원
(B) 애완동물 가게
(C) 개 사육자
(D) 전문 마구간

해설 송장의 구매 내역에서 단서를 얻어야 한다. 고객명에 그린 밸리 목장이라고 언급되어 있고 구매 물품에 가죽 말 안장과 동물 덮개가 있는 것으로 보아 해로프 씨는 전문 마구간을 운영하는 사람임을 유추할 수 있다. 정답은 (D).

2 주문에 대해 암시된 것은?
(A) 맞춤 제작이 요청되었다.
(B) 미불액이 결제되어야 한다.
(C) 10%의 인터넷 할인이 적용되었다.
(D) 7월 말에 처리되었다.

해설 양식의 마지막 부분에 있는 단서(2)의 특별 주문 사항을 보면 동물 덮개에 따로 문구를 새겨 달라고 했으므로 맞춤 제작이 요청되었음을 알 수 있다. 정답은 (A).

[3-4] 스포츠 용품 구매 영수증

SydneySports.com – Customer Receipt		SydneySports.com – 고객 영수증	
Bill to: Marie Ellis 865 Newbury Lane, Chicago, IL 60604	**Ship to:** Jan Eagan 394 Holloway Road, Seattle, WA 98116	**구매인:** 마리 엘리즈 뉴베리 가 865, 일리노이 주, 시카고, 60604	**수령인:** 젠 이건 홀로웨이 가 394 워싱턴 주, 시애틀 98116
(3C)**Order date:** April 7	**Estimated delivery:** April 10	(3C)**주문일:** 4월 7일	**예상 배송일:** 4월 10일

117

Hylon tennis racket	$135.99
(3A)Sydney Sports sweatshirt	$19.99
Delivery charge	$5.65

Payment type:	Subtotal: $161.63
Credit card [ ]	
Bank transfer [✔]	(4)**Frequent shopper discount:** $16.50
(3D)Please note that all listed prices include the applicable sales tax.	Total: $145.13

하일론 테니스 라켓	135.99달러
(3A)시드니 스포츠 운동복 상의	19.99달러
배송료	5.65달러

결제 방법:	소계: 161.63달러
신용카드 [ ]	
은행 이체 [✔]	(4)**단골 고객 할인:** 16.50달러
(3D)기재된 가격에는 모두 해당 판매세가 포함되어 있습니다.	총계: 145.13달러

어휘 estimated delivery 예상 배송일 delivery charge 배송료 payment 결제, 지불 applicable 해당[적용]되는 sales tax 판매세 frequent 잦은, 빈번한

3 주문에 대해 사실이 아닌 것은?

(A) 옷을 포함하고 있다.
(B) 시카고로 보내질 것이다.
(C) 4월 7일에 주문되었다.
(D) 세금 납부가 포함되어 있다.

해설 영수증의 각 항목과 선택지를 대조하여 (A), (C), (D)를 소거할 수 있다. 시카고는 배송 수령지가 아닌 청구지이므로 정답은 (B).

4 엘리즈 씨에 대해 추론할 수 있는 것은?

(A) 신용카드로 지불했다.
(B) 새로운 곳으로 이사할 계획이다.
(C) 익일 배송을 위해 추가 비용을 지불했다.
(D) 이전에 구매를 한 적이 있다.

해설 단서(4)에 나온 단골 고객 할인이라는 항목을 통해 구매자인 엘리즈 씨가 과거에도 이 사이트에서 구매를 한 적이 있다는 것을 유추할 수 있다. 따라서 정답은 (D).

FINAL STEP   p.138

1 (B)   **2** (A)   **3** (C)   **4** (A)   **5** (C)

[1-2] 철물점 영수증

```
           833 Park Street
           Phoenix, AZ 85034
```
Date: August 19	Store ID: 082
Reference #: 57934	Cashier: Jenny

Item	Description	Price
304943	#8 x 2 in. (1)screws (box of 80)	$7.95
859606	1/8 in. x 48 in. x 96 in. prefinished (1)wood paneling	$10.97
859606	1/8 in. x 48 in. x 96 in. prefinished wood paneling	$10.97
395821	16 oz. (1)wood glue	$6.95
	Subtotal	$36.84
	Tax	$2.27
	Total	$39.11

Amount Tendered: $39.11
Credit Card: XXXX XXXX XXXX 7964

```
              파크 가 833
          애리조나 주, 피닉스 85034
```
날짜: 8월 19일	매장 번호: 082
참조 번호: 57934	계산원: 제니

물품	물품 설명	가격
304943	#8 x 2인치 (1)못 (80개 들이 상자)	7.95달러
859606	1/8인치 x 48인치 x 96인치 가완성된 (1)목재 패널	10.97달러
859606	1/8인치 x 48인치 x 96인치 가완성된 목재 패널	10.97달러
395821	16온스 (1)목공풀	6.95달러
	소계	36.84달러
	세금	2.27달러
	총계	39.11달러

지불 금액: 39.11달러
신용카드: XXXX XXXX XXXX 7964

Delk's Deals: (2)Retain this receipt and present it the next time you visit Delk's to get 10% off your purchase (excludes (1)power tools).

어휘　retain ~을 계속 지니다, 간직하다　　exclude 제외하다

델크스의 정책: (2)이 영수증을 보관하셨다가 다음 번 델크스 방문 시에 제시하셔서 물건을 10% 할인 받으십시오 ((1)전동 공구 제외).

1　델크스의 사업 유형은?
　　(A) 옷가게
　　(B) 철물점
　　(C) 가구점
　　(D) 보석상

해설　구입한 물품의 목록으로 델크스의 업종을 유추할 수 있다. 영수증에 기재된 못, 목재 패널, 전동 공구 등으로 미루어 보아 정답은 (B).

2　고객들에게 영수증 보관이 권장되는 이유는?
　　(A) 할인 받는 데 쓸 수 있다.
　　(B) 보증을 받는 데 필요하다.
　　(C) 경품 추첨에 응모할 수 있다.
　　(D) 설문 조사에 참여할 수 있다.

해설　단서(2)에 영수증을 보관했다가 다음 방문 시에 할인을 받으라고 안내되어 있으므로 정답은 (A).
패러프레이징　지문의 retain과 get 10% off your purchase가 문제와 정답에서 각각 keep과 get a discount로 패러프레이징되었다.

[3-5] 업무 평가 양식

On March 1 our head office will dispatch a team of employees to visit our site and conduct performance appraisals on all employees. This assessment is done annually. However, (3)it is of particular importance this year because we have never been assessed under the new policies that were implemented in January. Please see the sample evaluation form below.

Name:
Department:

Category	Maximum Point Value
Overall contributions to the company – Includes review of work tasks to date	30
(4)Teamwork – Both with team members and other departments	15
Attendance and punctuality – Penalty for unexplained absences	10
Professional development training – Workshops, seminars, conferences, etc.	10
Productivity – Ability to meet output targets	25
Job suitability – Possessing necessary skills and knowledge	10
Assessor 1: Assessor 2:	Total: ___/100

3월 1일, 저희 본사는 우리 현장을 방문하여 모든 직원을 대상으로 업무 평가를 실행하기 위해 한 팀의 직원들을 파견할 것입니다. 이 평가는 매년 실시됩니다. 하지만, (3)올해는 특히 중요한데, 1월에 시행된 새 정책하에서는 한 번도 평가된 적이 없기 때문입니다. 아래에 있는 샘플 평가표를 봐 주세요.

이름:
부서:

항목	최대 점수
회사에 대한 전반적인 기여 – 현재까지의 업무 검토 포함	30
(4)팀워크 – 팀원 및 다른 부서와의 관계 모두	15
근태와 시간 엄수 – 사유 없는 결근에 대한 불이익	10
전문성 개발 교육 – 워크숍, 세미나, 학회 등	10
생산성 – 생산량 목표를 달성하는 능력	25
직무 적합성 – 필수 기술과 지식 보유	10
평가자 1: 평가자 2:	총점: ___/100

The results of the appraisal will be announced on March 20. (5)As an incentive, anyone who receives a score of 95 or more will receive special compensation for their extraordinary performance. You may choose either a cash bonus or extra paid vacation.

평가 결과는 3월 20일에 발표될 것입니다. (5)장려책으로서, 95점 이상의 점수를 받는 직원은 누구나 뛰어난 실적에 대해 특별한 보상을 받게 될 것입니다. 현금 보너스와 추가적인 유급 휴가 중 하나를 선택할 수 있습니다.

어휘 head office 본사(= headquarters) dispatch 파견하다 conduct 실행하다 appraisal 평가(= assessment, evaluation) implement 시행하다 contribution 기여 punctuality 시간 엄수 penalty 불이익; 벌금 absence 결근 possess (자질 등을) 지니다, 갖추고 있다 announce 발표하다 incentive 장려책 compensation 보상 extraordinary 뛰어난

3 이번 평가가 더욱 중요한 이유는?
(A) 새 소유주에 의해 요구되었기 때문에
(B) 누가 승진될지 결정할 것이기 때문에
(C) 정책 변화 후 첫 번째 평가이기 때문에
(D) 해고 결정을 내리는 데 사용될 것이기 때문에

해설 단서(3)에 따르면, 이번 업무 평가는 새 정책이 시행된 후 첫 번째 평가라서 더 중요하다고 했으므로 정답은 (C).
패러프레이징 본문의 we have never been assessed 이하가 정답에서 It is the first assessment after a policy change로 패러프레이징되었다.

4 직원들이 최대 15점을 받게 될 자질은?
(A) 협동심
(B) 창의성
(C) 태도
(D) 리더십

해설 샘플 평가표를 참고하여 문제를 풀어야 한다. 평가 항목 중 최대 15점을 받을 수 있는 항목은 팀워크뿐이므로 정답은 (A).
패러프레이징 본문의 Teamwork가 정답에서 Cooperation으로 패러프레이징되었다.

5 장려책에 대해 언급된 것은?
(A) 팀원들 간에 균등하게 분배될 것이다.
(B) 각 부서별로 한 명씩에게 주어질 것이다.
(C) 재정적인 보상과 추가적인 휴가 중 하나일 수 있다.
(D) 만점의 평가 점수를 받는 직원들을 위한 것이다.

해설 단서(5)에 따르면 업무 평가의 총점이 95점 이상인 직원은 누구나 현금 보너스나 유급 휴가의 형태로 보상받게 될 것이라고 했으므로 정답은 (C).

FURTHER STEP
p.140

1 (A) **2** (C) **3** (A) **4** (B) **5** (B)

[1-5] 미술 대회 안내 전단지 & 대회 참가 양식 & 쇼핑몰 쿠폰

Delgado Amateur Art Contest

Residents of Delgado are invited to attend (1B)the city's inaugural art contest. The contest is open to all ages, and artists can enter pieces in the categories of Portrait, Nature, or Abstract. (1C)Thanks to sponsorship from a number of shops and restaurants in the area, we are pleased to offer the following prizes (four per category):
1st Place: $300 voucher from Vox Electronics
(4-2)2nd Place: $150 voucher from Pennington Mall
3rd Place: 2 one-year memberships to the Benson Art Museum
4th Place: $50 voucher from Sam's Steakhouse

Entries will be accepted on June 14 at the Delgado Community Center from 9 A.M. to 4 P.M. (2-2)Paintings will be displayed in the main hall

델가도 아마추어 미술 대회

델가도 주민들께서는 (1B)우리 시의 첫 번째 미술 대회에 참가해 주시기 바랍니다. 대회는 모든 연령에 열려 있으며, 초상화, 풍경화, 추상화 부문에 출품할 수 있습니다. (1C)지역 상점 및 식당 여러 곳의 후원 덕분에, 다음과 같은 상품을 수여할 수 있게 되어 기쁘게 생각합니다 (각 부문당 넷):
1등: 300달러 상당의 복스 전자 제품 상품권
(4-2)2등: 150달러 상당의 페닝턴 몰 상품권
3등: 벤슨 미술관 1년 회원권 2장
4등: 50달러 상당의 샘스 스테이크하우스 상품권

출품작은 델가도 커뮤니티 센터에서 6월 14일 오전 9시부터 오후 4시까지 받습니다. (2-2)회화는 본관에 전시될 것이며

while the auditorium's stage will accommodate the sculptures. The artwork can be viewed by the public until June 25, on which day (1D)the entries will be assessed by a judging panel made up of faculty from the Hillview University Art Department.

One entry per person. Registration fee of $15. For more information, or to register, visit www.delgadoart.org.

---

www.delgadoart.org/register

Name: Jeremy Ellington
Phone number: (495) 555-9094
E-mail address: j.ellington@dci9.com
Title of entry: *Waterfalls in Spring*
Type of entry: (2-1)[✔] Painting   [   ] Sculpture
Age: [   ] Youth (under 18)   [✔] Adult
Category: [   ] Portrait   [✔] Nature   [   ] Abstract

(3)**Special instructions:** Painting should be lit from the back instead of using the usual track lighting. I will provide the lamp for this.

(4-1)**Pennington Mall Voucher**

Value: $150
Issued to: Jeremy Ellington   **Issue date:** June 27

This voucher can be used at any store in Pennington Mall. Change will be given in the form of another voucher if the amount is over $10. Change that is $10 or less will be given in cash.

Valid until December 31. (5)See reverse side for restrictions.

강당 무대에는 조각품이 놓일 것입니다. 미술작품은 6월 25일까지 대중에게 전시되며, 그날 (1D)힐뷰 대학 미술과 교수진으로 구성된 심사위원단이 출품작들을 평가할 것입니다.

1인당 1점의 출품작을 받습니다. 등록비는 15달러입니다. 더 자세한 정보나 등록을 원하시면, www.delgadoart.org를 방문하십시오.

---

www.delgadoart.org/register

이름: 제레미 엘링턴
전화번호: (495) 555-9094
이메일 주소: j.ellington@dci9.com
출품작 제목: 〈봄의 폭포〉
출품작 유형: (2-1)[✔] 회화   [   ] 조각
연령: [   ] 청소년(18세 미만)   [✔] 성인
부문: [   ] 초상화   [✔] 풍경화   [   ] 추상화

(3)**특별 지시 사항:** 그림은 일반적인 트랙 조명을 사용하지 말고 뒤쪽에서 조명을 비추어야 합니다. 이를 위해 조명을 제가 제공하겠습니다.

(4-1)**페닝턴 몰 상품권**

금액: 150달러
발행 대상: 제레미 엘링턴   **발행일:** 6월 27일

본 상품권은 페닝턴 몰의 어떤 매장에서든 사용할 수 있습니다. 해당 액수가 10달러를 초과할 경우 잔액은 또 다른 상품권의 형태로 받게 됩니다. 10달러 이하의 잔액은 현금으로 받게 됩니다.

12월 31일까지 유효. (5)제약 조건은 뒷면 참조.

어휘 inaugural 첫, 개시의   sponsorship 후원   voucher 상품권, 쿠폰   entry 출품(작)   auditorium 강당   accommodate 공간을 제공하다, 수용하다   assess 평가하다   judging panel 심사위원단   faculty 교수진   registration fee 등록비   instruction (보통 복수형) 지시 (사항)   track lighting 트랙 조명 (조명 장치를 천정, 벽 등의 레일에 달아 이동시키는 방식)   issue 발행하다   change 잔돈, 거스름돈   in cash 현금으로   valid 유효한   reverse side 뒷면   restriction 제약 조건, 제한

---

1 대회에 대해 시사되지 않은 바는?
 (A) 수상자들은 이메일로 통지를 받게 될 것이다.
 (B) 처음으로 열리는 것이다.
 (C) 지역 업체들의 후원을 받는다.
 (D) 대학 교수들이 심사할 것이다.

해설 광고 전단에서 (A)를 제외한 나머지 선택지들의 내용을 확인할 수 있다. 수상자에게 통지하는 방법에 대해서는 나와 있지 않으므로 정답은 (A).

2 〈봄의 폭포〉에 대해 사실인 것은?
 (A) 추상화 작품이다.
 (B) 6월 25일에 전시되었다.
 (C) 본관에 전시되었다.
 (D) 전문 미술가가 만들었다.

해설 두 지문 연계 문제이다. 참가 양식에서 〈봄의 폭포〉는 회화 작품이라고 했는데, 전단에서 회화는 본관에 전시된다고 했으므로 정답은 (C).
오답 피하기 〈봄의 폭포〉는 풍경화이며, 6월 25일에 전시된 것이 아니라 25일까지 전시된 것이고, 전단지 제목에 '아마추어' 미술 대회라고 나와 있으므로 나머지 선택지는 모두 오답이다.

3 엘링턴 씨가 요청하는 것은?
 (A) **조명의 위치 바꾸기**
 (B) 미술품을 유리 뒤편에 배치하기
 (C) 더 밝은 조명 제공하기
 (D) 미술품을 평소보다 더 높은 곳에 매달기

해설 참가 양식의 특별 지시 사항을 보면 엘링턴 씨는 앞에서 비추는 조명 대신 뒤쪽 비추는 조명을 사용해야 한다고 요구 사항을 명시하고 있다. 따라서 정답은 (A).

4 엘링턴 씨가 자신의 출품 부문에서 받은 등수는?
 (A) 1등
 (B) **2등**
 (C) 3등
 (D) 4등

해설 두 지문 연계 문제이다. 엘링턴 씨가 받은 상품은 페닝턴 몰 상품권인데, 이를 안내 전단지에서 확인해 보면 2등 상품에 해당하므로 정답은 (B).

5 상품권 뒷면에서 찾아볼 수 있는 것은?
 (A) 매장 목록
 (B) **약관**
 (C) 만기일
 (D) 특별 할인 행사

해설 상품권 뒷면에 대한 질문이므로, 바로 see reverse side for restrictions 부분을 찾아가야 한다. 상품권 뒷면에 나온 restrictions(제약 조건)를 참조하라고 했는데, 이를 달리 표현한 (B)가 정답이다. terms and conditions는 '약관, 계약 조건' 등을 뜻하는 표현이다.

UNIT 18 정보문

PRE-STEP
p.143

A 1 (B) 2 (A) 3 (A) 4 (B) 5 (A) 6 (B) 7 (A) 8 (B) 9 (B)
10 (A) 11 (A) 12 (B) 13 (A) 14 (A) 15 (B)

B 1 (B) 2 (B)

A
1 (B) ready, 이제 사용 준비가 된
2 (A) free, 무료 샘플을 받다
3 (A) steps, 절차를 따르다
4 (B) duration, ~의 투숙 기간
5 (A) spending, ~의 월 지출을 줄이다
6 (B) satisfaction, 고객 만족도 평가
7 (A) association, 협회의 회원이 되다
8 (B) extend, ~의 투숙을 하룻밤 연장하다
9 (B) directions, 호텔까지의 자동차 약도
10 (A) attractions, 인기 관광 명소
11 (A) charge, 신규 가입비를 부과하다
12 (B) cater, ~의 요구에 하나하나 부응하다
13 (A) renovated, 새롭게 보수된 객실
14 (A) accommodate, 세 명까지 수용하다
15 (B) period, 조기 등록 기간

B
1 We urge you to sign up for a membership before January 31 so that you can receive two complimentary tickets to the Annual Florida Boat Show.
(A) Take advantage of the discount on boat show tickets before January 31.
(B) Register for membership by January 31 in order to get free tickets.

1월 31일 전에 회원 가입을 하셔서 연례 플로리다 보트쇼의 무료 티켓 2장을 받으시길 권고 드립니다.
(A) 1월 31일 전에 보트쇼 티켓 할인을 누리십시오.
(B) 1월 31일까지 회원 등록을 하시고 무료 티켓을 받으십시오.

2 We have several rooms for large gatherings, such as retirement parties, awards ceremonies, banquets, and conferences. We also have two on-site restaurants to suit even the most discerning tastes.
(A) Our staff can handle large groups, and there are several good restaurants in the area to choose from.
(B) We have facilities for a variety of events, including dining options that will appeal to everyone.

은퇴식이나 시상식, 연회, 학회 같은 대규모 모임을 위한 객실도 여럿 마련되어 있습니다. 또한 가장 수준 높은 입맛까지 맞출 수 있는 구내 식당 두 곳도 갖추고 있습니다.
(A) 저희 직원들이 대규모 그룹을 다룰 수 있으며, 지역에는 선택할 수 있는 괜찮은 식당이 여러 군데 있습니다.
(B) 저희는 모든 분들의 흥미를 끌 만한 식사 옵션을 포함한 다양한 행사 시설을 보유하고 있습니다.

MAIN STEP 1
p.144

 커피 메이커 사용설명서

Thank you for purchasing a Westover coffee maker. ①To keep your device in top condition, we

웨스트오버 커피 메이커를 구매해 주셔서 감사합니다. ①기계를 최상의 상태로 유지하기 위해, 다음의 세척과 예방 관리 팁을

123

recommend the following cleaning and preventive maintenance tips:

– Use filtered water to decrease mineral buildup.
– Regularly wipe down the machine with a cloth.
– ②Remove used coffee grounds after brewing.

③To order our exclusive Westover unbleached coffee filters, visit www.westoverappl.com.

권장해 드립니다:

– 무기물 침전을 줄이기 위해 여과수를 사용하세요.
– 정기적으로 기계를 천으로 닦아 주세요.
– ②커피를 내린 뒤 커피 찌꺼기를 제거해 주세요.

③저희의 독점적인 웨스트오버 무표백 커피 필터를 주문하시려면, www.westoverappl.com을 방문해 주세요.

어휘 preventive 예방을 위한 maintenance 관리, 보수 buildup 축적, 비축 ground 찌꺼기 brew (커피 등을) 만들다, 내리다 exclusive 독점적인, 유일한 unbleached 표백하지 않은

① 이 정보문을 발견할 수 있을 것 같은 곳은?
→ 제품 사용설명서

해설 해당 정보문은 커피 메이커 사용법에 대해 나열하고 있기 때문에 제품 사용설명서에 적합한 내용이다.

② 권고 사항으로 언급되지 않은 것은?
→ 커피를 내리기 전에 커피콩 갈기

해설 커피를 내린 후 커피 찌꺼기를 제거하라는 말은 있지만 커피를 내리기 전에 커피콩을 갈라는 언급은 없다.

③ 커피 필터에 대해 사실인 것은?
→ 별도로 구매해야만 한다.

해설 마지막 단락에 표백하지 않은 커피 필터를 구매하기 위해서는 웹사이트를 방문하라고 나와 있는 것으로 보아 커피 필터는 따로 구매해야 한다는 것을 알 수 있다.

MAIN STEP 2

p.145

1 (D)   **2** (A)   **3** (D)   **4** (C)

[1-2] 전자레인지 제품 사용설명서

Thank you for purchasing the Topeka-3E microwave oven from Geo Appliances. We hope you enjoy using this product. (1)When unpacking and setting up your microwave, please follow these steps:

(2B)1. Take off all materials used for shipping, such as paper and foam pieces.
(2D)2. Wipe the interior of the microwave with a damp cloth.
3. Place the device on a countertop or a steady shelf. (2C)It should be at least three inches away from a wall to allow for proper ventilation.
Your microwave is now ready for use.

To report any problems with your microwave, please call our Customer Care Hotline at 1-800-555-2940.

지오 전자에서 토페카-3E 전자레인지를 구매해 주셔서 감사합니다. 저희는 귀하께서 이 제품을 즐겨 사용하시기를 바랍니다. (1)포장을 풀고 전자레인지를 설치하실 때 다음의 절차를 따라 주십시오:

(2B)1. 종이나 발포 고무 조각 등, 배송에 사용된 모든 재료를 떼어 내십시오.
(2D)2. 젖은 천으로 전자레인지 내부를 닦으십시오.
3. 기기를 조리대나 튼튼한 선반 위에 놓으십시오. (2C)적절한 통풍을 위해 기기는 벽에서 최소 3인치 정도 떨어져 있어야 합니다.
귀하의 전자레인지는 이제 사용 준비가 되었습니다.

전자레인지의 문제를 알리시려면, 고객 관리 직통 전화 1-800-555-2940으로 전화해 주십시오.

어휘 unpack (짐을) 풀다 set up ~을 설치하다[세우다] material 재료 foam 발포 고무 wipe 닦다, 훔치다 damp 젖은, 축축한 device 기기, 장치 proper 적절한 ventilation 통풍 hotline 직통 전화

1 이 정보가 인쇄되어 있을 것 같은 곳은?

   (A) 기기 측면
   (B) 직원 안내서
   (C) 소매점의 간판
   (D) 제품 사용설명서

해설 도입부에 구매자를 대상으로 사용 방법을 설명하는 글임이 드러나 있어 이것이 전자레인지의 제품 사용설명서임을 알 수 있다. 따라서 정답은 (D).

2 토페카-3E에 관한 절차로 언급되지 않은 것은?

   (A) 시간을 기기에 입력해 놓기
   (B) 포장재 제거하기
   (C) 장치를 배출구에서 떨어뜨려 놓기
   (D) 전자레인지 내부 닦기

해설 지문에 제시된 세부 이용 방법과 보기들을 하나씩 대조해 가며 풀어야 하는 문제이다. (A)의 경우 언급된 바가 없으므로 정답이다.

[3-4] 보트 협회 회원 모집

(3)**Join the Landis Sailing Association!**

(3)Enjoy these amazing benefits by becoming a member of the association.
* A free subscription to the *Sail the World* monthly magazine
* A 15% discount on all sailing clothes and equipment at Landis Heads retail store
* Free use of the Landis Sailing Club facilities throughout the year

Moreover, (4)we urge you to sign up for a membership before January 31 so that you can receive two complimentary tickets to the Annual Florida Boat Show (valued at $150 each).

Call 1-800-555-0982 or visit us at www.landissailing.org.

(3)랜디스 항해 협회와 함께하세요!

(3)협회의 회원이 되어 이러한 놀라운 혜택을 누려 보세요.
*월간 잡지 〈세계로의 항해〉 무료 구독
*랜디스 헤즈 소매점에서 항해 의류 및 장비 15% 할인
*랜디스 보트 클럽 시설 연중 무료 사용

또한, (4)1월 31일 전에 회원 가입을 하셔서 연례 플로리다 보트쇼의 무료 티켓 2장을 받으시길 권고 드립니다. (장당 150달러 상당)

1-800-555-0982로 전화 주시거나, www.landissailing.org을 방문해 주세요.

어휘 association 협회 | benefit 혜택 | subscription 구독 | retail store 소매점 | facility 시설 | throughout the year 일년 내내 | complimentary 무료의

3 이 정보문의 목적은?
   (A) 지역의 항해 의류 매장을 광고하기 위해
   (B) 구독료 변경을 안내하기 위해
   (C) 새롭게 재개장한 요트 클럽을 홍보하기 위해
   (D) 협회에 새로운 회원을 구하기 위해

해설 지문의 제목에는 글의 목적이 드러나 있으므로 반드시 읽어 보자. 제목에서 협회에 합류할 것을 권하고 있고, 첫 번째 문장에서 회원이 될 경우 받게 되는 혜택을 언급하고 있으므로 정답은 (D)이다.

4 읽는 사람들이 요청받은 것은?

   (A) 정기적으로 행사에서 자원 봉사하기
   (B) 사전에 티켓 구매하기
   (C) 특정일 전에 회원 되기
   (D) 월말에 공연 관람하기

해설 단서(4)에서 무료 티켓을 제공하니 1월 31일 전에 가입할 것을 권장하는 문구가 나오므로 정답은 (C).
패러프레이징 지문의 sign up for a membership이 정답에서는 Become a member로 패러프레이징되었다.

FINAL STEP   p.146

1 (B)   2 (C)   3 (B)   4 (C)   5 (D)

[1-2] 휴대 전화 요금제에 관한 정보문

Family Cell Phone Plans

Find the right plan for you and your family! Bundling the accounts of several family members can significantly reduce your monthly spending on smartphone services. Compare and save today!

	R&C	Metro 5	Conway Mobile	Atlas Communications
One-time start-up fee	(1A) None	$20 per line	$25 total	$15 per line
Monthly service cost (up to 4 lines)	$120/month	$100/month	$160/month	$100/month
Data usage limit	(1C)12GB	8GB	10GB	4GB
Talk minutes	Unlimited	3,000/month	Unlimited	Unlimited
Text messages	(1D) Unlimited	Unlimited	Unlimited	500/month
Percentage of dropped calls	4.2%	2.5%	1.8%	2.1%
(2) Customer satisfaction rating	59%	72%	(2)93%	76%

Note: Prices listed do not include taxes or device cost.

가족 휴대 전화 요금제

귀하와 귀하의 가족에게 맞는 요금제를 찾아보십시오! 여러 가족 구성원들의 계정을 묶으면 스마트폰 서비스에 대한 여러분의 월 지출을 상당히 줄일 수 있습니다. 오늘 비교해 보고 절약하십시오!

	R&C	메트로 5	콘웨이 모바일	아틀라스 통신
일회성 신규 가입비	(1A)없음	회선별 20달러	총 25달러	회선별 15달러
월 서비스 요금 (4개 회선까지)	120달러/월	100달러/월	160달러/월	100달러/월
데이터 이용 제한	(1C) 12기가바이트	8기가바이트	10기가바이트	4기가바이트
통화 시간	무제한	3,000분/월	무제한	무제한
문자메시지	(1D) 무제한	무제한	무제한	500통/월
통화 끊김 현상 비율	4.2%	2.5%	1.8%	2.1%
(2)고객 만족도	59%	72%	(2)93%	76%

주의: 목록에 있는 금액에는 세금이나 단말기 비용이 포함되어 있지 않습니다.

어휘 plan 요금제; 계획 bundle 묶다, 꾸리다 account 이용 계정; 계좌 significantly 상당히, 두드러지게 reduce 줄이다, 낮추다 start-up fee 신규 가입비 dropped call 통화 끊김 현상 satisfaction 만족 device 장치, 기구

1 R&C에 대해 사실이 아닌 것은?
 (A) 신규 가입비를 부과하지 않는다.
 (B) 월 요금이 가장 비싼 요금제이다.
 (C) 가장 많은 데이터 이용량을 제공한다.
 (D) 무제한 문자메시지를 제공한다.

2 가장 우수한 고객 서비스를 제공할 것 같은 회사는?
 (A) R&C
 (B) 메트로 5
 (C) 콘웨이 모바일
 (D) 아틀라스 통신

해설 R&C 요금제에 관한 질문이므로 표에서 R&C와 관련된 부분을 집중적으로 보아야 한다. 선택지 (A), (C), (D)는 표에서 모두 확인할 수 있지만, 월 요금제는 R&C가 월 120달러, 콘웨이 모바일이 월 160달러로 콘웨이 모바일이 가장 비싸다. 따라서 정답은 (B).

해설 표의 '고객 만족도' 항목이 고객 서비스와 연결되는 것을 의미상 유추하는 것이 핵심이다. 네 회사 중 고객 만족도가 가장 높은 곳은 콘웨이 모바일이므로 정답은 (C).

[3-5] 포럼 참가 안내문

4th Annual Human Resources Management Forum: Rates and Other Information

Pre-Forum Workshops on Monday, October 7
Registration includes a full-day workshop led by HR consulting gurus John Wang and Leah Fuentez, complimentary lunch and beverage breaks, and an e-document packet full of useful tips and links.

Forum from Tuesday to Thursday, October 8-10
Registration includes three days of conference sessions, (3D)complimentary lunch and beverage breaks, (3A)the conference dinner (October 9), and (3C)free admission to the exhibition area.

Rates

(4)**Early-Bird***	**Standard**
Member of IHRA Workshop only: $500 (4)Conference only: $800 Workshop and conference: $1,100	**Member of IHRA** Workshop only: $650 Conference only: $950 Workshop and conference: $1,450
Non-member Workshop only: $650 Conference only: $950 Workshop and conference: $1,450	**Non-member** Workshop only: $750 Conference only: $1,050 Workshop and conference: $1,650

(4)(5)* The early-bird registration period begins July 13 and ends August 12.

어휘 registration 등록 guru 전문가 complimentary 무료의 admission 입장 exhibition 전시(회) early-bird 조기 신청의, 일찍 오는 사람을 위한

---

3 포럼 등록에 포함되어 있지 않은 것은?
(A) 특별 저녁 식사
(B) 정보 묶음
(C) 전시회 입장권
(D) 무료 다과

해설 두 번째 문단에 포럼 등록 시 제공되는 혜택들이 언급되어 있다. (B)는 포럼 사전 워크숍 등록 시 받을 수 있는 자료이므로 (B)가 정답.

패러프레이징 the conference dinner가 (A) A special dinner로, free admission to the exhibition area가 (C) Entry to the exhibitions로, complimentary lunch and beverage breaks가 (D) Free refreshments로 패러프레이징되었다.

4 회원이 7월 31일 학회만 등록 시 지불하는 금액은?
(A) 500달러
(B) 650달러
(C) 800달러
(D) 950달러

해설 먼저, 문제에서 제시하고 있는 조건은 세 가지이다. 7월 31일, 학회만 등록 시, 회원에 해당하는 정보를 찾아보자. 지문의 마지막 줄에서 볼 수 있듯이, 7월 31일은 조기 등록 기간이다. 따라서 조기 등록 참가비를 보면, 회원이 학회만 등록할 경우 800달러임을 알 수 있다.

5 8월 13일에 일어날 일은?
   (A) 서류가 배포될 것이다.
   (B) 포럼이 끝날 것이다.
   (C) 온라인 등록이 마감될 것이다.
   (D) 할인 금액을 이용할 수 없을 것이다.

해설 지문에 흩어진 단서를 종합해서 풀어야 하는 문제이다. 참가비 요금표를 보면 포럼에 조기 등록 시 일반 요금에서 할인된 가격을 적용받을 수 있는데, 조기 등록 기간은 8월 12일까지이므로 정답은 (D)이다.

FURTHER STEP

p.148

1 (C)   **2** (C)   **3** (A)   **4** (B)   **5** (C)

[1-5] 호텔 광고 & 객실 요금 정보 & 예약 변경 요청 이메일

Make Memories at the Almeida Hotel

A memorable and pleasurable vacation starts with a remarkable hotel. At Almeida Hotel, we strive to ensure that you rest in comfort and luxury while our staff caters to your every need.

(1)Known for having the most breathtaking vistas in the region, as many of our rooms overlook Vanna Beach's crystal-clear waters and white sand, our facility has modern amenities and a contemporary atmosphere. (5-1)For $20 per person, our hotel will send a private car to pick you up from the airport and drive you into the city to our hotel. The charge also includes a return trip to the airport at the end of your stay.

Our spacious, newly renovated guest rooms are priced based on double occupancy, although most rooms can accommodate up to three people (or five for the largest suite).

Additionally, we have several rooms for large gatherings, such as retirement parties, awards ceremonies, banquets, and conferences. We also have two on-site restaurants to suit even the most discerning tastes. All guests may purchase a $15 voucher that entitles them to access our breakfast buffet each day of their stay. The buffet is served from 7 A.M. to noon every morning and features made-to-order options.

(2)Almeida Hotel Spring Rates

Book a room for any date between March 1 and May 30 to take advantage of the off-peak rates listed below.

Room Type	Rate per Night*	Amenities Provided
Platinum Suite	$460	King-size bed, 50-inch HD flat-panel TV, high-speed Internet access, large balcony, fully equipped kitchen

알메이다 호텔에서 추억을 만드세요

기억에 남을 만한 즐거운 휴가는 훌륭한 호텔에서 시작합니다. 저희 알메이다 호텔은 직원들이 고객들의 요구 하나하나에 부응하여 고객들이 편안하고 고급스럽게 휴식을 취하실 수 있도록 하기 위해 노력하고 있습니다.

(1)저희 객실 대다수는 반나 해변의 수정같이 맑은 바다와 백사장을 내려다보고 있기에 지역에서 경치가 가장 뛰어난 것으로 알려져 있으며, 저희 호텔 건물은 최신 편의시설과 현대적인 분위기를 갖추고 있습니다. (5-1)1인당 20달러면, 개인 자가용을 보내어 여러분을 공항에서 태워 시내에 있는 저희 호텔까지 모셔 옵니다. 이 요금에는 숙박 마지막 날 공항까지 돌아가시는 차편도 포함되어 있습니다.

새롭게 보수된 널찍한 객실은 가격이 2인 1실을 기본으로 하지만, 대부분의 객실은 최대 3인(가장 큰 스위트룸은 5인)까지 수용할 수 있습니다.

게다가, 은퇴식이나 시상식, 연회, 학회 같은 대규모 모임을 위한 객실도 여럿 마련되어 있습니다. 또한 가장 수준 높은 입맛까지 맞출 수 있는 구내 식당 두 곳도 갖추고 있습니다. 모든 투숙객은 투숙하는 동안 매일 조식 뷔페를 이용할 수 있는 15달러짜리 쿠폰을 구입하실 수 있습니다. 뷔페는 매일 오전 7시부터 정오까지 제공되며, 맞춤식 메뉴를 선택하실 수 있습니다.

(2)알메이다 호텔 춘계 요금

3월 1일부터 5월 30일 사이의 어느 날짜에든 객실을 예약하셔서 아래에 열거된 비수기 요금을 이용하십시오.

객실 종류	1박당 요금*	제공되는 편의시설
플래티넘 스위트	460달러	킹사이즈 침대, 50인치 HD 평면 TV, 초고속 인터넷 접속, 대형 발코니, 완벽하게 구비된 주방

(4-2) Diamond Suite	$400	King-size bed, 50-inch HD flat-panel TV, high-speed Internet access, in-room safe, medium balcony
Gold Suite	$360	Queen-size bed, 37-inch HD flat-panel TV, high-speed Internet access, in-room safe
Silver Suite	$320	Queen-size bed, 37-inch HD flat-panel TV, high-speed Internet access

*If more than two people will be staying in the room, a surcharge of $85 will be added per person to have a portable cot in the room. Visit www.almeidahotel.com (2)for a list of summer season rates, driving directions to the hotel, and details on popular tourist attractions.

To: Almeida Hotel <service@almeidahotel.net>
From: Bruno Pinto <brunop@usernet.mail>
Date: April 2
Subject: Upcoming stay

Dear Hotel Agent,

I recently reserved a room at your hotel for May 4 through May 20, and I need to make some minor changes to that booking. (3)When I first called to make the reservation, I thought my return flight was on May 20, but I've just discovered that it is actually on May 21. I would like to extend my stay by one night. (4-1)Does the rate of $400 still apply?

Also, (5-2)my wife and I have decided to bring our ten-year-old son with us on this trip. We will need a cot in our room for the entire duration of our stay, and (5-2)we also plan on using your airport transportation service. Please add the necessary charges to our bill.

Thank you for accommodating these changes.

I look forward to staying at your hotel,

Bruno Pinto

1 광고에 따르면, 알메이다 호텔의 유명한 점은?
(A) 세심한 직원들
(B) 우아하게 장식된 스위트룸
(C) 멋진 바다 풍경
(D) 구내 식당

해설 알메이다 호텔은 맑은 바다와 백사장을 내려다보고 있어 뛰어난 경치로 잘 알려져 있다고 했으므로, 정답은 (C).
패러프레이징 지문의 Known for가 문제에서 famous for로 바꾸어 표현되었다.

2 객실 요금에 대해서 암시된 것은?
(A) 호텔 클럽 회원들에게는 더 저렴하다.
(B) 날짜가 임박해서 예약하면 더 비싸다.
(C) 연중 시기에 따라 변동된다.
(D) 보수 비용을 지불하기 위해 인상되었다.

해설 요금 정보에 단서가 흩어져 있으므로 주의 깊게 보아야 한다. 호텔 요금을 안내하는 지문의 제목과 마지막 단락에서 각각 Spring Rates와 summer season rates라는 표현을 통해 객실 요금이 계절별로 달라진다는 것을 알 수 있다. 따라서 정답은 (C).

3 핀토 씨에 대해 시사된 것은?
(A) 처음 예약을 전화로 했다.
(B) 친구를 통해 이 호텔에 대해 알게 되었다.
(C) 처음에 계획했던 것보다 더 일찍 떠나야 한다.
(D) 이 호텔을 다른 사람들에게 추천할 의향이 있다.

해설 이메일에서 핀토 씨는 처음에 전화를 걸어 예약했다고 했으므로, 정답은 (A).
오답 피하기 호텔을 알게 된 경위나 추천할 의향이 있는지 여부는 알 수 없으며, 처음에 계획했던 것보다 하루 더 늦게 떠나야 한다고 했으므로, 나머지는 모두 오답이다.

4 핀토 씨가 예약했을 가능성이 가장 큰 객실은?
(A) 플래티넘 스위트
(B) 다이아몬드 스위트
(C) 골드 스위트
(D) 실버 스위트

해설 요금 정보와 이메일을 보고 풀어야 하는 연계 문제이다. 단서(4-1)에서 핀토 씨가 400달러 요금이 여전히 적용되냐고 묻는 것으로 보아, 처음에 예약한 객실의 1박 요금이 400달러였다고 짐작할 수 있다. 객실 요금 정보를 보면 요금이 400달러인 객실은 다이아몬드 스위트이므로 정답은 (B).

5 핀토 씨가 교통 서비스에 대해 지불할 액수는?
(A) 20달러
(B) 40달러
(C) 60달러
(D) 85달러

해설 호텔 광고에 따르면 공항에서 호텔까지 개인 자가용을 이용하는 요금은 1인당 20달러인데, 이메일에서 핀토 씨 일행은 아내와 아들까지 포함해 3명이므로, 총 60달러를 지불해야 한다. 정답은 (C).

CHAPTER TEST 2

p.150

1 (A)	2 (B)	3 (D)	4 (D)	5 (D)	6 (A)	7 (C)	8 (D)	9 (A)
10 (B)	11 (B)	12 (C)	13 (B)	14 (A)	15 (B)	16 (D)	17 (D)	18 (C)
19 (D)	20 (C)	21 (C)	22 (D)	23 (D)	24 (B)	25 (C)	26 (C)	27 (A)

[1-2] 연구소 출입 암호에 대한 공지

Biotech Laboratories

Welcome to the Biotech Laboratories family! We are very happy to have you join us. In accordance with company regulations, our laboratories are locked at all times of the day. (1)Employees are issued a personalized five-digit passcode that they must type into the keypad before entering or exiting any laboratory. These codes take two weeks to process, however, so until yours has been granted, we request that you please use the temporary access code provided below. (2)After your orientation has completed on November 4, you should be able to use your new code.

Temporary Access Information
Employee name: Stella Wilpstra
Password: 1234#
Valid through: November 4

바이오테크 연구소

바이오테크 연구소의 가족이 되신 것을 환영합니다! 귀하가 일원이 되셔서 매우 기쁩니다. 사내 규정에 따라, 우리 연구소는 하루 종일 잠겨 있습니다. (1)직원들은 연구실에 들어가거나 나오기 전 키패드에 입력해야 하는 개인 맞춤형의 다섯 자리 암호를 발급받게 됩니다. 그러나 이 암호를 처리하는 데 2주가 걸리므로, 귀하의 암호가 승인될 때까지 아래에 제공된 임시 출입 암호를 이용해 주시기를 요청 드립니다. (2)11월 4일에 귀하의 오리엔테이션이 완료되면, 귀하의 새로운 암호를 사용하실 수 있게 될 것입니다.

임시 출입 정보
직원 이름: 스텔라 윌프스트라
암호: 1234#
유효 기간: 11월 4일

어휘 in accordance with ~에 따라, ~에 부합되게 regulation 규정, 규제 issue 발급[발행]하다 personalize 개인의 필요에 맞추다 passcode 암호 exit 나가다, 떠나다 process 처리하다 grant 승인[허락]하다 temporary 임시의, 일시적인 access 입장, 접근 valid 유효한

1 공지의 주요 내용은?
   (A) 제한 구역 출입을 위한 절차
   (B) 신입 직원을 위한 오리엔테이션 일정
   (C) 컴퓨터 암호 설정에 대한 지시
   (D) 승인을 위한 사내 규정 작성

해설 공지에서 다뤄지는 전반적인 주제를 골라야 하는 문제이다. 연구실에 출입하기 위한 방법을 안내하는 내용이므로 정답은 (A).

2 임시 암호에 대해 추론할 수 있는 것은?
   (A) 모든 직원들에게 동일하다.
   (B) 추후 업데이트될 것이다.
   (C) 직원들에 의해 선택된다.
   (D) 격주로 변경된다.

해설 임시 암호를 쓰다가 11월 4일에 새로운 암호를 사용할 수 있을 거라 했으므로 정답은 (B).

[3-4] 부재중 전화 관련 문자메시지

JILL BRAME   11:25 A.M.
My phone shows a missed call from you. What's up?

질 브레임   오전 11:25
전화하셨는데 제가 못 받았네요. 무슨 일이세요?

131

LANDON COLE	11:26 A.M.	랜던 콜	오전 11:26

Oh, I had my annual health checkup earlier this morning.

LANDON COLE	11:27 A.M.	랜던 콜	오전 11:27

(3)I needed to write down the company's insurance coverage number on the form, but I didn't know what it was.

(3)서류에 회사의 보험 번호를 적어야 했는데, 그게 뭔지 몰라서요.

JILL BRAME	11:28 A.M.	질 브레임	오전 11:28

But it's all sorted out now?

그런데 지금은 다 해결됐나요?

LANDON COLE	11:29 A.M.	랜던 콜	오전 11:29

Yeah, I called Bert when you didn't answer. He was able to look up the information for me.

네, 당신이 전화를 받지 않아서 버트에게 전화했어요. 그가 필요한 내용을 찾아줄 수 있었어요.

JILL BRAME	11:30 A.M.	질 브레임	오전 11:30

Oh, good. Sorry I wasn't available.

아, 잘됐네요. 못 받아서 미안해요.

JILL BRAME	11:31 A.M.	질 브레임	오전 11:31

I've been in meetings all morning. (4)I had my phone set to silent mode, so I didn't hear it ring.

오전 내내 회의 중이었거든요. (4)휴대 전화를 무음으로 설정해 두어서, 울리는 걸 못 들었어요.

LANDON COLE	11:32 A.M.	랜던 콜	오전 11:32

I completely understand. I do the same thing. (4)It's never good to have a phone call interrupt a meeting.

충분히 이해해요. 저도 똑같이 하는걸요. (4)전화 때문에 회의에 지장을 주는 건 결코 좋지 않죠.

어휘 missed call 부재중 전화 annual 연례의 health checkup 건강검진 insurance coverage 보험 sort out ~을 해결[처리]하다 completely 완전히 interrupt 방해하다

---

3 콜 씨가 처음에 브레임 씨에게 연락한 이유는?
(A) 건강검진 일정을 잡기 위해
(B) 버트 씨의 연락처를 요청하기 위해
(C) 보험에 대해 문의하기 위해
(D) 계정 번호를 요청하기 위해

해설 단서(3)에서 콜 씨는 건강검진에 서류에 필요한 회사의 보험 번호를 몰라서 전화한 것이라고 처음에 전화했던 이유를 밝히고 있다. 은행이나 보험사 등 서비스를 제공하는 업체에서 고객에게 부여하는 번호를 account number라고 하므로 정답은 (D).
패러프레이징 지문의 company's insurance coverage number가 정답에서 account number로 패러프레이징되었다.

4 오전 11:32에, 콜 씨가 "저도 똑같이 하는걸요"라고 하는 의도는?
(A) 연속으로 회의 일정을 짠다.
(B) 자주 휴대 전화를 잊어버리고 두고 온다.
(C) 통화보다 문자메시지를 선호한다.
(D) 종종 휴대 전화의 벨소리를 꺼 둔다.

해설 주어진 표현 "I do the same thing" 앞의 단서(4)에서 브레임 씨는 휴대 전화를 무음으로 설정해서 벨소리를 듣지 못했다고 했고, 뒤의 단서에서 콜 씨는 회의에 지장을 주어서는 안 된다고 했다. 따라서 "저도 똑같이 하는걸요"라는 콜 씨의 말은 자신도 회의 중에는 휴대 전화를 무음으로 설정해 둔다는 뜻임을 알 수 있다.

[5-7] 피트니스 센터 광고

Fitness World: Practically a Brand-new Gym!

After six long weeks of renovations, we have finally reopened! (5)Fitness World remains in the same location where it started a decade ago, but it is now three times bigger. We kept the size of the sauna the same, but expanded the upstairs workout spaces used for yoga, kickboxing, and aerobics classes. We also added all new equipment on the main floor. These classes are offered several times

피트니스 월드: 사실상 새로운 체육관으로!

6주간의 긴 공사를 마치고, 저희가 마침내 재개장을 했습니다! (5)피트니스 월드는 10년 전 개업할 당시와 같은 장소에 그대로 위치해 있지만 3배 더 커졌습니다. 저희는 사우나의 크기는 똑같이 유지했으나 요가, 킥복싱 그리고 에어로빅 수업에 쓰이는 위층의 운동 공간을 확장했습니다. 또한, 본관에 새로운 기구를 더 가져다 놓았습니다. 이 수업들은 단체로 운동하면서 자극과 지지를 얻는 것을 즐기는 분들을 위해 일주일에 여러 번 제공됩니다. 대조적으로, (6C)만약 개인적인 도움을 받는 것을 선호하신다면, 저희의 개인 트레이너들이 1주일에 5일간 지도

a week for individuals who enjoy the motivation and support of working out in a group. Conversely, (6C)if you prefer to have individual assistance, (6A)our personal trainers are present five days a week. However, they're not available on weekends. (6B) Although personal trainers can be expensive, (6D)we have a trial policy that allows people to work out with a trainer once for free so they can see if it is worth the cost.

(7)What our members like best about our gym is that we are open 24 hours a day for individuals who do not like to work out during regular hours. To see our membership rates, go to www.fitnessworld.org.

가능합니다. (6A)하지만 그들은 주말에는 출근하지 않습니다. (6B)비록 개인 트레이너들의 비용이 비쌀 수 있지만, 저희는 그 비용의 가치를 여러분들이 느끼도록 하기 위해 (6D)무료로 한 번의 트레이너 시범 이용 기회를 드리는 정책을 취하고 있습니다.

(7)저희 회원님들께서 저희 체육관에 대해 가장 좋아하시는 부분은 정규 시간에 운동하고 싶지 않아 하는 분들을 위해 하루 24시간 문을 연다는 것입니다. 회원제 요금을 보시려면, www.fitnessworld.org를 방문하십시오.

어휘 renovation 공사, 개조   equipment 기구, 장비   motivation 자극, 동기 부여   support 지지   conversely 대조적으로
prefer to do ~하는 것을 선호하다   assistance 도움, 지원   available 이용 가능한   trial 시범 이용, 도전   allow (~하는 것을) 가능하게 하다   regular hours 정규 시간, 정상 영업 시간   rate 요금, 비율, 속도

---

5 피트니스 월드가 영업을 해 온 기간은?
 (A) 3년
 (B) 5년
 (C) 6년
 (D) 10년

해설 단서(5)를 보면 피트니스 월드가 10년 전 개업했다는 사실이 직접적으로 언급되어 있으므로 정답은 (D)이다.
패러프레이징 지문의 a decade라는 숫자의 단위 표현이 정답에서 Ten years로 패러프레이징되었다.

6 개인 트레이너에 대해 사실이 아닌 것은?
 (A) 주중에는 이용이 불가능하다.
 (B) 서비스 비용이 저렴하지 않다.
 (C) 1:1 교육을 제공한다.
 (D) 시범 이용 수업을 제공한다.

해설 개인 트레이너 서비스를 이용할 수 없는 때는 주중이 아니라 주말이므로 정답은 (A)이다.

7 피트니스 월드의 인기 있는 특징은 무엇인가?
 (A) 요금이 다른 체육관보다 저렴하다.
 (B) 편리한 곳에 위치해 있다.
 (C) 아무 시간에나 사람들이 운동할 수 있게 한다.
 (D) 강사들이 전직 운동선수 출신이다.

해설 단서(7)에서 회원들이 체육관이 24시간 영업하는 것을 좋아한다고 했으므로 정답은 (C)이다.
패러프레이징 본문의 24 hours a day가 정답에서 at any times로 바뀌어 표현되었다.

[8-10] 식당 소개 웹사이트

http://www.themunchbox.com

Home | **About**

(8)The Munch Box is an all-American chain of diners across the United States. Primarily serving truck drivers and other cross-country commuters, each branch of our restaurant is open 24 hours a day, 7 days a week. We are also open on holidays and even offer special meals for travelers on these days. (9)Our diners are located at unusual stopping points along major highways to provide travelers on long trips with the ability to stop where other facilities are not present. (10)Click on the link below to be redirected to the section of our Web site that identifies all Munch Box diner locations on an interactive map:

http://www.themunchbox.com

홈 | 회사 소개

(8)먼치 박스는 미국 전역에 있는 미국 전통의 식당 체인입니다. 주로 트럭 운전기사들과 기타 전국을 가로지르는 통근자들에게 음식을 제공하는데, 우리 식당의 각 지점은 하루 24시간, 일주일 내내 문을 엽니다. 우리는 휴일에도 영업을 하고, 이때는 여행객들에게 특별식도 제공합니다. (9)먼 길을 가는 여행객들이 다른 시설들이 없는 지역에서도 정차할 수 있도록 우리 식당들은 주요 고속도로상의 흔치 않은 정차 지점에 위치하고 있습니다. (10)아래 링크를 클릭하여 우리 웹사이트의 쌍방향 지도 상에서 모든 먼치박스 식당의 위치를 확인할 수 있는 페이지로 이동해 보세요. http://www.themunchbox.com/locations.

http://www.themunchbox.com/locations.

어휘 **all-American** 미국 전통의, 미국을 대표하는 **primarily** 주로, 우선적으로 **cross-country** 전국을 가로지르는, 국토를 횡단하는 **commuter** 통근자 **branch** 지점, 지사 **redirect** 이동시키다, (다른 주소로) 보내다 **identify** 식별[확인]하다 **interactive** 쌍방향의, 상호적인

8 무엇에 관한 웹사이트인가?
 (A) 저렴한 호텔 체인
 (B) 유명한 주유소 브랜드
 (C) 잘 알려진 길가의 대형 건물들
 (D) 미국 전역에 있는 음식점

해설 지문 첫 문장의 chain of diners에서 먼치 박스가 식당 체인임을 알 수 있다. 따라서 정답은 (D).

9 먼치 박스에 대해 추론할 수 있는 것은?
 (A) 사업을 여행자들에게 맞춤화했다.
 (B) 휴일에는 영업하지 않는다.
 (C) 주요 고속도로에서 멀리 떨어져 있다.
 (D) 트럭 운전기사들에게 할인을 제공한다.

해설 단서(9)에 따르면, 먼치 박스는 먼 길을 가는 여행객들을 위해 고속도로의 흔치 않은 정차 지점에 위치해 있다고 했으므로 여행자들에게 맞춤화된 식당임을 알 수 있다. 따라서 정답은 (A).

10 제공된 링크에서 이용 가능한 정보는?
 (A) 주간 고속도로의 사진
 (B) 식당 위치에 관한 지도
 (C) 예약 시 사용할 전화번호
 (D) 특별 가격 할인

해설 링크가 언급된 부분을 찾아서 단서를 얻어야 한다. 단서(10)을 보면 링크를 통해 웹사이트에 들어가면 지도로 식당의 위치를 확인할 수 있다고 했으므로 정답은 (B).

[11-13] 회의 준비 관련 온라인 채팅 대화문

Paula Noelle 10:01 A.M. (11)Thank you both for agreeing to help me with the customer feedback panel this afternoon. After the main demonstration, you'll both be leading small group discussions.	폴라 노엘 오전 10:01 (11)두 분 모두 오늘 오후에 고객 평가단 일을 도와주시기로 해주셔서 감사드려요. 주요 시범 설명 후에, 두 분은 소규모 토론을 이끌게 되실 겁니다.
Vera Simmons 10:02 A.M. Okay. I got the list of questions that you e-mailed. They are fairly straightforward. (11)It seems that we just need to get the customers talking and find out what they think.	베라 시몬즈 오전 10:02 알겠어요. 이메일로 보내 주신 질문 목록을 받았어요. 아주 간단하네요. (11)우리는 고객들이 발언을 하도록 유도하여 그들이 생각하는 바를 알아내기만 하면 될 것 같아요.
Doug Gilmore 10:03 A.M. Right. Paula, do you still need help setting up the conference room?	더그 길모어 오전 10:03 맞아요. 폴라, 회의실 준비에 아직 도움이 필요한가요?
Paula Noelle 10:03 A.M. Yes. There are 23 participants on our list, our biggest group yet. (12)The conference room is supposed to have 25 leather chairs, but there are only 21 in there.	폴라 노엘 오전 10:03 네. 우리 명단에 23명의 참가자가 있는데, 여태까지 그룹 중에 가장 큰 규모예요. (12)회의실에 25개의 가죽 의자가 놓이기로 되어 있는데, 거기에 21개밖에 없어요.
Doug Gilmore 10:04 A.M. (12)Don't worry. I'll get them. People sometimes take them out to use in other rooms.	더그 길모어 오전 10:04 (12)걱정 말아요. 내가 가져갈게요. 사람들이 가끔 다른 방에서 사용하려고 가져가거든요.
Vera Simmons 10:06 A.M. And I've put up some signs to direct participants where to go. They should be able to make their way to the 3rd floor conference room on their own.	베라 시몬즈 오전 10:06 그리고 참가자들이 어디로 가야 하는지를 알려주는 표지판을 몇 개 걸었어요. 직접 3층 회의실까지 찾아갈 수 있을 거예요.

Doug Gilmore　　　　　　　　10:08 A.M.
How will they get into the 3rd floor offices without the door code?

Paula Noelle　　　　　　　　10:09 A.M.
Employees should leave the door open until everyone has arrived.

Vera Simmons　　　　　　　　10:10 A.M.
(13)In that case, I'd better hurry up and post something about that near the door. Otherwise, participants might get locked out.

더그 길모어　　　　　　　　오전 10:08
출입문 비밀번호 없이 3층 사무실에 어떻게 들어갈 수 있죠?

폴라 노엘　　　　　　　　오전 10:09
모두가 도착할 때까지 직원들이 문을 열어 두어야 해요.

베라 시몬즈　　　　　　　　오전 10:10
(13)그렇다면, 서둘러 현관 근처에 그에 관해 뭔가를 게시해야겠네요. 그렇지 않으면, 참가자들이 문이 잠겨 들어오지 못할 수도 있으니까요.

어휘 demonstration 시범 설명　fairly 꽤, 상당히　straightforward 간단한, 쉬운　set up ~을 준비[설치]하다　participant 참가자　be supposed to do ~하기로 되어 있다　put up ~을 (내)걸다　sign 표지판　direct 길을 알려주다, 안내하다　make one's way to ~로 나아가다　otherwise 그렇지 않으면　get locked out 문이 잠겨 들어가지 못하다

11 오후 행사의 목적은?
(A) 사업 계약을 협상하기 위해
(B) 고객 의견을 알아내기 위해
(C) 신입 직원들을 교육하기 위해
(D) 정책 변경에 대해 논의하기 위해

해설 오후에 고객 평가단이 모여 토론을 하게 되는데, 고객들과의 대화를 통하여 그들의 의견을 알아내는 것이 행사의 목적이라고 볼 수 있으므로 정답은 (B).

12 오전 10:04에, 길모어 씨가 "내가 가져갈게요"라고 하는 의도는?
(A) 일부 서류를 찾고 있다.
(B) 참가자를 더 모집하는 것을 도울 수 있다.
(C) 의자들을 찾아볼 계획이다.
(D) 명단을 준비할 것이다.

해설 주어진 표현 "I'll get them" 앞의 단서(12)에서 노엘 씨는 회의실에 가죽 의자가 모자란다고 걱정했고, 이에 대해 길모어 씨는 걱정 말라고 하고 있다. 따라서 "내가 가져갈게요"라는 길모어 씨의 말은 필요한 의자를 찾아보겠다는 뜻임을 알 수 있다. 정답은 (C).

13 시몬즈 씨가 다음에 할 것 같은 일은?
(A) 출입문 비밀번호 확인하기
(B) 공지 붙이기
(C) 방 장식하기
(D) 자물쇠 수리하기

해설 다음에 할 일을 묻고 있으므로, 시몬즈 씨의 마지막 말을 주의 깊게 보아야 한다. 단서(13)에서 시몬즈 씨가 현관 근처에 직원들을 위한 공지를 게시하겠다고 했으므로, 정답은 (B).
패러프레이징 지문의 post something이 정답에서는 Put up a notice로 패러프레이징되었다.

[14-17] 전시회에 대한 기사

Contam Corp. Sponsors Blue Glass Gallery
By Marissa Sagese

Contam Corp. recently announced its first-time sponsorship of the Blue Glass Gallery of Contemporary Art. The gallery's upcoming exhibit is a retrospective of works by the distinguished artist Eligio Calabrese. Opening night for the much-anticipated exhibit is scheduled for Saturday, April 20.

Mr. Calabrese is a world-renowned sketch artist. (14)Although he first entered the art world several decades ago as a watercolorist, it is his gray pencil drawings that eventually won him critical acclaim internationally. In particular, his abstract approach to objects alters the way people typically interpret drawings, and allows them to see everyday scenes in a completely new light. (15)As with all of our

콘탬 사가 블루 글래스 미술관을 후원하다
마리사 사지스 작성

콘탬 사는 최근 블루 글래스 현대 미술관을 처음으로 후원하기로 했다고 발표했다. 그 미술관에서 곧 있을 전시회는 뛰어난 화가 엘리지오 칼라브레스 씨의 작품 회고전이다. 많은 기대를 모으고 있는 이 전시회가 개막하는 밤은 4월 20일 토요일로 예정되어 있다.

칼라브레스 씨는 세계적으로 유명한 데생 화가이다. (14)비록 그는 몇십 년 전 수채화 화가로 예술계에 처음 입문했지만 궁극적으로 그에게 전 세계적으로 비평가들의 찬사를 받게 해준 것은 그가 회색 연필로 그린 데생 작품들이다. 특히, 사물에 대한 그의 추상적 접근은 사람들이 전형적으로 그림을 해석하는 방식을 바꾸어 주고 일상적인 장면들을 완전히 새로운 견지에서 보게끔 해준다. (15)석 달간 치러지는 우리의 모든 전시들과 마찬가지로 이 전시회는 그의 25년간의 경력 동안 칼라브레스 씨가 다루었던 많은 주제들을 조명하도록 기획되었다.

three-month exhibits, this collection has been designed to highlight the many themes used by Mr. Calabrese throughout his twenty-five year career. (16)(17)In gratitude for sponsoring the exhibition, the Blue Glass Gallery of Contemporary Art is extending free admission to Contam Corp. employees on opening night. All ushers will possess a copy of the staff directory, so employees need only identify themselves by name. <u>Ticket pricing will return to the regular $21.00 amount for the remainder of the exhibit's run.</u> Anyone interested in viewing the exhibit can purchase tickets on the gallery's Web site at www.blueglassgallery.com or through the box office at 555-329-2814. You won't want to miss this must-see event.

(16)(17)전시회 후원에 대한 감사로, 블루 글래스 현대 미술관은 전시회가 시작되는 밤에 콘탐 사의 직원들에게 무료 입장을 제공할 예정이다. 모든 안내원들은 직원 명부를 한 부씩 가지고 있을 것이기 때문에 직원들은 자신이 누구인지 이름을 밝히기만 하면 된다. <u>남은 전시회 기간에는 입장권 가격이 다시 정가인 21달러가 된다.</u> 전시회를 관람하고자 하는 사람이면 누구나 미술관 웹사이트 www.blueglassgallery.com에서 또는 555-329-2814로 매표소에 전화하여 티켓을 구매할 수 있다. 당신은 꼭 봐야만 하는 이 행사를 놓치고 싶지 않을 것이다.

어휘 contemporary 현대의, 동시대의 upcoming 곧 있을, 다가오는 exhibit 전시회, 전람회 retrospective 회고하는, 회상하는 distinguished 뛰어난, 눈에 띄는 world-renowned 세계적으로 유명한 critical 비평(가들)의; 중대한 acclaim 찬사, 칭찬 in particular 특히, 특별히 approach 접근 (방식) alter 바꾸다, 전환시키다 interpret 해석하다, 이해하다 in gratitude for ~에 대한 감사로 staff directory (직원들의 이름이 나열되어 있는) 직원 명부 identify 신원을 밝히다 remainder 나머지, 남은 것

14 칼라브레스 씨에 대해 언급된 것은?
(A) 시간이 지나면서 예술적 스타일을 바꿨다.
(B) 4월 20일에 참석할 것이다.
(C) 밝은 색상을 이용한 그림으로 알려져 있다.
(D) 사실주의적 예술을 한다.

해설 특정 인물에 대한 문제이므로 칼라브레스 씨가 언급된 기사의 두 번째 문단을 보아야 한다. 단서(14)에 따르면 그가 수채화에서 데생으로 예술적 스타일을 바꿨음을 알 수 있다. 따라서 정답은 (A).

15 블루 글래스 미술관에 대해 추론할 수 있는 것은?
(A) 특정 그룹을 위한 사설 전시를 주관한다.
(B) 전시는 일반적으로 90일 동안 한다.
(C) 전시회를 통해 큰 수익을 낸다.
(D) 콘탐 사와 지속적인 관계를 맺고 있다.

해설 단서(15)를 통해 이 미술관의 다른 모든 전시회들도 석 달간 진행된다는 것을 유추할 수 있으므로 정답은 (B).
패러프레이징 지문의 three-month가 정답에서 90 days로 패러프레이징되었다.

16 직원들이 무료로 입장할 수 있는 방법은?
(A) 단체로 표를 구매함으로써
(B) 웹사이트에서 쿠폰을 출력함으로써
(C) 미술관 직원에게 신분증을 보여줌으로써
(D) 특정일 밤에 미술관을 방문함으로써

해설 미술관은 전시회가 시작되는 밤에 직원에게 무료 입장을 제공한다고 했으므로 정답은 (D).
오답 피하기 신분증을 보여줄 필요까지는 없고 이름만 말하면 된다고 했으므로 (C)는 오답.

17 [1], [2], [3], [4]로 표시된 위치 중 다음 문장이 들어가기에 가장 알맞은 곳은?
"남은 전시회 기간에는 입장권 가격이 다시 정가인 21달러가 된다."
(A) [1]
(B) [2]
(C) [3]
(D) [4]

해설 주어진 문장은 나머지 전시회 기간에는 입장권 가격이 정가로 돌아간다는 내용으로, 이를 통해 특정 기간에는 입장권 가격에 변동이 있음을 유추해야 한다. 단서(17)에서 전시회가 시작되는 밤에 콘탐 사 직원들이 무료 입장 혜택을 받는다고 했으므로, 이때가 지나면 입장권 가격이 원래대로 돌아갈 것임을 알 수 있다. 정답은 (D).

[18-22] 주문 송장 & 배송 오류 문의 이메일

CUSTOMER INVOICE

Date of Order: January 2
Invoice #: 959110

고객 송장

주문 일자: 1월 2일
송장 번호: 959110

Customer Name/Address: Clifford Elston, 4650 Oakmound, Lombard, IL 60148

(18A) Origin of Order	(18C) Shipping Method	Estimated Delivery Date	(18D) Payment Type	Rewards Member
Web site	Standard	January 7	Credit Card	No

Quantity	Item #	(19) Description	Unit Price	Line Total
1	A394	Revica Men's Thermal Ski Jacket – Large	$149.99	$149.99
1	S596	Revica Insulated Gloves – Large	$25.99	$25.99
2	P439	Woodland Co. Protective Ski Goggles	(21-2) $15.99	(21-2) $31.98

Thank you for your purchase! We stand by all products sold at Harrison Co. If you are dissatisfied with your merchandise, please contact us at service@harrisonco.com.

Subtotal	$207.96
Discounts/ Coupons	-$0.00
Sales Tax	$12.49
(18B) Delivery	$8.95
Total	$229.40

To: Harrison Co. <service@harrisonco.com>
From: Clifford Elston <elstonc@wondermail.com>
Date: January 7
Subject: Invoice #959110

To Whom it May Concern:

I placed an order with your company on January 2 and received the merchandise this morning. (20)Unfortunately, I purchased a large jacket, but I was sent a medium instead. (22)I was planning on wearing the jacket on a ski trip this weekend. Because of this trip, I can receive a delivery at my house no later than January 9, after which time I will not be there. I hope you can use a courier that offers two-day or overnight delivery instead of using your usual shipping company because I need it exchanged as soon as possible.

In addition, I ordered two pairs of protective goggles. (21-1)The flyer I received in the mail said that all goggles were buy-one-get-one-free this month without a coupon. (20)(21-1)However, I was charged for both, so the price of one of them should have been deducted on the invoice.

고객 이름/주소: 클리포드 엘스턴, 일리노이 주 60148, 롬바르드, 오크마운드 4650

(18A) 주문 방식	(18C) 배송 방법	배송 예정일	(18D) 지불 방법	회원 보상
웹사이트	보통	1월 7일	신용카드	없음

수량	품번	(19)품목 기술	단가	품목 총액
1	A394	레비카 남성용 보온 스키 재킷 – 라지 사이즈	149.99달러	149.99달러
1	S596	레비카 단열 장갑 – 라지 사이즈	25.99 달러	25.99 달러
2	P439	우드랜드 보호용 스키 고글	(21-2) 15.99달러	(21-2) 31.98달러

구매에 감사드립니다! 저희는 해리슨 사에서 판매하는 전 제품에 대해 책임을 집니다. 상품에 만족하지 않으셨다면, service@ harrisonco.com 으로 연락주세요.

소계	207.96달러
할인/쿠폰	-0.00달러
판매세	12.49달러
(18B)배송비	8.95달러
총액	229.40달러

수신: 해리슨 사 <service@harrisonco.com>
발신: 클리포드 엘스턴 <elstonc@wondermail.com>
날짜: 1월 7일
제목: 송장 번호 959110

관계자 분께:

저는 1월 2일에 귀사에 주문을 했고 오늘 오전에 물품을 받았습니다. (20)불행히도, 저는 라지 사이즈 재킷을 구매했지만 대신 미디엄 사이즈를 받았습니다. (22)이번 주말 스키 여행에 그 재킷을 입을 계획이었습니다. 이 여행 때문에, 저는 늦어도 1월 9일까지만 집에서 배송을 받을 수 있는데, 그 이후에는 집에 없을 것입니다. 가능한 한 빨리 교환을 해주셨으면 하므로 평소의 배송 업체를 이용하지 마시고 이틀 혹은 익일 배송을 해주는 택배회사를 이용해 주시길 바랍니다.

게다가, 저는 두 개의 보호용 고글을 주문했습니다. (21-1)우편으로 받았던 전단지에는 이번 달에는 쿠폰 없이도 모든 고글 하나를 사면 하나를 무료로 준다고 되어 있었습니다. (20)(21-1)하지만 저는 두 개에 모두 비용이 청구되었는데 두 개 중 한 개의 가격이 송장에서 제해졌어야 합니다. 이 메시지를 받으셨다는 확인과 함께 이메일을 회신해 주시고 이 문제들을 어떻게 해결하실지에 대해 설명해 주시기 바랍니다.

클리포드 엘스턴 드림

Please e-mail me back with confirmation that you have received this message and explain how these issues will be resolved.

Sincerely,

Clifford Elston

> **어휘** invoice 송장 insulated 단열 처리를 한 protective 보호의 merchandise 물품 place an order 주문하다 purchase 구매하다 no later than 늦어도 ~까지 courier 택배회사, 배달원 overnight delivery 익일 배송 exchange 교환하다 charge (요금·값을) 청구하다 deduct 공제하다, 빼다 confirmation 확인 resolve 해결하다

18 엘스턴 씨의 주문에 대해 사실이 아닌 것은?
(A) 온라인으로 이루어졌다.
(B) 배송비가 포함되었다.
(C) 빠른 배송으로 보내졌다.
(D) 신용카드를 이용하여 결제되었다.

> **해설** 엘스턴 씨의 주문에 관한 문제이므로 송장을 주의 깊게 살펴야 한다. 엘스턴 씨의 주문은 빠른 배송이 아닌 보통 배송으로 보내졌기 때문에 정답은 (C).

19 해리슨 사가 판매하는 것 같은 제품은?
(A) 의료 기기
(B) 난방 설비
(C) 캠핑 장비
(D) 스키 용품

> **해설** 송장은 해리슨 사의 제품 구매 내역이다. 고객이 주문한 물품 ― 스키 재킷, 단열 장갑, 스키 고글 ― 을 통해서 해리슨 사가 스키 용품을 판매하는 회사임을 추론할 수 있다. 따라서 정답은 (D).

20 엘스턴 씨가 이메일을 보낸 이유는?
(A) 파손된 제품에 대해 항의하기 위해
(B) 상품을 주문하기 위해
(C) 주문의 문제점을 알리기 위해
(D) 지불 기한에 대해 문의하기 위해

> **해설** 엘스턴 씨가 보낸 이메일에 집중하여 문제를 풀어야 한다. 그는 잘못된 치수의 재킷을 배송받았고, 그가 지불한 고글 가격에서 한 개 가격은 공제돼야 한다고 했으므로 주문의 문제점을 알리려고 이메일을 썼음을 알 수 있다. 따라서 정답은 (C).

21 엘스턴 씨의 지불금에서 공제될 액수는?
(A) 8.95달러
(B) 12.49달러
(C) 15.99달러
(D) 25.99달러

> **해설** 송장과 이메일을 모두 확인해 가며 단서를 찾아야 하는 연계 문제이다. 엘스턴 씨가 보낸 이메일에 따르면, 고글이 1+1 행사를 한다는 것을 보고 고글을 2개 주문했다고 했는데, 송장에 보면 2개 금액이 청구되었으므로, 스키 고글 한 개의 가격인 15.99달러가 공제되어야 한다. 따라서 정답은 (C).

22 엘스턴 씨에 대해 암시된 것은?
(A) 필요한 쿠폰을 잃어버렸다.
(B) 스키 여행을 위해 바지를 구매했다.
(C) 장갑에 대해 더 많이 청구되었다.
(D) 1월 10일에 도시에 없을 것이다.

> **해설** 엘스턴 씨는 1월 9일까지는 집에서 물건을 받을 수 있지만, 그 이후에는 스키 여행을 가서 못 받는다고 했으므로, 그가 1월 10일에는 여행을 간 상태라는 걸 추론할 수 있다. 따라서 정답은 (D).

[23-27] 채용 공고 & 채용 이메일 & 신입사원 오리엔테이션 일정표

Job Openings at Willow Co.

Willow Co., the leading supplier of corporate credit card services, is looking for motivated individuals to join its team. We have a solid reputation for excellence, and (23)we offer some of the highest base salaries and commission rates in the industry. For applicants to be considered, we require (24C) excellent speaking and writing skills, (24D)the capacity to work well with others, and a positive attitude. Previous sales experience is preferred, but we are willing to train the right people. (24A)Please

윌로우 사의 일자리 공석

기업 신용카드 서비스 선두 공급업체인 윌로우 사에서 팀에 합류할 의욕 넘치는 인재를 찾습니다. 우리는 탁월성으로 탄탄한 명성을 갖고 있으며, (23)업계 최고의 기본 급여와 성과급을 제공합니다. 지원자 선정 조건으로, (24C)뛰어난 화술과 글쓰기 능력, (24D)다른 사람들과 잘 협업할 줄 아는 능력, 그리고 긍정적인 태도가 요구됩니다. 이전의 영업 경력을 우대하지만, 우리는 기꺼이 적절한 인재를 교육시킬 용의가 있습니다. (24A)직접 방문을 위해 본인 차량이 있어야 한다는 것을 알려드립니다.

note that you must have your own vehicle for in-person visits.

To apply, please send a résumé and cover letter to Claire Harper at harper.c@willow-co.com by June 18. Interviews will be held from June 21 to 25. (25-2) Successful candidates will report to their assigned branches for orientation sessions on July 6 (Lake City), July 7 (Winston), July 8 (Sherwood), and July 9 (Dawsonville).

To: Anthony Burris <a.burris@ridgepost.net>
From: Claire Harper <harper.c@willow-co.com>
Date: June 28
Subject: Contract

Dear Mr. Burris,

Welcome to the Willow Co. team! We are pleased you accepted the position. I will send you the sample employment contract sometime this week. Please look it over and let me know if you have any questions about it. You should bring a signed copy to (25-1)the orientation session, which your branch is scheduled to hold on July 8. (26-1)You should arrive at 8 A.M. and report to the head of human resources. You will train with various staff members throughout the day. I have attached a copy of the orientation schedule so you know in advance what will be covered. I look forward to working with you.

Warmest regards,

Claire Harper
Administrative Assistant, Willow Co.

Willow Co. New Employee Orientation

Time	Activity	Led by
8:00 A.M.	Arrival and Introductions	Administrative Assistant Claire Harper
8:30 A.M.	Welcome and Company Overview	Vice President Kevin Yoon
9:00 A.M.	Expectations and Company Policies	(26-2)HR Director Margaret Daniels
10:30 A.M.	Break	
10:45 A.M.	Employee Benefits and Compensation	Finance Director Stephanie Lowe
11:15 A.M.	Security Procedures and ID Photos	Security Manager Dennis Mallory
noon	Lunch	

(27)Please have a notebook or day planner with you to take notes during the orientation. After lunch, employees will receive training from their team leaders.

어휘 job opening 채용 공고 | leading 선두적인 | supplier 공급업체 | motivated 의욕 있는 | solid reputation 탄탄한 명성 | base salary 기본급 | commission 성과급 | applicant 지원자 | capacity 능력 | positive 긍정적인 | in-person 직접의 | cover letter 자기소개서 | assigned 배정된 | employment contract 고용 계약서 | look over ~을 살펴보다 | throughout ~내내 | attach 첨부하다 | in advance 미리 | cover 다루다 | overview 개요 | expectation 기대 | benefit (보통 복수형) (직원) 복지 혜택 | compensation 급여, 수당 | procedure 절차

23 이 일자리의 장점으로 언급된 것은?
(A) 전속 계약금
(B) 탄력적인 근무 일정
(C) 넉넉한 휴가 기간
(D) 경쟁력 있는 급여

해설 채용 공고에서 업계 최고의 급여 및 성과급을 제공한다고 했으므로, 정답은 (D).
오답 피하기 (A) A signing bonus는 고용 계약 시 일회성의 인센티브로 지불하는 보너스로, 실적에 따라 받는 commission과는 다른 개념이다.
패러프레이징 지문의 highest base salaries가 정답에서 Competitive wages로 패러프레이징되었다.

24 이 일자리의 자격 요건으로 시사되지 않은 것은?
(A) 개인 차량
(B) 마케팅 분야 경력
(C) 뛰어난 커뮤니케이션 능력
(D) 협업할 수 있는 능력

해설 채용 공고에서 excellent speaking and writing skills는 (C)에, the capacity to work well with others는 (D)에 해당하는 내용이다. 단서(24A)에 자신의 차량이 있어야 한다는 조건도 나와 있다. 영업 경력을 우대하긴 하지만 마케팅 경력에 대한 언급은 없으므로 정답은 (B).

25 버리스 씨가 근무하게 될 곳은?
(A) 레이크 시
(B) 윈스턴
(C) 셔우드
(D) 도슨빌

해설 이메일과 채용 공고에서 단서를 찾아야 하는 연계 문제이다. 이메일에서 버리스 씨가 일하게 될 지점은 7월 8일에 오리엔테이션이 예정되어 있다고 했고, 채용 공고에서 이날 오리엔테이션을 하는 지점은 셔우드임을 확인할 수 있다. 따라서 정답은 (C).

26 버리스 씨가 오리엔테이션에 도착해서 맨 처음 찾아야 하는 사람은?
(A) 클레어 하퍼
(B) 케빈 윤
(C) 마가렛 대니얼즈
(D) 데니스 말로리

해설 이메일과 일정표에서 단서를 찾아야 하는 연계 문제이다. 이메일에서 버리스 씨는 지점에 도착해서 인사부장에게 보고해야 한다는 지시를 받았는데, 오리엔테이션 일정표에서 인사 책임자는 마가렛 대니얼즈 씨임을 확인할 수 있다. 따라서 정답은 (C).

27 오리엔테이션 프로그램에 대해 시사된 것은?
(A) 참가자들은 쓸 것을 가져와야 한다.
(B) 매 시간 사이에 휴식 시간이 있다.
(C) 단 한 명의 인솔자가 이끈다.
(D) 팀장들이 다음날 신입 직원들을 만날 것이다.

해설 오리엔테이션에 관한 내용이므로 일정표에서 단서를 찾는다. 일정표의 끝부분에 메모를 할 수 있는 공책이나 일일 계획표를 가져와 달라고 했으므로 정답은 (A).
패러프레이징 지문의 a notebook or day planner with you to take notes가 정답에서 something to write on으로 패러프레이징되었다.

CHAPTER 3 실전 모의고사
ACTUAL TEST 1

p.162

147 (C)	148 (C)	149 (A)	150 (C)	151 (B)	152 (A)
153 (C)	154 (C)	155 (A)	156 (C)	157 (D)	158 (B)
159 (C)	160 (A)	161 (A)	162 (C)	163 (D)	164 (B)
165 (A)	166 (D)	167 (C)	168 (D)	169 (B)	170 (B)
171 (C)	172 (C)	173 (D)	174 (C)	175 (B)	176 (C)
177 (D)	178 (D)	179 (A)	180 (A)	181 (A)	182 (D)
183 (B)	184 (A)	185 (D)	186 (C)	187 (D)	188 (D)
189 (D)	190 (A)	191 (B)	192 (D)	193 (B)	194 (A)
195 (D)	196 (B)	197 (C)	198 (A)	199 (D)	200 (B)

[147-148] 행사 일정에 관한 회람

MEMO

Dear staff:

(147)This memo is to share with you the updated schedule for the final quarter of our fiscal year. We request that you make note of the following special occasions and record these events in your agendas. If you are aware of any scheduling conflicts, please inform the management staff.

– Holiday in honor of the company's anniversary ... May 7
– Computer system upgrade ... June 19
– (148)Pharmaceutical development convention ... July 24–26
– Year-end financial audit ... August 3

회람

직원 여러분들께:

(147)이 회람은 우리 회계 연도 마지막 분기의 최신 일정을 공유하기 위함입니다. 다음 특별 행사들을 숙지하시고 의제로 이 행사들을 기록해 두시기를 요청 드립니다. 만약 일정이 겹치는 것이 발견되면 관리 직원에게 알려주시기 바랍니다.

– 회사 창립기념일 휴무 ... 5월 7일
– 컴퓨터 시스템 업그레이드 ... 6월 19일
– (148)제약 개발 총회 ... 7월 24–26일
– 연말 회계 감사 ... 8월 3일

어휘 updated 최신의, 갱신된 quarter (1년의 4분의 1인) 분기 fiscal 회계의 make note of ~에 대해 숙지하다 occasion 행사, (어떤 일의) 때 agenda 의제, 회의 안건 be aware of ~을 알다[자각하다] scheduling conflict 일정이 겹침 audit 회계 감사, (품질 등의) 검사

147 회람의 목적은?
(A) CEO의 퇴임을 알리기 위해
(B) 직원들에게 컴퓨터 교체를 지시하기 위해
(C) 직원들에게 예정된 행사를 알리기 위해
(D) 휴일 일정을 보여주기 위해

해설 지문의 목적을 묻는 문제이므로 회람 도입부를 읽도록 한다. 일정을 공유하기 위해 회람을 보낸다고 했으므로 정답은 (C).

148 제약 총회가 시작하는 때는?
(A) 5월 7일
(B) 6월 19일
(C) 7월 24일
(D) 7월 26일

해설 단서(148)을 보면, 제약 개발 총회가 7월 24일부터 26일까지라고 했으므로 정답은 (C).
패러프레이징 지문의 Pharmaceutical이 문제에서 drug로 바꾸어 표현되었다.

[149-151] 결혼식장 예약 확인 이메일

To: Felicity Caparulo <felicitycaparulo@capcorporation.com>
From: Mike Yard <mike.yard@trafalgarhall.com>
Date: February 20
Subject: Hall reservation confirmation
Attachment: Electronic receipt

Dear Ms. Caparulo,

First of all, I wish to congratulate you on your engagement! Second, I am writing to (149)confirm receipt of your deposit for the wedding that you have booked with us at Trafalgar Hall. According to your file, you are taking advantage of (150A)our catering services in addition to (150B)our in-house party planner. To accommodate your 150 dinner guests, there will be eighteen round tables with eight people placed at each. Your head table will then seat the remaining six members of the wedding party. (150C)Be aware that our furniture arrangement is fixed and will not be changed.

I've attached an electronic copy of the receipt for the $1,000 deposit that you have already paid. The outstanding balance will be confirmed once you have determined your decoration preferences. The prices will then be calculated accordingly. (151) Please visit our Web site www.trafalgarhall.com/decorations to view pictures of decoration choices we have available. Included on the same page are also (150D)photos of our floral centerpieces.

Warm regards,

Mike Yard, Reservation Director
Trafalgar Hall

수신: 펠리시티 카파룰로 <felicitycaparulo@capcorporation.com>
발신: 마이크 야드 <mike.yard@trafalgarhall.com>
날짜: 2월 20일
제목: 홀 예약 확정
첨부 파일: 전자 영수증

카파룰로 씨께,

우선, 귀하의 약혼을 축하 드립니다! 둘째로, (149)귀하께서 저희 트라팔가 홀에 예약하신 결혼식 예치금이 저희 측에 수령 확인되었음을 알려드리기 위해 이메일을 씁니다. 귀하의 파일에 의하면, 귀하께서는 저희 (150B)사내 파티 플래너와 더불어 저희 (150A)케이터링 서비스를 이용 예정이십니다. 150명의 귀하 측 저녁식사 손님을 수용하기 위해 각 8명씩 앉는 18개의 원탁 테이블이 제공될 것입니다. 그리고 가장 앞쪽 테이블에는 나머지 6명의 결혼식 하객 인원이 앉게 될 것입니다. (150C)가구 배치가 확정되었으며 이는 변경되지 않음을 유념하시기 바랍니다.

귀하께서 이미 지불하신 1,000달러 예치금의 영수증에 대한 전자 사본을 첨부했습니다. 미납 잔액은 귀하께서 선호하는 장식을 결정하시면 확정될 것입니다. 가격은 그러고 나서 그에 따라 계산될 것입니다. (151)이용 가능한 장식 사진을 보시려면 저희 웹사이트 www.trafalgarhall.com/decorations를 방문해 주십시오. 같은 페이지에 (150D)저희 중앙부 꽃 장식 사진들이 포함되어 있습니다.

트라팔가 홀, 예약 담당자
마이크 야드 드림

어휘 electronic 전자의, 온라인상의 engagement 약혼, 약속 confirm receipt of ~의 수령을 확인하다 deposit 예치금, 보증금 book with ~에 예약하다 in-house 사내 accommodate (인원을) 수용하다 remaining 나머지의, 남은 be aware that ~을 유념하다[자각하다] fix 확정하다, 고정하다 outstanding balance 미납 잔액 preference 선호하는 것 calculate 계산하다, 산정하다 accordingly 그에 맞춰, 부응하여 available 이용 가능한 centerpiece 중앙부 장식, 가장 중요한 작품

---

149 행사의 목적은?
 (A) 결혼 축하연
 (B) 결혼식 전날 만찬
 (C) 신부 축하 점심식사
 (D) 약혼식

해설 이메일에서 논의되는 행사의 종류를 봐야 한다. 카파룰로 씨가 결혼식을 위해 트라팔가 홀을 대여하였고, 내빈들에게 케이터링 서비스가 제공된다고 했으므로 정답은 (A).

150 트라팔가 홀에서 제공하는 서비스가 아닌 것은?
 (A) 음식 케이터링
 (B) 파티 구상
 (C) 가구 재배치
 (D) 방 장식

해설 NOT 문제는 선택지 4개를 모두 지문과 하나하나 대조해 가며 풀어야 한다. 가구 배치는 한번 확정되면 다시 변경되지 않는다고 했으므로 정답은 (C).

151 웹사이트에서 이용할 수 있는 정보는?
  (A) 저녁식사 및 후식 메뉴
  (B) 선택 가능한 장식 이미지들
  (C) 연회장의 도면
  (D) 좌석과 테이블 배치도

해설 웹사이트에서 이용 가능한 정보를 찾기 위해 사이트 주소가 언급된 부분을 재빨리 찾아 읽도록 한다. 웹사이트에 장식 사진들이 있다고 했으므로 정답은 (B).

패러프레이징 지문의 pictures of decoration choices가 정답에서는 Images of decoration options로 패러프레이징 되었다.

[152-153] 근무 요청 문자메시지

LEAH BORDERS   08:12 A.M.
(152)My alarm didn't go off this morning, so I just woke up! I'm so sorry to ask you this, but could you open the café for me?

LEAH BORDERS   08:13 A.M.
With traffic, I'll never make it across town by 9:00 A.M. and you're the only other manager who has a key.

KEVIN JESTER   08:16 A.M.
Okay, Leah. I can do that for you.

KEVIN JESTER   08:17 A.M.
(153)The only problem is that I can't stay for your entire shift. I have a dentist appointment at 10 A.M.

LEAH BORDERS   08:18 A.M.
That's fine! (153)I just need someone to open the doors and be there when the first customers arrive. I should be there by 9:30 A.M.

KEVIN JESTER   08:20 A.M.
Okay. I'll work for you until then.

LEAH BORDERS   08:20 A.M.
Thank you. I'm glad that you live so close to the café!

KEVIN JESTER   08:21 A.M.
Yeah, it works out perfectly.

레아 보더즈   오전 08:12
(152)오늘 아침에 알람이 울리지 않아서 이제서야 깼어요! 이런 부탁 드려서 정말 미안하지만, 제 대신 카페 문을 좀 열어줄 수 있겠어요?

레아 보더즈   오전 08:13
차가 밀려서, 저는 오전 9시까지 시내를 지나 절대 도착하지 못할 텐데, 저 말고 당신이 열쇠를 가지고 있는 유일한 매니저라서요.

케빈 제스터   오전 08:16
알았어요, 레아. 제가 그렇게 해 드릴게요.

케빈 제스터   오전 08:17
(153)단 한 가지 문제는 제가 당신 근무 시간 내내 있을 수는 없다는 거예요. 오전 10시에 치과 예약이 있거든요.

레아 보더즈   오전 08:18
그건 괜찮아요! (153)누군가 문을 열고 첫 번째 손님이 올 때 그곳에 있어 주기만 하면 돼요. 오전 9시 30분까지는 제가 도착할 테니까요.

케빈 제스터   오전 08:20
알겠어요. 그때까지 제가 대신 일할게요.

레아 보더즈   오전 08:20
고마워요. 당신이 카페에 그렇게 가까이 살아서 다행이에요.

케빈 제스터   오전 08:21
네, 더할 나위 없이 잘된 거죠.

어휘 **go off** (경보 등이) 울리다   **make it** 시간 맞춰 가다   **shift** 교대 근무   **dentist appointment** 치과 예약   **work out** (일이) 잘 되어가다

---

152 보더즈 씨에 대해 시사된 바는?
  (A) 늦게 일어났다.
  (B) 교통 체증에 갇혀 있다.
  (C) 열쇠를 잊고 안 가져왔다.
  (D) 근무 일정표를 분실했다.

해설 단서(152)에서 보더즈 씨는 알람이 울리지 않아서 이제서야 깼다고 상황을 설명하고 있으므로 그녀가 늦게 일어났다는 것을 알 수 있다. 따라서 정답은 (A).

153 오전 08:18에, 보더즈 씨가 "그건 괜찮아요"라고 하는 의도는?
  (A) 제스터 씨와 근무를 바꿔 줄 것이다.
  (B) 치과 예약을 변경할 수 있다.
  (C) 자신의 근무 시간 중 일부만 대신해 주면 된다.
  (D) 제스터 씨에게 기꺼이 초과 근무 수당을 지불할 것이다.

해설 보더즈 씨가 제스터 씨에게 대신 카페 문을 열어 줄 것을 부탁했는데, 보더즈 씨의 근무 시간 내내 대신 일해 주기는 어렵다고 제스터 씨가 대답했다. 이에 "그건 괜찮아요"라고 말한 것은 근무 시간 내내 있을 필요는 없다는 의미이므로 정답은 (C).

[154-156] 기업 확장 계획에 대한 기사

Mexico Weekly
Business Reports

MEXICO CITY, July 8—(154)Developer Jordan Callen has purchased additional land upon which he plans to begin expanding his dairy factory in Mexico City. Callen's aim is to triple the current size of his factory's internal space in order to install sophisticated new equipment. In addition to multiplying the number of Callen's assets, (156) the new machinery will also enable him to create one of the first "zero water" manufacturing sites in the world. Callen Ltd. will be implementing these new processes at its Factory Viridiana in the water-deprived area of Mexico City. (156)After the construction has been completed, the facility will be able to use water that has been recycled from its dairy operations. This then creates a location in which zero water is wasted. (155)Callen Ltd. plans to perfect this process and then replicate the approach in many of its other global factories. It is an important step toward creating sustainability in the industry.

〈멕시코 위클리〉
비즈니스 보도

멕시코 시티, 7월 8일—(154)개발업자 조던 캘런 씨는 멕시코 시티에 있는 자신의 유제품 공장을 확장하려고 계획하는 추가 부지를 구입했다. 캘런 씨의 목적은 새로운 정교한 장비를 설치하기 위해 현재 공장의 내부 공간을 세 배로 확장하는 것이다. 캘런 씨의 자산 규모가 증가하는 것은 물론이고, (156)그 새로운 기계는 그가 세계 최초의 "수분 제로" 제조 지역 중 하나를 만들 수 있게 할 것이다. 캘런 사는 멕시코 시티의 물 부족 지역에 있는 비리디아나 공장에서 이 새로운 공정을 시행할 예정이다. (156)공사가 끝나면 이 시설은 유제품 공정으로부터 재활용된 물을 이용할 수 있게 된다. 그러고 나서 물이 한 방울도 낭비되지 않는 장소가 생기는 것이다. (155)캘런 사는 이 공정을 완벽하게 한 후 전 세계의 다른 공장들 다수에서 이 처리 방식을 재현할 계획이다. 이는 산업 내에 지속 가능성을 이루어 내기 위한 중요한 한 걸음이다.

어휘 dairy 유제품, 낙농업 aim 목적, 목표 triple 세 배로 만들다 install 설치하다 multiply 증가시키다, 증대시키다 asset (보통 복수형) (기업 등이 보유한) 자산 enable ~ to do ~가 …할 수 있게 하다 implement 시행하다, 실행하다 deprived 부족한, 빈곤한 operation (기업의) 운영, (공장의) 가동 replicate 재현하다, 복제하다 approach 처리[접근] 방식

---

154 기사의 주제는?
(A) 다국적 기업가의 약력
(B) 공장 내부 묘사
(C) 확장 계획의 세부 내용
(D) 멕시코로의 기업 진출

155 캘런 사에 대해 시사된 바는?
(A) 세계 곳곳에 공장을 가지고 있다.
(B) 정수 회사이다.
(C) 재정 자원이 한정되어 있다.
(D) 경쟁사의 아이디어를 모방한다.

156 [1], [2], [3], [4]로 표시된 위치 중 다음 문장이 들어가기에 가장 알맞은 곳은?
"그러고 나서 물이 한 방울도 낭비되지 않는 장소가 생기는 것이다."
(A) [1]
(B) [2]
(C) [3]
(D) [4]

해설 공장 확장 예정인 캘런 사의 세부 계획에 대해 설명한 기사이므로 정답은 (C)이다.
오답 피하기 물을 낭비하지 않는다는 것 외에 공장 내부에 대해 드러난 바가 없으므로 (B)는 오답. 멕시코로 처음 진출하는 기업이 아니라 이미 멕시코에 있는 유제품 공장 확장에 관한 내용이므로 (D) 역시 오답.

해설 캘런 사가 전 세계에 다른 많은 공장을 갖고 있다고 했으므로 (A)가 정답임을 알 수 있다.
패러프레이징 지문의 global factories가 정답에서 factories around the world로 패러프레이징되었다.

해설 주어진 문장은 물이 한 방울도 낭비되지 않는 시설이 생긴다는 내용으로, 연결사 then이 쓰인 것으로 미루어 보아 그 앞에는 물 절약이 가능한 새로운 시설 설립에 관한 내용이 와야 한다. 첫 번째 단서(156)에서 "수분 제로"를 가능하게 하는 방법이 제시되고, 두 번째 단서(156)에서 유제품 공정에 재활용된 물을 이용한다고 했으므로 주어진 문장은 이 뒤에 와야 자연스럽다. This는 주어진 문장의 앞 문장 전체를 가리킨다.

[157-158] 발레 공연 광고

Adelphi Performances
Presents…
(157)*Moonlight Wishes*
A ballet written and choreographed by Madame Cannato

The Bovim Ballet Company
Starring: Penelope Ramirez, Leo D'Avanzo, Tammy Matarese, and Leah Bonnema
February 19 at 8 P.M.
Cautley Hall
Auerspergstrasse 4, Salzburg 5020, Austria

General admission as well as VIP tickets can be purchased through the box office or online at www.cautleyhall.com until 12 P.M. on the day of the performance. (158)VIP passes allow patrons to receive autographs from the dancers after the show.

아델피 공연단에서
(157)마담 카나토가 작곡하고 안무를 짠 발레 〈달빛 기원〉을 선보입니다.

보빔 발레단
주연: 페넬로페 라미레즈, 레오 다반조, 태미 마타리스, 레아 본네마
2월 19일 저녁 8시
코틀리 홀
오스트리아, 잘츠부르크 5020, 아우어슈페르크슈트라쎄 4번지

VIP 입장권을 비롯한 일반 입장권은 공연 당일 오후 12시까지 매표소나 www.cautleyhall.com에서 온라인으로 구매하실 수 있습니다. (158)VIP 입장권은 고객분들로 하여금 공연 후 무용단에서 사인을 받을 수 있게 해드릴 것입니다.

어휘 **performance** 공연, 수행 **choreograph** 안무를 짜다 **star** (영화·연극 등에서) 주연을 맡다 **admission** 입장, 허가 **patron** 고객, 후원자 **autograph** 사인

157 어떤 공연에 대한 정보인가?
(A) 교향악단
(B) 합창단
(C) 뮤지컬
(D) 무용

해설 발레 공연 광고이므로 정답은 (D).
패러프레이징 지문의 ballet가 정답에서 상위어인 dance로 패러프레이징되었다.

158 참가자들이 사인을 받을 수 있는 방법은?
(A) 매표소를 방문함으로써
(B) 특권을 제공하는 표를 구매함으로써
(C) 연기자 개개인과 만남으로써
(D) 공연에 일찍 도착함으로써

해설 단서(158)에 언급되어 있듯이, 무용단에서 사인을 받으려면 VIP 입장권을 구매해야 하므로 정답은 (B).
패러프레이징 지문의 VIP passes가 정답에서 privileged tickets로 패러프레이징되었다.

[159-160] 버스 시간표

Destination	Departure Time	Arrival Time	Platform	Status
Calgary, AB	9:00 A.M.	11:55 A.M.	2	Boarding
Banff, AB	9:15 A.M.	1:20 P.M.	11	(160) Delayed
Red Deer, AB	10:20 A.M.	(159) 12:05 P.M.	8	On schedule

Passenger instructions:
1) Travelers are encouraged to arrive at the bus terminal 45 minutes before their departure time. Tickets are sold without specific seats assigned, so passengers who arrive at the last minute may

목적지	출발 시간	도착 시간	승강장	상황
앨버타 주, 캘거리	오전 9시	오전 11시 55분	2번	탑승 중
앨버타 주, 밴프	오전 9시 15분	오후 1시 20분	11번	(160)지연
앨버타 주, 레드디어	오전 10시 20분	(159) 오후 12시 5분	8번	정시 운행

승객 지침:
1) 여행하시려는 분들은 출발 시간 45분 전에 버스터미널에 도착하실 것을 권유 드립니다. 승차권에 특정 좌석이 지정되지 않고 판매되므로, 마지막에 도착하신 승객 분들께서는 객차가 이미 꽉 차 있는 것을 보실 수도 있습니다.

discover that the coach is already full.
2) Please line up at your designated platform with your ticket ready.

2) 승차권을 준비하시고 지정된 승강장에 줄을 서 주시기 바랍니다.

어휘 boarding 탑승, 승차   delayed 지연된, 기한을 넘긴   on schedule 정시에, 예정대로   be encouraged to do ~하도록 권유[장려]되다   line up 줄 서다   designated 지정된

159 레드디어행 버스가 도착하는 시간은?
  (A) 오전 10시 20분
  (B) 오전 11시 55분
  (C) 오후 12시 5분
  (D) 오후 1시 20분

해설 시간표에서 목적지가 Red Deer라고 쓰인 차편의 도착 시간을 보면 된다. 정답은 (C).

160 뱀프행 버스에 대해 암시된 것은?
  (A) 정시에 출발하지 않을 것이다.
  (B) 고장 났다.
  (C) 좌석이 이미 꽉 찼다.
  (D) 가장 먼저 출발할 것이다.

해설 뱀프행 버스와 관련된 부분을 찾아본다. 버스가 지연될 것이라고 시간표에 나와 있으므로 일정대로 출발하지 않을 것임을 유추할 수 있다. 따라서 정답은 (A).
패러프레이징 지문의 Delayed가 정답에서 not leave on schedule로 바꾸어 표현되었다.

[161-163] 수하물 규정에 관한 공지

Attention West Wing Airlines Passengers

(161)We require that all of our passengers familiarize themselves with the West Wing Airlines baggage policy. The total baggage allowance for all domestic flights is two checked bags and two carry-on bags per passenger. (162)Any traveler who exceeds the acceptable number of bags is subject to a $50 fee to be charged at the discretion of the ticket agent. All small carry-on items, such as purses, must be stowed underneath the seat in front of you. Larger luggage items should be placed in the overhead compartments. Unidentified liquids in unmarked containers, firearms, and sharp objects are not allowed on the plane. (163)For more information on the carry-on and checked baggage rules, please call us at 1-800-937-8946.

웨스트윙 항공사 탑승객들께서는 주목해 주세요.

(161)모든 탑승객들께 웨스트윙 항공사의 수하물 규정을 숙지하시기를 요청 드립니다. 모든 국내선 비행의 총 수하물 허용량은 탑승객 1인당 부치는 가방 두 개와 기내용 가방 두 개입니다. (162)허용된 가방 수를 초과하는 여행자 분께서는 발권 직원의 재량으로 50달러의 비용을 부과받게 됩니다. 핸드백과 같은 작은 기내용 물품들은 여러분 앞에 있는 좌석 아래에 보관하셔야 합니다. 더 큰 짐은 머리 위 보관함에 보관하셔야 합니다. 표시되지 않은 용기 안에 담긴 정체 불명의 액체, 화기, 날카로운 물체들은 모두 기내 반입이 금지됩니다. (163)기내용 짐과 부치는 짐 관련 규정에 대해 더 궁금한 점이 있으시면 1-800-937-8946으로 전화해 주시기 바랍니다.

어휘 familiarize oneself with ~을 숙지하다[잘 알고 있다]   allowance 허용, 허가   domestic 국내의; 가정의   check (비행기 등을 탈 때 수하물을) 부치다   carry-on bag 기내 휴대용 가방   exceed 초과하다   acceptable 허용된, 용인되는   be subject to ~이 부과되다   at the discretion of ~의 재량으로   stow 보관하다, 잘 넣어두다   compartment 보관함, 칸   unidentified 정체 불명의, 알아볼 수 없는   firearm (총, 포 등의) 화기   ban 금지하다

161 공지의 목적은?
  (A) 관련 정책을 알리기 위해
  (B) 대피 절차를 요약해 주기 위해
  (C) 안전 규정을 명시하기 위해
  (D) 가격 변동을 안내하기 위해

해설 글의 목적을 찾는 문제이므로 지문의 앞부분에 주목해야 한다. 위 공지는 수하물 규정을 알리기 위해 보내진 것이므로 정답은 (A).
오답 피하기 지문은 주로 수하물 정책과 관련된 내용이므로 (C)는 오답.

162 탑승객들에게 50달러의 비용이 부과되는 이유는?
(A) 비행기에 동물을 데려오기 위해 지불했다.
(B) 좌석 아래쪽에 기내용 짐을 보관하지 않았다.
(C) 명시된 수하물 허용량을 초과했다.
(D) 부친 짐에 금지된 물품들을 넣었다.

[해설] 지문에서 50달러가 언급되는 부분을 찾는다. 단서(162)에 허용된 가방 수를 초과하는 여행자들에게 50달러의 비용이 부과될 것이라고 했으므로 정답은 (C).
[패러프레이징] 지문의 exceeds the acceptable number of bags가 정답에서 surpassed the stated baggage allowance로 패러프레이징되었다.

163 사람들이 정보를 더 얻을 수 있는 방법은?
(A) 정보 제공 비디오를 시청함으로써
(B) 안전 안내 책자를 읽음으로써
(C) 비행 승무원에게 문의함으로써
(D) 항공사에 직접 연락함으로써

[해설] 단서(163)에서 궁금한 점이 있으면 전화로 문의하라고 했으므로 정답은 (D).
[패러프레이징] 지문의 call us가 정답에서 contacting the airline으로 패러프레이징되었다.

[164-167] 미용실 이전에 관한 편지

Deidra Herndon
234 Cambine St.
Vancouver, BC V5A 4S3

Tiny Tots Hair Salon
849 Burrad Blvd.
Vancouver, BC V5A 0A1

1 November

Dear loyal customer:

Tiny Tots Hair Salon is moving to Burrad Blvd. (166A)Our new building is twice the size of our old one, which allows us to book more appointments and service more customers than we could in the past.

(166B)The new space will have a specifically designed area full of magazines and picture books available to keep children occupied and busy while they are waiting for their appointments. Reading materials will also be available for accompanying adults.

To celebrate the opening of our new salon, (164)we will be having a customer loyalty party on Saturday, November 20. Starting the next day, we will extend our hours. (167)Previously, our salon had been closed on Tuesdays, but now—in response to the high customer demand—it will be open every day of the week from 9 A.M. to 6 P.M. We're trying to make it easier for customers to get appointments that fit their busy schedules.

(166C)Additionally, we have created our own line of children's hair-care products. (165)Enclosed is a pamphlet with pictures of the entire line of Tiny Tots merchandise that we will be selling at our new location. (166C)All of these items will be offered at 30% off the normal price until November 30. Thus, even if you can't attend our party on the twentieth, be sure to drop by to check out these high-quality, chemical-free items.

데이드라 헌던 씨
캠바인 가 234
브리티시 컬럼비아 주, 벤쿠버 V5A 4S3

타이니 타츠 미용실
버라드 대로 849
브리티시 컬럼비아 주, 벤쿠버 V5A 0A1

11월 1일

항상 애용해 주시는 고객 여러분께:

타이니 타츠 미용실이 버라드 대로로 자리를 옮깁니다. (166A)저희의 새 건물은 이전 건물보다 두 배로 크며, 그로 인해 예전보다 더 많은 예약을 받을 수 있고 더 많은 고객 분들께 서비스를 제공해 드릴 수 있게 되었습니다.

(166B)또한, 새 공간에는 어린이들이 예약 시간을 기다리는 동안 그들을 집중하느라 바쁘게 해 줄 잡지들과 그림책으로 가득 찬 특별히 고안된 공간이 있을 것입니다. 읽을거리는 함께 오시는 어른들도 이용하실 수 있습니다.

저희의 새로운 미용실의 개장을 축하하기 위해 (164)11월 20일 토요일에 고객 만족 다과회를 열고자 합니다. 그다음 날부터 영업 시간을 연장할 것입니다. (167)전에는 저희 미용실이 화요일에 휴무였지만 이제는—고객들의 요구에 응답하여—매일 오전 9시부터 저녁 6시까지 일주일 내내 문을 열게 됩니다. 저희는 고객 여러분께서 바쁘신 일정에 맞춘 예약을 더 수월하게 잡으실 수 있도록 노력하고 있습니다.

(166C)또한, 저희 미용실의 독자적인 어린이 모발 케어 제품군을 출시했습니다. (165)동봉된 것은 새 지점에서 판매하게 될 모든 타이니 타츠 제품군의 사진이 있는 책자입니다. (166C)모든 제품들은 11월 30일까지 정가에서 30%가 할인되어 제공될 것입니다. 따라서, 20일에 저희 다과회에 참석하지 못하셔도 이 고품질의, 화학물질이 들어 있지 않은 제품들을 확인하러 꼭 들러 주시기 바랍니다.

We hope to see you at our new location sometime soon.
Tiny Tots Hair Salon

조만간 새로운 미용실에서 귀하를 뵙게 되기를 바랍니다.
타이니 타츠 미용실

어휘 appointment 예약, 약속 specifically 특별히, 중요하게 occupied 집중한, 정신이 팔린 reading material (보통 복수형) 읽을거리 accompanying 동반[수반]하는 loyalty 충실, 충성 enclosed 동봉된, 포함된 merchandise 제품 drop by 잠깐 들르다

164 영업 시간이 연장되는 때는?
(A) 11월 1일
(B) 11월 21일
(C) 11월 25일
(D) 11월 30일

해설 단서(164)에서 11월 20일에 다과회가 열리고, 그 다음날부터 영업 시간이 연장된다고 했으므로 정답은 (B).

165 편지에 동봉된 것은?
(A) 광고 책자
(B) 할인 쿠폰
(C) 주문서
(D) 명함

해설 단서(165)에서 제품 사진을 볼 수 있는 책자를 편지에 동봉했다고 했으므로 정답은 (A).
패러프레이징 지문의 Enclosed와 pamphlet이 문제와 정답에서 각각 included와 advertising brochure로 패러프레이징되었다.

166 가게에 일어난 변화로 언급되지 않은 것은?
(A) 규모 확장
(B) 독서 구역 마련
(C) 신상품 할인
(D) 2층 증축

해설 NOT 문제이므로 선택지 4개를 지문 내용과 하나하나 비교해야 한다. 2층 증축에 대한 내용은 나와 있지 않으므로 정답은 (D).

167 [1], [2], [3], [4]로 표시된 위치 중 다음 문장이 들어가기에 가장 알맞은 곳은?
"저희는 고객 여러분께서 바쁘신 일정에 맞춘 예약을 더 수월하게 잡으실 수 있도록 노력하고 있습니다."
(A) [1]
(B) [2]
(C) [3]
(D) [4]

해설 주어진 문장은 고객의 일정에 맞춘 예약을 더 쉽게 할 수 있도록 노력 중이라는 내용으로, 그 앞에는 이를 위한 구체적 노력이나 방법에 관한 내용이 오는 것이 자연스럽다. 단서(167)을 보면 전에는 화요일에 휴무였다가 일주일 내내 문을 열게 되었다고 했으므로 주어진 문장은 이 뒤에 와야 한다. 정답은 (C).

[168-171] 동료의 퇴사 및 채용에 관한 온라인 채팅 대화문

Marsha Hudspeth   4:25 P.M.
You two missed the announcement in the staff meeting, but I'm sure you've already heard that, (168)on November 2, we will be saying goodbye to our beloved director of operations, Keith Winfield.

James Ambrosino   4:27 P.M.
I'm so sad to see him leave. I'll miss having him in the office.

Alphie Dorado   4:29 P.M.
Me too. (169)But we all knew that he had to retire eventually. It's the right decision.

James Ambrosino   4:31 P.M.
I agree. Anyway, his role will be taken over by Ed Culler, who is currently the head of the production department. Ed is a great fit for that position. He'll begin training soon, right?

마샤 허즈페스   오후 4:25
두 분은 직원 회의의 발표 내용을 못 들었지만, (168)11월 2일에 존경하는 우리 회사 경영 책임자이신 키스 윈필드 씨와 작별하게 된다는 것은 이미 들었을 겁니다.

제임스 앰브로시노   오후 4:27
그분이 떠나신다니 너무 섭섭해요. 그분이 재직하실 때가 그리울 거예요.

알피 도라도   오후 4:29
저도 그래요. (169)하지만 우리 모두 그분이 결국 퇴직하실 수밖에 없다는 걸 알고 있었잖아요. 그건 옳은 결정이에요.

제임스 앰브로시노   오후 4:31
저도 같은 생각이에요. 어쨌든, 그분의 역할은 현재 생산부 부서장이신 에드 컬러 씨에게 인계될 거예요. 에드 씨는 그 자리에 최고의 적임자. 에드 씨는 조만간 연수를 시작할 거예요, 그렇죠?

Alphie Dorado	4:33 P.M.

Yes. Ed will train under Mr. Winfield in October. We wanted him to have a full month in the position while Mr. Winfield was still here.

James Ambrosino	4:35 P.M.

But Ed's position is still unfilled, which worries me. We need to locate a suitable candidate as soon as possible.

Marsha Hudspeth	4:37 P.M.

(170)(171)I'm going to send out an e-mail this afternoon to the entire production department letting all senior staff members know that they are invited to send their résumés to Alphie for consideration.

Alphie Dorado	4:39 P.M.

(171)Please indicate that the deadline is the end of the month. We don't have a lot of time to spare.

Marsha Hudspeth	4:41 P.M.

Of course. I'll be sure to include all the relevant deadline information as well as a copy of the job description.

알피 도라도	오후 4:33

네, 에드 씨는 10월에 윈필드 씨 밑에서 연수를 받을 거예요. 우리는 윈필드 씨가 아직 회사에 계시는 동안 에드 씨가 온전히 한 달 동안 그 자리를 겪어보기를 원했거든요.

제임스 앰브로시노	오후 4:35

그런데 에드 씨의 자리가 아직 공석이라, 걱정이에요. 가능한 한 빨리 적합한 후보를 찾아야 해요.

마샤 허즈페스	오후 4:37

(170)(171)제가 오늘 오후에 생산 부서 전체에 이메일을 보내서 모든 상급 간부들에게 알피 씨가 살펴보도록 각자의 이력서를 보내 달라고 알릴 예정이에요.

알피 도라도	오후 4:39

(171)마감은 이번 달 말까지라는 걸 명시해 주세요. 우리에게는 할애할 시간이 많지 않으니까요.

마샤 허즈페스	오후 4:41

물론이죠. 직무 설명서 사본과 함께 관련된 마감 안내 정보를 모두 포함시키도록 할게요.

어휘 beloved 존경하는, 사랑하는 director of operations (최고) 경영 책임자 retire 퇴직[은퇴]하다 eventually 결국 take over 인수하다 currently 현재 fit 적임자 unfilled (일자리 등이) 비어 있는 locate 찾다 suitable 적합한 candidate 후보자 senior staff 상급 간부 relevant 관련 있는 job description 직무 설명서

---

168 회사를 떠나는 사람은?
  (A) 제임스 앰브로시노
  (B) 에드 컬러
  (C) 마샤 허즈페스
  (D) 키스 윈필드

[해설] 단서(168)에서 키스 윈필드 씨와 작별을 하게 된다고 하고 있고, 그가 은퇴해서 회사를 떠나게 된다는 언급이 이어지고 있다. 따라서 정답은 (D).

169 오후 4:29에, 도라도 씨가 "그건 옳은 결정이에요"라고 하는 의도는?
  (A) 앰브로시노 씨의 제안에 동의한다.
  (B) 변화에 대한 이유를 이해한다.
  (C) 신임 책임자가 일을 잘 해 낼 것이라고 생각한다.
  (D) 회사의 현재 지도부를 신임한다.

[해설] 동료의 퇴사를 아쉬워하고 있음에도 불구하고, 단서(169)를 통해 화자들은 윈필드 씨가 결국 떠날 것을 예상하고 있었다는 것을 알 수 있다. 따라서 정답은 (B).

170 허즈페스 씨가 하겠다고 말한 것은?
  (A) 직무 설명서 작성하기
  (B) 특정 부서에 이메일 보내기
  (C) 지원 마감일 결정하기
  (D) 연수 세션 준비하기

[해설] 단서(170)에서 허즈페스 씨는 오후에 생산 부서 전체에 이메일을 보내겠다고 하고 있다. 따라서 정답은 (B).
[오답 피하기] 직무 설명서를 작성하겠다는 것이 아니라 사본을 이메일에 첨부하겠다고 했으므로 (A)는 오답이다.

171 이달 말에 있을 일은?
  (A) 은퇴식이 열린다.
  (B) 연수 프로그램이 시행된다.
  (C) 지원 기간이 끝난다.
  (D) 채용 공고가 게시된다.

[해설] 단서(171)을 종합해 보면, 생산부서 간부들이 이력서를 제출하여 부서장직에 지원할 수 있는 기간이 이달 말까지이므로 정답은 (C).

[172-175] 강의 일정 변경에 관한 회람

To: Graphic Design Team
From: Ella Parkinson
Date: March 2

Hello Everyone,

(172)I am writing to inform you of an adjustment to the design workshop, (174)which was originally scheduled for 9 A.M. on Friday, March 6, in conference room 3 of the Square Media headquarters building. (173)Unfortunately, Jacqueline Wallace has to fly to Beijing to meet with a client, so she will not be able to attend the workshop. As a result, (174)her 90-minute talk on using the Macrex Illustrator software program will be canceled because we were unable to find a replacement speaker. (174)Since this was the first session of the talk, we have decided to start the workshop from the second session, which will be Joseph Bennett's talk. Please refer to the handout distributed earlier for the complete timetable and description of topics.

The workshop will cover a variety of topics including specific software programs, design trends, and common mistakes. (175)All graphic design team employees at Square Media's three branches are expected to attend the workshop. If you are unable to do so for any reason, please e-mail me at ellap@squaremedia.net as soon as possible. This is so we can arrange for you to obtain the information in another way and also to have an accurate head count for the caterer. Any other questions may be directed to your immediate supervisor. They also have additional copies of the schedule should you need one. Please note that it is not necessary to bring your own laptop computer to the workshop.

This workshop was made possible by Square Media's Professional Development Fund. Should you have suggestions for future events that you believe would improve the skills of you and your colleagues, please send them to Amal Sykes at amals@squaremedia.net.

수신: 그래픽 디자인팀
발신: 엘라 파킨슨
날짜: 3월 2일

안녕하세요, 여러분,

(172)디자인 워크숍의 변경 사항에 대해 알려드리고자 이메일을 보냅니다. (174)디자인 워크숍은 원래 스퀘어 미디어 본사 건물 3회의실에서 3월 6일 금요일 오전 9시에 열릴 예정이었습니다. (173)공교롭게도 재클린 월러스 씨가 고객을 만나기 위해 베이징으로 가야 해서, 워크숍에 참석하지 못하게 되었습니다. 그 결과, Macrex 일러스트레이터 프로그램 사용에 관한 (174)그녀의 90분짜리 강의는 대신할 연사를 찾지 못한 이유로 취소될 것입니다. (174)이 강의가 첫 세션이기 때문에, 조셉 베넷 씨의 강의가 있을 두 번째 세션부터 워크숍을 시작하기로 결정했습니다. 전체 시간표와 주제 설명은 전에 나눠 드린 인쇄물을 참조하시기 바랍니다.

워크숍에서는 특정 소프트웨어 프로그램과 디자인 경향, 흔히 저지르기 쉬운 실수 등 다양한 주제를 다룰 것입니다. (175)스퀘어 미디어의 지점 세 곳에 근무하는 그래픽 디자인팀 직원들은 모두 워크숍에 참석하기로 되어 있습니다. 어떤 이유로든 그럴 수 없는 경우에는, 가능한 한 빨리 ellap@squaremedia.net으로 저에게 이메일을 주시기 바랍니다. 여러분이 다른 방법으로 정보를 얻을 수 있도록 조정하기 위해서일 뿐만 아니라 식사를 제공할 업체를 위해 정확한 인원수를 알기 위해서이기도 합니다. 기타 질문은 여러분의 직속 상사에게 하시면 됩니다. 여러분이 필요로 할 경우, 직속 상사에게도 여분의 일정표가 있습니다. 워크숍에 여러분의 노트북 컴퓨터를 가져올 필요가 없다는 것을 알려드립니다.

이번 워크숍은 스퀘어 미디어의 전문성 개발 기금의 지원을 받아 가능해졌습니다. 향후 여러분 및 동료들의 능력을 향상시킬 것으로 여겨지는 행사에 대한 제안이 있으시면, amals@squaremedia.net으로 아말 사이크스 씨에게 보내 주십시오.

어휘 adjustment 수정, 조정 originally 원래 headquarters 본사 replacement 대신할 사람 refer to ~을 참조하다 handout 배포 자료, 인쇄물 cover 다루다 obtain 얻다 accurate 정확한 head count 인원수 caterer (행사) 음식 공급업체 immediate supervisor 직속 상사 additional 추가의 colleague 동료

172 회람의 목적은?
(A) 신제품을 홍보하기 위해
(B) 회사 규정을 설명하기 위해
(C) 일정 변경을 알리기 위해
(D) 신임 관리자를 소개하기 위해

해설 공지의 목적은 주로 첫 부분에서 언급된다. 단서(172)에서 워크숍의 변경 사항을 알리기 위해서라고 목적을 밝히고 있으며, 이어지는 내용을 보면 일정상 변경이 있음을 알 수 있다. 따라서 정답은 (C).

173 월러스 씨에 대해 추론할 수 있는 것은?
(A) 더 나중 시간대에 강의를 할 것이다.
(B) 베이징 지점으로 옮길 계획이다.
(C) 강의 주제 변경을 요청했다.
(D) 막판에 출장이 잡혔다.

174 월러스 씨의 강의가 원래 끝나기로 되어 있던 때는?
(A) 오전 9:30
(B) 오전 10:00
(C) 오전 10:30
(D) 오전 11:00

175 일부 수신인들이 파킨슨 씨에게 이메일을 보내야 하는 이유는?
(A) 노트북을 예약하기 위해
(B) 불참을 알리기 위해
(C) 일정표를 요청하기 위해
(D) 제안을 하기 위해

[해설] 단서(173)에서 월러스 씨는 베이징에서 고객을 만나야 하기 때문에 워크숍에 참석하지 못한다고 했는데, 이를 통해 워크숍 일정이 모두 정해진 후에 월러스 씨의 출장이 잡힌 것임을 유추할 수 있다. 따라서 막판에(at the last minute) 출장이 생긴 것이므로 정답은 (D).

[해설] 지문에 흩어진 정보를 종합해야 풀 수 있는 문제이다. 월러스 씨의 강의는 원래 오전 9시에 시작하는 워크숍의 첫 시간이었으며, 90분짜리였음을 알 수 있으므로, 예정되었던 강의 종료 시간은 오전 10시 30분이다. 따라서 정답은 (C).

[해설] 파킨슨 씨는 회람 작성자로, 단서(175)에서 워크숍에 참석하지 못하는 직원들은 자신에게 이메일을 보내 달라고 하고 있다. 따라서 정답은 (B).
[오답 피하기] 마지막 단락의 이메일 주소를 보고 (D)를 답으로 고르지 않도록 주의한다. 마지막 단락에서 직원들이 제안하고자 하는 내용을 이메일로 받을 사람은 아말 사이크스 씨이지, 파킨슨 씨가 아니다.

[176-180] 시 주차 정책 안내 이메일 & 주차권 영수증

To: Evangeline Hong <eviehong@netmail.com>
From: City of Saskatoon Parking Authority <noreply@cospa.com>
Subject: Obligatory parking pass
Date: March 2

Dear Ms. Hong:

Thank you for updating your address with the city database!

We hope you are settling into your new location comfortably. (176)This e-mail is intended to inform you of a parking policy for people who own property in your current complex. All cars parked in the attached lots must have a parking permit displayed in their dashboard windows.

(177)These parking passes are easily purchased through the City of Saskatoon. However, since your complex contains both residential as well as commercial units, there are two distinct types of parking passes. Business owners and their employees must apply for a $1,000/year purple parking pass. Purchasers of purple passes must keep their receipts if they wish to be reimbursed for this expense by their employers. Conversely, (179-2) yellow passes are granted exclusively to residents. The cost of a yellow pass is $600/year. Each parking pass—regardless of category type—has the number of an assigned parking spot labeled on it. A $15 fine will be charged to the owner of any vehicle found parked in a spot that does not correspond to the number on the parking pass displayed.

수신: 에반젤린 홍 〈eviehong@netmail.com〉
발신: 새스커툰 시 주차 당국 〈noreply@cospa.com〉
제목: 의무 주차권
날짜: 3월 2일

홍 씨께:

시의 데이터베이스에 귀하의 주소를 갱신해 주셔서 감사합니다!

귀하께서 새로운 곳에서 편안히 정착하시기를 기원합니다. (176)이 이메일은 귀가가 현재 살고 계신 복합 단지에 부동산을 소유하고 있는 분들께 해당되는 주차 정책을 알려드리기 위함입니다. 부설 주차장에 주차된 모든 차량은 자동차 계기판 위 유리창에 주차권을 보이게 두어야 합니다.

(177)이 주차권은 새스커툰 시에서 손쉽게 구매할 수 있습니다. 그러나, 귀하의 복합 단지에는 상업 단지뿐만 아니라 주거 단지도 있기 때문에 2가지의 서로 다른 종류의 주차권이 발행됩니다. 사업 소유주들과 직원들은 연 1,000달러의 보라색 주차권을 신청하여야 합니다. 보라색 주차권의 구매자 분들께서는 고용주에게 비용을 환급을 받고자 할 경우 반드시 영수증을 보관하셔야 합니다. 반대로 (179-2)노란색 주차권은 거주자들에게만 독점적으로 주어집니다. 노란색 주차권의 비용은 연간 600달러입니다. 종류와 상관없이 각 주차권에는 지정된 주차공간의 번호가 그 위에 적혀 있습니다. 부착된 주차권의 번호가 주차되어 있는 공간과 일치하지 않는 차량들에는 15달러의 벌금이 부과될 것입니다.

Payments can be made by credit card, debit card, or check. Be aware that city employees are prohibited from accepting cash payments. (180-2) When applying for a parking permit, you can select whether you would prefer to have your pass delivered to your home or be picked up at the City of Saskatoon Parking Authority center on Broadway Avenue. All passes are valid for one year from the date of purchase. An expiry date will be printed clearly on each pass.

Should you have any questions about the information details above, please call 555-567-1194. This is an automated message. Do not reply to this e-mail.

Regards,

City of Saskatoon Parking Authority

City of Saskatoon Parking Permit Receipt

Issue Date: March 4

Vehicle Information	Permit Information
Owner: Evangeline Hong **Address:** 221 Idylwyld Dr. N, Saskatoon, SK **License plate number:** 247 IVT **Payment Information** (179-1)**Amount Paid:** $600 (178)**Payment Method:** Credit card **Signature:** Evangeline Hong	(179-1)**Pass Type:** Yellow **Issue Type:** New (180-1)**Delivery Method:** Mail **Card Number:** XXXX XXXX XXXX 5465

Thank you for taking advantage of the City of Saskatoon's public parking service.

주차권은 신용카드, 체크카드나 수표로 지불하실 수 있습니다. 시의 공무원은 현금으로 지불 처리를 할 수 없다는 것을 알아두시기 바랍니다. (180-2)주차권을 신청하실 때 귀하의 주차권을 집으로 배송 받으실지, 브로드웨이 가에 있는 새스커툰 시의 주차 관리소에서 수령하실지 선택하실 수 있습니다. 모든 주차권은 구매일로부터 1년간 유효합니다. 만료일은 각 주차권에 명확히 인쇄되어 있습니다.

위에 안내된 세부 사항에 대해 질문이 있으시면 555-567-1194로 전화 주시기 바랍니다. 이는 자동 메시지입니다. 이 이메일로 답신하지 마시기 바랍니다.

새스커툰 시 주차 당국 드림

새스커툰 시 주차권 영수증

발행일: 3월 4일

자동차 정보	주차권 정보
소유자: 에반젤린 홍 주소: 새스캐처원 주 새스커툰 아이다일와일드 가 북쪽 221 자동차 번호판: 247 IVT 지불 정보 (179-1)지불액: 600달러 (178)결제 방법: 신용카드 서명: 에반젤린 홍	(179-1)종류: 노란색 발행 종류: 신규 (180-1)배송 방법: 우편 카드번호: XXXX XXXX XXXX 5465

새스커툰 시의 공공 주차 서비스를 이용해 주셔서 감사합니다.

어휘 settle into (새 집, 직장 등에) 자리를 잡다) 정착하다 property 부동산, 건물 attached 부속의 lot 주차장, 터 dashboard 자동차 계기판 residential 주거용의, 주거지의 commercial 상업용의 distinct 다른, 구분되는 reimburse (비용을) 환급해 주다 grant 주다, 수여하다 exclusively 독점적으로, 배타적으로 regardless of ~와 상관없이 label 라벨을 붙이다, (필요 정보를) 적다 correspond to ~에 응하다, ~와 일치하다 valid (법적, 공식적으로) 유효한, 타당한 expiry date 만료일, 만기일 automated 자동화된 issue 발행; 발행하다 license plate 자동차 번호판

---

176 이메일이 작성된 이유는?
(A) 새로운 이웃을 환영하기 위해
(B) 주소를 갱신하기 위해
(C) 정책을 설명하기 위해
(D) 결제를 요청하기 위해

177 주차권에 대해 언급된 것은?
(A) 구매는 선택 사항이다.
(B) 매달 갱신된다.
(C) 상업용 가격이 더 저렴하다.
(D) 결제는 새스커툰 시에 해야 한다.

해설 이메일의 앞부분에서 This e-mail is intended to inform you of(이 메일은 귀하께 ~을 알리기 위함입니다) 이하의 내용에 집중해야 한다. 이메일은 건물 단지의 주차 정책을 설명하기 위한 것이므로 정답은 (C).

해설 단서(177)에 따르면 주차권은 새스커툰 시를 통해 구매할 수 있다고 했으므로 정답은 (D).
오답 피하기 모든 주차 차량이 계기판에 주차권을 두어야 한다고 했으므로 (A)는 오답. 상업용 주차권은 연간 1,000달러, 거주자용 주차권은 연간 600달러라고 했으므로 (B)와 (C)도 각각 오답.

178 홍 씨가 주차권을 구매한 방법은?
(A) 현금으로
(B) 은행 이체로
(C) 수표로
(D) 신용카드로

해설 영수증에서 홍 씨의 지불 수단을 봐야 한다. 신용카드로 결제했으므로 정답은 (D).

179 홍 씨가 신청한 주차권의 종류는?
(A) 거주자용 주차권
(B) 상업용 주차권
(C) 임시 주차권
(D) 방문자용 주차권

해설 두 지문을 모두 보아야 풀 수 있는 연계 문제이다. 영수증에서 홍 씨가 신청한 주차권이 노란색이라는 것과, 결제액이 600달러라는 힌트를 얻은 후 이메일을 보아야 한다. 이메일에 따르면 노란색이고 연간 비용이 600달러인 것은 거주자용 주차권이므로 정답은 (A).

180 홍 씨에 대해 추론할 수 있는 것은?
(A) 그녀의 주차권을 집으로 배송시켰다.
(B) 결제액을 환불받았다.
(C) 주차권 종류를 바꿀 것이다.
(D) 주차권을 갱신할 것이다.

해설 두 지문을 모두 보아야 풀 수 있는 연계 문제이다. 영수증의 배송 방법란을 보면 주차권은 우편으로 배송되었는데, 이메일에 주차권을 집으로 배송받을지 직접 수령할지 선택할 수 있다고 했다. 이는 곧 홍 씨가 주차권을 집으로 배송시켰다는 것을 뜻하므로 정답은 (A).

[181-185] 다리 보수 공사를 공지하는 웹사이트 & 최신 정보 공지

www.cityofbrooklyn.org

| **Home** | Residents | Business | Event |

(181)Brooklyn Bridge Renovation Project

City of Brooklyn engineers have raised concerns about the structural soundness of the Brooklyn Bridge. (181)(185-2)In response, the bridge will be closed for construction for four months from May 1 to August 31. (182B)During this time, no public access will be granted to the bridge. Bridge use will be restricted solely to construction personnel and their equipment. Several detours will be established to help address any resulting traffic congestion in the surrounding area. (182C)Signposts for these alternate routes will be prominently displayed before entering the construction zone. Barring any unforeseen circumstances, we anticipate that this work will be completed before the first of September. (182A)Once it has begun, the City of Brooklyn will provide regular updates on the construction progress and any ensuing road closures throughout the repair period. To find these updates, simply click on the Brooklyn Bridge Renovation Project link here on the City of Brooklyn home page.

NOTICE: Brooklyn Bridge Renovation Project **UPDATE**

June 1

As part of our weekly updates on the Brooklyn Bridge Renovation Project, this notice is to confirm that construction has begun. (184)Because of the severe weather conditions experienced by the

www.cityofbrooklyn.org

| **홈** | 거주민 | 기업체 | 행사 |

(181)브루클린 다리 보수 공사 계획

브루클린 시 공학자들은 브루클린 다리의 구조적 안전성에 대해 우려를 제기해 왔습니다. (181)(185-2)이에 대응하고자 다리는 5월 1일부터 8월 31일까지 4개월 동안 공사로 인해 폐쇄됩니다. (182B)이 기간 동안에는 일반인들이 다리에 접근하는 것이 허용되지 않습니다. 다리의 이용은 공사 인력과 그들의 장비에만 국한될 것입니다. 주변 지역에 이에 따른 교통 혼잡을 해결하기 위해 여러 개의 우회로가 설치될 것입니다. (182C)이러한 대체 경로를 알려주는 표지판들이 공사 구역에 진입하기 전에 눈에 잘 띄도록 배치될 것입니다. 예상치 못한 상황이 발생하지 않는다면, 이 작업이 9월 첫째 날 이전에 완료될 것이라고 예상하고 있습니다. (182A)일단 시작이 되면 브루클린 시는 보수 기간 내내 공사 진행 상황과 그에 따른 도로 폐쇄에 대한 최신 정보를 정기적으로 제공해 드릴 것입니다. 이러한 최신 정보를 보시려면 이곳 브루클린 시 홈페이지의 브루클린 다리 보수 공사 계획 링크를 클릭하시기 바랍니다.

공지: 브루클린 다리 보수 공사 계획 **최신 정보**

6월 1일

브루클린 다리 보수 공사 계획의 주간 업데이트의 일환으로, 이 공지는 공사가 시작되었음을 확정하기 위함입니다. (184)5월 내내 브루클린 시가 겪었던 궂은 날씨로 인해 브루클린 다리의 수리 작업을 시작하기 위한 그 모든 노력이 불가능해졌습니다.

City of Brooklyn throughout the month of May, any efforts to commence repair work on the Brooklyn Bridge were rendered impossible. However, yesterday's clear skies enabled work crews to finally complete their first full day of work. (183)(185-1)Because of the late start, we anticipate that work efforts will continue exactly a month longer than originally estimated. The Brooklyn Bridge will then be opened for use the very next day. All of the previous instructions and information remain in effect.

그러나 어제의 맑은 하늘 덕분에 작업반원들이 마침내 처음으로 전일 작업을 완료할 수 있었습니다. (183)(185-1)시작이 늦어져서 우리는 작업이 원래 예상했던 것보다 정확히 한 달 더 길게 지속될 것으로 예상합니다. 브루클린 다리는 그후 바로 다음날 이용이 가능하도록 공개될 것입니다. 이전에 드린 모든 설명과 정보는 그대로 유효합니다.

어휘 raise concerns about ~에 대해 우려를 제기하다 structural 구조적인, 구조상의 soundness 안전성, 튼튼함 in response 대응하여, 응답하여 public access (특정 건물, 지역에 대한) 일반인의 접근[출입] be restricted to ~으로 국한되다[제한되다] detour 우회로 address (문제나 어려운 상황을) 해결하다 alternate route 대체 경로 prominently 두드러지게, 현저히 barring ~만 없다면, ~을 제외하면 ensuing 그에 따른, 뒤이은 commence 시작하다, 착수하다 render (어떤 상태가 되게) 만들다 in effect 유효한, 효과적인

---

181 웹사이트에서 설명하는 것은?
 (A) 보수 공사 계획
 (B) 경관 조성 제안
 (C) 새로운 다리 건설
 (D) 교통 사고

해설 웹사이트 게시물의 제목에서도 알 수 있듯이 이 글은 보수 공사로 인한 다리의 폐쇄를 알리고 있으므로 정답은 (A).
패러프레이징 지문의 Renovation Project가 정답에서 repair project로 패러프레이징되었다.

182 일반 대중에 대해 언급된 것이 아닌 것은?
 (A) 일정의 진행에 대한 정보를 계속 듣게 될 것이다.
 (B) 특정 지역에의 접근이 제한될 것이다.
 (C) 대체 운행 경로가 제공될 것이다.
 (D) 운전할 때 지체를 경험할 것이다.

해설 NOT 문제이므로 지문 전체에 걸쳐 흩어져 있는 단서들을 각 선택지와 하나씩 대조해 가면서 정답을 찾아야 한다. 교통 혼잡을 방지하기 위해 우회로를 설치한다고 했으므로 (D)가 정답이다.

183 공지에서 알 수 있는 것은?
 (A) 다리는 이제 이용하기에 안전하다.
 (B) 일정 지연이 있었다.
 (C) 최신 정보가 매월 제공된다.
 (D) 비용이 예상했던 것보다 많이 든다.

해설 공지에 따르면 공사 시작이 늦어져 작업 기간이 길어진다고 했으므로 정답은 (B).

184 공지에 따르면 문제의 원인은 무엇인가?
 (A) 악천후
 (B) 기계적인 결함
 (C) 인력 부족
 (D) 자재 부족

해설 문제에서 가리키는 problem이 보수 공사 지연을 의미하는 것임을 알아야 한다. 단서(184)에 따르면, 궂은 날씨로 시작이 늦어졌다고 하였으므로 정답은 (A).
패러프레이징 지문의 severe weather conditions가 정답에서 Poor weather conditions로 패러프레이징되었다.

185 브루클린 다리가 재개장하는 때는?
 (A) 5월 1일
 (B) 8월 30일
 (C) 9월 20일
 (D) 10월 1일

해설 연계 문제는 지문 간 연결 고리를 찾아야 한다. 공지에서 공사가 한 달 더 지속된다는 것을 확인하고 웹사이트에서 공사 일정을 보면, 보수 공사가 완료되는 시점은 기존의 8월 31일에서 한 달 미뤄진 9월 30일임을 알 수 있다. 공지에서 다리가 개장하는 것은 공사 완료 다음 날이라 했으므로 정답은 (D).

[186-190] 뮤지컬 공연 광고 전단 & 공연 비평 & 동행 권유 이메일

Spinnaker Theater Presents
Snowflakes and Silk

(186)September 12–(189-2)25 at 7:30 P.M. nightly

스피네커 극장에서 〈스노우플레이크 앤 실크〉를 상영합니다

(186)9월 12일–(189-2)25일 매일 저녁 7:30

154

Starring: Wei Ku
Directed by: Sofia Gilman
Music and lyrics by: Yong Huang
(187-2)Choreography by: Arnoldo Trentino

"Musical theater at its finest!" — Kent Wilson, *New York Artists Association*

(186)Actors will be signing posters and CDs after the September 12 performance. Donations for the Willow Children's Hospital will be collected after the September 14 performance.

Purchase tickets at www.spinnakertheater.com. Discounts on refreshments for all Spinnaker Theater members.

Weekly Theater Review: *Snowflakes and Silk*
4.5/5 Stars
Reviewed by: Richard Perez

This dramatic musical tells the story of a young boy who loses his family and becomes a trader along the Silk Road in China during the Han Dynasty. His journey to success teaches him lessons about love, fortune, and fate.

Lead actor Wei Ku's performance seemed tentative at first, but found his stride later in the show and let his voice ring out. The heartwarming story is accompanied by enchanting music and superb directing. (187-1)I was particularly impressed with the choreography. The dance routines were the best and most unique I've seen in a long time. Viewers would benefit from reading up on the time period before attending the show, as it is useful for (188)following what is going on. *Snowflakes and Silk* is currently playing at the Spinnaker Theater.

To: Madison Aguilar <m.aguilar@ggcmail.com>
From: Kate Hayes <hayeskate@meridian1.com>
Date: September 14
Subject: *Snowflakes and Silk*

Dear Madison,

I'm wondering if you are still interested in going to see *Snowflakes and Silk* at the Spinnaker Theater. Most critics have really liked the show, so I think it's worth seeing. I know you had originally suggested going on September 18, but I just checked the Web site, and there are no tickets available for that night. (189-1)In fact, the final performance is the only one that isn't sold out yet. So, I think we should go then and get our tickets as soon as possible. (190)You're the perfect person to accompany me since you often go to shows like this. You can tell me how it compares to others you've seen!

Let me know if you're available,

Kate

어휘 dramatic 극적인 trader 무역상 fortune 부, 재산 lead actor 주연 배우 tentative 머뭇거리는, 자신 없는 find one's stride 자신감[원래의 페이스]을 찾다 ring out 울리다 heartwarming 흐뭇한, 감동적인 accompany 동행[동반]하다 enchanting 매혹적인 superb 최상의 particularly 특히 dance routine 정해진 춤 동작 benefit from ~로부터 이득을 보다 read up on ~에 대해서 많이 읽다[공부하다] critic 비평가 worth doing ~할 만한 가치가 있는 be sold out 매진되다 available 시간이 나는

186 관객들이 개막 공연에서 할 수 있는 것은?
(A) 기부하기
(B) 공연 감독 만나기
(C) 사인 받기
(D) 할인 티켓 구매하기

해설 지문에 개막 공연(opening performance)이라는 키워드가 바로 나타나 있지 않으므로, 공연 홍보 전단지의 날짜 정보들을 종합해 풀어야 하는 문제이다. 공연이 시작되는 9월 12일에 배우들이 사인을 해 준다고 했으므로 정답은 (C).
패러프레이징 지문의 signing이 정답에서 an autograph로 패러프레이징되었다.

187 페레즈 씨는 누구의 작업을 가장 마음에 들어 했는가?
(A) 웨이 쿠의 작업
(B) 소피아 길먼의 작업
(C) 용 황의 작업
(D) 아놀도 트렌티노의 작업

해설 두 지문을 보아야 풀 수 있는 연계 문제이다. 페레즈 씨는 비평 작성자로, 공연에 대해서 안무가 특히 인상적이었으며 이제까지 본 것 중 최고라고 칭찬하고 있다. 홍보 전단지에서 안무가는 아놀도 트렌티노 씨임을 확인할 수 있으므로 정답은 (D).

188 비평에서, 2단락, 여섯 번째 줄의 어휘 "following"과 의미상 가장 유사한 것은?
(A) 추구하다
(B) 이해하다
(C) 감시하다
(D) 지지하다

해설 지문에서 follow는 '(무슨 일이 일어나고 있는지를) 이해하다'라는 뜻으로 쓰이고 있다. 따라서 정답은 (B). follow는 '따라가다'라는 의미에서 확장되어, 맥락을 놓치지 않고 내용을 잘 따라간다는 의미에서 '이해하다'라는 뜻으로 쓰이기도 하니 잘 알아두도록 하자.

189 헤이즈 씨가 공연에 가자고 제안하는 때는?
(A) 9월 15일
(B) 9월 18일
(C) 9월 20일
(D) 9월 25일

해설 선택지가 모두 시간이나 날짜로 이루어진 경우 연계 문제이다. 이메일에서 헤이즈 씨는 매진되지 않은 유일한 공연은 마지막 공연뿐이므로 그날 가자고 제안하고 있다. 홍보 전단지에서 공연은 9월 25일에 끝나는 것을 알 수 있으므로 (D)가 정답이다.

190 아귈라 씨에 대해 추론할 수 있는 것은?
(A) 뮤지컬을 자주 보러 간다.
(B) 여럿이 가는 것을 선호한다.
(C) <스노우플레이크 앤 실크>를 이미 보았다.
(D) 헤이즈 씨에게 비평을 보냈다.

해설 아귈라 씨는 이메일의 수신자이므로 you와 관련된 내용을 주의 깊게 본다. 헤이즈 씨는 아귈라 씨가 이런 공연을 자주 보러 간다고 했는데, 여기서 공연은 뮤지컬을 가리키므로 정답은 (A).

[191-195] 인물에 대한 기사 & 만찬 프로그램 & 축하 이메일

Collins, Inc.—November Newsletter

Spotlight on Achievement: Thomas Briggs

Sales Director Thomas Briggs is an integral part of the success of Collins, Inc., and we'd like to highlight his fine work in this month's column. (191C)Mr. Briggs first got to know Collins, Inc., during a summer internship with us ten years ago. Thanks to his hard work and his dedication to continually learning more about the market, he took on positions of increasing responsibility. He is now the head of the sales department, where his strong leadership and valuable insights have served the position well. In addition to growing the customer

콜린즈 사 – 11월 회보

업적 집중 조명: 토마스 브릭스

영업 이사인 토마스 브릭스 씨는 콜린즈 사의 성공에 없어서는 안 되는 존재로, 이달의 칼럼에서는 그의 뛰어난 업적을 조명해 보고자 합니다. (191C)브릭스 씨는 10년 전에 우리 회사의 하계 인턴 사원 근무 동안 처음으로 콜린즈 사를 알게 되었습니다. 성실하고 시장에 대해 더 많이 배우는 데 끊임없이 전념한 덕분에, 그는 점점 더 많은 책임이 따르는 자리를 맡게 되었습니다. 그는 현재 영업부 부서장으로, 강한 리더십과 귀중한 통찰력으로 이 자리를 잘 수행해 왔습니다. 고객층을 늘린 것 외에도, 그는 협동심과 생산성을 증진하기 위해 (191A)영업부를 재편하였습니다.

base, (191A)he has restructured the sales staff to promote cooperation and productivity.

Mr. Briggs will be presented with the prestigious Employee of the Year Award at the company's annual banquet. He is truly deserving of this honor, as he has spent his career working to (192)meet the needs of Collins, Inc., and its investors. We can't thank him enough for his amazing work.

Collins, Inc., Annual Banquet
December 11, Sacramento Convention Hall

6:00 P.M. Cocktail Reception, live music by the Archie Jazz Trio
7:00 P.M. Welcome Speech by Vice President Carol Polk
7:30 P.M. Best New Employee Award Presented to Brenda Bohn by Latanya Perry
7:45 P.M. Best Team Award Presented to Human Resources by Emma Shaw
(193)8:00 P.M. Dinner Service and Year-in-Review Video
9:00 P.M. (191D)Employee of the Year Award Presented to Thomas Briggs by President Troy Logan
(195-2)9:15 P.M. Future Projects Speech by President Troy Logan

---

To: Thomas Briggs <t.briggs@collinsinc.net>
From: Evelyn Wade <e.wade@collinsinc.net>
Date: December 12
Subject: Just a note

Hi Thomas,

I'm sorry I didn't have a chance to speak with you after the event last night. I had to catch a flight for a business trip, so (195-1)I left right after your award presentation. (194)I just want you to know how proud of you I am for this achievement. Great job! I can't think of anyone who deserves it more. It's a pleasure working with you on the management team, and I look forward to seeing more success from you in the years to come.

All the best,

Evelyn

어휘 achievement 업적, 성취 integral 필수적인 highlight 강조하다 dedication 헌신, 전념 take on (일을) 떠맡다 insight 통찰력 in addition to ~외에도 customer base 고객층 restructure 재편하다 promote 증진하다, 촉진하다 productivity 생산성 prestigious 명망 있는 banquet 연회 meet the needs 요구를 충족시키다 reception 환영 연회 award presentation 시상식 management 관리, 경영

191 브릭스 씨에 대해 시사되지 않은 것은?
(A) 자기 부서원들을 재조직하였다.
(B) 현재 승진 고려 대상이다.
(C) 콜린즈 사에서의 최초 일자리는 인턴 사원이었다.
(D) 콜린즈 사 회장으로부터 상을 받았다.

해설 단서가 두 지문에 걸쳐 흩어져 있으므로 각 선택지와 지문을 빠르게 대조해야 한다. 기사에서 (A)와 (C)를, 만찬행사 프로그램에서 (D)를 확인할 수 있지만, 현재 그의 승진이 논의된다는 언급은 없으므로 (B)가 정답.

192 기사에서, 2단락, 세 번째 줄의 어휘 "meet"과 의미상 가장 유사한 것은?
(A) 연결하다
(B) 우연히 마주치다
(C) 모이다
(D) 충족시키다

해설 지문에서 meet은 needs(요구)와 함께 '요구를 충족시키다'라는 뜻으로 쓰이고 있다. 따라서 '채우다, 충족시키다'라는 뜻의 fulfill이 가장 유사한 의미를 갖는다. 정답은 (D).

193 콜린즈 사의 연례 만찬 행사에 대해 사실인 것은?
(A) 작년과 같은 장소에서 열렸다.
(B) 식사는 저녁 행사 도중에 나왔다.
(C) 각 수상자의 영상이 상영되었다.
(D) 저녁 행사는 재즈 연주로 끝났다.

해설 만찬 행사 프로그램을 보면 행사 도중에 저녁 식사가 나오므로 정답은 (B).
오답 피하기 작년과 같은 장소에서 열렸는지 여부는 알 수 없으며, 영상은 수상자들에 대한 것이 아니고, 재즈 연주는 행사 끝이 아닌 시작 때 있었으므로 나머지는 모두 오답이다.

194 이메일의 목적은?
(A) 동료를 축하하기 위해
(B) 부탁을 하기 위해
(C) 감사를 표하기 위해
(D) 초대를 하기 위해

해설 웨이드 씨는 시상식 당일에 브릭스 씨에게 축하 인사를 할 기회가 없었기에, 늦게나마 브릭스 씨의 수상을 축하하기 위해 이메일을 보낸 것이다. 따라서 정답은 (A).

195 프로그램 중 웨이드 씨가 놓친 것은?
(A) 칵테일 연회
(B) 최고 신입 직원상
(C) 올해를 되돌아보는 영상
(D) 사업 계획 연설

해설 두 지문을 보아야 풀 수 있는 연계 문제이다. 이메일에서 웨이드 씨는 동료의 시상식 후에 바로 만찬회장을 떠나야 했다고 했는데, 만찬 행사 프로그램을 보면 시상식 후에 남은 일정은 회장의 사업 계획 연설뿐이므로 정답은 (D)이다.

[196-200] 봉사 활동 소개 웹페이지 & 사내 공지 & 감사 이메일

---

www.dixoncity.gov

| HOME | ANNOUNCEMENTS | EVENTS | CITY COUNCIL |

September is Homeless Assistance Month

The city council of Dixon City wants to raise awareness about homelessness and poverty in our region and to provide opportunities for the community to get involved. Below, you will find some suggested volunteer opportunities. More will be added at a later time.

Dixon City Outreach Association: Assist in cooking and serving a meal at one of our four locations throughout the city. Meals are served at the Webster Center (Mondays & Thursdays), **(196-2) Dawson Shelter (Tuesdays** & Fridays), House of Hope (Wednesdays & Saturdays), and the 5th Street Soup Kitchen (Sundays). Contact Lena Becker at lena@dixoncityoa.org.

Helping Hands Warehouse: Volunteers are needed to sort the clothing **(197)gathered** in our warehouse

---

www.dixoncity.gov

| 홈 | 공지 | 행사 | 시의회 |

9월은 노숙인 지원의 달입니다

딕슨 시 시의회에서는 우리 지역의 노숙 및 빈곤에 대한 인식을 높이고 공동체가 참여할 기회를 제공하고자 합니다. 아래에 자원봉사 기회를 제안하고 있습니다. 나중에 더 추가될 예정입니다.

딕슨 시 봉사활동 모임: 시 곳곳에 위치한 네 군데 장소에서 요리 및 식사 제공을 도와주세요. 식사가 제공되는 장소는 웹스터 센터(매주 월요일과 목요일), **(196-2)도슨 쉼터(매주 화요일과 금요일)**, 희망의 집(매주 수요일과 토요일), 5번가 무료 급식소(매주 일요일)입니다. lena@disoncityoa.org로 레나 벡커 씨에게 연락 주세요.

구호 물품 창고: 창고에 **(197)모인** 의류를 분류하여 기부용과 중고 매장 판매용으로 정리하는 데 자원 봉사자들이 필요합니다. w_tirado@helpinghands1.org로 월터 티라도 씨에게 연락 주세요.

and organize it for both donations and for sale at our thrift store. Contact Walter Tirado at w_tirado@helpinghands1.org.

(199-2)Dixon City Job Center: Assist those affected by homelessness and unemployment by tutoring them in reading, computer skills, interview skills, and more. Contact Angela Nichols at nichols.a@jobcenterdc.com.

To: Almazan, Inc., Staff
From: Andrew Bristow, Office Manager

September 5

In support of Homeless Assistance Month, (196-1)our staff will work with the Dixon City Outreach Association to serve a meal to the homeless on Tuesday, September 14. Everyone is welcome to participate, and we need at least 20 people to volunteer. We will leave the office at 5 P.M. together, and we should be finished by 7:30 P.M. We will rent a charter bus to take us to the site so that everyone can ride together. You will be dropped off back at the office afterwards. (198)Employees who take part in the activity do not have to come into the office the following day (September 15) until after lunch. This is our way of showing our appreciation for your support of this important project.

Please sign up with Jane in the HR office by September 10. You may also want to visit the Announcements page on the city's Web site to find other volunteer opportunities that you can do on your own.

Thank you.

To: Eric Canton <canton.e@almazaninc.com>
(199-1)**From:** Angela Nichols <nichols.a@jcenterdc.com>
Date: September 21
Subject: Thank you
Attachment: timetable_sept-dec.pdf

(199-1)Dear Mr. Canton,

Thank you for volunteering at our site this week. Your assistance truly makes a difference in the lives of others. While we've had a lot of volunteers so far this month thanks to the city's support of Homeless Assistance Month, (200)we do need volunteers on an ongoing basis. If you'd like to visit us again, please feel free to contact me anytime. I've attached a timetable of our services, with the most short-staffed time slots marked in red. (200)I hope you will consider working with us again soon.

Warmest regards,

Angela Nichols

어휘 assistance 도움 raise awareness 인식을 높이다 poverty 빈곤 get involved 관여하다 outreach 봉사 활동 warehouse 창고 sort 분류하다 gather 모으다; 모이다 thrift store 중고 할인 매장 unemployment 실업 tutor 가르치다 charter bus 전세 버스 drop off (차로 태워서) 내려주다 appreciation 감사 make a difference 변화[영향]를 주다 so far 지금까지 on an ongoing basis 지속적으로 short-staffed 직원[일손]이 부족한 time slot 시간대 mark 표시하다

196 알마잔 사 직원들이 자원 봉사를 할 가능성이 가장 큰 곳은?
(A) 웹스터 센터
(B) 도슨 쉼터
(C) 희망의 집
(D) 5번가 무료 급식소

해설 두 지문 연계 문제이다. 회람을 보면 알마잔 사 직원들은 화요일에 딕슨 시 봉사 활동 모임을 돕고 노숙인들에게 식사 제공을 할 예정이라고 했는데, 웹페이지를 보면 화요일은 도슨 쉼터에서 봉사 활동이 이루어지는 날이므로 정답은 (B).

197 웹페이지에서, 3단락, 첫 번째 줄의 어휘 "gathered"와 의미상 가장 유사한 것은?
(A) 건설된
(B) 만난
(C) 수집된
(D) 추정되는

해설 gather는 '(사람들이) 모이다'라는 뜻의 자동사와 '~을 모으다'라는 뜻의 타동사 둘 다로 쓰인다. 지문에서는 앞의 명사 clothing을 수식하여 '모인[수집된] 의류'라는 뜻으로 쓰이고 있다. 따라서 '모으다, 수집하다'라는 뜻의 동사 collect가 의미상 가장 유사하다. 정답은 (C).

198 알마잔 사 직원들에 대해 사실인 것은?
(A) 참여하는 데 대해 반나절의 휴가가 주어질 것이다.
(B) 봉사 활동 장소까지 각자의 차로 운전해 갈 것이다.
(C) 봉사 활동에 의무적으로 참여해야 한다.
(D) 신청하려면 브리스토우 씨에게 연락해야 한다.

해설 회람에서 봉사 활동에 참여한 직원들은 다음날 점심 시간 이후에 출근해도 된다고 했으므로, 오전 휴가가 주어진다는 것을 알 수 있다. 따라서 정답은 (A).
오답 피하기 봉사 활동 장소까지는 전세 버스를 대여해 다 같이 가고, 봉사 활동 참여는 선택 사항이며, 신청은 인사부의 제인 씨에게 하라고 했으므로 나머지는 모두 오답이다.

199 캔턴 씨가 자원 봉사로 했을 것 같은 일은?
(A) 의류를 정리했다
(B) 중고 매장에서 일했다
(C) 음식을 서빙했다
(D) 기술을 가르쳤다

해설 두 지문 연계 문제이다. 이메일의 단서(199-1)을 종합해 보면 안젤라 니콜즈 씨가 캔턴 씨의 자원 봉사에 대해 감사하는 것을 알 수 있고, 웹페이지의 단서(199-2)에서 니콜즈 씨가 딕슨 시 일자리 센터의 담당자임을 알 수 있다. 따라서 정답은 (D).

200 이메일을 보낸 이유는?
(A) 재정적 기부자에게 감사하기 위해
(B) 지속적인 참여를 장려하기 위해
(C) 정규직 일자리를 제안하기 위해
(D) 직원 채용 과정을 설명하기 위해

해설 첫 번째 문장의 Thank you만 보고 (A)를 답으로 고르지 않도록 주의한다. 단서(200)에서 지속적으로 자원 봉사자들이 필요한 상황임을 알리고, 다시 자원 봉사에 참여해 줄 것을 부탁하고 있으므로 정답은 (B).

ACTUAL TEST 2

p.182

147 (C)	148 (B)	149 (A)	150 (B)	151 (D)	152 (B)
153 (D)	154 (D)	155 (C)	156 (B)	157 (B)	158 (D)
159 (A)	160 (B)	161 (C)	162 (B)	163 (A)	164 (C)
165 (C)	166 (D)	167 (B)	168 (C)	169 (C)	170 (C)
171 (B)	172 (A)	173 (B)	174 (D)	175 (A)	176 (A)
177 (D)	178 (C)	179 (D)	180 (B)	181 (A)	182 (D)
183 (C)	184 (D)	185 (A)	186 (A)	187 (C)	188 (C)
189 (B)	190 (D)	191 (B)	192 (D)	193 (A)	194 (B)
195 (A)	196 (C)	197 (D)	198 (B)	199 (D)	200 (C)

[147-148] 재고 정리 행사 전단

Don't miss the biggest event ever at Oakland Home Center! (147)We're relocating to a nearby building, so we're marking down most of the items in the store to get rid of our excess stock. The most popular brand names are on sale, with discounts you won't see anywhere else.

(148)The sale starts this Saturday, September 6, and lasts through the weekend only, so stop by to browse our wide selection of items. Doors open at 8 A.M. Come early to get the merchandise you need before it sells out, and don't forget to keep your receipt to take advantage of the ten-year warranty on all products sold at Oakland Home Center. We hope you will take part in this great opportunity to add useful appliances to your home at a fraction of the cost. We thank you for your patronage, and we look forward to seeing you.

오클랜드 홈 센터의 가장 큰 행사를 놓치지 마세요! (147)저희는 인근 건물로 이전할 예정이라서 초과 재고 물품을 없애기 위해 가게에 있는 대부분의 물품들의 가격을 인하할 것입니다. 가장 인기 있는 브랜드들이 어디에서도 볼 수 없는 할인 가격으로 세일 중입니다.

(148)세일은 9월 6일 토요일에 시작해서 주말까지만 계속될 것이므로, 오셔서 다양한 품목들을 둘러보세요. 영업 시작 시간은 오전 8시입니다. 상품이 다 팔리기 전에 일찍 오셔서 필요한 물품을 구매하시고, 오클랜드 홈 센터에서 파는 모든 제품의 10년 보증을 이용하기 위해서 영수증을 보관하는 걸 잊지 마세요. 저희는 고객님이 이 좋은 기회에 참여해서 적은 비용으로 집에 유용한 가전제품을 가져가시길 바랍니다. 고객님의 애용에 감사 드리며, 고객님을 뵙기를 고대하겠습니다.

어휘 relocate 이전하다 mark down ~의 가격을 인하하다 get rid of ~을 없애다 excess 초과의 stock 재고 browse 둘러보다 merchandise 물품 sell out 다 팔리다 take advantage of ~을 이용하다 warranty 보증 take part in ~에 참여하다(= participate in) fraction 부분, 일부 patronage 애용

147 광고되고 있는 것은?
(A) 제품 출시
(B) 업주 변경
(C) 이전 세일
(D) 개점

해설 오클랜드 홈 센터는 근처 건물로 이전하면서 재고를 정리하기 위해 할인 판매를 한다고 했으므로 정답은 (C).

148 행사에 관해 사실인 것은?
(A) 1년에 한 번 진행한다.
(B) 일요일에 끝난다.
(C) 카드 소지자들을 위한 보상이다.
(D) 오전 9시에 시작한다.

해설 행사는 토요일에 시작해서 주말까지만 진행된다고 했으므로 일요일에 끝난다는 것을 알 수 있다. 따라서 정답은 (B).
오답 피하기 영업 시작 시간이 오전 8시라고 했으므로 (D)는 오답.

[149-151] 사내 교육 관련 회람

To: All Employees
From: Gloria Brown, HR Director
Date: October 20
Subject: Monthly Company Training

The monthly company training for November will take place on November 9 at 4 P.M. This month, we will have two programs rather than just one. As you know, (149)Upton Enterprises has recently changed its benefits package for full-time employees. Many of you have contacted me with questions about how this affects your working hours, sales incentives, and severance pay. There is also some confusion about who is eligible for the on-site daycare facilities. (149)The first program will allow me to give detailed information about these topics and offer clarification.

The second program will feature motivational speaker and business relations expert Jay Goulding. (150)Some of you may remember Mr. Goulding from his time of employment here. He has gone on to become a highly respected consultant on interpersonal skills. His first book, *Workplace Connections*, will be published later this year, and it will be accompanied by an international speaking tour.

(151)While the second session is scheduled to finish at 6 P.M., Mr. Goulding reports that the question-and-answer session following his talk has the tendency to go on for some time. If this happens, you will automatically be eligible for overtime pay. You will not need to fill out the usual paperwork, as this will be done for you by the accounting staff.

If you would like more information about the two programs, please view the detailed schedule posted on the company Web site.

수신: 전 직원
발신: 인사부 부장, 글로리아 브라운
날짜: 10월 20일
제목: 월별 사내 교육

11월 월별 사내 교육이 11월 9일 오후 4시에 있을 예정입니다. 이번 달에는 한 개가 아닌 두 개의 프로그램이 있습니다. 여러분도 아시다시피, (149)업톤 사는 최근에 정직원을 위한 복리 후생 제도를 바꾸었습니다. 많은 분들이 이것이 근무 시간, 판매 성과급 그리고 퇴직금에 어떤 영향을 미치는지에 대해 저에게 연락을 해서 질문을 주셨습니다. 또한 사내 보육 시설을 이용할 자격이 있는 사람은 누구인지에 대해 약간의 혼란도 있었습니다. (149)첫 번째 프로그램은 이러한 주제에 대해 제가 자세한 정보와 설명을 드릴 수 있도록 해 줄 것입니다.

두 번째 프로그램에는 동기 부여 연설가이자 사업 관계 전문가인 제이 골딩 씨가 와 주실 것입니다. (150)여러분 중에는 골딩 씨가 여기서 근무했던 때를 기억하는 분도 계실지 모르겠습니다. 그는 대인관계 기술 분야에서 매우 훌륭한 상담가가 되었습니다. 그의 첫 번째 책인, 〈직장 관계〉는 올해 말에 출간될 것이며 해외 강연 투어를 동반할 것입니다.

(151)두 번째 교육이 저녁 6시에 끝나는 것으로 예정되어 있지만, 골딩 씨는 강연 후에 있는 질의응답 시간이 조금 길어질 수도 있다고 하였습니다. 만일 이렇게 된다면, 여러분에게는 자동으로 초과 근무 시간에 대한 수당을 받을 자격이 생기게 될 것입니다. 평상시 작성하시던 서류를 작성하지 않아도 되는데, 이것이 회계부 직원에 의해 작성될 것이기 때문입니다.

두 프로그램에 대해 더 많은 정보를 원하신다면, 회사 웹사이트에 게시된 자세한 일정을 참고해 주세요.

어휘 benefits package 복리 후생 제도 full-time employee 정직원 contact 연락하다 affect 영향을 미치다 incentive 성과급 severance pay 퇴직금 confusion 혼란 be eligible for ~의 자격이 있다 day care facility 보육 시설 clarification 설명 motivational speaker 동기 부여 연설가 employment 고용 respected 훌륭한; 존경받는 interpersonal 대인 관계의

149 브라운 씨에 따르면, 첫 번째 프로그램의 목적은?
(A) 복리 후생 제도를 설명하기 위해
(B) 신입 사원들을 소개하기 위해
(C) 의사소통 능력을 향상시키기 위해
(D) 판매 성과급을 협상하기 위해

해설 복리 후생 제도가 바뀐 후 이에 대해 많은 문의가 있었고 제도를 자세히 설명하기 위해 첫 번째 프로그램을 진행할 것이라고 했으므로 정답은 (A).
오답 피하기 의사소통 기술을 향상시키기 위한 것은 두 번째 프로그램이므로 (C)는 오답.

150 골딩 씨에 대해 언급된 것은?
(A) 현재 해외 강연 투어 중이다.
(B) 업톤 사에서 근무했었다.
(C) 베스트셀러 책의 작가이다.
(D) 신문방송 학위가 있다.

해설 두 번째 교육 프로그램의 진행자 골딩 씨를 소개하면서 그가 업톤 사에서 근무했던 사실을 아는 직원들도 있을 것이라고 했으므로 정답은 (B).

151 강의가 저녁 6시 이후에 끝날 경우 일어날 일은?
(A) 직원들이 다음날 늦게 올 것이다.
(B) 골딩 씨가 비용을 청구할 것이다.
(C) 회사가 식사를 주문할 것이다.
(D) 직원들이 초과 수당을 받을 것이다.

해설 단서(151)에 따르면 강연 후에 있을 질의 응답 시간이 길어져서 근무 시간을 초과하게 될 경우 초과 근무 수당을 받게 될 것이라고 했으므로 정답은 (D).

패러프레이징 지문의 be eligible for overtime pay가 정답에서 be paid extra로 패러프레이징되었다.

[152-153] 문서 제출 요청 문자메시지

LUCAS YANCEY 07:02 A.M.
(152)Jackie, I'm afraid I'm feeling very ill today. I won't be coming into the office.

JACKIE KOVAR 07:03 A.M.
Oh, I'm sorry to hear that! I hope you feel better soon. Do you want me to let the department head know that you won't be here today?

LUCAS YANCEY 07:07 A.M.
Thanks, (152)but I've already phoned Ms. Luther to let her know.

LUCAS YANCEY 07:10 A.M.
I do have one favor to ask, though. I'm supposed to submit the monthly status reports today. Do you remember helping me work on those?

JACKIE KOVAR 07:11 A.M.
Of course. Do you need me to submit them for you?

LUCAS YANCEY 07:12 A.M.
Yes, please. You'll have to print them all first, though. They're on the shared server.

JACKIE KOVAR 07:15 A.M.
All right. I'll take a look.

JACKIE KOVAR 07:21 A.M.
(153)There's a folder under your name entitled *Monthly*.

LUCAS YANCEY 07:22 A.M.
That's the one. Thanks!

루카스 얀시 오전 07:02
(152)재키, 오늘 제가 몸이 아주 안 좋아요. 사무실에 못 나갈 것 같아요.

재키 코바 오전 07:03
아, 그렇다니 안됐네요! 곧 낫기를 바랄게요. 오늘 출근 못 하신다고 제가 부서장님께 알려드릴까요?

루카스 얀시 오전 07:07
고맙지만, (152)제가 벌써 루더 씨에게 전화해서 알려드렸어요.

루카스 얀시 오전 07:10
하지만 부탁할 게 하나 있어요. 제가 오늘 월례 현황 보고서를 제출해야 되거든요. 제가 그거 작업하는 걸 도와준 거 기억나요?

재키 코바 오전 07:11
물론이죠. 제가 대신 제출해 드릴까요?

루카스 얀시 오전 07:12
네, 부탁해요. 그런데 우선 그걸 모두 프린트해야 해요. 공유 서버에 있어요.

재키 코바 오전 07:15
알았어요. 찾아볼게요.

재키 코바 오전 07:21
(153)〈월례〉라는 제목으로 당신 이름 아래에 폴더가 하나 있네요.

루카스 얀시 오전 07:22
바로 그거예요. 고마워요!

어휘 department head 부서장 ask a favor 부탁하다 be supposed to do ~해야 된다, ~하기로 되어 있다 submit 제출하다 status report 현황 보고서 shared server 공유 서버 entitle 제목을 붙이다; 자격[권리]를 주다

152 얀시 씨가 루더 씨에게 연락한 이유는?
(A) 동료에게 연락을 부탁하기 위해
(B) 너무 아파서 출근할 수 없다는 것을 알리기 위해
(C) 제출 마감일을 재조정하기 위해
(D) 진료 예약 일정을 잡기 위해

해설 단서(152)에서 얀시 씨는 루더 씨에게 전화해서 자신이 아파서 출근할 수 없다는 것을 알렸다고 했으므로 정답은 (B).

패러프레이징 지문의 feeling very ill이 정답에서 too sick으로 패러프레이징되었다.

153 오전 07:22에, 얀시 씨가 "바로 그거예요"라고 하는 의도는?
(A) 코바 씨가 오류를 정정한 것에 대해 감사하고 있다.
(B) 보고서를 어디에 제출해야 하는지 설명하고 있다.
(C) 코바 씨에게 폴더를 삭제하라고 말하고 있다.
(D) 파일을 어디서 찾아야 하는지 확인해 주고 있다.

해설 단서(153)에서 코바 씨는 본인이 발견한 폴더를 언급하고 있다. 이에 얀시 씨가 곧이어 "바로 그거예요"라고 말한 것은 그 폴더가 바로 얀시 씨가 말한 폴더라는 의미이므로 정답은 (D).

[154-156] 업무 역량 강화 프로그램 안내 이메일

To: All employees <allstaff@rankmedia.com>
From: Noah Mecurio <mecurionoah@rankmedia.com>
Date: September 26
Subject: Professional development opportunity

The Rank Media Professional Development Team is starting a new initiative for our employees. (154)Because we require all staff members to regularly present marketing pitches and ideas to clients, communication is a critical skill for everyone employed here at Rank Media. To further develop this skill in our employees, I highly encourage each of you to join the "Talking Points" program, which is designed for staff members interested in enhancing their speaking ability. (156)Participants will meet weekly for six months and speak for five minutes on a randomly assigned topic pertinent to a corporate environment. During this time, participants will undoubtedly notice a dramatic improvement in their presentation effectiveness. (156)They will also increase their overall confidence while speaking in front of an audience.

Program meetings will be held on lunch breaks so that they don't interfere with work schedules. Additionally, because topics are assigned and delivered spontaneously, no 'homework' is necessary. For those who are curious about the program, we will hold a demonstration meeting to illustrate what it is all about and why it is so popular with other companies. After the demonstration on November 15, you will have an opportunity to sign up. If you determine that you are interested in participating at that time, (155)please contact the "Talking Points" coordinator, Regina Grimes at grimes@rankmedia.com. We hope you will all consider being a part of this program.

Noah Mecurio
Professional Development Leader

수신: 전 직원 〈allstaff@rankmedia.com〉
발신: 노아 메큐리오 〈mecurionoah@rankmedia.com〉
날짜: 9월 26일
제목: 경력 개발 기회

랭크미디어 사의 경력개발팀은 우리 직원들을 위해 새로운 계획을 추진하려고 합니다. (154)우리는 모든 직원 여러분들이 정기적으로 마케팅 홍보와 아이디어를 고객들에게 제시하도록 요구하고 있으므로, 의사 소통은 이곳 랭크미디어 사에 고용된 모든 이들이 갖추어야 할 중요한 기술입니다. 우리 직원들이 이 기술을 좀 더 개발하도록 하기 위해 저는 여러분 모두가 "요점 말하기" 프로그램에 참여하기를 강력하게 권고하는데, 이는 자신의 말하기 능력을 강화하는 데 관심이 있는 직원들을 위해 고안된 프로그램입니다. (156)참가자들은 6개월 동안 매주 만나서 임의로 주어지는 기업 환경과 관련된 주제에 대해 5분 동안 말하게 됩니다. 이 기간 동안에 참가자들은 발표 효율성이 놀라우리만큼 향상되는 것을 확실히 감지할 것입니다. (156)그들은 또한 청중 앞에서 말하는 동안 전반적인 자신감을 상승시키게 될 것입니다.

업무 일정에 방해가 되지 않도록 프로그램 모임은 점심시간에 열릴 것입니다. 또한 주제는 자율적으로 할당되거나 전달되므로 '숙제'를 하실 필요는 없습니다. 프로그램에 대해 궁금한 점이 있는 분들을 위해 우리는 프로그램이 어떤 것인지, 왜 이것이 다른 회사에서 그렇게 인기가 많은지 보여 드리는 시연회를 가질 예정입니다. 11월 15일 시연이 있은 후 여러분은 등록할 기회를 가지게 될 겁니다. 만약 그때 참가하는 데 관심이 있다고 결정하시게 되면 (155)〈요점 말하기〉 프로그램 책임자인 레지나 그림스 씨에게 grimes@rankmedia.com으로 연락 주시기 바랍니다. 여러분 모두가 이 프로그램의 일원이 되는 것을 고려해 주셨으면 합니다.

경력개발팀장
노아 메큐리오 드림

어휘 initiative 계획, 주도 require ~ to do ~에게 …할 것을 요구하다 pitch (판매) 홍보, 권유 critical 중요한 be designed for ~을 위해 고안되다[만들어지다] participant 참가자, 참석자 randomly 임의로, 무작위로 assigned 할당된, 배당된 pertinent 적절한, 관련 있는 corporate 기업의 undoubtedly 확실히, 의심할 바 없이 overall 전반적인, 전체의 confidence 자신감 spontaneously 자율[자발]적으로 demonstration 시연, 설명 coordinator 책임자, 조정인

154 랭크미디어 사의 업종은?
(A) 광고 대행사
(B) 기술 업체
(C) 홍보 회사
(D) 마케팅 회사

해설 도입부에서 회사의 사업에 대해 간략히 설명하고 있으므로 이 부분을 살펴보면 된다. 단서(154)에서 고객들에게 marketing pitches(마케팅 홍보)를 제시하도록 요구된다고 했으므로 정답은 (D).

155 레지나 그림스 씨는 누구인가?
(A) 잠재 고객
(B) 외부 직원
(C) 프로그램 책임자
(D) 개인 비서

해설 지문에서 레지나 그림스 씨의 이름을 재빨리 찾도록 한다. 마지막 단락에 그녀가 coordinator라고 나와 있으므로 정답은 (C).

156 [1], [2], [3], [4]로 표시된 위치 중 다음 문장이 들어가기에 가장 알맞은 곳은?
"이 기간 동안에 참가자들은 발표 효율성이 놀라우리만큼 향상되는 것을 확실히 감지할 것입니다."
(A) [1]
(B) [2]
(C) [3]
(D) [4]

해설 주어진 문장은 어떤 기간에 발표의 효율성이 향상된다는 내용으로, 해당 문장의 this time이 가리키는 것을 지문에서 찾아보면 첫 번째 단서(156)의 for six months이다. 문맥을 살펴보면 주어진 문장은 <요점 말하기> 프로그램의 효과에 관한 것으로, 프로그램의 또 다른 효과에 해당하는 두 번째 단서(156)의 also라는 표현을 통해 주어진 문장이 그 앞에 와야 함을 알아채야 한다. 따라서 정답은 (B).

[157-158] 직원 송별회 초대장

LIMBURI HOTEL

Mr. and Mrs. Brillon
11 Xuan Dieu Road
Hanoi, Vietnam

February 17

(157)We cordially extend an invitation for you to attend a farewell banquet being held in honor of Mr. Rudy Winslow. After 18 years of hard work and allegiance to serving the people here at the Limburi Hotel, Mr. Winslow is moving on to an exciting opportunity at another company. Please join us at the Haven Hill Country Club to celebrate his many years of service. Cocktail attire is mandatory. (158) Please respond with your attendance and number of accompanying guests to the party organizer, Kathleen Jobrani, at kathleen.jobrani@limburi.com prior to March 22.

Regards,

Limburi Hotel Management

림버리 호텔

브리용 부부 귀하
샹두 가 11
베트남, 하노이

2월 17일

(157)루디 윈슬로 씨를 기리기 위해 열리는 송별회에 귀하 부부를 정중하게 초대하는 바입니다. 18년간 이곳 림버리 호텔에서 열심히 근무하고 사람들에게 헌신적으로 봉사해 온 윈슬로 씨가 다른 회사에서 멋진 기회를 얻어 옮기게 되셨습니다. 헤이븐 힐 컨트리 클럽에서 저희와 함께 그의 오랜 기간의 근무를 기념해 주십시오. 비즈니스 복장 차림은 필수입니다. (158)연회 기획자인 케이틀린 조브라니 씨에게 kathleen.jobrani@limburi.com으로 3월 22일 전까지 귀하의 참석 여부와 동반 인원수를 알려주시기 바랍니다.

림버리 호텔 경영진 드림

어휘 cordially 정중하게, 성심으로 farewell banquet 송별회 in honor of ~를 기리어, ~을 축하하여 allegiance 충성, 헌신 move on to ~로 옮겨가다 cocktail attire 비즈니스 복장, 준 정장차림 mandatory 필수의, 반드시 지켜야 하는 respond with ~으로 응답[반응]하다 accompanying 동반하는, 함께하는

157 조브라니 씨가 준비하고 있는 행사의 종류는?
(A) 은퇴 축하연
(B) 송별회
(C) 시상식
(D) 칵테일 환영 연회

해설 이 초대장은 루디 윈슬로 씨의 송별회에 브리용 부부를 초대하기 위해 보내지는 것이므로 정답은 (B).
오답 피하기 지문의 Cocktail attire(비즈니스 복장)만 보고 정답을 (D)로 고르지 않도록 주의하자.
패러프레이징 지문의 farewell banquet이 정답에서 goodbye banquet으로 패러프레이징되었다.

158 행사에 대해 사실인 것은?
(A) 2월 전에 응답하여야 한다.
(B) 주최 장소는 호텔이다.
(C) 복장 규정은 자유로운 옷차림이다.
(D) 초대받은 이들은 손님을 동반할 수 있다.

해설 단서(158)에서 동반 인원수를 이메일로 보내 달라고 했으므로, 손님을 동반해도 된다는 것을 알 수 있다. 따라서 정답은 (D).

[159-160] 서점 보수 공사 공지

(159)Over the last 27 years, Malaprop Books has been a popular spot to buy used books and magazines in the East Park neighborhood. We are grateful for our many regular customers. However, we are sorry that we will soon be closing our doors temporarily to conduct some much-needed renovations. For three days, from April 22 to 24, we will be repairing some damaged pipes, repainting walls, rearranging furniture, and adding more shelving. (160)Visit us again on April 25 when we reopen for business and show off our new interior. For one day only, we will be handing out free coffee to adults and chocolate milk to children with every book purchase.

(159)지난 27년간 맬러프랍 서점은 이스트파크 인근 지역에서 중고 서적과 잡지를 살 수 있는 인기 있는 장소였습니다. 저희의 많은 단골 고객 분들께 깊은 감사를 드립니다. 그러나, 많이 필요로 했던 일부 보수 공사를 진행하기 위해 곧 한시적으로 휴업을 할 것이란 점에 대해 사과 드립니다. 4월 22일부터 24일까지 3일 동안, 저희는 손상된 배관을 수리하고 벽을 새로 칠하고, 가구를 재배치하며, 더 많은 선반을 설치하게 됩니다. (160)저희가 다시 영업을 시작하고 새로운 실내 장식을 선보이게 될 4월 25일에 다시 방문해 주세요. 하루 동안만, 모든 도서 구매마다 어른에게는 무료 커피를, 아이들에게는 초코 우유를 나눠 드릴 예정입니다.

어휘 be grateful for ~에 대해 감사하다 regular customer 단골 (고객) temporarily 한시적으로, 임시로 conduct 진행하다, 수행하다 much-needed 많이 필요로 했던, 꼭 필요한 rearrange 재배치하다 shelving (붙박이) 선반 show off ~을 선보이다[과시하다] hand out ~을 나눠 주다[배포하다]

---

159 맬러프랍 서점에 대해 암시된 것은?
(A) 찾는 사람이 많은 동네 서점이다.
(B) 계속 같은 사람이 소유주였다.
(C) 매주 일주일에 3일 문을 연다.
(D) 만화와 그래픽 소설 전문이다.

해설 첫 문장에서 단서를 찾을 수 있는 문제이다. 서점이 인근 지역에서 인기 있는 장소라고 했으므로 정답은 (A).
패러프레이징 지문의 popular spot이 정답에서 heavily visited neighborhood store로 패러프레이징되었다.

160 공지에 따르면 매장이 재개업하는 날짜는?
(A) 4월 24일
(B) 4월 25일
(C) 4월 26일
(D) 4월 27일

해설 단서(160)에 따르면, 가게가 4월 25일에 다시 영업을 시작한다고 했으므로 정답은 (B).

[161-163] 서비스 이용 후 감사 편지

The Pelican
107 Pearse Street
Dublin, Ireland

(162)January 15

더 펠리칸
피얼스 가 107
아일랜드, 더블린

(162)1월 15일

Dear Pelican Management,

(161)I just wanted to send a note to extend a sincere thank you to the Pelican for hosting our banquet last week. I was impressed at how easily your team serviced our group in the ballroom while still ensuring that sufficient staff members were present to check in and care for your regular guests in the lobby downstairs. As you know, (162)last month, we celebrated our twenty-fifth year in business. We consider this to be an important milestone. Thankfully, The Pelican made sure everything went according to the plan.

The most notable part of the evening was the decorations. Your decorators made the Starlight Ballroom look absolutely stunning. Specifically, (163)I want to single out Declan Castor, who is a wonderful event coordinator. Having a very professional manner and polite tone, he addressed all of my questions fully over the phone. He made the whole planning process a delight for me. Overall, I'd have no hesitation in recommending the Pelican to others for similar events.

Again, thank you all so much!

Michael Calhoun
Venture Insurance

펠리칸 사 경영진께,

(161)지난주에 저희의 연회를 주최해 준 더 펠리칸 사에게 진심으로 감사 인사를 전하기 위해 편지를 보냅니다. 저는 귀하의 팀이 충분히 많은 직원이 아래층 로비에서 일반 손님을 신경 쓰고 체크인하는 걸 도와주면서, 대연회장에서 저희에게 수월하게 서비스를 제공하는 것에 대해 감명받았습니다. 아시다시피, (162)지난달에 저희는 창사 25주년을 기념했습니다. 저희는 그것을 중요한 사건으로 생각하고 있습니다. 감사하게도, 더 펠리칸 사는 모든 일이 계획에 따라 진행되도록 해주었습니다.

행사일 저녁에 가장 눈에 띄는 부분은 장식이었습니다. 귀사의 실내 장식가는 스타라이트 대연회장을 굉장히 아름답게 보이게 만들었습니다. 특히, (163)저는 훌륭한 행사 책임자인 데클란 캐스터 씨를 지목하고 싶습니다. 그는 매우 전문가적인 태도와 친절한 어조로 전화를 통해 저의 모든 질문들을 완전히 해결해 주었습니다. 그는 저에게 계획 단계 전체를 기쁨으로 만들어 주었습니다. 종합적으로, 저는 유사한 행사를 위해 더 펠리칸 사를 다른 회사에 추천하는 것을 주저하지 않을 것입니다.

다시 한 번, 정말 감사 드립니다!

벤처 보험 회사
마이클 캘훈 드림

어휘 extend 연장[확장]하다 sincere 진심의 banquet 연회 be impressed at ~에 감명받다 sufficient 충분한 milestone 중요한 사건 notable 눈에 띄는 ballroom 대연회장 stunning 굉장히 아름다운 single out ~을 지목하다 hesitation 주저, 망설임 recommend 추천하다

161 편지가 보내진 목적은?
(A) 직원을 축하하기 위해
(B) 준비 시간을 정하기 위해
(C) 서비스에 대해 업체에게 감사하기 위해
(D) 필수 지시 사항을 제공하기 위해

162 12월에 벤처 보험 회사에 일어난 일은?
(A) 두 번째 지사가 문을 열었다.
(B) 기념일이 있었다.
(C) 사업 거래가 마무리되었다.
(D) 중요한 판매 기록이 갱신되었다.

163 캐스터 씨에 대해 사실인 것은?
(A) 질문에 친절히 답했다.
(B) 연회장을 장식했다.
(C) 펠리칸 호텔을 추천했다.
(D) 감사 쪽지를 썼다.

해설 편지 본문 첫 번째 문장에 목적이 언급되어 있다. 더 펠리칸 사에 감사 인사를 전하기 위해 편지를 썼다고 했으므로 정답은 (C).
패러프레이징 지문의 extend a sincere thank you가 정답에서 thank a business로 바뀌어 표현되었다.

해설 특정한 기간에 대해 묻는 질문이므로 지문에서 날짜 정보가 등장하는 부분을 집중해서 보아야 한다. 두 개의 단서(162)를 종합해 보면 편지가 쓰인 달이 1월이고 창사 25주년이 지난달이라고 했으므로 12월에 벤처 보험 회사의 창사 25주년이었음을 알 수 있다. 정답은 (B).

해설 캐스터 씨가 언급된 단서(163)을 통해 그가 친절한 태도로 전화 응대를 했음을 알 수 있으므로 정답은 (A).

[164-167] 의류 생산업체의 구인 공고

Everest Inc. offers a broad assortment of brand-name sporting equipment, apparel, and footwear in

에베레스트 사에서는 광범위한 종류의 유명 스포츠 장비, 의류, 신발들을 전문점에서 공급하고 있습니다. 저희 회사는

a specialty store environment. Our corporate office is headquartered in Binghamton, New York; (165)our production plant is located in the nearby city of Ithaca; and our two most successful stores can be found in Madison, Wisconsin, and Frankfort, Kentucky. However, we haven't finished expanding yet! We are hiring for the positions detailed below:

(164)**Administrator, Payroll (1 position):** The payroll administrator helps the human resources manager with all functions related to maintaining personnel records and making salary payments. (164)Specifically, s/he prepares and processes the biweekly payroll for nearly 15,000 employees.

Associate, Sales (1 position): The sales associate organizes and displays merchandise according to company standards. Associates must also keep all pricing, clearance discounts, and special promotions up-to-date.

Director, Public Relations (1 position): (167)The public relations director develops and executes strategies intended to create a positive public image for Everest, Inc. S/he forms relationships with the media, the government, and the community. Managing crisis operations to protect Everest, Inc.'s reputation after negative incidents have occurred is an essential part of the role.

Operations Supervisor (1 position): The operations supervisor oversees and ensures the smooth and efficient performance of the operations department. Because s/he is responsible for directing a large team, supervisory experience is required.

(165)**Plant Mechanic (2 positions):** Working in the production plant, the mechanic performs skilled work related to building maintenance, such as welding, cutting, and electrical work. S/he also conducts preventive maintenance procedures throughout the building and must be available on call as needed.

(166)If you wish to apply for any of the above positions, please do so online by completing the fields at www.everest.com/careers. You will need to upload an updated résumé and a cover letter. Applications received by fax or e-mail will not be considered.

뉴욕 주 빙햄턴에 본사가 있으며 (165)생산 공장은 이타카 시 근처에 위치해 있고, 가장 성공적인 두 곳의 점포는 위스콘신 주 메디슨과 켄터키 주의 프랭크포트에서 찾을 수 있습니다. 그러나 우리는 아직 확장이 끝나지 않았습니다! 우리는 아래에 열거된 직책을 채용하고 있습니다:

(164)**급여 사무원 (1명):** 급여 사무원은 직원들의 인사 기록을 관리하고 급여 지급과 관련된 모든 일을 하는 데 있어 인사과장을 돕게 될 것입니다. (164)특히 거의 15,000여 명에 이르는 직원들의 격주 급여를 준비하고 처리할 것입니다.

판매 직원 (1명): 판매직 사원은 회사의 기준에 맞춰 상품들을 정리하고 진열합니다. 직원들은 또한 모든 가격, 재고 정리 할인, 특별 행사가 등을 계속해서 최신 상태로 유지해야 합니다.

홍보 이사 (1명): (167)홍보 이사는 에베레스트 사의 긍정적인 대외 이미지를 창출하기 위한 전략을 개발하고 실행합니다. 그/그녀는 언론, 정부, 지역사회와 관계를 형성합니다. 불상사가 발생했을 경우 에베레스트 사의 평판을 보호하기 위한 위기 관리를 총괄하는 것은 이 역할의 중요한 부분입니다.

운영 관리자 (1명): 운영 관리자는 운영 부서의 원활하고 효율적인 업무 수행을 감독하고 보장합니다. 큰 팀을 감독하는 책임이 있기 때문에 관리상의 경력이 요구됩니다.

(165)**공장 정비사 (2명):** 생산 공장에 근무하면서 정비사는 용접, 절단, 전기 작업과 같은 건물의 유지 보수와 관련된 숙련된 작업을 수행합니다. 또한 건물 전체에 예방적인 보수 작업을 실시하며 필요할 경우를 대비해 항상 대기 중이어야 합니다.

(166)위에 언급된 직책 중 하나에 지원하고자 하시면 www.everest.com/careers에서 온라인으로 칸을 작성하심으로써 그렇게 해주시기 바랍니다. 최신 이력서와 자기 소개서도 올려 주셔야 합니다. 팩스나 이메일로 수령된 지원서는 고려하지 않습니다.

어휘 assortment (같은 품목을 여러 가지 종류로 모은) 모음, 종합   specialty store 전문점   be headquartered in ~에 본사가 있다, ~에 본부를 두고 있다   payroll 급여 대상자 명단   associate 직원, 같이 일하는 사람   clearance 창고 정리   strategy 전략, 계획   crisis 위기   reputation 평판, 명성   incident 사건, 일   occur 발생하다, 일어나다   operation 운영, 활동   supervisor 관리자, 감독자   ensure 보장하다, 확실히 하다   supervisory 관리상의, 감독상의   mechanic 정비사, 자동차 정비공   welding 용접 (기술)   preventive 예방적인, 사전에 실시하는   on call (항상) 대기 중인   cover letter 자기 소개서   application 지원(서)

164 급여 사무원에 대해 암시된 것은?
   (A) 재무 관련 컴퓨터 소프트웨어를 운영한다.
   (B) 출장 일정을 세운다.
   (C) 2주마다 급여를 지급한다.
   (D) 직원들의 금융 정보를 수집한다.

165 공장 정비사가 일하게 될 곳은?
   (A) 빙햄턴
   (B) 프랭크포트
   (C) 이타카
   (D) 매디슨

166 구직 희망자가 지원하기 위한 방법은?
   (A) 이메일을 보냄으로써
   (B) 모집자에게 전화함으로써
   (C) 팩스를 보냄으로써
   (D) 온라인상의 서식을 작성함으로써

167 [1], [2], [3], [4]로 표시된 위치 중 다음 문장이 들어가기에 가장 알맞은 곳은?
   "그/그녀는 언론, 정부, 지역사회와 관계를 형성합니다."
   (A) [1]
   (B) [2]
   (C) [3]
   (D) [4]

해설 단서(164)에 명시된 급여 사무원의 업무에 대한 설명을 통해 (C)가 정답임을 알 수 있다.
패러프레이징 지문의 biweekly가 정답에서 every two weeks로 패러프레이징되었다.

해설 두 개의 단서(165)를 종합해서 풀어야 한다. 공장 정비사의 직무가 서술된 부분의 단서(165)에서 정비사는 생산 공장에서 근무하게 될 것이라 했으며, 첫 단락의 단서(165)에서 생산 공장이 이타카 시 근처에 위치해 있다는 것을 알 수 있으므로 정답은 (C).

해설 단서(166)에서 구직 희망자는 온라인으로 웹사이트에서 양식을 작성하라고 했으므로 정답은 (D).

해설 주어진 문장은 누군가가 언론, 정부, 지역사회와 같은 외부 기관과 관계를 형성한다는 내용이며, 지문이 구인 공고인 것으로 미루어 보아 특정 직무를 기술하는 문장임을 알아채야 한다. 단서(167)에 보면 홍보 이사직이 회사의 대외 이미지 창출을 위한 전략을 실행한다고 했으며, 주어진 문장 또한 이와 관련 있는 내용이므로 해당 문장은 단서(167) 뒤에 와야 알맞다. 따라서 정답은 (B).

[168-171] 열차 지연에 대한 온라인 채팅 대화문

Joel Forrest　　　　　　　　　3:39 P.M.
Good afternoon, everyone. (168)Let's talk about the planned train drivers' strike on February 5 and how it is going to affect us at Oakridge Station.

Brenda Muse　　　　　　　　　3:43 P.M.
Obviously, some services will be canceled, and others will be delayed because of this. Has the management team determined what particular routes will be impacted?

Richard Dunnellon　　　　　　3:45 P.M.
Yes. (169)The cancellations will be: the Poppe Line to Toronto at 14:00, the Locklear Line to Ottawa at 09:30, and the Hickory Line to Brantford at 08:00. Furthermore, the 11:00 train to Brantford will be delayed by 15 minutes.

Joel Forrest　　　　　　　　　3:47 P.M.
The good news is that it affects fewer train lines than we initially feared, so that's encouraging.

Brenda Muse　　　　　　　　　3:49 P.M.
That's true, but one of the things we must keep in mind—and remind passengers about too—is that an event like this will also influence the services that are still running.

조엘 포레스트　　　　　　　　　오후 3:39
안녕하세요, 여러분. (168)2월 5일로 예정된 열차 기관사들의 파업과 그것이 우리 오크리지 역에 어떤 영향을 미칠지에 대해 얘기를 나눠 봅시다.

브렌다 뮤즈　　　　　　　　　오후 3:43
분명히, 그로 인해 일부 운행은 취소될 거고 또 다른 일부는 지연될 거예요. 어떤 특정 노선이 영향을 받을지 관리팀에서 파악했나요?

리차드 더넬론　　　　　　　　오후 3:45
네. (169)취소되는 것은 14시 토론토행 포프 노선, 9시 30분 오타와행 로크리어 노선, 8시 브랜트포드행 히코리 노선이에요. 또 브랜트포드행 11시 기차는 15분 지연될 거예요.

조엘 포레스트　　　　　　　　　오후 3:47
좋은 소식은 우리가 애초에 걱정했던 것보다는 더 적은 기차 노선에 영향을 준다는 건데, 그래서 그나마 위안이 되네요.

브렌다 뮤즈　　　　　　　　　오후 3:49
그렇긴 하지만, 우리가 명심해야 할 것은, 그리고 승객들에게도 주지시켜야 할 것은, 이와 같은 사건은 여전히 운행 중인 노선에도 영향을 미친다는 거예요.

Joel Forrest 3:51 P.M.
Brenda's right. (170)Many of the regular train departures will become jammed with passengers because people will be compensating for other routes that are not available.

Brenda Muse 3:53 P.M.
(171)We should post a notice at the station reminding passengers to go to their platforms much earlier than the scheduled departure times in order to ensure that they get on their trains.

Richard Dunnellon 3:55 P.M.
That's a good plan. Obviously, we need to post the amended schedule as well. I can take care of both of those things.

어휘 strike 파업 affect 영향을 미치다(= impact) obviously 분명히, 확실히 particular 특정한 cancellation 취소 encouraging 고무적인 keep in mind (that) ~을 명심하다 become jammed with ~으로 붐비다 compensate for ~을 보상[만회]하다

조엘 포레스트 오후 3:51
브렌다 말이 맞아요. 사람들이 이용할 수 없는 다른 노선들을 만회하려고 할 것이기 때문에 (170)정기 열차 출발편 다수가 승객들로 붐빌 거예요.

브렌다 뮤즈 오후 3:53
(171)역에 공지를 게시해서 승객들에게 기차를 확실히 타려면 예정된 출발 시간보다 훨씬 이전에 승강장으로 가라고 알려야겠어요.

리차드 더넬론 오후 3:55
그거 좋은 계획이네요. 분명히, 수정된 운행 일정표도 게시해야 하고요. 제가 그 둘 다 처리할게요.

---

168 오크리지 역의 운행 일정 변경을 초래한 것은?
(A) 일부 열차가 정기 점검에 빠져 있다.
(B) 새로운 운행 노선들이 도입되고 있다.
(C) 직원들이 일하러 가기를 거부하고 있다.
(D) 몇몇 철로를 새로 건설하고 있다.

해설 단서(168)에서 train drivers' strike (열차 기관사들의 파업)가 운행 일정에 지장을 주는 원인임을 알 수 있다. 따라서 정답은 (C).

169 브랜트포드행 기차가 출발하게 될 시간은?
(A) 08:00
(B) 09:30
(C) 11:15
(D) 14:00

해설 단서(169)에서 브랜트포드행 기차가 두 번 언급되는데, 8시 출발편은 취소되고, 11시 출발편은 15분 지연될 것이라고 했으므로 정답은 (C).

170 포레스트 씨가 언급한 문제점은?
(A) 일부 직원들은 경험이 많지 않다.
(B) 문제를 해결할 자금이 충분하지 않다.
(C) 일부 운행 노선은 매우 붐빌 것이다.
(D) 승객들이 불만을 제기할 것으로 예상된다.

해설 단서(170)에서 포레스트 씨는 정기 열차편 다수가 승객들로 붐비게 될 것을 우려하고 있으므로 정답은 (C).
패러프레이징 지문의 jammed with passengers가 정답에서 overcrowded로 패러프레이징되었다.

171 오후 3:55에, 더넬론 씨가 "그거 좋은 계획이네요"라고 하는 의도는?
(A) 수정된 열차 운행표를 게시할 것을 제안한다.
(B) 승객들에게 일찍 도착하라고 권고하기를 원한다.
(C) 시간표를 수정하려고 한다.
(D) 신규 직원을 채용하자는 의견을 지지한다.

해설 단서(171)을 보면, 뮤즈 씨가 승객들에게 예정 시간보다 더 일찍 도착하라는 내용을 알리자고 했으므로 더넬론 씨의 말은 이에 찬성하는 뜻임을 알 수 있다. 따라서 정답은 (B).

[172-175] 규정 변경을 알리는 편지

August 26

Dear Staff,

On behalf of the management team at Cheshire Consulting, I would like to tell you about a decision that was recently made. (172)Starting from September 1, we will implement a new regulation

8월 26일

직원 여러분께,

체셔 컨설팅 사의 경영진을 대표해서, 최근에 이루어진 결정 사항에 대해 말씀 드리고자 합니다. (172)9월 1일부터, 인터넷 사용에 관해 새로운 규정을 시행합니다. 현재는 직원들에게 업무와 관련 없는 사이트 방문과 근무 시간 중에 개인 이메일

regarding Internet usage. Currently, employees are permitted to visit Web sites not related to work and to use personal e-mail accounts during working hours. Under the new policy, this will not be allowed. The decision was made in an effort to boost productivity, as we believe that employees are spending too much time on personal matters while at the office. I apologize for the short notice of this announcement. (173)I planned to send this letter earlier but was delayed because a work crew is renovating my branch, which resulted in temporarily having no access to company records.

Details about the policy are outlined in Form 4861. We encourage all employees to read the information carefully so that they may be in compliance with the new rules. (174B)If you would like a copy of the new policy, you may request one by e-mailing Joshua Decker at j.decker@limaco.com. (174C)This form can also be downloaded from the company Web site, which you can access with your employee number and password. Please talk to your supervisor if you have problems logging in. Alternatively, (174A)we can mail you a printed copy to keep for your records, which can be done by making a formal request in writing to Mr. Decker.

We thank you in advance for complying with the new policy. We also value employee feedback about this and other matters. Therefore, (175) Thomas Neely is forming a task force to monitor employee morale and elicit feedback from the staff. If you would like him to consider you for this group, please give him a call at extension 34.

Sincerely,

Elizabeth Simon

계정 사용이 허용되어 있습니다. 새로운 정책하에서는, 이것이 허용되지 않습니다. 이 결정은 생산성을 높이기 위한 일환으로 내려진 것으로, 직원들이 회사에 있는 동안 개인적인 일에 너무 많은 시간을 소비하고 있다고 여겨지기 때문입니다. 이런 안내를 갑작스럽게 드리게 된 것에 대해 사과 드립니다. (173)이 편지를 더 일찍 보낼 계획이었으나 작업반이 제 지점을 보수 공사하고 있어, 일시적으로 회사 기록에 접근할 수 없게 되어 지연되었습니다.

이 정책에 대한 세부 사항은 양식 4861번에 약술되어 있습니다. 새로운 규정을 따를 수 있도록 모든 직원들이 안내 사항을 주의 깊게 읽어 주실 것을 당부 드립니다. (174B)새로운 정책의 사본을 원하시는 경우, j.decker@limaco.com으로 조슈아 데커 씨에게 이메일을 보내서 한 부 요청하실 수 있습니다. (174C)이 양식은 여러분의 직원 번호와 패스워드로 접속하여 회사 사이트에서도 다운받으실 수 있습니다. 로그인하는 데 문제가 있을 경우 여러분의 상사에게 말씀하십시오. 또는, (174A)여러분이 기록으로 보관할 수 있도록 인쇄본을 우편으로 보내 드릴 수도 있는데, 이는 데커 씨에게 정식 요청서를 작성해서 보내면 됩니다.

새로운 정책을 따라 주시는 것에 대해 미리 감사 드립니다. 회사에서는 또한 이것 및 기타 문제에 대한 직원들의 의견을 소중히 여기고 있습니다. 그래서 (175)토마스 닐리 씨가 직원들의 사기를 살피고 직원들로부터 의견을 이끌어내기 위해 프로젝트팀을 꾸리고 있습니다. 닐리 씨가 여러분을 그 팀원으로 고려해 주기를 바라신다면, 내선번호 34번으로 그에게 전화 주십시오.

엘리자베스 사이먼 드림

어휘 implement 시행하다 regulation 규정 regarding ~에 관하여 boost 북돋우다 productivity 생산성 short notice 갑작스러운 통보 work crew 작업반 temporarily 일시적으로 have no access to ~에 접근[접속]하지 못하다 in compliance with ~에 따라, ~에 응하여 alternatively 또는, 그렇지 않으면 in advance 미리 comply with ~을 따르다 morale 사기 elicit 이끌어내다 extension 내선, 구내전화

172 편지의 목적은?
(A) 직원들에게 규정 변경을 알리기 위해
(B) 직원들에게 일부 서류를 요청하기 위해
(C) 인터넷 접속과 관련된 문제를 보고하기 위해
(D) 다가오는 경영 회의를 안내하기 위해

173 사이먼 씨가 편지를 늦게 보내게 된 원인은?
(A) 컴퓨터 오류
(B) 보수 공사
(C) 파일 분실
(D) 직원 결근

해설 편지 본문 첫 문장에서 최근에 내려진 결정 사항을 알리는 것이 편지의 목적임을 밝히고 있는데, 단서(172)에서 인터넷 사용에 관한 새로운 규정 시행이 그 구체적인 내용임을 알 수 있다. 따라서 정답은 (A).

패러프레이징 지문의 new regulation이 정답에서 rule change로 패러프레이징되었다.

해설 단서(173)에서 지점 보수 공사 때문에 편지 발송이 지연되었다고 밝히고 있으므로 정답은 (B).

174 양식 4861번에 담긴 정보에 접근할 수 있는 방법으로 시사되지 않은 것은?
  (A) 인쇄본 요청하기
  (B) 이메일 보내기
  (C) 인터넷 계정에 접속하기
  (D) 데커 씨 사무실로 전화하기

해설 NOT 문제는 선택지를 지문과 하나하나 대조해 보아야 한다. (D)를 제외한 선택지들은 각각 지문에서 확인 가능하지만 데커 씨의 사무실로 전화하라는 내용은 없다. 따라서 정답은 (D).

175 닐리 씨가 맡고 있는 일은?
  (A) 신임 매니저 임명하기
  (B) 교육 자료 인쇄하기
  (C) 위원회 팀원 선정하기
  (D) 회의 일정표 작성하기

해설 단서(175)에서 닐리 씨가 프로젝트팀을 꾸리고 있는데, 그 팀원이 되고 싶으면 닐리 씨에게 연락하라는 것으로 보아 닐리 씨가 팀원 선정을 맡고 있음을 알 수 있다. 따라서 정답은 (C).
패러프레이징 지문의 task force가 정답에서 committee로 패러프레이징되었다.

[176-180] 환경 보호 대회 광고 & 대회 수상 기업 관련 기사

Going Green with the Unozim Environmental Grant

Unozim is a company extremely concerned about the environment. (176)Therefore, we are once again hosting an environment-preservation contest for businesses called the 'Unozim Grant.' The purpose of this contest is to provide businesses with an incentive to protect nature and reduce the environmental impact of their daily actions. All companies who register for the contest must develop a program in their communities that is related in some way to environmental preservation. (178-1)The first-place winner will be awarded $100,000; second place, $50,000; and third place, $10,000. The prize money given should be used to fund the proposed initiative. (177)The recipient of last year's grant was a law firm who assigned a team of lawyers to work with Congress to enact a new environmental policy. The legislation discourages water pollution through harsher penalties for corporations who get rid of chemical waste by dumping it into our water system. This year's applications must be received no later than June 18. The contest results will be e-mailed to all participating organizations by July 5.

Wegryn Enterprises Earns Congratulations!
By Whitney Caldwell

(180C)Congratulations should be extended to our very own local technology development company, (178-2)Wegryn Enterprises, on becoming a recipient of the Unozim Grant. Wegryn Enterprises was awarded $10,000 to finance an electronic-waste management program. (180D)The company sells large volumes of technological devices and is therefore aware of the consumer trash that is produced when customers regularly upgrade their devices. Most of these items — used computers, cell phones, etc. — are simply thrown into the

우노짐 환경 기금으로 친환경적이 되자

우노짐 사는 환경에 매우 관심을 갖는 기업입니다. (176)그래서 우리는 다시 한 번 기업들을 대상으로 '우노짐 기금'이라고 불리는 환경 보호 대회를 개최합니다. 이번 대회의 목적은 자연을 보호하고 그들의 일상적인 활동을 통해 자연에 주는 피해를 경감시키고자 기업들에게 보상을 드리는 것입니다. 대회에 등록한 모든 회사는 환경 보호와 어느 정도 관련이 있는 지역사회 프로그램을 개발하여야 합니다. (178-1)1등 수상자는 10만 달러, 2등은 5만 달러, 3등은 1만 달러를 수여받게 됩니다. 상금은 제안된 계획을 위한 자금으로 사용되어야 합니다. (177)지난해 기금 수상자는 새로운 환경 정책을 입안하기 위해 자사의 변호사 한 팀을 의회와 함께 일하도록 파견한 법률회사입니다. 제정법은 우리의 상수원 시스템에 화학 폐기물을 버리는 회사들에 혹독한 벌금을 물리는 것을 통해 수질오염을 억제하고 있습니다. 올해의 신청은 6월 18일까지만 받습니다. 대회 결과는 7월 5일까지 모든 참가 단체들에게 이메일로 보내질 것입니다.

위그린 사 경사를 얻다!
휘트니 콜드웰 작성

(180C)지역의 기술 개발 회사인 위그린 사가 우노짐 기금의 수상자가 되어 축하의 말을 전하는 바이다. (178-2)위그린 사는 전자 폐기물 관리 프로그램에 자금이 될 1만 달러를 수여받았다. (180D)이 회사는 대량의 기술 장비들을 판매하는데, 이로 인해 고객들이 자신들의 장비를 정기적으로 업그레이드 할 때 생겨나는 소비자 폐기물에 대해 인지하고 있다. 이러한 물건들의 대부분인 중고 컴퓨터, 휴대 전화 등은 그저 쓰레기통으로 버려지지만 이 기술 폐기물들은 적절하게 폐기되지 않으면 환경에 위험이 될 수 있다. (179)이러한 사안을 방지하기 위해 위그린 사는 개인이 낡은 기기들을 버릴 수 있도록 점포 외부에 수거함을 설치할 것이다. 그러고 난 후 (180A)수백 명의 위그린 사 직원들 중 한 명이 제품들이 제대로

garbage, but this technological waste can be hazardous to the environment if it is not disposed of appropriately. (179)To combat this issue, Wegryn Enterprises will place a dumpster outside its store for individuals to drop off outdated devices. Afterward, (180A)one of the hundreds of workers at Wegryn Enterprises will ensure that the items are discarded correctly. We should all be very proud of (180B)our local environmental heroes who entered this contest for the first time this year. What a pleasant surprise to see them win one of the top prizes.

폐기되도록 할 것이다. (180B)우리는 올해 처음으로 대회에 참여하는 우리 지역의 환경 영웅들을 매우 자랑스러워해야만 한다. 그들이 최고의 상 중 하나를 받는 것을 보는 것이 얼마나 즐겁고 놀라운 일인지 모르겠다.

어휘 grant 보조금 extremely 매우, 대단히 preservation 보호, 보존 incentive 장려 정책 first-place 1등의, 선두의 award 수여하다, 상을 주다 fund 자금을 대다 discourage 억제시키다, 말리다 harsh 혹독한, 가차 없는 get rid of ~을 제거하다 dump A into B A를 B에 버리다[떠넘기다] extend 확장하다, 연장하다 finance 자금을 지원하다, 돈을 융통하다 be aware of ~을 인지하다 be hazardous to ~에 위험하다 combat (안 좋은 일이 일어나지 않도록) 방지하다, 싸우다 dumpster 수거함 ensure 확인하다, 확실히 하다 discard 폐기하다, 버리다

176 광고의 목적은?
(A) 대회 참가를 독려하기 위해
(B) 회사 프로젝트를 홍보하기 위해
(C) 수상자를 발표하기 위해
(D) 개인적 환경 보호 운동을 장려하기 위해

해설 광고의 제목과 앞부분을 보면 기업들을 상대로 열리는 환경 보호 대회를 알리는 것임을 알 수 있다. 전체에 걸쳐 상금, 일정, 이전 수상 기업 등에 대해 설명하고 있으므로 정답은 (A)이다.

177 지난해 보조금을 받은 프로그램은?
(A) 조직화된 나무 심기 운동
(B) 다 쓴 배터리 수집
(C) 고속도로 쓰레기 제거 프로그램
(D) 수질 오염을 방지하는 법안

해설 단서(177)을 보면, 화학 폐기물 무단 투기에 벌금을 물릴 수 있는 법이 제정되었고, 이 정책을 입안하기 위해 변호사를 파견한 기업이 상을 받았다고 했다. 따라서 정답은 (D).

178 위그린 사의 등수는?
(A) 1등
(B) 2등
(C) 3등
(D) 꼴찌

해설 두 개의 지문을 모두 읽어야 풀 수 있는 문제이다. 광고를 통해서 1, 2, 3등의 각각의 상금 금액을 알 수 있는데, 기사에서 위그린 사가 1만 달러의 상금을 받았다고 했으므로 단서를 종합해 보면 정답은 (C).

179 위그린 사가 계획하는 것은?
(A) 화학 물질 의존도 낮추기
(B) 에너지 효율 전기로 전환하기
(C) 직원들이 카풀을 하도록 권장하기
(D) 소비자들의 폐기된 전자 제품 수거하기

해설 단서(179)를 보면, 위그린 사는 전자 폐기물들이 환경에 악영향을 미치는 것을 막기 위해 수거함을 설치할 것이라고 했으므로 정답은 (D).
패러프레이징 지문의 outdated devices가 정답에서는 discarded electronic items로 패러프레이징되었다.

180 위그린 사에 대해 사실이 아닌 것은?
(A) 수백 명의 직원들이 있다.
(B) 전에도 이 대회에 참가한 적이 있다.
(C) 신기술을 창조하는 회사이다.
(D) 매장에서 기술 장비를 판매한다.

해설 NOT 문제는 선택지 4개를 모두 지문과 대조해 가며 풀어야 한다. 위그린 사는 위 대회에 처음으로 출전한 것이므로 정답은 (B)이다.

[181-185] 재정 관리 강좌 공지 & 강좌 신청 이메일

Attention Sailex Company

(181)Are you a recent college graduate? Are you working your first permanent full-time job? If you

사일렉스 사 직원 여러분 주목하세요.

(181)최근에 대학을 졸업하셨나요? 처음으로 계속 일할 수 있는 정규직으로 근무하고 있습니까? 만약 이 두 가지 질문에 모두

answered yes to both of these questions, NOW is the time to start thinking seriously about your financial future. Learning the necessary skills to budget, save, and eliminate student debt should be your priority. Miskatonic College can do that for you! We offer a number of evening classes in financial planning and financial management. (181)We will teach you how to make the most out of your new paycheck. Our goal is to position you well for a successful financial future.

Most of our classrooms are located in the Conniff Building on the south side of campus. (182)However, there are some exceptions, so be sure to check the rooms indicated on the class schedule to verify where you must go.

Course title	(185-2) Debt repayment planning	Learning how to save	The basics of budgeting	The need for investments
Dates	December 6, 8, 10	January 13, 15	January 20, 22, 24	January 20
Times	6 P.M.– 9 P.M.	7 P.M.– 10 P.M.	6 P.M.– 9 P.M.	7 P.M.– 10 P.M.
Pricing	$150	$100	$150	$50
Special notes		Held in Webb Hall		

(Due to classroom constraints, enrollment is limited to 30 people per class.)

Please submit a completed registration form to the recruitment coordinator James Cunningham at jcunningham@miskatoniccollege.com. Registration must be done a minimum of one month prior to the start date of your selected class. Once your enrollment has been confirmed, you must provide payment by either credit card or bank transfer within seven days of your first class.

To: James Cunningham <jcunningham@miskatoniccollege.com>
From: Elmira Monroe <emonroe@sailexcompany.net>
Date: November 17
Subject: Becoming a student
Attachment: Registration form

Dear Mr. Cunningham:

I noticed recently that a flyer for your school was displayed in my office break room. I am interested in joining your college. (183)I've attached the registration form that I downloaded from your Web site. Although I like all of the courses listed, (185-1) at the moment, I can only take the one offered in December. Could you please verify whether or not there is still an available (184)seat in this class? Once I have received your confirmation I will proceed with my tuition payment. I'm very excited about taking a course from your institution.

Thank you,

Elmira Monroe

이 수업에 아직 이용 가능한 (184)자리가 있는지 없는지 확인해 주실 수 있을까요? 확인을 받는 즉시 수강료 결제를 진행하겠습니다. 귀하의 기관에서 강좌를 수강하는 것에 대해 매우 기대감에 차 있습니다.

감사합니다.

엘미라 먼로 드림

어휘 **permanent** 영구적인, 불변의 **full-time** 정규직의 **budget** 예산을 세우다; 예산 **eliminate** 없애다, 제거하다 **priority** 우선 순위, 우선 사항 **make the most out of** (기회, 여건을) 최대한 활용하다 **pay check** 급료, 봉급 **exception** 예외 **verify** 확인하다, 입증하다 **enrollment** 등록 **at the moment** 지금은, 당장은 **take a course** 강좌를 수강하다 **institution** 기관, 단체

181 공지가 가장 의도된 대상은?
(A) 신입사원
(B) 재학 중인 대학생
(C) 대학 교수
(D) 미취업 구직자

해설 공지의 첫 번째 줄을 통해 공지의 대상이 사회초년생, 즉 신입사원이라는 것을 유추할 수 있다. 따라서 정답은 (A).

182 강좌에 대해 시사된 바는?
(A) 낮 시간 대에 제공된다.
(B) 강의 규모는 25명으로 제한되어 있다.
(C) 전부 같은 가격이다.
(D) 위치가 가끔씩 바뀐다.

해설 강의실이 주로 콘니프 빌딩에 위치하고 있지만 바뀔 수도 있다고 했으므로 정답은 (D).
오답 피하기 강의 규모는 30명으로 제한이라고 했으므로 (B)는 오답. 모두 저녁 시간대에 제공되고 수강료도 각기 다르므로 (A)와 (C)도 오답이다.

183 이메일에 따르면, 먼로 씨가 첨부 양식을 얻은 곳은?
(A) 대학에서 집어왔다.
(B) 그녀가 요청한 후 우편으로 보내졌다.
(C) 웹사이트에서 출력했다.
(D) 사무실에 게시되어 있었다.

해설 단서(183)을 통해서 먼로 씨가 웹사이트에서 직접 양식을 내려받아 작성한 것을 알 수 있으므로 정답은 (C).

184 이메일에서, 1단락 다섯 번째 줄의 어휘 "seat"과 의미상 가장 유사한 것은?
(A) 뒤
(B) 시간
(C) 지하
(D) 자리

해설 여기서 seat은 문맥상 수강 참가가 가능한 '자리'의 의미이므로 (D)가 정답.

185 먼로 씨가 등록하길 원하는 강좌는?
(A) 부채 탕감 계획
(B) 저축하는 법 배우기
(C) 예산 책정의 기본
(D) 투자의 필요성

해설 먼로 씨의 이메일에서, 그가 12월 강의를 수강하고자 함을 알 수 있다. 공지에서 강의 일정표를 확인하면 12월에 열리는 수업은 부채 탕감 계획 하나뿐이므로 정답은 (A).

[186-190] 예약 확인 이메일 & 여행 일정표 & 여행객 대상 공지

To: Carla Lambert <lambertc@fresnopost.net>
From: Kenny Warren <kenny@ace-travel.net>
Date: May 14
Subject: Your upcoming vacation

Dear Ms. Lambert,

수신: 칼라 램버트 〈lambertc@fresnopost.net〉
발신: 케니 워렌 〈kenny@ace-travel.net〉
날짜: 5월 14일
제목: 귀하의 다가오는 휴가

램버트 씨께,

Thank you for booking your vacation through Ace Travel! I have made all of the arrangements for your trip to White Sands Island. I was unable to book a suite for you and your husband for the entire trip, so (186-1)you will be staying in a double room on your first night at Bay Resort. After that, you will be moved to a suite. As a result, the total price of the package will be slightly reduced.

All tickets for your activities on the island have been purchased, and these will be sent to you by mail this week. If anything gets canceled, just let me know when you get back, and I can help you to process a refund request. You do not need paper tickets for your flight. Simply show your passport at the time of check-in.

(187)The deposit has already been paid, so there is a balance of $1,750. Please take care of this by May 30.

If I can be of service in any other way, please do not hesitate to contact me.

Sincerely,

Kenny Warren
Travel Agent, Ace Travel

Ace Travel Itinerary: White Sands Island
Customer: Lambert, Carla
Other Traveler(s): Lambert, Paul

(186-2)**DAY 1 [Saturday, June 3]**
- 8:35 A.M. Everton Air Flight EV304 departure from Walsh Airport
- 10:43 A.M. Arrival at White Sands Island, take shuttle to (186-2)Bay Resort
- 8:00 P.M. Banquet dinner, Bay Resort

(188B)**DAY 2 [Sunday, June 4]**
- 9:00 A.M. Snorkeling Lesson at Vitali Beach
- 7:30 P.M. Lyndon Folk Singers Concert, Upland Hall

DAY 3 (189-2)**[Monday, June 5]**
- 2:00 P.M. Guided hike through Comet Park
- 4:30 P.M. (189-2)Traditional basket-making lesson, Kerns Building
- 5:00 P.M. Tour local art exhibit, Pearl Center

DAY 4 [Tuesday, June 6]
- (188D)9:00 A.M. Two-person spa package, Bay Resort
- (188A)3:35 P.M. Everton Air Flight EV650 departure from Mojica Airport

---

NOTICE TO ALL VISITORS

(189-1)The Kerns Building will be closed from June 2 to June 10 due to unforeseen circumstances. All activities scheduled for these days have been canceled, and (190)you should contact the ticket provider directly to seek a refund. The reason for this unexpected closure is the recent hurricane, which caused structural damage to a section of a building while passing through the area. This damage needs to be repaired for a safety inspection before the building can be reopened. We apologize for any inconvenience this may cause.

– The Management Team

받으십시오. 예기치 못한 폐쇄의 이유는 최근 허리케인이 이 지역을 통과하면서 건물 한 구역에 피해를 끼쳤기 때문입니다. 건물을 다시 열기 전에 안전 점검을 위해서는 이 피해를 보수해야 합니다. 이로 인해 불편을 끼쳐드려 죄송합니다.

– 관리팀 드림

어휘 make arrangements for ~을 준비하다 slightly 약간 by mail 우편으로 refund request 환불 요청 deposit 예약금, 보증금 balance 잔액 take care of ~을 처리하다 be of service 도움이 되다 itinerary 여행 일정표 unforeseen 예기치 못한(= unexpected) directly 직접, 바로 closure 폐쇄 structural damage 건물의 피해 safety inspection 안전 점검 inconvenience 불편

---

186 램버트 씨가 2인실에 묵게 되는 때는?
(A) 6월 3일
(B) 6월 4일
(C) 6월 5일
(D) 6월 6일

해설 두 지문 연계 문제이다. 이메일에서 램버트 씨 부부가 베이 리조트에서의 첫날 밤은 2인실에서 묵게 될 것이라고 했는데, 여행 일정표를 보면 6월 3일이 여행 첫날로 이때 베이 리조트에 머문다는 것을 알 수 있다. 정답은 (A).

187 워렌 씨가 램버트 씨에게 요청한 것은?
(A) 주소 확인하기
(B) 여권 사본 보내기
(C) 최종 결제 완료하기
(D) 여행 보험 구매하기

해설 이메일에서 워렌 씨는 램버트 씨에게 예약금을 제외한 나머지 금액을 기한 내에 결제해 줄 것을 요청하고 있다. 따라서 정답은 (C).

188 램버트 씨의 여행에 대해 사실이 아닌 것은?
(A) 돌아오는 비행편은 오후에 출발한다.
(B) 스노클링 강습은 주말로 예정되어 있다.
(C) 여행 일정상 매일 오전에 활동이 포함되어 있다.
(D) 그녀의 리조트는 구내에 스파가 있다.

해설 여행 일정표에서 (A), (B), (D)에 해당하는 내용을 확인할 수 있다. 하지만 여행 3일차에는 오전 일정이 잡혀 있지 않기 때문에 정답은 (B).

189 램버트 씨가 참여하지 못하게 될 활동은?
(A) 자연 속 하이킹
(B) 공예 강습
(C) 음악 공연
(D) 미술품 관람

해설 두 지문 연계 문제이다. 공지에서 컨즈 빌딩이 6월 2일부터 6월 10일까지 문을 닫게 되어, 이 기간에 예정된 행사는 모두 취소된다고 알리고 있다. 램버트 씨의 여행 일정표를 보면, 6월 5일에 컨즈 빌딩에서 바구니 만들기 강습이 있는데 이 활동은 하지 못하게 됨을 알 수 있다. 바구니 만들기는 공예에 속하므로 정답은 (B).

190 공지에 따르면, 일부 방문객들에게 요청된 것은?
(A) 일기 예보 듣기
(B) 재개장 후 다시 오기
(C) 보수 작업 상태 확인하기
(D) 환불 요구하기

해설 단서(190)에서 티켓 판매자에게 직접 연락하여 환불을 요구하라고 했으므로 정답은 (D).
패러프레이징 지문의 seek a refund가 정답에서는 Request a reimbursement로 패러프레이징되었다.

[191-195] 통역 서비스 광고 & 서비스 의뢰 이메일 & 업체 일정표

**Global Interpretation Enterprises –
We speak your language!**

At Global Interpretation Enterprises (GIE), we offer in-person professional interpreters for a variety of settings. We understand that in business situations,

글로벌 통역 회사 –
우리는 여러분의 언어로 말합니다!

저희 글로벌 통역 회사 (GIE)에서는 다양한 환경을 위한 개인 전문 통역사를 제공합니다. 저희는 비즈니스 상황에서는 정확성이 (192)중요하다는 것을 알고 있습니다. 그래서 저희는

accuracy (192)counts. That's why we only hire native speakers of the target language. All our interpreters are fully trained and have experience in a number of professional fields in addition to their language skills. Our services are perfect for negotiations, seminars, conferences, court hearings, and more.

Check out our competitive rates below:

Two-hour session	$290
(191-2)Four-hour session	$560
Six-hour session	$780
Eight-hour session	$960
More than eight hours	Please contact us.

To book an interpreter for your next event, call (493) 555-7792 or e-mail us at booking@ginterpretation.com.

To: Global Interpretation Enterprises <booking@ginterpretation.com>
From: Shirley Lowry <lowrys@lumiomfg.com>
Date: October 3
Subject: RE: Lumio Manufacturing Conference

Dear Mr. Metz,

Thank you for your prompt reply. I am glad that your company will be able to supply an interpreter for our upcoming event. As I said in my original request, (191-1)we would like a 4-hour session (194-1)with a native English speaker who can translate French. Our own staff members will cover the Spanish and Mandarin sessions.

(194-1)The interpreter's first talk will be at the Pomona Hotel on October 27 at 3 P.M. Someone at the registration booth will direct him or her where to go. (193)Please also let the person know that he or she is welcome to come to the dinner after the final talk. This would, of course, be off the clock, but we would provide a complimentary ticket to get in.

Sincerely,

Shirley Lowry
Event Coordinator, Lumio Manufacturing

Lumio Manufacturing Conference
October 27, Pomona Hotel

Title	Speaker	Time	Location	Language*
Applying for Government Grants for Research Projects	Rachelle Uribe	3 P.M.	Pine Hall	Spanish

---

대상이 되는 언어의 모국어 사용자만 채용합니다. 저희의 모든 통역사들은 충분한 훈련을 받았으며 언어 능력뿐만 아니라 여러 전문 분야의 경험도 갖추고 있습니다. 저희는 협상, 세미나, 회의, 법정 심리 등에서 완벽한 서비스를 제공합니다.

아래에서 저희의 경쟁력 있는 요금을 확인하십시오:

2시간	290달러
(191-2)4시간	560달러
6시간	780달러
8시간	960달러
8시간 이상	저희에게 연락 주십시오.

여러분의 다음 행사에 통역사를 예약하시려면, (493) 555-7792번으로 전화 주시거나 booking@ginterpretation.com으로 저희에게 이메일을 주십시오.

수신: 글로벌 통역 회사 〈booking@ginterpretation.com〉
발신: 셜리 로우리 〈lowrys@lumiomfg.com〉
날짜: 10월 3일
제목: 회신: 루미오 제조사 회의

메츠 씨께,

신속한 답변에 감사 드립니다. 저희 회사의 다가오는 행사에 통역사를 보내주실 수 있다니 다행입니다. 처음에 요청할 때 말씀 드렸듯이, (194-1)저희는 프랑스어를 통역할 수 있는 영어 원어민으로 (191-1)4시간을 원합니다. 스페인어와 중국어 세션은 저희 회사 직원들이 맡을 것입니다.

(194-1)통역사가 맡을 첫 번째 연설은 10월 27일 오후 3시에 포모나 호텔에서 있습니다. 등록 부스에서 통역사에게 어디로 가야 할지 알려줄 것입니다. 또한 (193)통역사에게 마지막 연설 후에 저녁식사에 얼마든지 와도 좋다고 알려주시기 바랍니다. 물론, 이는 근무 시간에 포함되지는 않겠지만, 입장할 수 있는 무료 식사권을 제공할 수 있습니다.

루미오 제조사, 행사 담당자
셜리 로우리 드림

루미오 제조사 회의
10월 27일, 포모나 호텔

제목	연사	시간	장소	언어*
연구 프로젝트를 위한 정부 보조금 신청하기	레이첼 유리베	오후 3시	파인 홀	스페인어

Trade Agreements and How They Affect You	Amabella Legault	(194-2) 3 P.M.	Oak Hall	French
Environmentally-Friendly Manufacturing	Timothy Bartlett	3 P.M.	Spruce Hall	English
The Key to Teamwork among Employees	Phillip Paradis	5 P.M.	Willow Hall	French
(195) Making the Most of Modern Machinery	Lisa Stevens	5 P.M.	Spruce Hall	English
Waste Reduction in Materials Processing	Lei Chiang	5 P.M.	Pine Hall	Mandarin
Buffet Dinner - Ticket Required		7 P.M.	Main Ballroom	N/A

*All non-English talks will be translated into English.

무역 협정 및 그것이 끼치는 영향	아마벨라 르골트	(194-2) 오후 3시	오크 홀	프랑스어
환경 친화적 제조	티모시 바레트	오후 3시	스프루스 홀	영어
직원들 간 팀워크의 비결	필립 파라디스	오후 5시	윌로우 홀	프랑스어
(195)현대 기계 장비 최대한 활용하기	리사 스티븐스	오후 5시	스프루스 홀	영어
재료 공정 중 폐기물 감량	레이 창	오후 5시	파인 홀	중국어
저녁 뷔페 – 티켓 필요		저녁 7시	본관 연회장	해당 없음

*모든 비영어 강연은 영어로 통역됩니다.

어휘 interpretation 통역, 해석 in-person 개인적인, 직접의 setting 환경 accuracy 정확성 target language (통역 등에서) 대상 언어 interpreter 통역사 negotiation 협상 court hearing 법정 심리 competitive 경쟁력 있는 prompt 신속한 cover 맡다, 다루다 registration 등록 off the clock 근무 시간 외의 complimentary 무료의 grant (정부나 단체에서 주는) 보조금 trade agreement 무역 협정 environmentally-friendly 환경 친화적인 make the most of ~을 최대한 활용하다 machinery (집합적) 기계류 reduction 감소 translate 번역하다, 통역하다

191 루미오 제조사가 서비스 대가로 지불할 액수는?
(A) 290달러
(B) 560달러
(C) 780달러
(D) 960달러

해설 루미오 제조사는 이메일 작성자인 로우리 씨의 회사이다. 이메일에서 루미오 제조사가 통역사를 필요로 하는 시간은 4시간이라고 했고, 광고의 요금표에서 4시간에 해당하는 요금을 찾으면 (B)가 정답이다.

192 광고에서, 1단락, 두 번째 줄의 어휘 "counts"와 의미상 가장 유사한 것은?
(A) 허락하다
(B) 고려하다
(C) 계산하다
(D) 중요하다

해설 count는 여러 가지 뜻으로 쓰이는 대표적인 다의어로, 사실상 선택지에 나오는 의미로 모두 쓰이므로 문맥을 읽어야 어느 뜻으로 쓰였는지 알 수 있다. 지문에서는 뒤에 목적어 없이 자동사로 '중요하다'라는 뜻으로 쓰이고 있다. 따라서 정답은 (D).

193 로우리 씨는 무슨 일에 GIE의 통역사를 초대했는가?
(A) 무료로 식사에 참석하기
(B) 단체 사진 찍기
(C) 호텔에서 하룻밤 묵기
(D) 미리 연사 만나기

해설 이메일의 마지막 단락에서 로우리 씨는 통역사에게 무료 식사권을 제공할 테니 저녁식사에 참석하라는 말을 전해 달라고 하고 있으므로 정답은 (A).

194 GIE의 통역사가 10월 27일 오후 3시에 가야 할 곳은?
(A) 파인 홀
(B) 오크 홀
(C) 스프루스 홀
(D) 윌로우 홀

해설 두 지문 연계 문제이다. 이메일에서 루미오 제조사는 10월 27일 오후 3시에 포모나 호텔에서 프랑스어 통역사가 필요하다고 했고, 일정표에 따르면 오후 3시에 프랑스어 연설이 있는 곳은 오크 홀이다. 따라서 정답은 (B).

195 스티븐스 씨의 연설 내용은?
(A) 기술 활용
(B) 환경 문제
(C) 공공 기금 확보
(D) 직원 협력

해설 스티븐스 씨의 연설 주제인 Making the most of modern machinery의 의미를 가장 잘 포함하고 있는 선택지를 고르면 된다. 이 경우 주제를 좀더 포괄적으로 표현한 것이 보통 정답이 된다. 따라서 정답은 (A).
오답 피하기 (B), (C), (D)는 각각 Environmentally-Friendly Manufacturing, Applying for Government Grants for Research Projects, The Key to Teamwork among Employees에 해당하는 내용이므로 모두 오답.
패러프레이징 지문의 Making the most of가 정답에서 Using으로, modern machinery가 technology로 각각 패러프레이징되었다.

[196-200] 구인 광고 & 면접 관련 이메일 & 장소 이용 관련 회람

Salesperson Needed

Grelton Pharmaceuticals, a leading supplier of prescription medications, is seeking self-motivated salespeople to join its team. The ideal candidate will want to develop a long-term career with us. (196C)The main responsibility of the position is maintaining our existing relationships with clinics and other medical facilities. A bachelor's degree in any field is required, and (196A)you must have worked in a sales environment for at least two years. You will often visit clients in person, so (196B) you must be able to go out of town regularly, often for a few days at a time.

We offer a competitive compensation package, which includes medical insurance, use of a company car, and a generous amount of paid vacation time. In addition, (196D)salespeople are eligible for a raise every three months, far sooner than most other companies.

To apply, send a résumé and cover letter to Adam Atwood at a.atwood@greltonpharma.com by March 28. (197-1)If you are selected for an interview, you must also submit two letters of recommendation, a copy of your valid driver's license, and a copy of your university transcripts.

To: Suzanne Hirsch <suzanneh@securepost111.com>
From: Adam Atwood <a.atwood@greltonpharma.com>
Date: April 5
Subject: Interview with Grelton Pharmaceuticals

Dear Ms. Hirsch,

영업사원 구합니다

처방약의 선두 공급업체인 그렐턴 제약회사에서 우리 팀에 합류할 의욕적인 영업사원을 찾고 있습니다. 이상적인 지원자는 우리 회사에서 오랫동안 경력을 쌓아가기를 원하는 사람입니다. (196C)주요 업무는 병원 및 기타 의료 시설과의 기존 관계를 유지하는 것입니다. 어떤 분야든 학사 학위가 요구되며, (196A)최소 2년간 영업 분야에서 일한 경험이 있어야 합니다. 고객을 직접 방문하는 일이 종종 있어서, 대개 한 번에 2~3일 동안, (196B)정기적으로 출장을 갈 수 있어야 합니다.

우리 회사는 경쟁력 있는 급여 수준을 제공하는데, 의료 보험과 회사 차량 이용, 넉넉한 유급 휴가가 포함됩니다. 또한 (196D)영업사원은 대부분의 다른 회사들에 비해 훨씬 더 빠른, 3개월마다의 급여 인상을 받을 자격이 주어집니다.

지원하시려면, 3월 28일까지 a.atwood@greltonpharma.com으로 애덤 앳우드 씨에게 이력서와 자기 소개서를 보내십시오. (197-1)선발되어 면접을 보시게 될 경우, 추천서 2부와 유효한 운전 면허증 사본, 대학 성적 증명서 사본도 제출해야 합니다.

수신: 수잔 히어쉬 <suzanneh@securepost111.com>
발신: 애덤 앳우드 <a.atwood@greltonpharma.com>
날짜: 4월 5일
제목: 그렐턴 제약회사 면접

히어쉬 씨께,

It was a pleasure speaking to you on the phone this morning, and I'm pleased that you are available for an interview. (198)Our hiring committee was especially impressed with your cover letter. We believe that you can express yourself clearly in writing, and this is an important part of the job.

Your interview is scheduled for 10:30 A.M. on April 10 with sales director Paula Jakin and office manager Wendell Beckwith. I have attached a map to our office building. And you should come to the third floor. (199-2)The office administrator, Jesse Tucker, will be in the reception area to direct you where to go.

(197-2)Of the documents you need to submit prior to the interview, I still need the copy of your driver's license and your university transcripts. Feel free to send these to me anytime. I look forward to meeting you in person!

Sincerely,

Adam Atwood
HR Director, Grelton Pharmaceuticals

To: All Employees
From: Wendell Beckwith

April 6

The third-floor meeting room will be unavailable to employees from 9 A.M. to 4 P.M. on Tuesday, April 10, due to interviews for the open sales positions. Several rooms are available on other floors, but they must be reserved in advance. (199-1)If you need to find a meeting space elsewhere in the building, please e-mail the office administrator, who will help you to make the necessary arrangements. (200)For those of you working on the 3rd floor, please try to speak quietly and avoid using the copiers while interviews are being held. Thank you for your understanding.

오늘 오전에 전화 통화를 하게 되어 반가웠으며, 면접에 시간을 내실 수 있으시다니 기쁩니다. (198)회사 채용위원회에서는 특히 히어쉬 씨의 자기 소개서에 깊은 인상을 받았습니다. 히어쉬 씨는 글로 자신을 분명히 표현할 줄 아는 능력이 있다고 여겨지는데, 이것이 이 일에 중요한 요소입니다.

면접은 폴라 제킨 영업 이사, 웬델 벡위스 사무소장과 4월 10일 오전 10시 30분으로 예정되어 있습니다. 우리 회사 건물로 오는 약도를 첨부했으니, 3층으로 오시면 됩니다. (199-2)사무행정 담당 직원인 제시 터커 씨가 접수대에서 어디로 가야 할지 알려드릴 겁니다.

(197-2)면접 전에 제출해야 할 서류 중에, 운전 면허증 사본과 대학 성적 증명서를 아직 못 받았습니다. 언제든지 저에게 보내 주십시오. 직접 만나 뵙게 되기를 고대하고 있겠습니다!

그렐턴 제약회사, 인사부장
애덤 앳우드 드림

수신: 전 직원
발신: 웬델 벡위스

4월 6일

3층 회의실은 4월 10일 화요일 오전 9시부터 오후 4시까지, 공석인 영업직 면접으로 인해 직원들이 이용할 수 없게 됩니다. 다른 층에 있는 몇몇 회의실을 이용할 수 있지만, 미리 예약해야 합니다. (199-1)건물 내 다른 곳에서 회의 장소를 찾으셔야 할 경우, 사무행정 담당 직원에게 이메일을 보내면, 필요한 준비를 하는 걸 도와줄 겁니다. (200)3층에서 근무하는 직원들께서는 인터뷰가 진행되는 동안에는 말씀을 조용히 해주시고 복사기 사용을 자제해 주시기 바랍니다. 이해해 주셔서 감사합니다.

어휘 prescription medication 처방약 self-motivated 의욕적인 candidate 지원자, 후보자 long-term 장기간의 maintain 유지하다 existing 기존의 bachelor's degree 학사 학위 regularly 정기적으로 competitive 경쟁력 있는 compensation package (급여와 복리후생을 포함한) 급여 수준, 보상 generous 넉넉한, 후한 be eligible for ~의 자격이 있다 raise 급여 인상 letter of recommendation 추천서 valid 유효한 transcript 성적 증명서 office administrator 사무행정 담당 직원 reception area 접수대 prior to ~ 이전에 in person 직접 unavailable 이용할 수 없는 open position 공석, 빈자리 reserve 예약하다 in advance 미리

---

196 일자리에 대해 언급되지 않은 것은?
  (A) 이전 경험을 요구한다.
  (B) 많은 출장이 수반된다.
  (C) 신규 고객 확보를 필요로 한다.
  (D) 급여가 빠르게 인상될 수 있다.

해설 (C)를 제외한 나머지 선택지는 모두 첫 번째 지문인 구인 광고에서 언급되어 있다. 주요 업무는 신규 고객 확보가 아닌 기존 고객 관리라고 했으므로 (C)가 정답.

197 히어쉬 씨가 이미 보낸 것은?
 (A) 운전 면허증 사본
 (B) 영업 전략 개요
 (C) 대학 성적 증명서
 (D) 추천서

198 채용위원회가 히어쉬 씨에 대해 인상 깊게 여긴 것은?
 (A) 학력
 (B) 글을 통한 커뮤니케이션 능력
 (C) 독특한 영업 전략
 (D) 이전 직장

199 사람들이 회의실 이용 여부에 대해 연락해야 하는 사람은?
 (A) 애덤 앳우드
 (B) 웬델 벡위스
 (C) 폴라 제킨
 (D) 제시 터커

200 4월 10일에 3층 직원들에게 요청된 것은?
 (A) 스낵 먹지 않기
 (B) 지원자들을 열렬히 환영하기
 (C) 소음을 최소한으로 줄이기
 (D) 컴퓨터 함께 쓰기

해설 두 지문 연계 문제이다. 구인 광고 마지막 문장에서, 면접에 필요한 서류로 추천서, 운전면허증 사본, 성적 증명서를 요구하고 있는데, 이메일에서 히어쉬 씨에게 아직 못 받은 운전 면허증 사본과 성적 증명서를 보내 달라고 요청하고 있다. 따라서 히어쉬 씨가 이미 보낸 것은 추천서이므로 (D)가 정답이다. (B)는 언급되지 않았다.

해설 이메일에 따르면 채용위원회가 히어쉬 씨의 자기 소개서에 깊은 인상을 받았다고 했는데, 그 이유가 글로 자신을 표현할 줄 아는 능력 때문이라고 했다. 이를 바꾸어 표현한 (B)가 정답이다.

해설 두 지문 연계 문제이다. 회람의 단서(199-1)에서 회의실을 구해야 할 경우, 사무행정 담당 직원에게 이메일을 보내라고 지시하고 있는데, 이 직원의 이름은 이메일의 단서(199-2)에 언급되어 있는 대로 제시 터커 씨이다. 따라서 정답은 (D).

해설 회람 끝부분에 3층 직원들에게 당부하는 내용이 나온다. 대화를 조용히 하고 복사기 사용을 자제하라고 한 것은 소음을 내지 말라는 뜻이므로 정답은 (C).

ACTUAL TEST 3

p.202

147 (C)	148 (B)	149 (B)	150 (D)	151 (C)	152 (C)
153 (C)	154 (B)	155 (A)	156 (D)	157 (D)	158 (D)
159 (B)	160 (D)	161 (B)	162 (D)	163 (C)	164 (D)
165 (D)	166 (D)	167 (C)	168 (A)	169 (B)	170 (C)
171 (D)	172 (B)	173 (C)	174 (A)	175 (A)	176 (C)
177 (D)	178 (A)	179 (B)	180 (C)	181 (B)	182 (D)
183 (D)	184 (C)	185 (A)	186 (B)	187 (C)	188 (C)
189 (C)	190 (D)	191 (A)	192 (C)	193 (B)	194 (C)
195 (C)	196 (B)	197 (A)	198 (D)	199 (A)	200 (B)

[147-148] 배송 지연 안내 편지

Tamara Lissow
66 Tunali Hilmi Caddesi
Ankara, Turkey 6680

May 21

Dear Ms. Lissow,

According to our records, you recently purchased a new, high-quality water filtration pump for your fish tank. After ordering it, we originally promised that the device would arrive within a week. Unfortunately, there was an error with the manufacturer who sends us products. (147)I wanted to update you on your order and let you know that there will be a delay. I promise that your pump will be available for pickup sometime next week. (148)To compensate you for the wait, please accept a complimentary bag of goldfish food. This is our gift to you.

Best wishes,

Caleb Mandelbaum
Manager, Pennington Pet Supply

타마라 리소우
투날리 힐미 카데시 66
터키, 앙카라 6680

5월 21일

리소우 씨께,

저희 기록에 따르면 귀하께서는 최근에 수족관에 사용하기 위해 새로 출시된 고급 여과 펌프를 구매하셨습니다. 그것을 주문하신 후에 저희는 원래 일주일 내로 그 장비가 도착할 것이라고 약속 드렸습니다. 안타깝게도 저희에게 상품을 보내주는 제조업체에서 실수가 있었습니다. (147)귀하의 주문에 대한 최근 상태를 말씀 드리고 귀하께 배송 지연에 대해 알려드리고 싶었습니다. 귀하의 펌프가 다음주 중으로는 수령 가능할 것이라는 점을 약속 드립니다. (148)기다리시게 한 것에 대한 보상으로 드리는 무료 금붕어 사료 한 봉지를 받아주십시오. 이것은 귀하께 드리는 저희의 사은품입니다.

페닝튼 펫 서플라이, 운영자
칼렙 만델바움 드림

어휘 high-quality 고급의, 고품질의 filtration 여과 (과정) manufacturer 제조업체, 제조사 delay 지연, 지체 pickup (화물, 우편물 등의) 수령, 집배 compensate for ~에 대해 보상하다[보상금을 주다] complimentary 무료의, 사은품의

147 만델바움 씨가 편지를 보낸 이유는?
   (A) 고객에게 매장을 방문해 달라고 부탁하기 위해
   (B) 서비스 상기 메모를 보내기 위해
   (C) 주문에 대한 세부 정보를 제공하기 위해
   (D) 연락처 정보 일부를 갱신하기 위해

해설 단서(147)의 I wanted to 이하를 통해 만델바움 씨가 편지를 보낸 이유를 파악할 수 있다. 리소우 씨가 주문한 물품의 배송이 늦어질 것임을 알리기 위해 편지를 보낸 것이므로 정답은 (C).

183

148 리소우 씨가 무료로 받게 될 것은?
(A) 수족관 장식품 견본
(B) 물고기 사료 비축분
(C) 정수용 펌프
(D) 새로운 유리 세정 제품

> **해설** 편지 뒷부분에서 고객이 받게 될 것에 대한 언급을 찾아보도록 한다. 배송 지연에 대한 보상으로 금붕어 사료를 한 봉지 줄 것이라 했으므로 정답은 (B).

[149-151] 연극 광고

Acclaimed novelist Jade Harvey has left the world of literature and successfully entered the realm of theater. Harvey's first-ever play, entitled *Portrait of a Lady*, is receiving compliments from audiences and critics alike. (149)Inspired by the real-life story of artist Amelia Cotter, Harvey has written a play about a woman who becomes a famous painter after a car accident leaves her bedridden. Even the title, *Portrait of a Lady*, was taken from the name of one of Cotter's paintings. The show is two-hours long with a twenty-minute intermission.

(150)The closing night performance will be on October 18 at 7 P.M. For this one night only, we have partnered with the nearby Savio Restaurant, known for its vegetarian dishes and exclusive use of local ingredients. After watching the play, simply present your theater ticket as a complimentary dinner voucher. The limit is one free meal per table.

With few show times remaining, seats at the box office are selling out fast. Get yours before they are all gone!

Rates:

Section	(151)Child	Adult	Group Discount*
Dress Circle	$17.99	$39.99	$35.99
Balcony	$17.99	$49.99	$44.99
Orchestra	$17.99	$59.99	$50.39

*Groups of 20 or more will receive a 10% discount.

호평 받는 소설가 제이드 하비 씨가 문학 세계를 떠나 성공적으로 연극계에 입성했습니다. 〈여인의 초상화〉라는 제목의 하비 씨의 최초의 연극이 관객들과 비평가 모두로부터 찬사를 받고 있습니다. (149)하비 씨는 예술가 아멜리아 코터 씨의 실화에 영감을 받아서, 차 사고가 그녀를 몸져 눕게 한 후 유명한 화가가 된 한 여성에 관한 연극을 썼습니다. 〈여인의 초상화〉라는 제목도 코터 씨의 그림 중 하나의 이름에서 따온 것입니다. 공연은 2시간이며, 20분의 중간 휴식 시간이 있습니다.

(150)마지막 날 밤 공연은 10월 18일 저녁 7시에 있을 예정입니다. 오직 이날 저녁에만, 저희는 채식 요리와 현지 재료만을 독점적으로 사용하는 것으로 유명한 근처 세비오 레스토랑과 제휴를 맺었습니다. 연극을 보고 난 후에 연극 티켓을 무료 식사 쿠폰으로 제시하세요. 무료 식사는 한 테이블당 하나로 제한됩니다.

공연이 몇 번 안 남았고, 매표소에서 좌석이 빠르게 팔리고 있습니다. 매진되기 전에 표를 마련하세요!

가격:

구역	(151)어린이	성인	단체 할인*
2층 특별석	17.99달러	39.99달러	35.99달러
발코니석	17.99달러	49.99달러	44.99달러
오케스트라석	17.99달러	59.99달러	50.39달러

*20명 이상의 단체는 10% 할인을 받을 수 있습니다.

어휘 acclaim 호평하다 literature 문학 realm 영역, 세계 entitle 제목을 붙이다; 자격[권리]를 주다 compliment 찬사, 칭찬 audience 관객 critic 비평가 inspire 영감을 주다 bedridden 아파서 누워 있는 intermission 중간 휴식 시간 partner with ~와 제휴를 맺다[협력하다] exclusive 독점적인 ingredient 재료 remain 남아 있다 voucher 쿠폰 dress circle (극장의 2층에 있는) 특별석

---

149 아멜리아 코터 씨는 누구인가?
(A) 허구의 인물
(B) 실제 화가
(C) 유명한 소설가
(D) 매표소 직원

> **해설** 지문에서 해당 인물이 언급된 부분을 재빨리 찾아본다. 연극이 예술가 아멜리아 코터 씨의 실화를 영감을 받아서 쓰였다고 했으므로 정답은 (B).
> **오답 피하기** 유명한 소설가는 아멜리아 코터 씨가 아니라 제이드 하비 씨이므로 (C)는 오답.

150 10월 18일에 일어날 일은?
(A) 〈여인의 초상화〉의 초연이 있을 것이다.
(B) 매표소가 닫혀 있을 것이다.
(C) 단체 할인이 적용되지 않을 것이다.
(D) 극장이 레스토랑과 제휴를 맺을 것이다.

해설 단서(150)에 따르면, 마지막 공연일인 10월 18일에만 세비오 레스토랑과 제휴를 맺어 식사를 무료로 제공한다고 했으므로 정답은 (D).

151 티켓의 가격에 대해 시사된 바는?
(A) 발코니석이 가장 저렴하다.
(B) 단체는 15%의 할인을 받는다.
(C) 어린이 티켓의 가격은 변하지 않는다.
(D) 학생들은 특별가를 제공받는다.

해설 티켓의 가격에 관한 질문이므로 가격 정보가 나와 있는 표 부분을 집중해서 보아야 한다. 어린이 티켓의 가격은 특별석, 발코니석, 오케스트라석 모두 17.99달러로 동일하므로 정답은 (C).
오답 피하기 가장 저렴한 좌석은 특별석이고, 단체는 10%의 할인을 받을 수 있으며, 학생 할인에 대해서는 언급된 바가 없기 때문에 (A), (B), (D)는 모두 오답이다.

[152-153] 결근을 알리는 문자메시지

KIERA WADE 9:02 A.M. Hi, Reese. (152)Sorry for the short notice, but would it be all right if I didn't come into the office today? There's a water leak in my house, and I'm waiting for the plumber to arrive. I was hoping to work from home instead.	키이라 웨이드 오전 9:02 안녕하세요, 리즈. (152)갑작스럽게 통보하게 돼서 죄송하지만, 오늘 제가 출근하지 않아도 괜찮을까요? 집에 누수가 있어서 배관공이 도착하기를 기다리고 있거든요. 대신에 집에서 일했으면 하는데요.
REESE BENTLEY 9:03 A.M. That's fine as long as you're able to get your project done on time.	리즈 벤틀리 오전 9:03 맡은 프로젝트를 제시간에 끝낼 수만 있다면 괜찮아요.
KIERA WADE 9:06 A.M. Of course. My plan is to work on it all day.	키이라 웨이드 오전 9:06 물론이죠. 하루 종일 그 작업을 할 계획이에요.
KIERA WADE 9:08 A.M. I've just logged into my work desktop through the remote server, but I can't access the folder with our subscriber information.	키이라 웨이드 오전 9:08 방금 원격 서버를 통해 제 사무실 데스크탑에 로그인했는데, 우리 구독자 정보가 있는 폴더에 접속할 수가 없어요.
REESE BENTLEY 9:10 A.M. Oh, that's because yesterday I asked Drake to clean up some of the files and update the spreadsheet. So the folder will be locked until he's finished with it.	리즈 벤틀리 오전 9:10 아, 그건 어제 제가 드레이크 씨에게 파일 일부를 정리하고 스프레드시트를 업데이트해 달라고 요청했기 때문이에요. 그래서 그가 그 일을 마칠 때까지 폴더가 잠겨 있을 거예요.
KIERA WADE 9:12 A.M. Well, I just need to get the address for one particular subscriber. (153)Is it possible to have him change the settings to "view only" just long enough for me to get the information I need?	키이라 웨이드 오전 9:12 음, 전 특정한 구독자 한 명의 주소만 있으면 되거든요. (153)제가 필요한 정보를 얻을 때까지만 그에게 설정을 "열람 전용"으로 바꿔 달라고 할 수 있을까요?
REESE BENTLEY 9:14 A.M. Let me check with him, but I think that's possible.	리즈 벤틀리 오전 9:14 그에게 물어볼게요, 그런데 제 생각에는 가능할 것 같아요.
KIERA WADE 9:15 A.M. Thank you so much!	키이라 웨이드 오전 9:15 정말 감사합니다!

어휘 **short notice** 갑작스러운 통보 **water leak** 누수 **plumber** 배관공 **on time** 제시간에 **remote server** 원격 서버 **subscriber** 구독자 **particular** 특정한

152 웨이드 씨가 벤틀리 씨에게 연락한 이유는?
(A) 마감일 연장을 요청하기 위해
(B) 업무에 관한 설명을 얻기 위해
(C) 예상되는 결근을 알리기 위해
(D) 직원 회의 일정을 다시 잡기 위해

해설 단서(152)에서 웨이드 씨는 출근하지 않아도 되는지 양해를 구하고 있으므로 정답은 (C).

153 오전 9:14에, 벤틀리 씨가 "그에게 물어볼게요"라고 하는 의도는?
(A) 드레이크 씨에게 그의 주소를 웨이드 씨에게 주라고 부탁할 것이다.
(B) 드레이크 씨에게 폴더를 일반인이 접속할 수 있도록 해달라고 말할 것이다.
(C) 드레이크 씨에게 일시적으로 파일 설정을 바꿔 달라고 지시할 것이다.
(D) 드레이크 씨에게 집에서 일해도 된다는 허락을 구할 것이다.

해설 벤틀리 씨의 "Let me check with him"은 웨이드 씨의 부탁에 대한 응답이다. 웨이드 씨는 필요한 정보를 얻는 동안만 파일 설정을 바꿔 달라고 요청하고 있으므로 정답은 (C).

[154-155] 구내 식당 폐쇄 공지

NOTICE

(154)For the next eight weeks, this cafeteria will be closed for renovations. The construction is anticipated to last from September 1 to October 31. We understand that this is an inconvenience to employees who will not be able to use the facilities during this time. Therefore, we have negotiated relationships with several nearby restaurants. (155) Until our cafeteria reopens, all employees will receive a 50% discount at all of the establishments listed on the attached document. At the time of order, just present your employee ID card to receive the discount.

공지

(154)앞으로 8주간 이 구내 식당은 보수 공사를 위해 폐쇄될 예정입니다. 공사는 9월 1일부터 10월 31일까지 지속될 것으로 예상됩니다. 이 기간 동안 시설을 이용할 수 없을 직원분들께 불편함이 있을 것이란 점을 잘 압니다. 그리하여 저희는 일부 인근 레스토랑들과 협의했습니다. (155)저희 구내 식당이 다시 문을 열 때까지 모든 직원은 첨부된 문서에 나열된 모든 식당에서 50% 할인을 받게 됩니다. 주문하실 때 할인받기 위해 그저 여러분의 사원 카드를 제시하시면 됩니다.

어휘 temporarily 임시로, 한시적으로 be anticipated to do ~할 것으로 예상되다 last 지속되다 inconvenience 불편, 애로 negotiate 협의[협상]하다 establishment 식당, 점포 display 제시하다, 보여주다

154 이 공지를 발견할 수 있을 것 같은 곳은?
(A) 창고 안
(B) 구내 식당 외부
(C) 주차장 안
(D) 엘리베이터 안

해설 단서(154)를 통해 이 공지가 구내 식당의 임시 폐쇄를 알리기 위한 것임을 알 수 있으므로 이 공지를 구내 식당의 외부에서 발견할 수 있을 것이라고 유추할 수 있다. 따라서 정답은 (B).

155 직원들에게 제공되는 것은?
(A) 지역 식당 할인
(B) 무료 식사 배달
(C) 식품 구입비 환불
(D) 대체 시설 이용

해설 단서(155)에서 구내 식당이 재개장할 때까지 근처 식당에서 할인된 가격으로 식사를 할 수 있다고 했으므로 정답은 (A).
패러프레이징 지문의 establishments가 정답에서는 eateries로 패러프레이징되었다.

[156-158] 마케팅 책임자의 경력에 대한 정보문

Employee Profile: Tammy Wyatt

Tammy Wyatt currently serves as the director of marketing here at Indigo Apparel. She joined our

직원 프로필: 태미 와이어트

태미 와이어트 씨는 현재 이곳 인디고 어패럴 사에서 마케팅 부장으로 재직하고 있습니다. 그녀는 15년 전에 석사 학위를

company fifteen years ago as a summer intern while she was completing her master's degree. Over the years, she has taken on positions of increasing responsibility, eventually working her way to the top of the department. She took over the director of marketing role four years ago. (156)During this time, the company expanded internationally, creating unique marketing needs for each region. Ms. Wyatt was able to handle these challenges with creativity and strong leadership, developing ad campaigns that suited the tastes of different audiences. This has helped us to increase our market share by as much as 30% in some areas.

Indigo Apparel has benefited greatly from Ms. Wyatt's hard work and expertise. (157)She developed an online system for customers that allowed them to enroll in weekly competitions at the touch of a button by sharing their ideas on social media. This helped to build brand awareness among our target demographic of young consumers. (158)Her forward thinking also led to the company's creation of its own channel on the popular video-sharing Web site *Fashion View*. We were one of the first companies in the industry to do so. (158)Though it has now become common practice, this was innovative when she first came up with the idea, and popular videos with fashion tips and interviews with Indigo Apparel's designers have been viewed millions of times.

It is clear that Ms. Wyatt is an essential part of the Indigo Apparel team, and we look forward to seeing her latest ideas in marketing and public relations.

이수하는 동안 하계 인턴 사원으로 우리 회사에 입사했습니다. 수년간 그녀는 점점 책임이 가중되는 직책들을 맡아 왔으며, 결국 부서장 자리까지 올랐습니다. 그녀는 4년 전에 마케팅 부장 직책을 맡게 되었습니다. (156)이 시기 동안, 회사는 국제적으로 사업을 확장하여 각 지역마다 고유의 마케팅 요구가 생겨났습니다. 와이어트 씨는 창의력과 강한 리더십으로 이러한 난제를 처리할 수 있었으며, 각기 다른 대중들의 취향에 맞는 광고 전략을 개발했습니다. 그 덕분에 우리는 일부 지역에서 시장 점유율을 30%나 늘릴 수 있었습니다.

인디고 어패럴 사는 와이어트 씨의 노고와 전문성으로부터 대단한 혜택을 입었습니다. (157)그녀는 고객들을 위한 온라인 시스템을 개발하여 고객들이 소셜 미디어에서 그들의 의견을 공유함으로써 버튼만 누르면 주간 경연 대회에 등록할 수 있도록 했습니다. 이는 우리의 광고 타겟층인 젊은 소비자들 사이에 브랜드 인지도를 구축하는 데 도움을 주었습니다. (158)그녀의 진취적인 사고는 또한 회사가 유명한 동영상 공유 사이트인 "패션 뷰"에서 독자적인 채널을 만드는 데까지 이어졌습니다. 우리 회사가 업계에서 그렇게 한 최초의 회사들 중 하나였습니다. (158)지금은 일반적인 관행이 되었지만, 그녀가 처음 그 아이디어를 내놓았을 당시 이것은 혁신적인 것이었으며, 패션에 대한 조언 및 인디고 어패럴 사 디자이너들과의 인터뷰를 담은 인기 동영상들은 수백만 번이나 시청되었습니다.

와이어트 씨가 인디고 어패럴 팀에 필수적인 존재라는 것은 분명하며, 마케팅 및 홍보 분야에서 그녀의 최신 아이디어들을 보게 되기를 고대합니다.

어휘 master's degree 석사 학위 take on (일을) 맡다 take over ~을 떠맡다, 인수하다 region 지역 suit ~에 맞다[어울리다] market share 시장 점유율 benefit from ~로부터 혜택을 입다[이득을 얻다] enroll 등록하다 competition 경연 대회 brand awareness 브랜드 인지도 target demographic 광고 타겟층 forward thinking 진취적인 사고 innovative 혁신적인 come up with (생각을) 내놓다, 제안하다 essential 필수적인 public relations 홍보

156 인디고 어패럴 사에 대해 사실인 것은?
(A) 현재 신입 디자이너들을 모집하고 있다.
(B) 마케팅 부장이 조만간 은퇴할 것이다.
(C) 업계 최대의 의류 매장이다.
(D) 한 국가 이상에서 영업을 하고 있다.

157 와이어트 씨가 고객들이 하기에 편하게 만들어 준 것은?
(A) 온라인 주문하기
(B) 매장 지점 찾기
(C) 비디오 교환하기
(D) 경연에 참가 신청하기

해설 단서(156)에서 인디고 어패럴 사가 국제적으로 사업을 확장했다는 언급이 있으므로 정답은 (D).
패러프레이징 지문의 internationally가 정답에서 in more than one country로 패러프레이징되었다.

해설 단서(157)에서 와이어트 씨가 개발한 온라인 시스템 덕분에 고객들은 버튼만 누르면 주간 경연 대회에 등록할 수 있게 되었다고 했으므로 정답은 (D).
오답 피하기 지문의 online system만 보고 정답을 (A)로 고르지 않도록 주의하자.
패러프레이징 지문의 enroll in weekly competitions가 정답에서 Sign up for contests로 패러프레이징되었다.

158 [1], [2], [3], [4]로 표시된 곳들 중, 다음 문장이 들어가기에 가장 알맞은 곳은?

"우리 회사가 업계에서 그렇게 한 최초의 회사들 중 하나였습니다."

(A) [1]
(B) [2]
(C) [3]
(D) [4]

해설 주어진 문장은 회사가 어떤 일을 업계 최초로 했다는 내용이므로, 이 앞에는 회사가 이룬 혁신적인 성과에 대한 내용이 와야 알맞다. 지문의 첫 번째 단서(158)에 보면 와이어트 씨가 회사의 고유 채널를 만드는 데 기여했다고 하고, 두 번째 단서(158)에서는 이것이 혁신적이었다고 하고 있으므로 주어진 문장은 이 사이에 와야 알맞다. 정답은 (D). 주어진 문장의 do so는 앞 문장의 creation of its own channel on the popular video-sharing Web site를 가리킨다.

[159-160] 비영리 단체를 소개하는 웹사이트

| HOME | **ABOUT US** | LECTURE SERIES | PRESS | CONTACT US |

(159C)Right Start Education (RSE) is a nonprofit educational organization founded by middle school teacher Lynn Flores. Throughout her career, Ms. Flores saw firsthand how students with learning difficulties fell further and further behind their peers. Many of these students came from low-income families who did not have the resources to provide the necessary additional support. **(159A)(159B)(159D)RSE's mission is to offer one-on-one tutoring to students aged 5 to 14 at its head office downtown and at various learning centers throughout the area.**

RSE relies on support from the public, as funding is not provided by the government. **(160)If you would like to donate to RSE, please click HERE and complete the donation form.** Credit cards and bank transfers are accepted. If you are interested in becoming a volunteer for RSE, please contact Annette McGuire at amcguire@rightstartedu.org.

| 홈 | **단체 소개** | 강의 시리즈 | 보도 | 연락처 |

(159C)라이트 스타트 에듀케이션(RSE)은 중학교 교사 린 플로레스 씨에 의해 설립된 비영리 교육 단체입니다. 그녀는 경력 내내 학습 장애를 가진 학생들이 그들의 또래보다 어떻게 점점 뒤떨어지는지를 직접 관찰하였습니다. 이러한 학생들 대다수는 필요한 추가적인 지원을 제공할 자산을 가지지 않은 저소득 가정 출신이었습니다. (159A)(159B)(159D)RSE의 사명은 시내에 있는 본사와 지역 도처에 있는 학습 센터에서 5~14세 정도의 학생들에게 일대일 개인 교습을 해주는 것입니다.

RSE는 정부로부터 기금을 제공받지 않기 때문에 대중들의 후원에 의존합니다. (160)만약 RSE에 기부하고 싶으시다면, 여기를 눌러서 기부 신청서를 작성해 주세요. 신용카드와 계좌이체가 가능합니다. 만약 RSE의 자원 봉사자가 되는 것에 관심이 있으시다면, 아네트 맥과이어 씨에게 amcguire@rightstartedu.org로 연락 주세요.

어휘 **nonprofit** 비영리적인 **organization** 단체 **found** 설립하다 **firsthand** 직접 **learning difficulties** 학습 장애 **fall behind** ~에 뒤떨어지다 **peer** 또래 **low-income** 저소득층 **resource** (보통 복수형) 자산, 부 **one-on-one** 일대일 **head office** 본사(= headquarters) **throughout** ~ 도처에 **rely on** ~에 의존하다 **funding** 기금 **donation** 기부 **volunteer** 자원 봉사자

159 RSE에 대해 사실이 아닌 것은?
(A) 개인 교습을 제공한다.
(B) 고등학생들을 대상으로 한다.
(C) 교사에 의해 시작되었다.
(D) 본사가 도시 중심에 있다.

해설 RSE는 5~14세의 학생들을 대상으로 하기 때문에 고등학생은 포함되어 있지 않다. 따라서 (B)가 정답이다.
오답 피하기 RSE는 학생들에게 일대일 개인 교습을 해 준다고 하였고, 한 중학교 교사에 의해 설립된 비영리 단체라 하였으며, 본사가 시내에 있다고 하였으므로 (A), (C), (D) 모두 오답이다.

160 웹사이트에 따르면, 사람들이 재정적인 기부를 할 수 있는 방법은?
(A) 수표를 보냄으로써
(B) 연회에 참석함으로써
(C) 맥과이어 씨에게 이메일을 보냄으로써
(D) 온라인 양식을 작성함으로써

해설 단서(160)에 따르면, RSE에 기부를 원하는 사람들은 웹페이지에서 기부 신청서를 작성하면 된다고 하였으므로 정답은 (D).
패러프레이징 지문의 complete the donation form이 정답에서 filling out an online form으로 패러프레이징되었다.

[161-163] 기술 지원 직원 구인 광고

Opening: Technical Support Representative

TP Recruiting is filling a full-time position in the field of technology.

(161)Working in an inbound call center environment, the technical support representative will be in charge of answering customer phone calls and providing resolution to technical and network problems. Technical support representatives are considered computer specialists and are expected to diagnose various problems through a series of questions and answers. Simultaneously, representatives must guide users step-by-step through solutions to various technological problems. These problems include—among other issues—recovering usernames and passwords, uninstalling/reinstalling basic software applications, and troubleshooting e-mail issues.

(162B)The ideal candidate will have a friendly attitude, a tendency toward the positive, (162C)and be able to clearly communicate technical solutions in a straightforward, professional manner. (162A)Candidates with previous call center experience are preferred and will be put at the top of the shortlist for consideration.

(163)Interested individuals should apply for this position by e-mailing their credentials (cover letter, résumé, and one written recommendation) to the human resources director, Virgil Samuels, at vsamuels@tprecruiting.com by March 4. After carefully reviewing the qualifications and receiving verification of previous employment, candidates selected for an interview will be contacted.

공석: 기술 지원 직원

TP 채용은 기술 분야의 상근직을 모집 중입니다.

(161)기술 지원 직원은 착신 콜센터에서 근무하며, 고객 문의전화에 응대하고 기술적 문제와 통신망 문제에 대해 해결책을 제시하는 업무를 담당하게 될 것입니다. 기술 지원 직원은 컴퓨터 전문가여야 하며 일련의 질문과 답변을 통하여 다양한 문제를 진단할 수 있도록 기대됩니다. 동시에, 직원은 다양한 기술적 문제들에 대한 해결책을 통해 단계적으로 그들을 안내해야만 합니다. 이러한 문제들은 여러 사안 중에서도 사용자명과 비밀번호 복구, 기본 소프트웨어의 삭제 및 재설치 그리고 이메일 문제를 해결하는 것을 포함합니다. .

(162B)가장 적합한 지원자는 친화력 있는 태도와 긍정적인 성향, (162C)쉽고 전문적인 태도로 기술적인 해결책을 분명히 이야기할 수 있는 사람입니다. (162A)이전에 콜센터에서의 경험이 있는 지원자는 선호될 것이며 최종 후보자 명단의 상위로 우대될 것입니다.

(163)관심 있는 개인은 자격 사항(자기소개서, 이력서, 한 통의 추천서)을 인사담당자 버질 사뮤엘스 씨에게 3월 4일까지 vsamuels@tprecruiting.com으로 이메일로 보내세요. 자격 사항들을 상세히 검토하고 이전 근무지의 확인을 마친 뒤에 면접에 선발된 지원자들에게는 연락이 갈 것 입니다.

어휘 representative 직원; 대표 be in charge of ~를 담당하다 resolution 해결책 consider 여기다, 고려하다 be expected to do ~할 것으로 기대되다 diagnose 진단하다 simultaneously 동시에 recover 복구하다 troubleshoot 수리하다 candidate 지원자 straightforward 간단한 previous 이전의 shortlist 최종 후보 명단 credential 자격 증명서 recommendation 추천(서) qualification 자격 (증명서) verification 확인

161 기술 지원 직원의 업무가 행해지는 방법은?
(A) 실황 회의를 통해
(B) 전화를 통해
(C) 이메일 서신을 통해
(D) 서류를 팩스로 보냄으로써

해설 광고의 첫 단락에 기술 지원 직원은 수신 콜센터에서 일하게 될 것이며 고객 전화에 응대하는 업무를 할 것이라고 나와 있으므로 정답은 (B).

162 공석에 대한 바람직한 자격 조건으로 언급되지 않은 것은?
(A) 콜센터 근무 경험
(B) 친근한 태도
(C) 분명한 의사 소통 능력
(D) 컴퓨터 기술 자격증

해설 NOT 문제는 선택지를 하나씩 소거해 가면서 풀어야 한다. 지원자의 자격 조건이 언급된 두 번째 문단을 주의 깊게 보면 컴퓨터 기술과 관련된 자격증은 언급되지 않았음을 알 수 있다. 따라서 정답은 (D).

163 지원자들이 지원서에 포함하도록 지시받은 것은?
(A) 그들의 학력을 증명하는 서류
(B) 잠재적인 추천인들의 명단
(C) 공식적인 자기 소개서
(D) 완성된 지원서 양식

해설 단서(163)에 따르면 관심 있는 지원자는 인사 담당자에게 자기소개서, 이력서, 추천서를 이메일로 보내야 한다고 했으므로 정답은 (C).

[164-167] 성공한 사업체에 대한 기사

(166)April 8 — (164)Washing, drying, and folding clothes is a chore that few people enjoy. That's where Ryan Co. comes in. The company was founded by two brothers, Douglas and Johnathan Ryan, who wanted to apply their entrepreneurial spirit to an everyday problem. Their company has storage lockers for rent in apartment buildings and other sites all over town. Customers are assigned a locker on a monthly, quarterly, or annual basis. They put their dirty clothing in the secure locker and use a smartphone app to request the service. The clothes are then laundered by the company and returned to the locker. A text message informs the customer that their clothes are ready to be picked up.

(165)"We came up with the idea one day when looking at the lockers after working out at the gym," says Douglas Ryan. "We were talking about how convenient it would be to have a drop-off point closer to home rather than making a special trip to the dry-cleaners."

(167)The two brothers originally tried a business model that offered dry-cleaning only, but they had trouble attracting customers because so many dry cleaning businesses offer free delivery. The business ended in failure. However, this didn't stop the brothers from trying again. The new business model, which became the basis for Ryan Co., focused on everyday clothing. (167)It had a price point that was affordable for a larger number of people.

Ryan Co. has been in operation for just three months but has already become one of the hottest new businesses in town. In fact, the lockers are at full capacity, and there is a waiting list. Since the current customers aren't expected to give up their lockers anytime soon, (166)the Ryan brothers are looking for more sites to place lockers next month.

(166)4월 8일 — (164)의류를 세탁하고 건조시키고 개는 것은 즐기는 사람이 거의 없는 집안일이다. 이 지점이 바로 라이언 사가 개입하는 곳이다. 이 회사는 더글라스 라이언과 조나단 라이언, 두 형제가 설립했으며, 그들은 자신들의 기업가 정신을 일상의 문제에 적용시키고자 했다. 그들의 회사는 시내 전역에 걸쳐 아파트 건물 및 기타 장소에 보관함을 대여하고 있다. 고객들은 월 단위나, 분기별로, 혹은 연 단위로 보관함을 배정받는다. 그들은 안전한 보관함에 자신들의 더러워진 의류를 넣고 스마트폰 앱을 이용하여 서비스를 요청한다. 그러고 나면 의류는 회사에서 세탁하여 보관함으로 돌려보낸다. 문자메시지 한 통이 고객들에게 그들의 의류가 찾아갈 준비가 되었음을 알려준다.

(165)"우리는 어느 날 헬스클럽에서 운동을 한 후에 물품 보관함을 보다가 이 아이디어를 떠올렸습니다."라고 더글라스 라이언 씨는 말한다. "우리는 딱히 세탁소를 오가는 대신에 집 가까이에 전달 장소가 있으면 얼마나 편리할지에 대해 얘기를 나누고 있었습니다."

(167)두 형제는 원래 드라이클리닝만 제공하는 업체를 시도했지만, 너무 많은 드라이클리닝 업체들이 무료 배달을 제공하는 까닭에 고객을 끌어모으는 데 어려움이 있었다. 그 사업은 실패로 끝났다. 하지만 이것이 형제가 다시 시도하는 것을 가로막지는 못했다. 라이언 사의 기반이 된 새로운 사업 모델은 일상적으로 입는 옷에 초점을 두었다. (167)그것은 더 많은 사람들에게 적당한 가격대를 마련했다.

라이언 사는 영업을 시작한 지 불과 3개월밖에 되지 않았지만 벌써 시내에서 가장 인기 있는 신규 업체 중 하나가 되었다. 실제로, 보관함은 전면 가동중이고 대기 명단이 있다. 현재 고객들이 조만간 자신들의 보관함을 내놓을 것으로 보이지 않기 때문에, (166)라이언 형제는 다음 달에 보관함을 놓을 장소를 더 찾고 있다.

어휘 **fold** 개다, 접다 **chore** 집안일 **found** 설립하다 **entrepreneurial spirit** 기업가 정신 **storage locker** 보관함 **assign** 배정하다 **on a monthly[quarterly, annual] basis** 월 단위[분기별, 연 단위]로 **launder** 세탁하다 **work out** 운동하다 **drop-off point** 전달 장소 **price point** 가격대, 기준 가격 **affordable** (가격이) 알맞은 **at full capacity** 전면 가동중인

164 라이언 사의 업종은?
(A) 의류 매장 체인점
(B) 음식 배달업체
(C) 의류 촬영소
(D) 세탁 서비스 업체

해설 단서(164)에서 나열한 의류를 세탁하고 건조시키고 개는 것이 바로 라이언 사에서 하는 일임을 알 수 있다. 한마디로 세탁 서비스를 제공하는 일이므로 정답은 (D).

165 회사 설립자들이 사업체에 대한 아이디어를 얻은 곳은?
(A) 비즈니스 강좌
(B) 텔레비전 광고
(C) 친구의 권유
(D) 헬스클럽 방문

해설 단서(165)에서 헬스클럽에서 운동을 하다가 사업체에 대한 아이디어가 떠올랐다고 했으므로 정답은 (D).
패러프레이징 지문의 gym이 정답에서 fitness facility로 패러프레이징되었다.

166 회사가 5월에 할 가능성이 가장 높은 것은?
(A) 직원 교육 제공
(B) 스마트폰 앱 개선
(C) 가격 인상
(D) 더 많은 지점 추가

해설 단서를 종합해서 풀어야 하는 문제이다. 기사가 작성된 날짜가 4월 8일인데, 기사의 마지막 문장에 있는 단서(166)에서 라이언 형제가 다음 달에 보관함을 놓을 장소를 더 찾고 있다고 했으므로, 정답은 (D).
패러프레이징 지문의 more sites가 정답에서 more locations로 패러프레이징되었다.

167 [1], [2], [3], [4]로 표시된 곳들 중, 다음 문장이 들어가기에 가장 알맞은 곳은?
"라이언 사의 기반이 된 새로운 사업 모델은 일상적으로 입는 옷에 초점을 두었다."
(A) [1]
(B) [2]
(C) [3]
(D) [4]

해설 주어진 문장은 라이언 사의 새로운 사업 모델이 일상적인 옷에 초점을 맞추었다는 내용으로, 앞에는 새로운 사업 모델을 구상하게 된 배경이, 뒤에는 그에 따른 결과가 오는 것이 자연스럽다. 지문의 첫 번째 단서(167)에서 형제가 드라이클리닝 서비스 업체를 시도했다가 실패했으나 포기하지 않았고, 두 번째 단서(167)에서 그것이 많은 사람들에게 적당한 가격대를 제공했다고 했으므로 주어진 문장은 이 사이에 와야 알맞다. 따라서 정답은 (C).

[168-171] 지역 행사 계획에 대해 논의하는 온라인 채팅 대화문

Dominic Ruckman   10:02 A.M.
Hi, Scarlett and Morgan. I'm hoping you two can update me on your plan for upcoming community events.

Scarlett Hawkins   10:04 A.M.
Of course. (168)The first proposal we have is to host a series of community workshops that will help new residents get settled in the city and find appropriate housing and childcare.

Morgan Cameron   10:06 A.M.
Each workshop will cover the same information about city parks, public facilities, voter registration, and local services.

Dominic Ruckman   10:08 A.M.
Do residents need to register or buy tickets in advance to attend the sessions?

Scarlett Hawkins   10:10 A.M.
No. Tickets will be free, and people just need to go to their chosen sessions at the designated time. We were thinking something like Session A: October 2, 10:00 A.M.; (169)Session B: October 3, 7:00 P.M.; Session C: October 4, 1:00 P.M.; and Session D: October 5, 2:00 P.M.

도미닉 루크만   오전 10:02
안녕하세요, 스칼렛 씨, 모건 씨. 다가오는 지역사회 행사를 위한 두 분의 계획에 대한 근황을 알려주셨으면 해요.

스칼렛 호킨즈   오전 10:04
물론이죠. (168)우리의 첫 번째 제안은 일련의 지역사회 워크숍을 열어서 새로운 주민들이 우리 시에 정착하고 적절한 주택과 보육시설을 찾는 데 도움을 주자는 거예요.

모건 카메론   오전 10:06
각각의 워크숍은 도시 공원, 공공 시설, 유권자 등록, 지역 서비스 업체들에 관한 동일한 정보를 다룰 거예요.

도미닉 루크만   오전 10:08
주민들은 워크숍에 참석하기 위해 등록을 하거나 미리 입장권을 구입해야 하나요?

스칼렛 호킨즈   오전 10:10
아뇨. 입장권은 무료일 것이고 사람들은 그냥 지정된 시간에 본인이 선택한 워크숍에 가기만 하면 돼요. 우리가 생각하고 있는 것은 대략 이래요. 세션 A는 10월 2일 오전 10시, (169)세션 B는 10월 3일 저녁 7시, 세션 C는 10월 4일 오후 1시, 그리고 세션 D는 10월 5일 오후 2시요.

Morgan Cameron	10:12 A.M.	모건 카메론	오전 10:12

(169)You'll notice that there's only one evening session. We're expecting that it will be popular, but seating is limited. We will need to warn people to arrive early to ensure entry.

(169)저녁 시간은 한 번밖에 없다는 것을 알아차리실 거예요. 그 워크숍이 인기가 있을 것으로 예상되는데, 좌석이 한정되어 있어요. 사람들에게 확실히 입장하려면 일찍 도착하라고 주의를 줘야 할 것 같아요.

Dominic Ruckman	10:14 A.M.	도미닉 루크만	오전 10:14

(170)What about potential venues? Have you looked into any possible locations yet?

(170)행사 장소로 가능성이 있는 곳은요? 벌써 가능한 장소를 조사해 봤나요?

Scarlett Hawkins	10:16 A.M.	스칼렛 호킨즈	오전 10:16

It's taken care of. All sessions will be held at Spette Hall at Ridge Drive and Lowes Road. We made the session suggestion based on its availability.

그건 해결됐어요. 모든 워크숍은 리지 로와 로우즈 로에 있는 스페티 홀에서 열릴 거예요. 그곳의 이용 가능성에 근거하여 워크숍을 제안했어요.

Morgan Cameron	10:18 A.M.	모건 카메론	오전 10:18

If you like this idea, (171)I'll add all of these details to our Web site as well.

이 아이디어가 마음에 드시면, (171)제가 이 세부 내용 전부 저희 웹사이트에도 추가할게요.

어휘 upcoming 다가오는 get settled 정착하다 appropriate 적절한 housing 주택 childcare 보육 (시설) voter registration 유권자 등록 designated 지정된 potential 가능성 있는 venue (행사) 장소 look into ~을 조사하다 take care of ~을 해결[처리]하다 based on ~에 근거하여 availability 이용[입장] 가능성

168 워크숍의 대상은?
(A) 최근에 이주한 사람
(B) 어린 아이들의 부모
(C) 일을 찾는 주민
(D) 시내 관광을 계획하는 방문객

해설 단서(168)에서 워크숍의 목적이 새로운 주민들이 시에 정착하는 데 도움을 주기 위함이라고 밝히고 있으므로 정답은 (A).
패러프레이징 지문의 new residents가 정답에서 People who have recently relocated로 패러프레이징되었다.

169 자리가 다 찰 것으로 예상되는 워크숍 세션은?
(A) 세션 A
(B) 세션 B
(C) 세션 C
(D) 세션 D

해설 단서(169)를 종합해 보면 저녁 시간에 열리는 워크숍은 인기가 많은 반면 좌석이 한정되어 있다고 했으므로 이 워크숍이 자리가 다 찰 것으로 예상할 수 있다. 저녁 시간에 배정된 세션은 세션 B이므로 정답은 (B).

170 오전 10:16에, 호킨즈 씨가 "그건 해결됐어요"라고 하는 의도는?
(A) 각 세션의 연사들을 확실히 확인했다.
(B) 행사 광고를 만들었다.
(C) 워크숍 장소를 선정했다.
(D) 입장권을 이미 따로 챙겨두었다.

해설 호킨즈 씨의 "It's taken care of"는 단서(170)에 있는 루크만 씨의 질문에 대한 대답이다. 루크만 씨는 행사 장소 선정의 진행 상황에 대해 묻고 있는데 호킨즈 씨가 해결됐다고 이야기했으므로 정답은 (C).

171 카메론 씨가 하겠다고 제안한 것은?
(A) 웹사이트에 사진 추가하기
(B) 가능한 행사 장소 둘러보기
(C) 입장권 인쇄하기
(D) 인터넷에 정보 게시하기

해설 카메론 씨는 대화의 마지막 부분에서 웹사이트에 세부 내용 전부를 추가하겠다고 제안하고 있으므로 정답은 (D).
패러프레이징 지문의 add all of these details to our Web site가 정답에서는 Post information online으로 패러프레이징되었다.

[172-175] 미납 요금 안내 편지

Heather Ingram
1950 Jarvis Street
Buffalo, NY 14214

November 1

Dear Ms. Ingram,

헤더 잉그램
자비스 가 1950
뉴욕 주 버팔로, 14214

11월 1일

잉그램 씨께,

I would like to bring to your attention an urgent matter regarding your account with Vine Satellite Television Services (VSTS). (172)You have an outstanding balance of $59.50, which was due on October 15. This charge is for services you received at your residence at 1950 Jarvis Street. (173)Our records show that you requested a service cancellation on September 14 and that the service was cut off on September 28, as two weeks' notice is required for all account changes. Therefore, the remaining charge is for the services rendered in September along with a $15 late fee.

(174)I tried to contact you several times over the past few weeks. At first, I kept getting no answer at the phone number you provided when you signed up for the service last year. In the most recent call, I got a recorded message saying that the number was no longer in service. I do hope this letter reaches you, as it is important for you to settle this bill as quickly as possible.

Enclosed you will find an updated bill with the summary of the charges. This is the same as your previous bill but with the $15 late fee added. Please pay the amount in full to VSTS immediately. You can do so by visiting our Web site at www.vinests.com or by making a bank transfer. Detailed instructions are included on the back of the bill. (175)If you do not make the payment by November 30, your account will be charged another late fee of $15. Therefore, I urge you to resolve the matter promptly.

Sincerely,

Leon Frost
Customer Service Agent, Vine Satellite Television Services

귀하의 바인 위성 텔레비전 서비스 (VSTS) 계정과 관련된 긴급한 문제를 알려드리고자 합니다. (172)귀하께서는 59.50달러가 미납되어 있으시며, 이는 10월 15일이 납부 기한이었습니다. 이 요금은 귀하의 자택이신 자비스 가 1950번지에서 받으신 서비스에 대한 것입니다. (173)저희 기록상으로는 귀하께서 9월 14일에 서비스 해지를 요청하셨고 9월 28일에 서비스가 중단되었는데, 이는 모든 계정 변경에 대해서는 2주 전 통지가 요구되기 때문입니다. 따라서 잔여 요금은 9월에 제공된 서비스에 대한 것에 15달러의 연체료가 더해진 것입니다.

(174)지난 몇 주 동안 여러 차례 귀하에게 연락을 드리고자 시도했습니다. 처음에는 귀하께서 작년에 서비스를 신청하실 때 제공해 주신 전화번호로 계속 응답을 받을 수 없었습니다. 가장 최근의 전화에서, 그 번호가 더 이상 사용되지 않는다는 음성 녹음 메시지를 받았습니다. 귀하께서 이 청구서를 가능한 한 빨리 해결하는 것이 중요하기 때문에, 이 편지가 귀하에게 도착하기를 간절히 바랍니다.

요금에 대한 간략한 요약이 담긴 업데이트된 청구서를 동봉합니다. 이것은 지난번 청구서와 동일하지만 15달러의 연체료가 추가된 것입니다. 즉시 VSTS로 전액 납부해 주시기 바랍니다. 저희 웹사이트인 www.vinests.com을 방문하시거나 계좌 이체를 통해서 결제하실 수도 있습니다. 자세한 안내사항은 청구서 뒷면에 나와 있습니다. (175)만일 11월 30일까지 납부하지 않으실 경우, 15달러의 연체료가 별도로 부과됩니다. 그러므로 조속히 이 문제를 해결하실 것을 당부합니다.

바인 위성 텔레비전 서비스, 고객서비스 담당자
레온 프로스트 드림

어휘 bring to *one's* attention ~에게 알리다   urgent 긴급한   outstanding balance 미납액   be due on ~까지 마감이다   charge 요금; 요금을 청구하다   render 주다, 제공하다   late fee 연체료   sign up for ~을 신청[가입]하다   settle 해결하다, 정착하다   Enclosed you will find ~을 동봉합니다   bank transfer 은행 이체   resolve (문제 등을) 해결하다   promptly 신속히

172 잉그램 씨가 편지를 받은 이유는?
 (A) 회사 안내자료를 요청했다.
 (B) 최종 결제를 하지 못했다.
 (C) 신제품에 관심이 있을 수도 있다.
 (D) 서비스에 불만을 제기했다.

173 편지에 따르면, 잉그램 씨가 9월에 한 일은?
 (A) 수리를 요청했다.
 (B) 서비스 패키지를 업그레이드했다.
 (C) 서비스를 해지했다.
 (D) 새 집으로 이사했다.

해설 단서(172)에서 잉그램 씨가 납부 기한을 넘겨 미납된 요금이 있음을 알리고 있으므로 정답은 (B).

패러프레이징 지문의 have an outstanding balance가 정답에서 failed to make a final payment로 패러프레이징되었다.

해설 단서(173)에서 잉그램 씨가 9월 14일에 서비스 해지를 요청한 기록이 있다고 했으므로 정답은 (C).

174 프로스트 씨가 어려움을 겪은 일은?
(A) 잉그램 씨에게 전화로 연락하기
(B) 설치 예약 일정 잡기
(C) 잉그램 씨의 우편 주소 알아내기
(D) 온라인 계정에 접속하기

해설 단서(174)에서 프로스트 씨는 몇 주 동안 잉그램 씨에게 전화 연락을 시도했으나 연락이 닿지 않았다고 했으므로 정답은 (A).

175 잉그램 씨가 11월 말까지 조치를 취하지 않을 경우 일어날 일은?
(A) 추가 요금이 청구될 것이다.
(B) 프로스트 씨로부터 다시 연락을 받을 것이다.
(C) 서비스가 중단될 것이다.
(D) 특별 판촉행사를 놓칠 것이다.

해설 단서(175)에서 11월 말까지 미납금을 납부하지 않을 경우, 연체료가 또 부과될 것이라고 했으므로 정답은 (A).
패러프레이징 지문의 another late fee가 정답에서 additional fee로 패러프레이징되었다.

[176-180] 도서관 관련 기사 & 도서관 이용 서약서 양식

Oxford (December 5)—(176)(177A)(177C)The archives of prominent legal scholar and university professor Landon Fry are available in the Paragon Law Library, a research library located on Broad Street. The archives, which contain thousands of pages of documentation, are housed in the Brontë room. "Landon Fry was one of our nation's most brilliant legal minds," announced (178) the archives facilitator, Ms. McDonald. (177B) His works analyzing the most significant aspects of constitutional law have been invaluable to law students and professors alike. The Paragon Law Library has recently compiled all his works into one large viewable assembly. Within the Paragon Law library is a massive collection of case studies, legal briefs, rare legal books, and notable legal commentaries like that of Landon Fry.

(179)This library is designed solely for on-site research purposes. It is mandatory for all new visitors to go to the reception desk to read and sign a form declaring that they understand the regulations of the library. Failure to follow the rules outlined in that declaration will result in confiscation of any banned items, (180-2B)immediate escort off the property, and possible (180-2D)fines or (180-2A) long-term suspensions.

Paragon Law Library Declaration Form

Name: Caroline Burr

As a library patron, I agree not to remove from the library archives—or to mark, deface, or injure in any way—any volume, document, or other object in their custody.

I promise to promote and protect an environment in the library that is conducive to legal research and study. I will do so by refraining from any activity or behavior that could disrupt and/or distract from the academic work of others. (180-1)I will refrain from eating, smoking, or drinking in the library and will

옥스포드 (12월 5일)—(176)(177A)(177C)저명한 법학자이자 대학 교수인 랜든 프라이 씨의 기록보관소가 브로드 가에 위치한 연구 도서관인 파라곤 법학 도서관에서 이용 가능하다. 보관소는 수천 페이지에 달하는 문서들을 보유하고 있는데, 이는 브론테 실에 보관되어 있다. (178)기록보관소 운영자인 맥도날드 씨는 "랜든 프라이 씨는 이 나라의 가장 뛰어난 법학 지성인 중 한 명이었습니다,"라고 말했다. (177B)헌법의 가장 중요한 측면들에 대해 분석한 그의 저술은 법대 학생과 교수 모두에게 똑같이 매우 귀중한 가치가 있다. 파라곤 법학 도서관은 최근 그의 저술들을 한데 엮어 방대한 양의 가치 있는 자료로 만들었다. 파라곤 법학 도서관은 랜든 프라이 씨의 것과 같은 판례 분석, 변론 취지서, 희귀 법학 도서, 눈에 띄는 법률 논평 등을 방대하게 수집하고 있다.

(179)이 도서관은 현장 연구만을 위해 고안되었다. 모든 방문객들은 의무적으로 안내 데스크로 가서 도서관의 규정을 이해한다고 선언하는 양식을 읽고 서명해야 한다. 서약서에 설명된 규정을 따르지 않을 경우 금지된 물건을 압수당하고, (180-2B)도서관에서 퇴실 당하거나 (180-2D)벌금형 또는 (180-2A)장기간의 입장 금지 제재가 내려질 수도 있다.

파라곤 법학 도서관 서약서

이름: 캐롤린 부어

도서관 이용자로서, 저는 도서관에서 관리하고 있는 도서나 문서, 기타 소장 목록을 어떠한 식으로든 절취하거나 표시하거나, 훼손하거나 손상시키지 않을 것에 동의합니다.

저는 법학 조사와 연구에 도움이 되는 도서관의 환경을 장려하고 보호할 것을 약속합니다. 다른 이들의 학문 활동을 방해하거나 흐트러뜨릴 수 있는 어떠한 활동이나 행동을 삼가는 방식으로 이를 시행하겠습니다. (180-1)도서관 내에서는 음식물 섭취, 흡연, 음주를 하지 않을 것이며 이야기를 하거나 음악 듣기, 또는 그 외의 방식으로 소음을 내지 않도록 자제하겠습니다.

abstain from making noises through speech, music, or otherwise.

I, *Caroline Burr*, have read, understood, and agreed to the above terms and conditions. I further acknowledge and agree to the corresponding punishments for breaking these conditions.

Signature: *Caroline Burr*

저 캐롤린 부어는 상기 규정들을 읽고, 이해했으며, 이에 동의합니다. 또한 이 규정들을 어길 시 상응하는 처벌을 인지하고 동의합니다.

서명: 캐롤린 부어

어휘 archive 기록보관소 prominent 저명한, 중요한 house 보관하다, 수용하다 mind 지성인, 지적인 인물 facilitator 운영자, 조력자 compile A into B A를 엮어[편찬하여] B를 만들다 viewable 볼 수 있는, 볼 만한 massive 방대한 양의, 대규모의 case study 판례 분석 brief (변호인의) 변론 취지서 notable 눈에 띄는, 주목할 만한 mandatory 의무의, 필수의 declaration 선언, 공표 confiscation 압수, 몰수 escort A off B A를 B 밖으로 데리고 나가다 suspension (일정 기간 동안) 중단, 정지 deface 훼손하다 in custody 관리하고 있는, 보호 중인 conducive to ~에 도움이 되는, ~에 이득인 refrain from ~을 삼가다[자제하다] (= abstain from) terms and conditions (계약 등의) 조건, 규정 acknowledge 인지하다 corresponding 상응하는, 대응하는 break (규칙 등을) 어기다

176 기사의 주제는?
(A) 법률 학회의 조직
(B) 재판에 필요한 조사
(C) 뛰어난 인물의 저술들
(D) 기록물의 폐기

해설 일반적으로 기사의 주제는 도입부에 등장한다. 기사의 도입부인 단서(176)에 저명한 법학자이자 대학 교수였던 랜든 프라이 씨의 저술들이 파라곤 법학 도서관에 소장되어 있다는 내용이 나오는 것으로 보아 정답은 (C).

177 프라이 씨에 대해 언급되지 않은 것은?
(A) 인정받는 법학자이다.
(B) 헌법에 대해 저술했다.
(C) 대학에서 강의한다.
(D) 학계에서 은퇴했다.

해설 NOT 문제는 선택지와 지문을 비교해서 선택지를 하나씩 소거해가며 풀어야 한다. 단서(177A), (177B), (177C)를 통해서 보기의 내용들을 모두 찾아볼 수 있다. 하지만 프라이 씨가 은퇴했다는 언급은 없으므로 (D)가 정답이다.

178 맥도날드 씨는 누구인가?
(A) 도서관 직원
(B) 연구 조교
(C) 법률 비서
(D) 단골 고객

해설 단서(178)에서 맥도날드 씨는 기록보관소 운영자라고 했으므로 정답은 (A).
패러프레이징 지문의 archives facilitator가 정답에서 library employee라는 상위어로 패러프레이징되었다.

179 파라곤 법학 도서관에 대해 사실인 것은?
(A) 직원들은 법학 관련 배경을 갖고 있다.
(B) 모든 문서들은 도서관 안에 있어야 한다.
(C) 도서들은 모두 온라인으로 이용 가능하다.
(D) 도서관 이용객들은 복사하는 것이 허용된다.

해설 도서관에서는 현장 연구만 가능하다고 했으므로 정답은 (B)이다.
패러프레이징 지문의 solely for on-site research purposes가 정답에서 All of its documents must remain in the library.로 바꾸어 표현되었다.

180 도서관에서 흡연할 경우 부어 씨가 받을 위험이 있는 처벌이 아닌 것은?
(A) 도서관에 입장 금지
(B) 건물 밖으로 즉시 추방
(C) 개인 도서관 회원증 압수
(D) 벌금 부과

해설 두 지문 연계 문제로, 먼저 서약서에서 흡연이 규정 위반임을 확인하고 기사를 보아야 한다. (A), (B), (D)는 모두 기사에서 찾아볼 수 있지만, 도서관 회원증을 압수한다는 내용은 언급되어 있지 않으므로 정답은 (C).

[181-185] 공연 개최 기사 & 공연 티켓 할인 적용 문의 웹사이트

Dance is Back at the Majesty
By Loretta Benderly

(181)Majesty Theater has announced its twelfth annual dance spectacle, entitled *The Festival of Movement*. In the springtime each year, the theater gathers dancers from around the world. (182)Together, they showcase all that dance has to offer, encompassing all genres from tap to hip hop.

(183)(184-2)The highlight of this year's three-day festival will be a wordless play scheduled for May 9. This unique performance is entirely void of dialogue. Without any narrative, the story is told through the artistry of dance and music alone. The festival performances are traditionally held in Waltman Hall every year. However, the stage was closed earlier this year for some reconstructive work, and all shows were switched to one of the three smaller halls—McManus Hall, Gilderton Hall, and Alexandra Hall. This renovation project was expected to continue until June 15, but the work has progressed more rapidly than anticipated. As a result, (183)all performances throughout the month of May will be moved back to Waltman Hall as originally planned.

As an exclusive privilege to Majesty Theater members, festival tickets can be purchased in advance and at 25% off the standard price. To take advantage of the discount, members must buy tickets before March 31. Starting of April 1, tickets to *The Festival of Movement* will be open to the general public.

---

www.majestytheater.com

| Home | Schedule | Ticket Info | **Contact** |

Name: Janet Vandersoek
Date: March 25
Subject: Ticket purchase

Message: (184-1)I just completed my purchase of two tickets for the wordless dance performance. I followed the Web site's instructions, completed the order, and was able to print tickets without any difficulty. (185)However, while looking at them I realized that I paid full price even though I should have received the 25% discount. I don't remember that being an option on the screen when I was processing the payment. Obviously, I have not missed the deadline, so I'm hoping someone can advise me on how to resolve the problem.

Thank you,

Janet Vandersoek

마제스티에 댄스가 귀환하다
로레타 밴덜리 작성

(181)마제스티 극단은 〈움직임의 축제〉라고 제목이 붙은 제12회 연례 대규모 댄스 공연을 열겠다고 발표했다. 매년 봄철이 되면 극단은 전 세계의 무용수들을 불러모은다. (182)다 함께 그들은 탭 댄스에서 힙합까지 모든 장르를 망라하여 춤이 보여줄 수 있는 모든 것을 공연한다.

(183)(184-2)3일 동안 열릴 올해 축제의 하이라이트는 5월 9일로 예정된 무언극이다. 이 독특한 공연에는 대화가 완전히 배제되어 있다. 어떠한 서사도 없이 이야기는 춤과 음악의 기교로만 전해진다. 축제의 공연들은 전통적으로 매년 월트먼 홀에서 개최되었다. 그러나, 올해 초 어떤 복원 작업으로 인해 무대가 폐쇄되어 모든 공연들은 좀 더 소규모의 강당인 맥매너스 홀, 질더튼 홀, 알렉산드라 홀 세 곳 중 한 곳으로 변경되었다. 이 보수 공사는 6월 15일까지 계속될 것으로 예정되었으나 예상보다 공사가 빠르게 진행되었다. 그 결과, (183)5월에 있을 모든 공연들은 원래 계획대로 다시 월트먼 홀로 옮겨질 것이다.

마제스티 극단의 회원들에게 독점적으로 주어지는 특권으로, 축제 입장권을 정가에서 25% 할인된 금액으로 미리 구매할 수 있다. 할인을 받으려면 회원들은 3월 31일 이전에 표를 구매해야 한다. 4월 1일부터 〈움직임의 축제〉 입장권이 일반 대중들에게 판매되기 시작할 것이다.

---

www.majestytheater.com

| 홈 | 일정 | 티켓 정보 | **연락처** |

이름: 재닛 반데르섹
날짜: 3월 25일
제목: 티켓 구매

전달 내용: (184-1)저는 방금 무언극 공연 표 2장을 구매했습니다. 웹사이트에 적혀 있는 지시대로 주문을 마쳤고 어려움 없이 표를 출력할 수 있었습니다. (185)그러나, 표를 살펴보던 중 제가 25%의 할인을 받았어야만 했음에도 불구하고 정가를 전부 지불했다는 것을 알게 되었습니다. 제가 결제를 진행할 때 그것이 화면상에서 선택사항이었는지 기억이 나지 않습니다. 마감 기한을 놓친 것은 분명히 아니므로 이 문제를 어떻게 해결해야 할지 누군가 알려주시기를 바랍니다.

감사합니다.

재닛 반데르섹 드림

어휘 **spectacle** 대규모 행사, (굉장한) 구경거리   **entitle** 제목을 붙이다   **encompass** 아우르다, 망라하다   **wordless** 무언의, 말이 없는   **be void of** ~이 없다   **dialogue** 대화, 담화   **narrative** (특히 소설 속 사건들에 대한) 서사, 이야기   **artistry** (예술적) 기교   **reconstructive** 복원하는, 재건하는   **switch** 변경하다, 바꾸다   **progress** 진행되다, 진척이 이루어지다   **exclusive** 독점적인, 단독의   **privilege** 특권, 특혜   **without any difficulty** 어려움 없이, 별문제 없이   **process payment** 결제를 진행하다   **obviously** 분명히, 명백하게   **resolve** 해결하다, 풀다

181 기사가 쓰인 이유는?
(A) 보수 공사를 설명하기 위해
(B) 연례 행사를 광고하기 위해
(C) 무용 수업을 홍보하기 위해
(D) 후원자들에게 자금 지원을 요청하기 위해

해설 기사의 앞부분에서 공연 일정을 간략히 소개하고 이에 대해 자세한 설명을 덧붙이고 있으므로 정답은 (B).

182 〈움직임의 축제〉에 대해 시사된 바는?
(A) 사교 댄스가 핵심이다.
(B) 모든 무용수들은 인근 도시 출신이다.
(C) 공연은 나흘 동안 진행된다.
(D) 아주 다양한 종류가 다뤄질 것이다.

해설 단서(182)에 따르면 탭 댄스, 힙합 등 여러 장르의 춤을 공연할 것이라 하였으므로 정답은 (D).
패러프레이징 지문의 encompassing all genres가 정답에서 A wide range of styles will be featured.로 패러프레이징되었다.

183 무언극이 열리는 곳은?
(A) 알렉산드라 홀
(B) 질더튼 홀
(C) 맥매너스 홀
(D) 월트먼 홀

해설 단서(183)을 종합해 보면 5월 공연들은 계획대로 월트먼 홀에서 한다고 했으므로 정답은 (D).

184 반데르섹 씨가 극장에 가게 될 날은?
(A) 3월 31일
(B) 4월 1일
(C) 5월 9일
(D) 6월 15일

해설 두 지문의 단서를 함께 보아야 정답을 찾을 수 있는 연계 문제이다. 반데르섹 씨의 문의글에 따르면 그녀는 무언극 표를 구매했다고 하였으며 기사를 통해 무언극이 5월 9일로 예정되어 있음을 알 수 있다. 따라서 정답은 (C).

185 반데르섹 씨에 대해 암시된 것은?
(A) 표를 사는 데 돈을 더 지불했다.
(B) 구매를 취소하기를 원한다.
(C) 표를 출력하는 데 문제가 있었다.
(D) 회원 마감 기한을 놓쳤다.

해설 반데르섹 씨는 표를 할인되지 않은 금액으로 산 것에 대해 문의글을 올린 것이므로 정답은 (A).
패러프레이징 지문의 paid full price ~ discount까지가 정답에서 overpaid for her tickets로 패러프레이징되었다.

[186-190] 영화 개봉 안내 기사 & 영화 예매 웹사이트 & 영화 관람에 대한 공지

War of the Mountains Opens Friday
Dean Ziegler

(186)The much-awaited second installment of the action-adventure *Mountaineer* has arrived! *War of the Mountains*, the second in a trilogy, opens in cinemas on Friday. Audiences have waited over a year for the release of this film. Although Padilla Studios spent a great (187)deal of money on trailers and posters to promote the movie, very few details have been released about what will actually occur during the film's two hours and forty-five minutes. There has been much speculation that there will be one major death in this movie, but that claim remains unconfirmed by anyone involved with the film. When questioned, director Kristin Gaudet remained very tightlipped. "It's a rollercoaster ride

〈워 오브 마운틴즈〉, 금요일에 개봉하다
딘 지글러

(186)간절히 기다리던, 액션 어드벤처 〈마운티니어〉의 2편이 나왔다! 3부작 중 2편인 〈워 오브 마운틴즈〉가 금요일에 극장에서 개봉한다. 관객들은 이 영화의 개봉을 일년 넘게 기다려 왔다. 파딜라 스튜디오가 이 영화를 홍보하기 위해 예고편과 포스터에 많은 (187)양의 돈을 썼음에도 불구하고, 영화가 상영되는 2시간 45분 동안 실제로 어떤 일이 벌어지는지에 대해서는 알려진 바가 거의 없다. 이 영화에서 중요한 죽음이 한 건 있을 것이라는 추측이 무성했지만, 이 주장은 아직까지 영화 관계자들에 의해 확인되지 않고 있다. 질문을 받고도, 크리스틴 고데 감독은 여전히 입을 꼭 닫았다. "액션과 감정이 롤러코스터를 타는 것 같을 겁니다. 관객들이 예상하지 못한 많은 것이 있습니다. 제가 밝힐 수 있는 것은 그뿐입니다."라고 그녀는 말했다.

of action and emotions. There is a lot that viewers won't see coming. That's all I'll reveal," she said.

Despite the lack of information about what will happen in the movie, fan anticipation is high, and the movie is expected to surpass the original in opening weekend ticket sales. Tickets for *War of the Mountains* are available online at www.movietickets.org or can be purchased at individual theaters. Prices vary according to the movie type, four of which are being offered for this film: 2D: $9.99, Imax: $12.99, (188-2)3D: $15.99, and 4D: $22.99.

영화에서 어떤 일이 벌어질지에 대한 정보가 부족함에도 불구하고, 팬들의 기대치가 높아 영화는 개봉 주말 티켓 판매에 있어서 1편을 능가할 것으로 예상된다. 〈워 오브 마운틴즈〉의 티켓은 www.movietickets.org에서 온라인으로 구입하거나 각 극장에서 구입할 수 있다. 가격은 영화의 종류에 따라 다르며, 이 영화에 대해 다음과 같은 네 가지 종류가 제공되고 있다: 2D: 9.99달러, 아이맥스: 12.99달러, (188-2)3D:15.99달러, 4D: 22.9달러.

---

www.movietickets.org

MOVIE SELECTION SCREEN

Name	Cell phone number	E-mail address
Daphne Dorsey	---	dapdorsey@netmail.org

■ (189)I don't have a cell phone, so please send the reservation to my e-mail instead.

THEATER AND TICKET INFO

Bisenzio Cinema
War of the Mountains, (188-1)(190-1)3D
April 2, 8:10 P.M., (190-1)**Cinema 9**
Be sure to check your show time again before moving to the payment screen.

I prefer seats that are:

Column	☐ right side	■ center block	☐ left side
Row	☐ front	■ middle	☐ back

Proceed to payment

---

www.movietickets.org

영화 선택 화면

이름	휴대전화 번호	이메일 주소
대프니 도시	---	dapdorsey@netmail.org

■ (189)저는 휴대 전화가 없으므로, 대신 제 이메일로 예약 내역을 보내 주십시오.

상영관 및 입장권 정보

비센지오 시네마
〈워 오브 마운틴즈〉, (188-1)(190-1)3D
4월 2일 저녁 8:10, (190-1)9관
결제 화면으로 넘어가기 전에 반드시 다시 한 번 상영 시간을 확인해 주십시오.

선호 좌석:

열	☐ 오른쪽	■ 가운데	☐ 왼쪽
줄	☐ 앞쪽	■ 중간	☐ 뒤쪽

결제 진행

ATTENTION, MOVIEGOERS

Due to a technical issue, (190-2)Cinemas 8 and 9 are unavailable for movie showings this evening.

Because we have another theater that can accommodate 3D movies, ticket holders for the 3D showings should go to Cinema 12 instead.

Unfortunately, Cinema 8 is our only 4D theater, so ticket holders for this film should visit the customer service desk. We apologize for the inconvenience and will not only refund these tickets in full, but will also give patrons free ticket passes to see this film at a later date.

영화 관람객들에게 알립니다

기술적인 문제로 인해, (190-2)8관과 9관은 오늘 저녁 상영 영화의 이용이 불가합니다.

3D 영화를 상영할 수 있는 다른 영화관이 있기 때문에, 3D 영화 입장권을 소지하신 분들은 대신 12관으로 가십시오.

유감스럽게도, 8관은 유일한 4D 상영관이라서, 이 영화의 입장권을 소지하신 분들은 고객 서비스 데스크를 방문해 주십시오. 불편을 끼쳐 드려 죄송하며 이 입장권을 전액 환불해 드릴 뿐만 아니라, 나중에 이 영화를 보실 수 있는 무료 입장권도 고객님들께 드리겠습니다.

어휘 **much-awaited** 간절히 기다리던　**second installment** (시리즈의) 2편　**trilogy** 3부작　**release** 공개[발표](하다)　**a great deal of** 많은　**trailer** (영화) 예고편　**speculation** 추측　**unconfirmed** 확인되지 않은　**tightlipped** 입을 꼭 다문　**reveal** 밝히다　**anticipation** 기대; 예상　**surpass** 능가하다, 뛰어넘다　**vary** 다르다　**payment** 결제, 지불　**refund in full** 전액 환불하다　**patron** 고객

186 〈워 오브 마운틴즈〉에 대해 시사된 바는?
(A) 저예산 영화이다.
(B) 인기 있는 영화의 후속작이다.
(C) 아동용 애니메이션 영화이다.
(D) 인기 스타가 총출연했다.

해설 기사 첫머리에서 〈워 오브 마운틴즈〉는 〈마운티니어〉라는 영화의 후속작임을 알 수 있으며, 기사 내용으로 보아, 〈마운티니어〉가 매우 흥행한 영화였음을 알 수 있으므로 정답은 (B).

187 기사에서, 1단락, 네 번째 줄의 어휘 "deal"과 의미상 가장 유사한 것은?
(A) 동의
(B) 합의
(C) 양
(D) 대우

해설 지문에서 deal은 a great deal of라는 관용적 표현을 이루고 있는데, 이는 '많은, 다량의'라는 뜻이다. 이때 deal은 '양'이라는 뜻으로 쓰인 것이므로 정답은 (C).

188 도시 씨가 입장권 값으로 지불할 가능성이 가장 큰 금액은?
(A) 9.99달러
(B) 12.99달러
(C) 15.99달러
(D) 22.99달러

해설 웹페이지를 보면, 도시 씨는 3D 영화를 선택했는데, 기사에 3D 영화의 가격이 15.99달러라고 나와 있으므로 정답은 (C).

189 도시 씨에 대해 사실인 것은?
(A) 저녁 8시 10분 이후에 도착할 것으로 예상된다.
(B) 전화로 예약했다.
(C) 이메일 통지를 선호한다.
(D) 뒤쪽 근처에 앉기를 원한다.

해설 단서(189)에서 도시 씨는 휴대 전화 대신 이메일로 예약 내역을 보내 달라고 요청하고 있으므로 정답은 (C).

190 도시 씨가 영화를 관람하게 될 상영관은?
(A) 5관
(B) 8관
(C) 9관
(D) 12관

해설 웹사이트의 단서(190-1)에 따르면 도시 씨가 예매한 영화는 3D 영화이며, 이 영화를 관람할 상영관은 9관이다. 그런데 공지의 단서(190-2)에서 9관이 이용 불가능하여 다른 3D 상영관인 12관으로 가라고 안내하였으므로, 도시 씨는 12관에서 영화를 관람하게 될 것이다. 따라서 정답은 (D).

[191-195] 강의 평가 웹사이트 & 강의 평가 양식 & 강의 요청 이메일

www.barnettcollege.edu

HOME	MY COURSES	MY ACCOUNT	CONTACT US	LOG OUT

We are excited to announce that your course instructor evaluations are now available under the "My Courses" section of your online account. While you will still receive an evaluation link via e-mail as usual, as a distance education student, you will also have the option to simply log into your online student account to complete and submit your course evaluation in a few simple steps. Our intention was to make the process of filling out evaluations for your classes easier and more convenient.

(191)We wish to thank you in advance for your participation. Student feedback plays an essential role in helping Barnett College continue to improve its course offerings. We use the information to ensure that we're providing both courses and instructors that fit your educational needs and goals. Because your responses have a direct

www.barnettcollege.edu

홈	나의 강의	나의 계정	연락처	로그아웃

여러분의 온라인 계정의 "나의 강의" 항목 아래에서 여러분이 듣는 강의의 강사 평가가 이제 이용 가능하다는 것을 알려드리게 되어 기쁩니다. 평소처럼 이메일을 통해 평가 링크를 수신하게 되겠지만, 원격 교육을 받는 학생들은 또한 온라인 학생 계정에 로그인만 하면 몇 단계 만에 강의 평가서를 작성하여 제출하는 방법도 선택할 수 있게 됩니다. 우리의 목적은 강의에 대한 평가서를 작성하는 과정을 더 쉽고 더 편리하게 만들기 위함입니다.

(191)여러분의 참여에 대해 미리 감사 드립니다. 학생들의 평가는 바넷 대학이 지속적으로 강의 개설을 향상시키는 데 매우 중요한 역할을 합니다. 우리는 이 정보를 이용하여 여러분의 교육적 요구와 목표에 걸맞은 강의 및 강사를 확실히 제공할 수 있도록 하겠습니다. 여러분의 응답이 바넷 대학의 미래에 직접적인 영향을 미치기 때문에, 시간을 내어 솔직하고 정확한 평가를 해 주시기 바랍니다.

impact on the future of Barnett College, please take the time to give honest and accurate feedback.

TEACHING EVALUATION

Student Name: (192-1) Cliffe Fonseca
Course Title: Medieval Poetry
Instructor Name: Dr. Susan Borre
Course Code: 3116E

	Strongly disagree	Disagree	Neutral	Agree	Strongly Agree
The syllabus was comprehensive, clear, and accurate.	☐	☐	☐	☐	■
The content of tests and assignments was consistent with content of lectures and readings.	☐	☐	☐	☐	■
The grading policies were clear and consistently followed.	☐	☐	☐	☐	■
The instructor showed concern for student learning and development.	☐	☐	■	☐	☐

Would you recommend this instructor to others? Why or why not?

Yes, I would recommend Dr. Borre. (195D)I've been in one of her classes on campus before (Restoration Literature). I thought both that class and my recently completed class were worthwhile and inspiring.

Please identify the aspects of the course you found most useful or valuable for learning.

The lectures were quite interesting and full of details that expanded upon the readings.

What suggestions would you make to the instructor for improving the course?

It's difficult to interact through distance studies courses, but overall, Dr. Borre did a great job. (193)I think it might help if she encouraged more online discussions.

강의 평가서

학생 이름: (192-1)클리프 폰세카
강의명: 중세 시대의 시
강사명: 수잔 보레 박사
강의 코드: 3116E

	매우 그렇지 않다	그렇지 않다	보통 이다	그렇다	매우 그렇다
강의 계획표가 포괄적이고 명확하며 정확했다.	☐	☐	☐	☐	■
시험 및 과제의 내용이 강의 및 교재의 내용과 일치했다.	☐	☐	☐	☐	■
채점 규정을 명확하고 일관되게 따랐다.	☐	☐	☐	☐	■
강사가 학생들의 학습과 발전에 관심을 보였다.	☐	☐	■	☐	☐

이 강사를 다른 학생들에게 추천하겠습니까? 그 이유는 무엇입니까?

네, 보레 박사님을 추천하겠습니다. (195D)전에 학내에서 보레 박사님의 강의 중 하나를 수강한 적이 있습니다(왕정복고 시대의 문학). 그 강의와 최근에 이수한 강의 둘 다 수강할 가치가 있고 고무적이었다고 생각했습니다.

강의의 어떤 면이 배움에 가장 유익하고 중요하다고 여겼는지 밝혀 주세요.

강의는 매우 흥미로웠고 교재에 대해 부연하는 자세한 설명로 가득 차 있었습니다.

강의 개선을 위해 강사에게 어떤 제안을 하겠습니까?

원격 강의를 통해 서로 소통하는 것이 어렵지만, 전반적으로 보레 박사님은 강의를 매우 잘하셨습니다. (193)온라인 토론을 더 장려하신다면 도움이 될 것 같습니다.

To: Susan Borre <borre@barnettcollege.edu>
From: Wanda Ringler <ringler@barnettcollege.edu>
Date: May 26
Subject: Returning next semester

Dear Dr. Borre,

As you are aware, at the end of each course, students are obligated to complete course evaluations that indicate their opinions of the course itself as well as of the instructor. We use these evaluations to help us recognize extraordinary members of our faculty. You have consistently received very positive teaching evaluations. (194) We would, therefore, like to invite you to add another class, British Authors, to your teaching schedule for next semester. (192-2)This would be in addition to the online course, Medieval Poetry. (195A)(195B)Since you've taught both of these classes before, I think the preparation time would be minimal.

We have tentatively scheduled the class for Tuesdays and Thursdays at 2 P.M. It would take place in room 207, which was originally scheduled for the Modern Shakespeare class taught by Professor Brian Rocco. We expect very low enrollment for that class, so we plan to move it to the spring semester next year.

If you are able to accept this additional responsibility, please let me know as soon as possible so that we may include the information in the course catalog.

Best wishes,

Wanda Ringler
HR Recruitment Manager,
Barnett College

수신: 수잔 보레 <borre@barnettcollege.edu>
발신: 완다 링글러 <ringler@barnettcollege.edu>
날짜: 5월 26일
제목: 다음 학기 복귀

보레 박사님께,

알고 계시듯이, 매 강좌가 끝나면, 학생들은 강사뿐만 아니라 강의에 대해서도 의견을 나타내는 강의 평가서를 작성해야 합니다. 이 평가서는 뛰어난 교수진을 파악하는 데 도움이 됩니다. 박사님은 지속적으로 매우 긍정적인 강의 평가를 받아 오셨습니다. (194)그래서 다음 학기에는 박사님의 강의 일정에 '영국 작가들'이라는 강의를 하나 더 추가하셨으면 합니다. (192-2)이것은 온라인 강의인 '중세 시대의 시'에 추가되는 것입니다. (195A)(195B)이 강의들 둘 다 전에 가르치신 적이 있기 때문에, 준비 시간은 별로 걸리지 않을 거라고 생각합니다.

잠정적으로 이 강의는 화요일과 목요일 오후 2시로 일정을 잡았습니다. 207호실에서 진행될 것인데, 이곳은 원래 브라이언 로코 교수가 가르치는 '현대 셰익스피어'가 진행될 예정이었습니다. 그 강의의 등록이 매우 저조할 것으로 예상되어, 그것은 내년 봄 학기로 옮길 계획입니다.

이 추가되는 업무를 받아들이실 수 있다면, 강의 목록에 안내를 포함시킬 수 있도록 가능한 한 빨리 제게 알려주시기 바랍니다.

바넷 대학
인사 채용 담당자
완다 링글러 드림

어휘 evaluation 평가 via ~을 통해 distance education 원격 교육 intention 목적, 의도 play a role 역할을 하다 fit 적절하다, 들어맞다 comprehensive 포괄적인, 종합적인 be consistent with ~와 일치하다 grading 등급 매기기, 채점 consistently 일관되게, 지속적으로 on-campus 학내의 restoration 왕정 복고 시대 worthwhile 가치 있는 inspiring 고무적인 identify 밝히다 expand upon ~에 대해 부연하다 be obligated to do ~할 의무가 있다 recognize 인정하다 extraordinary 뛰어난 faculty 교수진 tentatively 잠정적으로 enrollment 등록; 등록자 수

---

191 평가서를 작성하도록 요청받고 있는 사람은?
  (A) 대학생
  (B) 강사
  (C) 조교
  (D) 인사부 직원

해설 웹사이트의 앞부분에서는 강의 평가서를 작성하는 새롭고 간편한 방법을 소개하고 있고, 뒷부분에서는 강의 평가서 작성을 적극적으로 요청하고 있다. 뒷부분에서 강의 평가서 작성을 요청하는 대상이 바넷 대학 학생들임을 알 수 있으므로 정답은 (A).

192 폰세카 씨에 대해 추론할 수 있는 것은?
(A) 이메일 기반 평가서를 요청했다.
(B) 최근에 바넷 대학으로 옮겼다.
(C) 온라인으로 강의를 이수했다.
(D) 보레 박사의 강의를 또 수강할 계획이다.

해설 두 지문 연계 문제이다. 단서(192-1)에서 폰세카 씨는 수잔 보레 박사의 '중세 시대의 시'라는 강의를 수강했다고 했는데, 단서(192-2)에서 이 강의가 온라인 강의임을 확인할 수 있으므로 정답은 (C).

193 폰세카 씨에 따르면, 보레 박사가 앞으로 강의를 개선할 수 있는 방법은?
(A) 과제물을 더 공정하게 채점함으로써
(B) 토론의 양을 늘림으로써
(C) 강의를 더 재미있게 만듦으로써
(D) 더 체계적인 강의 계획표를 작성함으로써

해설 강의 평가서 마지막에서 폰세카 씨는 강의를 개선하기 위한 방법으로 온라인 토론을 장려할 것을 제안하고 있다. 결국 토론을 더 많이 하게 해 달라는 것이므로 정답은 (B).

194 이메일의 주된 목적은?
(A) 새로운 규정을 소개하기 위해
(B) 보레 박사에게 설문조사 작성을 요청하기 위해
(C) 강사직을 제안하기 위해
(D) 평가 결과를 분석하기 위해

해설 단서(194)에서 평가를 높게 받은 강사에게 추가로 강의를 맡기겠다는 결정을 알리고 있으므로 정답은 (C).
오답 피하기 이메일의 앞부분만 보고 강의 평가서 결과를 분석하기 위해 보내진 것으로 착각하면 안 된다. (D)는 오답.

195 보레 박사가 가르친 강의로서 시사되지 않은 것은?
(A) 영국 작가들
(B) 중세 시대의 시
(C) 현대 셰익스피어
(D) 왕정 복고 시대의 문학

해설 두 지문에 단서가 흩어져 있으므로 각 선택지를 재빨리 지문과 대조한다. (A)와 (B)는 이메일에서, (D)는 강의 평가 양식에서 보레 박사가 가르친 강의로 언급되고 있지만, (C)는 브라이언 로코 교수의 강의라고 했으므로 정답은 (C).

[196-200] 워크숍 불참 통보 이메일 & 강연 취소 안내 이메일 & 워크숍 일정

To: Ryan Ashcroft <ashcroftr@newburncollege.net>
From: (196-1)Anastasia Cusack <cusack@inspirekey.com>
Date: March 18
Subject: Scheduling Conflict

Dear Mr. Ashcroft,

I am writing to notify you that due to unforeseen circumstances, (196-1)I will no longer be able to give the Wednesday afternoon talk at the 2nd Annual Newburn College Online Business Workshop Series. Unfortunately, I have been given a mandatory work assignment to meet with a client overseas, so I will be out of the country for the week during which you are holding the workshop. I would be happy to suggest some possible replacements for my talk, as I have several colleagues who might be interested in participating in your event.

I deeply regret that I cannot (197)keep the commitment I made, especially since I so thoroughly enjoyed my participation in these workshops last year. I hope that you will still consider me as a speaker for next year.

My apologies again,

Anastasia Cusack
Inspirekey Marketing

수신: 라이언 애쉬크로프트
〈ashcroftr@newburncollege.net〉
발신: (196-1)아나스타샤 쿠잭 〈cusack@inspirekey.com〉
날짜: 3월 18일
제목: 일정 겹침

애쉬크로프트 씨께,

예상치 못한 상황으로 인해 (196-1)제2회 연례 뉴번 대학 온라인 비즈니스 워크숍 시리즈에서 수요일 오후 강연을 하지 못하게 됨을 알려드리고자 메일 드립니다. 유감스럽게도, 반드시 해야 하는 업무로 해외에서 고객을 만나는 일을 맡게 되어서, 워크숍이 열리는 주 동안 제가 외국에 있을 예정입니다. 강연을 대신할 수 있는 사람을 기꺼이 추천해 드릴 수도 있는데, 몇몇 동료가 이 행사에 참여할 의향이 있을 수도 있기 때문입니다.

제가 한 약속을 (197)지키지 못하게 되어 정말로 유감이며, 작년에 이 워크숍에 참여한 것이 대단히 즐거웠기 때문에 특히 더 그렇습니다. 내년에도 강연자로 저를 고려해 주시기를 바랍니다.

다시 한 번 사과 드립니다.

인스파이어키 마케팅
아나스타샤 쿠잭 드림

To: Leila Wortham <leilawortham@inbound.plus>
From: Ryan Ashcroft <ashcroftr@newburncollege.net>
Date: March 22
Subject: Workshop Series
Attachment: Amended Schedule

Dear Ms. Wortham,

(198)I want to inform you about some changes in the upcoming 2nd Annual Newburn College Online Business Workshop Series. I've attached the new schedule to this e-mail.

(196-2)I'm disappointed to tell you that the Wednesday afternoon talk that you registered for, "Mobile Marketing," has been replaced with "Designs that Work." The original talk was canceled due to problems with the speaker's schedule. I apologize for any inconvenience this change may cause. Unfortunately, it was out of our control. You have been automatically enrolled in the replacement lecture. However, if you prefer not to attend it, please e-mail me back, and I will process a refund for you.

The rest of the talks on the schedule will remain the same, (199-1)so there are no issues with the talk by Linda Rinaldi that you also signed up for on March 10. You may direct questions to my office at 555-2342.

Thank you for your understanding,

Ryan Ashcroft
Newburn College Workshops Organizer

Second Newburn College Online Business Workshop Series

AMENDED SCHEDULE

Time	Lecture	Speaker
(199-2)Monday, 8 A.M.–12 P.M.	Customer Care	Customer Service Supervisor, Linda Rinaldi
Monday, 1 P.M.–5 P.M.	Planning Your Budget	Finance Manager, Iliza Waldron
Tuesday, 8 A.M.–12 P.M.	(200) Maximizing Social Media	Advertising Director, Elsie Ocampo
Tuesday, 1 P.M.–5 P.M.	Measuring Results	Consultant, Larry Palmer
Wednesday, 8 A.M.–12 P.M.	Trends and Planning	Web Analyst, Cassandra Valle

| Wednesday, 1 P.M.–5 P.M. | Designs that Work | Graphic Designer, Jean Breaux |

어휘 scheduling conflict 일정이 겹침 notify 알리다 unforeseen 예상치 못한 mandatory 의무적인 assignment 일, 임무 overseas 해외에서 replacement 대신할 사람[것] commitment 약속 thoroughly 대단히; 철저히 amend 수정하다 inform 알리다 register for ~을 신청하다, ~에 등록하다(= enroll in, sign up for) be replaced with ~로 대체되다 out of one's control ~의 통제[능력] 밖인 automatically 자동으로 supervisor 관리자, 감독 maximize 극대화하다, 최대한 활용하다 measure 평가하다, 측정하다 analyst 분석가

196 쿠잭 씨 강연의 제목은?
(A) 예산 책정하기
(B) 모바일 마케팅
(C) 효과적인 디자인
(D) 결과 평가하기

해설 두 지문을 모두 보아야 풀 수 있는 연계 문제이다. 첫 번째 이메일에서 쿠잭 씨는 수요일 오후 워크숍에서 강연을 하지 못하게 됐음을 알리고 있다. 두 번째 이메일에서 강연자의 사정으로 취소된 수요일 오후 강연의 제목이 "모바일 마케팅"이라고 했으므로 정답은 (B).

197 첫 번째 이메일에서, 2단락, 첫 번째 줄의 어휘 "keep"과 의미상 가장 유사한 것은?
(A) 이행하다
(B) 보관하다
(C) 보유하다
(D) 막다

해설 지문에서 keep은 약속을 '지키다'라는 뜻으로 쓰이고 있다. 따라서 '이행하다, 따르다'라는 뜻의 fulfill이 가장 유사한 의미를 갖는다. 정답은 (A).

198 두 번째 이메일의 목적은?
(A) 교육 프로그램을 광고하기 위해
(B) 워크숍에 사람을 초대하기 위해
(C) 강연 참석을 확인하기 위해
(D) 행사에 관한 최신 소식을 전하기 위해

해설 이메일을 보낸 목적은 주로 첫 부분에 나오기 때문에 첫 문장을 주의 깊게 읽어야 한다. 워크숍 일정의 변동 사항을 알리고자 한다고 했으므로 (D)가 정답이다.
패러프레이징 지문의 inform you about some change가 정답에서 give an update로 패러프레이징되었다.

199 워섬 씨가 3월 10일에 신청한 강연 중 일부의 시간대는?
(A) 월요일 오전
(B) 월요일 오후
(C) 화요일 오전
(D) 화요일 오후

해설 두 번째 이메일에서, 워섬 씨가 3월 10일에 린다 리날디 씨의 강연을 신청했다고 하였는데, 워크숍 일정표에 따르면 린다 리날디 씨 의 강연은 월요일 오전에 있으므로 정답은 (A).

200 온라인 네트워킹 사이트에 관심 있는 사람들에게 가장 적합할 강연은?
(A) 일리자 월드론의 강연
(B) 엘시 오캄포의 강연
(C) 래리 팔머의 강연
(D) 카산드라 발리의 강연

해설 강연 제목 중에서 질문의 online networking sites와 관련 있는 것을 고르면 된다. Social Media가 이와 가장 관련이 깊으므로 정답은 (B).

NE 능률

토마토 토익 공식 홈페이지
www.tomatoclass.com

토마토 TOEIC 실전 1000제만의
따라 올 수 없는 혜택!

■ 토마토 TOEIC 실전 1000제 RC　　　　■ 토마토 TOEIC 실전 1000제 LC

해설집 무료 제공	테스트별 & 문항별 MP3 (온라인/모바일 제공)	복습어휘리스트 어휘 MP3 제공	토익 모의테스트 성적표 + 약점분석

스크립트, 해설, 해석, 어휘 등 토마토 TOEIC 실전 1000제 교재 한 권이면 이 모든 것을 다 보실 수 있습니다.	실전 테스트 보듯 한 번에 들을 수도, 복습 시 문항별로 들을 수도 있는 MP3를 제공합니다. 다운로드는 물론 모바일로도 들을 수 있습니다.	문제에서 풀었던 단어들을 복습할 수 있도록 해당 단어들의 어휘리스트와 MP3를 제공합니다. 따로 단어장을 구매할 필요가 없습니다.	토익 성적 예측과 나만의 약점 분석도 해 보실 수 있도록 온라인 모의고사 1회분을 제공합니다.

토마토 클래스 | www.tomatoclass.com　　　지금 토마토 클래스를 방문하시면
다양한 무료 혜택을 받으실 수 있습니다.

NE 능률

● 토익 점수 마구 올려주는 토익 ●

토마토 토익

최신 출제 경향 완벽 반영

토익 기초 단기 완성 라인업

1등 영어 학습 브랜드의 40년 전문성과 노하우를 담아
최단 시간 목표 점수 달성을 약속합니다.

― 중급 기본서 ―　― 파트별 전략서 ―　― 실전 모의고사 ―

토마토 토익 공식 홈페이지
www.tomatoclass.com

하루 30분씩 3주 만에
완성하는
PART 7 · VOCA
주제별 어휘리스트

01 BUSINESS
02 PRODUCTS
03 DAILY LIFE
04 ECONOMY & SOCIETY
05 JOBS & PERSONNEL

01 BUSINESS

🎧 Part7_Topic_01

회의 및 공식 모임

☐☐ **scheduling conflict**
일정 **충돌**
🔹 주로 회의 일정이 겹쳐 이를 변경하는 내용의 지문에 종종 등장한다.

☐☐ **in honor of** an achievement
성과를 **기념하여**
🔹 동사 commemorate(기념하다)로 선택지에서 품사를 바꾸어 표현되는 경우도 있다.

☐☐ **postpone** the meeting
회의를 **연기하다**
🔹 동사 put off, delay와 동의어로 패러프레이징된다.

☐☐ express **unanimous** support for the offer
그 제안에 대해 **만장일치의** 지지를 표하다

☐☐ a **venue** for the next seminar
다음 세미나 **장소**

☐☐ **on behalf of** our staff
우리 직원을 **대표하여**

☐☐ **head** the committee
위원회를 **이끌다**
🔹 동사 lead(이끌다)가 유의어로 쓰인다.

☐☐ **endorse** a proposal
제안을 **지지하다**
🔹 동사 advocate(지지하다)가 유의어로 쓰인다.

☐☐ **discrepancy** over issues
안건에 대한 의견 **불일치**

☐☐ be at the top of the **agenda**
가장 중요한 **안건**이다

공지 및 보고

☐☐ send an interoffice **memorandum**
사내 **회람**을 보내다

☐☐ **implement** a new policy
새 정책을 **시행하다**

> 전략: -ment로 끝나지만 동사임에 유의할 것. carry out, conduct는 일을 '수행하다'의 의미에 가깝고, implement는 '정책', '계획' 등을 '시행, 실행하다'의 의미이다.

☐☐ **relocate** the business
회사를 **이전하다**

> 전략: 동사 move(이사하다), transfer(옮기다)가 유의어로 쓰인다.

☐☐ **alert** all employees to a security issue
모든 직원들에게 보안 문제를 **알리다, 경고하다**

> 전략: alert A to B(A에게 B를 알리다, 경고하다)의 형태로 자주 쓰인다.

☐☐ **announce** A to B
B에게 A를 **발표하다**

> 전략: announce that S+V(that이하를 발표하다)의 형태로도 자주 쓰인다.

☐☐ New regulations will **take effect**.
새 규정의 **효력이 발생**할 것이다.

☐☐ **inform** A of B
A에게 B를 **알리다**

> 전략: inform A that S+V(A에게 that 이하를 알리다)의 형태로도 쓰이며, notify A of B(A에게 B를 알리다), report B to A(A에게 B를 알리다)와 유사 구문으로 패러프레이징된다.

☐☐ enhance the company's **reputation**
회사의 **명성**을 높이다

☐☐ a **spokesperson** for the company
회사 **대변인**

> 전략: 동사구 represent the company(회사를 대표하다)로 품사를 달리하여 패러프레이징 되는 경우가 있다.

☐☐ **turn in** the report
보고서를 **제출하다**

> 전략: 자주 출제되는 유의어 file(제출하다)도 기억해둘 것.

업무 관련

- **collaborate** with
  ~와 **공동으로 일하다**
  > 전략: collaborate on 뒤에는 협력 내용이 나와서 '~에 대해 협력하다'의 의미가 되므로 구분해서 알아두어야 한다.

- increase employee **involvement**
  직원 **참여**를 높이다
  > 전략: encourage employee participation(직원 참여를 독려하다)로 패러프레이징된다.

- monthly sales **quotas**
  월간 판매 **할당량**

- make an **adjustment**
  조정하다

- **assign** the work
  일을 **부여하다**
  > 전략: assign A to B(B에게 A를 부여하다)의 형태로도 자주 쓰이며 유의어로 allocate(부여하다, 할당하다)가 있다.

- **assume** *one's* duty
  ~의 임무를 **맡다**
  > 전략: 동의어로 be in charge of, take over, undertake 등이 있다.

- a **cooperative** working environment
  협조적인 업무 환경

- a project **coordinator**
  프로젝트 **담당자**

- a day **shift**
  주간 **교대 근무**

- make a **revision**
  수정하다

- examine the **attached** document
  첨부된 문서를 검토하다

- **deal with** the documents
  서류들을 **처리하다**

사무기기 및 사무 용품 수리

□□ **under repair**
수리 중인

□□ less expensive to **maintain**
유지하기에 덜 비싼

□□ **equip** A with B
A에게 B를 설치해주다

□□ **out of order**
고장난

□□ orders for **office supplies**
사무 용품 주문

□□ replace the **damaged** part
손상된 부분을 교체하다

회계 및 재무

□□ increase **expenditures**
비용을 늘리다
전략 사업 상의 지출 비용을 의미하며 동의어로는 expense, cost가 있다.

□□ **overhead expenses[costs]**
간접 비용
전략 기업의 비용 중 임대료, 전기료, 수도, 광열비 등의 간접비를 의미한다.

□□ **estimate** the charge
비용을 추산하다

□□ an **outstanding** balance
미결제된 잔액

□□ **cut back** on spending
소비를 줄이다
전략 유의어로 reduce(축소하다), decrease(감소하다), lower(낮추다)가 자주 쓰인다.

□□ **settle** an account
거래를 청산하다, 갚다
전략 유의어로 pay(지불하다), make a payment(값을 치르다)가 자주 쓰인다.

기업 거래 및 계약

☐☐ be **affiliated** with
~와 **제휴하다**

🔵 전략 비슷한 표현으로 go into partnership(협력하다, 제휴하다)가 자주 쓰인다.

☐☐ **negotiate** with
~와 **협상하다**

🔵 전략 '논의하다'의 뜻인 discuss로 자주 패러프레이징되며, 간혹 거래할 때 가격을 '흥정하다'의 의미를 가진 bargain으로 바뀌어 쓰이기도 한다.

☐☐ **contract out** A to B
A를 B에게 **하청 주다**

🔵 전략 명사인 contract의 '계약'이라는 의미와 다르므로 잘 알아 두자.

☐☐ **confidential** papers
기밀 문서

🔵 전략 비슷한 표현으로 classified document(기밀 문서)가 자주 쓰인다.

☐☐ make a **bid**
입찰하다

☐☐ give written **consent** for a proposal
제안서에 서면 **동의**하다

☐☐ make a financial **transaction**
금융 **거래**를 하다

🔵 전략 비슷한 표현으로 do business with(~와 거래하다)가 자주 쓰인다.

☐☐ **renew** a subscription
구독을 **갱신하다**

🔵 전략 유의어로 update(갱신하다)가 있다.

☐☐ **merge** with another company
다른 회사와 **합병하다**

🔵 전략 합병 관련 표현은 주로 기사문에서 자주 나오며 유의어로 consolidate(통합하다), amalgamate(합병하다) 등이 자주 출제된다.

☐☐ **acquire** a competitor
경쟁사를 **인수하다**

🔵 전략 유의어인 take over(인수하다)로 패러프레이징된다. M&A(merge & acquisition 인수합병)에서 명사형인 acquisition이 쓰이며 기업 거래 관련 소재로 자주 출제된다.

02 PRODUCTS

🎧 Part7_Topic_02

제조 및 생산

- ☐☐ store goods in the **warehouse**
  제품을 **창고**에 보관하다

- ☐☐ the high **yields** and profits
  높은 **생산량**과 수익

- ☐☐ an electronic **device**
  전기 **기구**
  - 전략 appliance(가전기기), gadget(소형가전) 등이 유의어로 자주 쓰인다.

- ☐☐ **assemble** the components
  부품을 **조립하다**

- ☐☐ **restricted** area
  제한 구역

- ☐☐ a **patent** on the new technology
  신기술에 대한 **특허**

- ☐☐ manufacturing **plant**
  제조 **공장**

- ☐☐ **refurbished** facilities
  재단장된 시설
  - 전략 renovated(개조된)로 패러프레이징된다.

- ☐☐ an electrical power **outage**
  전력 **공급 중단**, 정전
  - 전략 '정전'을 의미하는 동의어로 power cut, blackout이 자주 출제된다.

- ☐☐ a **defective** item
  결함 있는 제품

- ☐☐ **operate** the machinery
  기계를 **작동하다**

- ☐☐ **facilitate** each process
  각 과정을 **편리하게 하다**

공장 및 안전수칙

☐☐ wear **protective** gear
보호 장비를 착용하다

☐☐ prevent workplace **injury**
작업장 내 **상해**를 예방하다

☐☐ under the **supervisor**'s direction
감독자의 지시 하에

> 전략 supervisor는 일반적인 감독자, 상사를 의미하는 반면 foreman은 공장, 건설 현장 등에서 여러 명의 근로자를 감독하는 사람을 의미한다는 차이가 있다.

☐☐ **observe** the safety instructions
안전 사항을 **준수하다**

> 전략 comply with(지키다), obey(따르다), adhere to(고수하다)가 유의어로 자주 쓰인다. observe의 명사형에는 observance(준수)와 observation(관찰)이 있는데 서로 그 의미가 다르니 혼동하지 않도록 주의할 것.

☐☐ **designated** section
지정된 구역

☐☐ follow the safety **precautions**
안전 **예방 수칙**을 따르다

☐☐ **outdated** system
낡은 시스템

> 전략 obsolete(구식의)와 old(낡은)로 선택지에서 패러프레이징 되는 경우가 많다.

☐☐ equipment **malfunction**
장비의 **오작동**

> 전략 trouble(문제)이나 breakdown(고장)으로 패러프레이징된다.

제품 출시 및 광고

- [ ] **be for sale** starting tomorrow
  내일부터 **판매된다**
  - 전략: be available(이용 가능하다)로 바꾸어 표현될 수 있다.

- [ ] **reasonable** price
  적당한 가격
  - 전략: affordable price(저렴한 가격), low price(낮은 가격)로 패러프레이징될 수 있다.

- [ ] follow the **latest** trend
  최신 유행을 따르다

- [ ] **innovative** design
  혁신적인 디자인

- [ ] **mark down** some items
  몇몇 물품의 **가격을 인하하다**
  - 전략: at discounted price(할인된 가격에)라는 유사 표현도 자주 출제된다.

- [ ] quality of **merchandise**
  상품의 품질
  - 전략: 유의어로 products(생산물), items(물품), goods(제품)가 있다.

- [ ] **demonstrate** the new functions
  새 기능을 **시연하다**

- [ ] distribute a **flyer**
  전단지를 배포하다

- [ ] have **distinguishing** features
  뛰어난 특징을 지니다
  - 전략: 유의어로는 outstanding(뛰어난), distinctive(독특한)가 자주 쓰인다.

- [ ] **launch** a new product line
  신제품 라인을 **출시하다**
  - 전략: 유의어인 release는 상품의 '출시' 뿐만 아니라 영화의 '개봉'이나 음반의 '발매'를 의미하기도 한다.

- [ ] attract **potential customers**
  잠재 고객을 끌어 모으다

- [ ] read a **pamphlet**
  소책자를 읽다

제품 구매 및 주문

☐☐ **be out of stock**
재고가 없다

☐☐ **browse** the selection
물품을 **구경하다**
- 전략: look around(둘러보다)로 패러프레이징될 수 있다.

☐☐ offer **customized** packages
맞춤형 패키지를 제공하다
- 전략: 유의어로 personalized(개인화된), tailored(맞춤의)가 자주 쓰인다.

☐☐ read an **instructions manual**
사용설명서를 읽다

☐☐ the **receipt** for some goods
제품에 대한 **영수증**
- 전략: receipt는 '영수증'의 의미 외에도 '수령(받음)'을 의미하기도 한다.

☐☐ pay for the product in **installments**
할부로 물건 대금을 지불하다
- 전략: 비슷하게 생긴 단어인 installation(설치)과 혼동하지 말자.

배송

☐☐ **behind** schedule
예정보다 **늦게**
- 전략: 반의어로는 ahead of schedule(예정보다 일찍)이 있다.

☐☐ **no later than** eight o'clock
늦어도 8시 정각**까지는**

☐☐ send documents by **courier**
배달원에 의해 서류를 보내다
- 전략: 유의어로는 delivery man(배달부)이 쓰인다.

☐☐ **overnight** delivery
익일 배송

고객서비스

☐☐ **strive** to provide the best service
최고의 서비스를 제공하기 위해 **노력하다**

> 전략) 보통 strive to do(~을 위해 노력하다)의 형태로 자주 쓰이며 고객서비스를 광고하는 지문에 자주 등장하는 표현이다.

☐☐ **redeem** a coupon
쿠폰을 **상품으로 교환하다**

> 전략) 불만이 있는 고객에게 사과의 의미로 추후에 물건으로 교환 가능한 상품권을 제공하는 소재에서 자주 등장한다.

☐☐ a product with an expired **warranty**
보증이 만료된 제품

☐☐ **expedite** the processing of a claim
불만 처리 절차를 **신속하게 하다**

☐☐ **complimentary** items
무료 상품

> 전략) for free(공짜로), at no cost(무료로), without charge(비용 없이)로 패러프레이징된다. complementary(보완적인)와 구분하여 알아두자.

☐☐ respond to *one's* **inquiry**
~의 **문의 사항**에 답변하다

> 전략) question(질문), request(요청)로 패러프레이징되며 고객의 문의 사항에 답변하는 지문에 자주 등장하는 표현이다.

☐☐ Thank you for your **patronage.**
애용에 감사드립니다.

> 전략) Thank you for your loyalty.가 유사 표현으로 쓰인다.

☐☐ offer a 30-day money-back **guarantee**
30일 이내 환불 **보장**을 제공하다

☐☐ **encounter** a problem with a client
고객과의 문제에 **직면하다**

☐☐ improve customer **satisfaction**
고객 **만족도**를 향상시키다

> 전략) 형용사인 content(만족한)로 패러프레이징된다. 반의어로는 complaint(불만), dissatisfaction(불만족)과 claim(불만)이 있다.

03 DAILY LIFE

🎧 Part7_Topic_03

관광 및 숙박

☐☐ receive a **travel itinerary**
여행 일정표를 받다
🔹 travel schedule과 동의어로 패러프레이징된다.

☐☐ **make a reservation** for a room
방을 **예약하다**
🔹 book an accommodation(숙소를 예약하다)으로 패러프레이징된다.

☐☐ during the **peak season**
성수기 동안

☐☐ enjoy impressive **scenery**
인상적인 **경치**를 즐기다

☐☐ a tourist **attraction**
관광 **명소**
🔹 landmark(명소, 주요 지형지물)가 유의어로 사용된다.

☐☐ the **privilege** of club membership
클럽 회원의 **특권**

☐☐ nightly **rate**
숙박 **요금**
🔹 rate는 정해진 단위당 기준 가격을, charge는 판매하는 것에 부과하는 요금을, cost는 원가를, fee는 수수료를, fare는 교통수단을 이용하고 지불하는 요금을 의미한다.

☐☐ high-quality **hospitality** services
양질의 **접객** 서비스
🔹 숙박업소를 홍보하는 지문에서 서비스를 강조하거나, 만족한 고객이 이용 후기를 보내는 상황의 지문에서 종종 등장한다.

여행 수단 및 출입국

□□ **issue** a visa
비자를 **발급하다**

전략 동사일 때는 '발급하다', '발표하다'를 의미하지만 명사일 때는 논의되어야 하는 '쟁점'이나 잡지의 '호'라는 의미이다.

□□ Keep your **personal belongings** with you.
개인 소지품을 휴대하십시오.

전략 personal possessions가 동의어로 쓰인다.

□□ get through **customs**
세관을 통과하다

□□ *one's* final **destination**
~의 최종 **행선지(목적지)**

□□ visit the **duty-free shop**
면세점을 방문하다

전략 duty-free는 tax-free(면세의)로 패러프레이징된다.

□□ lose the **luggage**
짐을 잃어버리다

전략 baggage(수하물), suitcase(여행 가방)로 패러프레이징된다.

□□ show *one's* **boarding pass**
~의 **탑승권**을 보여주다

□□ fill out the **immigration** form
출입국 신고서를 작성하다

□□ reserve an **aisle seat**
통로 쪽 좌석을 예약하다

□□ **retrieve** a lost item
잃어버린 물건을 **되찾다**

전략 reclaim(되찾다)으로 패러프레이징된다.

□□ a long **layover**
긴 **경유** 시간

전략 stopover와 유의어로 패러프레이징된다.

□□ submit visa application forms to the **embassy**
대사관에 비자 신청서를 제출하다

레스토랑 및 쇼핑

□□ use better **ingredients**
더 좋은 **재료**를 사용하다

□□ receive a five-star **rating**
별 5개의 **평점**을 받다

□□ a **voucher** for a free meal
무료 식사 **상품권**
🔵전략 free coupon(무료 쿠폰)으로 패러프레이징되며 빈출 어휘이므로 반드시 알아둘 것.

□□ an **inexpensive** item
비싸지 않은 물건
🔵전략 cheap(값싼), economical (경제적인), affordable(감당할 수 있는), low-cost(가격이 낮은)로 다양하게 패러프레이징된다.

□□ a famous restaurant in a **suburban** area
교외 지역에 있는 유명한 레스토랑

□□ a front desk **receptionist**
안내 데스크 **접수원**

□□ add **flavor** to food
음식에 **맛**을 더하다

□□ advertisement for the **retail outlet**
소매점의 광고

□□ **serve** authentic dishes
정통 음식을 **제공하다**
🔵전략 serve는 '(음식을) 차리다', '대접하다', '제공하다'의 의미로 서비스 업종 관련 지문에서 자주 쓰인다.

□□ informal **attire** for women
여성을 위한 편한 **의복**
🔵전략 clothes, garment와 유의어로 쓰이지만, clothes는 옷, 의류를 전반적으로 지칭하며 garment, attire는 보다 격식을 갖춘 표현이다.

부동산 계약 및 공과금 납부

☐☐ call a **real estate** agent
부동산 중개인에게 전화하다

전략 property(부동산)와 동의어로 패러프레이징되며, 주택 임대 광고문 등에 자주 등장한다.

☐☐ **a tenant** of an apartment complex
아파트 단지의 **입주자**

전략 resident(거주자), inhabitant(주민), leaseholder(임차인)로 패러프레이징된다.

☐☐ **terminate** the lease
임차 기간을 **종결하다**

☐☐ available **for lease**
임대로 사용 가능한

☐☐ pay a **deposit**
보증금을 지불하다

전략 계약을 하기 전에 먼저 지불하는 보증금이나, 서비스나 상품을 이용하기 전에 내는 예치금을 의미한다.

☐☐ incur heavy financial **penalties**
무거운 **위약금**을 물다

전략 fine(벌금)으로 패러프레이징된다.

☐☐ provide the **amenities**
편의시설을 제공하다

전략 facility(시설), accommodation(수용시설)으로 패러프레이징될 수 있다.

☐☐ **overdue** utility bill
연체된 공과금

전략 선택지에서 outstanding(미불의), delinquent(체납된)가 유의어로 쓰이며, 공과금이나 도서 연체료 등과 관련하여 쓰인다.

☐☐ decide on a 15% **commission**
수수료를 15%로 결정하다

전략 물건이나 서비스를 제공한 것에 대해 지불하는 '수수료'를 의미한다.

☐☐ deliver a **reminder**
독촉장을 보내다

전략 연체된 공과금을 독촉하는 '독촉장'이나 '이전의 공지를 상기시키는 것'을 의미한다. 스펠링이 비슷한 remainder(나머지)와 혼동하지 말자.

04 ECONOMY & SOCIETY

🎧 Part7_Topic_04

경기 상황

☐☐ **anticipate demand**
수요를 예측하다
> 전략 기업의 계획 수립과 관련하여 customer demand(고객의 수요)로 자주 쓰인다.

☐☐ **during a recession**
불황기 동안에
> 전략 economic downturn(경제 불황)으로 패러프레이징된다.

☐☐ **business forecast**
경기 예측
> 전략 유의어로 outlook(전망), prospect(가망)가 있다.

☐☐ **impede economic development**
경제 발전을 저해하다
> 전략 hinder(저해하다), disrupt(방해하다), interfere(개입하다)로 패러프레이징된다.

☐☐ the **domestic** market
국내 채권 시장

☐☐ **short** of oil
석유 부족

☐☐ positive **economic indicators**
긍정적인 경제 지표

☐☐ **unemployment** rate
실업률

☐☐ fluctuations in **exchange rates**
환율의 변동

☐☐ create a **vicious cycle**
악순환을 만들다

정책 관련

☐☐ **under current policy**
현 **정책** 하에서

☐☐ **mediate** contract disputes
계약 분쟁을 **중재하다**

☐☐ government **authorities**
정부 **당국**

전략 (어떠한 일을 할) 권한이라는 뜻도 가진다.

☐☐ **municipal** government
지방 자치 정부

전략 '도시의'의 의미일 땐 civic으로 패러프레이징될 수 있다.

☐☐ **on strike**
파업 중인

전략 strike는 동사로 '치다'라는 의미가 있지만, 토익의 기사문에서는 '파업'의 뜻으로 자주 출제된다.

☐☐ the **controversial** issues
논쟁적 문제

전략 비슷한 의미인 '논란의 여지가 있는'을 뜻하는 debatable, disputable로 패러프레이징된다.

☐☐ come to a **compromise**
타협에 이르다

전략 동사 reach가 쓰여서 reach a settlement(협상을 타결하다)로 패러프레이징되며 노조의 파업이나 정책 결정에서 결론에 도달하였음을 의미할 때 자주 쓰인다.

☐☐ settle a **dispute**
분쟁을 해결하다

전략 dispute가 조직, 정당, 국가 간의 심각한 논쟁을 뜻하는 반면 argument(논의)는 개인 간의 의견 차이, 논쟁을 의미한다. disagreement(의견 충돌)보다 좀 더 격식을 갖춘 단어라는 점도 알아두자.

은행 업무 및 금융

☐☐ **open a bank account**
은행 **계좌**를 개설하다
전략 account는 동사로 쓰이면 account for의 형태로 '~을 설명하다'의 뜻으로도 쓰인다는 점에 유의할 것.

☐☐ **payable** to A
A에게 금액을 **지불해야 하는**
전략 payable to 다음에 지불 상대가 오는 것이 일반적이며, 회계 관련 지문에서는 accounts payable(미지급금)로도 자주 쓰인다.

☐☐ the date of **maturity**
만기일
전략 금융상품(적금, 투자)과 관련하여 사용되며, expiration date(유효기간)로 패러프레이징된다.

☐☐ apply for a **loan**
대출 신청하다
전략 loan이 동사로 '대출하다'로 쓰일 땐 동의어인 lend(빌려주다)로 패러프레이징된다.

☐☐ home **mortgage**
주택 **저당**

☐☐ bankruptcy **creditor**
파산 **채권자**

☐☐ **accrue** interest
이자가 **붙다**
전략 earn(벌다, 얻다)으로 패러프레이징된다.

☐☐ **lucrative** investment opportunities
수익성 있는 투자 기회
전략 profitable(이익이 되는)로 패러프레이징된다.

☐☐ introduce a new **remittance** service
새로운 **송금** 서비스를 도입하다
전략 '돈을 보내다'라는 의미인 send money, transfer money 등의 표현으로 패러프레이징될 수 있다.

☐☐ review a **bank statement**
은행 거래 내역서를 검토하다
전략 statement는 '내역서, 명세서'의 의미 말고도 '진술서'의 의미가 있어서 사고나 상황에 대한 공식적인 발표와 관련하여 쓰인다.

보험 및 세금

- ☐☐ file the **insurance claim**
  보험 청구(서)를 제출하다

- ☐☐ **be deducted** from the account
  계좌에서 **공제되다**

- ☐☐ **impose** a tax **on** imported goods
  수입품**에** 세금을 **부과**하다

- ☐☐ receive the **tax rebate**
  세금 환급을 받다

- ☐☐ be entitled to **tax exemptions**
  면세의 자격이 있다

- ☐☐ a monthly **premium** of $10
  월 **보험료** 10달러

사회 전반 및 공동체

- ☐☐ provide **grant** funding
  보조금 재정지원을 제공하다

- ☐☐ **donate** money to a foundation
  재단에 돈을 **기부하다**

- ☐☐ **found** a nonprofit organization
  비영리 단체를 **설립하다**

- ☐☐ **observe** the general rule
  일반 규칙을 **준수하다**

- ☐☐ charity **fundraiser**
  자선 **기금 모금자**

- ☐☐ **legal** advice on business law
  상법에 대한 **법률** 상담

- ☐☐ **volunteer** at a hospital
  병원에서 **자원봉사하다**

- ☐☐ **solicit** sponsors
  후원자를 **구하다**

방송 및 출판

☐☐ **subscribe** to a newspaper
신문을 **정기구독하다**

☐☐ check out **periodicals**
정기간행물을 대출하다
> 전략 -al로 끝나지만 형용사가 아니라 명사라는 점에 주의하자.

☐☐ **exclusive** interview
독점 인터뷰

☐☐ **censorship** of the program
프로그램 **검열**
> 전략 be monitored closely(면밀히 감시받다)로 패러프레이징될 수 있다.

환경 관련

☐☐ **endangered** species
멸종위기에 처한 동식물
> 전략 in danger of extinction(멸종위기에 처한)으로 패러프레이징되며 환경단체와 관련된 지문에 출제된다.

☐☐ protect wildlife **habitats**
야생동물의 **서식지**를 보호하다

☐☐ household waste **disposal**
생활 폐기물 **처리**

☐☐ release **pollutants** into the air
오염물질을 대기 중으로 방출하다.
> 전략 -ant로 끝나서 형용사 같아 보이지만 명사라는 점에 유의할 것.

☐☐ **hazardous** materials
위험한 물질

☐☐ remove a **toxic** substance
유독성 물질을 제거하다

05 JOBS & PERSONNEL

🎧 Part7_Topic_05

구인구직

- highly qualified **candidate**
  상당한 자격을 갖춘 **후보자**

- fill a **vacancy**
  공석을 채우다

- **be on** a three-month **probation**
  3개월간의 **수습 기간 중인**

- flexibility in the **labor** market
  노동 시장에서의 유연성

급여 및 복지 혜택

- a high **salary** level
  높은 **급여** 수준

- 20 days of **paid vacation**
  20일의 **유급 휴가**

- make the company's new **payroll**
  회사의 새 **급료 지급 명부**를 만들다

- a competitive **benefits package**
  경쟁력 있는 **복지 혜택**

- provide her with an **incentive**
  그녀에게 **추가 수당**을 제공하다

- the **working conditions** and remuneration
  근무 환경과 보수

자격 요건

- **qualifications** in accounting
  회계 분야의 **자격 요건**
  > 전략 형용사형으로 be qualified for (~할 자격을 갖추다)라는 표현이 자주 쓰인다. (= be eligible for, be entitled to)

- **adept** at working with the computers
  컴퓨터를 **능수능란하게 다루다**
  > 전략 전치사 at과 함께 자주 쓰이며, 유의어인 proficient(능숙한)은 전치사 in과 함께 쓰인다는 점에 유의하자.

- review an applicant's **credentials**
  지원자의 **자격**을 검토하다
  > 전략 구인 자격 요건/지원 자격을 통틀어 일컫는 말이 qualifications, requirements이고 지원자가 보유한 자격이나, 자격 증명서 등을 일컫는 말이 credentials이다.

- **be experienced in** marketing
  마케팅에 **경력이 있다**

- request a letter of **reference**
  추천서를 요청하다
  > 전략 recommendation letter와 동의어로 쓰이며, 구인 광고 지문에서 자격 요건 중 하나로 추천서를 요구하는 경우가 많다.

- **preference** to a candidate with experience
  경력이 있는 지원자에 대한 **선호**
  > 전략 자격 요건 관련하여, '선호'나 '우대사항'을 의미하는 단어로 advantage(우대)도 자주 쓰인다.

- accounting **certification**
  회계 **자격증**
  > 전략 certification은 직업 등을 얻기 위한 조건으로 자격, 자격증을 의미하며 불가산 명사이다. 명사 certificate도 '자격증'의 의미를 가지지만 가산 명사라는 점에 유의할 것.

- praise his kind **demeanor**
  그의 친절한 **태도**를 칭찬하다

인사 업무

☐☐ **retire** from the company
회사에서 **퇴직하다**

🔹 retire가 보통 정년에 도달하여 직위에서 은퇴하는 것을 의미한다면, resign은 어떠한 이유로 본인의 의지를 가지고 퇴직하는 것을 의미한다.

☐☐ improve **interpersonal skills**
대인 관계술을 향상시키다

☐☐ **motivate** the staff to work overtime
직원들이 초과 근무를 하도록 **동기를 부여하다**

☐☐ **dismiss** her from her post
그녀를 직위에서 **해고하다**

🔹 layoff, fire 등의 표현으로 패러프레이징될 수 있다.

☐☐ high **morale** in the company
회사에서의 높은 **사기**

☐☐ **assess** the work
업무를 **평가하다**

🔹 명사로 '평가'를 의미하는 appraisal, evaluation, estimate와 같은 유의어들로 패러프레이징되며, 직원들의 인사 평가, 성과 관리와 관련한 지문에서 자주 쓰인다.

☐☐ reduce **labor costs**
인건비를 줄이다

☐☐ the **dispatch** from headquarters
본사로부터의 **파견**

☐☐ announce **job cutbacks**
인력 감축을 알리다

🔹 reduce manpower(인력을 감축하다)로 패러프레이징될 수 있다.

☐☐ be on **sick leave** for two days
이틀간 **병가**를 내다

🔹 참고로 maternity leave는 '출산 휴가'를 의미한다.

05 JOBS & PERSONNEL

하루 30분씩 3주 만에 완성하는
PART 7·VOCA

UNIT별 복습 어휘리스트

UNIT 01	의도 파악 문제	**UNIT 12**	이메일/편지
UNIT 02	문장 위치 찾기 문제	**UNIT 13**	광고문
UNIT 03	목적/주제 문제	**UNIT 14**	기사문 (1)
UNIT 04	대상/출처 문제	**UNIT 15**	기사문 (2)
UNIT 05	세부 정보 문제	**UNIT 16**	회람/공지
UNIT 06	NOT/TRUE 문제	**UNIT 17**	표/양식
UNIT 07	추론 문제	**UNIT 18**	정보문
UNIT 08	유의어 문제	**UNIT 19**	ACTUAL TEST 1
UNIT 09	단서를 종합하는 문제	**UNIT 20**	ACTUAL TEST 2
UNIT 10	연계 문제	**UNIT 21**	ACTUAL TEST 3
UNIT 11	문자메시지/SNS		

UNIT 01 의도 파악 문제

🎧 Part7_U01_Vocab

☐☐	expect	예상하다
☐☐	approximately	대략
☐☐	presentation	발표, 프레젠테이션
☐☐	go ahead	진행하다
☐☐	be familiar with	~에 대해 잘 아는, 익숙한
☐☐	respond to	~에 대답하다
☐☐	book	예약하다
☐☐	retirement party	은퇴 기념 파티
☐☐	set up	~을 준비하다
☐☐	put up decorations	장식을 하다
☐☐	reserve	예약하다
☐☐	preference	선호하는 것
☐☐	land	착륙하다
☐☐	connecting flight	연결 항공편
☐☐	confirmation	확인(서)
☐☐	notice	알아채다, 인지하다
☐☐	glitch	작은 문제, 결함
☐☐	available	이용 가능한
☐☐	overlap	중복, 겹침
☐☐	postpone	연기하다, 미루다
☐☐	propose	제안하다
☐☐	contract	계약
☐☐	casual	가벼운, 격식을 차리지 않은
☐☐	conduct	수행하다
☐☐	fix	고치다

UNIT 02 문장 위치 찾기 문제

🎧 Part7_U02_Vocab

☐☐	fiscal year	회계연도
☐☐	productivity	생산성
☐☐	express concern	우려를 표하다
☐☐	relevant	적절한, 관련 있는
☐☐	personnel	직원, 인사(과)
☐☐	extra	추가의, 별도의
☐☐	permanent	영구적인, 지속적인
☐☐	initially	처음에
☐☐	make one's mark	명성을 떨치다
☐☐	commemorate	기념하다, 축하하다
☐☐	recommendation	추천
☐☐	previously	이전에
☐☐	high-quality	고품질의, 고급의
☐☐	transportation	교통수단, 교통기관
☐☐	existing	기존의
☐☐	accommodate	수용하다
☐☐	passenger	승객
☐☐	access	입장[접근]
☐☐	suburb	교외
☐☐	population	인구
☐☐	relieve	완화하다
☐☐	automate	자동화하다
☐☐	investment	투자
☐☐	implement	시행하다
☐☐	commuter	통근자

UNIT 03 목적/주제 문제

🎧 Part7_U03_Vocab

☐☐	construction	공사
☐☐	landscape	조경, 경치
☐☐	facility	(보통 복수형) 편의 시설
☐☐	requirement	요건
☐☐	participate in	~에 참가하다
☐☐	expert	전문가
☐☐	field	분야
☐☐	valuable	귀중한
☐☐	confirm	확정하다
☐☐	make it to	~로 나아가는 데 성공하다
☐☐	informative	설명하는, 정보를 제공하는
☐☐	preliminary	예비의, 예선의
☐☐	qualify	자격을 부여하다
☐☐	competition	경연, 경합
☐☐	contestant	(대회, 시합 등의) 참가자, 경연자
☐☐	scheduling conflict	일정상의 충돌
☐☐	uncomfortable	불편한
☐☐	malfunction	고장 나다
☐☐	management	관리(팀)
☐☐	take steps	조치를 취하다
☐☐	remedy	개선하다
☐☐	belongings	소지품
☐☐	debris	쓰레기, 잔해
☐☐	possession	(주로 복수형) 소지품
☐☐	disruption	혼란
☐☐	patience	이해, 인내심

UNIT 04 대상/출처 문제

🎧 Part7_U04_Vocab

☐☐	initiate	시작하다
☐☐	voluntary	자발적인
☐☐	recall	회수, 리콜
☐☐	manufacture	제조하다
☐☐	freezer	냉동실
☐☐	refund	환불
☐☐	process	가공하다
☐☐	intermission	중간 휴식 시간
☐☐	permit	허용하다, 허락하다
☐☐	admit	입장시키다
☐☐	at least	최소한
☐☐	short-term	단기의
☐☐	assistant	보조
☐☐	register with	~에 등록하다
☐☐	fill out	작성하다
☐☐	form	양식
☐☐	accurately	정확하게
☐☐	provide	제공하다
☐☐	valid	유효한
☐☐	account number	계좌번호
☐☐	detail	(보통 복수형) 세부 사항
☐☐	receive	받다
☐☐	pay statement	급여 명세서
☐☐	ensure	확인하다
☐☐	in order	제대로 된

UNIT 05 세부 정보 문제

🎧 Part7_U05_Vocab

☐☐	material	직물, 천
☐☐	lightweight	경량의, 가벼운
☐☐	guarantee	보장하다
☐☐	offer	제공하다; 할인
☐☐	exclusive	고급의; 독점적인
☐☐	dedication	헌신
☐☐	erupt	나다, 분출되다
☐☐	warehouse	창고
☐☐	insurance investigator	보험 조사원
☐☐	present	참석한
☐☐	cover	보장하다; 씌우다
☐☐	outstanding	미처리된; 미불의
☐☐	disclose	밝히다
☐☐	cope with	대처하다
☐☐	superintendent	관리자
☐☐	on behalf of	~을 대표하여
☐☐	management team	경영진
☐☐	attend	참석하다
☐☐	conference	회의
☐☐	be scheduled for	~로 일정이 잡혀져 있다
☐☐	venue	장소
☐☐	arrangement	준비, 합의
☐☐	outline	대략적으로 설명하다; 개요
☐☐	enhance	높이다
☐☐	reputation	명성
☐☐	refreshment	(보통 복수형) 다과

UNIT 06 NOT/TRUE 문제

🎧 Part7_U06_Vocab

☐☐	former	이전의
☐☐	complete	끝마치다
☐☐	obtain	획득하다
☐☐	promising	유망한
☐☐	emergency	긴급
☐☐	expedite	신속히 처리하다
☐☐	reimbursement	상환
☐☐	approach	다가오다, 접근하다
☐☐	simultaneous	동시의, 같이 일어나는
☐☐	evolve into	~으로 발전[진화]하다
☐☐	entire	전체의
☐☐	admission	입장료
☐☐	recognized	인정된, 알려진
☐☐	manufacturer	제조사
☐☐	establishment	설립
☐☐	expand	확장하다
☐☐	merchandise	상품
☐☐	operation	운영
☐☐	unload	(짐을) 내리다
☐☐	shipment	수송품, 적하물
☐☐	certify	자격증을 교부하다
☐☐	equipment	장비
☐☐	assign	할당하다
☐☐	supervise	감독하다
☐☐	candidate	지원자, 후보자
☐☐	significant	상당한; 중요한

UNIT 07 추론 문제

🎧 Part7_U07_Vocab

☐☐	acquisition	구매, 구입
☐☐	identification	신분증
☐☐	board	탑승하다
☐☐	timely	적시의, 시기 적절한
☐☐	supplier	공급 업체
☐☐	effectively	효과적으로
☐☐	attention	주목, 관심
☐☐	demonstrate	(기계나 전자 제품 등의) 시연을 하다
☐☐	secondary	부차적인, 또 다른
☐☐	indoor	실내의
☐☐	inquiry	문의
☐☐	brief	간략한, 짧은
☐☐	description	설명
☐☐	finance	자금을 대다; 자금
☐☐	interest rate	이자율
☐☐	application	신청서
☐☐	submit	제출하다
☐☐	bank statement	은행 명세서
☐☐	license	등록증; 면허증
☐☐	collateral	담보물
☐☐	scrutinize	면밀히 조사하다
☐☐	handle	다루다
☐☐	delinquent	연체된
☐☐	deny	거부하다
☐☐	deposit	예치하다
☐☐	hesitate	주저하다

UNIT 08 유의어 문제

🎧 Part7_U08_Vocab

☐☐	satisfaction	만족도
☐☐	outstanding	뛰어난
☐☐	dependable	신뢰할 수 있는
☐☐	appoint	임명하다
☐☐	retain	보유하다
☐☐	stability	안정성
☐☐	struggle to *do*	~하려고 고군분투하다
☐☐	support	부양하다
☐☐	pay off	~을 갚다
☐☐	enroll	등록하다
☐☐	outcome	결과
☐☐	edge	유리함
☐☐	manage	관리하다
☐☐	profit	수익, 이익
☐☐	broad	넓은
☐☐	tracking	추적, 탐색
☐☐	component	(구성) 요소
☐☐	challenging	어려운, 도전적인
☐☐	functionality	기능
☐☐	conversely	반대로, 역으로
☐☐	formerly	이전에, 예전에
☐☐	undergo	겪다, 경험하다
☐☐	transformation	변화, 전환
☐☐	estimate	예상치, 견적
☐☐	sophisticated	수준 높은, 세련된
☐☐	operate	운영하다; 조작하다

UNIT 09 단서를 종합하는 문제

🎧 Part7_U09_Vocab

☐☐	announce	알리다, 발표하다
☐☐	acquire	인수하다
☐☐	labor	노동력
☐☐	affordable	(가격이) 저렴한, 알맞은
☐☐	numerous	수많은
☐☐	throughout	전역에[도처에]
☐☐	sufficient	충분한
☐☐	capital	자본
☐☐	secure	확보하다
☐☐	workforce	인력
☐☐	apply for	~에 지원하다
☐☐	ideal	이상적인
☐☐	candidate	지원자
☐☐	promote	승진시키다
☐☐	negotiate	협상하다
☐☐	lucrative	수익성이 좋은
☐☐	reliability	믿음직함
☐☐	exceed	초과하다
☐☐	consistently	지속적으로
☐☐	positive	긍정적인
☐☐	attitude	태도
☐☐	possess	소유하다
☐☐	invaluable	귀중한
☐☐	asset	자산
☐☐	qualification	**(보통 복수형)** (특정 분야에 대한) 약력, 기술, 지식
☐☐	resilient	탄력성 있는, 회복력 있는

UNIT 10 연계 문제

🎧 Part7_U10_Vocab

☐☐	notify A of B	A에게 B를 알리다[공지하다]
☐☐	revolutionary	혁신적인, 혁명적인
☐☐	aisle	(진열대 사이의) 통로
☐☐	place an order	주문하다
☐☐	charge	(금액, 수수료 등을) 부과하다
☐☐	regular	일반의, 보통의
☐☐	time-sensitive	긴급한, 분초를 다투는
☐☐	extract	추출액, 엑기스
☐☐	seasonal	계절의, 기간 한정적인
☐☐	transition to	~로 위치를 옮기다, ~로 이동하다
☐☐	hospitality	(호텔 서비스 등의) 접객업; 환대
☐☐	reference	추천서, 추천인
☐☐	full time	상근직의, 정규 근무시간에 일하는
☐☐	enforce	(강제적으로) 실시하다, 집행하다
☐☐	comply with	(법이나 규정 등을) 따르다, 준수하다
☐☐	establish	확립하다
☐☐	strategically	전략적으로, 계획적으로
☐☐	found	창설하다
☐☐	decade	10년
☐☐	suggestion	제안
☐☐	necessary	필수인
☐☐	rent	대여하다
☐☐	hire	고용하다
☐☐	private	개인적인, 사적인
☐☐	audience	관객

UNIT 11 문자메시지/SNS

🎧 Part7_U11_Vocab

☐☐	head	향하게 하다; 향하다
☐☐	present	발표하다
☐☐	foster	발전시키다
☐☐	cooperation	협동심
☐☐	at the last minute	막판에, 임박해서
☐☐	board meeting	이사회
☐☐	give a hand	도와주다
☐☐	reimbursement	환급
☐☐	hand in	~을 제출하다
☐☐	budget	예산
☐☐	alternative	대안
☐☐	reasonable	합리적인
☐☐	request	요청하다
☐☐	cover	처리하다
☐☐	specialty	전문가
☐☐	treatment	치료, 요법
☐☐	respectively	각각
☐☐	check in	수속하다, 등록하다
☐☐	representative	대표, 대리인
☐☐	brochure	안내책자
☐☐	count on	~을 믿다
☐☐	latest	최신의
☐☐	commercial	상업적인
☐☐	fascinating	대단히 흥미로운

UNIT 12 이메일/편지

🎧 Part7_U12_Vocab

☐☐	missing	없어진
☐☐	replacement	교환(대체)품
☐☐	displeasure	불쾌감, 불만
☐☐	in response to	답하여, ~에 응하여
☐☐	wire	(전자 시스템을 이용하여) 송금하다
☐☐	vary	다르다, 다양하다
☐☐	as a token of	~의 표시로
☐☐	enterprise	기업, 회사
☐☐	institute	도입하다
☐☐	donation	기부, 기증(품)
☐☐	participation	참여, 참가
☐☐	mandatory	의무적인
☐☐	in need	어려움에 처한, 궁핍한
☐☐	undertaking	일, 프로젝트
☐☐	separate from	~와는 별도인
☐☐	bilingual	두 언어를 사용하는
☐☐	satisfactory	만족스러운
☐☐	term	(계약) 조건; 용어
☐☐	look forward to *doing*	~하기를 고대하다
☐☐	get together	만나다, 모이다
☐☐	catch up	못다 한 얘기를 나누다
☐☐	networking	인적 네트워크 형성
☐☐	appliance	가전제품
☐☐	landscaping	조경
☐☐	denote	의미하다, 나타내다

UNIT 13 광고문

🎧 Part7_U13_Vocab

☐☐	supervisor	관리자
☐☐	advantage	유리한 점, 장점
☐☐	position	(일)자리, 직위
☐☐	track	추적하다
☐☐	expenses	비용, 경비
☐☐	verification	증명, 입증, 검증
☐☐	restore	복구하다
☐☐	charge	청구하다, 요금
☐☐	quote	견적
☐☐	assorted	갖가지의
☐☐	combine	결합하다
☐☐	following	다음[아래]에 언급되는
☐☐	disposable	일회용의
☐☐	prototype	원형, 샘플
☐☐	desirable	바람직한
☐☐	compensation	보상(금)
☐☐	particular	특별한, 특정한
☐☐	retirement	퇴직, 은퇴
☐☐	previous	이전의
☐☐	ownership	소유(권)
☐☐	expire	만료되다
☐☐	schedule	일정을 잡다
☐☐	avoid	방지하다, 피하다
☐☐	separately	따로따로, 별도로
☐☐	administer	관리하다

UNIT 14 기사문 (1)

🎧 Part7_U14_Vocab

☐☐	alter	바꾸다, 고치다
☐☐	measure	조치, 정책
☐☐	mark	(중요 사건을) 축하하다
☐☐	recognize	인식하다, 인정하다
☐☐	take advantage of	~을 이용하다, 기회로 활용하다
☐☐	regarding	~에 관해
☐☐	merge	합치다, 병합하다
☐☐	amenities	오락 시설
☐☐	go into effect	발효하다, 효력이 발생되다
☐☐	state-of-the-art	최신식의, 최첨단의
☐☐	resident	주민
☐☐	allocate	배정하다
☐☐	attraction	명소, 명물
☐☐	boast	자랑하다, 뽐내다
☐☐	on-site	현장의, 현지의
☐☐	engage in	~에 참여[관여]하다
☐☐	interactive	쌍방향의, 상호적인
☐☐	organization	조직
☐☐	accomplish	달성하다, 완수하다
☐☐	pursue	추구하다
☐☐	a range of	여럿의, 다양한
☐☐	accordingly	그에 맞춰
☐☐	undisclosed	밝혀지지 않은
☐☐	recipient	수신인, 수령인
☐☐	be in charge of	~을 책임지다

UNIT 15 기사문 (2)

🎧 Part7_U15_Vocab

☐☐	traffic congestion	교통 정체
☐☐	duration	(지속되는) 기간
☐☐	unveil	발표하다
☐☐	feature	~의 특징을 이루다
☐☐	corporate	기업의
☐☐	contemporary	현대의
☐☐	cutting-edge	최첨단의
☐☐	increasingly	점점 더
☐☐	leading	선두적인
☐☐	acquisition	인수
☐☐	utilize	활용하다
☐☐	downsize	축소하다
☐☐	immediate	즉시의, 즉각적인
☐☐	strike	파업
☐☐	seek to *do*	~하는 것을 추구하다
☐☐	controversial	논란이 많은
☐☐	arise	발생하다
☐☐	reflect	반영하다; 숙고하다
☐☐	regulation	규제
☐☐	take effect	효력을 발휘하다
☐☐	release	발표하다
☐☐	outdated	구식인
☐☐	quarterly	분기별의
☐☐	staffing	직원 채용
☐☐	individually	개별적으로

UNIT 16 회람/공지

🎧 Part7_U16_Vocab

☐☐	registration	등록
☐☐	accessible	이용[접근] 가능한
☐☐	stand out	눈에 띄다, 두드러지다
☐☐	no later than	늦어도 ~까지는
☐☐	make arrangements for	~을 준비하다
☐☐	renovation	보수
☐☐	deal with	~을 처리하다; 다루다
☐☐	contribute to	~의 원인이 되다, ~에 기여하다
☐☐	defective	결함이 있는
☐☐	thoroughly	완전히
☐☐	malfunction	오작동
☐☐	refurbish	재단장하다
☐☐	designate	지정하다
☐☐	alert	알리다; 기민한
☐☐	expenditure	지출(= spending)
☐☐	unanimous	만장일치의
☐☐	urge	강력히 권고하다
☐☐	collaborate with	~와 협업하다
☐☐	assume	맡다
☐☐	turn in	제출하다(= submit)
☐☐	effort	수고, 노력
☐☐	tenant	세입자
☐☐	maintenance	유지 보수, 관리
☐☐	at *one's* convenience	~가 편리한 때에
☐☐	aware	알고 있는

UNIT 17 표/양식

🎧 Part7_U17_Vocab

☐☐	temporary	임시의, 일시적인
☐☐	clearance	허가, 승인
☐☐	extension	내선번호
☐☐	report to	~에게 알리다
☐☐	wholesale	도매의
☐☐	distributor	도매업자
☐☐	payment	결제, 지불
☐☐	applicable	해당[적용]되는
☐☐	frequent	잦은, 빈번한
☐☐	exclude	제외하다
☐☐	dispatch	파견하다
☐☐	appraisal	평가(= assessment, evaluation)
☐☐	contribution	기여
☐☐	punctuality	시간 엄수
☐☐	penalty	불이익; 벌금
☐☐	absence	결근
☐☐	incentive	장려책
☐☐	extraordinary	뛰어난
☐☐	inaugural	첫, 개시의
☐☐	voucher	상품권, 쿠폰
☐☐	entry	출품(작)
☐☐	assess	평가하다
☐☐	faculty	교수진
☐☐	instruction	**(보통 복수형)** 지시 (사항)
☐☐	change	잔돈, 거스름돈
☐☐	restriction	제약 조건, 제한

UNIT 18 정보문

🎧 Part7_U18_Vocab

☐☐	preventive	예방을 위한
☐☐	exclusive	독점적인, 유일한
☐☐	proper	적절한
☐☐	ventilation	통풍
☐☐	association	협회
☐☐	subscription	구독
☐☐	plan	요금제; 계획
☐☐	account	이용 계정; 계좌
☐☐	significantly	상당히, 두드러지게
☐☐	complimentary	무료의
☐☐	exhibition	전시(회)
☐☐	remarkable	훌륭한, 놀라운
☐☐	cater to	~에 부응하다, 충족시키다
☐☐	atmosphere	분위기
☐☐	overlook	(건물 등이) 내려다보이다
☐☐	spacious	널찍한
☐☐	additionally	게다가
☐☐	gathering	모임
☐☐	banquet	연회
☐☐	suit	~에 맞추다
☐☐	entitle	자격[권리]를 주다
☐☐	fully equipped	완비된
☐☐	surcharge	추가 요금
☐☐	upcoming	다가오는, 곧 있을
☐☐	extend	연장하다
☐☐	bill	계산서, 청구서

UNIT 19 ACTUAL TEST 1

🎧 Part7_U19_Vocab

☐☐	updated	최신의, 갱신된
☐☐	quarter	(1년의 4분의 1인) 분기
☐☐	engagement	약혼, 약속
☐☐	deprived	부족한, 빈곤한
☐☐	replicate	재현하다, 복제하다
☐☐	allowance	허용, 허가
☐☐	appointment	예약, 약속
☐☐	eventually	결국
☐☐	suitable	적합한
☐☐	adjustment	수정, 조정
☐☐	obtain	얻다
☐☐	settle into	(새 집, 직장 등에 자리를 잡고) 정착하다
☐☐	property	부동산, 건물
☐☐	expiry date	만료일, 만기일
☐☐	commence	시작하다, 착수하다
☐☐	render	(어떤 상태가 되게) 만들다
☐☐	fortune	부, 재산
☐☐	tentative	머뭇거리는, 자신 없는
☐☐	superb	최상의
☐☐	integral	필수적인
☐☐	restructure	재편하다
☐☐	prestigious	명망 있는
☐☐	outreach	봉사활동
☐☐	gather	모으다; 모이다
☐☐	unemployment	실업

UNIT 20 ACTUAL TEST 2

🎧 Part7_U20_Vocab

☐☐	mark down	~의 가격을 인하하다
☐☐	warranty	보증
☐☐	patronage	애용
☐☐	initiative	계획, 주도
☐☐	randomly	임의로, 무작위로
☐☐	undoubtedly	확실히, 의심할 바 없이
☐☐	demonstration	시연, 설명
☐☐	coordinator	책임자, 조정인
☐☐	cordially	정중하게, 성심으로
☐☐	allegiance	충성, 헌신
☐☐	accompanying	동반하는, 함께하는
☐☐	regular customer	단골 (고객)
☐☐	cover letter	자기소개서
☐☐	productivity	생산성
☐☐	short notice	갑작스러운 통보
☐☐	discourage	억제시키다, 말리다
☐☐	priority	우선 순위, 우선 사항
☐☐	exception	예외
☐☐	verify	확인하다, 입증하다
☐☐	institution	기관, 단체
☐☐	unforeseen	예기치 못한 (= unexpected)
☐☐	closure	폐쇄
☐☐	interpretation	통역, 해석
☐☐	accuracy	정확성
☐☐	complimentary	무료의
☐☐	reduction	감소

UNIT 21 ACTUAL TEST 3

🎧 Part7_U21_Vocab

☐☐	acclaim	호평하다
☐☐	compliment	찬사, 칭찬
☐☐	critic	비평가
☐☐	partner with	~와 제휴를 맺다, 협력하다
☐☐	ingredient	재료
☐☐	be anticipated to *do*	~할 것으로 예상되다
☐☐	take on	(일을) 맡다
☐☐	region	지역
☐☐	innovative	혁신적인
☐☐	come up with	(생각을) 내놓다, 제안하다
☐☐	firsthand	직접
☐☐	rely on	~에 의존하다
☐☐	funding	기금
☐☐	resolution	해결책
☐☐	simultaneously	동시에
☐☐	recover	복구하다
☐☐	appropriate	적절한
☐☐	potential	가능성이 있는
☐☐	promptly	신속히
☐☐	archive	기록보관소
☐☐	terms and conditions	(계약 등의) 조건, 규정
☐☐	patron	고객
☐☐	evaluation	평가
☐☐	identify	밝히다
☐☐	automatically	자동으로